THE FIRM AS A COLLABORATIVE
COMMUNITY

The Firm as a Collaborative Community

Reconstructing Trust in the Knowledge Economy

CHARLES HECKSCHER AND PAUL S. ADLER

OXFORD

UNIVERSITY PRESS

OXFORD
UNIVERSITY PRESS

Great Clarendon Street, Oxford OX2 6DP

Oxford University Press is a department of the University of Oxford.
It furthers the University's objective of excellence in research, scholarship,
and education by publishing worldwide in

Oxford New York

Auckland Cape Town Dar es Salaam Hong Kong Karachi
Kuala Lumpur Madrid Melbourne Mexico City Nairobi
New Delhi Shanghai Taipei Toronto

With offices in

Argentina Austria Brazil Chile Czech Republic France Greece
Guatemala Hungary Italy Japan Poland Portugal Singapore
South Korea Switzerland Thailand Turkey Ukraine Vietnam

Oxford is a registered trade mark of Oxford University Press
in the UK and in certain other countries

Published in the United States
by Oxford University Press Inc., New York

British Library Cataloguing in Publication Data
Data available

Library of Congress Cataloging in Publication Data
Data available

Typeset by SPI Publisher Services, Pondicherry, India
Printed in Great Britain
on acid-free paper by
Biddles Ltd., King's Lynn,
Norfolk

ISBN 0-19-928603-5   978-0-19-928603-4

1 3 5 7 9 10 8 6 4 2

Contents

Contents

Introduction

Charles Heckscher and Paul S. Adler

A central tension has run through social analysis for well over a century: community and trust seem increasingly necessary in a complex interdependent world, but they are also less available. At the same time that markets and polities have drawn people into tighter webs of relations, traditional communities have been greatly weakened, and the unifying institutions of previous eras—dominant religions, labor unions, major political parties—have lost much of their credibility. The resulting sense of fragmentation and anomie has led some to despair and others to call for the revival of community, including conservative appeals to traditional values and liberal explorations of dialogue and participation.

What is less known is that the corporate sphere has faced the same essential problem and has engaged in considerable practical innovation in dealing with it. Complex knowledge-based production requires high levels of diffuse cooperation resting on a strong foundation of trust. Contrary to the claims of neoliberal approaches, neither markets nor hierarchies are sufficient for coordination in such conditions: bonds of trust are essential. Yet the old corporate communities based on a culture of loyalty, which have been the basis for commitment for a century now, have been taken apart by three decades of economic turbulence, downsizing and restructuring. These developments raise the fear that the foundations of organizational trust are eroding when they are most needed.

Some look back with nostalgia, and argue that we should respond by reconstructing a culture of loyalty. Yet that culture had its own problems: it proved unable to encompass the increasing scope, diversity, and flexibility of interactions in business and other arenas. The traditional form of community was often narrow in its parochialism and deadly in its conformism—the antithesis of what is needed in our increasingly knowledge-intensive economy.

A growing group of theorists has been exploring the possibility of a new form of trust that would enable interdependent activity in the more fluid, open contexts characteristic of knowledge production, reconciling choice with community. The past few years have seen a proliferation of work on non-traditional forms of trust: 'studied,' 'deliberate,' 'swift,' and 'reflective.' And an emerging body of research focuses on new forms of organization among professionals and in 'post-bureaucratic' firms and markets.

The contributors to this volume have come together around a shared sense that a distinctively new form of community is being developed in the womb of the most advanced business organizations today. The claim at the core of the current study is that leading-edge organizational innovations, driven by pragmatic business considerations, offer a glimpse of this community, one that is collaborative and open rather than traditionalistic and closed. When firms and the business networks within which they operate become more knowledge intensive and more solutions oriented, they find it increasingly necessary for people to 'work things out' flexibly through discussion rather than relying either on arm's-length market exchange or bureaucratic authority. Thus while many companies have dismantled traditional relations of loyalty, many of the most successful of them have *not* simply retreated to some combination of self-interest and hierarchical command; rather they have gone at least some distance towards putting into practice a form of trust that overcomes the rigidities of traditional communities.

Studying these companies we can learn a great deal about why trust is needed, why traditional forms have broken down, and how new forms have begun to fill the gap. This emergent collaborative community rests on three major institutional pillars:

1. A shared ethic of interdependent contribution, fundamentally different both from traditional ethics of honor and loyalty, and from the modern individualist ('Protestant') ethic;

2. A formalized set of norms of interdependent process management, supplementing and often replacing the informal relations of traditional communities. These process approaches include iterative co-design, metaphoric search, and systematic mutual understanding; and

3. An interactive social character, formed by changes in family, childhood, and workplace patterns, that grounds an interdependent social

identity. This motivational pattern enables people to manage multiple group affiliations and peer relationships; they are less tied to motivations of autonomy or paternalistic dependence.

This volume is itself a result of an extensive collaboration among diverse specialists. The contributors fall into two main groups: those who are based in academia, and those who make their living primarily as consultants to large companies. The 'academics' bring to the table a theoretical perspective grounded not primarily in the business world, but in other social institutions; the 'business' writers bring a rich knowledge of what is going on in companies right now, and a 'feel' for what makes sense. Of course, the collaboration would be impossible if the line were as clear as that: the dialogue has depended on the fact that everyone has spent considerable time in both camps.

The group met three times over the course of a year and a half under the auspices of the Center for Workplace Transformation at Rutgers University. In the first session participants presented their initial understandings of how trust and community work in the best firms and inter-firm networks. The second meeting focused especially on drafts of the main theoretical concepts. The third was organized around close discussion and collective critiques of chapter drafts. We also greatly benefited throughout from an 'independent auditor': Paul DiMaggio made very valuable and generous contributions through detailed critiques in all the sessions.

The flow of the volume is as follows:

- The opening section is primarily theoretical, sketching the main concepts of collaborative community.
  - Paul Adler and Charles Heckscher provide an overview, including the historical evolution and future prospects of this way of relating. They sketch the basic elements of the emerging form of community—values, organization, and identity. They also review the counter-forces that work against community and trust, but conclude that the evolution of production towards complex interdependent knowledge-based services and products will continue to foster collaboration in spite of these obstacles.
  - Charles Sabel focuses on the level of organization, on the workings of 'interdependent process management.' In particular he shows how the mechanisms of iterative co-design and disentrenching search, when put into motion, can generate trust through a

dynamic process of learning. Finally, he extends this organizational argument from the level of the workplace to the level of governance, showing that even highly complex systems (including governments) can build trust through properly designed incentives and forums that create cumulative understanding.

- Michael Maccoby focuses on character and identity, arguing that collaborative interactions are based on a transformation of social character that has been under way for several decades. He traces the roots of this change in the evolution of family systems as well as transformations at work. He analyzes ways in which the interactive character develops through the life cycle—including both the positive potential for intimacy and leadership based on mutual development, and the negative potential for superficiality and loss of integrity.

• The next set of chapters develop these concepts through studies of the internal structure of firms:

- Jay Galbraith examines the organization of firms, arguing that they are becoming complex combinations of multiple types of networks: in addition to the traditional dichotomy of informal relations and formal organization, there is increasing dependence on e-coordination, formal teams, integrators, and matrices. This creates new challenges for leadership, which must foster and manage differentiated systems of relationships through network design.

- Adler takes up the software design industry. In the past software developers were united by a 'guild' form of professional community—a form that united them in a common identity as independent 'hackers.' The recent drive to process management has destroyed that pattern: it has meant greater specialization, formalization, and control. This control initially took a coercive form, but more recently it has taken a more participative and enabling form. Professional community has also taken a more interdependent, collaborative form. The result is a highly efficient and innovative combination of bureaucracy and community with new internal contradictions.

- Maccoby considers the health care industry, which is under enormous pressure from the rapid development of medical knowledge and technology, but which has not moved nearly as far as the software industry. The craftlike tradition of independent practice is more deeply embedded and has created walls between special-

ties and levels that are hard to overcome. The more recent bureaucratic control systems have brought some cost efficiencies but
at the cost of patient focus. The Mayo Clinic provides some indication of how collaboration might work to combine knowledge in
the service of patient outcomes; but it has not yet proved its
ability to work on large scales.

- Annabel Quan-Haase and Barry Wellman analyze the use of
computer-mediated communication in a small software company.
They conclude that the company is in effect a hybrid: both hierarchy and collaboration (networking) are extremely important features of daily operations, and they form complex combinations.
Computer-mediated communication adds a capability for wider
ranges of problem solving across departments with differing
cultures; but it also helps strengthen more localized and personal
relations.

- Saul Rubinstein takes up the issue of employee voice in collaborative companies by examining a set of attempts at labor–management cooperation in team-based work organizations. He finds that
in some instances unions can add value to companies by increasing
the degree of collaboration—in effect creating an environment
where management lets go enough to get the full advantages of
interactivity. However, these cases also require deep changes in the
internal functioning of unions, which pose significant challenges.
In the end most companies have been content with part-
way solutions rather than full institutional collaboration.

• A pair of chapters looks at systems that cross firm and industry
boundaries.

- Lynda Applegate compares three sets of trans-firm relations: in the
financial services, health care, and automotive industries. This
level presents particular problems of governance: the more successful cases have evolved innovative inter-firm organizational
solutions and ownership structures that reinforce a sense of common membership rather than locking in status hierarchies. The
cases show not only the benefits, but also the difficulties and
vulnerabilities of such inter-firm arrangements as they struggle
to extend the limits of traditional systems.

- John Paul MacDuffie and Sue Helper show that auto supplier relations are being driven inexorably towards greater collaboration,
but finds that this move is being shaped into two patterns based

on prior history: 'collaboration without trust' with the USA's 'Big Three' auto companies, and 'collaboration with trust' with Japanese manufacturers. Close examination of case material suggests the first of these may not be sustainable, and that trust adds clear value to the partners and to production outcomes.

- The final section focuses on the issues involved in the deliberate creation of collaborative relationships.
  - Maccoby and Heckscher note the challenges posed for leadership by this shift—especially the move from appealing to motives from father transference, which is the archetypal relationship embodied in paternalist bureaucracies, to drawing on horizontal sibling transferences.
  - Heckscher and Nathaniel Foote take up a set of interventions that aim to create within-firm dialogues around shared purpose, strategy, and the barriers to execution. These often reveal the power of the iterative learning model sketched by Sabel, but they also frequently run into obstacles from leaders and hierarchical mechanisms that are not easily overcome. One key to success is the development of a team of mid-level managers representing the core value of contribution rather than deference, and committed to reporting the unvarnished truth.
  - Mark Bonchek and Robert Howard discuss initiatives to bring together stakeholders of firms in leader-to-leader networks. The development of forums between companies and customers must overcome tensions between 'learning' and 'selling,' between 'intimacy' and 'reach,' and between hierarchy and collaboration; but it is capable of modifying market-based choices in a way that increases value for all parties.

Though the contributors came to considerable agreement, there remain differences in emphasis and areas of uncertainty which might be worth outlining at the outset. First, and probably most intensively discussed, is the independent importance of values as distinct from the structures of process management. Some argued that a well-designed process eventually creates higher levels of trust and community through the repeated experience of good results; others insisted on the independent importance of new values—the ethic of contribution—and the need to deliberately foster them. As we worked through individual cases there was no irrefutable resolution. There was, however, general agreement that change efforts need to start with a process focus, if only because this brings people together around a common, external task, and that shared values change significantly in the move to collaboration. The remaining question is how much *independent* attention should be paid to values.

A similar debate arose around the role of identity and character. There was general agreement that there was a significant shift away from the 'bureaucratic personality' outlined by Merton in the 1940s; but there was a range of views about how much this shift was grounded in childhood experiences and how much it could be brought about through adult resocialization via the experience of collaborative work organization. Working through the various case studies, it appeared that individuals differed on this dimension: while many individuals seem capable of shifting from one mode to the other, there are always some who seem characterologically incapable of functioning in a collaborative system.

A third dimension of debate had to do with the continuing role of bureaucracy within collaborative organizations. Once again, the debate shaped up as a matter of nuance rather than of fundamental disagreement. Some argued that collaborative community is emerging in the corporate world in a form that is intertwined with core features of bureaucracy such as formalization, standardization, specialization, and hierarchy. Others argued that while these structural features are indeed essential to the effective functioning of collaborative community, they assume such a radically different meaning in the new context that it would be misleading to call them bureaucratic.

Finally, there was also a degree of difference in the overall assessment of the prospects for collaboration. Certainly strong forces are arrayed against it: the neoliberal swing towards unfettered markets, the widespread fundamentalist retreats towards traditional values, the increased exercise of naked power by corporations in their relations to employees and suppliers. It was clear that the movement we analyze towards collaboration is a contested one, and that many companies have gone down the 'low road' of tighter control. Nevertheless, all the group members agreed that the long-term competitive and human advantages afforded by collaborative community ensured that it would continue to attract proponents.

It should also be added that the publication of this volume does not, in our eyes, mean the end of our work. Many ideas were proposed for further chapters, many concepts have yet to be properly nailed down, and many issues need to be further explored. For example, we touched on the problem of collaborative *accountability* frequently, but did not go further. We have not paid sufficient attention to possible distortions and inequities *within* the collaborative model, such as the tendency of reputations to become highly centralized and exclusive. We surfaced, in the last meeting, a sense that the formalized process management which is crucial to our analysis must still be grounded, even in the most advanced cases, in a network of personal trust and friendship; but we have not worked through the connections between personal networks and more formal process relations. We began to sketch a typology of different versions of collaborative forms—but that will have to wait for future work.

Our thinking developed considerably through these discussions and debates. We hope this publication is a way of launching the continuing discussion in a wider field.

Part I

Framing Concepts

1

Towards Collaborative Community

Paul S. Adler and Charles Heckscher

Introduction

In the last thirty years the celebration of the unfettered market has gained considerable momentum. There has been a sustained attack on collective institutions—on government, large bureaucracies of all kinds, worker associations, and communal norms of equity and solidarity—and a growing chorus celebrating competition and its association with individual freedom and choice. This chapter, and indeed the whole volume that it introduces, voices a counterpoint to that chorus.

From a long-term perspective, the recent ascendance of the market is but the latest phase in a long-running tug-of-war of competing ideologies. At least since Adam Smith praise for the dynamism of markets has oscillated with anxiety about the decline of community. And indeed, the communal side continues to be heard today: the appeal of communitarianism and the power of fundamentalist and values-based movements are testimony to the continuing widespread concern that alienation has been the dark corollary of market individualism.

This debate has focused not only on society as a whole, but also on the corporate arena, which is the center of our analysis here. Recent years have witnessed a clear challenge to corporate community and its commitments to lifetime employment. Widespread attempts to shake up bureaucratic hierarchies have been buttressed by the ideology of individualistic 'free agency.' Concurrently, on the other side of the debate, we have also heard much about the need for more collaboration and teamwork, and about the dangers of losing employees' loyalty and commitment.

A basic tension marks these developments: on the one hand, a desire for progress, choice, and dynamic change; on the other, a desire for community and stability of values. We argue that it is the inability to conceptualize 'post-modern' types of community that has led many observers into a nostalgia—sometimes enthusiastic, sometimes uncomfortable—for vanishing forms of social relationships.

The academic literature has struggled to deal effectively with these tensions. Analyses based on economics have been hamstrung by an a priori commitment to self-interest as the only salient motive of human action and exchange as the only bond. Some economists have sought to incorporate power and authority, yielding a literature on markets versus hierarchies; but efforts to conceptualize trust and solidarity bonds have been rare and clumsy. Sociologists, meanwhile, have paid far more attention to the strains on community—indeed, this trope might be considered constitutive of sociology as a field—but without achieving anything close to consensus.

Broadly speaking, sociological views have been divided into three camps. A first camp develops a pessimistic critique of capitalist growth and of modernization more generally as leading to the progressive erosion of community—a 'tragic' vision we can trace back to Weber and Tönnies, and extending forward to Putnam, Sennet, and others. A second camp, drawing from conservative theorists like Tocqueville, seeks hope in a revival of pre-modern community through support for the remnants that have survived the onslaught of the market—traditional forms such as family, friendship networks, church groups. Both these camps encounter sharp criticism and diffuse discomfort, in particular because they assume—to mourn or to promote—a form of community that stifles individual autonomy and development.[1]

A third camp, however, has explored the possibility that a new and possibly higher form of community might emerge, offering a framework for trust in dynamic and diverse relationships, and reconciling greater degrees of both solidarity and autonomy. These ideas have for the most part remained philosophical and abstract.[2] A few have attempted to find empirical grounding for the new form of community in relatively peripheral social forms such as science and (to a lesser extent) the professions.

The present essay lies within this third camp. We argue that capitalist development does indeed corrode traditional forms of community, but also that the demand for complex, knowledge-based and solutions-oriented production in the modern capitalist economy has stimulated significant progress towards a new form of community. Rather than focusing on institutions like science and the professions, we direct attention to the very center of capitalist society—the structure of large corporations and the nature of inter-firm relations. We argue that in the last few decades, a form of community—we call it *collaborative community*—has emerged that points the way beyond the classic antinomy of individual vs. collective, of tradition vs. freedom, of *Gemeinschaft* vs. *Gesellschaft*, and begins to embody the intuition behind Durkheim's notion of 'organic solidarity.'

Such a diagnosis may appear perverse, given the rise of market-oriented neoliberalism and the associated phenomena of outsourcing and employment insecurity. We do not deny the importance of these counter-tendencies; but we argue that capitalism and its concomitant pressures for competitive advantage and profit *simultaneously* stimulate progress toward collaborative community *and* retard and distort this progress. The result, we suggest, is a zigzag path, jerky and halting, but pointing nevertheless over the longer term towards the emergence of the new form of community as an increasingly central principle of social organization. This is not an ineluctable trend, however: it has resulted from myriad human choices and social struggles that have favored social advance over narrow interests of elite groups.

Community: beyond *Gemeinschaft* and *Gesellschaft*

The classical formulation and its limits

Community is essential to the human condition. Fundamentally, people need to be able to rely on others. *Trust* is a willingness to act on the basis of such reliance. *Community* is the set of institutions that give a basis for this confidence, by establishing and enforcing mutual expectations—so that when I do something I have some idea of how you are likely to react, and how it will all come out.

A 'thick' kind of trust, in which members have a high degree of confidence in their expectations of others' behaviors, is found in very structured and stable communities with powerful mechanisms of socialization. In the sociological tradition such community has been known since Tönnies's seminal writings as *Gemeinschaft*. 'Thin' trust relies on relatively few rules and only generic assumptions about others—mostly that others will act rationally in their own self-interest; this is the basis of trust in what Tönnies called *Gesellschaft*—often translated as business but also denoting association.

Sociologists have long postulated that *Gesellschaft* is too weak to sustain real human relations and moral order. Many writers have argued that capitalism has undermined the *Gemeinschaft* conditions for true community, provoking fear that such a shift will destroy the order that is the basis of cultural meaning, personal integrity, and social peace. In this view, the dominance of the market and the emergence of an order based entirely on rational self-interest produces anomie (Durkheim 1893/1984), alienation (Marx 1844/1975), lack of civic involvement (Putnam 2000), personal instability (Fromm 1973), corrosion of character (Sennett 1998), moral disorientation, and a host of other evils:

> Things fall apart, the center cannot hold
> Mere anarchy is loosed upon the world ... [3]

Marx was among the early writers to argue that capitalism systematically destroys the affective links of pre-capitalist communities, leaving only relations of naked self-interest. At the end of the nineteenth century Max Weber expressed the fear that the 'iron cage' of rationality would imprison mankind by its instrumental efficiency, driving out all communal forms of organization. Fifty years later David Riesman's *Lonely Crowd* touched a nerve among many feeling the anomie of our cities and enterprises. The economist Joseph Schumpeter formulated a similarly gloomy assessment: capitalism, he argued, both lives off and destroys the remnants of community derived from pre-capitalist societies, and therefore inevitably undermines the conditions for its own survival.[4]

The second, more traditionalist, camp in sociology has sought to moderate this critique by pointing to the survival of traditional *Gemeinschaft* ties at the interstices of modern *Gesellschaft*. Family, local community, voluntary associations, and churches still bring people together. However, the evidence is hard to ignore that over the past century—to borrow Habermas's formulation—such 'lifeworld' spaces have been progressively 'colonized' by the 'system world' of business and government.

More fundamentally, both the pessimistic and traditionalistic discourses suffer a fatal flaw: analysis of *real* communities of the kind to which they refer often reveals communities as restrictive, oppressive to minorities, hierarchical, and resistant to change. Such community is not only inimical to the freedoms we moderns take for granted, but would also be ineffective as a matrix for dynamic, flexible, economic development. The positive side of the rise of modern society and the market economy was the *liberation* of the individual from the dead weight of custom and narrow loyalties. Marx and Engels were eloquent in the Communist Manifesto:

In place of the old local and national seclusion and self-sufficiency, we have inter-course in every direction, universal interdependence. ... National one-sidedness and narrow-mindedness become more and more impossible ... The bourgeoisie ... has rescued a considerable part of the population from the idiocy of rural life.[5]

While the rise of capitalism lent enormous momentum to it, the impetus for escape from traditional communities began in many spheres even before the consolidation of the new mode of production, and before Hobbes and Smith provided a theoretical framework for it. In commerce, the escape from *Gemeinschaft* was manifest in the legitimization of usury and the growth of entrepreneurialism in Italy and the Low Countries; in art, in the development of ideas of individual genius superseding traditional themes and motifs; in religion, in the sudden eruption of Protestant challenges, based on individual faith, to the Catholic Church's control of dogma; in politics, in the development of national identities distinct from the prior religious and limited local communities. The exhilaration of breaking free is one of the central emotional tones of history since the Renaissance.[6]

Thus modern society is caught in a contradictory self-representation—an antinomy of individualism and community, with neither side sufficient to ground relations in an increasingly interdependent and dynamic society. The thick forms of *Gemeinschaft* trust are comforting but stifling; the thin forms of *Gesellschaft* trust are liberating but alienating; and their combin-ation is unstable, with the latter progressively corroding the former.

History, however, does not pose problems it cannot solve.[7] We submit that the resolution of this conundrum is taking shape 'below the radar' of most social analysts, in the corporate sphere. We argue that within and between firms, community has been evolving towards a new form we call *collaborative*—one that can be interpreted as a dialectical synthesis of the traditional opposites *Gemeinschaft* and *Gesellschaft*.[8]

Three organizing principles and three forms of community

Abstractly speaking, we can identify three primary principles of social organization.[9] *Hierarchy* uses authority to create and coordinate a horizon-tal and vertical division of labor—a bureaucracy in Weber's ideal-type form. *Market* relies on the price mechanism to coordinate competing and anonymous suppliers and buyers. *Community* relies on shared values and norms.[10] Table 1.1 summarizes the key contrasts.

Real collectivities embody variable mixes of these principles. Moreover, real collectivities may best be mapped using the principles as three orthog-onal dimensions rather than as three apexes of a two-dimensional triangle:

Table 1.1. Three Principles of Social Organization

	Hierarchy	Market	Community
Coordinating mechanism	Authority	Price	Trust
Primary benefits	Control	Flexibility	Generation and sharing of knowledge
Resources produced	Organizational capital	Economic capital	Social capital
Fits tasks that are	Dependent	Independent	Interdependent

the fact that one principle is a powerful factor shaping a particular collectivity does not preclude one or both of the other principles from also being powerful factors. However neither hierarchy nor market can actually function without at least some underpinning of community. Neither can function without a stable set of expectations shared by its members—that, for example, contracts will be honored and doing one's duties will be rewarded.

The form of community differs depending on its relation to the other two principles of social organization. When the dominant principle of social organization is hierarchy, community takes the form of *Gemeinschaft*. When the dominant principle shifts to market, community mutates from *Gemeinschaft* into *Gesellschaft*. We postulate that when community itself becomes the dominant organizing principle, it will take a form quite different from either *Gemeinschaft* or *Gesellschaft*.

Aspects of this new form of community can be discerned in the organization of science and the professions. Today, we argue, this new form is also emerging in the heart of the corporate realm. To summarize the argument below, we can contrast the new form of community with the two earlier ones on three fundamental dimensions:

1. *Values*: Community is first a set of value orientations shared (more or less) by all members of a group. Everyone can assume that the others will orient to those values and can therefore predict their actions and responses. This forms the basis for trust among individuals and order in social interaction. Collaborative community is distinctive in its reliance on value-rationality—participants coordinate their activity through their commitment to common, ultimate goals. Its highest value is *interdependent contribution*, as distinct from loyalty or individual integrity.
2. *Organization*: Community is also a social structure, specifying the boundaries of reference groups, the appropriate forms of authority, and the division of labor. Collaborative community is distinctive in

social structures that support *interdependent process management* through formal and informal social structures.

3. *Identity*: Community cannot be effective as an organizing principle if it is merely an external constraint on people or a socially sanctioned set of values: it must become internalized in personalities and motivational systems. Collaborative community is distinctive especially in its reliance on interactive social character and *interdependent self-construals*: rather than orienting to a single source of morality and authority, the personality must reconcile multiple conflicting identities and construct a sense of wholeness from competing attachments and interactions.[11]

Table 1.2 summarizes the argument that we lay out in the subsequent subsections.

Table 1.2. Three Forms of Community

	Gemeinschaft community in the shadow of hierarchy	*Gesellschaft* community in the shadow of market	*Collaborative* community as the dominant principle
Values	*Trust based on*: • loyalty • honor • duty • status deference	• integrity • competence • conscientiousness • integrity	• contribution • concern • honesty, • collegiality
	Legitimate authority based on: • tradition or charisma	• rational-legal justifications	• value-rationality
	Values: • collectivism	• consistent rational individualism	• simultaneously high collectivism and individualism
	Orientation: • particularism	• universalism	• simultaneously high particularism and universalism
Organization	• mechanical division of labor coordinated by common norms	• organic division of labor coordinated by price and/or authority	• organic division of labor coordinated by conscious collaboration
	• organization through vertical dependence	• organization through horizontal independence	• enabling (horizontal and vertical) interdependence
	• tie structure is local, closed	• global, open	• 'glocalization'
Identities	• status-dependent	• independent	• interdependent • self-construal, interactive • social character

Gemeinschaft: *traditional community*

In its traditional (*Gemeinschaft*) form, community itself had a sacred quality. As Tönnies (1887) argued, *Gemeinschaft* had a hierarchical structure, in which individuals and subunits are related in clear chains of subordination to the superordinate leader whose authority derives from tradition or charisma (per Weber).[12] The core values are therefore those of loyalty and deference.

In such a social structure, horizontal relations, such as the relations of husband and wife, of doctor and patient, even of merchant and client, are defined indirectly, in terms of status obligations and their 'fit' within the larger system rather than through direct interaction or negotiation. In effect, the proper relationship between two parties can be read directly from their respective social roles. Challenges to status or violations of obligations of deference are a deeply feared threat to order. Shakespeare expressed this world view with customary power, frequently linking disruptions of the status order—violations of 'degree'—not only to social but even to cosmic chaos:

> Take but degree away, untune that string,
> And, hark, what discord follows!
> What plagues and what portents! what mutiny!
> What raging of the sea! shaking of earth!
> Commotion in the winds! frights, changes, horrors ...[13]

The bedrock of trust in the traditional order is honor, or duty—the fulfillment of a status role defined by the social order. Those who are honorable, in other words, are trustworthy. A large system of sanctions, especially the force of reputation in the community, centers on the performance of these obligations.

This form of community is necessarily closed and particularistic, and this closure is reflected in the nature of social identities. Identities under *Gemeinschaft* typically trace a sharp differentiation between insiders and outsiders. They are conformist, because conformity defines insider status. They have hierarchy built in. Friendships and romantic relationships do exist in traditional societies, but if they cross the boundaries of the status system they are seen as grave threats to order.

Clearly such a form of community leaves little room for modern markets, let alone systematic innovation. Under *Gemeinschaft* conditions, these processes must be organized informally and in the interstices of the system.

Gesellschaft *and the limits of association*

The development of individualism was an upheaval that shook apart the traditional order. It 'took degree away,' freeing people from the strictures of status and therefore destroying the basis of trust in the status order. In its place it put as the basis of trust the *integrity* of the individual; trust became based on the consistency—the rational instrumental consistency —of action. It led to the necessity of forming an independently coherent sense of the self, distinct from social roles and institutions.

One core insight in both Weber and Durkheim is that the move to individualism did not mean the elimination of the shared moral beliefs, or even a relaxation of them. It involved rather the development of a new *content* to the moral order. Both associated this change with Protestantism, which created a moral imperative for individualism. Both stressed that individualism in this sense was not a matter of the expression of an essential 'human nature,' but quite the contrary, a socially determined obligation which created heavy burdens on personality: an *obligation* to be rational, self-interested, and consistent. It is in this sense that *Gesellschaft* is not the negation of community but a form of it. The individualism in Protestantism produced enormous pressures for the rationalization of motivation and the acceptance of individual responsibility, and (as Durkheim noted) the overload could easily lead to pathologies such as suicide.

On the one hand, this value system—of which Protestantism is only one manifestation—supported and framed a market economy by freeing action from the constraints of status and by requiring a consistent moral person who can be responsible for promises and contracts.[14] On the other hand, the second insight we take from Durkheim and Weber, as well as from Marx and other critics of modernity, is that this modern value is inherently incomplete and contradictory because it disconnects values from relationships. It breaks the communal ties of traditional society by separating people from each other. It does not provide a framework for lateral relationships of colleagueship and collaboration; indeed, it radically separates individuals from each other and connects them (in the Protestant version) directly to God or (in secular versions) to their own private grounding of values. Values aside from individualism itself thus become personal and private rather than ways of connecting to others.

Gesellschaft is thus inevitably associated with subjective alienation. The communal dimension cannot be removed from human relationships without a loss of sense of self and of meaning. It is not surprising, then, that traditional community has continued to flourish in the interstices of the larger, cooler set of *Gesellschaft* associations, nor surprising that the two remain in tension. National and local communities draw people together, but they also limit the scope of markets and are essentially contradictory to the ethic of individualism.

The main solution in modern times has been to wall off community, especially the family, in a 'private' sphere, where it can provide comfort and solidarity without threatening the larger system.[15] But this way of dealing with social interaction—through the separation of public from private and the reliance on informal links for community—is adequate only when the density of interaction is low enough that people can distinguish a large realm in which their actions do not affect others, and when there is no need for intensive collaboration. As these conditions change—as the intensity of interdependence and the needs for collaborative effort increase—the separation breaks down. Then there is a need for a socially ordered form of lateral, cooperative relationships. That change has been visible both at the societal level and within the economic sphere.

The emergence of collaborative community

Neither the traditional nor modern forms of community are adequate for groups that seek high levels of adaptiveness and complex interdependence. In such situations trust is particularly *important*, because people depend a great deal on others whose skills and expertise they cannot check; autonomy and 'rugged individualism' give way to an increasingly dense web of interdependence, and there is a growing need for stable cooperative relations among highly differentiated actors. But in such situations trust is also particularly *difficult* to achieve, because it can no longer be based on tradition or on personal acquaintance and experience.[16] We believe that close scrutiny of contemporary firms reveals the emergence of a new type of community that can square this circle.

Collaborative community forms when people work together to create shared value. This increasingly characterizes societies in which the generation of knowledge, often involving many specialists, has become central to economic production. In this it is fundamentally unlike the two forms we have described above: the traditional, where values are assumed to be eternally embodied in the existing community, without the need for shared 'work' to achieve them; and the modern, where values are removed from the public realm and left to individuals, with community being merely a place where individuals can pursue their own ends by participating in a shared game. In a collaborative community, values are not individual beliefs, but the object of shared activity; they have to be discussed and understood in similar ways by everyone. The basis of trust is the degree to which members of the community believe that others have contributions to make towards this shared creation.[17] Adler's chapter invokes this idea under the label 'object': a collaborative community emerges when a collectivity engages cooperative, interdependent activity towards a common object.

The institutions of collaborative community are centered on defining the core purposes and regulating interactions so that the right people can contribute at the right time to advance the process of value-creation. In a dynamic environment purpose must be distinguished from eternal 'values,' which are timeless statements of what the group *is*. Purpose is a relatively pragmatic view of what the group is trying to achieve, given the environmental challenges, in the foreseeable future. Agreement on purpose or strategy is crucial: members of the community need to both understand it in depth and be committed to its achievement. This means that rather than being left to a small cadre of leaders, the purpose must become a matter for widespread discussion. One can see this result clearly in corporations: in the last few decades strategy has often moved from a confidential preserve of top management to a key desideratum for all employees.

When value and purpose are discussed, they may also be contested. This is possibly the most difficult aspect of the difficult move to collaboration: finding ways to debate core orientations while still working together. Whereas in the *Gesellschaft* community working together is a more or less accidental by-product of an interplay of individual interests—coordination achieved by an invisible hand of the market or by a nexus of employment contracts—in the collaborative community it involves a deliberate and deliberated commitment to shared ends. But deliberation at this level is hard to manage. Even in voluntary organizations, it can easily slide into polarization or factionalism which shuts off discussion.

Moreover, in the capitalist firm, there are deep structural challenges to collaborative community. First, the power asymmetry between managers and employees generates anxiety, deference, and resentment. Second, the external goals of the firm are deeply contradictory—to produce useful products and services ('use-value' in the parlance of classical political economy) and to create monetary profit ('exchange-value'). In capitalist firms, collective purpose is therefore contradictory in its very nature. Nevertheless, there has been a slow elaboration of mechanisms for deliberation—forums in which employees are invited to 'push back' against their superiors, and where the contradictory nature of the firms' goals is acknowledged and confronted.

Theoretical antecedents

Several writers have sought to define forms of community that somehow squared the circle of solidarity and flexibility, community and autonomy. In recent decades these themes have been central to the political debate in the United States and to academic debates among communitarians, Rawlsians, traditionalists, and other strands of social and ethical theory. Despite their differences, they have all been searching for a kind of community that would provide stability of expectations, security of relationships, safety against opportunism, without the conformism, insularity, status oppression, and other problematic characteristics of traditional communities—one that would reconcile freedom with constraint, individualism with collectivism.

The ones who have come closest to the cooperative form have been those who have focused on discourse and deliberation. The most articulate among them is probably Jürgen Habermas, who has attempted to characterize this form of legitimization in terms of the 'ideal speech situation.'[18] His argument is that it is possible, indeed necessary, to organize society as a genuine dialogue among differentiated groups.

These writers have had to fight strong pessimistic currents from both the left and the right. 'Realists' in both camps believe that ideals of participation and cooperation ignore the reality of power and conflict. Max Weber, the great theorist of power, is best known for his pessimism about the 'iron cage' of bureaucratic domination, which, he said, 'is superior to every form of mass and even of "communal" action. And where the bureaucratization of administration has been completely carried through, a form of power relation is established that is practically unshatterable.'[19] And for most of the nineteenth and twentieth centuries Weber seemed to be right: large formal organizations expanded at the expense of small organizations and informal associations.

Yet even in that period some effective institutions were based on different principles. In particular, scientific and professional communities have long been characterized by a normative commitment to values (e.g. health, scientific progress) and these commitments have enabled these relatively large collectivities to govern themselves. Their norms have been radically different from the rational individualism of modern society as a whole. They have emphasized obligations of sharing, of mutual help, of focus on collective goals and purposes. They have developed elaborate mechanisms regulating horizontal relations, including peer review and accountability, that have been based on distinctive occupational identities.

Weber noted the distinctiveness of science and the professions and suggested that they were governed by 'value rationality' (*Wertrationalität*), that is, by a shared belief in the values and purposes of a group. Value-rationality is expressed in collegial forms of decision making: it accords no legitimacy to commands as such, since each member is assumed to be equal in their exclusive orientation to the 'absolute value' to which they are all devoted.[20]

But Weber remained skeptical that value-rationality could support a robust form of organization.[21] Like many other commentators, he believed that a reliable administration requires a more solid foundation— that subordinates accept the legitimacy of orders from authorized superiors. Collegiality, he argued, is viable only within small or loosely structured groups: it is difficult to see how it can serve as a principle of organization in large and disciplined bodies.

At about the same time, Emile Durkheim was also exploring the possibility of collegial relations with his concept of 'organic solidarity.' Durkheim argued that the hugely complex division of labor wrought by capitalist development implied an 'organic' form of solidarity based on the interdependence of specialized roles. The web of interdependence in organic solidarity enabled people to build trust and to bank on the future notwithstanding the absence of the traditional values and ordered statuses of pre-capitalist societies. But Durkheim struggled to understand how such a community could keep from flying apart into the fragmented state of 'anomie.' His best answer, like Weber's, focused on occupational groupings or professions,[22] but it remained sketchily developed and problematic.[23]

Our thesis is that Weber and Durkheim were ahead of their time in these explorations—that the forms of collaboration that they turned to for models were as yet underdeveloped for the task of resolving the major problem of modern community. It is only in recent decades that community based on organic solidarity and value-rationality has become a practical economic imperative. Today, as corporations struggle to adapt to an increasingly knowledge-intensive world, they have begun to develop forms of organization that reflect these principles. Corporations have a growing practical need for a new kind of community and trust that breaks the *Gemeinschaft/Gesellschaft* antinomy, and they have made significant—though still far from complete—progress in achieving it. By observing this progress we can flesh out the abstractions that Weber and Durkheim sketched, and begin to build a more complete sense of how such an order might develop the strength and solidity to overcome the iron cage of bureaucracy.

Thus we revive the Weberian and Durkheimian analysis to help us understand how people can organize themselves and build needed levels of trust in a society that is increasingly interdependent and knowledge intensive. Value-rationality is the core value base, and organic solidarity the core organizing principle, of the emerging collaborative community.[24]

Community and the firm

Community in the shadow of hierarchy

The pre-industrial era—that is, prior to the growth of large corporations in the late nineteenth century—was marked by the rapid growth of market relationships and individual entrepreneurship. It was nevertheless already clear that to the extent that economic activity involved working together within or across firms, some form of relational connection other than markets was needed. In this period, relations within firms were often coordinated by the traditional mechanisms of craft guilds, with their long-standing systems of deference and status. Inside contracting often leveraged similarly traditional family ties. Where workers lacked craft traditions and family ties, where work was more 'proletarianized,' managers often instituted some form of paternalistic 'welfare' provisions. These modeled the firm on the pattern of the family. Between firms, relational community was typically strong because business ties were deeply embedded within traditional, spatially bound, communities.

Such forms of community, however, depended essentially on face-to-face relationships and provided little support for cooperation on a large scale. As the economy developed to a point where production and distribution could be sustained on a mass basis, these clusters of small firms were progressively supplanted by large corporations built on principles of rational bureaucracy, modern individualism, and *Gesellschaft* association. Rational bureaucracy too, however, proved insufficient. Purely bureaucratic structures, even when buttressed by a strong ethos of professionalism in workplace relations, often led to rigidity, unresponsiveness, and conflict.[25] Corporate managers thus recognized fairly early that they needed some form of trust and active, intentional collaboration—that is, some form of community.

Confronted with the inadequacy of the purely formal rationality of *Gesellschaft*, corporate managers continued to reach backward for remedies, and tried to recreate elements of *Gemeinschaft* in the form of a loyalty-based ethos. Whereas the earlier generation of 'welfare' provisions typically focused on the non-work lives of workers—sickness and death provisions, social activities, libraries, etc.—a new generation of 'human relations' proponents attempted to restore community to the workplace relations between workers and managers. Chester Barnard, whose experience as president of New Jersey Bell gave him unusually practical insight, emphasized the responsibility of the executive in creating loyalty through communication and leadership: 'The most important single contribution required of the executive, certainly the most universal qualification, is loyalty, domination by the organization personality.'[26] The Human Relations stream of research and practice pursued the deliberate development of loyalty-based corporate community.[27]

By the 1940s, leading corporations—partly under the pressure of sustained conflict and resistance to the new forms of management from workers and unions, partly under the influence of personnel management ideas inherited from both scientific management and human relations schools of thought—had developed an elaborate form of community that enabled them to avoid some of the worst excesses of purely rational bureaucracy. This mix of hierarchy and community was often embodied in the institution of the 'internal labor market.'[28] As a structural dimension of community, internal labor markets represented a commitment to filling higher-level positions by promotion from within. They thus increased the employee's economic dependence on the firm. The value counterpart to this structure was loyalty: employees owed a duty to do their best for their corporations and to obey orders, and the corporations had a reciprocal duty to offer care and lifetime security to those who did their best to fulfill these obligations. These values were preached by leaders, embodied in daily expectations, and supported by mechanisms of self-interest such as company-dependent pension plans and a strong link between pay and seniority. Many successful large companies in the decades from 1940 to 1980—whether in America, Europe, or Japan; whether in the auto industry, steel, or telecommunications—embraced the community of loyalty, creating a hybrid structure that could be described as a 'paternalist bureaucracy.'[29]

This loyalty-based community was powerful because it allowed managers to elicit commitments beyond individual interests and beyond the boundaries of rational authority. However it was not modern, and certainly not rational, but rather *traditional* in its nature, structured around similarities and vertical relations of deference.

The content of the traditional ethic of large bureaucratic firms can be summarized under a set of interrelated obligations: respecting the structure, conscientiousness in performance, and loyalty:

- Respecting the structure means observing hierarchical distinctions: don't skip levels, don't take responsibility beyond your mandate. It also has a correlative set of duties to respect others' turf, the logic being that everyone is supposed to be responsible for his or her own domain. Thus the norms include not challenging others on their own turf; always trying to figure out whose responsibility a problem is and everyone else getting out of the way; and in general an avoidance of conflict. Any type of conflict involves some breakdown in the structure and should simply be referred to the appropriate higher level for resolution.

- Conscientiousness in performance means (as Merton 1940 put it) 'devotion to one's duties, a keen sense of the limitations of one's authority and competence, and methodical performance of routine activities'—a secularized version of the Protestant notion of calling. Some typical correlatives include avoidance of risk (anything outside the routine should be referred to higher levels) and a focus on following the rules and procedures rather than concern about the results—the latter being the responsibility of the higher-ups who make the rules.

- Loyalty, as discussed above, centers on deference to authority and status order. A major correlative is conformity (fitting within the dominant value pattern). Rosabeth Kanter's classic study of IBM in its heyday used the striking phrase 'homosocial reproduction' to explain the basis of trust: that is, within this order it was important to be seen as similar to others in order to be trusted. This is precisely the basis of traditional loyalty, as discussed earlier. The Human Relations writers, such as Mayo, used the medieval community as their reference point, and observers of corporate cultures have frequently used the term 'feudal' in their descriptions,[30] primarily because of this element of deference, dependence, and loyalty.

These norms are interrelated because they all support a structure of nested hierarchy with closely defined job responsibilities, which is the core of bureaucracy. Such an organization is strong in its vertical coordination, but weak in lateral, horizontal coordination. This latter was assured mainly by the fabric of the 'informal' organization.[31] The stability of the large, bureaucratic corporation certainly allowed for the formation of these informal relations, but since these relations were private and invisible to the formal control structures, they only sometimes supported these latter structures, and could equally work at cross-purposes to them.

The bureaucratic character type, as elaborated by Merton and others, has a strongly individualist side—one that takes great pride in doing a defined job well, that seeks a sphere of autonomy and a clear objective, and wants to be held accountable as an individual for meeting that objective. Success from this viewpoint is marked by the solidification of organizational position, because that means that people leave you alone and do not challenge your competence in your sphere. This kind of character expresses respect for peers by leaving them their own sphere of autonomy, by not criticizing or 'second-guessing' them. But in practice corporate employees cannot operate as individualistic monads. They are part of a collective effort and a hierarchical social order, which means that the craftlike motivation to do a job is not sufficient. Thus alongside the strongly individualistic and craftsmanlike self there is a simultaneous sense of self as subsumed under the corporate community. It is this side that is stressed by writers like Mills, Kanter, and Jackall: all these authors have found that members of *Gemeinschaft*-inflected bureaucratic hierarchies in fact behave in an extremely conformist way, 'looking up and looking around' (in Jackall's phrase) for signals about what is acceptable, avoiding conflict and risk, accepting with few questions the moral authority of their superiors.[32]

This systematic conflict between individualist self-images and subordinated identities is very apparent in water-cooler conversations. Among their peers people will often claim to act with total integrity and fearlessness towards their bosses—'I'm the kind of person who isn't afraid to tell the truth'; but when given the opportunity to actually voice criticisms through open doors or feedback forums or other mechanisms that trumpet 'empowerment,' very few will act out their individualist dreams.

The growing need for community in industry

Given the limitations of loyalty and conscientiousness as a basis for community, some suggest that the way forward for corporate organization is simply to cast aside all vestiges of community and allow the market to assert more thorough control, perhaps complemented by rational bureaucracy.

However, the requirements of knowledge production increase rather than reduce the need for community and trust; the pure market path is even less viable than a combination of market and hierarchy.

In the industrial era the dominant companies were those that could organize scale and scope, producing in high volume reliably and efficiently, distributing to large enough markets to reduce unit costs. The organization of production in this economy required that large numbers of people perform consistently on defined tasks. Though things never became completely routinized, there was relatively little need for innovation and adaptation. When market demands moved out of sync with organizational systems, companies reorganized, changing tasks and responsibilities within a continuing bureaucratic frame. Such reorganizations happened infrequently, with long stretches of stability in between.

Since the 1970s two fundamental and interconnected developments have made this way of organizing inadequate: the growth of knowledge and the increased sophistication of consumers.

KNOWLEDGE

In the most economically advanced countries, the 'mysteries' of effective commodity production have become common knowledge; they are now merely tickets for entry rather than keys to winning in competition. In place of strategies of scale and scope, companies are looking increasingly to draw value from knowledge, in the form of product and process innovation and customer responsiveness. They draw on the abilities of a more-educated and more-skilled workforce,[33] and they cater to the needs of a sophisticated consumer base that already owns most basic commodities and increasingly seeks novelty and customization. Knowledge has moved to the center as margins have fallen in commodity production, as the educational levels of the workforce have risen, and as scientific and technical knowledge has accelerated.[34]

The large corporation combining rational bureaucracy and loyalty-based community meets its limits in organizing the production of knowledge. Bureaucracy, as has been frequently documented, is very effective at organizing routinized production, but it does very poorly at these complex interactive tasks involving responsiveness and innovation.[35] Under bureaucracy, knowledge is treated as a scarce resource and is therefore concentrated, along with the corresponding decision rights, in specialized functional units and at higher levels of the organization. However, in organizations that are competing primarily on their ability to respond and innovate, knowledge from all parts of the organization is crucial to success, and often subordinates know more than their superiors. Innovation and responsiveness cannot be rigorously preprogrammed, and the creative collaboration they require cannot be simply commanded. The vertical differentiation of bureaucracy is effective for routine tasks, facilitating downward communication of explicit knowledge and commands, but less effective when tasks are non-routine, since lower levels lack both the knowledge needed to create new knowledge and the incentives to transmit new ideas upward.

Many economists argue that, given these difficulties, bureaucracies should be replaced by markets. But this argument encounters a fundamental difficulty: a substantial body of modern economic theory has shown that the market mechanism fails to optimize the production and distribution of knowledge.[36] Knowledge is a 'public good'; that is, like radio transmission, its availability to one consumer is not diminished by its use by another. With knowledge, as with other public goods, reliance on the market/price mechanism forces a trade-off between production and distribution. On the one hand, production of new knowledge would be optimized by establishing strong intellectual property rights that create incentives to generate knowledge. On the other hand, not only are such rights difficult to enforce, but, more fundamentally, they block socially optimal distribution. Distribution of knowledge would be optimized by allowing free access because the marginal cost of supplying another consumer with the same knowledge is close to zero. Economists have established that neither markets nor hierarchies (in the form of central planning) nor any intermediate forms (such as regulated markets and market socialism) can simultaneously optimize incentives to produce knowledge and to disseminate it.[37] The same dilemma characterizes options for knowledge management within firms: neither market-based transfer pricing nor bureaucratic fiat nor any combination of the two suffices in the face of current technological and competitive challenges.

In response to the difficulty posed by the public goods characteristics of knowledge, much recent economics scholarship has argued for the acceptance of a second-best solution. In the absence of other alternatives, pure or mixed markets and hierarchies are seen as the best feasible way of organizing production.[38] This resignation is, however, not warranted. Hierarchy and market are not the only possible organizational forms, and for this purpose they are not the best ones. Community is an alternative form of coordination—one that is essential to knowledge creation.

Compared to hierarchy and market, community makes possible an enlarged scope of simultaneous knowledge generation and sharing.

Community can dramatically reduce both transaction costs—replacing contracts with handshakes—and agency risks—replacing the fear of shirking and misrepresentation with mutual confidence. Community can thus greatly mitigate the coordination difficulties created by knowledge's public good character. And insofar as knowledge takes a tacit form, community is an essential precondition for effective knowledge transfer.[39]

The key requirement for effectiveness in complex knowledge work is the combining of different kinds of expertise and information in both the generation and dissemination processes. This may involve, for instance, the knowledge of the marketer and that of the product designer, or that of the salesperson and the strategic planner, or that of the assembly-line worker and the mechanical engineer. In each of these cases and a growing number of others, the parties have understandings that could help each other in improving production, but they speak different languages and have different interests. The problem is to bring them together to find the interactions that will benefit each other and the whole.

For this markets and bureaucracies are not the answer. Markets involve an exchange of the products of knowledge: individuals get the output of specific expertise but not the ability to interact with it and improve it. Bureaucracies, similarly, structure interactions so that each person performs in a box and 'throws' the output 'over the wall' to the next; the only combination occurs by moving up the hierarchy, where the superiors are supposed to know everything their subordinates know. This system crumbles when superiors no longer can grasp the full scope of the problems on which their subordinates are working.

Knowledge work thus requires that each party offer something with no guarantee that they will get anything specific in return. They must *trust* that the other has useful competence and knowledge that will help in their joint effort; that the other can understand her own ideas well enough to engage them productively; and that the other is motivated to help her and contribute to the joint effort.

The critical role of trust in knowledge production has long been emphasized in the sociology of science. The advance of the capacity for discovery has gone hand in hand with the advance of mechanisms for the generation of trusting social relations. Here trust is grounded not in informal ties but in formalized systems of assessment and exchange: from making experiments and notes public, in the eighteenth and nineteenth centuries; to systems of peer review; to the regularization of independent replication as a key test of validity; to the use of cross-disciplinary teams; and finally to the recent growth of large-group scientific projects with at times hundreds of authors, in which no single authority can judge and manage the breadth of knowledge involved.[40]

Similarly, corporations are finding that to produce the complex forms of knowledge increasingly needed for economic growth—bringing together the expertise of multiple specialists—they need to move beyond the informal links of the paternalist community. Indeed, they have begun to reinvent many of the same mechanisms discovered by the scientific community over the past two centuries: posting the outcomes of experiments and projects in public form on intranets; developing a form of peer review through multisource feedback mechanisms; organizing in increasingly large and diverse project teams.

'Knowledge' does not refer in this context only to technical or abstract information gained in higher education. Management theorists have often argued that where cost rather than quality or innovation is the dominant concern—that is, in more routine, repetitive operations— front-line employees' knowledge and innovative capacity can safely be sacrificed. Recent research, however, has shown that this was a comforting and comfortable illusion, plausible only when competitive rivalry was muted by monopoly conditions. When more aggressive competitors appear, even routine operations must learn the discipline of continuous improvement—thus learn to mobilize all the organization's available intelligence, not only that of staff experts. Blue- and pink-collar workers also have knowledge that is critical to firm performance. The automobile production process functions better if the knowledge of the line workers is combined with that of the design engineers and quality inspectors: this is the lesson of (among others) NUMMI, which introduced Japanese methods of collaborative quality analysis and learning to General Motors through an alliance with Toyota.[41] The arena of low-end services— McDonald's and Wal-Mart—has often focused on cost control, but there is also evidence here that drawing the front-line workers into participative relations with their bosses and coworkers helps to improve service and create competitive advantage.[42] The challenge at all levels is to combine different forms of knowledge: the relatively concrete, practical experience of those in contact with customers with the technical expertise of engineers and the abstract conceptualizations of strategists and marketers.

CUSTOMER FOCUS AND SOLUTIONS STRATEGIES

A second key factor undermining traditional community, and at the same time raising the stakes for a new level and form of community, is the growing sophistication and complexity of industrial and consumer markets. This is apparent on at least two levels: users in advanced economies have moved beyond the stage of 'black box' consumption and are increasingly looking for customized products that distinguish them from the mass; and business-to-business markets have greatly expanded, and in these markets, the customer is in many cases far more demanding and powerful than an individual consumer.

As a result, many large companies have been pressed to turn outward. In the older mass-production market companies were distinguished primarily by internal capabilities—cost control and efficiency—and much less by their customer or supplier relations. On the customer side, they could generally 'push' products out the door and expect the market to absorb them. As consumers become more demanding, however, the push is less likely to work: it becomes imperative to develop ongoing and deep *understanding* of customers and to gear production around it. On the supplier side, firms are increasingly dependent on a broadening range of specialized suppliers of equipment, materials, subassemblies, and services: firms therefore need to develop a more nuanced understanding of suppliers' capabilities. Thus 'customer focus,' 'outsourcing,' and 'supply chain management' have become widespread mantras for cultural change in large companies—and the magnitude of the challenge is indicated by the difficulty of implementing this way of operating.[43]

Under the pressure of these forces, businesses in an increasing range of industries are seeking to make an even more profound change: moving away from commodity production focused on scale and scope and embarking on strategies which provide customized solutions—tailored mixes of services and products that respond to the changing needs of the customer.[44] IBM is one marquee company that has reorganized itself on this basis, shifting from a focus on selling its products to a focus on providing answers to customer problems—which may mean combining its products with those of other companies, or bringing together resources from different parts of the firm.

This move towards outsourcing and solutions requires the organizational capability to combine resources flexibly both inside and outside the company walls. Hierarchy and market mechanisms do not suffice: market mechanisms do not suffice because the holders of resources tend to compete with each other and to hoard their capabilities rather than sharing them; bureaucratic mechanisms do not suffice because coordination requires moving resource decisions up and down long ladders of authority that end distant from the actual problem. *Gemeinschaft* forms of community are increasingly inadequate too, because they make it very hard to develop trust with an ever-changing array of people outside the enterprise.

Collaborative community, as we have defined it, is powerfully stimulated by the shift to knowledge and solutions strategies.[45] One very clear manifestation is the growth of alliances, which fall in the space between markets and hierarchies: the Citibank Esolutions case which we will describe shortly created an alliance unit specifically to draw in capabilities from outside the bank that could not be found internally.[46]

The inadequacy of the community of loyalty

Although trust and community are, as we have argued, vital to the organization of knowledge work, the form they have traditionally taken in corporations of the industrial era is inadequate to the task. The first and most obvious problem is that the foundation of this kind of collaboration is the expectation of long-term employment. This expectation creates both emotional and self-interested bases for trust: the emotional base is a widely shared sense of loyalty; the self-interested base is that one's dealings with fellow employees are likely to be repeated, so good and bad acts will not be forgotten. But leading companies in the last thirty years have been unable to sustain employment security, even in cases like IBM or Delta Airlines where they tried explicitly to do so, and even in countries like Japan with a very strong tradition of and commitment to employment stability. The dynamism of the economic change has broken through attempts to hold this dike. As the expectation of long-term employment in large companies declines, people's identity and self-interest both have tended to become disconnected from their companies, undermining the traditional foundation of collaboration.

Second, collaborative relations in the loyalty-based system tend to be personal and linked to the hierarchy, rather than cutting across it. This is particularly evident in the management ranks: subordinates develop a loyalty to bosses, who bring their employees with them as they are promoted. Employees feel a solidarity with others in their functional group, tied to disdain for and rivalry with other groups. This structure of the informal organization reinforces the near-universal phenomenon of 'empire building,' and it strengthens rather than weakens the barriers between functions and divisions. Collaborative relationships across boundaries, where they emerge, are largely serendipitous rather than based on organizational needs. That is, someone in production may have a friend in marketing, which might lead to some useful exchanges of information;

but this relationship is not generated by the organization itself. It is likely to result from their having attended a training program together, or having children at the same school, or being members of the same club. The probability that the *right* connections (from the organizational perspective) will be made is low.[47]

Third, while the paternalist community distributes resources in a slightly more fluid way than that prescribed by pure rational bureaucracy, it is not yet fluid enough. The trust based on the community of loyalty allows middle managers and line workers often to barter exchanges without reference to collective goals, as a way of avoiding cumbersome bureaucratic procedures: these take the form 'I'll do this for you now (for instance, I'll lend you one of my people for a few weeks) in the expectation that you'll do something for me later.' Such bilateral trust can sometimes help organizations deal with crises and small fluctuations of demand, but it is inadequate to the task of organizing new resources reliably and rapidly around complex problems: that would require a more generalized reciprocity.

Finally, the paternalist community reinforces bureaucratic divisions in another important way: it is based heavily on the norm that each person is expert in her own domain, and no one should challenge anyone else's knowledge territory. Thus instead of promoting engaged discourse and working through disagreements, this version of community suppresses conflict and encourages 'getting along'—a conclusion also common to the various observational studies of traditional corporations cited above. In this culture 'teamwork' means not pushing others but rather avoiding fights.

The community of loyalty is particularistic. A knowledge-intensive economy needs a more universalistic orientation. It needs teamwork based on commitment to the principles of teamwork—not based on loyalty to particular others in the team. It needs 'swift trust'[48]—not blind trust based on long-standing familiarity.

THE LIMITS OF LOYALTY: AN ILLUSTRATION

Task forces are a common organizational form of knowledge work, grouping people from across functions, areas, levels, and sometimes companies, focused around solving a problem. In a nutshell, the problem of community in the current business world is this: task forces have become increasingly necessary for competitive success in an increasingly knowledge-intensive economy; but the ties of paternalist community interfere with their functioning rather than facilitating them. Members are more concerned with protecting their own 'turf' than with achieving common objectives. They are both unable and unwilling to enter into real dialogue with other parts of the organization, since a crucial norm within bureaucracies is that each part should 'respect' the expertise of others in their own areas.

Task forces have proliferated enormously in the last few decades. In automobile production, the sequential design process characteristic of bureaucracies has been shown to be vastly inferior in time and quality to 'simultaneous engineering,' in which engineers and production people form task forces. The Total Quality movement consists essentially of forming task forces crossing traditional lines to analyze processes throughout organizations. Almost every one of the movements that has swept through management in recent years, from Re-engineering to Alliance Management, has had task forces at the core, bringing together people with varied experiences and knowledge for direct dialogue outside the normal hierarchy.[49]

At the same time, it has become clear that task forces face enormous resistance from the existing organization because they challenge the basis of loyalty and community in traditional corporations: the supervisor–subordinate unit. In the paternalist structure, as sketched above, this unit formed a tight, mutually protective and interdependent, family-like bond of solidarity (though, like any family, there could often be internal battles and dysfunctions). Employees depended entirely on their supervisor for rewards and advancement as well as for the quality of their daily work life; the supervisor's prestige depended almost entirely on the performance of the subordinates. When someone goes off to work on a task force, the superior loses control, and the task force member is left in limbo in terms of future sponsorship and influence. The only way of sustaining the relationships in which so much has been invested is for the employees to view their task force service in terms of protecting the interests of their 'home' units, and to show their boss that they have protected them; but this, of course, undermines the effectiveness of the task force.

These ways in which knowledge-intensive production puts strain on the structure of paternalist bureaucracy can be seen clearly in a publicly available case, 'Mod IV,' which is typical of many other situations we have observed.[50] The case involves a product development team at Honeywell trying to make a transition from the traditional sequential development to simultaneous cross-functional decision making. The core problems involve a tug-of-war among three perspectives: marketing, which focuses on customers' buying preferences; engineering, which is concerned primarily with quality and functionality of the product; and corporate leadership, focused on improving financial performance in order to fend off the threat of takeovers. Traditionally these differences in perspective and priority had been resolved, as in most bureaucracies, through methods that involved relatively little interaction: the case uses the widely known phrase 'throwing things over the wall.' At Honeywell, marketing was king: it generally started the product development process and laid out specifications from the customer perspective; engineering then tried to design to those and in turn tossed designs to manufacturing; and higher leadership would intervene sporadically using their authority to enforce particular priorities. When on occasion engineering felt that marketing's demands were infeasible, higher authority was again called in to make a binding decision.

But this traditional process was clearly too slow and unresponsive to meet the company's competitive demands. Product development was therefore restructured as a collaborative task force that would bring different viewpoints together simultaneously. The new process fundamentally changed the familiar dynamics. As the participants put it: 'The team system does not allow people to single-mindedly defend the position of their functional area, of what's easiest, or best, or cheapest for their own functional area. It forces people to look at a bigger picture' (Margolis and Donnellon 1990: 4). This shift, however, involved a large number of difficult transformations in attitudes and relations that greatly hampered the process:

- The different groups lacked 'credibility' with each other: engineering was seen by marketing as cavalier about deadlines; marketing was seen by engineering as careless about quality; higher management feared that no one on the team understood the real importance of the project to the business.

- There was a tug-of-war around respect. Marketing's self-image was as the driver and leader of company success. This project, however, had been initiated by engineers, and marketing was being asked to play an equal role in a peer process. They naturally resisted this demotion. Meanwhile, engineering was resentful of their past subordination and convinced that marketing did not take them seriously enough.

- There were no consensual grounds for prioritization. Each player felt its own priorities—quality, customer satisfaction, etc.—were key. Traditionally marketing's priorities were always put first; but when the parties had to work them out in dialogue there was no basis for decision. As a result, as one person put it, '*All* work is high priority.' This created intolerable stress in the system.

- In general, there were no legitimate decision rules. The champion of the project was concerned that if he played his usual role of bureaucratic direction he would stifle initiative, so he tried to be hands-off and leave people a great deal of autonomy. At the same time he fretted that his concerns were not being given sufficient weight. The team members, meanwhile, seemed to be trying to read the tea leaves in interpreting slight signals from their leader, since this would give them at least something solid to hang onto; when they could not, they were unable to work out a way to actually reach decisions in the face of conflicting views about the solution.

These are, in our terms, indicators of the breakdown of the paternalist bureaucracy. Modir's problems are typical, not unusual. Despite the flowering of books trumpeting task forces as the key to success, such teams continue to face many resistances and difficulties in most companies.[51] Our interviews in a wide range of companies have shown that most employees—to this day—resist joining task forces and believe that they are ineffective; and too often even task forces that succeed we disbanded prematurely. Even the most successful cases rarely achieve what the buzzword promises, 'simultaneous' planning; the auto industry's successes have moved only partially away from the linear model, achieving overlapping problem solving but not true concurrent discussion among units.[52] It is these problems that constitute the data for our claim that without a rebuilding of communal institutions, the potential of a knowledge economy cannot be realized.

Yet we must also recognize that the glass is half full: there has been a tremendous amount of social invention facilitating the operation of task forces, from the techniques of brainstorming to the elaborate 'technology' of process management, with 'process champions' and 'process leaders' helping shepherd these new units outside the usual bureaucratic roles. While we cannot confidently cite a single lasting instance of an organization that can reliably produce effective task forces, we do see many partial or temporary or recent examples; the following section discusses one such organization, in order to characterize more specifically the form of community that could support the new knowledge economy.

The emergence of a collaborative corporate community

Our central thesis is that an increasingly knowledge-intensive, solutions-oriented economy requires collaborative community. We are not, however,

Pollyannas: while the capitalist nature of our economy greatly stimulates this trend, it is also evident that market forces have had a destructive effect on many communities in the last twenty years, and that few companies have achieved anything like the sense of coordinated contribution that we describe. Firms are caught between conflicting imperatives: they must both draw people into a common, collaborative endeavor, and simultaneously deal with the fact that this endeavor risks being undermined at any time by the market imperative of profitability or by managerial autocracy. Thus while we begin with a focus on positive developments, we will return to the negative ones below.

The past three decades have witnessed an extraordinary burst of innovation in corporations centered around the notion of teamwork. The word itself has evolved in meaning with these developments of practice. Within the bureaucratic culture, as mentioned earlier, 'teamwork' largely referred to a sociable and informal willingness to help out and a general disposition to avoid conflict. In the 1970s it became focused on small, face-to-face teams working collaboratively rather than merely implementing orders from a boss. In the last decade it has further evolved, to cover complex processes spanning multiple levels, parts of the organization, and indeed firms—centered in middle management, though sometimes involving front-line workers. Such elaborated collaborative processes involve far more than market exchange, but also far more than paternalist deference, and therefore far more than the historically familiar form of community.

It is our contention that these, more advanced forms of corporate organization are tending towards a novel, collaborative form of community more suited to higher levels of interdependence, as distinct from *Gemeinschaft*-like dependence and *Gesellschaft*-like independence. We can characterize the new form under three headings: values, structure, and identity.

These three dimensions are discussed throughout the essays in this volume. Here we will draw our evidence primarily from the Esolutions group in Citibank, which was studied by Charles Heckscher in 2000–2. While we focus on this case to build at least one rich picture, other cases referred to in other chapters are consistent with these points: GHX (Chapter 9), IBM (Chapter 4), Cisco (Chapter 2), Delphi (Chapter 10), the Mayo Clinic (Chapter 6), Veridian (Chapter 12), Nestlé (Chapter 4), various software services companies (Chapter 5), and others.

The Esolutions case was one of a long series of efforts by Citibank over twenty-five years to break the old 'fiefdoms' (as they were referred to internally) of the geographic divisions and create capabilities for cross-unit coordination of experts that would bring the global strengths of the bank to bear on customer solutions. Esolutions, a unit of about 150 people within the cash management division, was established to integrate the bank's customer management and global products on the internet. The unit emerged from a unit with a different name which had been marginal and isolated; it gradually built its connections to the cash management structure; and after three years it was folded more tightly into the larger division while still retaining many of its innovative ways of operating.

The work was organized in a very fast-moving and free-wheeling way. The basic orientation was to listen to customer needs and to try to create technological platforms for meeting them as rapidly and flexibly as possible. Initiatives were not only new forms of information flow to customers; Esolutions also introduced many new products—electronic bill presentment, credit instruments, investment infrastructure—that could be facilitated through an integrated digital interface.

Many of these initiatives were generated by middle managers who pushed them as far as they could, negotiating for resources with their peers and superiors. They therefore frequently needed to create task forces on the fly, bringing in not only other members of their own unit but people from the more established product and marketing divisions. They also needed to create alliances with companies that had capabilities not available within Citibank at all. For example, it would have taken years for the company's in-house computer staff to develop software platforms for the customer interface; but a whole network of small dot-coms had already built major parts of it. Thus representatives of these outside companies had also to be drawn into relationships, and sometimes into ongoing task forces, with people from various parts of Citibank.

THE ETHIC OF INTERDEPENDENT CONTRIBUTION

In collaborative firms or parts of firms an ethic is emerging that contrasts sharply with the loyalty ethic described above. It can be summarized around two elements: contribution to the collective purpose, and contribution to the success of others. We can see it in Esolutions.

- Contribution to the group's purpose contrasts with focus on one's own job responsibilities; it particularly legitimizes going 'above and beyond' the duties of the job—not in terms of effort but in terms of trying to solve a problem regardless of the formal responsibilities involved. But it also implies working with others as part of a group effort, rather than trying to gain total control or responsibility as would be the expectation in a bureaucratic framework. An important corollary is that this value legitimizes the taking of risks, in the sense of assuming responsibilities beyond one's mandate—though not to the exclusion of the need to build teamwork and agreement. Another is it does not require or legitimize deference to higher-status positions, but to the contrary requires the surfacing of conflict and engagement of differences:

[How do you decide whom to trust?] 'I look for someone who would be open to criticism or suggestions as opposed to someone who would get defensive, be scared by people meddling around. Some people are just content with just managing their piece of turf and don't want anyone mucking around in it. In this business a lot of the role is to find out how pieces of the business are run if you don't already know. So it's important that the people you're talking to are open, and you not be overbearing and say 'Here's how you have to do things.'

- Contribution to the success of others, an equally important part of this ethic, implies the need to understand the concrete interests and identities of others in a collaborative relationship, and to help them achieve their own goals as well as those of the group:

Focusing on the alignment and focusing on values—I mean value-generation, not values—is the way you get trust.

It legitimizes attention to factors other than the immediate goal or task; in general, it is more accepting than the loyalty ethic of the validity of competing claims such as family and career.

In other words, the responsibility of the individual extends to helping maintain the strength of the set of collaborative relationships in which he functions, rather than just to fulfilling the obligations of the job. Both of these dimensions imply an obligation to openness and sharing of information, which is treated in the traditional bureaucratic ethic as a preserve of job holders.

The ethic of contribution does not entail long-term loyalty; employees of Esolutions had no expectation of lifetime employment. The focus is on existing projects and relationships, with an assumption that these will evolve and change. It is not founded on the essentially traditional notion that people can be trusted to the extent that they are locked in to the same order; it is founded instead on an assessment of personality attributes, in a modern sense, independent of any particular social order—attributes that include the ability and motivation to help group efforts.[53]

The radical nature of the concept of contribution can be seen in the problems it poses for accountability. Traditional bureaucratic accountability assumes that people are rewarded for performances for which they are clearly responsible, and for which they control the resources. When those conditions are absent, the system of material rewards is thrown into disarray. As a result, in Citi Esolutions and other units moving towards collaboration, people are often driven by the value of contribution even when the reward system does not line up with it:

Q: Does [the head of this task force] have any input into your evaluation?
A: As far as I know probably not.
Q; So why do you spend time on it?
A: Because I think it is an important function that we must fulfill in order to achieve our goal of being leading e-business provider in the world.[54]

The contrasts between this ethic of contribution, or collaborative ethic, and the traditional ethic of loyalty produce mutual scorn and tension. Loyalists see the collaborative ethic, paradoxically enough, as just a version of naked individualism, because it rejects lifelong commitment. They know that the kind of deal that is common within the loyalist community—long-term log-rolling, with a favor now repaid with favors next year—has no value for the ethic of contribution, which values only a mutual helping-out on the current shared purpose. Those who have internalized the collaborative norms, on the other hand, are equally scornful of the loyalists for avoiding risks and conflict, submitting to demands for conformity instead of pushing their distinctive competencies as part of the larger effort, seeking to build their personal empires, and generally failing to take responsibility for outcomes beyond their immediate job responsibilities:

In an alliance, when we talk about sharing value, there's no culture problem. But if you talk about [traditional companies] having an alliance you will have some culture issues: people want to do it internally, people want to build empires and get bigger responsibilities.

Thus the two types look for different signals to see whether others are trustworthy. In traditional bureaucratic organizations people look for cues that someone is a part of the particular shared culture: at IBM for many years it involved the kind of hat you wore, at UPS where you drank your coffee, and so on; clothes and manners are generally highly important indicators of who can be trusted. In those contexts people also shy away immediately from those who come across as 'abrasive' or 'impatient.' Contributors, by contrast, reject this kind of symbolism as completely irrelevant; rather, they see the tendency to be sociable, to talk about relationships rather than the task, as a sign of *un*trustworthiness, because it means that the other will probably fail to take the risks and make the commitments needed for success:

Everyone has their own signals that they look for. If someone comes into the first meeting and starts throwing around names my hackles go up—because that means rather than focusing on capabilities and market proposition they're trying to establish credibility in terms of who they know and who they've talked to. That at the end of the day doesn't move you an inch down the line. People who hedge— who don't share information, who say 'I can't tell you this, or I've got to go talk to somebody'; or sometimes even more damning is when you ask for a piece of information that they should look for every day as part of their performance indicators and they've never looked at it. People who exaggerate—people who have had an elevator discussion with someone and say we're deep in negotiations with him—that kind of exaggeration is pretty easy to spot. It all comes down to what you can contribute, what is your business proposition.

I don't buy into the cultural thing—the hard part is finding the people who do what you need done. At the end of the day it's a matter of what you contribute to them, articulate what the proposition is and what you need from them, and form a one-to-one relationship around the proposition rather than any culture hocus-pocus stuff.

Thus contributors are far more open than loyalists to diversity on gender, race, and other outward presentational signs, because trust in their view of the world does not depend on 'fitting in' or being similar to others; on the contrary, difference is valuable to contribution to the group effort. People look for *distinctive* competencies, and very often look for 'new ways of thinking' to enhance the range of organization capability. Where the traditional organization culture emphasized conformity to values, the collaborative ethic emphasizes 'value-generation, not values.'

At the same time, contributors also reject with equal moral sharpness the free-agent definition of responsibility, which is essentially *Gesellschaft* individualism without a group component. The free-agent ethic values breaking out of the constraints of both community and bureaucracy, sees it as the moral responsibility and right of individuals to push as far as they can and to maximize their individual potential. What is lacking is a con-comitant obligation to the success of the group or the shared task.[55]

The ethic of interdependent contribution as a set of values fits well with the demands of tasks that call for different types of knowledge and competency to be brought to bear in a fluid way. It also adds complexity

to moral choices because it involves two dimensions of responsibility—
'vertically' to the collectivity and 'horizontally' to the success of peers—
and because these responsibilities are not nested in a simple hierarchy,
but can conflict with each other. There is not one boss to please, but an
entire network of collaborating partners. Thus there are very subtle
elements of judgement that cannot be resolved by a rule of thumb as
simple as deference to the boss: how far to take responsibility beyond
one's formal scope when a customer or crisis demands it; how far to
push one's particular knowledge competence when others fail to recognize
it; and so on.

'Contribution,' of course, requires something to contribute *to*: that is,
people must understand the value that they are creating in the same way
and they have to be committed to achieving it. On both scores, collaborative community in the corporate world encounters fundamental
limits: capitalist purpose is, as we indicated above, always dual, and the
commitment of employees to it must by nature be ambivalent as well.
Nevertheless, we observe firms creating novel mechanisms to connect
people far beyond the top management circle to strategic purpose (for an
example, see Chapter 12) and we observe firms defining their goals in
novel ways. In most corporate settings the focus of strategy is the success
of the firm defined by market performance. In collaborative settings this
is not enough: some therefore use the 'balanced scorecard' to identify
not only financial goals but also customer satisfaction, internal process,
and employee development goals; others rely on 'values-based leadership.' In these various forms, collaborative-community-oriented corporations are seeking ways to articulate goals that bring to the fore the use-
value aspects and in doing so, they often make visible the tensions
between the use-value and exchange-value aspects. IBM has recently
made explicit its conception that a 'great company' must motivate its
employees to pursue more than market success, to make a positive
contribution to social values; and it has conducted a major values initiative to draw out the social goals that employees at all levels want to
contribute to. This raises a question of what happens when the market
values and other social purposes conflict—a question to which we will
return in the last section.

INTERDEPENDENT PROCESS MANAGEMENT

In addition to this new value orientation, the collaborative community
requires a new way of organizing—ways of structuring how people relate
to each other and how sanctions are applied when they deviate.[56]

Collaborative community in modern industry needs to coordinate interactions that span a wide range of competencies and knowledge bases, and that shift constantly to accommodate the evolving nature of knowledge projects. The challenges it faces cannot be met through 'teamwork' in the usual sense of small, homogeneous, and informal groups. Process management coordinates large, diverse communities and high levels of complexity. It must solve several difficult problems of organization:

1. The boundaries of solidary groups must be far less fixed than in traditional communities, far more capable of being bridged and merged.

2. It must accommodate a very high level of technical division of labor and diversity of knowledge and skills.[57]

3. It must allow for authority based not on status but on knowledge and expertise—that is, 'value-rationality'—which means that people must in many cases be accountable to peers or to those below them in the hierarchy, rather than to their formal superiors.

4. It must bring values into the realm of public discussion, so that they can become common orienting and motivating elements for all the members of the community. Thus it must find a way past the modern assumption that values are personal and private, and find ways to build shared commitment and understanding around them.

These problems require the deliberate and formal organizing of cooperation; while informal relations cannot be replaced or repressed, they are (as discussed earlier) far from sufficient in scope and flexibility. Organized informality is sufficient to coordinate relations in traditional bureaucratic environments; but it breaks down when confronted with the challenges of knowledge production and solutions orientation.

'Process management' in corporations has therefore become an increasingly elaborated and technical matter, with strong accountability and where accountability is not only hierarchical. Rather than emerging spontaneously from personal ties, relationships and trust are often built deliberately through organized discussions and explorations of motivations. These new formalisms are sometimes experienced as oppressive, and indeed the language of process management can become a cover for coercive bureaucratic control; but when it is successful, people experience the rules of process management as enabling rather than constraining, as helping to structure new relations rather than limiting them (see Chapter 5).

Interdependent process management has two aspects: processes for building a shared sense of purpose, and processes for coordinating work relations among people who are pursuing this purpose from different bases of knowledge and skill. In the corporate context, building shared purpose means actively encouraging system-wide understanding and discussion of strategy; and coordination means building systems to structure discussion along 'value chains.' On both dimensions collaborative community 'controls' hierarchy, though it does not displace it.[58]

Processes for developing shared purpose

In traditional bureaucracies, strategy was the preserve of the top team; 'operational' layers were focused on day-to-day matters and explicitly removed from the strategy-making process. At times, particularly in firms that required more frequent strategy adaptations, top levels sought the informal involvement of lower, operational levels; but their involvement was conceived as a supplement to the top-down strategy process.[59] Even twenty years ago it was rare for companies to share with their employees strategic information or goals beyond the vaguest generalities. In the past couple of decades, this has radically changed: a growing number of firms are involving lower layers in a more 'dialogic' and collaborative strategy formulation process, and by now most large companies make determined efforts to make sure employees at all levels understand the competition, customer needs, and strategic challenges.[60]

The pragmatic reason for the shift is that so many companies have been forced to make major modifications in strategy and identity, and they are not able to wait until everyone has settled into new roles before moving ahead. In traditional corporations the 'mission' was eternal and defining; in collaborative ones the generation of shared purpose becomes, as it were, an ongoing task rather than a fixed origin. It is evolving and fluid, and organized systems are needed to renew shared understanding and commitment. This has been a major force behind the development of collaborative mechanisms.

In the Citibank case this focus on strategy was continuous and widespread. There was a slogan ('Connect, transform, extend'), but far more than that: 'Our internet strategy is well documented and communicated throughout the company. Twenty years ago a strategy document would have been in only certain hands within the company and kept very close. Now it's everywhere, on all the intranets.'

A detailed 'e-business road map' was available to everyone in the organization. It was organized around the three basic strategies, continuously updated and refined. Incoming managers were regularly briefed in groups by the division head, and other senior managers met regularly with various subunits to reinforce the same messages and to hear what issues were arising in implementation. New project teams usually spent two to three days at offsite meetings talking through their relation to the business strategy, with industry leaders and key partners inside and outside the business. The road map became a kind of 'lingua franca' through which different parts of the organization could communicate: presentations at all levels and in multiple combinations were organized around these categories, and intranet documents from all the subunits used the same organization. Because of this common core, any person could go to the intranet site of another group, understand it, and navigate through it.

The generation of strategic purpose, in other words, was a highly practical and interactive matter—not chiselled in stone and handed down from on high, but a topic of continuous argumentation and application. The top team had a central role in defining the strategy, but this role involved listening and synthesizing and encouraging debate. Such an approach was essential to transforming strategy into a living purpose that linked people in daily work.

With all of this it is not surprising that everyone we interviewed could talk about strategic issues with detail, passion, and clarity—not using rote words, but making creative connections to daily problems and issues. They were also quite capable of disagreeing with aspects of the strategy: several spoke of intense arguments they had had in one or another forum with top management around the nature of the business. Finally, they were capable of adjusting quickly with the market: 'We move fast when we need to. ... We opened the new year with a new strategy, and now it's on everyone's mind and in everyone's mind; everyone's talking about "solutions" and not talking about "internet" so much.'

Esolutions is an unusually advanced example of collaborative community, but far from isolated. In this book, the discussion of the Strategic Fitness Process in Chapter 12 revolves around the initiation of intensive conversations about strategic direction in companies like Hewlett-Packard and Merck; this becomes the trigger for fundamental transformation in relations and values. Other widely publicized instances include Ford under Nasser, GE under Welch, and IBM under Gerstner and Palmisano.[61]

At the same time we should not overstate the case: though this type of process for building agreement around a unifying purpose has moved a long way in the last few decades, it has not often—even in Esolutions reached the ideal-type model of a collaborative community. With rare exceptions, it remains limited in scope.

We can distinguish two basic types of process around purpose. The first, which has been quite widely developed in many large corporations, is the development of widespread understanding of the strategy, with discussion aimed mainly at clarifying and building commitment to it. This involves elaborated processes of communication, training, leadership reinforcement, and integration with appraisals and other organizational systems. The Citibank case exemplifies this level.

The second involves closing the loop: inviting diverse people throughout the organization to reflect on the strategic direction and, by highlighting issues from their perspective, to contribute to its reformulation. Here the record is much more limited. At Citibank Esolutions, for instance, interviewees sometimes had well-thought-out concerns about the strategy—as one would expect in an environment where there was so much discussion of it. One view was that the e-business model required a crucial shift from the traditional focus on large customers:

[We] are playing in a new environment: you have to very rapidly respond, handle transitions, and deal with small customers. ... Without solving this fundamental problem there'll be no e-business. It's a very deep problem—it is fundamentally important to the identity of the bank.

This kind of objection was voiced with a sense of frustration. If it were an operational problem, people would know the process for raising it, having it analyzed, and making improvements; but for a fundamental matter of strategic orientation the process was not well developed, and there was a sense of mystery about how it would be resolved.

This is a rather widespread experience: very few top management teams have been willing to loosen their authority over strategic direction so far as to suggest it might really be changed by discussion. Some have tried to organize forums in which members of the organization can genuinely 'push back,' but these rarely go beyond the level of sporadic and unsystematic conversations.

There are a few partial exceptions. One is detailed later in this volume: the 'Strategic Fitness Process' described in Chapter 12 can lead to organized debate on core strategic issues, and sometimes even pushes top management in directions they did not expect. At Veridian, for example, the mid-level team challenged management to move to a consistent 'high-end' strategy rather than playing it safe by continuing to develop small projects that could be done within existing subunits. Another instance which should be mentioned is a recent effort by IBM in redefining its core values: CEO Sam Palmisano broke with the previous practice of sending down values from top management; he staged a 'values jam' in which all employees were invited to debate, with a systematic synthesis of the discussions as a major input to the final product.

Charles Sabel, later in this volume (Chapter 2), also points to prototypes of a process of 'disentrenching search' that go to the next step: not only providing an opening for real debate, but systematically encouraging the continual questioning of strategic goals—'applying the core principle of iterated co-design to the choice of strategy or goals itself.' Companies such as Cisco and Illinois Tool Works, and (remarkably) certain regulatory agencies such as the US Securities and Exchange Commission, have developed processes which force members regularly to justify their strategic choices against possible alternatives.

Such efforts have begun to develop a set of technologies and techniques—how to organize discussion, how to handle major disagreements, how to synthesize a large number of inputs—that at least point the way towards a reliable process of value debate. How far they can go against the common resistance of leaders is an unresolved question. On the one hand these processes seem to result in a combination of flexibility and robustness that is hard to beat over time in the marketplace. On the other, the process of participative value discussion may push the limits of what is feasible within the constraints of a capitalist economy. We will return to these longer-term issues in the final section.

Processes for coordinating work (value chains)

The shared purpose is meaningless without organized ways for people with different skills and competencies to contribute to it and to interact with each other. Traditional bureaucracies coordinated sequences of actions through pre-established standards and plans; formally, each part focused on its job and 'threw it over the wall' to the next. Inevitable problems were smoothed to a greater or lesser degree 'on the fly' through informal mechanisms of mutual adjustment.[62] These informal systems, however, are limited, functioning reliably only on a local scale. With growing knowledge intensity and solutions orientation, with the escalating intensity and scale of interdependence, companies have therefore sought to organize these lateral connections through formal analysis and coordination of the steps in the movement from raw material to final output—what has come to be called the 'value chain.'

This coordination has been based on a rapidly evolving set of systems and techniques for organizing collaborative discussions—that is to say, making it possible for people to exchange views and knowledge and to reach agreements on action without relying on a hierarchical superior. At the first level, such techniques of process management organize the functioning within small groups. Innovations have included techniques for consensual prioritization of goals and purposes of the group; procedures to encourage listening and understanding the diversity of views and knowledge (brainstorming being one key technique for this purpose), including criteria for bringing in new players as the core issues develop; methods of interactive research to build shared understanding of the emerging options; and decision rules for building agreement on courses of action.

The next level, which has evolved more recently, involves structuring interdependencies beyond the team, with other parts of the organization and environment—typically using the metaphor of a 'chain' of value moving towards the ultimate purpose or output of the organization. In the case of the Citibank Alliance group the value chain was sketched in the way shown in Fig. 1.1.

The next step is to elaborate the value chain in terms of the interdependencies to all the parts of the organization. The Citibank alliance group had a checklist of all the authorities and experts that are needed in shepherding the formation of a new relationship—lawyers, accountants, and so on. This was then 'mapped' into a sequence of connections and links needed to move the process forward (see Fig. 1.2).

To 'move fast' enough, key processes are continuously redefined and actively managed. Various teams and individuals have developed elaborate process maps for their own work, often looking to others for help and advice on the key steps. The alliance group's influence, as its leader points out, is based in part on being 'smart about process' in its particular area; those we interviewed outside the group say they go to the alliance team to

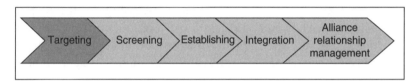

Fig. 1.1 Citibank Esolutions process map: key subprocesses

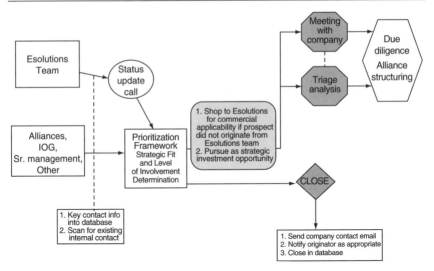

Fig. 1.2 Citibank Esolutions detailed process map for alliance screening

make sure they do not miss important steps in working out agreements with partners. In this approach process is a resource to be used, shared, and developed on an as-needed basis:

We document it on paper; when we make a change on it it gets communicated to everybody; everybody knows about it, we've had team meetings to discuss it; everyone understands their role. We did that twice—originally it was just me and a couple of other people; then when we split responsibilities from delivery and execution we had to redo the exercise.

A key quality of an interdependent process map is its horizontality: that is, it cuts across the divisions of the formal organization. Whereas the principle of hierarchy as reflected in the traditional bureaucracy resolves unforeseen issues in interdepartmental coordination by referring them upwards for decision making by hierarchical superiors, interdependent process management defines ways in which the peers in their respective departments can collaborate directly to resolve these issues. An investment banker may deal with a marketer in this process without necessarily going through their common boss, which would be a violation of a central principle of bureaucracy. Indeed, because the standard of contribution applies to everyone, even relations that cross vertical levels in the hierarchy have a spirit of peer dialogue within these processes: everyone has the right to speak at whatever level they can contribute, regardless of formal position.

The hierarchy does not disappear, of course, remaining central particularly in the allocation of resources. In order to ensure that processes remain aligned with overall missions, organizations typically define a set of roles that link the process structure with the formal hierarchy: Table 1.3 is an excerpt from one used at AT&T.

The principles underlying these interdependent processes can be derived from their essential purpose: they aim to respond to outside demands or to develop innovative ideas by combining specialized knowledge into larger patterns. In the terms just sketched, they are norms that facilitate contribution—in other words, that help to ensure that all can contribute to their maximum capacity. These processes therefore cannot rely on authority, which does not often enough correspond with the value of knowledge or the capacity to contribute to solutions; they must free up people to speak openly and to contribute fully. Overlaying the structure of authority, they seek to create conditions for the effective functioning of influence, which is based on the capacity to contribute to the collective effort.[63]

The monitoring of performance cannot be done only through the hierarchical superior, as in traditional bureaucracies, because in collaborative orders the boss does not have close enough knowledge of how his subordinates are performing in teams and task forces of which he is not a part. Thus peer assessment becomes increasingly central—not just peers in the abstract, but those with whom the person has worked and who are in a

Table 1.3. Process-Centric Roles and Responsibilities

Process champion	Ensures process efforts are linked with overall business strategies and goals and advocates process breakthrough initiatives for one or more of the thirteen QMS (Quality Management System) processes
Process owner	Provides process vision, commits to customers' primary requirements, and is ultimately accountable for one or more of the QMS processes
Process leader	Charts PMT (process management team) activity, manages funding process, and interfaces with customers and suppliers
PMT leader	Leads effort to develop and implement initiatives to improve process capability and achieve process results
PMT member	Analyzes and recommends improvements to the process
Support manager	Manages the executing of current process and implements process improvements to achieve process results
Process associate	Executes current process and implements process improvements to achieve process results

Source: AT&T Total Quality Management materials, 1995.

direct position to judge how well he has contributed and managed commitments. 'Three hundred and sixty-degree' appraisal processes are therefore spreading rapidly. They encounter the usual obstacles: those with a bureaucratic ethic resist such spreading of information or distort it with subterranean politics. Nevertheless, there is growing evidence of its effectiveness in high-flexibility environments.[64]

A central issue is that performance goals are no longer neatly ordered through the hierarchical structure, but may often conflict. In a bureaucracy it is always clear, or should be, who is 'the boss' for any given situation; in a collaborative order people may be working on multiple tasks and initiatives with multiple accountabilities, and they frequently find themselves in situations where they are pulled in several directions at once. The ability to manage these tensions is one of the key capabilities required of individuals.

In recent years interactive process management has become an increasingly elaborated and technical matter (for further elaboration, see Chapters 2 and 5). This shift to flexible teamwork and collaboration does not mean the abandonment of bureaucratic hierarchy, but rather its combination with community:

[Do people feel frustrated by the growth of controls?] There's no frustration—it makes sense, it's not bureaucratic and controlling, it's normal good business... It does not mean now that the people who do have a lot of good ideas get stepped on. The only people who are uncomfortable are those who don't understand the business well enough to spot new opportunities. (Citibank)

A final level in process management is the ability to gather experiences into systematic learning. There has been much recent writing on the concept of a 'learning organization,' and considerable elaboration of mechanisms of review. Adler's chapter describes formalized process development in software coding. Charles Sabel, later in this volume, cites examples such as NUMMI and Cisco, which establish clear benchmarks and regularly revisit the success of the strategy in relation to those benchmarks, bringing together the experience of all the relevant actors. In some settings, particularly manufacturing operations where production goals are clear, these techniques have been developed to a high level of detail and reliability.

There has been less practical progress in more complicated areas and higher-level processes, where goals are fluid and multidimensional. A number of companies, including GE, Coca-Cola, Cigna, Hewlett-Packard, Monsanto, and Young & Rubican, have established a new position of 'chief learning officer' who is supposed to coordinate the flow of knowledge so as to draw out the key learnings for the organization. Our anecdotal evidence suggests that this has so far rarely developed beyond the level of ad hoc interventions to the level of systematic and effective organizational reviews.

Linking purpose and process: understanding and commitment

In order for diverse parts of the knowledge-intensive, solutions-oriented organization to work together they must understand each other.[65] The Mod IV case above illustrates the lack of understanding between functions like marketing and engineering in traditional bureaucracies—and the resulting difficulty of collaboration. In order to work effectively together the two functions must each believe the other has a contribution to make to their shared project: an engineer must understand why a simple focus on quality may be limited and why marketers' analyses of customer segments may help in achieving their shared goals.

Traditional cultures, including the corporate culture of loyalty, block such understanding: they are marked by jokes and rituals that express each group's sense of itself and denigrate outsiders as crazy or weird or bad. Collaborative relations have to overcome such stereotypes. But there is always resistance to such understanding because within traditional communities understanding is the same as commitment: understanding others in effect means one has to agree with them and to become one with them. A key aspect of collaborative community is that one can understand without committing—that one can take the perspective of others and gain a sense of their motivation without bonding to them and 'joining' them in a moral unity.

Interdependent process management thus involves deliberate mechanisms of understanding, and, distinct from those, mechanisms of commitment. A first step in process-based trust is to help participants to grasp the logic and sympathize with the feelings of other actors by putting them 'in their shoes.' This may involve listening exercises, informal retreats, and shared educational experiences[66]—all techniques which have spread widely in the last few decades.

The problem of commitment has more recently moved to the foreground. In a collaborative community commitments and their enforcement are neither part of the informal culture nor automatically linked to the hierarchy: they must be deliberately agreed to. Thus an important element of process management is the articulation of what people have agreed to do, and the specification of ways to make sure they do it. At a larger scale companies are still wrestling with the commitment problem, as illustrated by Citibank's experience. They developed a complex computer-based system called COMPASS which was intended to allow people from different parts of the organization to come together around strategic priorities and to record commitments in such a way that they could be monitored. There is considerable resistance to engaging in these recorded agreements, however, much of which derives from lack of trust between divisions: people still anchored in the bureaucratic culture are resistant to putting so much information into the public domain accessible to people outside their local units. IBM's elaborate 'commitment management system' has faced similar resistance. In both instances, however, there is a general sense of the need for some such process tool to enable people to trust the work of others in cross-unit initiatives, and in both cases development is continuing.

SOCIAL CHARACTER: THE INTERDEPENDENT SOCIAL SELF

Community requires the internalization of motives in a stable self, because only if one can grasp others' motivational patterns can one have confidence in how they will act in the future. Thus character is always central in the generation of trust. Social character is the core aspects of character produced within social groups, through common socialization mechanisms, that enable people to count on the fact that others will react predictably.[67]

The shift to modernity created new requirements for personality: a high level of independence and personal consistency. Enormous social changes were needed to establish this kind of psychology as a dominant type. E. P. Thompson showed the work that had to be done in the eighteenth century to instill 'modern' orientations of punctuality and responsibility in recalcitrant peasants, without which the emerging factory regime could not have succeeded.[68] The current emergence of a new ethic is today creating new strains, because it demands the ability to interact in multiple communities and to adapt to competing demands of interdependence.

Social character involves two major aspects of personality. Durkheim and Freud, among others, focused on the superego—the internalization of social values in individual motivations, so that people want to realize social values and feel guilty if they don't. This anchoring of values in personal motivations is essential to the stability of social orders: we can trust others in large part because they have more than a calculating relation to shared values. The second aspect, which is the focus of ego-psychology, involves the ways in which social identities are integrated into a coherent sense of 'self.' Someone with a strong ego can maintain consistency and stability in multiple groups and can deal with the tension and uncertainty of competing demands. Failure to act appropriately in a group leads to emotions not of guilt but of loss of self-esteem and embarrassment.

In a traditional community, proper behavior is a direct function of status position. The effect of *Gesellschaft*-oriented modernity is to liberate the person from the social order: 'in the formal psychological sense of the term,' says Weber, 'it tried to make [man] into a personality.'[69] It did this in the first instance by insisting on a direct connection between the individual and God, so that right behavior was defined and motivated by the individual's relation to a personal deity. Eventually, as Weber showed, it evolved into an expectation of instrumentally rational discipline: people could differ in their wants but they could relate to each other based on this common expectation of instrumental rationality.

The collaborative community demands more: it demands not only that a person be an individual, but that she draw on that individuality to make distinct contributions in multiple social projects and settings. It is not enough to be unique; uniqueness has value only in terms of its relations. Thus it requires a personality that has internalized an ethic of contribution and that is able to relate that to multiple identities in various groups.

This is a difficult balancing act, as can be seen by the common laments in modern literature and social science about anomie, depression, and loss of self-respect. A classic failure of this kind of personality is a loss of internal coherence—the kind of glad-handing, sociable, but empty and amoral type popularized in *The Music Man* or *Death of a Salesman*. These types have neither a superego sense of what they think is valuable, nor a sense of integration among their social relations: they can take any identity and behave without guilt or embarrassment in any way that the immediate situation demands. The line is thin, as Arthur Miller illustrated, between such seemingly irrepressible sociability and the disintegration of the person—with suicide as the ultimate marker.[70]

Our understanding of these linkages between social structure and personality is informed by the pragmatists'—Mead, Dewey, Cooley, et al.—discussion of the 'social self.'[71] On the pragmatist view, the self is fundamentally—constitutively—social, shaped by the individual's set of social interactions, and the inner sense of self-identity is forged in this interaction. Mead defined three basic types of social self which correspond closely to the three types of community we have sketched. In traditional societies, the social self was generated by uniting a social group through hostility to some outside group, and by subsuming individuals under preordained social statuses. In modern society, the social self derives primarily from a competitive battle with people within the social group. And he suggested, as early as 1918, the need for a third type of social self in advanced societies, one in which the assertion of self is in effect bounded and turned from aggressiveness towards the kind of collaborative social construction of the kind we have discussed.

Mead did not name these types; we can label them in a manner consistent with the terminology we have been using: *dependent, independent*, and *interdependent* social selves. The first is defined by social status and driven primarily by a sense of honor and shame; the second asserts autonomy and uniqueness and is driven primarily by feelings of guilt.[72] As for the third—what kind of self is needed to function effectively in a collaborative social order? Mead sketched it abstractly:

The test of success of this self lies in the change and construction of the social conditions which make the self possible, not in the conquest and elimination of other selves. His emotions are not those of mass consciousness dependent upon suppressed individualities, but arise out of the cumulative interest of varied undertakings converging upon a common problem of social reconstruction. (1918: 602)

To put it another way, this kind of self presents itself not in terms of its social status, nor as an independent and abstract 'individual'; people present themselves as interdependent with others, and are motivated to maintain and develop those relations.

What this means in a setting like the corporation is that people feel emotionally connected to the shared purpose; pride and self-valuation result from contributing to that purpose. This can be distinguished on one side from loyalists' attachment to the organization as such, and their pride in 'being part of' a powerful firm; and on the other from the individualist protestations of free agents who claim no emotional connection to the group and take pride only in their own accomplishments and rewards. In the case of Citibank Esolutions, which we use here as an (imperfect) example of collaborative community, we find people regularly saying things like: 'It's not about me succeeding or failing, it's about the multiple teams doing that' and 'In order to make the kind of thing we're working on happen, you can't do it by yourself; you have to work and play well with others or you won't get anything done.'

The interviewees in Citibank Esolutions frequently distinguished themselves sharply on several dimensions from what they called 'bureaucratic' types. One was in their willingness to engage in debate and to embrace disagreement and conflict:

Some people are just content with just managing their piece of turf and don't want anyone mucking around in it. ... [You want] someone who would be open to criticism or suggestions as opposed to someone who would get defensive, be scared by people meddling around.

Another important and recurring theme was that they did not seek to establish and protect an organizational position. Their sense of what they were about had to do with whether they made something happen, not whether they established a position of power. They spoke with scorn of 'empire builders' and those who 'are just content with just managing their piece of turf and don't want anyone mucking around in it.' When they spoke of the leader of the alliance group, by contrast, several people elaborated on the theme: 'He's a big influence player—he doesn't want to build an empire, doesn't want a large team.' One of those working with him had no formal organizational ties of accountability, but pitched in for other reasons: '... as far as I understand [the alliance leader] doesn't input into my performance evaluation. I don't have input into his evaluation either. I put time into this because I believe it is important to fulfill our goal of becoming the global leader of e-solutions.' In this interview the passion and detailed ideas this person expressed about how to develop the e-solutions approach made clear why he spent energy on an area which did not build his own organizational power.

In order to operate effectively in such an environment, they stressed, it was essential to be far more open about information and competencies than is usual in bureaucratic environments, especially with peers. The primary reward they sought was not a consolidation of their position, but a recognition of their ability to contribute: 'My approach is to be transparent with the peers about the value you are bringing.... If you've generated enough value recognition will come, people understand where the value is being generated.'

This sense of worth from contribution as opposed to position is novel enough that it is often hard even for its proponents to express— as can be seen in the struggle of this person to define the basis for his approach:

It's important that the people you're talking to are open, and you not be overbearing and say here's how you have to do things. It stems from security, being comfortable with your position—and I don't mean position from an organizational perspective, I mean it more that you don't feel that someone's going to come in and ... [pause] I'm trying to make a distinction between hierarchy and feeling comfortable that you know what you're doing.

Competence in this framework is not a matter of doing well in a position; you 'know what you're doing' not in the sense of executing a defined expertise or doing a defined job, but in the sense of being able to make a difference on the collective task.

This sense of self centrally involves another theme stressed by Mead: the ability to role-take with a wide variety of others. The traditional bureaucratic character type manages to reduce interaction with, and the need for understanding of, those who are different by on the one hand emphasizing conformity, and on the other building walls around different positions. The collaborative sense of self, by contrast, requires constant interaction, taking responsibility for the collective outcome rather than just for doing a job, and it therefore requires the ability to grasp the distinctive contributions that different types can make to a shared project. Individuals need a capacity to 'see it from the other's point of view'—far more than in either traditional or modern forms of community. The language for this at Citibank is consistent: people talk about analyzing value for others in building collaborative efforts:

I quickly brought my team together and said, 'Here's our chance to make a difference in the institution.' One-on-one I figured out what was in it for each of them; and I did a grid for myself ... on where the conflicts were. So in every meeting I made sure there was something important for every person.

And another:

I sat down in office and made a war map on the wall about who I needed to get involved within Citibank. I outlined under each of them what the alliance would bring to them: to a senior guy it will bring market share or revenue; for lower levels it should bring learning opportunities that could be added to their resume; and so on.

Finally, as can be seen in some of these quotes, the interdependent, interactive sense of self is comfortable with a relatively unstructured process involving a great deal of negotiation; in contrast, the bureaucratic character tends to seek authoritative rules and procedures and to avoid such fluid situations where responsibility is blurred.

We are cognizant of an important debate concerning how deeply identity is grounded, and thus how easily it can be changed. One view is that it can change quickly with social expectations; another is that it is grounded in personality dynamics set in childhood. We have observed in our own research people who seem to 'get it' rather quickly on moving from a traditional to a collaborative environment; on the other hand, there are some who remain unable to adapt to the new culture even after consider-able efforts. Adler's chapter describes some 'conversion' experiences among previously highly individualistic software developers, but that study also indicates that some developers cannot adapt to the more inter-dependent process.

Michael Maccoby's chapter makes an argument that the interactive sense of self is a matter of character, and that its spread in the last decades is connected to the transformation of early socialization, espe-cially the decline in stable traditional families, which creates from a very early age increased capability to view events from multiple perspectives and to negotiate among them. This pattern is then developed through schooling and other socializing agents through a lifelong series of stages. If this is right, then the full development of the collaborative commu-nity will be a slow business. Certainly the progress made in almost a century since Mead's outline has been very incomplete, and the trad-itional bureaucratic patterns of self remain strong. The high level of tension and mutual mistrust between those who hold to traditional ethics and those who have internalized a collaborative ethic is evidence of the magnitude of the change, and also suggests that it may take generations for robust trusting community to be possible on the basis of contribution.

COLLABORATIVE COMMUNITIES, HIERARCHIES, AND MARKETS

Collaborative community often appears in the research and business lit-erature in the guise of 'network relations' and is often treated as opposed to hierarchy and formal systems in general. Networks are frequently ana-lyzed in terms of purely associational and voluntary relations, and collab-oration is treated in terms of breaking free from the organizational hierarchy. This view appears in practice as well as in theory: many man-agers, like the division head in the Mod IV case described above, feel that if they want to foster collaboration they must abandon their tools of power and position, and they retreat into a passive position of 'letting people work it out.'

Yet this simple opposition is untenable in both theory and practice. Whenever a group is focused on shared instrumental activity (rather than mere coexistence or expressive activity), effective authority is essen-tial to success—to define direction, to allocate resources, and to resolve disputes. Without it communal groups inevitably fall victim to faction— the splitting of groups that do not agree with each other or who want to maintain their autonomy—and to inefficiencies resulting from the inability to make decisions that involve conflict among members.[73]

In reality hierarchy and collaborative community are combined in a wide spectrum of patterns. The history of science provides the broadest range of examples. The scientific community is highly collaborative in the sense we have discussed: the primary value is contribution to the common enterprise; there is an increasingly elaborated web of process rules that assure the integrity of the method and effective interaction among related projects; and there are thorough socialization processes to ensure that these values and norms are internalized and understood by all members. For the most part science involves hierarchy only in the definition and certification of educational requirements, and the long socialization of postgraduate education is the main mechanism of control. But wherever science becomes focused on the pursuit of complex projects it adopts a more strongly hierarchical form—without necessarily undermining the essential communal mechanisms. Large-scale research is generally performed in laboratories with very strong leaders and status orders. This is also the result when social pressures develop for targeted scientific efforts—the atomic bomb being a prototypical case. In more recent times government funding agencies have become a mechanism of centralized control to steer scientific research in particular directions, funding large laboratories.

Another current and highly relevant illustration is the open-source software movement, which is often portrayed by its advocates as the communal opposite of the hierarchical Microsoft approach to coding. The actual experience of open source, however, is more complicated: the need for disciplined coordination in complex projects has led to the introduction of mechanisms of authority, sometimes masked. Its most visible successes—Linux and Apache—have been strongly coordinated by central mechanisms: Linus Torvalds as benevolent despot in the case of Linux, a formalized committee in the case of Apache.[74]

On the other hand, it is also evident that hierarchy can interfere with the development of collaborative community. The expectation of deference built into traditional bureaucratic organization is a continual obstacle to collaboration; thus any assertion of power by those higher in the organization is likely to trigger these deeply ingrained expectations. The widespread experience of those who have tried to sponsor participation in corporations is, contrary to the hopes of radical reformers, that lower levels tend to be very cautious about pushing the limits of their familiar patterns and of challenging their leaders, even when they are strongly encouraged to do so.[75]

In short, community and authority are not mutually exclusive; they can and do need to fit together. The form of authority is closely related to the values of the community in which it operates. It can sustain itself only when it fits within these communal definitions of legitimacy. In traditional systems authority is justified on the basis of eternal order—'the way things have always been done'. In bureaucratic systems, as Weber showed, it is justified on the basis of legal rationality—its instrumental effectiveness and sanction from above. In a collaborative system, authority is justified on the basis of the value of contribution. Authority is frequently essential to the attainment of shared purpose. As long as the members of the community believe that it is playing this essential role, authority is compatible with the collaborative community. Conflict develops when it is used in the pursuit of purposes *not* shared by the community, or in ways seen by many as harming that purpose.

In practice, this means that authority in a collaborative order has to involve more engagement and dialogue than in other orders: whereas a bureaucratic leader can refer to abstract principles of rationality and a traditional leader can refer to eternal laws, the collaborative leader has to justify decisions in terms of helping the concrete community to work effectively. The exercise of authority in collaborative corporations therefore looks different from that in traditional bureaucracies:

- *Allocating resources*. In organizations like Citibank Esolutions, individuals may create networks to pursue an opportunity and cobble together resources for a while from their own banks of time and money; at a certain point they need to get others with broader control over resources to agree that the course is worth pursuing. This is not just a single boss, as it typically is in a bureaucracy, but generally consists of some sort of 'review team' that involves multiple parts of the organization. In one documented case at IBM, the CEO indicated his general support for a team that had been developing internet opportunities on their own hook, but he did not simply 'grant' them a pot of resources to work with or set them up as a new division. Instead, his approval served more indirectly to help their negotiations with division and other leaders who held needed resources.[76]

- *Performance appraisals.* Reputational feedback from coworkers, as discussed above, is crucial to process-based trust; but in a firm this cannot work entirely by the 'pure' collaborative method of gradually isolating those who do not contribute, moving them towards the margins of the group. At some point efficiency demands that decisions be made about firing or reassigning those who do not perform; peer networks are notoriously bad at such decisions. The balance struck at Citi and other organizations we have studied takes this form: formal bosses no longer function as in the past as the main assigners and monitors of tasks to 'their' people, nor are they the primary appraisers. Instead, they are the coordinators of a multisource appraisal system, gathering the data from coworkers, partners, and customers; feeding it back in a structured way; and making decisions about what to do in cases of problems.

- *Conflict resolution.* Even with the best process skills and internal mediation, people may end up with different views of how to proceed on difficult problems; higher management plays a key role in defining what path best contributes to the general mission and mandate. Typically in collaborative units leaders will be less willing to leap in to break deadlocks than in pure bureaucracies and will more frequently use their persuasive powers—bringing to bear their knowledge of strategic issues, making sure that the parties don't avoid the issues, enforcing deadlines, but avoiding in almost all instances simply taking the decision out of the hands of the contending parties. Nevertheless, the fact that bosses remain in the background as potential interveners is very important for pushing peers to resolve problems on their own.

The relations between community and markets have also been transformed with the rise of collaborative orientations. The most visible sign is the rise of complex alliances and network relations that combine market and hierarchy mechanisms with high levels of trust. The Citibank alliance group was specifically charged with responsibility for establishing ongoing relations with companies outside Citibank who could bring needed resources and skills to the Esolutions effort; rather than acquiring these companies or merely purchasing their products, Citi sought to create ongoing mutually beneficial relations which would retain flexibility and benefit both parties. The realm of supplier relations, further explored in Chapter 10, has evolved in a similar way. Toyota, for example, always makes its suppliers aware of the ultimate power of the market test: it tries to maintain at least two sources for any non-commodity inputs.

However, the relationships between Toyota and these suppliers are hardly composed of anonymous, arm's-length, spot-market transactions. These contracts embody a comprehensive set of documents specifying in detail product requirements and management processes, and they are embedded within a long-term, high-trust, mutual-commitment relationship. Finally, there is an increase in the importance of industry-level coordination—not just in terms of legislative lobbying, but in terms of charting strategic directions and standards. Toyota brings its key suppliers together in a supplier association to share ideas and learn from each other in a forum in which competitive rivalry is moderated by collaborative community.[77] Other examples include Intel, which includes contribution to the development of the industry as a part of its performance appraisal for managers; and the Tapestry Networks forums described later in Chapter 13. Lynda Applegate explores this terrain in more detail in Chapter 9. The major point is that the values governing collaborative community also govern the legitimization of markets and hierarchies, and thus transform the interaction among these coordination mechanisms.

The balance of this volume explores aspects of the development of collaborative community—the ways in which it has succeeded in transforming the corporate realm, and also the obstacles it has encountered and the limitations of its current form. In the following section, we address the question of how far it can develop within the constraints of current economic and social institutions, and what transformations may be needed at this broader level. We will focus on the seeds of positive development, but it is worth reiterating that they have grown as far as they have despite many hostile aspects of the environment: continuing pressure for cost cutting that has often led to increased control, growing inequality, and a wide trend of market worship that denies the importance of community and trust.

The overall course of development: the zigzag path

In the previous sections, we have argued that powerful economic and social forces are pushing towards collaborative relations; but this is hardly evident if one simply looks around. The 'neoliberal' movement of the past thirty years, which has spread through much of the industrial world, runs largely in the opposite direction. Based on the premiss that the market can solve all ills, neoliberalism cheerfully encourages the dismantling of communal institutions and values such as employment security, loyalty, labor–management accords, and other long-term relationships. Meanwhile, performance incentives have increasingly been used (both within firms and in government policy) to favor those who break free of the communal norms and show their independence, and to reject those who can't measure up.[78] The neoliberal impulse has a more ambivalent relation to hierarchy. On the one hand, markets replace hierarchies as the preferred mechanism for coordinating large production units, and the services previously supplied by government are outsourced to private, market-oriented firms. On the other hand, even though such shifts are often portrayed as an advance in individualism and a way of freeing people from the constraints of the big bureaucracy, in practice, within these smaller units they typically involve a strengthening of hierarchical control at the expense of any acknowledgement of community. It has become routine for new leaders to impose their will by fiat, deliberately disregarding shared culture and 'the way things are done around here'; part of the routine, of course, has also been frequent mass layoffs which, at least in the white-collar realm, have been seen as an unprecedented attack on long-held expectations. Not surprisingly, there is considerable polling evidence that job satisfaction has declined and the level of fear in corporations has risen.[79]

In this section, we put in broader perspective the trends towards collaborative community that the previous section claimed to discern.

Tendencies and counter-tendencies

While we believe we can see the resurgence and reconstruction of community, we should also note powerful counter-tendencies, even among firms that are focused on the challenges posed by growing knowledge intensity and solutions orientation. These trends and counter-trends are observable on multiple levels: in employment relations, in interdivisional relations within firms, and in inter-firm relations:

1. *Employment relations.* In dealing with increased competitive pressures, many companies have relied heavily on hierarchical or market mechanisms to the detriment of community. On the hierarchy side, we see companies that have depended on brilliant strategic plans or determined cost-cutting initiatives driven from the top, with little involvement from employees.[80] The market side is most clearly represented by firms that have radically decentralized and opened their divisions to outside competition, reducing not only hierarchical rules but also bonds of

cooperation with other divisions. Both these approaches have been found wanting by at least some scholars. The 'top-down' approach has been shown, not too surprisingly, to yield little lasting change in attitudes and values; more surprisingly, it also seems to yield little lasting cost reduction or efficiency improvement.[81] Radical decentralization has led to such duplication of effort and strategic incoherence that in cases ranging from ABB to Kodak to Lucent it has been quickly reversed.

The market path has been particularly popular. Many companies have increased the use of individual incentives,[82] and the use of contingent workers. The implementation of incentive plans has often set people in competition with each other rather than encouraging shared contribution; in Citibank, as in other cases we have examined, those engaged in collaboration have found that the incentive system did more harm than good. And contingent workers, for legal and organizational reasons, are often sharply cut off from collaboration with permanent employees and separated from the main management systems of the firm.

Nevertheless, there are numerous corporations who are rowing against the current in their commitment to community as a way to augment their knowledge and solutions capabilities. For every Wal-Mart, there is a Costco.[83] The following chapters discuss some of these cases in more depth.

2. *Interdivisional relations.* Large multi-business corporations are under increasing pressure from financial markets to show real benefits for purported synergies. The first result of this pressure is, once again, often the reassertion of hierarchy and market rather than community. Hierarchical moves include the trend to divest unrelated businesses in the interest of 'focus,' and to jettison any 'social contract' hesitations they may have had to sell off less profitable lines of business. Market logic drives a trend to strengthening market-style incentives to division managers.

But the fact remains that in related-diversified firms, if divisions seek only to meet their own divisional objectives, they will behave in ways that are detrimental to the firm's global objectives. A third result of the performance pressure on large corporations is, therefore, a cluster of innovations that appear to be pushing beyond the limits of market and hierarchy towards community. Many multidivisional firms are actively experimenting with new ways to stimulate collaboration among profit centers. The notion of core competencies, as articulated by Prahalad and Hamel (1990), is premissed on the insight that corporate competitiveness depends on bodies of expertise that are typically distributed across divisions rather than contained within them, and collaboration across divisions, therefore, is a critical, not a secondary issue.[84]

A panoply of collaborative mechanisms founded on community and trust has emerged to coordinate across independent units. 'Customer relations managers' are one relatively simple approach—individuals with enough prestige across multiple units that they can persuade people that there is mutual benefit to working together. More broadly, many companies have adopted what Jay Galbraith (2000) calls a 'front–back' structure, where the customer interface pulls together resources from a product back-end; such structures require intensive use of consensual coordinating units to thrash out the allocation of resources. Similarly, titles such as chief technology officer and chief knowledge officer have proliferated; these positions have broad responsibility for building cross-division knowledge and sharing but typically lack formal authority—they rely on trust in their attempts to build more trust.[85]

3. *Inter-firm relations*. Collaborative community is hardly the dominant ethos in inter-firm relations. We see some firms, to the contrary, imposing ever sharper market discipline on their suppliers by aggressively demanding lower prices and moving rapidly to cut off suppliers who cannot deliver.[86] We also see firms trying to force improvements in their supplier base by introducing more unilateral 'hierarchical contracts' into their market relations.[87]

At the same time, however, a growing number of firms are building long-term, trust-based partnerships with their suppliers. Though the issue is still hotly debated, a burgeoning body of research suggests that trust plays a critical role in successful inter-firm relations.[88] This research shows that when firms need innovation and knowledge inputs from suppliers rather than just standardized commodities, no combination of strong hierarchical control and market discipline can assure as high a level of performance as trust-based community.[89]

A particularly interesting and well-documented illustration of the resulting moves towards community has been the gradual adoption by US auto manufacturers of a model of close relations with suppliers rather than arm's-length market contracts. The percentage of US auto parts producers who provide sensitive, detailed information about their production process to their customers grew from 38 per cent to 80 per cent during the 1980s.[90] Though this approach was initially inspired by Japanese *keiretsu*, it has taken a very different form in this country—one much less bound by traditional links, much more open to discussion and negotiation, and therefore closer to the collaborative form of trust. Chapter 10 discusses this trend and its limits in more detail.

Evidence for a trend to inter-firm community is even stronger in the proliferation of collaborative network forms of organization for the most knowledge-intensive tasks and industries.[91] Patent pooling and cooperative R&D consortia have multiplied in recent decades. Formal professional and technical societies and informal community ties among scientists constitute other, less direct forms of inter-firm networking whose importance appears to be growing.

The countervailing forces are strong. These high-trust network forms may be more productive, but since the market principle is also present, they suffer the risk of opportunistic defection. Self-interested behavior can sometimes encourage trustworthiness, particularly when the 'shadow of the future' is long. But self-interest does not reliably ensure the diffusion and persistence of trust-based networks, and whole regions can find themselves stuck at low-trust and poor-performing equilibria. However, when these regions are subject to competition from regions that have attained a higher-trust, higher-performing equilibrium, one sometimes observes serious, sustained, self-conscious efforts to create trust.[92] Some of these efforts succeed. One might hypothesize that if efforts to create trust as a response to competition do not succeed, economic activity will tend to shift to higher-trust regions. In either case, the trend towards community seems likely to emerge, if only at a more global level.

The contradictory forces shaping capitalist development

What are we to make of the persistence of these counter-tendencies that reinforce market and hierarchy and that undermine community? What underlying forces do they reflect? Why should a prognosis of emergent community be accorded any credibility? We believe a fruitful approach to the answer can be found in Marx's work, which analyzed the evolving tension in capitalist society between the *forces* of production—the cumulative growth of productive knowledge embodied in equipment, skills, and techniques—and the *relations* of production—the persistence of the basic matrix of capitalist property relations.

On the one hand, the capitalist system of property relations greatly stimulates the development of technology and human productive capabilities, leading to growing knowledge intensity and to increasing interdependence and interconnection of human activity. Capitalism creates an increasingly extensive division of labor across and within firms and regions, and an ever-denser web of interdependence in production and exchange—visible as globalization and the development of the world market. Marx called this tendency the 'socialization' of the forces of production—where socialization here means the development of the linkages that give individuals access to the wider capabilities of societies.

On the other hand, these same capitalist relations of production simultaneously divide people through exclusion and dependence—workers from employers, firms from competitors, countries from rivals—and impede the emergence of a collaborative management of this growing interdependence. Under capitalist relations, the increasingly interdependent economy is coordinated—in the first instance—not by a collaborative community, but by the coercive mechanisms of the market (coordinating across firms via the price mechanism) and of capitalist hierarchy (coordinating within firms via the employment relation).

As capitalism progresses, however, the pressure of competition forces firms to introduce more directly social, collaborative means of coordination and community. In their search for competitive advantage, firms learn to collaborate both with other firms and with their employees. The firm's ability to create use-values—and thus to valorize the capital invested in them—depends on ever more effective collaboration within the 'collective worker.'[93] The socialization of the forces of production thus also encompasses a tendency to greater conscious interdependence—and progressively prevails over the tendency of the relations of production to exacerbate divisions and domination. Capitalists, Marx and Engels write in the Communist Manifesto, are the 'involuntary promoters' of socialization.

The persistence of private ownership of means of production and the associated asymmetries of class power ensure that the movement towards socialization—towards greater conscious social connectedness and collaborative community—proceeds only in a halting, uncertain manner, prone to breakdowns. Moreover, alongside the 'high road' of collaborative community, the basic matrix of capitalist relations of production continually reproduces the 'low road' of super-exploitation and dispossession.[94]

A zigzag path

The net effect of the contradictory forces just described is to impart to the movement towards collaborative community a zigzag form. We can see this first, in the history of corporate management in the past century and a half.

Researchers who have studied the evolution of the popularity of various management techniques in management journals have consistently identified periods that alternate between a focus on employee commitment and a focus on managerial control:

1. Commitment, 1870s–1890s: welfare work.
2. Control, 1890s–1910s: scientific management.
3. Commitment, 1920–1940s: human relations.
4. Control, 1940s–1960s: systems rationalization.
5. Commitment, 1970–1990: employee involvement.
6. Control, 1990– : business process re-engineering and outsourcing.[95]

The surface pattern is one of alternation; but closer examination reveals an underlying progression. Starting from a situation of 'competitive capitalism' and 'simple control,'[96] the sequence of commitment approaches aims successively deeper; the sequence of control approaches aims successively broader; and the latter have become increasingly hospitable to the former.

First, relative to the commitment approaches, there is a clear shift from the earlier reliance on paternalism, to relatively impersonal, bureaucratic norms of procedural justice, to an emphasis on empowerment and mutual commitment, targeting progressively deeper forms of subjective involvement of the individual worker. And this sequence engaged progressively deeper layers of work organization: welfare work did not seek to modify the core of work organization; human relations addressed mainly supervision; employee involvement brought concern for commitment into the heart of work organization.

Second, the sequence of control innovations—from scientific management to systems rationalism to re-engineering—aims at successively broader spans of the value chain. Scientific management focuses on tasks and the flow of materials in the workshop. Systems rationalism aimed at a more comprehensive optimization of production and distribution activities. Re-engineering and outsourcing aimed at the rationalization of flows across as well as within firms.

Third, the relation between the commitment and control approaches seems to have changed: the control approaches seem to have become increasingly hospitable to commitment. Within two or three years of publishing a text popularizing a rather brutally coercive method of business process re-engineering, both James Champy and Michael Hammer published new volumes stressing the importance of the human factor and the need for job redesigns that afford employees greater autonomy.[97] The undeniably autocratic character of much early re-engineering rhetoric and its rapid 'softening' compares favorably with more unilateral and enduring forms of domination expressed in post-war systems rationalism. It compares even more favorably with the even more unilateral and rigid rhetoric in turn-of-the-century scientific management: scientific management only softened its relations with organized labor after nearly two decades of confrontation.[98]

The zigzag path of development in management technique appears to trace a vector that corresponds well to Marx's notion of 'socialization': conscious control, and in particular in the form of collaborative community, characterizes progressively broader spans of activity. Fig. 1.3 attempts to diagram this argument.

Beyond the economic sphere: a related zigzag

So far our discussion has focused on the economic sphere; but it should be obvious that progress towards collaborative community in that sphere depends to a considerable extent on buttressing from a 'superstructure' of political and societal institutions. In the USA, we have seen an oscillation from a *laissez-faire* period in the late nineteenth century, to the Progressive era in which societal regulation grew in strength; then another

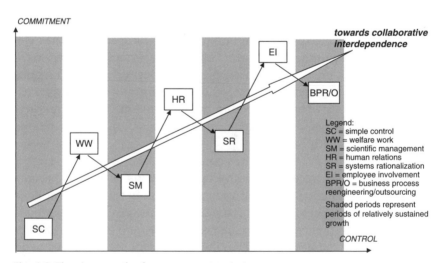

Fig. 1.3 The zigzag path of management technique

laissez-faire wave in the post-First World War period, giving way to a long period of growth of relatively strong unions and regulatory systems from the 1930s to the 1970s. The last three decades have been primarily a move towards dismantling those institutions by once again removing the communal limits on business activity.[99] Like many other writers in management and social sciences, we argue that continued vitality of US capitalism will require a reassertion of non-market forces. Successful businesses require trust among their employees and a supportive social infrastructure for everything from an educated work force to transportation networks to contract enforcement (Fig. 1.4).[100]

With this longer historical view, we can also see some characteristic patterns within the swings of the pendulum. The *laissez-faire* periods unleash great dynamism and innovation, but at the price of stability: in undermining the institutions that ground trust and mutuality of expectation, they allow new kinds of behaviors, some of which are productive but others of which are not. Inequality increases, as the 'winners' who catch the new wave outdistance the 'losers' still holding the expectations of the past. The loss of shared values leads to the spread of corruption, wider cynicism and alienation, retreat from the public arena, and varieties of fundamentalist reaction. Economic bubbles follow from the decline of stable expectations, as people trying to find their way in the new order follow the crowd.

Over time these problems bring the need for community to the forefront: there is a search for values and organizational systems that can stabilize and unify the economic order, reducing the instability and increasing commitment and justice. These institutions include government regulation, systems of representation, legal codes, and—most difficult—growing moral consensus that affects socialization in schools as well as the shape of public media.

Thus the 'Gilded Age' after the Civil War in the USA was a period of generally strong market expansion driven by the tremendous increase in transportation capacities, especially railroads and steamships, unleashing a manufacturing capacity that had just begun to grow before the war. The severe dislocation of communities and traditional relationships in this age, including the rise of an extremely wealthy class, led to a populist backlash and serious conflicts in the late part of the century which energized the Progressive movement.

A second long period of growth, starting about 1900, was based around electrification and automobile production, and further encouraged by the development of large corporations (though these were still in a crude stage

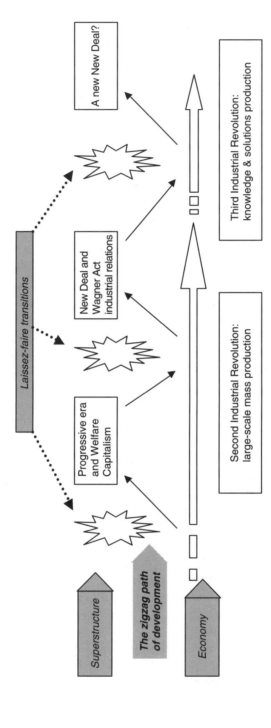

Fig. 1.4 The zigzag path of economy and society

of organization). Both unions and government regulation found themselves increasingly helpless in the face of these new market forces, and were increasingly seen as fetters on them; 'scientific management' began to spread widely and to dismantle earlier forms of worker control of the shop floor. The 'Roaring Twenties' were the culmination of this reassertion of the market: craft unions went into precipitous decline; economic inequality increased sharply, with captains of industry flaunting their unheard-of levels of wealth; the loss of moral unity was evident in everything from the hedonism of the flappers to the corruption of Harding and the many business scandals of the 1920s. The lack of coordinated expectations and shared sense of value contributed to the huge stock run-up prior to 1929. Then, starting with the election of Franklin Roosevelt, the nation entered a period of communal reconstruction, with new types of government regulation and the growth of industrial unionism as the most concrete manifestations. By the 1950s a considerable alignment of expectations and sharply reduced inequality had led to a relatively stable period of economic growth.[101]

There is a widespread sense, backed by some hard economic evidence, that the period since the mid-1970s has been the first part of a third such wave, starting with a *laissez-faire* reassertion of the market.[102] Certainly it has been a period characterized by political deregulation and union decline. In the 1990s signs of corruption began to increase; the growth of inequality became undeniable; and anxiety over the loss of shared values and fears of libertinism has become a potent political issue. The tension between economic transformation and traditional values is growing more fevered. It thus seems likely, on this analysis, that we will soon move towards institutional reconstruction, whether out of crisis (like the Depression) or through some more orderly process. The thrust of our argument is that this reconstruction will occur around collaborative community rather than *Gemeinschaft* or *Gesellschaft* patterns of community described above.

It is thus not surprising from this perspective that there are strong anti-collaborative elements in the current scene—rising efforts at managerial control, increased outsourcing, a sharp decline in labor–management cooperation, rising inequality, the selfish individualism manifest in the corruption at Enron. These are signs of the power of new market forces breaking through and overwhelming previous formal and informal accords. But if our essential claim is correct—that such an economy requires a high level of trust and collaboration—then these 'pure and simple' market logics must give way to institutions of mutual trust in some form.

The challenges ahead

We do not argue that the restoration of community is inevitable. So far the historical pattern confirms Marx's claim, which we have adopted, that capitalist productive forces cannot advance without also developing the institutions of social trust and cooperation—even if this linkage is riddled with tension. But those who have benefited from the trends of the last three decades are not likely to cede easily.

One major danger is the hardening of the current dualistic structures: strong mechanisms of collaboration and community for high-end 'knowledge workers' alongside coercive hierarchical and market control over the lower tier of the workforce. It can be argued that this would not be economically optimal, but that argument need not determine the course of history; a 'good-enough' compromise that preserves the privileges of the elite and avoids major disruption from below might well survive.

Today McDonald's and Wal-Mart stand as emblems of the possibility of a future of control rather than community. These companies have succeeded with a control strategy, squeezing huge savings out of traditional—and woefully inefficient—supply chains and work systems characteristic of a relatively backward retail sales world. Some business analysts have argued that this cannot last—that these approaches represent an old industrial model of organization applied to services, which must be replaced in time by a more collaborative one that re-engages front-line workers in interaction with customers.[103] These proposals, however, have not yet been widely adopted, and we cannot be certain that they will be.

The maximization of the value of knowledge production and collaborative community—the constellation of economic and social sketched in this volume—is not, in other words, a historical inevitability, but depends on action to address certain key challenges and take advantage of opportunities. The two key challenges that loom largest on the horizon are the reform of the stakeholder regime and the redefinition of property rights to accommodate knowledge production.

STAKEHOLDER REGIMES

A stakeholder regime is an ordered societal relation among groups representing different values.[104] The future of collaborative community in the economic sphere depends crucially on the elaboration of progressively more advanced stakeholder regimes.

The recent period since about 1970, which we label 'neoliberalism,' has been marked by a disarray similar to that seen at the beginning of the last century. The new force of knowledge production has led to a reordering of economic activity which escapes the control of the prior regulatory institutions. Both government and unions find themselves grasping at smoke as they try to manage it. The new conditions, like the earlier period of disarray, have opened the way to corporate corruption, growing inequality, and unpredicted cycles of boom and bust; they have also led to lower civic involvement and high levels of anxiety. Even the renewed growth period that (arguably) began in the 1990s is marked by this neoliberalism. The Wal-Mart model, and business process re-engineering more broadly, has torn at the social fabric, exacerbating rather than mitigating rampant 'winner take all' inequalities;[105] the erosion of regulation has led to a loss of moral consistency and confidence in business; and the instability of expectations has fueled a series of boom–bust cycles.

The logic of the new regulatory order in the first transitional period (before 1930) was 'modeled,' as it were, within the emergent economic institutions before they developed at the societal level. In that instance, the logic was one of bureaucratic rationality, following consistent rules, in place of the previous craft traditions. Corporations mastered the organization of bureaucracy first, but they were not able to harness it effectively on their own: studies from the 1920s show the degree to which managers tried to retain personal and arbitrary discretion within large organizations, which undermined the consistency and rationality needed for an effective bureaucracy. It was not until unions and government grasped the logic themselves and forced companies to be consistent with their own rhetoric that this powerful organizational form reached its potential for economic productivity as well as for other social goods.

Our argument suggests that an analogous sequence is playing out now: Companies understand the importance of collaboration but are unable to create it on their own. Their rhetoric trumpets the importance of participation and mobility; but their policies continually reassert control, and they also restrict mobility and the full development of knowledge capabilities by trying to draw a sharp line between the valuable employees that they want to keep and the others who are expendable.

If the neo-corporatist institutions are in disarray and the neoliberal ones are insufficient, there is a need for new forms of regulation that institutionalize a new balance between the contending social forces. This must clearly involve a structure of representation which is itself less rule based than industrial unionism, more open to flexible teamwork; it is likely also to involve many social groups that have found their voice in the period since the establishment of the neo-corporatist regime, such as minorities, women, environmentalists, and so on. In order to bring out the most productive aspects of the collaborative order we have described, it must find ways to pressure management once again into living up to its own rhetoric: to ensure true participation that is not subject to arbitrary interference, and to ensure true mobility that genuinely encourages the development of knowledge by most of the workforce and the opportunity to move with security and confidence to the firms and jobs where that knowledge can best be used. It is beyond the scope of this essay to go into more detail.[106]

PROPERTY LAW

The move to mass production involved a shift from individual ownership to the diffuse, socialized form embodied in publicly traded firms, with the correlative separation of management from ownership.[107] This deep shift was essential to the mass-production economy because it enabled the needed scale of investment in the massive new entities. The problem now is equally profound: the development of knowledge cannot be contained within the boundaries of bureaucratic firms, and it therefore presents problems of ownership that are so far unresolved.

Significant knowledge is created through long network processes of experimentation and critique, and it generally combines multiple insights. Assigning ownership rights to the knowledge almost always ignores large parts of this process—it 'cuts the network' arbitrarily.[108] More damaging, it encourages owners, whether companies or individuals, to keep their knowledge secret rather than sharing it as is necessary to realize its full social value.

The tension between traditional forms of ownership and the requirements of a knowledge economy is playing out on many fronts.

- Lawrence Lessig (1999, 2001) describes the internet as a battlefield between those who want to allow equal access to all and those who want to reshape the underlying code so as to distinguish among participants on the basis of ownership; the former is better for innovation, the latter for profit.

- A growing problem concerns the rights of corporations to restrict the use of knowledge by their employees through non-compete covenants or confidentiality restraints. This creates a huge obstacle to mobility: it often prevents people from leaving companies because they cannot use their knowledge and skills elsewhere. At the same time it severely restricts the exchange and development of knowledge. Litigation over these restraints has been growing in recent years, but courts have yet to find a consistent way through the thicket.

- Intellectual property in both entertainment and biotechnology as well as the broader realm of science and technology are posing acute problems in international relations. Different countries view property rights in these domains very differently, and the stakes are huge and growing.

The debate on what this means for ownership rights has just begun. Lessig proposes treating the basic infrastructure of the internet as a kind of commons, and Alan McAdams suggests customer ownership of networks.[109] More importantly, vast innovations are taking place in practice, in the form of alliances and consortia: the developing collaborative relations with competitors and contributors in many industries have spawned new types of contracts and agreements that parse ownership rights and returns in ways that have not yet been grasped by theorists.[110]

What is clear so far is that the conflict between knowledge production and the assigning of ownership rights is fundamental, and the trajectory is uncertain; and this brings us to our final and most speculative level of analysis.

Community beyond capitalism?

Our argument carries us to a deeper and broader question: Can the move to collaborative community be made within capitalist societies, or are there fundamental obstacles posed by the nature of capitalism that prevent it?

In the past two centuries, major changes in the nature of production have shaken but not sunk capitalism as a system. Notably, as we have discussed, the emergence of mass production and large corporations required deep changes in regulatory frameworks, stakeholder relations, and the legal framework of ownership, but not fundamental change in the core institutions of capitalism. So far in sketching the institutional needs for collaborative trust we have assumed that they could be established with a similar kind of reform.

But extrapolating the tendency sketched in Fig. 1.3 points to the historical limits of capitalism as a system. As production is reconfigured to allowed planful control over ever-larger aggregates—from individual tasks to whole work processes, larger firms, then entire supply chains—the role of the market as a coordinating mechanism is progressively subordinated. As production is reconfigured to support a higher level of interactivity and trust—collaborative relations between and within firms—the central roles of the market and hierarchy are challenged.

Over a century ago, capitalist relations of production morphed to accommodate a more-socialized form of production in large corporations through the remarkable legal fiction that a corporation is an 'artificial person.' Now these relations and their legal expression are facing a strong challenge once again due to the shift to greater knowledge intensity. We do not argue that capitalism is incapable of absorbing this challenge; but rather that in absorbing it, capitalism strengthens collaborative community and sharpens the conflict between collaborative community and the dominant market principle. Marx and Engels wrote in the Communist Manifesto that capitalism creates its own gravediggers: we see a growing challenge to the dominance of the market posed by the persistent minority of impoverished workers and the swelling ranks of knowledge workers.[111]

In the end a central question is: Can knowledge production be performed most effectively in the framework of capitalist institutions of ownership? In prior phases of productive advance, the equivalent question has had an affirmative answer: the capitalist form did survive the industrial revolution and the transition to mass production, but only at the cost of what conservative critics call 'creeping socialism.' As we transition to the knowledge economy, the creeping is likely to accelerate.

In any case, it is worth underlining that this analysis implies that we can neither do without community, nor go backward to familiar forms of community. The temptation is always strong, when patterns of expectation and relationships break down, to long for familiar models from the past that provided a unified sense of meaning and wholeness. We have seen this throughout the modern era in constant, though ultimately futile, attempts to sustain *Gemeinschaft* communities. As Schumpeter and Marx both pointed out, though from very different viewpoints, the advance of capitalism has steadily eroded these traditional remnants. Today many of those who criticize the heartlessness of neoliberalism draw their programs from past images of paternalist bureaucracy, which provided security and a sense of belonging. But that framework for trust is no longer adequate to an economy based on knowledge and continual responsiveness, nor to a society that continues to challenge fixed status distinctions. The way forward lies in the active development of the promise of collaborative community.

References

Abrahamson, Eric (1997). 'The emergence and prevalence of employee management rhetorics: the effects of long waves, labor unions, and turnover, 1875–1992.' *Academy of Management Journal*, 40/3: 491–533.

Academy of Management Review (1998). Special topic forum on trust in and between organizations, 23/3.

Adler, P. S. (1990). 'Marx, machines and skill.' *Technology and Culture*, 31/4: 780–812.

—— (1993). 'The learning bureaucracy: New United Motors Manufacturing, Inc.' In Barry M. Staw and Larry L. Cummings (eds.), *Research in Organizational Behavior*, 15: 111–94.

—— (1997). 'Work organization: from Taylorism to teamwork.' *Industrial Relations Research Association 50th Anniversary Magazine* (June): 61–5.

—— (2001). 'Market, hierarchy, and trust: the knowledge economy and the future of capitalism.' *Organization Science*, 12/2: 214–34.

—— (2005). 'The future of critical management studies: a paleo-marxist view.' Forthcoming in *Critical Sociology*.

—— and Borys, B. (1996). 'Two types of bureaucracy: coercive versus enabling.' *Administrative Science Quarterly*, 41/1: 61–89.

—— and Ferdows, K. (1992). 'The chief technology officer: a new role for new challenges.' In L. R. Gomez-Mejia and M. W. Lawless (eds.), *Advances in Global High-Technology Management: Top Management and Executive Leadership in High Technology*. Greenwich, Conn.: JAI Press: ii. 49–66.

—— Goldoftas, B., and Levine, D. I. (1999). 'Flexibility versus efficiency? A case study of model changeovers in the Toyota production system.' *Organization Science*, 10/1: 43–68.

Alchian, A. A., and Demsetz, H. (1972). 'Production, information costs, and economic organization.' *American Economic Review*: 777–95.

Anderson, Joel (2001). 'Competent need-interpretation and discourse ethics.' In James Bohman and William Rehg (eds.), *Pluralism and the Pragmatic Turn: The Transformation of Critical Theory*. Cambridge, Mass.: MIT Press.

Apel, K.-O. (1987), 'The problem of philosophical foundations in light of a transcendental pragmatics of language.' In K. Barnes, J. Bohnmann, and T. McCarthy (eds.), *After Philosophy: End or Transformation?* Cambridge, Mass.: MIT Press: 250–90.

Arrow, K. (1962), 'Economic welfare and the allocation of resources for invention.' In Universities-National Bureau Committee for Economic Research, *The Rate and Direction of Inventive Activity*. Princeton: Princeton University Press: 609–25.

—— and Hurwicz, L. (eds.) (1977). *Studies in Resource Allocation Processes*. Cambridge: Cambridge University Press.

Ashkenas, Ron, Ulrich, Dave, Jick, Todd, and Kerr, Steve (1993). *The Boundaryless Organization*. San Francisco: Jossey-Bass.

Barber, B. (1983). *The Logic and Limits of Trust*. New Brunswick, NJ: Rutgers University Press.

Barker, James R. (1993). 'Tightening the iron cage: concertive control in self-managing teams.' *Administrative Science Quarterly*, 38: 408–37.

Barley, Stephen R., and Kunda, Gideon (1992). 'Design and devotion: surges of rational and normative ideologies of control in managerial discourse.' *Administrative Science Quarterly*, 37: 363–99.

Barnard, Chester I. (1938). *The Functions of the Executive*. Cambridge, Mass.: Harvard University Press.

—— (1946). 'Functions and pathology of status systems in formal organizations.' In William F. Whyte (ed.), *Industry and Society*. New York: McGraw-Hill: 207–43.

Barnes, L. B. (1981). 'Managing the paradox of organizational trust.' *Harvard Business Review* (Mar.–Apr.): 107–16.

Barney, Jay B., and Hansen, Mark H. (1994). 'Trustworthiness as a source of competitive advantage.' *Strategic Management Journal*, 15, Special Issue: 175–216.

Baron, J. N., Dobbin, F. R., and Jennings, P. D. (1986). 'War and peace: the evolution of modern personnel administration in U.S. Industry.' *American Journal of Sociology*, 92/2 (Sept.): 350–83.

Bartlett, C. A., and Wozny, M. (2001). *GE's Two-Decade Transformation: Jack Welch's Leadership*. Harvard Business School case study 399150.

Beer, Michael, Eisenstat, Russell A., and Spector, Bert (1990). *The Critical Path to Corporate Renewal*. Boston: Harvard Business School Press.

Bell, Daniel (1973). *The Coming of Post-Industrial Society: A Venture in Social Forecasting*. New York: Basic Books.

—— (1993). *Communitarianism and its Critics*. Oxford: Clarendon Press.

Bennis, Warren G., and Nanus, Burt (1997). *Leaders: Strategies for Taking Charge*. 2nd edn. New York: HarperBusiness.

—— and Slater, Philip E. (1964), 'Democracy is inevitable.' *Harvard Business Review* (Mar.–Apr.).

—— —— (1998). *The Temporary Society*. San Francisco: Jossey-Bass.

Bensaou, M., and Venkatraman, N. (1995). 'Configurations of interorganizational relationships: a comparison between U.S. and Japanese automakers.' *Management Science*, 41/9: 1471–92.

Berle, A., and Means, G. (1933). *The Modern Corporation and Private Property*. New York: The Macmillan Co.

Bigely, G. A., and Pearce, J. L. (1998). 'Straining for shared meaning in organization science: problems of trust and distrust.' *Academy of Management Review*, 23/3: 405–21.

Birch, David L. (1987). *Job Creation in America*. New York: Free Press.

Blackburn, P., Coombs, R., and Green, K. (1985). *Technology, Economic Growth and the Labor Process*. New York: St Martin's Press.

Blair, M., and Kochan, T. (eds.) (2000). *The New Relationship: Human Capital in the American Corporation*. Washington, DC: Brookings Institution.

Blau, Peter M. (1963). *The Dynamics of Bureaucracy.* Chicago: University of Chicago Press.

Bloom, Paul N., and Perry, Vanessa G. (2001). 'Retailer power and supplier welfare: the case of Walmart.' *Journal of Retailing,* 77/3: 379–96.

Bohl, Don L. (1996). 'Minisurvey: 360-degree appraisals yield superior results, survey shows.' *Compensation & Benefits Review,* 28/5 (Sept.–Oct.): 16–19.

Bowles, S., Gintis, H., and Gustafsson, B. (1993). *Markets and Democracy: Participation, Accountability and Efficiency.* Cambridge: Cambridge University Press.

Bradach, Jeffrey L., and Eccles, Robert G. (1989). 'Markets vs hierarchies: from ideal types to plural forms.' *Annual Review of Sociology,* 15: 97–118.

Braverman, H. (1974). *Labor and Monopoly Capital.* New York: Monthly Review of Books.

Brockner, Joel, and Siegel, Phyllis (1996). 'Understanding the interaction between procedural and distributive justice: the role of trust.' In Roderick M. Kramer and Tom R. Tyler (eds.), *Trust in Organizations.* Thousand Oaks, Calif.: Sage: 390–413.

Bromiley, Philip, and Cummings, Larry L. (1995), 'Transaction costs in organizations with trust.' In Robert J. Bies, R. J. Lewicki, and Blair L. Sheppard (eds.), *Research on Negotiations in Organizations.* Greenwich, Conn.: JAI: 219–47.

Brown, John Seely, Durchslag, Scott, and Hagel, John, III (2002). 'Loosening up: how process networks unlock the power of specialization.' *McKinsey Quarterly,* Special Edition: Risk and resilience: 59–69.

Brynjolfsson, Erik, Malone, Thomas W., Gurbaxani, Vijay, and Kambil, Ajit (1994). 'Does information technology lead to smaller firms?' *Management Science,* 40/12: 1628–44.

Burawoy, Michael (1979). *Manufacturing Consent.* Chicago: University of Chicago Press.

Burns, T., and Stalker, G. (1961). *The Management of Innovation.* London: Tavistock.

Business Week (1982). 'TRW leads a revolution in managing technology.' (15 Nov.).

Butler, J. K., and Cantrell, R. S. (1984). 'A behavioral decision theory approach to modeling dyadic trust in superiors and subordinates.' *Psychological Reports,* 55: 19–28.

Carchedi, G. (1977). *The Economic Identification of Social Classes.* London: Routledge & Kegan Paul.

Carney, M. (1998). 'The competitiveness of networked production: the role of trust and asset specificity.' *Journal of Management Studies,* 35/4: 457–79.

Champy, James (1995). *Reengineering Management.* New York: HarperBusiness.

Ciborra, Claudio (1996). 'What does groupware mean for the organizations hosting it?' In Claudio Ciborra (ed.), *Groupware & Teamwork: Invisible Aid or Technical Hindrance.* Wiley Series on Information Systems. New York: John Wiley: Introduction.

Clark, Charles Hutchison (1958). *Brainstorming: The Dynamic New Way to Create Successful Ideas.* Garden City, NY: Doubleday.

Clark, Kim B., and Fujimoto, Takahiro (1989). 'Overlapping problem solving in product development.' In K. Ferdows (ed.), *Managing International Manufacturing*. Amsterdam: Elsevier: 127–52.

Cobble, Dorothy Sue (1991). 'Organizing the postindustrial work force: lessons from the history of waitress unionism.' *Industrial and Labor Relations Review*, 44/3 (Apr.): 419–36.

—— (1994). 'Making postindustrial unionism possible.' In Sheldon Friedman, Richard W. Hurd, Rudolph A. Oswald, and Ronald L. Seeber (eds.), *Restoring the Promise of American Labor Law*. Ithaca, NY: HR Press: ch. 20.

Cohen, Joshua, and Sabel, Charles (1997). 'Directly-deliberate polyarchy.' *European Law Journal*, 3/4 (Dec.): 313–42.

Coleman, James S. (1987). 'Social organization of the corporation.' University of Chicago: mimeo draft, 25 Feb.

Coleman, R. (1990). *Foundations of Social Theory*. Cambridge, Mass.: Belknap Press.

Collins, J. C., and Porras, J. I. (1994). *Built to Last*. New York: HarperCollins.

Comfort, Louise K. (1997). 'Toward a theory of transition in complex systems.' *American Behavioral Scientist*, 40/3 (Jan.): 375–83.

Crozier, Michel (1964). *The Bureaucratic Phenomenon*. Chicago: University of Chicago Press.

Daft, Richard L. (1998). *Essentials of Organization Theory and Design*. Cincinnati: South-Western College Publishing.

Dalton, Melville (1959). *Men Who Manage: Fusions of Feeling and Theory in Administration*. New York: John Wiley & Sons.

Davenport, T. H., and Prusak, L. (1998). *Working Knowledge*. Boston: Harvard Business School Press.

DeGrazia, Sebastian (1948). *The Political Community: A Study of Anomie*. Chicago: University of Chicago Press.

Dewey, John (1927). *The Public and its Problems*. New York: Henry Holt & Co.

DiMaggio, Paul (1992). 'Nadel's paradox revisited: relational and cultural aspects of organization structure.' In N. Nohria and R. G. Eccles (eds.), *Networks and Organization: Structure, Form, and Action*. Boston: Harvard Business School Press: 88–142.

Donnellon, Ann (1993). 'Cross-functional teams in product development: accommodating the structure to the process.' *Journal of Product Innovation Management*, 10: 377–92.

Dore, Ronald (1983). 'Goodwill and the spirit of market capitalism.' *British Journal of Sociology*, 34: 459–82.

Downs, Anthony (1967). *Inside Bureaucracy*. Boston: Little, Brown.

Drucker, Peter (1973). *Management: Tasks, Responsibilities, Practices*. New York: Harper & Row.

Dryzek, John (2001). 'Legitimacy and economy in deliberative democracy.' *Political Theory*, 29/5 (Oct.): 651–69.

Durkheim, Emile (1893/1984). *The Division of Labor in Society*, trans. W. D. Halls. New York: Free Press.

—— (1897/1951). *Suicide*, trans. John A. Spaulding and George Simpson. Glencoe, Ill.: The Free Press.

—— (1915/1995). *The Elementary Forms of the Religious Life: A Study in Religious Sociology*. London: George Allen & Unwin Ltd.

Dyer, J. H. (1996). 'Does governance matter? Keiretsu alliances and asset specificity as sources of Japanese competitive advantage.' *Organization Science*, 7/6: 649–66.

—— and Chu, W. (1998). 'The determinants of interfirm trust in supplier–automaker relationships in the U.S., Japan and Korea.' Wharton, unpublished.

Earl, Michael J., and Scott, Ian A. (1999). 'What is a chief knowledge officer?' *Sloan Management Review* (Winter): 29–38.

Eccles, R. (1985). *The Transfer Pricing Problem*. Lexington, Mass.: Lexington.

Edwards, Bob, and Foley, Michael W. (1998). 'Civil society and social capital beyond Putnam.' *American Behavioral Scientist*, 42/1: 124–39.

Edwards, Richard (1979). *Contested Terrain: The Transformation of Workplace in the Twentieth Century*. New York: Basic Books.

Eisner, Marc Allen (1993). *Regulatory Politics in Transition*. Baltimore: Johns Hopkins University Press.

Elderkin, Kenion W., and Bartlett, Christopher A. (1993). *General Electric: Jack Welch's Second Wave (A) and (B)*. Harvard Business School case study 9-391-248, 2 Apr.

Etzioni, A. (1988). *The Moral Dimension*. New York: Free Press.

—— (1991). *A Responsive Society: Collected Essays on Guiding Deliberate Social Change*. San Francisco: Jossey-Bass.

Evans, P. (1995). *Embedded Autonomy: States and Industrial Transformation*. Princeton: Princeton University Press.

—— (1996). 'Government action, social capital and development: reviewing the evidence on synergy.' *World Development*, 24/6: 1119–32.

Feldstein, Lewis, and Putnam, Robert (2003). *Better Together: Restoring the American Community*. New York: Simon & Schuster.

Fisher, Roger, and Ury, William (1981). *Getting to Yes: Negotiating Agreement without Giving In*. New York: Houghton Mifflin.

Foote, Nathaniel W., Galbraith, Jay, Hope, Quentin, and Miller, Danny (2001). 'Making solutions the answer.' *McKinsey Quarterly*, 3: 84–93.

Fox, Alan (1974). *Beyond Contract: Work, Power and Trust Relations*. London: Faber and Faber.

Freland, Robert F. (1996). 'The myth of the M-Form: governance, consent, and organizational change.' *American Journal of Sociology*, 102: 483–526.

Freidson, Eliott (1975). *Doctoring Together: A Study of Professional Social Control*. New York: Elsevier.

Freud, S. (1923/1960). *The Ego and the Id*. New York: Norton. (Norton edition of the 1960 Strachey translation of the German original.)

Fromm, E. (1973). *Anatomy of Human Destructiveness*. New York: Holt, Rinehart and Winston.

Fromm, Erich, and Maccoby, Michael (1970). *Social Character in a Mexican Village.* Englewood Cliffs, NJ: Prentice-Hall.

Fukuyama, F. (1995). *Trust: The Social Virtues and the Creation of Prosperity.* New York: Free Press.

Galbraith, Jay R. (1995). *Designing Organizations: An Executive Briefing on Strategy, Structure and Process.* San Francisco: Jossey-Bass.

—— (2000). *Designing the Global Corporation.* San Francisco: Jossey-Bass Publishers.

Gambetta, D. (ed.) (1988). *Trust: Making and Breaking Cooperative Relations.* Oxford: Basil Blackwell.

Gates, Henry Louis, Jr. (1998). 'The end of loyalty.' *New Yorker* (9 Mar.): 34–44.

Gerlach, Michael L. (1992). *Alliance Capitalism: The Social Organization of Japanese Capitalism.* Berkeley, and Los Angeles: University of California Press.

Gerstner, L. V. (2002). *Who Says Elephants Can't Dance? Inside IBM's Historic Turnaround.* New York: HarperCollins.

Gerth, H. H., and Mills, C. Wright (trans. and eds.) (1946). *From Max Weber: Essays in Sociology.* New York: Oxford University Press.

Giddens, A. (1990). *The Consequences of Modernity.* Stanford, Calif.: Stanford University Press.

—— (1994). *Beyond Left and Right: The Future of Radical Politics.* Cambridge: Polity Press.

Gomes-Casseres, Benjamin (1994). 'Group vs group: how alliance networks compete.' *Harvard Business Review* (July–Aug.): 4–11.

Gordon, David M. (1996). *Fat and Mean: the Corporate Squeeze of Working America and the Myth of Managerial 'Downsizing.'* New York: The Free Press.

Gordon, R. W., and Simon, W. H. (1992). 'The redemption of professionalism?' In R. L. Nelson, D. M. Trubek, and R. L. Solomon (eds.), *Lawyers' Ideals/Lawyers' Practice: Transformations in the American Legal Profession.* Ithaca, NY: Cornell University Press.

Gorz, A. (1967). *Strategy for Labour: A Radical Proposal.* Boston: Beacon Press.

Gouldner, A. W. (1954). *Patterns of Industrial Bureaucracy.* New York: Free Press.

—— (1957). 'Cosmopolitans and locals: toward an analysis of latent social roles I.' *Administrative Science Quarterly,* 2/3 (Dec.): 281–306.

Granovetter, M. (1985). 'Economic action and social structure: the problem of embeddedness.' *American Journal of Sociology,* 91: 481–510.

Greenwood, Jeremy (1997). 'The third industrial revolution: technology, productivity, and income inequality.' Washington, DC: AEI Press. Also downloaded from www.econ.rochester.edu/Faculty/GreenwoodPapers/third.pdf, 9/3/04; also *Economic Review* (1999): Q II: 2–12.

Grobstein, Clifford (1973). 'Hierarchical order and neogenesis.' In Howard H. Pattee (ed.), *Hierarchy Theory: The Challenge of Complex Systems.* New York: George Braziller: ch. 2.

Gupta, A. K., and Govindarajan V., (1986). 'Resource sharing among SBUs: strategic antecedents and administrative implications.' *Academy of Management Review*, 29/4: 695–714.

Guzzo, Richard A, and Dickson, Marcus W. (1996). 'Teams in organizations: recent research on performance and effectiveness.' *Annual Review of Psychology*, 47: 307–38.

Habermas, Jürgen (1975). *Legitimation Crisis*, trans. Thomas McCarthy. Boston: Beacon Press.

—— (1984). *The Theory of Communicative Action*. Cambridge: Polity Press.

—— (1990). *Moral Consciousness and Communicative Action*, trans. Christian Lenhardt and Shierry Weber Nicholsen. Cambridge, Mass.: MIT Press.

—— (1991). *Communication and the Evolution of Society*, trans. and introd. Thomas McCarthy. Cambridge: Polity Press.

—— (1993). *The Philosophical Discourse of Modernity*. Cambridge, Mass.: MIT Press.

—— (1994). 'Three normative models of democracy.' *Constellation*, 1/1: 1–10.

Häcki, Remo L., and Lighton, Julian (2001). 'The future of the networked company.' *McKinsey Quarterly*, 3: 26–39.

Hackman, J. Richard, and Wageman, Ruth (1995). 'Total quality management: empirical, conceptual, and practical issues.' *Administrative Science Quarterly*, 40/2 (June): 309–42.

Hamel, Gary (2000). 'Waking up IBM: how a gang of unlikely rebels transformed Big Blue.' *Harvard Business Review* (July–Aug.): 5–12.

Hammer, Michael (1996). *Beyond Reengineering*. New York: HarperBusiness.

—— and Champy James, (1993). *Reengineering the Corporation*. New York: Harper-Business.

Hancké, Bob (1997). 'Trust or hierarchy? Changing relationships between large and small firms in France.' *Small Business Economics*, 11/3: 237–52.

Handy, Charles (1995). 'Trust and the virtual organization.' *Harvard Business Review*, 73/3 (May–June): 40–50.

Hardin, R. (1992). 'The street-level epistemology of trust.' *Politics and Society*, 21: 505–29.

Harvey, David (1990). *The Condition of Modernity*. Cambridge, Mass.: Blackwell.

—— (2003). *The New Imperialism*. New York: Oxford University Press.

Hawthorn, Geoffrey (1988). 'Three ironies in trust.' In Diego Gambetta (ed.), *Trust: Making and Breaking Cooperative Relations*. New York: Basil Blackwell: ch. 7: 111–26.

Heckscher, Charles C. (1988). *The New Unionism: Employee Involvement in the Changing Corporation*. New York: Basic Books.

—— (1995). *White-Collar Blues: Management Loyalties in an Age of Corporate Restructuring*. New York: Basic Books.

—— Maccoby, Michael, Ramirez, Rafael, and Tixier, Pierre-Eric (2003). *Agents of Change: Crossing the Post-Industrial Divide*. Oxford: Oxford University Press.

Heimer, Carol (1992). 'Doing your job and helping your friends: universalistic norms about obligations to help particular others in a network.' In N. Noria and R. G. Eccles (eds.), *Networks and Organizations: Structure, Form, and Action*. Boston: Harvard Business School Press: 143–64.

Heisig, Ulrich, and Litteck, Wolfgan (1995). 'Trust as a basis of work organization.' In W. Littek and Tony Charles (eds.), *The New Division of Labour: Emerging Forms of Work Organization in International Perspective*. Berlin: de Gruyter: 17–56.

Helper, S. (1991). 'Strategy and irreversibility in supplier relations: the case of the US automobile industry.' *Business History Review*, 65/4: 781–824.

—— and Sako, M. (1995). 'Supplier relations in the auto industry in Japan and the USA: are they converging?' *Sloan Management Review* (Spring): 7–84.

Heskett, James L., Jones, Thomas O., Loveman, Gary W., Sasser, W. Earl, and Schlesinger, Leonard A. (1994). 'Putting the service–profit chain to work.' *Harvard Business Review* (Mar.–Apr.): 164–74.

Hill, C., Hitt, M., and Hoskisson, R. (1992). 'Cooperative vs. competitive structures in related and unrelated diversified firms.' *Organization Science*, 3/4: 501–21.

Hirschman, A. O. (1970). *Exit, Voice, and Loyalty*. Cambridge, Mass.: Harvard University Press.

—— (1982). 'Rival interpretations of market society: civilizing, destructive or feeble?' *Journal of Economic Literature*, 20: 1463–84.

—— (1992). *Shifting Involvements: Private Interests and Public Action*. Princeton: Princeton University Press.

Holland, C. P., and Lockett, A. G. (1997). 'Mixed mode network structures: the strategic use of electronic communication by organizations.' *Organization Science*, 8/5: 475–88.

Holton, Gerald (1996). *Einstein, History, and Other Passions*. Reading, Mass.: Addison-Wesley.

Hyde, Alan (1997). 'How Silicon Valley has eliminated trade secrets (and why this is efficient).' Draft. See web variant 'The wealth of shared information: Silicon Valley's high-velocity labor market, endogenous economic growth, and the law of trade secrets.' http://andromeda.rutgers.edu/~hyde/, 11 Mar. 2003.

Hyman. R. (1987). 'Strategy or structure? Capital, labour and control.' *Work, Employment and Society*, 1/1: 25–55.

Jackall, Robert (1988). *Moral Mazes: The World of Corporate Managers*. New York: Oxford University Press.

Jacoby, S. (2004). *Employing Bureaucracy*. Revised edition. Mahwah, NJ: Lawrence Erlbaum.

Kanter, Rosabeth Moss (1977). *Men and Women of the Corporation*. New York: Basic Books.

Kaplan, R. S. (1984). 'The evolution of management accounting.' *Accounting Review*, (July).

—— (1996). *The Balanced Scorecard: Translating Strategy into Action*. Boston: Harvard Business School Press.

Kern, H. (1998). 'Lack of trust, surfeit of trust: some causes of the innovation crisis in German industry.' In Cristel Lane and Reinhard Bachmann (eds.), *Trust within and between Organizations*. New York: Oxford University Press: 203–13.

Kim, Peter H. (1997). 'Working under the shadow of suspicion: the implications of trust and mistrust for information sharing in groups.' University of Southern California, unpublished.

Kirkpatrick, Frank G. (1986). *Community: A Trinity of Models*. Washington, DC: Georgetown University Press.

Korczynski, Marek (1996). 'The low trust route to economic development: inter-firm relations in the UK engineering construction industry in the 1980s and 1990s.' *Journal of Management Studies*, 33/6: 787–808.

Kotz, D. M, McDonough, T., and Reich, M. (eds.) (1994). *Social Structures of Accumulation: The Political Economy of Growth and Crisis*. Cambridge: Cambridge University Press.

Koza, Mitchell P., and Lewin, Arie Y. (1998). 'The co-evolution of strategic alliances.' *Organization Science*, 9/3: 255–64.

Kramer, Roderick M. (1999). 'Trust and distrust in organizations: emerging perspectives, enduring questions.' *Annual Review of Psychology*, 50: 569–98.

Kurland, Nancy B. (1996). 'Trust, accountability, and sales agents' dueling loyalties.' *Business Ethics Quarterly*, 6/3: 289–310.

Kusterer, Ken C. (1978). *Know-how on the Job: The Important Working Knowledge of 'Unskilled' Workers*. Boulder, Colo.: Westview Press.

Lakoff, George (1996). *Moral Politics: What Conservatives Know That Liberals Don't*. Chicago: University of Chicago Press.

Lawler, E. E., III, Mohrman, S. A., and Ledford, G. E., Jr. (1998). *Strategies for High Performance Organizations*. San Francisco: Jossey-Bass.

Lawrence, Paul R., and Lorsch, Jay W. (1967). *Organization and Environment*. Boston: Harvard Business School.

Lee, Dennis M. (1992). 'Management of concurrent engineering: organizational concepts and a framework of analysis.' *Engineering Management Journal*, 4/2 (June): 15–25.

Lessig, Lawrence (1999). *Code and Other Laws of Cyberspace*. New York: Basic Books.

—— (2001). *The Future of Ideas: The Fate of the Commons in a Connected World*. New York: Random House.

—— (2003). 'Fiber to the people: when customers own the network, everyone wins.' *Wired*, 11/12 (Dec.) (www.wired.com/wired/ archive/11.12/view.html?pg=5).

Levine, D. (1995). *Reinventing the Workplace: How Business and Employees Can Both Win*. Washington, DC: Brookings Institution.

Lewicki, Roy J., and Bunker, Barbara Benedict (1996). 'Developing and maintaining trust in work relationships.' In Roderick M. Kramer and Tom R. Tyler (eds.), *Trust in Organizations*. Thousand Oaks, Calif.: Sage: 114–49.

Liebeskind, J. L., and Oliver, Amalya Lumerman (1998). 'From handshake to contract: trust, intellectual property, and the social structure of academic research.' In Cristel Lane and Reinhard Bachmann (eds.), *Trust within and between Organizations*. New York: Oxford University Press: 118–45.

—— Zucker, L., and Brewer, M. (1996). 'Social networks, learning and flexibility: sourcing scientific knowledge in the new biotechnology firms.' *Organization Science*, 7/4: 428–43.

Lorsch, J. W., and Allen, S. A., III (1973). *Managing Diversity and Interdependence*. Boston: Division of Research, Graduate School of Business Administration, Harvard University.

Luhmann, Niklas (1973/1979). *Trust and Power*. New York: John Wiley & Sons (original German edns. 1973, 1975).

Lynd, Helen (1958). *On Shame and the Search for Identity*. New York: Harcourt Brace.

McAdams, Alan (2003). 'The case for end-user-ownership of advanced fiber networks (AFNs).' *Rural Telecon* 28 Sept.–(1) Oct.

Macaulay, Stuart (1963). 'Non-contractual relations in business.' *American Sociological Review*, 28: 55–70.

Maccoby, Michael (1976). *The Gamesman: The New Corporate Leaders*. New York: Simon & Schuster.

McEvily, Bill, Perrone, Vincenzo, and Zaheer, Akbar (2003). 'Trust as an organizing principle.' *Organization Science*, 14 (Jan.–Feb.): 91–103.

MacIver, R. M. (1917/1970). *Community: A Sociological Study—Being an Attempt to Set out the Nature and Fundamental Laws of Social Life*. 4th edn. London: Frank Cass & Co.

Macneil, Ian R. (1980). *The New Social Contract*. New Haven: Yale University Press.

Margolis, Joshua, and Donnellon, Anne (1990). *Mod IV product development team*. Harvard Business School case study 9-491-030.

Markus, H. R., and Kitayama, S. (1991). 'Culture and the self: implications for cognition, emotion, and motivation.' *Psychological Review* 98: 224–53.

Marx, K. (1844/1975). 'Estranged labor.' In *The Economic and Philosophical Manuscripts*, trans. Rodney Livingstone and Gregory Benton. New York: Vintage Books.

—— (1859/1977). *A Contribution to the Critique of Political Economy*. Moscow: Progress Publishers.

—— (1973). *Grundrisse: Foundations of Political Economy*. Harmondsworth: Penguin.

—— and Engels, Frederick (1848/1948). *The Communist Manifesto*. New York: International Publishers (1948, reprinted 1986).

Mashaw, J. L. (1983). *Bureaucratic Justice: Managing Social Security Disability Claims*. New Haven: Yale University Press.

Mayo, E. (1933). *The Human Problems of an Industrial Civilization*. London: Macmillan.

Mead, George H. (1918). 'The psychology of punitive justice.' *American Journal of Sociology*, 23: 577–602.

—— (1934). *Mind, Self, and Society*, ed. Charles Morris. Chicago: University of Chicago Press.

Merton, Robert K. (1940). 'Bureaucratic structure and personality.' *Social Forces*, 17: 560–8.

—— (1983). *The Sociology of Science*. Chicago: University of Chicago Press.

Meyerson, D., Weick, K. E., and Kramer, R. M. (1996). 'Swift trust and temporary groups.' In R. M. Kramer and T. R. Tyler (eds.), *Trust in Organizations: Frontiers of Theory and Research*. Thousand Oaks, Calf: Sage: 166–95.

Mill, John Stuart (1869). *On Liberty*. London: Longman, Roberts & Green.

Miller, Gary J. (1992). *Managerial Dilemmas: The Political Economy of Hierarchy*. New York: Cambridge University Press.

Mills, C. Wright (1951). *White Collar: The American Middle Classes*. London: Oxford University Press.

Mintzberg, Henry (1973). *The Nature of Managerial Work*. New York: Harper & Row.

—— (1979). *The Structuring of Organizations*. Englewood Cliffs, NJ: Prentice-Hall.

Mohrman, Susan Albers, Tenkasi, Ramkrishnan V., Lawler, Edward E., III, and Ledford, Gerald E. Jr. (1995). 'Total quality management: practice and outcomes in the largest US firms.' *Employee Relations*, 17/3: 26–41.

Nahapiet, J., and Ghoshal, S. (1998). 'Social capital, intellectual capital, and the organizational advantage.' *Academy of Management Review*, 23/2: 242–66.

Nasser, Jacques, and Wetlaufer, Suzy (1999). 'Driving change: an interview with Ford Motor Company's Jacques Nasser.' *Harvard Business Review* (Mar.–Apr.): 75–88.

Nelson, R. R. (1988). 'Institutions supporting technical change in the United States.' In G. Dosi, C. Freeman, R. Nelson, G. Silverberg, and L. Soete (eds.), *Technical Change and Economic Theory*. London: Pinter: 312–29.

Nove, Alec (1982). *The Economics of Feasible Socialism*. London: Allen and Unwin.

Nyland, Chris (1998). 'Taylorism and the mutual-gains strategy.' *Industrial Relations*, 37/4: 519–42.

OECD (1996). *Employment and Growth in the Knowledge-Based Economy*. Paris: Organization for Economic Co-operation and Development.

Organization Science (1998). Special issue on managing partnerships and strategic alliances, 9/3.

Ouchi, W. (1980). 'Markets, bureaucracies and clans.' *Administrative Science Quarterly*, 25, (Mar.): 125–41.

Pagden, Anthony (1988). 'Trust in eighteenth-century Naples.' In D. Gambetta (ed.), *Trust: Making and Breaking Cooperative Relations*. Oxford: Basil Blackwell: 127–41.

Paine, Thomas (1792/1951). *The Rights of Man*. New York: E. P. Dutton.

Palmisano, Samuel J., Hemp, Paul, and Stewart, Thomas A. (2004). 'Leading change when business is good: the HBR interview—Samuel J. Palmisano.' *Harvard Business Review* (1 Dec.): 60–70.

Parsons, Talcott (1937). *The Structure of Social Action*. New York: McGraw Hill.

Parsons, Talcott (1963). 'On the concept of influence.' *Public Opinion Quarterly*, 27: 37–62.

—— (1968). 'On the concept of value commitments.' *Sociological Inquiry*, 3/8 (Spring): 135–60.

—— (1969). 'On the concept of political power.' In Talcott Parsons, *Politics and Social Structure*. New York: The Free Press: ch. 14.

—— (1971). *The System of Modern Societies*. Englewood Cliffs, NJ: Prentice-Hall.

—— and Platt, Gerald (1973). *The American University*. Cambridge, Mass: Harvard University Press.

Pateman, Carole (1970). *Participation and Democratic Theory*. Cambridge: Cambridge University Press.

Peiperl, Maury A. (2001). 'Getting 360 feedback right.' *Harvard Business Review*, 79/1 (Jan.): 142–7.

Peyrefitte, Alain (1995). *La Société de confiance: essai sur les origines et la nature du développement*. Paris: Éditions Odile Jacob.

Phillips, Derek L. (1993). *Looking Backward: A Critical Appraisal of Communitarian Thought*. Princeton: Princeton University Press.

Piaget, Jean, and Inhelder, Barbel (1958). *The Growth of Logical Thinking from Childhood to Adolescence*, trans. Ann Parsons and Stanley Milgram. New York: Basic Books.

Piore, Michel J., and Sabel, Charles F. (1984). *The Second Industrial Divide: Possibilities for Prosperity*. New York: Basic Books.

Porter, M. E. (1985). *Competitive Advantage*. New York: Free Press.

Powell, W. (1990). 'Neither markets nor hierarchy: network forms of organization.' *Research in Organizational Behavior*, 12: 295–336.

Prahalad, C. K., and Hamel, G. (1990). 'The core competencies of the corporation.' *Harvard Business Review*, 86: 79–91.

Putnam, Robert (1993). *Making Democracy Work: Civic Traditions in Modern Italy*. Princeton: Princeton University Press.

—— (2000). *Bowling Alone: The Collapse and Revival of American Community*. New York: Simon & Schuster.

Quandt, Jean B. (1970). *From the Small Town to the Great Community: The Social Thought of Progressive Intellectuals*. New Brunswick, NJ: Rutgers University Press.

Ramirez, Rafael (1999). 'Value co-production: intellectual origins and implications for practice and research.' *Strategic Management Journal*, 20/1: 49–65.

—— and Wallin, Johan (2000). *Prime Movers: Define your Business or Have Someone Define it Against You*. Chichester: John Wiley & Sons.

Ramsay, Harvie (1977). 'Cycles of control: worker participation in sociological and historical perspective.' *Sociology*, 11/3: 481–506.

Reichheld, Frederick F. (1996). *The Loyalty Effect: The Hidden Force behind Growth, Profits, and Lasting Value*. Boston: Harvard Business School Press.

Ring, Peter S. (1996). 'Fragile and resilient trust and their roles in economic exchange.' *Business and Society*, 35/2: 148–75.

—— (1997). 'Transacting in the state of union: a case study of exchange governed by convergent interests.' *Journal of Management Studies*, 34/1: 1–25.

—— and Van de Ven, Andrew H. (1992). 'Structuring cooperative relationships between organizations.' *Strategic Management Journal*, 13: 483–98.

Rosenberg, Nathan (1964). 'Neglected dimensions in the analysis of economic change.' *Oxford Bulletin of Economics and Statistics*, 26/1: 59–77.

Rothschild-Witt, J. (1979). 'The collectivist organization: an alternative to rational-bureaucratic models.' *American Sociological Review*, 44: 509–27.

Sabel, C. F. (1993). 'Studied trust: building new forms of co-operation in a volatile economy.' *Human Relations*, 46/9 (Sept.): 1133–70.

—— and Zeitlin, Jonathan (eds.) (1997). *World of Possibilities: Flexibility and Mass Production in Western Industrialization*. Cambridge: Cambridge University Press.

Sako, M. (1992). *Prices, Quality and Trust: Interfirm Relations in Britain and Japan*. Cambridge: Cambridge University Press.

Salter, M. S. (1983). 'Tailor incentive compensation to strategy.' *Harvard Business Review* (Mar.–Apr.): 94–102.

Satow, Roberta Lynn (1975). 'Value-rational authority and professional organizations: Weber's missing type.' *Administrative Science Quarterly*, 20 (Dec.): 526–31.

Scheff, Thomas J (2000). 'Shame and the social bond: a sociological theory.' *Sociological Theory*, 18/1 (Mar.): 84–100.

Schindler, P. L., and Thomas, C. C. (1993). 'The structure of interpersonal trust in the workplace.' *Psychological Reports*, 73: 563–73.

Schlesinger, Leonard A., and Heskett, James L. (1991). 'The service-driven service company.' *Harvard Business Review* (Sept.–Oct.): 146–58.

Schumpeter, J. (1942/1976). *Capitalism, Socialism and Democracy*. New York: Harper.

Sciulli, D. (1986). 'Voluntaristic action as a distinct concept: theoretical foundations of societal constitutionalism.' *American Sociological Review*, 51: 743–66.

Scott, W. Richard (1992). *Organizations: Rational, Natural, and Open Systems*. Englewood Cliffs, NJ: Prentice Hall.

Seligman, Adam B. (1997). *The Problem of Trust*. Princeton: Princeton University Press.

Selznick, Philip (1992). *The Moral Commonwealth: Social Theory and the Promise of Community*. Berkeley and Los Angeles: University of California Press.

Sennett, Richard (1998). *The Corrosion of Character: The Personal Consequences of Work in the New Capitalism*. New York: W. W. Norton and Company.

Settersten, Richard A., Jr., Furstenberg, Frank F., Jr., and Rumbaut, Rubén G. (eds.) (2004). *On the Frontier of Adulthood: Theory, Research, and Public Policy*. Chicago: University of Chicago Press; Sponsored by the John T. and Catherine D. MacArthur Foundation Research Network on the Transitions to Adulthood and Public Policy.

Shapiro, Susan P. (1987). 'The social control of impersonal trust.' *American Journal of Sociology*, 93/3: 623–58.

Silver, Allan (1985). ' "Trust" In social and political theory.' In Morris D. Janowitz, Gerald D. Suttles, and Mayer N. Zald (eds.), *The Challenge of Social Control*. Norwood, NJ: Ablex: ch. 4.

Simmel, Georg (1950). *The Sociology of Georg Simmel*, trans. Kurt Wolff. New York: Free Press.

Simon, Herbert A. (1973). 'The organization of complex systems.' In Howard H. Pattee (ed.), *Hierarchy Theory: The Challenge of Complex Systems*. New York: George Braziller: ch. 1.

Solomou, Solomos (1988). 'Phases of economic growth, 1850–1973: Kondratieff & Kuznets.' *Business History Review* (Winter): 727.

Sparrow, Malcolm K. (1994). *Imposing Duties: Government's Changing Approach to Compliance*. Westport, Conn.: Praeger.

Spencer, Martin E. (1970). 'Weber on legitimate norms and authority.' *British Journal of Sociology*, 21/2: 123–34.

Starr, Paul (1982). *The Social Transformation of American Medicine*. New York: Basic Books.

Stiglitz, J. E. (1994). *Whither Socialism?* Cambridge, Mass.: MIT Press.

Stinchcombe, Arthur L. (1985). 'Contracts as hierarchical documents.' In Arthur L. Stinchcombe and Carol Heimer, *Organization Theory and Project Management*. Bergen: Universitetsforslaget.

Strathern, Marilyn (1996). 'Cutting the network.' *Journal of the Royal Anthropological Institute*, 2/3 (Sept.): 517–35.

Suttles, Gerald D. (1972). *The Social Construction of Communities*. Chicago: University of Chicago Press.

Tajfel, H., and Turner, J. C. (1979). 'An integrative theory of intergroup conflict.' In W. G. Austin and S. Worchel (eds.), *The Social Psychology of Intergroup Relations*. Monterey, Calif: Brooks-Cole: 33–47.

Tarrow, Sidney (1996). 'Making social science work across space and time: a critical reflection on Robert Putnam's *Making Democracy Work*.' *American Political Science Review*, 90/2: 389–401.

Thompson, E. P. (1967). 'Time, work discipline, industrial capitalism.' *Past and Present: Journal of Historical Studies*, 38: 56–97.

Thompson, James D. (1967). *Organizations in Action*. New York: McGraw-Hill.

Tönnies, Ferdinand (1957). *Community and Society (Gemeinschaft und Gesellschaft)*, trans. and introd. Charles P. Loomis. East Lansing, Mich.: Michigan State University Press. Original edn. 1887.

Unger, R. M. (1975). *Knowledge and Politics*. New York: Free Press.

Uzzi, Brian (1997). 'Social structure and competition in interfirm networks: the paradox of embeddedness.' *Administrative Science Quarterly*, 42/1: 35–67.

Walton, R. E. (1985). 'Toward a strategy for eliciting employee commitment based on policies of mutuality.' In R. E. Walton and P. R. Lawrence (eds.), *HRM Trends and Challenges*. Boston: Harvard Business School: 35–65.

Walzer, Michael (1999). 'Rescuing civil society.' *Dissent*, 46/1: 62–7.

Wanguri, Deloris McGee (1995). 'A review, an integration, and a critique of cross-disciplinary research on performance appraisals, evaluations, and feedback: 1980–1990.' *Journal of Business Communication*, 32/3 (July): 267–93.

Waters, Malcolm (1989). 'Collegiality, bureaucratization, and professionalization: a Weberian analysis.' *American Journal of Sociology*, 94/5 (Mar.): 945–72.

Weber, Max (1904/1958). *The Protestant Ethic and the Spirit of Capitalism*. New York: Scribner's Press.

—— (1947). *The Theory of Social and Economic Organization*. New York: Free Press.

Wenger, Étienne (1998). *Communities of Practice*. New York: Oxford University Press.

Whyte, William H., Jr. (1956). *The Organization Man*. New York: Simon and Schuster.

Wicks, A. C., Berman, S. L., and Jones, T. M. (1999). 'The structure of optimal trust: moral and strategic implications.' *Academy of Management Review*, 24/1: 99–116.

Williamson, O. E. (1975). *Markets and Hierarchies*. New York: Free Press.

—— (1981). 'The economics of organization: the transaction cost approach.' *American Journal of Sociology*, 87: 548–77.

—— (1991). 'Economic institutions: spontaneous and intentional governance.' *Journal of Law, Economics and Organization*, 7: 159–87.

—— (1993). 'Calculativeness, trust, and economic organization.' *Journal of Law and Economics*, 36: 453–502.

Womack, James P., Jones, Daniel T., and Roos, Daniel (1991). *The Machine that Changed the World*. New York: HarperCollins.

Wright, Erik Olin (2000). 'Working-class power, capitalist-class interests, and class compromise.' *American Journal of Sociology*, 105/4: 957–1002.

Zelizer, Viviana A. (1996). 'Payments and social ties.' *Sociological Forum*, 11/3: 481–96.

Zenger, Todd R., and Hesterly, William S. (1997). 'The disaggregation of corporations: selective intervention, high-powered incentives, and molecular units.' *Organization Science*, 8/3: 209–22.

Zucker, Lynne G. (1986). 'Production of trust: institutional sources of economic structure, 1840–1920.' *Research in Organizational Behavior*, 8: 53–111.

Notes

1. The 'Communitarian' school carries nostalgia for traditional morality and community into the modern era. Selznick (1992), Etzioni (1991), and others are sensitive to the criticism that their approach may constrain individual freedom and development, and they struggle mightily to overcome it—but with only partial success; see Habermas's (1994) analysis.
2. The literature proposing a new form of community can usefully be divided into two major chunks, though there is some overlap: works that approach it 'deductively' from a broad sociological or philosophical perspective, and those that

approach it 'inductively' by generalizing the lessons of some concrete community. In the first camp we would cite as Parsons (1971; Parsons and Platt 1973) and
Habermas (1990, 1984). In the second we would emphasize Parsons's (1973)
treatment of the professions, and Bell's (1973) emphasis on knowledge work.
Others have focused on the film industry (e.g. Meyerson et al. 1996), craft networks (e.g. Powell 1990), industrial districts (Piore and Sabel 1984). We have used
some works from the sociology of science as central to our own thinking, but are
not aware of this model in the existing general literature on community.
3. W. B. Yeats, 'The Second Coming.'
4. Artists have taken up the theme as well: those who merely escape from old
communities, without committing to new ones, are the subject of the great
modern tragedies of loss of self—Emma Bovary, Raskolnikov, Gatsby.
5. Marx and Engels (1848/1948/9).
6. Social theory has mirrored these internal contradictions of modern society.
Most writers have been bound to one idea of community—the traditional
form; they thus see societies as either high or low in trust. Since high trust is
(in this view) grounded in traditional community, their recommendations for
action involve confusing notions of balance, trying to offset the bad aspects of
capitalism through a little tradition but without destroying its good aspects,
trying to go a little backwards but not too far. A perfect representative of this
type of theory is Francis Fukuyama (1995): his attempt to divide the world into
'high-trust' and 'low-trust' societies produces strange results such as the USA
standing alongside Germany and Japan as high trust, and France alongside
Korea and China as low trust; his recommendations fall precisely into the
uncomfortable a-little-more-of-this-but-not-too-much kind of reasoning.
Much of Robert Putnam's earlier work (2000) runs into the same problem,
though in his most recent writings (Feldstein and Putnam 2003) he is clearly
reaching, if tentatively, for a conception of a post-modern type of trust.

A somewhat more sophisticated strand has made a core distinction between
'personal' and 'impersonal' trust—notably in Luhmann (1973/1979) and many
influenced by him like Silver (1985) and Shapiro (1987), as well as in an important analysis by Zucker (1986). In its essence, however, this is simply a version of
the opposition of *Gemeinschaft* and *Gesellschaft*; impersonal trust is based on
rational-bureaucratic institutions and fails to create the conditions for active
cooperation or coherent identities.

There has been a recent spate of research on trust, much of it encouraged by
the Russell Sage Foundation, which has detailed many aspects of trust dynamics
in various situations and has tried to extend game theory by adding relational
concepts. The overall picture, however, continues to be as described in a review
article by Kramer (1999): the field has a lot more mid-level richness than it did
just a few years ago, but still no overarching story line. The exceptions are those
that we have underlined, and seek to join, as sketching the move *beyond* the
personal–impersonal, *Gemeinschaft–Gesellschaft* contrast.

7. 'Mankind thus inevitably sets itself only such tasks as it is able to solve, since closer examination will always show that the problem itself arises only when the material conditions for its solution are already present or at least in the course of formation' (Marx 1859/1977: preface).

8. Parallel developments can be discerned in the realms of political practice and theory: 'deliberative democracy' is perhaps the strongest thread. See Dryzek (2001); Cohen and Sabel (1997).

9. This threefold division has appeared in many works of the last twenty years, though often the authors seem unaware of the other instances: see Bradach and Eccles (1989), Ouchi (1980), Powell (1990), Adler (2001). As argued below (n. 10), it is also consistent with the Parsonian four-part model.

10. Since this chapter uses a Parsonian framework in part, we should explain the relationship between this three-part formulation and the four-part Parsonian analysis of societies. Markets and hierarchies correspond closely to Parsons's adaptive and goal-attainment subsystems. 'Community' *combines* his other two categories (integration and pattern maintenance). The current social phase as we are describing is really about the redefinition of both those subsystems through differentiation and relinking: what we describe as the 'ethic of contribution' is the pattern-maintenance aspect of the emerging community, and 'interdependent process management' is its integrative aspect. In this work we are analyzing the development of both aspects and the dynamics of their interchanges.

11. The relation between social values and personality runs in two directions. The internalization of values in personality is necessary to stabilize social relations and trust, as we have emphasized; but it is also necessary to stabilize personalities. Durkheim (and, from a different direction, Freud) analyzed the ways in which hierarchical values provided needed constraints and direction to otherwise formless needs; lacking them the personality becomes inchoate and, in Durkheim's (1897/1951) analysis, tends towards self-destruction (suicide). Mead (1934) analyzed the ways in which social relations and associations formed and stabilized the ego, or self-identity.

12. The structure is formally a semi-lattice, which is used by Piaget (Piaget and Inhelder 1958) to model the operations that maintain stable order in cognitive systems. He sees it as one of the fundamental patterns of human action systems, and indeed it seems to have this kind of significance in the maintenance of systems of trust. On the sacred nature of *Gemeinschaft* community, see also Durkheim (1915/1995).

13. William Shakespeare, *Troilus and Cressida*, i. iii, Ulysses' speech. To maximize the readability for this context, the text has been slightly abridged and rearranged without being marked with elisions. The full text can easily be found in any edition of Shakespeare.

14. The individualist morality also supports or frames the nation-state, which is not dependent on a status order but treats each individual as equally connected to the whole by the rights of citizenship. From this structural perspective, the nation-state is the equivalent of the Protestant God in terms of creating universal obligations of good citizenship—as opposed to particularistic status obligations—but leaving it largely up to the individual how this obligation will be integrated into a consistent personality.

15. John Stuart Mill (1869) treated the distinction between public and private realms as the 'one simple principle' that was the key to modern morality. It is a distinction that, however, is not tenable in more developed modern societies, as discussed below.

16. We expand below (in the section 'The growing need for community in industry') on the limitations of rational economic motives and reasoning for this purpose.

17. The concept of a community of purpose has some roots in existing literature, though it has not emerged clearly. We should note that theorists centered on *Gemeinschaft* have explicitly denied that shared purpose is necessary (e.g. MacIver 1917/1970: book II, ch. I). Some of the community thinkers around 1900 like John Dewey and Robert Park, grappling for a concept of community in modernity, stressed the centrality of purpose (see Quandt 1970: 24 ff.). It has often re-emerged in more recent theories that approach the idea of a 'new' type of community, such as Selznick (1992) and Heckscher (1995); also Comfort (1997) on purpose in dynamics of non-linear systems theory.

    We should be more systematic about the relation between *cooperative* and *collaborative* communities: Cooperative community is the general concept, and collaborative community—our focus here—is a subset of it specified to goal-oriented groups. Thus collaborative community adds some restrictions to the general concept. In particular, first, it adds a definition of *purpose* as the key coordinating element of community. Second, it specifies general norms of discourse and cooperation to norms that encourage cooperation *towards the purpose*—what we call here an 'ethic of contribution.' Third, it specifies the general *processes* of dialogue to particular processes organized around 'chains' of value-creation. We do not here analyze in detail the general notion of 'cooperative community' because our base of data and evidence comes from the collaborative form. We argue that the knowledge of collaborative community can illuminate the more general case; and, like others (e.g. Pateman 1970) we argue that the new social character called into being by collaborative interdependent activity in the economic sphere provides both a resource for and a stimulus to emergent cooperative community in the broader social sphere. But a full development of these points would require another essay.

18. Habermas (1990); see also Apel's (1987) treatment of the 'ideal community of communication.'

19. Gerth and Mills (1946: 228).

20. See Satow (1975) on professions as prototypes of Weber's 'missing type' of administration; also Sciulli (1986) on the professions as collegial organizations that exemplify non-authoritarian and non-bureaucratic social order. Spencer (1970) and Rothschild-Witt (1979) focus on other forms of *Wertrational*-governed collectivities: respectively, the USA under its Constitution, and cooperatives. Without going into too much detail, we must recognize the fact that science is more advanced in these dimensions than the older institutions of the professions. First, it is far more centered on collective enterprise, the building of a pool of shared knowledge, whereas the professions for the most part remain centered on individual implementation of the pool of knowledge. Second, science has gone much further in developing institutions to order interaction, including peer review and replicability of results.

21. Spencer (1970), Satow (1975), and Rothschild-Witt (1979) point out that only three of the four types of social action and associated normative bases identified by Weber (affectual, traditional, purposive-rational) were associated with corresponding forms of authority and administration (respectively: charismatic, traditional, and bureaucratic): value-rationality is conspicuous in its absence. In defense of Weber, it might be countered that the history of the professions hardly justifies optimism. Following Waters (1989) and generalizing from the accounts of the case of medicine offered by Starr (1982) and Freidson (1975), Weberians might respond that the collegial form of governance does not appear to have allowed the professions to steer their members through difficult trade-off choices to embrace policies that privilege broader social interests when these conflict with parochial self-interest. See chapters by Adler and Maccoby on the emergence of new forms of professionalism.

22. Weber, as we just pointed out, did not embrace the 'professional' solution as enthusiastically as Durkheim did in the famous Second Preface of *The Division of Labor in Society*—he remained skeptical that this could overcome the power of bureaucracy. But it remained nevertheless his best hope for the future. One of his most sustained discussions for the future, 'Science as a vocation,' is torn between the hope for the triumph of a scientific ethos and doubt about its ultimate value.

23. This is a point made in Parsons's (1937) discussion of Durkheim. Later Durkheim thought the 'corporations' (occupational associations) could serve as the structural forms needed to give substance to organic solidarity. Fascism gave this idea a bad odor. Daniel Bell's celebration of the professions as new 'axes of social organization' is one effort to revive the idea.

24. There has been a great deal of other sociological writing that has explored the notion of deliberate, purposive, dialogic community that breaks out of the *Gemeinschaft–Gesellschaft* dichotomy. The American pragmatists such as John Dewey (1927) were certainly moving in this direction, but they (like Durkheim and Weber) were too early to be able to see the developments we have focused on: in general they remained stuck in seeking for signs of the new community

in unlikely corners that did not develop far (e.g. Dewey's educational experiments), or in remnants of tradition like the small town (Quandt 1970). The recent stream of writing on post-*Gemeinschaft* community might possibly be traced to Suttles's (1972) extraordinary analysis of constructed communities. Habermas (e.g. 1991) has arguably been its most profound and influential spokesperson in his theories of discursive interaction and ethics; and there are other recent efforts in this line like Sabel (1992) and Meyerson et al. (1996). Our treatment falls in this stream but is distinctive in using a *central* social institution, that of corporate organization, as its source of evidence.

We have stuck with Weber and Durkheim rather than these intervening theorists because no one since them, in our view, has stated so clearly the core institutional dimensions and requirements for modern community. Habermas's work is immensely valuable, but most of it has abstracted from real social structures. We find our analysis largely consistent with his at an abstract level, and the treatment of ideal speech appears to provide an ethical frame for collaboration; but we have not found much discussion in his works of the institutional developments in the corporate sphere.

25. Observational studies such as Crozier (1964) and Blau (1963) have vividly shown the pathologies of organizations that approach pure bureaucracy.
26. Barnard (1938: 220). Barnard also emphasized the significance of status and deference in this form of organization, noting both its positive and negative aspects (see Barnard 1946). Note: Barnard's term 'organizational personality' is opaque. It is best understood as signifying what more recent scholarship by Tajfel and Turner (1979) calls 'social identity' as distinct from 'personal identity': they point out that we all have several overlapping social identities as members of various groups, and the salience of each form of identity depends on the circumstances. Organizational personality can be understood as the identity that defines us as members of the organization.
27. See Mayo (1933).
28. The idea of the internal labor market goes back to the early part of the century, but it was not fully put in place until unions embraced it and government legitimized it (in particular in the course of The Second World War)—see Baron et al. (1986), Jacoby (2004).
29. See more extended discussions of paternalist bureaucracy in Heckscher (1995).
30. See Whyte (1956: 32 ff.); also Drucker (1973); Mayo (1933); Jackall (1988). The legal order during this period also based its concept of the rights and duties of employees on master–servant law.
31. The informal organization was extremely strong: most observational studies suggest that middle managers and blue-collar workers alike spent the majority of their time interacting with peers (to whom they had no *formal* connection) rather than with their superiors and subordinates (see Mintzberg 1973; Kusterer 1978; Dalton 1959). Our point here is that these informal relations were not *organized* well enough for knowledge production.

32. Mills (1951); Kanter (1977); and Jackall (1988).
33. The fraction of US 17-year-olds who had completed high school grew from 6% in 1900, to 57% in 1950, to over 80% by the end of the century.
34. These trends have been well documented as early as Bell (1973). The growth of knowledge value in the economy is suggestively highlighted in a startling figure developed by Margaret Blair: As of 1978, plant, property, and equipment (PP&E)—the core of production in the mass-production economy—accounted for 83% of market value of debt plus equity in the non-financial corporate sector, but by 1998, PP&E had fallen to only 31% of market value of debt plus equity (Blair and Kochan 2000: 1).
35. See, e.g., Burns and Stalker (1961); Bennis and Slater (1964); Lawrence and Lorsch (1967); Mintzberg (1979); Scott (1992); Daft (1998).
36. Arrow (1962); Stiglitz (1994).
37. Arrow and Hurwicz (1977); Stiglitz (1994); Miller (1992).
38. Alchian and Demsetz (1972); Williamson (1975).
39. For elaboration of and evidence for these large claims, see Adler (2001) and citations therein.
40. This account of the advance of institutions of science is adapted from Holton (1996: 58–77).
41. Re NUMMI and similar cases see Adler (1993), and Chapter 10 in this volume.
42. See, e.g., Schlesinger and Heskett (1991).
43. See, e.g., Reichheld (1996).
44. A study by a large consulting firm in 1999, based on 230 companies, found that their leaders were predicting that the percentage of sales through solutions would grow markedly in the four industries examined: telecommunications, media and entertainment, electronics, and banking. For example, the percentage of companies with 25% or more of sales through solutions was predicted to grow from 19% to 67% in electronics, and commensurately in the others.
45. See Foote et al. (2001). A similar argument with slightly different language is made by Ramirez (1999) and Ramirez and Wallin (2000).
46. The literature on alliances and business networks has grown very large over the last few years. See, for example, Brown et al. (2002); Gomes-Casseres (1994); Ring and Van de Ven (1992); *Organization Science* (1998).
47. Some firms did establish systematic rotational policies for their 'fast-trackers,' with the intention that they would know all parts of the company before advancing to senior management. This, however, never affected more than a small number of employees, and had little impact on the strength of interdivisional barriers.
48. The best-known paper on 'swift trust' is probably Meyerson et al. (1996); see also Sabel (1993) ('studied trust'); Giddens (1994) ('active trust'), Eccles (1985) ('rational trust'), Adler (2001) ('reflective trust').
49. On simultaneous and sequential engineering in auto production, see Clark and Fujimoto (1989); Womack et al. (1991). On Total Quality Management, see

Hackman and Wageman (1995); Mohrman et al. (1995). Cf. also Bennis and Slater (1998): they reflect the imperative discussed above for increasingly complex recombination of knowledge.

50. Margolis and Donnellon (1990).

51. While the rate of task force success is very hard to measure broadly—since task forces come in very different flavors and success has many forms—the difficulty in implementing them has been well documented in a number of observational studies: see Donnellon (1993); Heckscher (1995).

52. See Lee (1992).

53. In a sense these employees are 'cosmopolitans' as defined by Gouldner (1957); but unlike Gouldner's category they were intensely involved in the local community and held great influence in it—an indicator of the profound change in the nature of trust and relationships.

54. The emergence of collaborative community requires some moderation of the market principle in compensation policy: the interdependent nature of contributions in a collaborative community make it impossible to identify very precisely individual contributions and therefore impossible to tailor rewards sharply to individual performance.

55. Note that 'individualism' comes in two types: one is an absence of morality, a simple refusal to 'conform' to any superordinate obligations; the other, the individualism described by Weber, is a moral obligation to develop and maintain personal integrity and consistency. All sociologists and almost everyone else would argue that the first, non-moral form of individualism is unsustainable. Our claim is that the second kind of individualism, which has been crucial in defining Western culture at least since the Reformation, is (gradually) giving way to a new obligation of contribution.

On attitudes towards free agents, see Heckscher (1995: 152 ff.).

56. In traditional communities (as Durkheim points out) organizing was directly a moral matter, with deviance leading immediately to moral outrage. This is a limited and rigid way of organizing. In the modern community, by contrast, Durkheim pointed to the realm of restitutive law—rules of interaction whose violation leads not to moral outrage, but rather to corrective action and learning. Process management is an extension of this kind of rule, operating increasingly beyond the economic sphere and extending into all public situations that involve knowledge-based collaboration.

57. Many early efforts in teamwork and participation tried to eliminate these sorts of differences by broadening everyone's skills so as to reduce knowledge differentiation; this has proved to be an impractical route.

58. Underlying this notion of 'control' is a cybernetic view drawn from Parsons. In a traditional bureaucracy the hierarchy controls the community in this cybernetic sense—the former frames and directs the latter—in a collaborative community the cybernetic relation is reversed. We want to underline, however, that this does not mean that community *replaces* hierarchy.

59. The prototypical case is GM: see Freeland (1996).
60. Examples of widespread strategic dialogue are cited below in n. 61.
61. For Ford, see Nasser and Wetlaufer (1999). For GE, see Bartlett and Wozny (2001); Elderkin and Bartlett (1993). For IBM, see Gerstner (2002); Palmisano et al. (2004).
62. See the classic formulation of J. D. Thompson (1967), building on March and Simon.
63. Parsons (1963). It is worth remarking that matrix management was a precursor of the kind of process management we are discussing, though it took only a first step: it recognized the existence of processes not mapped directly to formal hierarchy, but it tried to lock those processes into limited fixed structures rather than allowing them to be reconstituted as needed.
64. See Peiperl (2001); Bohl (1996); Wanguri (1995).
65. The notion of 'understanding' in this sense draws on many sources. Simmel (1950) in general was the master sociologist of understanding and its relation to trust. Habermas has more recently made it a centerpiece of his notion of communicative action, though he remains at a fairly abstract level. (Habermas 1984). In the recent literature on networks, Paul DiMaggio treats 'sympathy' as a key in building networks under uncertainty (1992: 126–7). Claudio Ciborra (1997), an important theorist of process, treats understanding as the most developed form of 'taking care,' which is critical to the success of group dialogues. Simmel notes that understanding can derive from motives other than personal caring: 'Innumerable times, [competition] achieves what usually only love can do: the divination of the innermost wishes of the other.'
66. The negotiation literature has developed this distinction of understanding from commitment, in the form of a phase of *discussing interests without commitment* (Fisher and Ury 1981).
67. On the concept of social character, see Fromm and Maccoby (1970).
68. Thompson (1967).
69. Weber is referring specifically to Calvinism as part of his general analysis of 'the spirit of capitalism' (1904/1958: ch. 4, section A: 'Calvinism').
70. Durkheim (1897/1951) conducted a famous sociological analysis of the connection between loss of social integration and suicide. Michael Maccoby's (1976) description of the dangers of loss of self in modern corporate leaders is very similar; see also his chapter in this volume.
71. Thus we will treat 'social self' and 'social character' as two sides of the same coin, and we will use both terms depending on the focus of analysis. 'Social character' focuses on psychological dynamics, 'social self' on the connection of those dynamics to social situations—both how they are generated by particular communities, and how they can be observed in relationships.

A related term that has been used in an extensive literature is 'self-construal' (e.g. Markus and Kitayama 1991). This is very similar to the idea of the 'social self,' though somewhat less connected to the psychological dynamics. We have chosen to use 'social self' mainly because it is more intuitively sensible and because it has a longer history going back to Mead.

72. On the theory of shame and guilt, see Scheff (2000); Parsons (1968); Lynd (1958).

73. Rothschild-Whitt (1979).

74. Furthermore, they have in practice been composed not of large associational networks but of very small groups who contribute almost all the code and who develop their own norms and enforcement mechanisms through constant interaction. Finally, open source has often failed in the absence of such forms of discipline: it has not worked in areas that are considered 'boring' by the hacker community. For an extended discussion of the limitations (as well as the strengths) of the open-source approach, see Nikolai Bezroukov, 'An annotated webliography on open source software development problems' (www.softpanorama.org/OSS/webliography.shtml, viewed 31 Aug. 2004).

75. As in all these patterns of expectations, a mutually reinforcing cycle helps hold it in place. Those lower show deference in part out of ingrained habit and belief, and in part from the rational expectation that if they don't they will be harmed by higher-ups who themselves expect deference. From the other end, those higher believe in the value of deference, but also believe that if it were given up those lower down would be rebellious or incapable of performing.

76. Hamel (2000).

77. See Chapter 10 in this volume.

78. On the rise of performance-based pay, see Lawler et al. (1998).

79. See, for example, 'Fears force employees to take initiative,' *USA Today*, 2 Mar. 1999. Steven Greenhouse, 'Workers are angry and fearful this Labor Day,' *New York Times*, 2 Sept. 2002.

80. See, e.g., Gordon (1996).

81. For evidence of failure of restructuring initiatives to lead to sustained performance improvement, see Chapter 12, n. 4. On the failure of top-down changes to affect culture, see Beer et al. (1990).

82. See Lawler et al. (1998).

83. See Stanley Holmes and Wendy Zellner, 'Commentary: the Costco way,' *Business Week*, 12 Apr. 2004.

84. See also Porter (1985: pt. III on 'horizontal strategy').

85. Adler and Ferdows (1992); Earl and Scott (1999); Collins and Porras (1994); and Davenport and Prusak (1998) document many techniques designed to encourage a bond of common identity and a norm of sharing needed for the easy flow of ideas across divisional boundaries.

86. e.g. Ashkenas et al. (1993: 240).

87. Stinchcombe (1985). Such hierarchical elements control not only product specifications but also the supplier's internal processes. Korczynski (1996), for example, documents a trend toward a low-trust combination of market and hierarchical relations between management contractors and building contractors in the UK engineering construction industry in the 1980s and 1990s. Hancké (1997) makes a similar diagnosis of the evolution of subcontracting relations in the French automobile industry.

88. e.g. *Organization Science* (1998).

89. Dyer (1996); Sako (1992); Helper (1991); Bensaou and Venkatraman (1995); Ring (1996, 1997). Korczynski's (1996) study, meanwhile, shows the converse: low-trust relations in the UK construction industry enabled schedule and cost improvements but not the creation of new knowledge.

90. Helper and Sako (1995).

91. Nelson (1988); Powell (1990); Liebeskind et al. (1996).

92. Sabel (1992).

93. 'An increasingly perfect division of labour objectively reduces the position of the factory worker to increasingly "analytical" movements of detail, so that the complexity of the collective work passes the comprehension of the individual worker; in the latter's consciousness, his own contribution is devalued to the point where it seems easily replaceable at any moment. At the same time, work that is concerted and well organised gives a better "social" productivity, so that the entire work-force of a factory should see itself as a "collective worker." ' A. Gramsci, *Selections from the Prison Notebooks*, online at Marxist Writers Archives www.marxists.org/archive/index.htm.

94. For further elaboration of this argument, see Adler (2005). See also Harvey (2003), for discussion of accumulation by dispossession alongside accumulation by expanded reproduction.

95. For the period up to 1990, see Abrahamson (1997); Barley and Kunda (1992). These cycles can arguably be linked to long waves of the economic cycle: periods of rapid economic expansion correspond roughly to periods of management emphasis on control (scientific management to the post-1900 boom; systems rationalization to the expansion around the Second World War), and the periods of decline correspond roughly to an emphasis on commitment (welfare work to the crisis of the 1880s and 1890s, human relations to the Depression, employee involvement to the stagflation of the 1970s).

96. Relying here on Edwards (1979).

97. Hammer and Champy (1993) represents the 'anti-communal' phase; Champy (1995) and Hammer (1996) see a revisiting of the need for trust and commitment.

98. Nyland (1998).

99. See, e.g., Eisner (1993); Piore and Sabel (1984).

100. This analysis of the tension between economic forces and values has a long pedigree in sociological theory. Marx represented this as the interplay between the base and superstructure; Weber called it the economic and value spheres. The bulk of Weber's vast work was devoted to showing that, contrary to Marx's view, the value sphere or superstructure was not a mere reflection of economic interests but had an independent dynamic. He did not, however, disagree about the basic tension and interaction of the two spheres. Parsons's model of social development also reflects this tension: he sees a constant cycling from adaptive primacy (economic) through goal attainment (political) to the communal functions of integrating and pattern maintenance. Another interesting treatment of this same oscillation or cycling is Hirschman (1992), which posits a pendulum swing between public action and private interest.

101. Re inequality, see the historical tracing of the Gini index in 'Income and poverty,' *Left Business Observer*, 9 May 2000: www.leftbusinessobserver.com/ Stats_incpov.html 16 Apr. 2004, 5:03:51 p.m. On the recent rise in inequality and income volatility, see also Andrew Hacker, 'The underworld of work,' *New York Review of Books*, 51/2, (12 Feb. 2004).

   The sequence in the USA is somewhat different from that in England and Western Europe. In the latter regions industrialization advanced rapidly in the first half of the nineteenth century, leading to strong anti-capitalist movements in the middle part of the century. In the USA, industrialization was slower to emerge and intertwined with the battle over slavery, so that the mid-century war was much less clearly about capitalism. Thus in the USA the 'first' and 'second' industrial revolutions overlapped more than in Europe: the great expansion of the Gilded Age was entwined with the growth of large corporations such as Standard Oil and the railroads. The main first major reform wave in the USA, the Progressive movement, was directed against corporations, or 'trusts,' whereas in Europe it was directed against factory abuses. But these differences are just variations on the pattern of economic–social oscillation described here.

102. See Greenwood's (1997) argument that the technological pattern resembles that of the earlier period.

103. Heskett et al. (1994); Schlesinger and Heskett (1991).

104. For more elaboration on stakeholder regimes, see Heckscher et al. (2003: ch. 12).

105. Bloom and Perry (2001).

106. Some efforts to envision a new stakeholder regime can be found in Heckscher (1988), Cobble (1991, 1994), and Heckscher et al. (2003). On the ways in which working-class association can stimulate capitalist productivity, see Wright (2000).

107. Berle and Means (1933).

108. Strathern (1996).

109. Lessig (2001, 2003); McAdams (2003).
110. Coleman (1987) on sharing of ownership rights to knowledge as creating new kinds of interdependency, challenging markets.
111. The thesis is hardly new. Gorz (1967) was a well-known proponent in the 1960s. We think he, like Durkheim, was too early.

2

A Real-Time Revolution in Routines

Charles F. Sabel

Introduction

We are living in an age of institutional revolution and democratic doubt. Our institutional capacity to solve complex problems—including especially the problem of providing ever more crucial services, such as education, to an ever more differentiated public—is increasing. But this capacity seems disconnected from, perhaps even at odds with our capacity for self-rule by familiar, parliamentary means.

Pessimism about a mismatch between our problem-solving capacities and our capacity for self-rule is congenital to organizational theory and a recurrent theme in modern reflection on democracy. Weber famously saw our passion for practical mastery of the world leading down the path lit by purposive reason to an inescapable, iron cage of bureaucracy (Weber 1958).[1] John Dewey, writing in *The Public and its Problems* (1927) in the late 1920s, worried that the American republic was threatened by the rise of the large organization controlled by manipulative elites. Democracy might save republican freedom, he thought, but only if the public could learn to organize itself to challenge again and again its own habits of thought. Public primary schools in which pupils, alone and together, learned to make independent sense of immediate experience became in this program a key bulwark against propagandistic manipulation (Dewey 1915). Writing twenty years later and deeply sympathetic to Dewey, Herbert Simon seemed to close

* This essay benefited greatly from incisive comments by Michael Cohen, Gary Herrigel, Peer Hull Kristensen, Karim Lakhani, William Simon, Yane Svetiev, Duncan Watts, Jonathan Zeitlin. The root cause of failures in error detection and correction is me.

the door on such reflective independence. In *Administrative Behavior* he showed that modern organizations were efficient precisely because they built on, indeed reinforced habits and routines (Simon 1947). At the end of his career Simon did raise, wistfully, the possibility of creating a universal language of design by which technical elites could coordinate organizational choices with each other while learning from and reporting to the public at large (Simon 1969). But the very need for such a political lingua franca underscored the background assumption of a disjuncture between the constraints of organization and the constraints of public choice—an assumption that has remained largely unquestioned down to the present.

And yet, and yet. The organizational revolution of today is different. It seems to tie organizational success to the very ability to challenge habit and routine that Weber could not imagine at all and Dewey and Simon could intuit as theoretical perspectives with, at best, limited practical prospects. In so doing today's revolution in organizations opens the way to a reconsideration of our pessimism about democracy, if not a democratic renewal. Such, at least will be my conclusion. To arrive there I will have to make good on the claim that this organizational revolution is different from the one that produced the huge public and private bureaucracies that came to define 'modern' organizations a century ago, and different because it makes a kind of permanent uprising against habit the key to survival in an otherwise unmanageably turbulent world. To show this I will have to present a theory of the new organizations that supplies new answers to the key questions that classical organizational theory taught us to ask. That will be my main task.

To begin, consider this schematic contrast between the canonical form of organization in the period from the late nineteenth century to roughly 1980, and their canonical form thereafter. In the first period organizations are hierarchical and closed. Headquarters sets goals. Successively lower levels of managers decompose the broad goals into narrower and narrower ones. Eventually organizational routines specify in great detail how to parse and execute tasks, and verify their execution. The organization is thus a vast machine for generating one set of rules for decomposing a broad goal into countless small, easily mastered steps, and another set of rules for checking compliance with the first. Subordinates are rewarded for following the rules (Chandler 1977).

After roughly 1980, the canonical organization is federated and open. Decisions of higher units are shaped by lower ones and the lower units can be formally outside the organization. Or, to capture the idea that information in the new organization flows up and down as well as sideways, organizations are said to be networked. General designs are set provisionally by the highest level and revised in light of proposals by internal and external 'lower'-level units responsible for executing key modules or subsystems. The organizational routines define methods for choosing provisional, initial designs and production set-ups, and revising them in the light of further review and operating experience. Collaborators are rewarded for achieving broad goals according to standards defined as part of the process by which the goals themselves are set. Rule following entails—paradoxically, given the older understanding of compliance—the obligation to propose a new rule when the current one arguably defeats its purpose (Nohria and Eccles 1992).

Network organizations manifestly outperform hierarchies in volatile environments, where goals change so quickly that reducing them to a seamless set of task specifications is highly risky, if it is possible at all. Specifically, in such environments the open, federated organization can produce a more useful and resilient design for a product or service by canvassing more alternatives in less time than a hierarchy with a like purpose (Eisenhardt and Tabrizi 1995; Ward 1995). Put another way, the network organization can achieve simultaneously three goals—cutting development time while increasing the utility and reliability of designs—which hierarchies, we will see, are thought to have to trade against each other, and that only in stable environments.

The new organizations, moreover, can be built in widely different settings. They were pioneered in the rich countries, beginning, of course, in Japan, with its highly explicit culture of reciprocity and trust, understood as a moral prohibition on exploiting the vulnerabilities created by intimate collaboration (Dore 1983; Nishiguchi 1994). But network organizations have been mastered and in some ways improved by Americans exalting individualism (MacDuffie 1997), Danes with social democratic solidarities rooted in Protestantism (Kristensen and Zeitlin 2004), and Irish with traditions of social inclusion derived from Catholicism (OECD 1996). The new organizations have diffused rapidly from the rich countries to developing and transition economies: some of Volkswagen's most advanced factories, for example, are in Brazil (Ramalho and Santana 2002) and the Czech Republic (Dörr and Kessel 1997). The network organizations are found in virtually every industry in the private sector, from capital-intensive automobile plants (Womack et al. 1990) to labor-intensive garment factories (Abernathy et al. 1999), and in many firms providing design, engineering, or computing services to business or consumers (Spreenberg et al. 1995). They are also, as we will see in the example of the reform of US public schools, playing an increasingly important role in the reorganization of the public sector. There is nothing new in such institutional iso-morphism across the public–private divide: The large bureaucracy emerged in Europe first in public administration and the military, then became a model for private firms (Kocka 1981), while the sequence was, by and large, reversed in the USA (Chandler 1977).

To say that the network organization is potentially as generally applic-able as the hierarchy is not, however, to say that there is 'one best way' to build the requisite class of network, any more than there was 'one best way' to build the classic hierarchy. The large German organization could make do with fewer layers of hierarchy and less precise rules than its French counterpart, because the German school system, to a greater extent than the French, prepared the workforce to fill gaps in the formal instruc-tions (Maurice et al. 1982). Given many analogous and persistent differ-ences in institutional context we should thus expect that there will be local, regional, and national variants of the network firm as well.

Some limits of the new organizations are, finally, as conspicuous as their competitive advantages over hierarchies in many settings. For all their counterintuitive accomplishments, and notwithstanding their propensity to empower subordinates and outsiders in ways that hierarchies systemat-ically limited, these organizations are not utopia realized. Suppliers and customers cooperate more intimately in the new organizational world than in the old; but despite the intimacy, and the heightened mutual vulnerabilities it creates, suppliers rightly fear their customers will some-times betray them (Herrigel 2004; Whitford forthcoming). Subsidiaries of multinational firms cooperate with, but also scheme against, each other, and strife frequently interrupts their cooperation with headquarters (Kris-tensen and Zeitlin 2004). Newspapers periodically report on reforming schools that cheat on test scores to outperform peers from whom they should be learning. Although, as we will see, the form of the power struggles in these organizations is in some ways as novel as the institu-tional routines whose control is their object, they are selfish and mean struggles none the less.

These stylized facts about the new, networked organizations prompt two immediate questions. First, how do networked organizations work? At a minimum, how do they manage to cut development times and errors while increasing the quality of designs through extensive canvassing of possibilities? Second, how are networked organizations governed? How, in other words, can they survive without the task specifications and compli-ance checking that controlled opportunism in the hierarchical corpor-ation? Some form of governance must control betrayal and the fear of it, or the institutions would not function at all; but whatever governance there is must be imperfect, or the risk of opportunism would not be widely registered as worrisome.

The task of this essay is to furnish elements of a response to these questions. The starting point is the classic theory of the organization developed by Simon in *Administrative Behavior* as supplemented by the work of Oliver Williamson on transaction costs (Williamson 1975; Coase 1937). This work provides a model for linking analysis of individual and institutional behavior to form a theory of organizations. It has also provided, almost as an afterthought, an explanation of the current organization revolution. Looking at what is wrong with that explanation will help clear the way to an alternative. As my aim is to put this body of work to explanatory use, not contribute to its intellectual history, I present the classic theory as augmented by the research it provoked, not as originally formulated.

'Dual' organization theory: human, all too human hierarchy and its flexibly informal twin

Classic organization theory was ahead of its time in being resolutely behavioral or human oriented. Where much economics of the 1950s (and of course still today) assumes that human agents are, for their purposes, practically omniscient and have limitless foresight, organization theory more plausibly assumes that humans have limited abilities to acquire and process the information needed to choose ends given means. This is the condition that Simon calls bounded rationality (Simon 1982). Where important currents in law, philosophy, and political theory assume human agents are powerfully motivated by principles of fairness and justice, organizational theory takes human agents to be appetitive and self-interested (with the calculation of individual self-interest itself limited by bounded rationality).

Important counter-currents within mainstream organization theory of course went even further, asserting that so bounded is the rationality of organizations that they are incapable of learning in the sense of improving decisions by deliberation on experience. Thus the assumption that decision makers 'survey' only the first feasible choice immediately accessible to them at the moment of decision, and 'prefer' that choice to any other or inaction, yields 'garbage-can' models of organizations, in which decisions result from collisions between decision makers and solutions (Cohen et al. 1972). The assumption that decision makers can compare only a few current solutions to their problem, and prefer the one that best meets their needs, but cannot draw from this decision any analytic conclusions regarding subsequent choices, turns organized decision making into muddling through (Lindblom 1959). The assumption that circumstances impose one and only one choice on decision makers at crucial moments, and that, once made, these choices are long unalterable because of self-reinforcing effects (network externalities or other increasing returns) or because of 'lock-ins' due to technical interdependencies, yields path dependency: where you come from determines where you go (Perrow 1984; Arthur 1994; David 1985). At the limit mainstream theory was challenged by the assumption that organizations are not engaged in problem solving at all. Rather, on the institutional isomorphism view, they are themselves locked in the iron cage of national or global capitalism, whose structural logic and moral imperatives they are powerless to resist, let alone influence (Zucker 1987).

Models of organizations as irrational had some currency in the study of the public sector, where, until recently, many important decisions, whether capriciously changeable or practically immutable, seemed equally impervious to learning.[2] But this qualification notwithstanding, classical organization theory was able convincingly to portray large institutions as capable of purposive behavior: less the plaything of fate than some sociologists and political scientists feared, though hardly the sovereign masters of all their possibilities that many economists took them to be. Indeed the grand achievement of organizational theory and transaction cost economics is to show how, in relatively stable environments, agents with human features can construct institutions—principally hierarchies—capable of 'satisficing': achieving by joint action an acceptable minimum of some goal beyond their individual reach, without being undone by the opportunism of individuals pursuing selfish interests at the cost of the organizational good (Simon 1955, 1956, 1957). In drastic synthesis the argument goes in these three steps.

The response to the problem of bounded rationality, under the important condition of relative stability, is the successive decomposition of complex tasks into ones simple enough for human agents to execute. At the limit the task is so simplified and routine that execution is habitual, requiring almost no conscious attention at all. This decomposition naturally yields an organizational hierarchy, where each subordinate takes instructions from, and passes the output of her efforts to, one superior. The assembly line is the emblem of this form of collective production, linear programming its mathematical counterpart.

The hierarchical decomposition of tasks is efficient because of economies of scale: The more a product is made or a service delivered, the lower the cost of producing it. 'Economies of scale' is the name of a complex bundle of efficiency-increasing elements whose nature singly and in interactive relation to each other is—still—very imperfectly understood. Some of the sources of these efficiency gains are direct: repetition or habituation increases dexterity, reducing the time to complete a task. Staying fixed on one or a few tasks also and obviously reduces the expenses associated with switching tasks—what Smith called the problem of 'sauntering,' and we would today count as a transaction cost—the cost of organization of a transaction. Others are indirect and complexly cognitive: simplifying tasks makes it easier to invent machines that replace human producers (Smith 1976; Williamson 1975). But whatever their exact source and interaction, the elements bundled as economies of scale demonstrate the enormous problem-solving capacities of individuals despite (in part even because of) their bounded rationality.

Hierarchical decomposition creates, but also provides the means for managing, a governance problem, where governance can be thought of as the system or method, with associated transaction costs, of giving all collaborators incentives to act in the joint interest. The governance problem arises because of the mutual specialization intrinsic to hierarchy. What I make only has value when combined with the part you make; my asset is dedicated or specific to yours. Hence if I can damage the organization without greatly harming myself by withholding my part or asset-specific investment, I can extort greater returns to my collaboration. This is the famous hold-up problem of non-vertically integrated but highly specialized mass producers (such as GM in the 1920s) with regard to specialized but external suppliers (such as Fisher Body) (Klein et al. 1978).[3] The opportunism or shirking of internal units or employees are attenuated variants of the same problem.

The workable response is for the principal—those in control of the hierarchy—to set the penalties for opportunism and the rewards for compliance so high that the subordinate agents will not forgo self-interested strategies. If the agents are outsiders, as in the classic hold-up case, the customer will have to acquire ownership of the independent supplier in order to exercise this discipline. Hence the drive for vertical integration or institutional closure. For insiders, the solution is a contractual arrangement rewarding compliance with, or sanctioning disregard of the principal's goals.

But notice that this solution is just workable or manageable; it is demonstrably imperfect. This is the inadvertent finding of economists initially bent on showing the reverse, namely that it is possible to set compatible incentives for the organization (or its owners) and its employees. In one version of these inadvertent impossibility theorems, each employee is promised the full return of her marginal unit of effort, and so has the incentive to act to the benefit of the whole organization. Of course all team members can't plausibly be promised the exclusive benefit of something they produce jointly—the marginal output of the organization as a whole. So all but one will have to be disappointed. You might think that the owner/CEO could sidestep the problem of joint or team production by signing a forcing contract with the team of employees in the hierarchy: The contract makes all (slightly) better off than otherwise if they successfully collaborate to meet the organization's goal, otherwise each suffers the same penalty. But this shifts the problem from ensuring the fidelity of the agents to the joint task to ensuring the fidelity of the principal. For under the forcing contract the owner/CEO has an incentive to bribe— make a side payment to—one of the team members to under-perform just enough to block the group from achieving its goal. This increases the owner's proceeds—the profit or residual—from the venture, but at the cost of limiting organizational performance (Holmstrom 1982). And so on.

The principal–agent governance conception of organization theory resonated with contemporaneous conceptions of society-wide, democratic governance. The public (conceived in the USA as the voters, in Europe as corporatist stakeholders) sets through its political or organizational representatives the goals of public policy and the attendant public administration, and periodically compares the promised platform to the results. Because efficiency requires hierarchy, and hierarchy can only (and, given the stability requirement, only occasionally) be controlled from the top, democratic participation in governance is necessarily limited to such periodic reviews. Hence the fears of Dewey and Simon, among many others, that a polity that has chosen to reap the rewards of efficient, large organizations can, at best, escape tyranny, not achieve true self-rule. Network governance, we will see below, offers a way beyond this minimalist or Schumpeterian view of democracy as the people's power to throw the bum rulers out, because it is rooted in forms of accountability that do not depend on the principal–agent relation (Schumpeter 1976).

Informality and flexibility—the elasticity of classical theory

Despite its preoccupation with hierarchy, classical organization theory, we saw, grew up in opposition to the Weberian idea of perfectly functioning bureaucracy. In addition to assuming lifelike agents with bounded rationality and a propensity for opportunism, the theory assumed from the start that few if any environments are stable enough to allow for perfect parsing of complex tasks; that the limits on parsability require improvisation; and that an understanding of how humans act in organizations—administrative behavior—requires attention to this endemic improvising.

Three settings regularly called for such improvisations. The first is at its inception or start up, when the organization does not have a goal (or, rather, it must choose which one to pursue among the many that are possible) (Simon 1958: 170–88). In this phase of self-programming it or its leaders are searching for and evaluating objectives, not parsing them. This search behavior is perceived as prior to and constitutive of the organization (the job of equity owners, CEO, and legislators is to have goals). The search is thus distinct from the organization's routine operation, except insofar as it is established as a separate activity—an industrial research laboratory, for example—outside the normal operating hierarchy.

But maturity—the second setting—does not eliminate the need for improvisation. Even in well-established hierarchies task definitions do not accurately specify what actually needs to be done. So individuals, moved by camaraderie, reciprocity, or other forms of sociability not reducible either to the functional imperatives of the organization or calculations of self-interest, must cooperate fluidly to correct the plan. This is in classical theory the realm of the informal; and social value—solidarity in one form or another—is its coin (Dalton 1948; Crozier 1964; Burawoy 1979). For Chester Barnard, one of the pioneers of the classic theory, the paramount task of the executive was precisely to coordinate the formal and informal organizations so as to achieve the organizational goal (Barnard 1938). Given what we just saw about the impossibility of writing incentive-compatible contracts or otherwise solving the governance problems of principal–agent organizations in principle, you might say we have worked our way back to a methodologically sophisticated, game-theoretic version of his position (Gibbons 2003).

The third setting is the volatile environment, where changes in background conditions call for so much adjustment that the organization is in effect always starting up. Already in the 1960s some niches in the ecology of large organizations were becoming so changeable that it was patently self-defeating to parse tasks hierarchically. The effective response, captured in Burns and Stalker's idea of the organic organization, was a kind of institutionally acknowledged informalism. In contrast to mechanic hierarchies, organic organizations are characterized by the adjustment and continual redefinition of individual tasks through interaction with others: a network structure of control, authority, and communication. The sanctions which apply to the individual's conduct in his working role derive more from presumed community of interest with the rest of the working organization in the survival and growth of the firm, and less from a contractual relationship between himself and a non-personal corporation, represented for him by an immediate superior; omniscience is no longer imputed to the head of the concern; knowledge about the technical or commercial nature of the here and now task may be located anywhere in the network, this location becoming the ad hoc centre of control authority and communication; a lateral rather than a vertical direction of communication through the organization, communication between people of different rank, also, resembling consultation rather than command (Burns and Stalker 1961: 121).

As the role of hierarchy decreases, there is a corresponding change in the values that bind the organization together. The loyalty of individuals to a particular institution, and the solidarity of those who share the same loyalties, declines. Instead 'commitment,' like 'that of the professional scientist to his work, becomes the glue of the organization.' So central is such 'commitment' to the direction of the institution that 'it becomes far less feasible to distinguish "informal" from the "formal" organization' (Burns and Stalker 1961: 122). Lawrence and Lorsch substantiate these claims with more detailed evidence some years later (Lawrence and Lorsch 1967).[4]

The upshot is that by the late 1960s the classic theory of organization became a close analog to the contemporaneous dual theory of labor markets and industrial organization (Doeringer and Piore 1971). Both identify a dominant or primary sector operating in stable environments. In the economic models this is the market segment where demand is growing predictably. This sector is complemented by a secondary one serving the remaining, volatile niches, where the nature and level of demand changes rapidly. In both cases the primary-sector organizations are hierarchically structured to take advantage of economies of scale. The secondary sector, more informal and fluid in both, is held together by professional commitments in large organizations and the craft ethos of small firms. In both cases too the informal, secondary sector is at once vanguard and rearguard of the primary. As vanguard it produces innovative products: think of the organic organization or the small firms that supply machine tools to the mass-production economy. But, as rearguard it also produces the shoddy goods and services that can be sold when transient peaks in demand allow small firms to sell inferior goods at high prices without inducing large firms/organizations to make long-term investments in expanding efficient production capacity.

When, as happened from the late 1970s, the self-reinforcing effects of what we now very loosely call globalization and technological change made the general environment abruptly more volatile, classic organization in its dual variant had a ready explanation for the institutional changes that ensued: The subordinate form of organization becomes more salient, if not dominant, and its informal fluidity—its routine rejection of routine— becomes, improbably, at least as much norm as exception.

Schematizing greatly, and leaving aside a detailed, descriptive literature aimed mostly at practitioners, research on this organizational 'insubordination' has gone in two directions. The sociological investigation has been directed towards a renewed appreciation of the suppleness of 'informal' coordination and the inventive capacity of human sociability. Consider the idea of 'communities of practice,' exemplified by the Xerox repairpersons who learn their craft while exchanging stories of difficult cases around the water cooler, not from the company's perpetually out-of-date and maddeningly incomplete service manuals (Lave and Wenger 1991; Brown and Duguid 1991). Or recall Weick's work on the mutual sense making at the heart of face-to-face interactions as an indispensable resource for 'organizing' (without need of a formal organization) a resilient response to especially unruly problems such as firefighting or launching planes from the pitching deck of an aircraft carrier (Weick 1995).[5] Weick likens organizing to jazz improvisation: the disciplined, aesthetically pleasing, and collaborative recombination of the familiar and the novel in changing circumstances, including of course circumstances created by improvisation itself. 'To watch jazz improvisation unfold is to have palpable contact with the human condition' (Weick 1998: 551). Contemporary organizations may 'redistribute improvisation rights' to speed response to an ever more changeable world (Sutcliffe and Sitkin 1996, quoted in Weick 1998: 549). But this only accentuates the deep sociological truth—long obscured by classic organization theory—that innovation can only become routine when the innovators are 'loosely coupled' (Weick 1976)—intimate enough to learn from nuance, but detached enough to break with convention and the habits of the group.

By taking humans to be inherently sociable, and sociability to include the capacity to make mutual sense of individual ambiguity, this line of sociological argument provides an important corrective to the relentlessly strategic characterization of human motivation in the behavioral assumptions of classic theory.[6] But, as we will see in a moment, by limiting the effective expression of inventive sociability to informal groups or communities, writers in this school discounted the possibility of 'sense making' in formal organizations, and so directed their key insight away from a domain where, I will argue, it is especially illuminating: the networked organization.

The second, business-school line of research is not concerned with the bedrock character of sociability, but rather the problem of managing the relations between formal and informal—mechanical and organic—organizations in a world where the need to balance the two, or switch rapidly from one to the other, is becoming ever more acute. As developed by the production-engineering wing of the Harvard Business School, the early versions of this literature focused on the emergence of cross-functional product development teams within the traditional hierarchical organization. Through the 1970s product development meant the execution, by narrowly specialized experts, of components specified in a master plan. At the limit, in some US and European automobile companies, for example, the latches for car doors were designed by engineers who did nothing but design door latches, model generation after model generation. The product manager in this setting chaired a committee whose members represented and liaised with—but had no authority over—the functional departments. This 'lightweight' product manager was thus in reality a 'glorified clerk,' who used formal meetings and reports to track the progress of events he could scarcely influence.

As market changes, often made visible by the success of Japanese firms, obstructed traditional forms of planning and made reliance on engineering tradition more dangerous, firms worldwide (often following the Japanese lead) shifted to 'heavyweight' product managers: high-ranking company officials with contacts to customers and marketing as well as production and testing, with a staff of rising stars from the functional departments who could intervene at all stages of development with bench-level engineers. Characteristically, however, the relation of both the 'heavyweight' team to the traditional organization and the 'heavyweight' product manager to his collaborators were informal: intervention in the functional departments was tolerated, even encouraged, but not formally authorized, and the 'heavyweight' managed by walking around selling ideas, discussing solutions—almost never holding meetings or writing reports (Clark and Fujimoto 1991).[7]

The current version of this approach turns the problem of balancing or hybridizing organizational forms into a near impossibility—a 'dilemma,' though not quite yet a tragedy. The argument, as developed by Clayton Christensen (Christensen 1997; Christensen and Raynor 2003),[8] begins with the now-familiar assumption that organizations adapted to routine, predictable, or 'sustaining' development require disciplines antithetic to those that must innovate or 'disrupt.' Managers risk tragedy because markets and firms built to address sustaining competition can always and (almost) unpredictably be disrupted by innovators (and vice versa, though we can ignore this limb of the argument here). The danger arises through the combination of a fact about technology and a fact about the cognition of incumbent managers: The most masterful producers and users of the dominant method know in the abstract that there is almost always a superior alternative to the currently dominant know-how (the technological fact). But given their routine disposition to improve on what they already know and find flaws in upstart challengers, the incumbents ignore the threat (the cognitive trap). Disruptive technologies therefore take hold in peripheral markets of no interest to the dominant players, as when electric-arc mini-mill steel producers started making low-grade rebar to reinforce concrete construction. Or they can arise from the 'non-consumption' of groups cut off from the existing markets for certain products, as when Sony sold the first, tinny transistor radios to teenagers who could not afford higher-fidelity, tube-powered sets, and in any case wanted to listen to music away from home. Once proven by 'outsider' firms, they are generalized to core domains of application, dislodging the established producers. Radical and generalizable production processes, such as lean production, can arise in the same way.

The managerial response to all this, in Christensen's view, is informalism at the highest level: He suggests that top managers, guided by elements of 'disruption theory,' can remain vigilant about the need to shift from one organization form to another, and even devise routines for facilitating the shift. But given the pervasiveness of the threat, the speed with which it can eventuate, and the hold of the cognitive trap, there is as much artful, on-the-spot fusing of old and new—improvisation in Weick's sense—as science in this response. Above all, and again characteristically, the repertoire of organizational forms remains unaltered: 'Institutions can't disrupt themselves,' Christensen writes (Christensen and Raynor

2003: 274). So, subtleties aside, the new world was generally taken to be the old one gone permanently out of tilt, if not topsy-turvy.

In retrospect this seems like an easily understandable mistake. It is easily understandable because the increasing weight of the 'subordinate' sector was just what contingency theory predicted in an increasingly volatile environment, and researchers don't often look a gift confirmation in the mouth. I say this from experience: Michael Piore and I reacted the same way to the developments of the 1980s, reworking the categories of dual labor market theory into the notion of flexible specialization: the use of general-purpose or craft skills and general-purpose machines (now pro-grammable and standardized, and therefore mass-producible) to respond to fragmented, volatile markets (Piore and Sabel 1984). The emphasis on craft community as the source and ultimate regulative of flexibility reson-ates with the new sociological informalism; the emphasis on the coexist-ence of and changing relation between mass and craft production at all levels of economic activity resonates with the attention to organizational hybrids and flip-flops in the managerial informalism.

But understandable or not, the move is a mistake. It saves the core of the old theory while illuminating some aspects of the new developments. But it does this at the price of obscuring those novel features in the current situation that most directly and profoundly challenge settled assump-tions. The tip-off is the formalism of the new organization. On anything but cursory inspection there are simply too many formal procedures—routines—to square with the notion of the networked organization as organized informality. But the routines of the new organization look counterintuitive or simply self-defeating from the vantage point of classic theory because they extend the organization's search for answers beyond familiar domains, rather than limiting the searches through detailed task parsing.[9] To show the generality of these routines, and thereby to under-score the need for a re-examination of the theoretical underpinnings of organizational sociology, I present three examples of these new discip-lines, drawn from separate strands of writing on the new organizations which quite obviously should at least talk to each other, but just as plainly do not.

Three types of pragmatist organization

Take first the deliberately innovative organization. This is the canonical case of the new, networked organization: the firm—it almost always is a firm—whose very purpose is to produce innovative products or services. A well-documented example is of design and production in the automobile industry (Helper et al. 2000).

The process starts when, say, the new-van design team in an automobile firm sets the general performance characteristics of the vehicle by benchmarking the best features of current vans and exploring which innovations under development can be incorporated in its design. To benchmark the potential of developmental work the team may ask for engineering simulations of possible outcomes, testmarket a product embodying a potentially valuable feature, or otherwise try to test the actual reaction of buyers to some approximation of the design they are exploring. Assessing the results of these probes, and again guided by reference to leading examples and comparison of possibilities, the team next provisionally subdivides or, to take a term from cognitive science, 'chunks'[10] its general goals into subtasks—the design of an engine, or heating, ventilation, and air-conditioning system—and chooses a specialist team from inside or outside the parent company to realize the initial specifications. It may seem unduly fussy to refer in this connection to 'chunking' rather than the more familiar 'modularizing,' especially since the latter is often used loosely in the automobile industry and elsewhere to mean the former. But modularization, more strictly speaking, aims at the creation of fixed, black boxes whose performance is durably defined in an interface listing the output returned for any input. Where the corrigible provisionality of design choices being described here is useful, modularization *strictu sensu* is, as we will see below, risky, even impossible (Sabel and Zeitlin 2004; MacDuffie and Helper, this volume).

After this initial chunking, separate project teams elaborate all the provisional subsystems concurrently, applying to that task the same kind of evaluation of competitors' successful efforts and developmental possibilities used in the van team's first round of benchmarking. In addition, they benchmark the production processes central to their eventual products to ensure that the methods employed will meet or surpass the efficiency of their most capable competitors. Engine plants, for instance, will have to produce engines that are at least as cheap and warrantable as those of competitors making similar engines in comparable volumes.

Then the initial overall goals are modified by the methods of simultaneous or concurrent engineering, e.g. the engine-design group may find a way to better its target specifications or to cut its manufacturing costs if it can persuade other component groups that design characteristics should be modified accordingly.

Refinement of this iterated co-design continues once production begins by means of just-in-time and the error-detection and correction methods associated with it. In just-in-time production, parts are supplied to each workstation only as needed: ideally, one at a time. Hence disruptions are immediately visible. A breakdown at one station halts production by stopping the flow of parts to downstream operations.

To assure the flow of production, therefore, the source of disruption must be identified. This typically requires tracing long causal chains back to improbable origins by insistent questions sometimes called the 'five whys.' For example:

Why is machine A broken?	No preventive maintenance was performed.
Why was the maintenance crew derelict?	It is always repairing machine B.
Why is machine B always broken?	The part it machines always jams.
Why does the jam recur?	The part warps from heat stress.
Why does the part overheat?	A design flaw. (MacDuffie 1997: 494)

Thus error detection and correction, like benchmarking and simultaneous engineering, reveal possibilities for improvement in unexpected (mis-) connections among the parts of complex endeavors; and the cumulative effect of these results is captured in improvements in the benchmark standards for various production processes.[11]

Benchmarking, simultaneous engineering, and error-detection methods like the 'five whys' are counterintuitive from the classical vantage point. In classical theory, we saw, routines are questioned only in exceptional circumstances. It is simply oxymoronic from this perspective to try to do what the new institutions do as a matter of course: routinely question the suitability of current routines for defining and solving problems. We can think of these new institutions as pragmatist in the sense of the philosophy of Peirce, James, and Dewey: They systematically provoke doubt, in the characteristically pragmatist sense of the urgent suspicion that our routines—our habits gone hard, into dogma[12]—are poor guides to current problems. Or we can think of benchmarking, simultaneous engineering, error detection, and the other disciplines grouped under the anodyne heading of 'continuous improvement' as institutionalizing, and so making more practically accessible, the deep pragmatist intuition that we only get at the truth of a thing by trying to change it (Unger forthcoming).

As a second instance of such pragmatist institutions consider the High Reliability Organizations (HROs) (Rochlin et al. 1987; La Porte and Consolini 1991).[13] HROs are well but incompletely designed to perform without fail such extraordinarily demanding tasks as generating electric power through nuclear fission, launching and recovering jet aircraft rapidly from and back onto pitching, greasy flight decks, launching and recovering space shuttles, or fighting forest fires as they race through rough terrain. The designs are necessarily incomplete because the conditions under which the specified tasks are to be accomplished are changing continuously in more or less subtle ways. If the organization is not adjusted accordingly, it fails, catastrophically. In the pragmatist terms just introduced, HROs become disastrously unreliable if they assume that routine, (nearly) invariant success is the result of following invariant routines; and the organizational challenge is to avoid accidents day after day without imperceptibly making this assumption (Weick et al. 1999).

Key to this are error-detection and root-cause analysis disciplines of the sort broadly familiar from the production/operations level of the innovative organization. In the setting of HROs, the most important and characteristic of these is near-miss reporting and analysis. Near misses of course are accidents that only accidentally didn't happen. So the near misses—and beyond that 'out-of-control' sequences that nearly produced near misses—are the urgent analog in the HRO to the line stoppages in a just-in-time system. Both trigger root-cause analysis meant not only to uncover the proximate cause of the incident, but to eliminate, through redesign of the organization if necessary, the background conditions which generated the immediate source of danger.

Note here a circumstance to which we return later when considering governance—the root-cause analysis regimes are often regarded as a key element in the governance of HROs, and when that is the case they are subject to regulatory scrutiny. For example nuclear power plants in the USA are rated in part on how effectively they respond to reports of anomalies at other plants that might be of relevance given their own set-up, and so on (Rees 1994; Perrin 2005).

New Public Services are a third case of pragmatist organizations. This type of institution is little discussed in the organizational sociology literature, but is receiving increasing attention in various domains of policy studies (Elmore and Burney 1997, 1998; Liebman and Sabel 2003, with references to the extensive literature). Well-documented examples are schools in Texas, Kentucky, North Carolina, and elsewhere in the USA that actually teach poor children of color to read and do mathematics with proficiency comparable to that attained by rich, white pupils. The new organizations are like HROs in being designed to achieve a single, complex task—teach children to read and use mathematics—and in relying on error detection to compensate for design deficiencies. But there is an important difference. Where the design gaps in HROs are, roughly speaking, small in relation to the overall structure (that is why we say it is well designed), in the new public service the situation is reversed: there is lots of 'gap' and little by way of consolidated design. No one, in other words, knows how to install a turn-key school system that produces the desired result. Instead the institutional solution is to build an organization that uses error detection and correction at the lowest (classroom) levels to find out what works, and then adjust the higher (school and district) level structures to generalize that behavior and encourage more refined error detection, and so on.

With regard to reading, for example, all students learn by some idiosyncratic combination of decoding strings of letters/phonemes (phonics) and derivation of the meaning of words and sentences from context (whole language method). Teachers identify the strengths and weakness of each student's mixture of strategies by sampling their skills in brief, daily sessions, and suggest improvements. (This might be called first-order error detection and correction.) The performance of students in the same grade is measured periodically state-wide by a standard test, allowing for the comparison of the performance of teachers, schools, and districts (second-order error detection).

The job of principals in this system is to create conditions in the school for generalizing the successes of the most successful teachers, and the job of the principals' superior—the district supervisor—is to create conditions for diffusing the successes of the most successful principals. By these means the reformed school is invented through the piecemeal, but eventually comprehensive improvement of an arbitrary, provisional structure, supposing only agreement on a very broad (but still non-vapid) goal: educational achievement (by mainstream measures) should not vary across groups in culturally salient hierarchies, and gaps should be closed by leveling up, not down.

Accepting now as a stylized fact that the new organizations operate successfully by application of these methods, and leaving for another time discussion of the morphology of and techniques for constructing the networks presumed in what follows, we return to the classic questions of bounded rationality, efficiency, and governance and try to provide a consistent and conceptually plausible account of this success.

Bounded rationality, efficiency, and governance in the pragmatist organization

Rethinking bounded rationality

The centrality of search routines to the new organizations suggests an alternative to the decomposition of tasks as a solution to the problem of bounded rationality: Under volatile conditions, when no one can know the whole answer to the design question we face, the response to bounded rationality is to find actors who are already solving (part of) the problem we will turn out to be trying to solve. On a very general level of course something of this sort must be possible: just as language is used to correct the defects of language, and thought the defects of thought, so the answers to current problems, even imprecisely defined ones, will eventually prove to be derivable from recombination of other, previous or current answers. But just as obviously this alternative search response can't be simply a matter of looking around, any more than parsing tasks hierarchically is simply a matter of breaking big problems into little pieces, or having new ideas is just a matter of thinking about old ones. Indeed, as a practical matter, the notion that the solution to our own limitations is to find collaborators who are less limited seems perilously close to wishful thinking, akin to the ridiculous strategy of the stranded economist who intends to open a can of tuna fish on a desert island by assuming there is a can opener at hand.

To be workable at all any such problem-solving search (regardless of where in the overall design or production sequence it is conducted) will have to (1) disentrench enquiry, directing attention away from habitual answers and towards unfamiliar solutions, while (2) it produces sufficient information about advantages and disadvantages of rival possibilities— the solution space—to suggest a (provisionally) acceptable solution, and so becomes, for the moment, self-limiting. If it is not disentrenching the search will be uselessly redundant: When you don't know what you are looking for, it is especially unproductive to look once more where you always look. If it is not fruitfully self-limiting the search will be outright destructive, sending the actors off on an endless fool's errand.

Benchmarking and error detection meet these conditions on solution-generating searches by obliging the actors to look for answers in a novel, initially open, but ultimately bounded space of possibilities. For benchmarking this is the set of best current or potential designs; for error detection it is the activity chains that might have caused a particular breakdown. The initial canvas of design solutions is necessarily novel and open because it must consider responses that are 'like,' but potentially better than, current practice on at least some of many dimensions, and 'like' has no determinate meaning in advance of a particular search. Indeed, to search for likes is to invite surprises. The point of the search is precisely to uncover an unsuspected but highly informative resemblance.

Consider by way of example this telling episode in the evolution of the modern paintbrush. A company is trying with little success to produce the traditional house painter's brush with artificial bristles. Even an accomplished artisan can't apply a smooth coat of paint with the synthetic bristles. The question arises: what is a paintbrush like? If a trowel, then the brush's performance is determined by the shape of the bristles' tip, and the company's problem is to find an artificial equivalent for the split ends of natural hairs. If, however, paintbrushes are like pumps, their performance is determined by the contours of the channels formed by the bristles, and the next step is to reposition the artificial bristles to channel paint correctly (Schoen 1979: 257–9). In this case the brush was more like a pump than a trowel—but this result, of course, is provisional. In more artfully inclined hands a brush may need to be less a pump than a trowel, sling-shot, or eyedropper.

As in this example, each possibility considered in metaphoric benchmarking provides a vantage point from which to evaluate the strengths and weakness of the others. Hence the search produces something 'like' a provisional taxonomy or map of accessible solution strategies in relation to each other. In this way it is self-limiting: Once you have a serviceable map of the solution space, you stop doing cartography and decide where you want to go.

Before turning the implications of this search solution to bounded rationality for the efficiency and governance of the new organization we need to consider a possible objection. The classical theory is, we said, insistently behavioral, and the notion of bounded rationality is its core. Is there any warrant to think that the account just given of learning through comparison is a characteristically human form of learning? Or is it only one of those 'just-so' stories that evolutionary biologists and functionalist social scientists invent to 'explain' outcomes that nothing else in their theoretical repertoire would have predicted? In responding it is useful to break the search process into two phases or stages.

The first, 'chunking,' or the initial subdivision of complex tasks into a manageable number of components or subsystems, is wholly uncontroversial. There is very good evidence that we are hard-wired to divide all complex tasks into no more than seven plus or minus two 'chunks' because that is the number of slots we have in short-term or working memory (Miller 1956). Complex tasks like designing a new van are thus chunked in both the classic approach and the alternative search method. The crucial and controversial issue is what happens next.

In the classic system the initial distinctions, once fixed, become the frame for subsequent ones. The model is traditional taxonomy in biology, where, say, each phylum contains families, each family genuses, and each genus species; and the proper definition of a species never perturbs the definition of higher-order sets. Hence in the classic view it is considered a grave design flaw when lower-level, finer-grained subdivisions force reconsideration of higher-level, coarser-grained ones. The analog to this view of classification in product design is of course the idea of perfect modularity: interfaces are so stable that components can be substituted within any module without disturbing the operation of the more encompassing system of which the altered module is itself a component (Ulrich 1995). Chomsky's generative grammar I (Chomsky 1965) and Simon's own closely related work on list processing in AI is a mathematical restatement and generalization of the traditional view of taxonomy.[14] Because categories have, in this view, a determinate meaning and unambiguous empirical referents, they can be represented by formal symbols. Any argument can in turn be represented as a string of symbols, and all reasoning by manipulation of such strings by appropriate rules.

In the alternative method, in contrast, chunking is heuristic—the goal of an initial partition is to see how, from the vantage point of each piece, it and the others might be reconfigured. The revision of categories is a desirable and expected outcome, not a failure of intelligence. On the contrasting, semantic holism or cognitive view, the categories of language and thought are inherently ambiguous. Members of each category share common features. But subsets of them have features common to members of other categories, and boundaries blur the same way among subsets. The only way to provide a usefully rich account of any one category, therefore, is to see it in relation to the web of likenesses and differences that connect it to the others: holistically (see generally Fodor and Lepore 1992). On this view metaphoric comparison is the essence of language, not a poetically licensed abuse of linguistic precision: Unless we engage in mutually clarifying 'sense making,' the ambiguities of our own thoughts render them too imprecise to be reliably useful. This view implies that interpretation of ambiguity within a language is in principle no different from conciliation of differences across languages—translation (Davidson 1974). So if

126

collaborative sense making and metaphoric comparison are indeed at the heart of language, we should be able to identify others already solving problems like our own, and having found them, construct jointly a language for collaboration—notwithstanding deep differences of original approach or paradigm, to use Kuhn's word.[15]

Though the social construction of meaning is less a finding in cognitive science than an assertion of philosophic anthropology (Markell forthcoming), an active research topic in cognitive anthropology (Hutchins 1995), and a fruitful hypothesis in the history of science (Galison 1997) and many other disciplines, recent work in semantics and cognitive psychology and classification in evolutionary biology (see Lakoff 1987 for a masterful summary) puts the metaphoric understanding of categories and language on substantial empirical foundations, suggesting that this revision of categories is as 'human' as chunking. The prototype effect is a seminal example of this research (Rosch 1978, 1983). Unless formally trained to do otherwise, we individuate categories, and categorize individuals, in relation to concrete prototypes or exemplars that embody in fullest form all the features for which a category stands. We experience an eagle as 'more' birdlike than a penguin, because eagles soar and glide while penguins flap their wings as they hop and waddle. But this means that to identify a bird as a bird we have to be thinking of winged creatures that are par excellence, just barely, and not quite birds—benchmarking the bird, if you like.[16]

Thus the search process by which networked organizations address the problem of bounded rationality seems if anything more native to our thought—more behaviorally accurate—than the symbolic processing of classical theory.[17]

Human problem-solving techniques are not, of course inherently efficient. On the contrary, behavioralists sometimes revel in the imperfections of human problem solvers revealed by comparison with the performance of truly rational beings. So having grounded the behavior plausibility of the new problem-solving methods, we have to ask after their efficiency as well.

Robustness as highly dynamic efficiency

Before we can ask how organizations can be efficient in high-volatility environments, however, we have to clarify the question. Efficiency is a static concept, or rather a concept for stable environments. The efficient solution is just the least-cost means of reaching a known end. When the ends are various, and by some measure closely related, it can still be meaningful to speak of 'an' efficient solution or a set of these. But when the ends become more various and less well specified it no longer makes sense to speak of optimum or efficient solutions. Instead we can ask whether our problem-solving technique is robust, meaning that it can be expected to produce workable answers in turbulent task environments. Think of robustness as highly dynamic efficiency.

To underscore this point let me note here the misleading incompleteness of Simon's well-known story about two watchmakers, Tempus and Hora, whose competition is intended to show the robustness (resilience in the face of disruption) of hierarchical modularization. Tempus and Hora made similarly complex watches of about 1,000 parts each. But Tempus, the craftsman, assembles each watch from 1,000 pieces, while Hora, the mass producer, makes subassemblies of ten pieces each and then combines these into the final product. Simon shows easily that unless the probability of disruption per unit time is extremely low, Tempus almost never completes a watch, and the typical disruption destroys an extremely valuable, nearly finished piece. Hora completes much more work and loses much less in each disruption, so modularization seems robust (Simon 1969: 90–2). And so it is in comparison with craft production of large numbers of extremely complex machines.

But modularization is plainly not robust in our current world, where key module makers—meaning here sole-source suppliers of indispensable components—are routinely destroyed by natural catastrophes or the complete devaluation of a core capacity through a competitor's innovation. The robust strategy in this world is one where there is no difference between setting up the production system and repairing or replacing it in case of disruption; or, put another way, where the same principles that generate the initial set-up also generate the capacity to respond to disruptions of the first design as circumstances require. These are the principles that our robust producer, Quaesitor, follows when she searches for collaborators who are good at searching for collaborators all the way down. In this system, if any of the producers 'breaks,' the broken one and its collaborators find at least one replacement or substitute.

Two pieces of anecdotal evidence from the automobile industry illustrate the fragility of module makers and, conversely, the robustness of Quaesitor-type re-chunkers. Thus it was until recently widely believed in the industry that the mega-module makers—producers of large systems such as complete power trains or complex seating—would be the great beneficiaries of the disintegration of the closed, hierarchical firm: Their capacity to integrate disparate components combined with the capacity to anticipate future developments would allow them to impose their design choices on their customers, the final assemblers, while their power as monopsonist purchasers would allow them to impose favorable terms on their own suppliers. But in fact the mega-module makers, having invested in the capacity to produce relatively fixed systems, are today constantly wrong-footed by the fluidity of actual designs (see MacDuffie and Helper, this volume). Federal Mogul is in bankruptcy, while Dana and Tenneco teeter on the brink. The real winners turn out to be firms that federate diverse and flexible makers of specialized components. These federated component producers are more robust in iterated-co-design settings than mega-module makers simply because components are ingredients in many systems while large systems—modules as they are, not as they are imagined to be in a world of interchangeable black boxes—must be tailored to only a few products. And flexible component makers can switch from one production process to another as innovation demands, hedging themselves and so their parent firms against the risk of technological obsolescence. Realizing the limits of modularization, the head of Dana's Automotive Systems Division recently announced the transformation of his unit 'from a component producer capable of supplying systems to a systems producer capable of supplying components' (Carol 2002).

The destruction, by fire, and the almost instantaneous, collaborative reconstruction of the capacity of a key Toyota supplier illustrates the robustness of networks of searchers seeking searchers (Nishiguchi and Beaudet 1998). When it burned down in 1997, Aisin's Kariya plant 1 in Kobe was the extraordinarily efficient, sole-source supplier to Toyota of P-valves, a relatively simple, but high-precision component of an anti-skid break-control mounted on all of the assemblers' makes and models. True to its just-in-time discipline, Toyota had only two-days' worth of P-valves in inventory on the day the fire broke out; when that stock was exhausted, the assembly lines stopped. But by three days after the fire a congeries of a few Aisin suppliers and many other firms in the Toyota group—very few with prior experience in manufacturing this particular part, all presumably motivated by solidarity and the self-interested desire to return to normalcy and distinguish themselves on the way—were producing more than a hundred types of P-valves in their own facilities. By five days after the fire two of Toyota's Kobe plants were reopened; three days later car production was at more than 90 per cent of the pre-fire level; a week later there was no shortage of P-valves at all. Ultimately 62 firms became emergency producers of P-valves; these producers themselves relied on more than 150 emergency suppliers. So devastating had been the fire that none of the participants had access to the precision tooling that Kariya plant 1 used to make the original part. Aisin did contribute to the recovery by installing thousands of additional phone lines to respond to requests for information. But neither it nor Toyota attempted to direct the reconstruction effort.

The key to the extraordinary success was the participants' vast, common experience of the Toyota variant of iterated co-design: Aisin could characterize the part and the production process in general terms—chunk them; the emergency producers could devise, starting from their own experience, many different ways (some quite innovative) of achieving these ends. Then they could chunk the processes they were contemplating so that their suppliers could do the same with respect to subtasks. So, as Quaesitor would have expected, the same disciplines that generated a network of 'module makers' continuously searching for ways to improve also generated the capacity to search out alternative solutions if one of the network's module-making nodes fails.

In a malign world this distinction between efficiency and robustness would translate into an impossible choice: we would have to either increase efficiency or increase robustness, without knowing from one day to the next which is called for. In a more benign world we would expect that increased robustness would increase efficiency as well, so that measures that help us enhance performance in a volatile environment also improve operations under more stable conditions. This is in fact what we observe with the new organization. I suspect that the overlap between robustness-enhancing and efficiency-enhancing mechanisms explains a good deal of the explosive diffusion of this new institutional type. Here is a list of some of these mechanisms; and like the list of mechanisms that contribute to economies of scale, it is illustrative, not exhaustive.

The first is benchmarking and the metaphoric learning associated with it. In a volatile environment we expect tomorrow's conditions to differ sharply from today's. So minimal prudence demands that we continuously benchmark new developments to avoid disastrous surprises. But we just saw that benchmarking searches inform us about all the possibilities in the—expanded—solution space. That means that so long as the environment has not cooled down to the organizational equivalent of absolute zero, where benchmarking itself is unnecessary because conditions never change, these comparisons tell us new things about solutions we already know even as they reveal solution strategies we had not foreseen at all. This is surely an important part of the reason why comparison of additional variants often improves the reliability of the eventual designs rather than degrading it.

Something similar is probably at work with the second mechanism: concurrency. Concurrent development—in which 'upstream' and 'downstream' steps proceed simultaneously, each taking account of the (changes in the) requirements of the other—is almost unavoidable when rapid change puts a prohibitive penalty on missing or being late for a market. But like benchmarking, concurrent development sheds new light on familiar designs and practices even while illuminating new environments. In particular concurrency calls into question taken-for-granted assumptions about the relation among components in any sub system by prompting chains of what-if questions about how perturbations in the environment would reverberate through the inner structure of the complex. So in all but the most stable settings, some concurrency probably leads to efficiency-improving discoveries about shortcomings in familiar arrangements while also increasing robustness.

A third class of mechanisms with advantages in stable as well as volatile worlds are the techniques of what might be called flexible formalization: the tools or methods for making tacit, lived knowledge explicit, but in a way that permits rather than discourages further exploration and revision. Metaphoric benchmarking and iterated co-design generally depend on, and generate, devices for characterizing imperfectly theorized alternatives well enough to allow comparison and provoke some combination of action and reflection that may eventually improve the characterizations. But this is of course also true of methods, such as the five whys, which are the production, or stable-world, analogs to these design disciplines. In the five whys each response clarifies an obscure circumstance and demands scrutiny of its own obscurities. Even the 'final' results of such iterated questions—the root causes of problems subjected to root-cause analysis—are frequently formulated as rebuttable constraints on practice. An example is the book of lessons learned often found in one or another variant in Toyota or Honda plants (MacDuffie 1997). These compilations log design or processing steps—stamping curves of more than a certain radius in sheet metal—that bump up against existing technical constraints. They mark the limits of current practice, not the limits of the possible. Aisin's astonishingly quick recovery from the destruction of its P-valve facility suggests, we saw, a close connection between the flexible formalisms used to characterize ongoing processes rigorously for purposes of continuous improvement in efficiency and the flexible formalisms that allow the on-the-fly assessment of design alternatives required for robustness. As we will see next, this kind of rule making as ruling in or out for now has important analogs in rule and law making by the state as well.

Governance

Governance in the classic organization, we saw, is on the principal–agent model, or its stakeholder variant. In this model the choice of projects is taken to be unproblematic. Principals are simply assumed to be endowed with the ability to identify the projects best for them. The task for governance, rather, is to motivate the agent's faithful execution of the project, punishing her for opportunistic, self-regarding use of gaps or imprecision in the principal's plan, and rewarding her for using her discretion to fill gaps and correct mistakes in the plan to achieve its goal.

In the pragmatist search organization the choice of goals is at least as great a concern of governance as the control of opportunism. In these organizations there can be no clear distinction between 'principals' who make initial plans and 'agents' who are expected to revise or remake those plans in the course of 'executing' them under volatile conditions. Choice of goals and the broad projects embodying them are as much the product as the starting point of organizational activity. In a world of fallible, appetitive decision makers, the stakeholders in the organization—those who stand to benefit from its success or suffer from its failures—will therefore surely want to establish some mechanism for checking that this goal-determination process has not been subverted by ignorance or greed. Likewise, taking broad goals or projects as at least temporarily fixed, the stakeholders will want institutionalized assurance that collaborators are not making opportunistic use of the wide discretion routinely granted them in pursuing current projects. Here I want to argue that, just as hierarchies call forth (in the threat of hold-ups) a distinctive governance concern, and furnish (in vertical integration) a correspondingly distinct response, so the pragmatist organization's error-detection and correction regimes afford responses to its characteristic governance risks.[18]

Take first the problem of controlling the opportunistic exploitation of discretion. By making each party's facility with shared and highly revealing problem-solving techniques transparent to the others, pragmatist organizations make current collaboration (or the exploration of possible joint work) richly informative about the potential and risks of partnership. Put another way, at least some of the information needed for the substance of collaborative problem solving in particular cases can be used for benchmarking the abilities and probity of current and potential partners. Thus a firm that easily ferrets out the source of errors with five-why methods will presumably do better at solving new problems, and hence be more a reliable collaborator, than one that gets lost in the maze of its own confusions. Similarly, the mutual transparency that results from co-design disciplines makes it possible to detect, and attempt to correct, potential problems before they become disasters. Call the fusion of substantive and evaluative knowledge that allows an organization to learn as it monitors accountability (and vice versa) learning by monitoring (Sabel 1996).

The explosive diffusion of pragmatist disciplines and the success of the new organization generally strongly suggest that such learning by monitoring is in fact workable at the level of individual projects or the operation of relatively small units, where 'workable' here means only that show-stopping opportunism and ineptitude are detected, not that all interests are perfectly aligned, eliminating every trace of power. On the contrary: In the real world, the immediate collaborators in any given project are seldom so buffered from the concerns of related activities, with perhaps conflicting goals, that their relations to partners reflect only their joint experience with them. Thus design engineers or purchasing managers may fully expect to build long-term, co-design relations with their current suppliers, yet come under irresistible pressure from marketing or other departments to cut costs in the short term, even at the price of subverting the collaborative relation. Fearing this kind of betrayal, suppliers may hedge their bets with customers, raising questions about their own dedication and loyalty, and so on.

But this turbulence, and the institutional fragilities it surely creates, no more excludes iterated co-design among pragmatist organizations than the impossibility of writing incentive-compatible contracts excludes the possibility of successful hierarchical organization in suitable environments. Just as managers used the camaraderie of the hierarchy to close the gap between formal instruction and actual need, so, we may suppose, the supervisors in the network organization are using the social values underpinning or generated by pragmatist institutions to 'manage' the dangers of a new kind of opportunism. What those values are is, to be sure, a very open question. Solidarity based on common, long-term membership in a stable organization which values the members' identification with one another and the institution is unlikely to flourish in a setting where entrance and exit from the organization is common at all levels, and where the organization's own identity or purposes, let alone the identity of its collaborators, are routinely in question. Professionalism in its traditional form, though not linked to boundaries of particular operating units, is also an unlikely source of mutual dedication in the pragmatist organization. Professionalism in disciplines such as medicine, law, and teaching is based on the mastery of particular tools and techniques through apprenticeship with master practitioners; professional mastery is precisely the ability to apply those tools and techniques independently to challenging problems. The mutual monitoring within and across professional groups inherent in iterated co-design and other pragmatist routines thus often affronts the dignity of professionals trained that only beginners and incompetents must continually account for themselves. I have used the term studied trust to characterize the mutual reliance—neither calculating *modus vivendi* nor blind allegiance—that emerges among actors who come, through repeated, closely monitored exchanges, to count regularly on another's probity and capacity (Sabel 1993). Mac-Duffie finds just such a process of repeated and repeatedly assessed exchange generating 'collaborative community,' as defined in this volume, whose 'core value or standard for trust is not performance to preset targets, but the willingness and capability to engage in discussion about how to work towards solutions of problems' (MacDuffie, this volume). But such nuance of characterization aside, if participation in the new disciplines, and the values to which it seems to give rise, did not facilitate detection of dangerously incapable or opportunistic partners, the spread of pragmatist organizations would have been quickly stopped by some variant of the hold-up—the collaboration-destroying use of collaborative discoveries—that classical organization theory long took to exclude just the sort of vertically disintegrated co-design commonplace today.

Yet the very connection between problem-solving substance and partner evaluation that makes learning by monitoring a—workable—instrument of governance on the project or small-unit level disqualifies it as a mechanism for governing large and complex institutions, such as multinational firms, public service providers, or regulatory systems, that must periodically reallocate resources among various, perhaps competitive projects, or add entirely new ones (Fujimoto 1997; Cusumano and Nobeoka 1998). The demonstration by each and every project group in such an organization that it and its collaborators can develop promising new goals from current ones plainly bears on, but cannot alone decide, which goals the encompassing organization should pursue.

By bringing disentrenching searches to bear on its choice of strategy or goals, however, the pragmatist organization can use the information generated by the lower-level exploration of possibilities to inform and discipline higher-level decisions. Recall that the aim of metaphoric benchmarking, and the self-limiting searches it generates, is precisely to encourage exploration of solutions beyond the boundaries marked by routine. The same device can be used to elaborate and reconsider the understandings and commitments underpinning the organization's goals. Alternative goals embodied in bundles of projects advance rival interpretations of the institution's purpose and values;[19] choosing amongst these alternatives the organization simultaneously considers, and fuses, questions of principle (ends) and questions of technical feasibility (means).[20]

The process of re-evaluating goals parallels the process of searching out and assessing narrower design choices. Thus the 'center' of the encompassing pragmatist institution—acting on behalf and with the help of representatives of the individual subunits—metaphorically or openly benchmarks its overall objectives, looking for goals 'like' the current ones, but arguably better on some dimension. Each of the federated units then does the same with respect to the broad subgoal for which it is responsible; and the general institutional goals are, if necessary, revised in the light of the interim results. Through iterated pooling of the benchmark goals the organization and its units set the general priorities with which to rank projects.

Accountable behavior in this setting no longer entails compliance in the sense of rule following, but rather provision of a compelling explanation for choosing, in the light of fresh knowledge, one way of achieving the common (sub)goal over others. At the limit principal–agent accountability gives way to peer review, in which decision makers learn from and correct each other even as they set goals and performance standards for the organization.

Notice that this theoretical response to the encompassing governance problem is not proof against manipulation, any more than learning by monitoring is an absolute bar to opportunism. The very existence of a goal-selection process of the kind described can tempt units and project groups to manipulate the center into adopting the rules that show their own efforts in the best possible light. If one succeeds, metaphoric benchmarking of goals will be a sham, and the organization's goals will depend on the outcome of struggles to gain control of the rule-making power. But, at least for now, it seems that this vulnerability too can be 'managed,' though, as noted a moment ago, the management necessary differs because the nature of the vulnerabilities does.

Brief accounts of a range of pragmatist governance mechanisms from the private and public sectors indicate how the general principles of pragmatist organizations (though not their managerial complements) apply in particular contexts. Take first the case of the Illinois Tool Works, a mid-size conglomerate with $9 billion in annual sales and nearly 50,000 employees worldwide. One of its divisions makes plastic and metal components, fasteners and assemblies, industrial fluids and adhesives, fastening tools, and welding products for the construction, automotive, and consumer durables markets. Another makes consumer and industrial packaging, as well as product identification and quality assurance equipment for the food retail and service, food and beverage, and capital goods industries. The firm is organized as a federation of some 600 units. These are financed by headquarters, which also provides corporate research and development facilities. But within these limits the units are largely independent. Each is responsible for setting its own goals, and is held accountable for outcomes. Because of this focus on components and small subsystems, and the flexibility of its individual units, ITW has flourished where mega-module makers, in their rigidity, have floundered.

The key governance rule for goal setting in ITW is derived from Pareto's rule of thumb that only a small fraction—about 20 per cent—of all the causes of an outcome account for some 80 per cent of the total effect. The 80/20 governance rule obligates the units to regularly redetermine which 20 per cent of their activities account for (roughly) 80 per cent of their profits. These disproportionately beneficial activities are to be generalized and developed, and the others spun off or abandoned. Generalizing the successful activities is not, however, straightforward. Each unit's sales to its customers bundle many different kinds of goods and activities: particular co-design services; unusually short product-development cycles: innovative use of particular materials or the processes by which they are worked. So, following the 80/20 rule, the unit's first task is in effect to do a root-cause analysis of the grounds of its own current successes, and redirect its strategy according to the results. That done, the unit must metaphorically benchmark the new strategy by exploring potential uses of its newly recharacterized capabilities that are 'like' the currently successful ones. Because judgements about the viability of strategies discovered in this way always contain a speculative element, a subsidiary governance rule provides that managers are not penalized for being wrong (once or twice), but face immediate sanctions if they are caught pursuing strategies that have not been disclosed and justified to headquarters. This second rule gives managers an incentive to (temporarily) immunize themselves against the risks of incorrect decisions by increasing the transparency of their decision making to headquarters, and so to other units in the firm and outside stakeholders.[21]

A second illustration is the governance system of Cisco Systems, the leading maker of network routers, switches, and interface devices. To remain competitive in one of the world's technologically and commercially most volatile markets, Cisco invests heavily in research (roughly 17 per cent of sales in recent years). But the distinctive aspect of its strategy is a policy of acquiring technologies or products pioneered by other, usually much smaller firms, and then working with the managers of acquired firms to develop them (Mayer and Kenney 2002: esp. 24). As of mid-2001, Cisco had incorporated some seventy-five units through A & D. This policy depends in turn on two governance rules. The first, disentrenching rule obligates business units to conduct a 'make or buy' review when preparing their annual business plan. This requires each unit to compare the strengths and weaknesses of its current produce or service, and closely related variants of these, to those alternatives under development or already produced by competitors. Because Cisco's headquarters has rich knowledge of the changing needs of end users through its sales force, and many ties to the research community, business unit managers have every reason to identify and evaluate potential acquisition targets before they come to general attention. In case of an acquisition, a second governance rule provides that the inside managers are rewarded for retaining the managers of the target firm, and integrating them into Cisco. Together the two rules not only encourage (as at ITW) regular reassessment and occasional brusque changes of strategy at the business-unit level, but also, by making outsiders into insiders, increase the cognitive diversity of management generally, and so facilitate the next rounds of assessment and change. And of course business-unit changes can in combination lead to large changes in overall strategy.

The public-sector equivalents of these disentrenching governance rules take the general form of an obligation that each unit measure itself against some general goal or performance standard—reliable and safe operations, continuous improvement in service provision—and correct shortfalls revealed by comparison with the performance of others facing similar situations. A straightforward regulatory application is the requirement to undertake near-miss analysis in the US nuclear power-generating industry. Utilities in the industry must report disruptions in their operations to the Institute for Nuclear Power Operation (INPO), an industry-funded entity ultimately responsible to the Nuclear Regulatory Commission. INPO officials sift these reports to distinguish harmless disruptions from dangerous ones. Thorough analyses of the causes of the dangerous disruptions, and ways of preventing them, are then circulated as Significant Operating Experience Reports, or SOERs. Industry Operating Experience Reviews then periodically assess the ability of particular plants to effectively use the SOERs and other means to improve their own affairs. For purposes of this review, a team of specialists in a variety of areas evaluates the plant's troubles since the last INPO inspection, paying particular attention to the plant's own reports on how it has responded to SOERs (Rees 1994, but see also Perrin 2005).

Where minute variations in daily operations are less likely to signal the possibility of substantial hidden risks, the government can require the regulated entity to scan periodically for possible hazards and present a plan for mitigating those that it identifies. A regulatory oversight body then evaluates the adequacy of the plans, and the steps to realize them, against the benchmarks set by the best performers. The shift in the USA in the 1990s from poke-and-sniff (organo-leptic) methods of ensuring food safety to the hazard analysis of critical control points (HACCPs) shows the drift of developments (US Department of Agriculture, Food Safety and Inspection Service 1996). In the organo-leptic method an inspector from the Federal Safety and Inspection Service examines every head of cattle or chicken being disassembled in a slaughterhouse for quality defects and especially signs of pathogens. The limitation of the method of course is that some pathogens may not be detectable by the usual examinations, so that meat products leaving the processing plant are not assuredly safe; and even if they are, pathogens introduced at later stages of the food supply chain would not be noticed. Under the HACCP regulations introduced by the US Department of Agriculture, meat and poultry processors have to identify all the points in their production processes where pathogens are likely to be introduced, detail how they will reduce these risks, and verify, by testing, the success of the adequacy of their measures. The HACCP plan must be complemented by a Standard Sanitation Operations Plan detailing the plant's regular housekeeping measures. The role of federal inspectors shifts from direct examination of animal carcasses to verification of the processors' hazard reduction systems. This verification starts with assessment of the adequacy of the HACCP plan (and the companion Standard Sanitation Operations Plan) and includes review of the plant's test results as well as independent testing by the inspectors. Eventually the HACCP system is to cover every link in the food supply chain from farm to plate.[22]

The US Securities and Exchange Commission is shifting the regime governing financial disclosures by publicly traded companies in an analogous direction. Having rediscovered in the recent stock-market bubble that complex rule systems are easily gamed by managers with powerful financial incentives to do so, the SEC is requiring firms to practice 'critical accounting': In reporting their financial results, firms will have to identify the critical accounting issues where their choice among arguably legitimate but rival methods of valuing results made a material difference to their statement of overall performance. For each of these issues the firm will have to document the alternatives considered; the valuation that would have resulted from the application of each; the reasons for the choice of the method actually used, and the key participants in the decision-making process that produced the final result; and even an assessment of the risks to the regulatory system as a whole that would eventuate if the firm's preferred method were broadly adopted.

With regard, finally, to complex public services, the disentrenching governance rules typically require operating units to formulate and periodically revise strategies for increasing rates of improvement towards a general end. In the case of pragmatist public school reform discussed above, for example, the general goal is to reduce and eventually eliminate the difference in performance in key subjects such as reading and mathematics between affluent, white students and poor students, who are also often of color. In Texas the state governance regime accordingly requires periodic testing in these subjects by means of sophisticated standard tests that (now) reward the ability to conceptualize rather than rote learning. Each school must report the results of these tests disaggregated by economic and ethnic groups, and the state pools the data so that parents with children in a particular school can compare the rate of improvement of the relevant subgroup in that school to the thirty-nine other schools in Texas demographically most similar to their children's. Further disaggregation at the district or school level then yields information about the performance of particular teachers and administrators that can guide further reorganization.

In elaborating these general features of pragmatist governance and illustrating their practicality the aim, again, is to make plausible the claim that the new search networks are governable in practice. This is not to suggest that such networks are, in virtue of the pragmatist institutions on which they are based, somehow proof in principle against all disruptions of governance, or that they are already well governed. In fact, leaving aside cases of egregious financial wrongdoing, it is striking that there is not a single, generally recognized example of sustained, organized, and well-characterized good governance in a multinational firm, including of course the many indisputably successful ones (Kristensen and Zeitlin 2004). One searches in vain for a canonical example of pragmatist governance in the public sector as well. The lesson, perhaps, is that behind the mask of prudence and sobriety, decision makers are irresponsibly reckless, all too eager to take a flyer on any promising fad without due consideration of the risks they are running. Or, as I suspect, the lesson may be that, in a world so volatile that failing to learn rapidly is almost surely fatal, it is more prudent to build the requisite kind of learning organization, and at the price of managing governance issues along the way, than to stay put until the governance of pragmatist institutions has been reduced to a textbook.

Democracy

A final contrast between classical organizations and pragmatist alternatives returns us to the opening theme of this essay: their relation to democracy. A fuller treatment would have to sketch in detail a pragmatist democracy, tracing the role of the legislature, administration, and judiciary in a polity that deliberately governed itself by framework laws intended to be revised in the light of diverse efforts to implement them (Sabel and Cohen 1997, 2003; Sabel and Dorf 1998; Sabel and Simon 2004). Here I only want to indicate how pragmatist institutions invert the very features of classic hierarchies that made them an encumbrance on, if not an outright obstacle to democracy: If the class organization reasonably occasioned pessimism about the prospects of democracy, then in its networked mirror image should, all else equal, occasion optimism about a democratic revival.

In classic theory, we saw, the routines of the large organization were the bane of democracy. Whether rooted in actual technical necessity, or imposed as technical necessities through the manipulations of self-interested, technically versed elites, these routines so limited individual and group autonomy as to reduce self-rule to the periodic power to change one set of rulers for another. Hence public school became (for Dewey) a kind of incubator of citizen autonomy, a last-ditch defense against the encroachment of the elites, while the idea of a universal language of design was (for Simon) a fanciful means of connecting fundamentally disparate technical elites, and allowing them at least to communicate with the masses.

But in the pragmatist organization, we saw, the questioning of routine at the level of individual projects and more generally has itself become institutionalized. In this sense the lesson of the Deweyan school and the world of work surely overlap, even if they are not identical: In both rule following elides with rule making, and individual autonomy is explicitly linked to group decision making. Reform of the current, bureaucratic public school system on pragmatist lines further blurs the distinction between education and other forms of problem solving. Meanwhile Simon's language of design has been transformed in pragmatist institutions from a forlorn, academic hope into an everyday necessity: the many, interconnected protocols of iterated co-design are in effect so many (partial, but intercommunicating) design languages, allowing actors with diverse expertise and different background assumptions not only to exchange ideas jointly but also to develop new tools for mutual understanding. More yet: in assuming all current expertise to be importantly limited, and hence the corresponding need to develop corrigible institutions through peer review and local experimentation informed by lay knowledge, pragmatist institutions directly challenge the traditional equation of efficiency with rule by unquestionable professionals and technical experts. By their nature, therefore, these institutions invite the individuals and groups that together form civil society to participate in new ways in the decisions that shape their lives. Long aware of the limits of principal–agent governance in volatile circumstances, and increasingly aware of emergent alternatives that allow for institutional learning in the absence of master plans, mayors and local administrators—in Denmark, for instance (Sørensen 2002)—and high civil servants and cabinet-level politicians—in, for example the Netherlands (Wetenschappelijke Raad voor het Regeringsbeleid 2004)—are beginning, but only just, to think openly about the implications of a shift to pragmatist public problem solving for parliamentary democracy (Engelen and Ho 2004).

Sidney Hook, one of the great philosophic wits of the last century, famously quipped that pragmatism was good in theory, not so good in practice. But his is almost surely not the last laugh. The deep surprise of the current organizational revolution is that pragmatism institutionalized—put rigorously into practice—for once, in the reality of our own time, seems to be confounding our inveterate theoretical pessimism, expanding our capacities for problem solving while inviting us to exercise our capacities for self-rule.

References

Abernathy, Frederick H., Dunlop, John T., Hammond, Janice H., and Weil, David (1999). *A Stitch in Time: Lean Retailing and the Transformation of Manufacturing— Lessons from the Apparel and Textile Industries*. New York: Oxford University Press.

Adler, Paul S., Goldoftas, Barbara, and Levine, David I. (1999). 'Flexibility versus efficiency? A case study of model changeovers in the Toyota production system.' *Organization Science*, 10/1: 43–68.

Anderson, E. G., Jr., Fine, C. H., and Parker, G. G. (2000). 'Upstream volatility in the supply chain: the machine tool industry as a case study.' *Production and Operations Management*, 9/3: 239–61.

Arthur, W. Brian (1994). *Increasing Returns and Path Dependence in the Economy*. Ann Arbor: University of Michigan Press.

Barnard, Chester I. (1938). *The Functions of the Executive*. Cambridge, Mass.: Harvard University Press.

Barnett, B., and Clark, K. (1996). 'Technological newness: an empirical study in the process industries.' *Journal of Engineering and Technology Management*, 13/3–4: 263–82.

Bendor, Jonathan, Moe, Terry M., and Shotts, Kenneth W. (2001). 'Recycling the garbage can: an assessment of the research program.' *American Political Science Review*, 95/1: 169–90.

Black, M. (1979). 'More about metaphor.' In A. Ortony (ed.), *Metaphor and Thought*. New York: Cambridge University Press: 19–45.

Brown, John Seely, and Duguid, Paul (1991). 'Organizational learning and communities of practice: toward a unifying view of working, learning, and innovation.' In M. D. Cohen and L. S. Sproull (eds.), *Organizational Learning*. London: Sage Publications: 59–82.

—— —— (2001). 'Creativity versus structure: a useful tension.' *MIT Sloan Management Review*, 42/4: 93–4.

Brown, Shona L., and Eisenhardt, Kathleen M. (1995). 'Product development: past research, present findings, and future directions.' *Academy of Management Review*, 20/2: 343–78.

—— —— (1997). 'The art of continuous change: linking complexity theory and time-paced evolution in relentlessly shifting organizations.' *Administrative Science Quarterly*, 42/1: 1–34.

Burawoy, Michael (1979). *Manufacturing Consent*. Chicago: University of Chicago Press.

Burns, Tom, and Stalker, G. M. (1961). *The Management of Innovation*. London: Tavistock Publications.

Carol, Bill (2002). 'Dana Corporation realigns automotive systems businesses: action leverages world-class resources to benefit customers.' *PR Newswire*, 19 June, at www.findarticles.com/cf_dls/m4PRN/2002_June_19/87471115/p1/article.jhtml, visited on 6 Jan. 2004.

Chandler, Alfred A. (1977). *The Visible Hand: The Managerial Revolution in American Business*. Cambridge, Mass.: Belknap Press of Harvard University Press.

Chomsky, Noam (1965). *Syntactic Structures*. The Hague: Mouton.

Christensen, Clayton M. (1997). *The Innovator's Dilemma*. Boston: Harvard Business School Press.

—— (2002). 'The rules of innovation.' *Technology Review*, 105/5: 32–8.

—— and Hart, S. L. (2002). 'The great leap: driving innovation from the base of the pyramid.' *MIT Sloan Management Review*, 44/1: 51–6.

—— and Raynor, Michael E. (2003). *The Innovator's Solution: Creating and Sustaining Successful Growth*. Boston: Harvard Business School Press.

—— Johnson, M. W., and Rigby, D. K. (2002). 'Foundations for growth: how to identify and build disruptive new businesses.' *MIT Sloan Management Review*, 43/3: 22–31.

Clark, Kim B., and Fujimoto, Takahiro (1991). *Product Development Performance: Strategy, Organization, and Management in the World Auto Industry*. Boston: Harvard Business School Press.

Coase, Ronald (1937). 'The nature of the firm.' *Economica*, 4: 386–405.

Cohen, Michael, March, James, and Olsen, Johan (1972). 'A garbage can model of organizational choice.' *Administrative Science Quarterly*, 17/1: 1–25.

Crouch, Colin, and Farrell, Henry (2004). 'Breaking the path of institutional development? Alternatives to the new determinism.' *Rationality and Society*, 16/1: 5–43.

Crozier, Michel (1964). *The Bureaucratic Phenomenon*. Chicago: University of Chicago Press.

Cusumano, Michael A., and Nobeoka, Kentaro (1998). *Thinking beyond Lean: How Multi-Project Management is Transforming Product Development at Toyota and Other Companies*. New York: Free Press.

Dalton, Melville (1948). 'The industrial "rate-busters": a characterization.' *Applied Anthropology*, 7 (Winter): 13–14.

David, Paul A. (1985). 'Clio and the economics of QWERTY.' *American Economic Review Papers and Proceedings*, 75: 332–7.

Davidson, Donald (1974). 'On the very idea of a conceptual scheme.' *Proceedings and Addresses of the American Philosophical Association*, 47: 5–20.

Dewey, John (1915). *The School and Society*. Chicago: University of Chicago Press.

—— (1922). *Human Nature and Conduct: An Introduction to Social Psychology*. New York: Holt.

—— (1927). *The Public and its Problems*. New York: Holt.

Doeringer, Peter B., and Piore, Michael J. (1971). *Internal Labor Markets and Manpower Analysis*. Lexington, Mass.: Heath.

Dore, Ronald (1983). 'Goodwill and the spirit of market capitalism.' *British Journal of Sociology*, 34/4: 459–82.

Dörr, Gerlinde, and Kessel, Tanja (1997). 'Das Restrukturierungsmodell Skoda-Volkswagen. Ergebnis aus Transfer und Transformation.' Publication of the project group Transformation und Globalisierung des Forschungsschwerpunkts Technik-Arbeit-Umwelt of the Wissenschaftszentrum Berlin für Sozialforschung, FS II 97–603, Berlin.

Dougherty, D. (1992). 'Interpretive barriers to successful product innovation in large firms.' *Organization Science*, 3/2: 179–202.

Doz, Y. L. (1998). *Alliance Advantage: The Art of Creating Value through Partnering*. Boston: Harvard Business School Press.

Eby, L. T., and Dobbins, G. H. (1997). 'Collectivistic orientation in teams: an individual and group-level analysis.' *Journal of Organizational Behavior*, 18/3: 275–95.

Eisenhardt, K. M., and Tabrizi, B. N. (1995). 'Accelerating adaptive processes: product innovation in the global computer industry.' *Administrative Science Quarterly*, 40/1: 84–110.

Elmore, Richard F., and Burney, Deanna (1997). 'School variation and systemic instructional improvement in Community School District #2, New York City.' High Performance Learning Communities Project, Learning Research and Development Center, University of Pittsburgh.

—— —— (1998). 'Continuous improvement in Community School District #2, New York City.' High Performance Learning Communities Project, Learning Research and Development Center, University of Pittsburgh.

Engelen, Ewald, and Ho, Monika Sie Dhian (eds.) (2004). *De Staat van de Democratie. Democratie voorbij de Staat*. WRR Verkenning 3. Amsterdam: Amsterdam University Press.

Ernst, Dieter (2004). 'Complexity and internationalisation of innovation: why is chip design moving to Asia?' Honolulu: East West Center, Working paper #64, 8 Nov.

Feller, J., Fitzgerald, B., Hissam, S., and Lakhani, K. (eds.) (2005). *Perspectives on Free and Open Source Software*. Cambridge, MA: The MIT Press.

Fine, C. H. (1996). 'Industry clockspeed and competency chain design: an introductory essay.' Proceedings of the 1996 Manufacturing and Service Operations Management Conference, Dartmouth College, Hanover, NH, 24–6 June.

—— (1997). 'Power diffusion in automotive supply chains.' Working draft.

—— and Whitney, D. E. (1996). 'Is the make–buy decision process a core competence?' Working draft.

—— Gilboy, G., Oye, K., and Parker, G. (1995). 'The role of proximity in automotive technology supply chain development: an introductory essay.' Working draft.

Fodor, Jerry, and Lepore, Ernest (1992). *Holism: A Shopper's Guide*. Oxford: Blackwell.

Foss, Nicolai J. (2003). 'Selective intervention and internal hybrids: interpreting and learning from the rise and the decline of the Oticon Spaghetti Organization.' *Organization Science*, 14/3: 331–49.

Fujimoto, Takahiro (1997). 'Capability building and over-adaptation: a case of "fat design" in the Japanese auto industry.' *Actes du GERPISA*, 19 (Feb.). See http://www.university.fr/PagesHtml/Laboratoires/ancien–gerpisa/actes/19/article1.html.

—— (1999). *The Evolution of the Toyota Manufacturing System*. Oxford: Oxford University Press.

Galison, Peter (1997). *Image and Logic: A Material Culture of Microphysics*. Chicago: University of Chicago Press.

Gallie, W. B. (1956). 'Essentially contested concepts.' *Proceedings of the Aristotelian Society*, 51: 167–98.

Garfield, J. L. (ed.) (1990). *Foundations of Cognitive Science: The Essential Readings*. New York: Paragon House.

Gibbons, Robert (2003). 'How organizations behave: towards implications for economics and economic policy.' Paper written for the Federal Reserve Bank of Boston Economic Conference, 'How humans behave: the implications for economics and economic policy' (8–10 June).

Gortner, H. F., Mahler, J., and Nicholson, J. B. (1987). *Organization Theory: A Public Perspective*. Chicago: Dorsey Press.

Hargadon, A., and Sutton, R. I. (1997). 'Technology brokering and innovation in a product development firm.' *Administrative Science Quarterly*, 42/4: 716–49.

Hatch, Mary Jo, and Weick, Karl E. (1998). 'Critical resistance to the jazz metaphor.' *Organization Science*, 9/5: 600–4.

Hedlund, G. (1999). 'The intensity and extensity of knowledge and the multinational corporation as a nearly recomposable system (NRS).' *Management International Review*, 39/1: 5–44.

Helper, Susan, MacDuffie, John Paul, and Sabel, Charles (2000). 'Pragmatic collaborations: advancing knowledge while controlling opportunism.' *Industrial and Corporate Change*, 10/3: 443–83.

Henderson, Rebecca M., and Clark, Kim B. (1990). 'Architectural innovation: the reconfiguration of existing product technologies and the failure of established firms.' *Administrative Science Quarterly*, 35/1: 9–30.

Herrigel, Gary (2004). 'Emerging strategies and forms of governance in high-wage component manufacturing regions.' *Industry and Innovation*, 11/1–2: 45–79.

von Hippel, Eric (2005). 'Open source software projects as "user innovation networks".' In J. Feller, B. Fitzgerald, S. Hissam, and K. Lakhani (eds.), *Perspectives on Free and Open Source Software*. Cambridge, MA: The MIT Press: 267–78.

Holmstrom, Bengt (1982). 'Moral hazard in teams.' *Bell Journal of Economics*, 13: 324–40.

Hutchins, E. (1995). *Cognition in the Wild*. Cambridge, Mass.: MIT Press.

Jehn, K. A., Northcraft, G. B., and Neale, M. A. (1999). 'Why differences make a difference: a field study of diversity, conflict, and performance in workgroups.' *Administrative Science Quarterly*, 44/4: 741–63.

Johnson, Stephen B. (2002). *The Secret of Apollo: Systems Management in American and European Space Programs*. Baltimore: Johns Hopkins University Press.

Jolls, Christine, Sunstein, Cass R., and Thaler, Richard (1998). 'A behavioral approach to law and economics.' *Stanford Law Review*, 50: 1471–550.

Katz, D., and Kahn, R. L. (1966). *The Social Psychology of Organizations*. New York: Wiley.

Keen, Peter G. W. (1981). 'Information systems and organizational change.' *Association for Computing Machinery*, 24/1: 24–33.

Keinan, G., and Koren, M. (2002). 'Teaming up type As and Bs: the effect of group composition on performance and satisfaction.' *Applied Psychology: An International Review*, 51/3: 425–45.

Kenagy, J. W., and Christensen, C. M. (2002). 'Disruptive innovation: a new diagnosis for health care's "financial flu".' *Healthcare Financial Management*, 56/5: 62–6.

Klein, Benjamin, Crawford, Alwin, and Alchian, Armen (1978). 'Vertical integration, appropriable rents and the competitive contracting process.' *Journal of Law and Economics*, 21/2: 297–326.

Koch, Christoph (2004). *The Quest for Consciousness: A Neurobiological Approach*. Englewood, Colo.: Roberts and Company Publishers.

Kocka, Jürgen (1981). *Die Angestellten in der Deutschen Geschichte 1850–1980: Vom Privatbeamten zum Angestellten Arbeitnehmer*. Göttingen: Vandenhoeck and Ruprecht.

Kristensen, Peer Hull, and Zeitlin, Jonathan (2004). *Local Players in Global Games: The Strategic Constitution of a Multinational Corporation*. New York: Oxford University Press.

Kuhn, Thomas S. (1962). *The Structure of Scientific Revolutions*. Chicago: University of Chicago Press.

—— (1979). 'Metaphor in science.' In A. Ortony (ed.), *Metaphor and Thought*. New York: Cambridge University Press: 409–19.

Kusunoki, K., Nonaka, I., and Nagata, A. (1998). 'Organizational capabilities in product development of Japanese firms: a conceptual framework and empirical findings.' *Organization Science*, 9/6: 699–718.

Lakhani, Karim, and Jeppeson, Lars Bo (work in progress). 'Broadcast search and solution attraction in scientific problem solving.'

Lakoff, George (1987). *Women, Fire, and Dangerous Things*. Chicago: University of Chicago Press.

Lam, A. (1997). 'Embedded firms, embedded knowledge: problems of collaboration and knowledge transfer in global cooperative ventures.' *Organization Studies*, 18/6: 973–96.

Lamaison, Pierre, and Bourdieu, Pierre (1986). 'From rules to strategies: an interview with Pierre Bourdieu.' *Cultural Anthropology*, 1/1: 110–20.

La Porte, Todd R. (1994). 'A strawman speaks up.' *Journal of Contingencies and Crisis Management*, 2/4: 207–11.

—— and Consolini, Paula M. (1991). 'Working in practice but not in theory: theoretical challenges of high-reliability organizations.' *Journal of Public Administration Research and Theory*, 1/1: 19–48.

—— and Rochlin, Gene (1994). 'A rejoinder to Perrow.' *Journal of Contingencies and Crisis Management*, 2/4: 221–7.

Larson, James R., Jr., Christensen, Caryn, Franz, Timothy M., and Abbot, Ann S. (1998). 'Diagnosing groups: the pooling, management and impact of shared and unshared case information in team-based medical decision making.' *Journal of Personality and Social Psychology*, 75/1: 93–108.

Lave, J., and Wenger, E. (1991). *Situated Learning: Legitimate Peripheral Participation*. New York: Cambridge University Press.

Lawrence, P. R., and Lorsch, J. (1967). *Organization and Environment*. Cambridge, MA.: Harvard University Press.

Levesque, L. L., Wilson, J. M., and Wholey, D. R. (2001). 'Cognitive divergence and shared mental models in software development project teams.' *Journal of Organizational Behavior*, 22/2: 135–44.

Levin, S. R. (1979). 'Standard approaches to metaphor and a proposal for literary metaphor.' In A. Ortony (ed.), *Metaphor and Thought*. New York: Cambridge University Press: 124–35.

Levitt, Barbara, and March, James G. (1988). 'Organizational learning.' *Annual Review of Sociology*, 14: 319–40.

Liebman, James S., and Sabel, Charles F. (2003). 'A public laboratory Dewey barely imagined: the emerging model of school governance and legal reform.' *NYU Review of Law and Social Change*, 28/2: 183–304.

Liker, J. K., Collins, P. D., and Hull, F. M. (1999). 'Flexibility and standardization: test of a contingency model of product design-manufacturing integration.' *Journal of Product and Innovation Management*, 16/3: 248–67.

—— Fruin, W. Mark, and Adler, Paul (1999). *Remade in America: Transplanting and Transforming Japanese Management Systems*. New York: Oxford University Press.

Lindblom, Charles, E. (1959). 'The science of "muddling through".' *Public Administration Review*, 19/2: 79–88.

MacDuffie, John Paul (1997). 'The road to root cause: shop-floor problem-solving at three automotive assembly plants.' *Management Science*, 43/4: 479–502.

Markell, Patchen (forthcoming). 'The potential and the actual: Mead, Honneth, and the "I".' In David Owen and Bert van den Brink (eds.), *Recognition and Power*. Cambridge: Cambridge University Press.

Maurice, Marc, Sellier, François, and Silvestre, Jean-Jacques (1982). *Politique d'éducation et organisation industrielle en France et en Allemagne: essai d'analyse sociétale*. Paris: Presses Universitaires de France.

Mayer, David, and Kenney, Martin F. (2002). 'Economic action does not take place in a vacuum: understanding Cisco's acquisition and development strategy.' Berkeley Roundtable on the International Economy, Working Paper 148, 16 Sept.

Mendelberg, Tali (2002). 'The deliberative citizen: theory and evidence.' In M. Delli Carpini, L. Huddy, and R. Y. Shapiro (eds.), *Political Decision-Making, Deliberation and Participation: Research in Micropolitics*. Greenwich, Conn.: JAI Press: vi. 151–93.

Miller, G. J. (1992). *Managerial Dilemmas: The Political Economy of Hierarchy*. Cambridge: Cambridge University Press.

Miller, George A. (1956). 'The magical number seven, plus or minus two: some limits on the capacity for processing information.' *Psychological Review*, 63: 81–97.

Neuman, G. A., Wagner, S. H., and Christiansen, N. D. (1999). 'The relationship between work-team personality composition and the job performance of teams.' *Group and Organization Management*, 24/1: 28–45.

Newell, A., and Simon, H. A. (1972). *Human Problem Solving*. Englewood Cliffs, NJ: Prentice-Hall, Inc.

Nicolaides, Phedon, Geveke, Arjan, and Teuling, Anne-Mieke den (2003). *Improving Policy Implementation in an Enlarged European Union: The Case of National Regulatory Authorities*. Maastricht: European Institute of Public Administration.

Nishiguchi, Toshihiro (1994). *Strategic Industrial Sourcing: The Japanese Advantage*. Oxford: Oxford University Press.

—— and Beaudet, A. (1998). 'The Toyota group and the Aisin fire.' *Sloan Management Review*, 40/1: 49–59.

Nohria, N., and Eccles, R. (1992). *Networks and Organizations: Structure, Form, and Action*. Boston: Harvard Business School Press.

OECD (1996). *Ireland: Local Partnerships and Social Innovation*. Paris: OECD.

Ortony, A. (1979*a*). 'Metaphor: a multidimensional problem.' In A. Ortony (ed.), *Metaphor and Thought*. New York: Cambridge University Press: 1–18.

—— (1979*b*). 'The role of similarity in similes and metaphors.' In A. Ortony (ed.), *Metaphor and Thought*. New York: Cambridge University Press: 186–201.

Perrin, Constance (2005). *Shouldering Risks: The Culture of Control in the Nuclear Power Industry*. Princeton: Princeton University Press.

Perrow, Charles (1984). *Normal Accidents: Living with High-Risk Technologies*. New York: Basic Books.

—— (1994). 'The limits of safety: the enhancement of a theory of accidents.' *Journal of Contingencies and Crisis Management*, 2/4: 212–20.

Petersen, Melody, and Drew, Christopher (2003). 'New safety rules fail to stop tainted meat.' *New York Times* (10 Oct.): A.1.

Piore, Michael, and Sabel, Charles (1984). *The Second Industrial Divide*. New York: Basic Books.

Polzer, J. T., Milton, L. P., and Swann, W. B., Jr. (2002). 'Capitalizing on diversity: interpersonal congruence in small work groups.' *Administrative Science Quarterly*, 47/2: 296–324.

Posner, M. I. (ed.) (1989). *Foundations of Cognitive Science*. Cambridge, Mass.: MIT Press.

Rainey, H. G. (1991). *Understanding and Managing Public Organizations*. San Francisco: Jossey-Bass Publishers.

Ramalho, José Ricardo, and Santana, Marco Aurélio (2002). 'VW's modular system and workers' organization in Resende, Brazil.' *International Journal of Urban and Regional Research*, 26/4: 756–66.

Rees, Joseph V. (1994). *Hostages of Each Other: The Transformation of Nuclear Safety since Three Mile Island*. Chicago: University of Chicago Press.

Rentsch, J. R., and Klimoski, R. J. (2001). 'Why do "great minds" think alike? Antecedents of team member schema agreement.' *Journal of Organizational Behavior*, 22/2: 107–22.

Rijpma, Jos A. (2003). 'From deadlock to dead end: the normal accidents–high reliability debate revisited.' *Journal of Contingencies and Crisis Management*, 11/1: 37–45.

Ripley, R., and Franklin, G. A. (1987). *Congress, the Bureaucracy and Public Policy*. Chicago: Dorsey Press.

Rochlin, Gene I., La Porte, Todd R., and Roberts, K. H. (1987). 'The self-designing high reliability organization: aircraft carrier flight operations at sea.' *Naval War College Review*, 90: 76–90.

Rosch, Eleanor (1978). 'Principles of categorization.' In E. Rosch and B. B. Lloyd (eds.), *Cognition and Categorization*. Hillsdale, NJ: Lawrence Erlbaum Associates: 27–48.

—— (1983). 'Prototype classification and logical classification: the two systems.' In E. Scholnick (ed.), *New Trends in Cognitive Representation: Challenges to Piaget's Theory*. Hillsdale, NJ: Lawrence Erlbaum Associates: 73–86.

Sabel, Charles (1982). *Work and Politics: The Division of Labor in Industry*. Cambridge: Cambridge University Press.

—— (1993). 'Studied trust: building new forms of cooperation in a volatile economy.' *Human Relations*, 46/9: 1133–70.

—— (1996). 'Learning by monitoring: the institutions of economic development.' In N. Smelser and R. Swedberg (eds.), *The Handbook of Economic Sociology*. Princeton: Princeton University Press: 137–65.

—— and Cohen, Joshua (1997). 'Directly-deliberative polyarchy.' *European Law Journal*, 3/4: 313–40.

—— —— (2003). 'Sovereignty and solidarity: EU and US.' In Jonathan Zeitlin and David Trubek (eds.), *Governing Work and Welfare in a New Economy: European and American Experiments*. Oxford: Oxford University Press: 345–75.

—— and Dorf, Michael C. (1998). 'A constitution of democratic experimentalism.' *Columbia Law Review*, 98/2: 267–530.

—— and Simon, William (2004). 'Destabilization rights: how public law litigation succeeds.' *Harvard Law Review*, 117/4: 1015–1101.

—— and Zeitlin, Jonathan (2004). 'Neither modularity nor relational contracting: inter-firm collaboration in the new economy. A critique of Langlois and Lamoreaux, Raff, and Temin.' *Enterprise and Society*, 5/3: 388–403.

Sagan, Scott D. (1994). 'Toward a political theory of organizational reliability.' *Journal of Contingencies and Crisis Management*, 2/4: 228–40.

Schoen, D. A. (1979). 'Generative metaphor: a perspective on problem-setting in social policy.' In A. Ortony (ed.), *Metaphor and Thought*. New York: Cambridge University Press: 254–83.

Schumpeter, Joseph A. (1976). *Capitalism, Socialism and Democracy*. New York: Harper & Row.

Searle, J. R. (1979). 'Metaphor.' In A. Ortony (ed.), *Metaphor and Thought*. New York: Cambridge University Press: 92–123.

Simon, H. A. (1947). *Administrative Behavior: A Study of Decision-Making Processes in Administrative Organization*. New York: Macmillan Co.

—— (1955). 'A behavioral model of rational choice.' *Quarterly Journal of Economics*, 69: 99–118.

—— (1956). 'Rational choice and the structure of the environment.' *Psychological Review*, 63: 129–38.

Simon, H. A. (1957). *Models of Man, Social and Rational: Mathematical Essays on Rational Human Behavior*. New York: Wiley.

—— (1958). *Organizations*. New York: John Wiley & Sons, Inc.

—— (1969). *The Sciences of the Artificial*. Cambridge, Mass.: MIT Press.

—— (1982). *Models of Bounded Rationality*. Cambridge, Mass.: The MIT Press.

Simon, William H. (2005). 'The crisis of the profession in the post-Enron era.' Unpublished paper presented as Annual Siegel Lecture on legal ethics, Duke University, 3 Mar.

Smith, Adam (1976). *The Wealth of Nations*, ed. Edwin Cannan. Chicago: Chicago University Press.

Sørensen, Eva (2002). *Politikerne og netværksdemokratiet: Fra suveræn politiker til meta-guvernør*. Copenhagen: Jurist-og Økonomforbundets Forlag.

Spreenberg, Peter, Salomon, Gitta, and Joe, Phillip (1995). 'Interaction design at IDEO product development.' *Proceedings of Conference on Human Factors in Computing Systems*. New York: ACM Press: 164–5.

Sunstein, Cass R., Kahneman, Daniel, Schkade, David, and Ritov, Ilana (2002). 'Predictably incoherent judgments.' *Stanford Law Review*, 54: 1153–214.

Sutcliffe, K. M., and Sitkin, S. (1996). 'New pesspectives on process management: Implications for 21st century organizations.' In C. Coopes and S. Jackson (eds.), *Handbook of Organizational Behavior*. Wiley, New York: 207–29.

Thelen, Kathleen (1999). 'Historical institutionalism in comparative politics.' *Annual Review of Political Science*, 2: 369–404.

Torrance, E. P. (1988). 'Creativity as manifest in testing.' In R. J. Sternberg (ed.), *The Nature of Creativity: Contemporary Psychological Perspectives*. New York: Cambridge University Press: 43–75.

Tsoukas, Haridimos, and Chia, Robert (2002). 'On organizational becoming: rethinking organizational change.' *Organization Science*, 13/5: 567–82.

Tushman, M. L., and O'Reilly, C. A. (1996). 'Ambidextrous organizations: managing evolutionary and revolutionary change.' *California Management Review*, 38/4: 8–30.

Ulrich, Karl (1995). 'The role of product architecture in the manufacturing firm.' *Research Policy*, 24/3: 419–40.

Unger, Roberto (forthcoming). 'The self-awakened: pragmatism unbound.' Unpublished manuscript.

US Department of Agriculture, Food Safety and Inspection Service, 9CFR Part 304, et al. (1996). 'Pathogen reduction; hazard analysis and critical control point (HACCP) systems; final rule.' Federal Register, Thursday, 25 July, 38805–50.

US Department of Agriculture, Office of Inspector General (2003). Great Plains region Audit Report, Food Safety and Inspection Service Oversight of Production Process and Recall at Conagra Plant (Establishment 969), report No. 24601-2-KC, Sept.

Vaughan, Diane (1997). 'Targets for firefighting safety: lessons from the Challenger tragedy.' *Wildfire* (Mar.): 29–40.

Verona, Gianmario, and Ravasi, Davide (2003). 'Unbundling dynamic capabilities: an exploratory study of continuous product innovation.' *Industrial and Corporate Change*, 12/3: 577–606.

Walsh, J. P., and Dewar, R. D. (1987). 'Formalization and the organizational life cycle.' *Journal of Management Studies*, 24/3: 216–31.

Ward, A. (1995). 'The second Toyota paradox: how delaying decisions can make better cars faster.' *Sloan Management Review*, 36/3: 43–61.

Weber, Max (1958). *The Protestant Ethic and the Spirit of Capitalism*, trans. Talcott Parsons. New York: Charles Scribner's Sons.

Weick, K. E. (1976). 'Educational organizations as loosely coupled systems.' *Administrative Science Quarterly*, 21: 1–19.

—— (1979). 'Cognitive processes in organization.' In B. Staw (ed.), *Research in Organizational Behavior*, i. Greenwich, Conn.: JAI Press: 41–74.

—— (1995). *Sensemaking in Organizations*. Thousand Oaks, Calif.: Sage Publications.

—— (1998). 'Improvisation as a mindset for organizational analysis.' *Organization Science*, 9/5: 543–55.

—— Sutcliffe, K. M., and Obstfeld, D. (1999). 'Organizing for high reliability: processes of collective mindfulness.' In B. Staw and R. Sutton (eds.), *Research in Organizational Behavior*, xxi. Greenwich, Conn.: JAI Press: 81–123.

Wetenschappelijke Raad voor het Regeringsbeleid (2004). *Bewijzen van goede dienstverlening*. Amsterdam: Amsterdam University Press.

Whitford, Josh (forthcoming). *The New Old Economy: Networks, Institutions, and the Organizational Transformation of American Manufacturing*. New York: Oxford University Press.

—— and Zeitlin, Jonathan (2004). 'Governing decentralized production: institutions, public policy, and the prospects for inter-firm collaboration in U.S. manufacturing.' *Industry and Innovation*, 11/1–2: 11–44.

Williamson, Oliver E. (1975). *Markets and Hierarchies: Analysis and Antitrust Implications*. New York: Free Press.

—— (1999). 'Strategy research: governance and competitive perspectives.' *Strategic Management Journal*, 20/12: 1087–108.

Winter, Sidney G. (1999). 'Organizing for continuous improvement.' In Robert E. Cole and W. Richard Scott (eds.), *The Quality Movement & Organization Theory*. Thousand Oaks, Calif.: Sage Publications, Inc.: 49–64.

Wisniewski, M. Y. L., Yashchin, E., Franch, R. L., Conrady, D. P., Fiorenza, G., and Noyan, I. C. (2003). 'Estimating the efficiency of collaborative problem-solving, with applications to chip design.' *IBM Journal of Research and Development*, 47/1: 77–87.

Womack, James P., Jones, Daniel T., and Roos, Daniel (1990). *The Machine that Changed the World*. New York: Rawson Associates.

Zingales, Luigi (2000). 'In search of new foundations.' *Journal of Finance*, 55: 1623–53.

Zucker, Lynne G. (1987). 'Institutional theories of organization.' *Annual Review of Sociology*, 13: 443–64.

Notes

1. Weber (1958: 181): 'In Baxter's view, the care for external goods should only lie on the shoulders of the "saint like a light cloak, which can be thrown aside at any moment". But fate decreed that the cloak should become an iron cage.'
2. For recent criticism of path dependency models for understating the capacity for large-scale institutional innovation, see Thelen (1999) and Crouch and Farrell (2004). For criticism of garbage-can models see Bendor et al. (2001).
3. For a reinterpretation of the Fisher Body acquisition as a forerunner of rather than alternative to pragmatist organizations, see Helper et al. (2000).
4. Here is how Lawrence and Lorsch summarize Burns and Stalker:

   In mechanistic systems the problems and tasks facing the concern as a whole are broken down into specialisms. Each individual pursues his task as something distinct from the real tasks of the concern as a whole, as if it were the subject of a subcontract ... Organic systems are adapted to unstable conditions, when problems and requirements for action arise which cannot be broken down and distributed among specialist roles within a clearly defined hierarchy of formal rules ... We have found ... that effective organizational units operating in stable parts of the environment are more highly structured, while those in more dynamic parts of the environment are less formal. (Lawrence and Lorsch 1967: 187–9)

5. See also Hedlund's idea of the Nearly Recomposable—not Decomposable—System. A key example is the university, with its flexible, project-based research groups and informal coordination mechanisms (deanship is a burden to be rotated; 'leading' positions confer honor, not the authority to boss others around), in Hedlund (1999).
6. This approach rehabilitates and applies to the explanation of highly organized activities the processual psychologies and ontologies of James and Bergson, with their emphasis on the dominance of intuition (now called tacit knowledge) over formal method, and of becoming (organizing) over being (organization). See Tsoukas and Chia (2002: 567).
7. Studies of the personal computer and industrial design industries from the mid-1990s come to similar conclusions, often characterizing the observed organizational form as a hybrid of the Burns and Stalker types. See the study of IDEO, a leading US industrial design firm, by Brown and Eisenhardt (1997); see also Brown and Eisenhardt (1995: 364); and Tushman and O'Reilly (1996: 8). In characterizing the new system not by its structure but rather by the respect the manager commands, this literature unwittingly anticipated the personalism that would prove a crucial flaw in the 'hybrid' regimes: Heavyweight managers

used their authority to advance their own projects, but also to obstruct inter-project coordination. On the relations between such and the later travails of the Japanese heavyweight project management see Fujimoto (1997).

8. For an antecedent argument breaking down the distinction between incremental and radical innovation, and thus between stable and volatile markets, see Hendersen and Clark (1990). They focus on the reconfiguration of familiar components to achieve new systemic effects, as in the repositioning and modifications of the motor, fan blades, and housing that change a ceiling fan into a portable floor fan.

9. Historians of one of the key precursors to iterated co-design—the 'systems management' used by the US military and civilian contractors to develop ballistic missiles and manned space-flight vehicles—have also been struck by the (new) formalism of the process of concurrent innovation. 'We have found that concurrency [in design] is as unforgiving to inept management principles as a high performance aircraft is to pilot error. In fact, it requires more formality, not less.' Lieutenant Colonel Benjamin Bellis (1962), cited in Johnson (2002: 47).

10. See below, pp. 125–7.

11. For examples of how NUMMI (the GM-Toyota joint venture) handles the tension between standard operating procedures and continuous improvement, see Adler et al. (1999).

12. Dewey (1922: 65–7) is careful to distinguish habit, as the creative disposition to respond, almost unselfconsciously, to new situations on the basis of long experience, from routine, as habit frozen into a compulsion to repeat prior responses despite novelty in the situations that typically trigger them. The difference between habit and routine is manifest in the difference between the artist and the mere technician: 'The artist is a masterful technician. The technique or mechanism is fused with thought and feeling. The "mechanical" performer permits the mechanism to dictate the performance. It is absurd to say that the latter exhibits habit and the former not. We are confronted with two kinds of habit, intelligent and routine. All life has its élan, but only the prevalence of dead habit deflects life into mere élan' (Dewey 1922: 66). What Dewey calls habits, modern cognitive neurobiology calls zombie agents: non-conscious but trainable processes directing purposive action such as tennis forehands or the darting, Saccadian motions by which the eye aquires its next target. Just as intelligence, or intelligent habit, is for Dewey the ability to reflect on and reshape habit, so cognitive neurobiology sees consciousness or awareness as an 'executive summary' of brain processes presented so as to enable choice among different plans of action. Learning achieved through conscious choice can then be 'automated' by training zombie agents to perform tasks that once required awareness. See Koch (2004: 233–7).

13. While early formulations of HRO theory just referenced made it seem that, given high enough stakes, organizations could almost always learn to learn,

normal accident theory (Perrow 1984), with its emphasis on tight, not loose, coupling and technical lock-ins, seemed to exclude learning regardless of the stakes. Later exchanges produced a judicious, if theoretically inconclusive outcome: Normal accident theorists conceded that complex technical systems could learn (Perrow 1994), while HRO theorists agreed that they did invariably do so (La Porte 1994 and La Porte and Rochlin 1994). This essay aims to advance understanding of how organizations learn without claiming that effective learning mechanisms cannot be thwarted, most especially by contests for power. See below, pp. 132–5.

14. Simon himself underscores the similar approach to formalization in Simon (1969).

15. See Galison (1997) for the view that scientists do indeed create pidgins to communicate across conceptual divides and that novel theories can emerge from these pidgins. For the contrary view of distinct languages and conceptual schemes as mutually unintelligible or incommensurate see Kuhn (1962). For Kuhn's extremely nuanced late views, which emphasize the role of metaphor in bridging 'paradigms,' see Kuhn (1979).

16. Debates over classification in evolutionary biology are particularly revealing. The traditional approach yields undecidable conflicts of classification: Cladists create categories on the basis of shared, historically derived features that reflect the sequence of evolutionary branching points. Pheneticists look to overall similarities in function, form, and biological role. Evolutionary biology aims for forms of categorization that anticipate the transformation of some sub-groups of one species into another, even if it is impossible to specify the transformations in advance (Lakoff 1987: 118–21).

17. More precisely we can say that our disposition for cognitive self-entrapment is just as natural as our capacity to extricate ourselves from the traps we create. Thus recent writing in behavioral law and economics focuses on the many ways human decision-making rules or heuristics are systematically biased by the context of decision making. Recent events, for instance, have an undue influence on our expectations of future occurrences simply because they are more accessible to our memory. We are inclined to risk more to recover losses than to earn equivalent gains because we are, unreasonably from the point of view of decision theory, attached to our endowments. Deliberating groups may sacrifice the potentially complementary knowledge of individual members to 'groupthink,' or ignore conclusions reached by groups deliberating about re-lated problems and so on. (For overviews see Jolls et al. 1998; Sunstein et al. 2002; and Mendelberg 2002.) But of course the extent of this context depend-ence is itself context dependent: Some contexts trigger biasing mechanisms, while others allow us to 'de-bias' judgements. In 'near real' experiments, for instance, teams of medical diagnosticians in which the team leader periodic-ally reminded the group of information dispersed among the members out-performed teams whose leaders periodically underscored common knowledge

(Larson et al. 1998). The shift to pragmatist organizations can be thought of as a deliberate effort to create an institutional context that allows for rapid detection and correction of context-induced cognitive biases.

18. For an incisive discussion of the challenges that the new, collaborative pursuit of innovative possibilities within and across firm boundaries poses for the traditional theory of the firm and finance economics, see Zingales (2000). If the principal—shareholders or CEO—can write contracts completely specifying the tasks of all agents, Zingales argues, then the firm is a nexus of contracts guaranteeing all the firm's input providers earnings equal to their opportunity costs. Assuming that initial investments are sunk, and can be disregarded, the value of the firm to its equity owners is then just the discounted value of future payouts minus contractual obligations. When innovation matters, so tasks cannot be specified precisely in advance, and exploration of profitable possibilities must be coordinated by implicit contracts, traditional theory can no longer be used to adjudicate conflicting claims on the firm's earnings. The firm's value to equity holders, moreover, depends less on its assets in place— current activities—than on the value of the 'real options'; or investment opportunities created by collaborative exploration. But, Zingales argues, traditional finance theory cannot evaluate these real options. The governance mechanisms described above can be thought of as the means institutions actually use to 'write' the implicit contracts postulated in Zingales's account to value the 'real options' they help generate.

19. Compare Simon's claim, founded not on Dewey but on logical positivism, that 'value elements' pertain to questions of policy, while 'factual elements' pertain to matters of administration (Simon 1947: 45–60).

20. From this point of view almost all broad organizational decisions are, like the idea of law or beauty, what Gallie calls 'essentially contested concepts' (ECC). In his 1956 formulation, essentially contested concepts are jointly defined by seven elements:

1. concept must be appraisive; accredits valued achievement;
2. achievement must be of an internally complex character, so its worth is attributed to the whole;
3. the accredited achievement is initially variously describable;
4. the accredited achievement must be of a kind that admits considerable modification in light of changing circumstances;
5. each party recognizes the fact that its use of the contested concept is contested by those of other parties;
6. ECC involve derivation from an original exemplar that conflicted parties agree on;
7. the claim of continuous contestation enables the original exemplar's achievement to be sustained or developed.

21. See Herrigel (2004). Notice that in casting about for an organizational solution to the innovator's dilemma of managing 'sustaining' or routine lines of business without being blindsided by 'disruptive' threats, Christensen seizes on the example of a company—Nypro—whose structure is similar to ITW's, but whose governance procedures are in crucial ways less formal and effective. What ITW is to metal components and small systems, Nypro is to plastics: a federation of many small units providing specialized products in various industries. Nypro, like ITW, provides central research and development services to its largely independent business units. The key difference is that Nypro has no equivalent to ITW's 80/20 disentrenching rule. Instead the firm uses periodic meetings among unit managers to spread ideas and develop a cooperative culture despite their rivalry for the headquarters' approval. In addition the CEO keeps close touch on innovations that diffuse among several units, and requires that the most successful of these be incorporated into the firm's standard operating procedures. There are, however, no systematic incentives, as there are at ITW, to scrutinize present practices for clues about new markets. This, for Christensen, remains the job of the CEO (Christensen and Raynor 2003: 271–5).
22. For the limits to the current implementation of the HACCP, see Petersen and Drew (2003). But for an illustration of the ways this system produces the information needed to pinpoint deficiencies in its own implementation, see US Department of Agriculture, Office of Inspector General (2003).

3

The Self in Transition

From Bureaucratic to Interactive Social Character

Michael Maccoby

The values and attitudes of the most highly educated and productive Americans are changing to fit a new economic and social environment. This chapter attempts to describe this change and its significance for the development of collaborative community.

The term social character was conceived by Erich Fromm (1941, 1955) to describe how the psyche adapts to the dominant mode of economic production and sociopolitical structure of a society. Social character refers to conscious or unconscious emotionally laden values and attitudes which determine behavior and are common to a group in a society. These elements of the social character may have both positive and negative aspects.

Human personality includes genetically determined qualities such as temperament and intelligence which are more inborn combined with character which is essentially learned. Social character is the part of character shared by people in a culture or social class. Social character is formed as a person internalizes the values and attitudes of a culture acting through family, school, workplace, and other institutions. These values which may or may not be conscious filter our experience and drive our behavior, so that we are not overwhelmed with the need to make decisions about every action we take, every reaction to threat or opportunity. Thus character is that part of personality which is a biological necessity for humans to adapt to their environment, the human equivalent of animal instinct.

Social character makes an individual want to do what is necessary to prosper in a particular environment. It also facilitates communication and social cohesion, since it sensitizes people about what is normal behavior in a society, what to expect from others who share the social character. For example, the peasant's cautious, independent, parsimonious, and hard-working attitudes and values are adaptive to an environment where no one can predict weather or market prices, but must prepare for the worst. A close-knit family with respect for paternal authority reinforced by a patriarchal religion strengthens an economic unit, provides emotional support, and security for old age.

The social character can be more active and productive or more passive and unproductive depending on historical circumstances. Social character changes more slowly than does the economy. Mexican villagers who were descendants of landless hacienda peons shared a fearful, submissive, and fatalistic social character, and a corresponding sense of a powerless self. This social character allowed them to survive in an oppressive plantation culture, but it kept them from prospering after the revolution of 1910–20 when they were given land.

Those people with the dominant social character who tend to be the most successful control a culture and shape its institutions and ideals. They therefore form the social character of the next generation. When Fromm and I (Fromm and Maccoby 1970; Maccoby 1995) studied Mexican *campesinos*, we found that those who were more entrepreneurial came from somewhat different economic backgrounds from either the traditional peasant farmers or hacienda peons. Their families might have had a store or been involved in delivering mail to other villagers. Both their social character and sense of self were social mutations. These entrepreneurs took advantage of new capitalist opportunities, and began accumulating money and power. The new economic conditions resulted in a form of 'social selection.' The entrepreneurs took over political, educational, and social institutions. They began to change the culture, and the more traditional peasants either adapted or fell behind.

When times change, those people whose social character fits the new conditions adapt easily, while those whose social character no longer fits feel alienated. They may become depressed or angry, vulnerable to political leaders who idealize the past, and demonize those who benefit from the changing world.

The decline of the bureaucratic character

Although national culture and language both make a difference to the sense of self, to the sense of identity, the social character of peasants in different countries is more alike than it is to that of their national urban counterparts. Likewise, with some cultural variations (Maccoby 2004), managers in corporations throughout the world share a social character, and their attitudes and values are changing national cultures as they change work and the education necessary to succeed at work.

The changing economy has had a major role in transforming the American social character during the past 150 years. In 1840, 70 per cent of Americans were farmers, and the dominant social character was in some ways similar to that of independent peasants throughout the world. Many of the others were craftsmen and women with similar social character traits.

The American social character in the nineteenth century came to exemplify the 'modern' ideal of strong individual integrity and autonomy. Tocqueville in the 1830s saw this as a major difference between Americans and Europeans: the latter still enmeshed in traditional systems of honor and deference, but Americans showing much more of the strong, adventurous, entrepreneurial spirit of people creating a democratic society. The democratic institutions were reinforced by the Protestant religion which emphasized both individualism and cooperation with those who shared religious beliefs. During the latter part of the nineteenth century, entrepreneurs and inventors built new industries. The social character of American business leaders after the Civil War became more exploitative, and more risk taking.

As companies and government agencies grew in the twentieth century, work became organized in bureaucracies, which required new values and attitudes. Schools and families began to shape the most competent young people to fit into bureaucratic hierarchies and get promoted by passing tests and pleasing bosses. The bureaucratic ideal modified that of the 'rugged individualist': it combined economic security with autonomy gained by moving up the hierarchy, running one's own department, and possibly reaching top management. Men took pride in identifying self with a great company or organization.

Typically, in the bureaucratic society, the social character of men was different from that of women. Men learned to be achieving careerists. This process took place in the family as a boy identified with the father. It continued at school, work, and outside work. Young men became part of informal bureaucratic organizations by bonding with other men at sports and later joining the right service clubs, e.g. Lions, Kiwanis, Rotary. Female values emphasized caring and mothering. However, wives were expected to support their husbands' careers not only in the home but also by joining clubs, churches, and voluntary organizations, preferably with the wives of men who could help their husbands' careers.

At the high point of the bureaucratic social character in the 1950s, 70 per cent of American families were headed by a single male wage earner with a wife at home. At this point in history, large American companies dominated the post-World War market. The prototypical bureaucrat, the organization man, appeared assured of lifetime employment in business or government.

The transformation of the bureaucratic character began when young people in the 1960s and 1970s identified themselves as rebels. They challenged extreme regimentation and stifling bureaucratic roles made more sinister by the vision of controlling information technology. Young men, afraid they would die in a meaningless war, questioned the legitimacy of authority and so-called expertise that had supported the war, maintained racial segregation, and kept women out of professions and leadership positions. Supported by a liberation movement, women rebelled against the limits of their roles and their dependency on men. More and more women entered the workforce and pursued careers. Birth control pills and availability of abortion freed them from unwanted childbearing. Furthermore, economic abundance and consumer needs stimulated by television were spurs to earn and spend more. The hoarding anal attitudes of the bureaucratic character were being replaced by consumerism and the search for unending pleasure.

The family changed and with it the forces shaping social character. By the mid-1990s, fewer than 20 per cent of families were headed by males as sole wage earners. Over 60 per cent of mothers with children under 6 were working outside the home. Children no longer identified father with achievement at work and mother with the values of caring. Authority in the dual career family was shared. Furthermore, children could no longer count on their parents to be at home for them when they returned from school. They had to learn to become more emotionally independent and to find emotional support from strangers or peers.

Changing work

While all of these factors weakened the institutions that formed the bureaucratic character, changing technology and modes of work in the 1980s and 1990s were also playing a major role in shaping a new social character. While jobs in manufacturing companies were shrinking, the service sector grew. (In 2001, it was almost 80 per cent of the workforce.) Service required enhanced interpersonal skills. The development of information and communication technology offered new business opportunities and favored entrepreneurial skills. These technologies further undermined traditional authority and bureaucratic seniority, since young people often knew more about them than did their elders. Continual development of technology resulted in the devaluation of the intellectual capital of older experts. Rather than accumulating knowledge and then applying it, success in the information age required that knowledge workers continually learn and unlearn.

In the middle to late 1980s, large companies 'downsized' to cut costs and to take advantage of automation. Loyalty and years of service no longer guaranteed lifetime employment. It became more cost-effective for companies to contract out services, sometimes to small entrepreneurial firms, or to reduce labor costs by exporting work to Asia and Latin America. No longer feeling protected by paternalistic companies, employees no longer felt loyal to them. Like professional athletes, managers and professionals had to reinvent themselves as 'free agents' who would work with whatever company offered the best deal. They began to identify themselves in terms of their skills and projects rather than as part of a company.

To become more productive and satisfy customers, the bureaucracies also began to redesign work. New modes of work required not only different skills but also new values. Organizational ideologies began to emphasize innovation, interactive networks, customer responsiveness, teamwork, and flexibility. The economic organizations creating the

Table 3.1. Organizational social character

	Bureaucratic	Interactive
Ideology and ideals	• Stability • Hierarchy/autonomy • Organizational loyalty • Moralism	• Innovation • Networks/independence • Free agency • Tolerance
Social character	• Inner directed • Identification with paternal authority and role; obsessive • Methodical, cautious, savers	• Interactive • identification with peers, siblings; marketing • Consumers, adventurers
Socioeconomic base	• Market-controlling bureaucracies • Slow changing technology • National markets • Lifelong employment • Traditional family	• Entrepreneurial companies • New technologies • Global markets • Employment uncertainty • Diverse family structures

greatest wealth had to become interactive instead of bureaucratic. They had to manage intelligence rather than energy. Instead of the paternalistic bureaucratic manager, the interactive managers were expected to be coaches of empowered individuals and teams, of young employees who knew more about technology than their elders. This change put a premium on team leaders able to get individuals to work collaboratively.

To summarize this shift, consider Table 3.1. It summarizes changes in socioeconomic base, the social character, and the ideals, ideology, or social self rooted in the bureaucratic and interactive social characters.

Table 3.2. Positive life-cycle development: bureaucratic and interactive social characters

Stage	Bureaucratic	Interactive
Basic trust	Focused on parents	Focused on parenting network
Autonomy	Self-directed conformity	Negotiating with parents
Initiative	Knowing your place, learning the role	Interpersonal competence, teamwork
Industry	Passing the tests	Learning to learn
Identity	Focusing on a career and belief system	Seeking a vocation at work or outside
Intimacy	Mutual care: forming a unit	Mutual development: building a network together
Generativity	Parenting, protecting	Coaching, facilitating
Ego integrity	Playing the bureaucratic role with dignity and effectiveness; resisting illegitimate commands and corrupting pressures	Pragmatic development of ideals. Living with contradictions and uncertainty without losing hope

Table 3.3. Typical developmental problems and causes

Stage	Bureaucratic	Interactive
Basic trust vs. basic mistrust	Dependency on mother—hothouse environment	Feeling abandoned—detachment
Autonomy vs. shame and doubt	Obsessive conformity	Lack of boundaries—impulsiveness
Initiative vs. guilt and anxiety	Oedipal struggle and over-identification with father	Anxiety about group acceptance causing over-conformity
Industry vs. inferiority	Loss of self-confidence—poor grades, performance	Overestimation of self as defense against loss of self-esteem
Identity vs. role confusion	Compulsive conformity to parental role model or peer group	Self-marketing and consumerism
Intimacy vs. isolation	Tribalistic relatedness	Superficial coupling
Generativity vs. stagnation	Becomes a narrow role	Nothing to teach
Ego integrity vs. despair	Tolstoy's *Death of Ivan Illich*—the lost self	Burn-out—anomie

Social character and the life cycle—bureaucratic vs. interactive

Fromm's concept of social character lacks a developmental framework. The social character does not appear full blown in childhood but is formed throughout the life cycle.

I have used Erik H. Erikson's (1950) eight stages of life to explore the development of social character. Erikson based his stages on the idea that people had to respond to the challenges of both their maturing bodies and the culture's expectations of them at different ages. How they met these challenges or accomplished these life tasks formed their competencies, values, emotional attitudes, and sense of identity or self.

What Erikson first wrote in 1950 and revised in 1963 now seems dated and somewhat mechanistic. The different cultural roles Erikson describes for men and women fit the bureaucratic, not the interactive era. Furthermore, the idea of psychosocial developmental stages can be misleading. First of all, Erikson, like most social scientists, uses the concept of development without defining it. What do we mean by development? Is it just maturation? Or growth? Maturation is a biological process that occurs in all living organisms. Growth can be either positive or chaotic as in cancerous growth. We would prefer to define human development as growth of competence, a process in which individuals and/or groups increase their ability to both determine and satisfy their needs. In terms of this definition, human development for an individual implies increased awareness and ability to frustrate compulsive needs that weaken a person, while reinforcing those needs that are consciously embraced and are strengthening. For the bureaucratic and interactive social characters, both the positive developmental outcomes and the typical psychological problems are different.

Optimal individual development for any social character requires a supportive community and ideals. Those ideals which have supported human development in Western society come from a tradition of democracy and a humanistic interpretation of religious teachings. They emphasize values of freedom; cooperation, even caring for strangers; creativity in work, and self-expression; and mature love between life partners. While no individual can fully realize these values, the effort to live them and with others to infuse them in society provides a deep sense of meaning and self-esteem. The more individuals live according to these ideals, the more they become individuated, strengthened in their sense of self.

While Erikson's eight stages can be a useful construct to think about psychosocial life tasks, these stages should not be considered mechanistically as though people move through life on a track, stopping at fixed stations to wrestle with these challenges. Development can be described more systemically in terms of complexity theory, as determining operating principles that direct a complex self-organizing system to adapt continually to both its environment and its biological maturation.[1]

Although success in mastering a life-cycle task increases the chances of success at the next level, failure at a particular stage does not mean that an individual has forever lost the chance to develop. Some people master psychosocial tasks or challenges despite early failure, with help from others. Correspondingly, the stresses of life may undermine development. The individual may be driven by unconscious needs and forced to wrestle with old issues, particularly those never fully resolved.

With these cautions in mind, Erikson's framework can be used to compare the bureaucratic and interactive social characters throughout the life cycle in terms of both positive developmental outcomes and typical psychological problems.

It should be stated that this is a speculative framework which integrates some established findings from developmental psychology[2] with the author's own observations and hypotheses.

Basic trust vs. basic mistrust

In the bureaucratic family, the infant is focused almost exclusively on the mother. The attitude of basic trust and love of life grows from connection with a loving mother and expectation that one's basic needs will be met by her. Ideally, the bond between mother and child includes a deep sense of knowing each other, sensing and responding to each other's needs.

The typical developmental problems at this stage have to do with over-dependency, inability to break the umbilical cord, sometimes because the mother who is so intensely attached to her children wants to maintain the relationship in which she feels needed by the child. Of course, problems with basic trust also stem from a cold, frightened, inadequate mother or a professionally frustrated mother who resents the mothering role which keeps her trapped at home.

In the interactive family, the mother usually starts out as the main infant caretaker, continuing the physical symbiosis of childbearing. But early on, others share this role, since she needs to return to her paid work. Ideally, the father also participates. As soon as is feasible, babies are put in day-care centers or in the care of hired nannies.

On the positive side, as infants receive care from others, the sense of trust is expanded beyond the mother. On the negative side, children may lack the security of deep maternal attachment. Feeling insecure and abandoned, they become more distrustful, anxious, and self-protectively avoidant. Later in life, this makes it harder for them to develop intimate relationships and accept the deep feelings of need for others that they've repressed.

Autonomy vs. shame and doubt

About the age of 2, children show a rebelliousness to adult authority that is the start of achieving a sense of autonomy. They want to be able to do things for themselves, to express themselves without losing loving support from parents. By this self-expression, children try to avoid the shame of being seen as babies who can't control their bodily functions, dress themselves, or handle a fork and spoon. They want to be able to do the right things to maintain a sense of dignity or self-esteem. Ideally, parents treat this rebelliousness with a combination of playful discipline and setting limits.

In the bureaucratic family, some parents respond to the child's self-expression with overly strict demands, such as too early toilet training. The danger is that the child will resolve the conflict between impulse and conformity by obsessive compliance, the uptight, super-clean, and humorless anal character described by Freud (1908). Alternatively, the child is plagued by doubt and needs constant reassurance that he or she is doing the right thing. Extreme shaming of a child at this age can cause deep hurt and anger which may be repressed. However, without some homeopathic shaming, the child does not learn to conform to social expectations and is vulnerable to more serious humiliations later in life.

The child in the interactive family is often faced with various parenting figures, less consistency in treatment, and less certainty on the part of authorities. Sensing the parents' insecurity about standards and their guilt about not being there when needed, the 2-year-old child learns to negotiate with parents for more freedom, things, or a later bedtime.

The danger is that lack of parental boundaries results in the child's failure to internalize adaptive elements of the social character. Uncontrolled impulsiveness and denial of shame makes it more difficult for the child to learn and to interact effectively with others. Ideally, the child starts to learn that increased freedom requires greater personal responsibility and that the grown-ups don't have all the answers.

Initiative vs. guilt and anxiety

Pre-school boys and girls separate for group play. Boys are more aggressive and hierarchical, while girls emphasize harmony and resolving conflicts (Maccoby 1999). This is an age where children must learn to control their competitiveness and envy. In the bureaucratic family, boys resolve their conflicts with authority by identifying with the father and his outlook on life, while girls identify with the mother and internalize her values. However, over-identification and obsessive conformity dampen spontaneity and flexibility and increase guilt.

Piaget (1932/1965) describes the moral development of children at this age. While the child accepts the commandments of authority as law, other children become rivals for the authority's love and approval. This authoritarian-egocentric attitude becomes prototypical for the bureaucrat, submissive to those up the hierarchy and competitive with peers. This attitude is strengthened by unconscious father transferences of childlike love for authority figures.[3]

Children of interactive families are less dependent emotionally on adults and already by this age more interactively competent, provided they have had secure attachments (Cortina and Marrone 2003). The psychological pitfall for these children is not fear of parents which becomes internalized as guilt, but rather anxiety about being accepted by the group. This anxiety is especially strong if secure attachment has not been achieved in infancy. Anxiety can cause over-conformity to peers, sacrifice of self in order to fit in. Or the child may reject the peer group or form alliances with other 'outcasts' who turn rejection into resentment and fantasies of revenge. These attitudes may return in adolescence with a vengeance as was the case in Littletown, Colorado, in the spring of 1999 when they resulted in a murderous and suicidal rampage.

While bureaucratic conformity results in identification with an older role model, the interactive child becomes increasingly alert to the changing fads and fashions of the peer group. In his 1950 book *The Lonely Crowd*, Riesman contrasted the inner-directed individual as having an internal gyroscope while the other-directed person developed interpersonal radar. When Riesman wrote his book, other-direction was a new phenomenon. By the 1990s, it had become the dominant form of social control.[4]

What Riesman did not predict was the growing diversity in American society. This is the age when children begin to identify themselves in terms of race or national origin. These identifications can separate groups of children from each other, increasing the feelings of resentment of those who do not fit into cliques. Nor could Riesman have predicted how the internet would provide a route of escape from failure at forming relationships into a world of unreal relatedness. The interactive child may find an identity with others by consuming 'cool' products advertised on TV and showcased by the fictional characters who have been adopted as the models of the moment by a peer group.

By the end of this stage, children of both sexes should be able to become more competent at maintaining cooperative relationships. Through play, they begin to work out their conflicts with oppressive authority. They should be able to win at games without being obnoxious and lose without feeling devastated.

Industry vs. inferiority

When children reach the age of 6 or 7, they are ready to become workers. The first work depends on the culture. In peasant villages, boys followed their fathers to the fields, while girls helped in the kitchen and cared for animals and younger siblings. In bureaucratic society, children must perform in school to get good grades and move up the scholastic ladder. Rather than learning to use agricultural tools, the challenge of this stage is to use the tools of the schoolroom. Development requires internal discipline, strengthening needs for learning and self-expression, deferring immediate gratification. This development can be stunted either by punishing authoritarian discipline on the one hand or, on the other, over-indulgence.

In bureaucratic society, boys also were expected to play team sports and develop what Piaget (1932/1965) called a sense of reciprocity, the ability to understand, follow, and design fair rules. This capability tempers egocentric competition and authoritarian hierarchy. It also introduces children to the principles that support a democratic society.

The ideals of American bureaucracy develop at this stage. They combine accepting the goals and objectives of authority with having autonomy in carrying them out. This includes the capability of forming teams to face a challenge, but returning to bureaucratic roles when the crisis is over. A prime example of these ideals in action was the Bell System, the telephone monopoly until 1984. The system was almost a caricature of extreme bureaucracy. At the front line, technicians had to follow strict rules and procedures. However, when there was a fire, flood, or hurricane which disrupted service, teamwork produced a quick, effective response (Heckscher et al. 2003).

By this stage, children of the interactive era are already prepared for teamwork with advanced interpersonal skills. Use of computers and the internet provides them with a greater scope to experiment. The line between work and play is blurred as they surf the net or engage in team projects.

Even in the interactive organization, there is still tension in the American social character about being a team player vs. individual achievement. In professional sports, this tension is resolved by maintaining both team and individual statistics, as well as evaluating individuals on their contribution to the team. Furthermore, competent coaching that both helps these young people sharpen their skills and establishes trust makes a significant difference. This kind of sophisticated management is also required in companies, so that interactive free agents will work cooperatively and feel rewarded for their work.

Industrious future bureaucrats risked becoming narrowly focused and unimaginative. Industrious interactive children risk becoming glib and shallow, with the illusion of knowing more than they do because knowledge seems the click of a mouse away. In the bureaucratic classroom, the unsuccessful child would lose self-confidence and self-esteem, triggering a vicious cycle of poor performance. While this might also happen to the interactive child, denial of failure is supported by the anti-bureaucratic popular culture and pop psychology which inflates the self and puts down authorities. Defending against the loss of self-esteem, these children overestimate their capabilities and become impervious to coaching. Teachers who care and help these children understand that the discipline required for learning and self-expression makes a huge difference in their future ability to learn and play a productive role in the interactive society.

Identity vs. role diffusion

Erikson (1950) writes that with the establishment of a good initial relationship to the world of skills and tools, and with the advent of puberty, childhood proper comes to an end. Youth begins. But in puberty and adolescence all samenesses and continuities relied on earlier are more or less questioned again, because of rapid body growth which equals that of early childhood and because of genital maturity. The growing and developing youths, faced with this physiological revolution within them, and with tangible adult tasks ahead of them, are now primarily concerned with what they appear to be in the eyes of others as compared with what they feel they are, and with the question of how to connect the roles and skills cultivated earlier with the occupational prototypes of the day.

Youth is a time of exuberance and experimentation, sometimes of grandiose ambitions, what might be termed a 'narcissistic moment' (Maccoby 2003). But inner discipline, acquired earlier, can guide a young person away from excessive and extreme behavior and toward an approach to life that balances work and play, that measures present enjoyment with future consequences.

Youth is also a time of connecting self with the larger society and its opportunities. In the bureaucratic age, the most competent young men of the middle class prepared themselves for careers in large business, government, or the professions of law and medicine. They paid attention to how one must behave and dress for success. A small percentage of women, usually identified with their fathers (Henning and Jardim 1978), did the same, but most thought about making themselves attractive to those men most likely to succeed.

Youth is a time of idealism, committing oneself to an ideology or religion. The enlarged cohort of baby boomer youth in the 1960s began the undermining of the bureaucratic character by contrasting dehumanizing rules, roles, and technology with ideals of freedom and democracy. Its winners avoided falling into the temptations of rigid ideology or drug-induced excess. They were able somehow to combine pleasure seeking and pragmatism. The losers were the ideological extremists, revolutionaries who became the disillusioned cynics, tribalistic cultists, and addicts.

The society that emerged in the 1980s and 1990s favored entrepreneurial free agents of both sexes. The challenge for youth was to turn vocations into careers, play into business, and to find meaning in work. For some, this involved caring for others in the helping professions like medicine and nursing. For others, it meant becoming experts who could work in many different organizations. For some future entrepreneurs, being a winner at the game of business and getting rich becomes the goal and meaning of their intense activity. Increasingly, for the interactive character, meaning is found in continual self-development, of both work and interpersonal competencies (Maccoby, 1988, 1995).

Large companies and government are now viewed by some young professionals as postgraduate training for more freewheeling careers. The identity of the interactive individual no longer emphasizes being part of a great company, but rather being a competent and respected professional, able to commit oneself to meaningful projects rather than powerful organizations.[5]

In the vibrant, dynamic labor market, those young people without strong values and sense of self have adapted by trying to be whatever the market has seemed to value. Those who are unable to adapt may seek an identity in cults, racial, ethnic, or religious extremism that demonizes the global economy and the winners. Many Americans appear to have lost their moral bearings, substituting a tepid tolerance for moral convictions (Wolfe 1998). Others have solved their doubts by embracing fundamentalist faiths.

Intimacy vs. isolation

Achieving an intimate relationship requires trust in oneself as much as in another person. Without a strong sense of self as an active agent, intimacy threatens loss of self-determination, being taken over by another person. An essential psychological task of maturity is to establish a loving relationship to overcome loneliness and create a family.

In the bureaucratic era, this meant forming a unit for mutual care and success, with clearly differentiated male and female roles. This intimate family might become isolated from the community, a tribalistic haven, held together by narcissistic self-inflation. 'We are better than everyone else.' In contrast, the developmental interactive family builds a network that goes beyond blood relations to connect with others who share values and aspirations.

The pathology of intimacy in the interactive era results from fears of the strong needs for mothering repressed in childhood. The detached, avoidant adult is both driven by these needs and repelled by their threat to flood the self with infantile yearnings. Because of this, there is superficial coupling and frequent break-ups.

Furthermore, two careers put pressure on a relationship and require mutual understanding and compromise. If the partners lack emotional security and trust, conflicts are more likely to break up the relationship, especially when women no longer need husbands to support them economically.

In the interactive era, each family must define its role and the role of its members. Ideally, the family supports positive development. I have defined human development as an individual's increased capability to determine and satisfy needs (Maccoby 1988, 1995). This means recognizing the difference between compulsive and developmental needs. Compulsive needs make a person less free, more driven. They include needs not only for substances and sex, but also for security, constant reassurance, and excessive control. Developmental needs expand freedom and choice. They include understanding, knowledge, creative self-expression, competence, and love. As individuals achieve maturity, they should become more conscious of their needs and values and more responsible for shaping them, therefore more committed not only to others, but to a concept of oneself, who I am, what I stand for, who I want to become.

Freud once described what a normal healthy person should be able to do as 'lieben und arbeiten,' to love and to work. Beyond normality, perhaps happiness requires love in one's work and some working at love. Fromm (1947) taught that there is a general lack of understanding about the kind of love which strengthens the self and deepens trust. This is different from falling in love or narcissistic love that makes the other an extension of the self. Many relationships collapse because they are built on mutual illusion. After a number of kisses the illusion dissolves; the prince and princess become frogs in each other's eyes.

In contrast, love as *agapé* means deeply knowing the other person and caring about what is best for that person. Love is itself kindled by the kind of love which not only includes affirmation, but also necessary criticism, refusal to collude when the other person strays from the path both believe is best.

Generativity vs. stagnation

With age and the achievement of a productive role at work and sustainable intimate relationships comes the challenge of bringing along the next generation, as a teacher, parent, or institution builder who articulates and defends values. This means taking responsibility for building one's society rather than merely enjoying one's rights and complying with the laws.

This role, at least at work, was clearer in the bureaucratic era, especially for men who could move up the hierarchy and expand their roles to mentor promising young men who in turn were attracted to them as father figures. The productive bureaucrat was an expert at something he could teach. Mentor and mentee enjoyed the emotional relationship and helped each other succeed. When women first entered bureaucracies, the ones able to create father–daughter relationships were best able to find mentors.

The interactive social character distrusts parental-type relationships, seeing them as stifling independence and threatening self-determination. Rather than transferring parental feelings to bosses at work, they feel closer to colleagues.[6] The interactive individual seeks those generative adults who can help and coach them without demanding submission or laying on them a 'heavy emotional trip' that demands they become like the coach. Furthermore, interactive people feel more comfortable separating relationships at work from those outside of work. They believe that mixing the two spheres detracts from good relationships in both.

The new social character has a hard time becoming generative. The traditional bureaucracy allowed, even encouraged, middle managers to be mentors at work and in volunteer organizations. There was less pressure, more time for bonding. The market pressure of the interactive organization leaves little time and even less energy for these forms of sociability.

The most generative individuals express and defend moral as well as productive values. Some create new institutions or companies. These generative individuals have faith in others and their capabilities. They experience deep satisfaction in helping others to realize their talents and vocations.

The interactive character responds to leadership that engages and involves a person in shaping an enterprise, but he or she is uneasy in the role of protective authority. Beyond success, these people place tolerance as their highest value. Their moral code: 'judge not that you be not judged.' They do not see themselves as defending organizational values they did not participate in framing. They say, 'those are not my values and I am not a policeman' (Maccoby 1995).

The most generative of the interactive may accept the role of coach or facilitator but this is generally limited to a particular project. The interactive philosophy is that each person is responsible for self-development.

Some interactive entrepreneurs treat their life and work like a game (Maccoby 1977). They enjoy the strategy, tactics, and the excitement of the contest. Winning becomes the overriding meaning of life, a kind of proof of God's favor. These people treat others as players to be moved around and replaced if need be.

Those of both social characters who fail the test of generativity stagnate. The bureaucrat became his narrow role, like a character in one of Kafka's novels. The interactive character never deepens knowledge and has nothing to teach. The well-being of the next generation and that of society as a whole will depend on whether those of the interactive generation understand and accept the challenge of generativity. So far, the signs are not good.

Ego integrity vs. despair

According to Erikson, the last stage of life has to do with accepting one's life as it has been lived and facing death without fear or regret. He wrote this when he was in his forties, and it now seems rather incomplete. People are living longer nowadays, and even after they retire from an active career, staying healthy calls for exercising mind and body. Generativity can last longer. W. Edwards Deming kept teaching when he was 90, and this world-renowned expert on quality management was still lecturing and learning.

Integrity means one has not betrayed one's ideal self, or if so, has repented and found the path again. Despair means losing one's way and losing the hope of finding it. Those who have betrayed themselves live with self-disgust and rationalizations that do not overcome their depression. But a sense of integrity is gained by a mature realism, a sense of what it has been possible to do, given one's opportunities and abilities and taking luck into account. It includes giving back to society more than one has received. Yet, the older person, or senior citizen, stays productive and vigorous so long as he or she remains engaged and generative, concerned and hopeful about the future as opposed to resigning from life and living in the past.

The integrity of the bureaucrat meant playing his role with dignity and effectiveness, resisting illegitimate commands and corrupting pressures. After retirement, it meant continuation of learning through reading, traveling, and voluntary activities. For women, it meant providing care and emotional support while maintaining an intellectual capability through participation in voluntary organizations and cultural activities.

The despairing bureaucrat was like Tolstoy's Ivan Illich who only realizes on his deathbed that he has never really been himself, only what others expected him to be. Perhaps, the despairing interactive character will be more like Ibsen's Peer Gynt, who confuses self-indulgence with self-expression, self-marketing with intimacy, and ends up alone and burnt out.

However, few with the new social character have reached old age. Maintaining integrity in the market-dominated world seems to call for a pragmatic attitude of continually testing one's views and values. For those who have been engaged in the complex market world, it means living with contradictions and uncertainty without losing hope. This requires a faith that gives meaning to individuation and creative engagement with one's community, which in the interactive age may include people throughout the world who share developmental values.

Society and the life cycle

Although the economic base of society, the dominant mode of production, is the major determinant of social character, social, political, and religious institutions also make a difference. The work ethic in America has remained robust, but it has changed from the bureaucratic careerism which supported stable institutions to an entrepreneurial, or self-marketing ethic, an ethic not of individuation but of individualism disconnected from the task of sustaining and strengthening democratic society. An essential key for America to maintain its vitality is generativity. The question we need to answer is how to best form the parents, teachers, and leaders who will articulate and implement values of both individual and social development.

The changing culture affects the developmental process in new ways. Increased freedom beginning in childhood requires increased understanding of alternatives, life choices, and their implications. The absence of strong parental identifications intensifies the need to discover personal meaning through self-development and, ideally, participation in the development of a fragmented society. Complexity requires intensified learning not only of facts, but, even more essentially, how to learn and how to create productive and sustainable relationships.

References

Beck, John C., and Wade, Mitchell (2004). *Got Game: How the Gamer Generation is Reshaping Business*. Boston: Harvard Business School Press.

Bellah, Robert Neelly, Madsen, Richard, Sullivan, William M., and Tipton, Steven M. (1985). *Habits of the Heart: Individualism and Commitment in American Life*. New York: Perennial Library.

Cortina, Mauricio, and Maccoby, Michael (eds.) (1996). *A Prophetic Analyst*. Northvale, NJ: Jason Aronson.

—— and Marrone, Mario (2003). *Attachment Theory and the Psychoanalytic Process*. London: Whurr Publishers Ltd.

Cushman, Philip (1995). *Constructing the Self, Constructing America: A Cultural History of Psychotherapy*. Boston: Addison-Wesley Pub.

Durkheim, E. (1951). *Suicide*. New York: The Free Press.

Erikson, E. H. (1950). *Childhood and Society*. New York: Norton.

Freud, Sigmund (1908). *Character & Anal Eroticism*. Standard Edition, vol. ix. London: The Hogarth Press.

Fromm, Erich (1941). *Escape from Freedom*. New York: Rinehart.

—— (1947). *Man for Himself: An Inquiry into the Psychology of Ethics*. New York: Rinehart.

—— (1955). *The Sane Society*. New York: Rinehart.

—— and Maccoby, Michael (1970). *Social Character in a Mexican Village*. Englewood Cliffs, NJ: Prentice-Hall. Reprinted with new introduction by Michael Maccoby. New Brunswick, NJ: Transaction Publishers, 1996.

Heckscher, Charles, Maccoby, Michael, Ramirez, Rafael, and Tixier, Pierre-Eric (2003). *Agents of Change: Crossing the Post-Industrial Divide*. Oxford: Oxford University Press.

Henning, Margaret, and Jardim, Anne (1978). *The Managerial Woman*. New York: Anchor/Doubleday.

Lasch, Christopher (1978). *The Culture of Narcissism: American Life in an Age of Diminishing Expectations*. New York: Norton.

Maccoby, E. E. (1999). *The Two Sexes: Growing up Apart, Coming Together*. Cambridge, Mass.: Harvard University Press.

Maccoby, Michael (1977). *The Gamesman: The New Corporate Leaders*. New York: Simon & Schuster.

—— (1988). *Why Work: Leading the New Generation*. New York: Simon & Schuster.

—— (1995). *Why Work*. 2nd edn. Alexandria, Va.: Miles River Press. Original edn. New York: Simon & Schuster, 1988.

—— (2003). *The Productive Narcissist: The Promise and Peril of Visionary Leadership*. New York: Broadway Books.

—— (2004), 'Why people follow the leader: the power of transference.' *Harvard Business Review* (Sept.).

Piaget, Jean (1932/1965). *The Moral Judgment of the Child*. New York: The Free Press. Original edn. *Le Jugement moral chez l'enfant*. Neuchâtel: Ed. Delachaux & Niestlé, 1932.

Riesman, David (1950). *The Lonely Crowd*. New Haven: Yale University Press.

Sigelman, Carol K., and Rider, Elizabeth A. (2003). *Life-Span Human Development*. Belmont, Calif.: Wadsworth/Thomson.

Tocqueville, Alexis de (1835/1990). *Democracy in America*. New York: Vintage Books.

Waldrop, M. Mitchell (1992). *Complexity*. New York: Simon & Schuster.

Whyte, William H. (1956). *The Organization Man*. New York: Simon & Schuster.

Wolfe, Alan (1998). *One Nation, After All: What Middle-Class Americans Really Think About: God, Country, Family, Racism, Welfare, Immigration, Homosexuality, Work, the Right, the Left and Each other*. New York: Viking.

Notes

1. Waldrop (1992).
2. Sigelman and Rider (2003).

3. Maccoby (2004).
4. There have been a number of attempts to chronicle shifts in social character, broadly defined, within the last fifty years in the United States. Riesman's (1950) *The Lonely Crowd* described a shift from a traditional inner-directed character, socially controlled by guilt, to an other-directed character controlled by anxiety. In *Man for Himself* (1947) and *The Sane Society* (1955), Fromm described the marketing character, making the self into a commodity that had to be pleasing and cooperative in order to get ahead in the hierarchical bureaucratic structures that dominated American business and government. About the same time, Whyte's *Organization Man* (1956) reinforced this portrait of the corporate character.

   Lasch's (1978) *Culture of Narcissism* proposed another shift in the American character from a more civic-minded attitude to self-centered consumerism following the collapse of liberalism, after the idealistic, war-torn decade of the 1960s. In *Habits of the Heart* (1985), Bellah and his associates added their observations of a growing alienation and extreme individualism in the American character.

   In *The Gamesman* (1977), Maccoby saw the first indications of a new social character among the top managers of some of the most innovative businesses in the United States. No longer the cautious, dependable Company Man of the 1950s, the new leaders were risk takers, thrilled by the game of winning or losing in the corporate world. They were creating both the technologies and attitudes at the frontier of social character change in America. However, Maccoby pointed out that while they were deeply related to their work, they were emotionally detached in their personal relationships.
5. A recent study (Beck and Wade 2004) reports that over 80% of professionals under age 35 played computer games as teenagers. These men and women express the traits of the interactive social character at work. They are critical of authority, more emotionally connected to peers, and identify themselves as free agents.
6. Maccoby (2004).

Part II

Community inside Firms

4

Mastering the Law of Requisite Variety with Differentiated Networks

Jay R. Galbraith

The key organizational aspect of 'collaborative community' as described in this volume by Adler and Heckscher (Chapter 1) and Sabel (Chapter 2) consists in formalized processes of interaction and learning, moving beyond the informal networks common in traditional firms. While this broad-brush description captures a core aspect of dynamic change under way in many large companies, it lacks an explanation of the full range of combinations that companies adopt in varying circumstances. Informal relationships and hierarchical line organizations have not disappeared as formalized processes have risen; rather, they have become integrated with a wider assortment of relational patterns that can be drawn on according to need in order to deliver a variety of resources.

These varied relational patterns can best be treated as types and combinations of *networks*. There is no consensus meaning of the term 'network': in social science research it is often used to denote egalitarian and voluntaristic association. But technically speaking that is just one specific type of network; hierarchies and markets are also network forms with other sets of norms, and informal friendships are as much networks as formal value chains.

My core proposition is that business success increasingly depends on the ability to manage *all* these types of networks appropriately. This capacity does require a high level of formalized process management skill, as argued by the authors above, and also a high level of trust; it also depends on the continued power of hierarchies and informal networks, as well as on new forms of relationships mediated by electronic communication.

Requisite complexity

The required complexity of networks results from the complexity of environmental demands. An enduring idea in organization theory is that an institution's organization must fit with its environment in order to be effective.[1] This fit is usually defined as matching external complexity in the environment with internal complexity in the organization; that is, an institution's organization must be as complex as its environment.[2] The challenge today arises from two sources. First, most institutional environments are increasing in complexity, and second, most organizations have difficulty in managing their current complexity. This chapter proposes that leaders think of their organizations as networks and use different kinds of networks to match the external constituencies that need managing.

The theoretical basis for thinking about complexity is cybernetics, the general theory of control systems.[3] A guiding principle in cybernetics is the law of requisite variety. That is, if an organism finds itself in an environment of twenty threats and opportunities, it needs to be capable of twenty responses to control its destiny. If it has fewer responses it will be vulnerable to threats or fail to capitalize on opportunities. If the environment has thirty threats and opportunities, the organism needs thirty responses and so on.

Organizational theorists have converted the organism to an organization and the law of requisite variety into requisite complexity.[4] Nohria and Ghoshal then applied this thinking to the increasing complexity faced by multinational corporations (MNCs). They suggested that we conceive of MNCs as a differentiated network of profit centers rather than any single archetype such as a regional structure, worldwide product divisions, or matrix. They found that a company's network was differentiated in that profit centers were sometimes country-based (developing countries) and sometimes product-based (developed world). Sometimes the profit centers were given autonomy (decentralized) and sometimes they were directed centrally. They showed the conditions under which this pattern of differentiation across the networks was appropriate and effective.

In this chapter the concept of differentiated network is expanded and further decomposed into an array of differentiated networks. Instead of a network of profit centers, this chapter will focus on a network for each strategic dimension. There are at least three types of networks in most organizations: a geographic network, a product or business unit network, and a functional network. For example, Nestlé is organized first around countries and regions as the basic profit centers. This geographic network, shown in Fig. 4.1, happens to be a hierarchy and serves as Nestlé's line organization.

There are two additional networks that extend across the geographic hierarchy. One is the network for the food business, which consists of the food business managers in each country and the corporate food manager. There are similar networks for each of Nestlé's other businesses, such as beverages, confection, and so on. These networks are active in managing global brands and new products. The second type of network is for functions like the R&D function. The network consists of R&D managers from each country that has an R&D function as well as the corporate R&D leader. There are similar networks for each of Nestlé's other corporate functions like finance, human resources, supply chain, etc. All three networks are shown in Fig. 4.2.

Nestlé illustrates the concept of requisite complexity. That is, Nestlé has a network for every strategically important dimension of its business. And when Nestlé diversifies into a new business area like pet foods, it adds another network. The pet food business network would consist of managers of the pet food business from every country that offers the pet food product line and the corporate business unit leader. In those countries

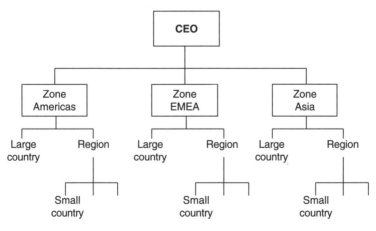

Fig. 4.1 Nestlé geographical structure

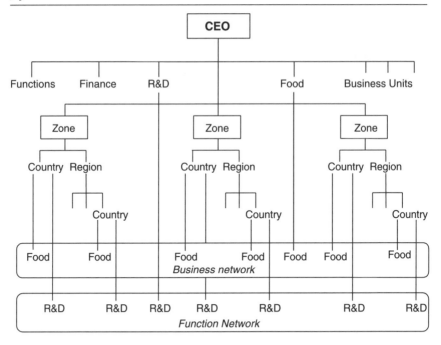

Fig. 4.2 Nestlé networks for businesses and functions

where there is an R&D unit for the pet food business, these units would join the R&D network and perhaps create a new subnetwork for animal science. In this manner, Nestlé evolves its organization to be as complex as its business.

The networks at Nestlé are also differentiated networks in terms of the amount of power and authority that is vested in them. For example, pet food is a new business for Nestlé that it built through the acquisition of stand-alone businesses. Since it is new and distributes its products through new and different channels, the pet food network is more autonomous from the country network than the beverages network. Beverages like Nescafé and Nestea are familiar products to country managers and are sold through the same channels as the products from the food, confection, and dairy businesses. Similarly the networks for functions are differentiated. The R&D function is more autonomous and powerful than the legal function. The laws of chemistry are more universal than the laws of governments, therefore the geographical network of country management is better able to manage the legal function network than the more global R&D function network.

The Nestlé example shows that we can conceive of organizations as a series of differentiated networks, one for each strategically important dimension. But why make the effort to do so? Because today, the three basic dimensions of organizations—businesses, geographies, and functions—are just the beginning. Most companies are facing two to three times that many important dimensions. However, not all dimensions are equally important. And not all dimensions can report to the CEO. We need even more differentiation in the types of networks in order to make the complexity manageable. In the next section the new complexity is articulated. The following section describes the full range of differentiated networks that can be employed to attain the requisite complexity.

Increasing complexity

The increasing complexity faced by companies is a continuation of the growth process identified by Chandler.[5] His historical perspective showed how companies grew from a single business functional organization to a diversified multi-divisional organization with functional staffs. This change from a single dimension (functions) to two dimensions (functions and business units) is repeated today by all types of companies. Stopford and Wells used Chandler's model to trace the expansion of American companies into international markets.[6] This growth added a third, geographic dimension to the business and functional structures. Indeed P&G, IBM, and Citibank all had three-dimensional structures like Nestlé's. Since 1990 there has been a proliferation of new strategically significant dimensions. One new focus was on business processes. A desire to reduce cycle times led companies to redesign and automate processes like supply-chain management (SCM) and customer relationship management (CRM). Then there was an attempt to integrate them into the accounting and finance systems with Enterprise Resource Planning (ERP) systems. Next came a focus on the customer. As companies moved from the mass market to segmented markets to personalized one-to-one markets, the customer dimension became more strategically important.[7] A third dimension is systems or solutions. Many customers prefer that a vendor integrate the stand-alone hardware and software products for them. For example, California schools are required to have video surveillance systems screening their premises. The school districts do not have the expertise to design and install these systems. They would prefer that

Cisco or Lucent do it for them. The solutions dimension arises at Lucent in order to integrate the products from the various business units. Yet another dimension is distribution channels. Most companies served their customers through a direct sales force. Today computer companies offer their products through their direct sales force, their internet store, call centers, value-added resellers, systems integrators, independent software vendors, application service providers, and, whether by choice or by chance, through eBay. So today most companies need to provide attention to processes, customer segments, solutions, and channels in addition to geography, functions, and business units.

In addition, there are numerous topics or knowledge areas about which companies need to stay current. The people interested in these topics are usually distributed across the organization. In the computer business people are interested in general topics like peer-to-peer computing, embedded or pervasive computing, wireless internet applications, and so on. Each of these topics could potentially become a strategically significant undertaking. Therefore these topics are also worthy of attention from the organization.

The concept of requisite complexity suggests that companies need a network for each of these strategic dimensions. Yet companies cannot implement six- or seven-dimensional matrix structures. Instead they apply differentiated networks to these dimensions. That is, companies differentiate the dimensions on the basis of their strategic importance and apply a type of network that is appropriate for the importance of the dimension. The next section describes the different types of networks and applies them to the customer dimension.

Differentiated networks

The networks described above were differentiated on the basis of the amount of power and authority that was vested in them. A complete range of networks is arrayed in Fig. 4.3.[8] At the bottom left-hand corner are the informal or voluntary networks, which possess the lowest amount of power and authority. As we move from the lower left to the upper right corner, we pass the different types of networks like formal teams. At the top is a line organization or hierarchy, which possesses the most power and authority. There are also other differentiating criteria that increase as we move from lower left to upper right. Costs increase due to more management time and effort that is invested into the dimension. And

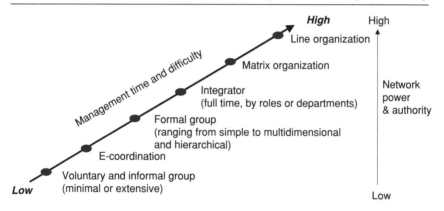

Fig. 4.3 Array of differentiated networks

conflicts and management difficulty in resolving them increase as more and more powerful points of view are put forth.

The implication of the array of differentiated networks is that management should choose the level of network power and authority that is appropriate for the strategic importance of the dimension. That is, a network may provide too much or too little of what is needed. Too much means that a network is more costly than the strategic benefits that it buys. Too little means that the chosen network lacks the power to coordinate the actors to produce the strategic benefit that is needed. When management is uncertain, it starts at the bottom with the cheapest and easiest network to use and moves up the list until the desired results are attained. Another implication is that the challenge of requisite variety can be met by stimulating the use of the most efficient networks at the bottom of the array. In the next section we will explore this issue of managing networks. But first, let us explain the different types of networks and how companies have employed them in engaging the customer dimension.

The customer dimension has increased in strategic importance along with the disappearance of mass markets. Companies now apply finer and finer segmentation schemes, which require greater and greater knowledge of the individual segments. Some of these customers want closer and longer-term relationships. And perhaps more importantly, the power in the buyer–seller transaction is moving to the customer. Vendors have adopted a variety of strategies to deal with these powerful customers. They vary from Nestlé treating all customers similarly on a global basis

185

to P&G which focuses on the top ten global retailers. As a result these vendors position themselves along the array of differentiated networks.

Informal networks

Informal networks are also called voluntary or emergent networks because they usually arise at the initiative of people on the front lines of action. They are often called self-organizing networks. They are the cheapest, easiest, and often the fastest form of networks. This is the type of network that was initially employed by Nestlé to coordinate across countries when serving the global retailers like Wal-Mart, Tesco, and Carrefour. Nestlé has chosen not to give special treatment, like global contracts, to the global retailers. However the account managers who call on these customers in the individual countries recognize a need to share ideas across borders in order to deal with these powerful and demanding customers. These front-line account managers began holding a dinner during the annual company sales meetings where all those responsible for Tesco from around the world would gather and share ideas. Then after the face-to-face meetings, these account managers could maintain contact throughout the year and better align their country strategies to these global giants. Nestlé believes these informal networks match the strategic importance that they have assigned to global retailers.

E-coordination

E-coordination is the use of the internet and electronic media to communicate and coordinate across functions, businesses, and countries around a strategic dimension like customers. Again Nestlé is an example. It recognized the efficiency of the internet and added it to its informal communication practices. The account managers now use email, chat rooms, and discussion groups to exchange ideas and information. In addition, the account manager in the customer's home country maintains a website and posts news and information about the customer. When a new CEO took over at Wal-Mart in 2002, the American account manager made an assessment of the change and what it might mean for Nestlé.

Newer software packages like Customer Relationship Management (CRM) systems allow more effective communication about a customer. Usually these packages identify all the touch points where the vendor meets the customer. People at these touch points record their experiences and all have access to the customer database and the results of the most recent interactions. These systems can be simple or rather elaborate as at some investment banks.[9]

The informal and e-coordination networks still leave the power to decide with the line organization. At Nestlé the communication across borders about Carrefour may be extensive. However each country management decides what to do with these customers based on the situation in their country. The customer network becomes more influential when the company chooses a network based on formal teams.

Formal teams

The network becomes more formal when top management plays a greater role in creating the team and staffing it. The team typically prepares a plan and its activities are more integrated into the company's day-to-day activities. These teams can vary from rather simple ones to complex hierarchies of teams.

An example of simple teams is the global account teams at ABB. These were formed when an important customer pointed out that ABB had 37 different sales people from 37 different profit centers calling on them and were delivering 37 different levels of service. ABB then created a global account team for this customer. The team consisted of all 37 salespeople calling on the customer. They were to create a global account plan for the customer. The plan was reviewed and approved by top management. The plan then served as the basis for setting goals for the salespeople and the country management where the customer was present. The program was expanded to five customers and then to twelve more.

A more complex team results when members from more functions are added to the salespeople. P&G started with a team of salespeople from across its product lines for Wal-Mart. However, Wal-Mart wanted a supply-chain partnership in order to reduce their joint costs. So members from manufacturing, distribution, marketing, finance, and IT were added to the team. The team of eighty people was located in Arkansas at Wal-Mart headquarters. A hierarchy of teams results when these large teams spawn subteams for various projects.

In the auto industry, suppliers to the original equipment manufacturers (OEMs) add the product development function to customer teams. The OEMs attain enough volume to justify the customizing of products for them. These teams are fully functional entities with the power and authority to make product design commitments. These teams also employ the lower-level networks already discussed. The design teams are all integrated into the OEMs' computer-aided design (CAD) system. And many vendors' teams are co-located with the OEM design team and maximize the face-to-face informal networking. So the use of networks is cumulative. Higher-level networks are added to—not substituted for—the lower-level ones. The customer dimension simply requires more communication and coordination to deliver the service that the customer requires.

Integrators

The next more powerful level for enhancing the customer dimension is the creation of a full-time integrating role for customer accounts and teams. When ABB grew its global account teams to more than fifty, a global accounts coordinator was created and reported to the Executive Committee. The integrator provides three new factors.

First the coordinator becomes a voice for the customer on the management team. These teams usually consist of managers of product lines, geographies, and functions. The coordinator gets the leadership thinking in terms of a portfolio of customers, customer priorities, and customer-centricity. Customer teams can also appeal to the coordinator in resolving conflicts.

The second task of the coordinator is to build and manage the infrastructure to support customer teams. The formal communications were mentioned earlier. The coordinators would assume the role of managing customer information systems and communications across customer teams. They usually create training programs for management and team members on the role and operation of key accounts. Many coordinators create a common planning system for customer plans. If fifty customer teams are creating plans, they are likely to create fifty planning formats. The coordinators simplify and speed up the process by agreeing on a single common format.

Another key addition to the infrastructure is a customer accounting system leading to customer profit and loss centers (P&Ls). Customer profitability is a key measure in setting customer priorities. In addition, asymmetries in costs and revenues always occur across geographies. That is, the customer account manager and team in the customer's home country put in extra efforts to make a sale to their customer. Often the initiative is successful but the customer's first purchases are for its subsidiaries in other countries. Thus the costs are incurrred in the home country and the revenues are booked in other countries. A global accounting system for customers can identify these asymmetries and management can correct for them.

The third addition is to provide industry expertise. When the number of major accounts grows, companies usually group them by industry. For example, Citibank grew its global accounts to around 250 and then grouped them into about ten industry groups. This industry specialization allows for the accumulation of more in-depth knowledge of the customers. All of these infrastructure additions can be combined in the planning process. The countries and product lines can then set customer-specific goals for key accounts, allowing customer teams, countries, and product lines to pursue an aligned set of goals.

Matrix organization

The next step in enhancing the power base of the customer dimension is to form customer- or customer segment-dedicated units within countries and product lines and have them report to the customer coordinator. The assumption is that the customer dimension has attained a strategic importance equal to the countries or business units. This importance is expressed by making the customer organization an equal partner in the decision-making process. In countries where the company may not control 100 per cent of the equity, joint ventures to serve multinational clients are often created between the parent company and local subsidiary.

Citibank created a matrix structure in emerging market countries for its customer teams. A global customer was frequently small and not profitable in a developing country but yet was a profitable and important customer on a global basis. Citi created a unit dedicated to the global customer in these developing countries. The customer unit leader worked for both the country manager and customer account manager. The country manager had two sets of goals: one for local customers and one for global customers.

Line organization

The final form of differentiated network is to convert the network into a line organization. In 1995 Citibank converted its customer teams into customer profit centers. It organized 1,100 customer teams into ten industry groups. The countries, in the developed world, were no longer profit centers. Country managers, most of whom were new, became integrators

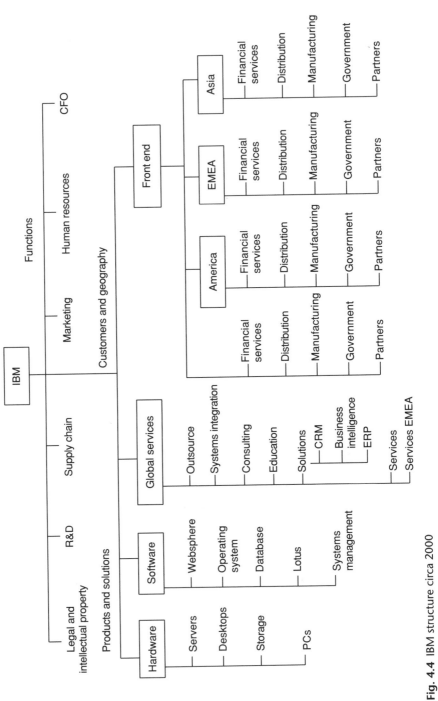

Fig. 4.4 IBM structure circa 2000

Source: Personal interviews.

and managed relationships in the countries with central banks and other institutions. Citibank maintained its matrix structure in developing countries.

The Citibank example illustrates a couple of points. The first is that it shows how Citibank moved from the bottom to the top of the array of differentiated networks. They started with informal coordination across countries for global customers. When global customers wanted more integrated service, Citibank created formal global account teams for them. Citi started with a few teams and moved to over 250. With many teams, they created a global account department to coordinate all of the teams and build the customer team infrastructure. The countries were still the profit centers, however. And then in 1995, Citibank increased the strategic priority assigned to global customers and decreased the priority for countries in Europe and North America. The customer teams became the profit centers. In the developing countries, customers and countries were both profit centers in a matrix structure. Citi differentiated the power assigned to country networks in different parts of the world.

The second point illustrated by this example is that strategic dimensions can be moved down as well as up the array of networks. Countries in the developed world were the line organization and profit centers. As customers moved across borders, countries became less important and country managers were downgraded to become integrators and more like ambassadors. So companies can move strategic dimensions up and down the array of networks and differentiate them as market conditions change.

The example of IBM can be used to summarize the ideas presented so far. Like Citibank, IBM eliminated countries as profit centers around the mid-1990s. They shifted the P&Ls to customer-centered units organized by industry groups. The IBM structure circa 2000 is shown in Fig. 4.4.

The structure is an illustration of how IBM has met the requisite complexity for its business. Reporting to the leadership are *functions* like marketing, *product lines* like hardware, software, and services, *geographies* like the Americas, *customer segments* like financial services, distribution, and so on, and *channel partners* like Siebel and SAP. Each of these five dimensions has a network of people that is distributed across the other dimensions of the structure. Also shown is the *solutions* unit in global services. Each solution that is selected by IBM has a 'solutions owner' in the unit and a network of people trained in delivering the solution distributed across the company. Not shown but important are the *process* owners. These people are typically in the functions. The owner for the new product development process is in R&D and supply-chain management process is in supply chain. Each owner has a network of people distributed across the company that work to maintain these processes.

More recently IBM has added two more networks to the seven described above. The new CEO has announced a new strategy called 'Business on Demand.' That is, companies can put their processes on the internet and let IBM run the data centers. The customers then buy as much computing time as they need. They buy computer time on demand rather than equipment from IBM. IBM has created a senior vice president (SVP) champion for Business on Demand. In turn the SVP has created a network of twenty-seven Business on Demand agents who are located in the product lines and industry groups. The network is to guarantee that all IBM products and solutions will work together in a grid-computing framework. A second network headed by a SVP is to convert all of IBM's own processes to the Business on Demand framework. They want to be their own reference account. This SVP has another network consisting of process owners, IT departments, and others.

So IBM has created one of the world's most complex organizations. There are at least nine types of networks across the company. There are also knowledge networks and various communities of practice. IBM seems to have an organization that is as complex as its environment. They struggle as all companies do to manage and coordinate all of these networks. They have been innovative in creating management decision processes to respond to this complexity.

IBM is not the only company that is attempting to act as 'one company.' The digital revolution is impacting companies around the world. In Europe one can find the TOP (Transformation to One Philips) program at Philips, the SiemensOne initiative, and OneUBS. Sony has created a broadband center that is charged with coordinating the transition of all of Sony's products to common standards so that they work together. The differentiated networks are being used by companies from all countries.

Building and managing networks: the role of trust

Describing these networks is only a first step towards creating them. The purposeful design of networks, especially the informal and e-coordination types, has a growing number of adherents. Success at employing the array of networks shown in Fig. 4.3 builds on a foundation of effective relational networks across functions, countries, and businesses. If functions and businesses are silos, cross-functional and business teams prove to be disappointing. But if there are cross-unit personal networks and people can work effectively with one another, focused teams can be powerful. As a result, leaders are investing time and effort in the building of broad-based trust.[10]

Although other chapters in this volume stress the importance of formalized processes transcending personal relationships, there is a good deal of evidence that personal relationships remain important as an aspect of network building. Nahapiet and Ghoshal, for example, define social capital in terms of three components: personal relationships, trusting relationships, and shared goals or mutual interest. The last two are generally consistent with notions of shared purpose and interdependent process management discussed in Chapter 1, but the stress on personal relationships harks back to more traditional organizations and suggests that remains an important foundation. Tsai and Ghoshal have found that divisions in an electronics company that measured high on these three dimensions produced more new products than those divisions that measured low.[11] Hansen found that business units in another electronics firm that were better connected than other business units got more information and used it to introduce new products in a shorter time period.[12] So interpersonal networks are both a foundation for the full array of differentiated networks and an interactive platform itself for coordinated action. Recall that Nestlé used these informal networks to communicate and coordinate actions for global retailers. Indeed many strategic dimensions can be coordinated or started at the informal level. Not all companies need to be as complex as IBM. It is the potential of these informal networks or communities of practice that has caught the interest of organization designers.

The design of these networks is not a trivial task. The reason, as mentioned above, is that the creation and maintenance of these networks takes time and effort. Social capital is created through investment and these investments should be made judiciously. Everyone-to-everyone networks in large organizations are neither possible nor desirable. The relationships need to be established at key interfaces. Sometimes these interfaces are clear as in the cross-functional linkages in the new product development process. There is evidence that close and frequent interaction across functions leads to timely integration and project effectiveness.[13] There is also a literature on how to eliminate barriers across functions by building networks using rotational assignments, co-location, and events and training programs.[14]

Some leaders have been quite skilled at the network-building process. Percy Barnevik, the former CEO of ABB, was one who invested heavily in creating cross-border networks, which, he believed, was a foundation for his cross-border matrix organization. Whenever a cross-border team was formed, he would ask the team leader to show him the staffing of the team. Usually if the team was led by a German, the team would consist of mostly Germans with perhaps a Swiss German and an Austrian thrown in for an international touch. Barnevik would then insist on a more diverse staffing consisting of a Norwegian, one British, an American, an Italian, a Japanese, and an Indian member rather than the Germans. After doing this review several times the word got out and team leaders would routinely recreate the organization in microcosm. One place that Barnevik believed that dense networks were desirable was at the top team level. Once a year, ABB would gather the top 100 (January) and the top 400 (August) for several days. Barnevik viewed the lunches and dinners at round tables as network-building and issue-raising opportunities. He and the HR managers planned the seating arrangements for each meal based on where they thought the links needed to be built and where conversations needed to take place. At dinner, typically a seven- to eight-course European affair, Barnevik would eat one course at seven different tables. The HR managers would hold his place and trade with him. He would initiate what he thought were the needed connections and conversations. So through cross-border teams, corporate events, as well as rotational assignments Barnevik would build cross-border networks and stimulate their use.

On other occasions, management may be unaware of the networks that form or where they should be forming. Many networks form spontaneously, like the Nestlé account managers for Wal-Mart. They recognized a mutual interest and initiated contacts. Management wants to make this type of network emergence to be easy, to assist in their formation, and to establish links with others who need to be included. One of the best network builders using both top-down and bottom-up networks is John Gage, the chief scientist at Sun Microsystems.[15] He stays on top of the computing area. He attends the computer conferences on supercomputing, massively parallel computing, grid computing, and so on. He visits the centers of advanced computing at universities, the Department of Energy, and the National Security Agency. He then visits all of Sun's R&D centers in Russia, Israel, the UK, Japan, India, China, Boston, and Silicon Valley. He finds out who is working on what and whether they are talking to others who are working on similar issues. He logs over one million air miles per year in doing his job, which he sees as 'keeping the smartest people at Sun thinking, talking and working together.' He essentially makes links across local networks where links are missing. He will bring key talent along with him and make introductions. But he also pays attention to emerging networks and what the topics of these networks are. He says, 'The best way to understand what's happening in a company is to get to its alias file—the master list of all its e-mail lists. Before the web, I used the alias file as my main mechanism for knowing what was going on at Sun. I didn't need anyone to tell me when we were working on a new chip project. Suddenly there's a new e-mail list, Sun Blazer, and I know what's happening. I didn't need anyone to tell me Java was getting hot. There used to be 35 people on the Java alias list, then there were 120. Something's happening.'

When 120 are too many to communicate with, John creates a new alias of the key players in Java and calls it Java Boss. He communicates with them and sees that they are aware and communicate with each other. John goes through the lists to see which individuals are on the most lists. It's a kind of local citation index. He makes sure that he knows who the peer-recognized people are, makes links between them when useful, and brings them to the attention of the leadership. In this way he keeps his finger on the pulse of the technical community, finds emerging hot topics and sees that they get funding when needed, removes barriers, and makes links where appropriate. He builds social capital at Sun.

Today there are software programs that do the same thing. The community structure can be determined by analyzing the email flow.[16] They determined the networks existing at HP Labs. Once the network is known, it can be analyzed and additional links made. Another program establishes networks. For people who enroll, the program searches their bookmarks and favorite bookmarks. When there are people who share favorite bookmarks, the program compiles a list and puts people in contact with each other. The program makes it easy for groups and networks to form.

Thus there is growing interest in building networks around the common interests and necessary issues facing organizations. These networks are adaptive responses to environmental complexity. They help organizations adapt to requisite complexity.

References

Ashby, W. R. (1956). *An Introduction to Cybernetics*. New York: Wiley.

Ashkenas, R., Ulrich, D., Jick, T., and Kerr, S. (2002). *The Boundaryless Organization*, Rev. edn. San Francisco: Jossey-Bass.

Chandler, A. D. (1962). *Strategy and Structure*. Cambridge, Mass.: MIT Press.

Clark, K., and Fujimoto, T. (1991). *Product Development Performance*. Boston: Harvard Business School Press.

Eisenhardt, K., and Tabrizi, B. (1995). 'Accelerating adaptive processes: product innovation in the global computer industry.' *Administrative Science Quarterly*, 40: 84–110.

Galbraith, J. R. (1994). *Competing with Flexible Lateral Organizations*. Reading, Mass.: Addison-Wesley.

—— (2002). *Designing Organizations*. Rev. edn. San Francisco: Jossey-Bass.

Hansen, M. T. (1999). 'The search-transfer problem: the role of weak ties in sharing knowledge across organizational subunits.' *Administrative Science Quarterly*, 44: 82–111.

—— (2002). 'Knowledge networks: explaining effective knowledge sharing in multi-unit companies.' *Organization Science*, 13/3: 232–48.

Lawrence, P., and Lorsch, J. (1967). *Organization and Environment*. Boston: Harvard Business School Press.

Nahapiet, J., and Ghoshal, S. (1997). 'Social capital, intellectual capital, and the creation of value in firms.' *Academy of Management Proceedings*: 35–9.

Nohria, N., and Ghoshal, Sumantra (1997). *The Differentiated Network*. San Francisco: Jossey-Bass.

Peppers, D., and Rogers, M. (1997). *Enterprise One to One*. New York: Currency-Doubleday.

Rapaport, R. (1996). 'The company is the network.' *Fast Company* (Apr.-May): 116.

Stopford, J., and Wells, L. (1972). *Managing the Multinational Enterprise*. London, Longmans.

Thompson, James D. (1967). *Organizations in Action*. New York: McGraw-Hill.

Tsai, W., and Ghoshal, S. (1998). 'Social capital and value creation: the role of intrafirm networks.' *Academy of Management Journal*, 41/4: 464–76.

Tyler, J. R., Wilkinson, D. M., and Huberman, B. A. 'E-mail as spectroscopy: automated discovery of community structure within organizations.' Available from www.huberman@hpl.hp.com.

Notes

1. An early reference can be found in Lawrence and Lorsch (1967). More of the fit theme has risen again in Nohria and Ghoshal (1997).
2. See Thompson (1967: ch. 6).
3. See Ashby (1956).
4. Nohria and Ghoshal (1997).
5. Chandler's historic study described how companies added new dimensions to their structures as they grew. See Chandler (1962).
6. See Stopford and Wells (1972).

7. Peppers and Rogers originated the one-to-one idea. Their best description of it is Peppers and Rogers (1997).
8. For a complete description of these types of networks, often called lateral forms, see Galbraith (2002).
9. For an example, see Galbraith (2002: ch. 7).
10. The definition used here is taken from Nahapiet and Ghoshal (1997: 35–9).
11. See Tsai and Ghoshal (1998: 464–76).
12. See his two articles: Hansen (1999: 82–111; 2002: 232–48).
13. See Clark and Fujimoto (1991); Eisenhardt and Tabrizi (1995: 84–110).
14. See Galbraith (1994); Ashkenas et al. (2002).
15. An interview with John Gage can be found in Rapaport (1996: 116).
16. For an example, see Tyler et al., 'E-mail as spectroscopy: automated discovery of community structure within organizations.' Available from www.huberman@hpl.hp.com.

5

Beyond Hacker Idiocy

The Changing Nature of Software Community and Identity

Paul S. Adler

Introduction

Professions are often taken as prototypical of a more collegial form of community, one that can be contrasted with both traditional *Gemeinschaft* and modern *Gesellschaft*. Indeed, the collegiality of professionals doing intrinsically meaningful work stands as a prefigurative model of the communist utopia of a 'free association of producers.'[1] The key features of professions giving them this status are their common professional socialization and their autonomy in economic status and in technical decision making.

In reality however, professionals' autonomy is increasingly restricted. First, a substantial and growing proportion of professionals work under heteronomous conditions, as employees of capitalist firms: engineers are the largest category of these 'organizational professionals.' Second, even without economic autonomy, professionals traditionally enjoyed considerable technical autonomy; but this technical autonomy too has been undermined by recent trends towards the bureaucratization of professional work.[2]

Many observers interpret the loss of economic and technical autonomy as a sign of abject proletarianization.[3] If such is indeed the future of professional work, the plausibility of the central thesis of this volume would be seriously undermined. After all, professions are the occupational category most directly implicated in the trends towards knowledge-intensive and solutions-oriented production that we have interpreted as driving the movement towards collaborative community.

This chapter challenges that pessimistic prognosis: I argue that it is precisely the loss of autonomy that is allowing professionals to move beyond the primitive, guild form of coordination towards a more advanced form—collaborative community. To ground my argument, this chapter examines the case of software developers.

Software is a fruitful field for this investigation. On the one hand, in the early years of the industry programmers—much like the physicians described by Maccoby in Chapter 6—resembled guild craftsmen, sharing elements of common socialization and enjoying great technical autonomy in their work. To quote one of them:

I remember that in the fifties and early sixties I was a 'jack of all trades.' As a programmer I got to deal with the whole process. I would think through a problem, talk to the clients, write my own code, and operate the machine. I loved it—particularly the chance to see something through from beginning to end.[4]

On the other hand, over the past few decades, a significant part of the software industry has undergone massive bureaucratization. A growing proportion of developers describe their work in terms more like these, taken from an interview with a developer who worked in a large systems-development consulting firm I will call GCC:

Where I used to work before I came to GCC, the development process was entirely up to me and my manager. What I did, when I did it, what it was going to look like when it was done, and so forth, was all up to me. It was very informal. Here everything is very different. It's much more rigid. It's much more formal. A lot of people lay out the schedule, the entire functionality, and what I'm going to be accountable for—before I even get involved. ...

When I got here I was kind of shocked. Right off, it was 'Here are your Instructions.' 'So what does this tell me?' 'It tells you how to do your job.' I thought I was bringing the know-how I'd need to do my job. But sure enough, you open up the Instructions, and they tell you how to do your job: how to lay the code out, where on the form to write a change request number, and so on. I was shocked.

Notwithstanding the development of powerful programming technologies over the recent decades, the guild model common in the industry's early years has proven grossly inadequate for the development of larger, more complex software systems. As systems have grown larger, so too has the proportion of projects that fail to meet their goals or fail entirely, creating what many observers call a state of 'crisis' and 'chaos.'[5] The effort to tame the chaos in software development has led to an increasing focus on 'process,' understood as the standardization, formalization, and management control of work processes. One popular vehicle for attaining greater process discipline is the Capability Maturity Model (CMM®) developed by the Software Engineering Institute (described in more detail below). At high levels of 'maturity,' software development should, its proponents argue, resemble a bureaucratic factory process in its disciplined operations, predictable results, and continuous improvement. The interviewee from GCC quoted above is from an organization at the highest CMM maturity level.

On the one hand, this bureaucratization promises considerably greater efficiency, timeliness, and quality.[6] On the other hand, concerns have been voiced about the CMM's bureaucratic nature. These concerns echo those addressed to the broader family of 'software factory' concepts of which the CMM is a part.[7] In particular, concern is often expressed that the discipline recommended by the CMM will reduce the autonomy of developers and will therefore be experienced by them as burdensome and coercive constraint. This would stifle the motivation and creativity that are, over the longer run, required for high-quality and innovative software development.[8] One software development manager interviewed in the present study expressed the concern this way: 'Programming has always been seen as more of an art form than a factory process. Programmers are supposed to be creative, free spirits, able to figure things out themselves. So the software factory idea was very alien to the culture of programmers.'

The debate about the future of software development, like the broader debate about the effects of bureaucratization on professional work, hinges crucially on our understanding of how professionals' communities and identities are reshaped by bureaucratic rationalization. So far, however, we have little research on these issues. Many observers simply assume that developers will reject this bureaucratization; but my interviews at GCC suggested a more complex picture. The developer quoted above—'I was kind of shocked'—went on to say:

But I can see the need now. Now I'm just one of 30 or 40 other people who may need to work on this code, so we need a change request number that everyone can use to identify it. It certainly feels restrictive at first. They explained the Instructions and the whole Program C process to us in our orientation seminar, but it's hard to see the value of it until you've been around a while. Now I can see that it makes things much easier in the long run. I hate to say it. As a developer, I'm pretty allergic to all this paperwork. It's so time-consuming. But it does help. You've got to keep in mind, too, that by the time we see the Instructions, they've been through a lot of revision and refinement. So they're pretty much on target.

The research reported here analyzes the experience of software developers in four software development units within GCC that have adopted the CMM and reached relatively high levels of maturity. My main findings are threefold: (*a*) under the influence of the CMM, the software development process had become more interdependent, and thus had been 'socialized' in the sense used by Marx and Engels;[9] (*b*) as a result, the structure of development organizations has shifted towards an 'enabling bureaucracy' form, one which combines high levels of community and hierarchy principles of organization, and creating a form of community that is collaborative rather than merely associational or guildlike; (*c*) the subjective identity of developers shifted from the individualistic 'hacker' form towards interdependent self-construal, in the sense used by cultural psychology;[10] and (*d*) these trends were simultaneously stimulated, distorted, and retarded by profitability pressures.

Theoretical starting points

My study takes as its theoretical starting point Marx's analysis of the capitalist production process. As discussed in Chapter 1, Marx saw capitalism as a system characterized by the production of 'commodities'— goods and services produced for sale on the market rather than for direct use by the producers. The commodity is thus a 'contradictory unity' of use-value (utility) and exchange-value (its value in exchange)— contradictory, because the imperatives of making something useful are not necessarily congruent with the imperatives that flow from the desire for profit.[11]

Within the capitalist production process, writes Marx, the basic use-value/exchange-value contradiction is expressed in the contradiction between the *labor process*, in which use-values in the form of working capacity, tools, and materials are combined to create new use-values, and the *valorization process*, in which these use-values appear in the monetary form of wages, fixed capital, and circulating capital, and are combined to create new exchange-value in the form of profit.[12] In Marx's view of the development of capitalism, the contradiction between these two aspects of the production process intensifies over time, as the labor process embodies a tendency towards what Marx called the 'socialization' of the forces of production, while the valorization process embodies the persistence of private-property-based relations of production. Valorization pressures simultaneously encourage, undermine, and distort the tendency towards socialization.[13] Let us unpack this summary formulation.

Socialization is commonly construed as the process whereby people new to a culture internalize its norms: Marx's use is broader. Marx's discussion of the socialization of the forces of production (as distinct from his arguments in favor of the socialization of property relations through nationalizations) suggests that this psychological internalization is just one form of a more general phenomenon: the forces of production are socialized insofar as they come to embody the capabilities developed in the larger society rather than only those that emerge from isolated, local contexts.[14]

The 'objective' socialization of the forces of production is visible at the societal level in the increasingly complex social division of labor—the specialization of industries and regions, and their increasing global interdependence.[15] At the enterprise level—where society's forces of production are instantiated as specific labor processes and specific collectivities—objective socialization was characterized by Engels in these terms:[16]

Before capitalist production. i.e. in the Middle Ages. . . . the instruments of labor—land, agricultural implements, the workshop, the tool—were the instruments of labor of single individuals, adapted for the use of one worker. . . [The bourgeoisie transformed these productive forces] from means of production of the individual into *social* means of production, workable only by a community of men. The spinning-wheel, the hand-loom, the blacksmith's hammer were replaced by the spinning-machine, the power-loom, the steam-hammer; the individual workshop, by the factory, implying the cooperation of hundreds and thousands of workmen. In like manner, production itself changed from a series of individual into a series of social acts.

Firms develop a whole panoply of management techniques to master what Marx calls the 'cooperation' necessary to coordinate this interdependent 'series of social acts.'[17] In this light, the emergence of bureaucracy can be seen as a key part of the socialization process.

To these objective dimensions of socialization corresponds a subjective dimension—to reprise the conventional meaning of socialization. When the effective subject of production is no longer an individual worker but the 'collective worker,'[18] workers' identities change—workers are resocialized. Socialization in this subjective sense can be understood as the emergence of more 'interdependent self-construals.'[19] The civilizing mission of capitalism is not only to stimulate enormously the quantitative development of the objective components of the forces of production, but also to take a decisive step in the realization of humankind's fundamentally social nature: 'When the worker cooperates in a planned way with others, he strips off the fetters of his individuality, and develops the capabilities of his species.'[20]

The development of the forces of production pulls workers out of what Marx and Engels call 'rural idiocy' and 'craft idiocy.'[21] Marx's use of the term idiocy preserves both its colloquial sense and the meaning from the Greek *idiotes*, denoting an asocial individual isolated from the polis. At the opposite end of the spectrum from the *idiotes*—in the form of the farmer or the craftsman—is the 'social individual,' described in the *Grundrisse* as the technician who accesses and deploys society's accumulated scientific and technological knowledge in a collaboratively organized production process.[22]

Under capitalism, this socialization tendency is simultaneously stimulated, retarded, and distorted by the prevailing relations of production. Competitive pressures force firms to break down parochialisms, to bring everyone into the world market, and to stimulate technological progress; but instead of a broadening association of producers progressively mastering their collective future, capitalism imposes the coercion of quasi-natural laws of the market over firms and the despotism of corporate bureaucracy over workers. The limitations on collective mastery that result from the dominance of the market over firms are visible in capitalism's inability to manage public goods and externalities. The limitations resulting from the coercion of the market are visible in the difficulties facing firms that attempt to establish collaborative relations with other firms up- and down-stream, only to find that competitive pressure destroys these high-trust relations. The limitations resulting from the despotic authority of managers over workers within firms is visible in the Sisyphean nature of corporate human resource management strategies—condemned to futility by the capitalist firm's need for workers who are simultaneously dependable and disposable.[23] With the increasing complexity of technology and the growing knowledge intensity of the economy, these handicaps become increasingly intolerable fetters on social development.[24]

In the overall dynamics of capitalism, these various constraints must and do slowly cede to the overall progress of socialization. In modern industry, competitive advantage often flows from skill upgrading and from greater collaborative interdependence within and between firms. The pursuit of those sources of competitive advantage makes capitalists the 'involuntary promoters' of socialization.[25] While at first, socialization appears in the alienated form of coercive market and bureaucratic control, the subsequent development of capitalism constantly brings forth new, more conscious and collaborative forms of socialization—forms which stand in ever-sharper contrast to the prerogatives of capital.

As a result of the persistence of capitalist relations of production, the path of socialization—the emergence of collaborative community—is halting and uneven. Globalization integrates markets, but by whipsawing regions against each other. Management mobilizes the collective worker, but then is seduced by the easy profits from downsizing and outsourcing. There is a long-term skill upgrading trend, but firms find the low road of deskilling and super-exploitation ever tempting.

The body of this chapter shows that this dialectic of socialization and valorization drives the evolution of software development and the mutations of professional communities and identities. First, however, I describe the context of the research and my research methods.

Some context

The Capability Maturity Model

In the 1980s, the US Air Force studied seventeen major software systems contracts and found that every project was late (by an average of 75 per cent) and over budget.[26] The chaos in large-scale commercial sector projects was (and still is) in general even worse.[27] In 1984, frustrated with such chaos, the Department of Defense (DoD) funded the Software Engineering Institute (SEI), based at Carnegie-Mellon University, to develop a model of a more reliable software development process. With the assistance of the MITRE Corporation, SEI developed a process maturity framework, releasing a preliminary description in 1987 and the first official version (version 1.1) in 1991.

A broad community of industry people helped shape the CMM. One of the CMM authors writes: 'Nearly 1000 external reviewers who were part of a "CMM Correspondence Group" had the opportunity to comment on the various drafts leading to CMM version 1.1. A CMM Advisory Board helped the SEI review and reconcile conflicting requests.'[28] The software CMM was subsequently complemented by CMM tools for systems engineering, people management, software acquisition, and engineering. In 2000, several of these were integrated into a broader tool called CMM-Integration.

This study focuses on the software CMM. This CMM distinguishes five successively more 'mature' levels of process capability, each characterized by mastery of a number of Key Process Areas (KPAs)—see Table 5.1. The

Table 5.1. The Capability Maturity Model

Level	Focus and description	Key process areas	Distribution of appraised organizations in: 1987–1991 (132 organizations)	2000–mid-2004 (1,543 organizations)
Level 1: Initial	**Competent people and heroics:** The software process is ad hoc, occasionally even chaotic. Few processes are defined, and success depends on individual effort and heroics.		80.0%	9.6%
Level 2: Repeatable	**Program management processes:** Basic program management processes are established to track cost, schedule, and functionality. The necessary process discipline is in place to repeat earlier successes on programs with similar applications.	• software configuration management • software quality assurance • software project tracking and oversight • software project planning • requirements management	12.3%	42.6%
Level 3: Defined	**Engineering processes and organizational support:** The software process for both management and engineering activities is documented, standardized, and integrated into a standard software process for the organization. All programs use an approved, tailored version of the organization's standard software process for developing and maintaining software.	• peer reviews • intergroup coordination • software product engineering • integrated software management • training program • organization process definition • organization process focus	6.9%	30.1%

Table 5.1. The Capability Maturity Model (*Cont'd*)

Level	Focus and description	Key process areas	Distribution of appraised organizations in: 1987–1991 (132 organizations)	2000–mid-2004 (1,543 organizations)
Level 4: Managed	**Product and process quality:** Detailed measures of the software process and product quality are collected. Both the software process and products are quantitatively understood and controlled.	• software quality management • quantitative process management • process change management	0.0%	8.6%
Level 5: Optimizing	**Continuous process improvement:** Improvement is enabled by quantitative feedback from the process and from piloting innovative ideas and technologies.	• technology change management • defect prevention	0.8%	9.6%

Sources: Paulk et al. (1993); Software Engineering Institute (2004).

CMM belongs to a class of improvement approaches that focus on 'process' rather than 'people.' It does not recommend any particular approach to organizational and behavioral issues: it focuses on the 'whats' and not the 'hows,' leaving CMM users to determine their own implementation approach. Level 1 represents an ad hoc approach—it corresponds to the traditional model of professional work. Level 2 represents the rationalization of the management of individual projects. Level 3 characterizes the way the organization manages its portfolio of projects. Level 4 addresses the quantification of the development process. Level 5 addresses the continuous improvement of that process. The underlying philosophy of this hierarchy was inspired by Crosby's five stages of TQM maturity—uncertainty, awakening, enlightenment, wisdom, and certainty.[29]

Early CMM assessments revealed a startlingly 'immature' state of software process, but one that conforms to the expectations of mainstream contingency theory: fully 80 per cent of the 132 organizations assessed during 1987–91 were found to be at the ad hoc Level 1. Over the subsequent years, there appears to have been significant shift (although it is difficult to tell given the changing and unrepresentative nature of the sample). This shift was assisted by the fact that the DoD and other government and private-sector organizations began using Software Capability Evaluations (SCEs) based on the CMM as part of their source selection process. The first evaluations pressed suppliers to reach Level 2, but before long the bar was raised to Level 3. Not surprisingly, the CMM has become the basis for numerous software service organizations' improvement efforts in both the government and commercial sectors. (The CMM is almost unknown among firms developing pre-packaged software products.)

Evidence is slowly accumulating that moving up the CMM hierarchy leads to improvements in product cost, quality, and timeliness. The SEI website lists several case studies of high-maturity organizations and the benefits they have achieved. According to one multi-organization statistical study, total development costs decreased by 5 to 10 per cent for every further level attained.[30] Another study examined thirty software projects in the systems integration division of a large IT firm over the period 1984–96, and estimated the effects of moving from Level 1 to 3 to be an increase of 578 per cent in the lines of code per error, a reduction of 30 per cent in cycle time, and a reduction of 17 per cent in person-months of effort.[31]

Skeptics remain unconvinced.[32] Critics of process approaches argue that these gains may be specific to the sampled organizations. More fundamentally, they may be earned at the expense of developer morale and commitment, and given the importance of developers' attitudes to performance, any performance gains may therefore be ephemeral.

However, we currently lack any reliable evidence on how developers actually respond to the discipline of CMM. Part of the problem is the inadequacy of most of the theoretical framings available for such research. The most common framing assumes that autonomy is a primordial psychological need—especially for professionals like software developers.[33] On reflection, however, it would beg the question to take autonomy as a key variable. It is surely insufficient to characterize the bureaucratization of software work only by what is lost: we also need to understand what replaces that lost autonomy. Abstractly speaking, autonomy is replaced by greater task interdependence and correspondingly more intensive coordination efforts. Autonomy theories assume that coordination is coercive, and that autonomy is thus replaced by dependence and domination. But this assumption needs to be tested against reality, since it is possible that autonomy is replaced by a more symmetrical and collaborative form of coordination—one that might be experienced very differently by employees.

Research methods

The research was conducted in a large, US-based professional service firm, which I will call GCC. With the support of senior management, interviews were conducted with staff in four programs in GCC's Government Systems group. ('Programs' at GCC were organizational units devoted to long-standing, multi-project client engagements.) The choice of these programs was guided by a research strategy that sought to understand how development staff experienced work at high CMM Levels. At the time of my research, Program A was at CMM Level 5; Program A's sister, Program B, was Level 3; Program C was almost Level 5 (it was certified Level 5 shortly after my study); and Program C's sister, Program D, was at Level 3.

In late 1999, I interviewed between fifteen and twenty-two people at various hierarchical levels and in various functions in each of these four programs. Interviews lasted approximately one hour. They were tape-recorded and interviewees were assured anonymity. The recordings were transcribed, and relevant excerpts were sent back to interviewees for review and correction. I also consulted voluminous internal documentation from each of these programs as well as documents from corporate entities supporting them.

To bring some order to these materials, I moved back and forth between existing theories and concepts derived inductively from the interview data. A draft report was circulated to interviewees and other interested parties at GCC, and their comments and corrections were incorporated in subsequent iterations. The present article distills some of the key arguments.

Building process at GCC

GCC is one of the largest software services firms in the world. Major players in this industry include Accenture, IBM, EDS, and CSC. In 2000, GCC's total sales exceeded $9 billion. It employed around 58,000 people. GCC had experienced double-digit annual revenue growth over most of the prior decade.[34]

At GCC, as in other large organizations, the term 'process' was used to refer to a whole hierarchy of standard operating procedures, from 'Policies' defining broad, corporate requirements down to 'Instructions' defining individual tasks. The 'granularity' of process at its finest levels can be gauged by the Instructions at one of the Level 5 programs, Program C. Amongst myriad other categories, there were separate Instructions that covered high-level design, two types of low-level design, two types of code reviews, one for testing, as well as Instructions for filling out change request implementation forms and root-cause analysis forms. Each Instruction was several pages in length. They often included the specific forms to be completed as well as flow charts detailing the sequence of associated tasks. Overall, the process documentation summed to some eight linear feet of shelf space. A sketch of the hierarchy of the Government Systems group's process documentation is given in Table 5.2. In recent years, almost all of this documentation had been put online, along with a host of other management information and communication tools. Prescribed work-flows were being built into automated document routing systems. Table 5.2 also describes this technology infrastructure.

If the documentation that developers were required to read was voluminous, so too was the documentation that they were required to write. In the words of one interviewee (perhaps exaggerating for dramatic effect):

I can write the code in two hours, but then I have to spend two days documenting it! It can be very frustrating. We have to document check-in and check-out, a detail design plan, a development plan. We have to print out all the differences between the old and the new code. There's documentation for inspection and certification. There's an internal software delivery form. A test plan. And all these need to be

Table 5.2. Process documentation and infrastructure

PROCESSES		INFRASTRUCTURE

Policies and procedures were listed under nine headings:
• General
• Organization
• Human resources
• Security and facilities
• Program development
• Legal/contracts
• Process definition and management
• Finance
• Procurement
	Process definition and management broke down into the following components. These mapped approximately onto the CMM Key Process Areas:
	• Process definition and management
	• Project planning
	• Project tracking
	• Requirements management
	• Intergroup coordination
	• Software acquisition and management and planning
	• Subcontract management
	• Quality assurance plan
	• Configuration management
	• Life-cycle engineering
	• Training management
	• Software quality management
	• Quantitative process management
	• Defect prevention
	• Process change management
	• Technology change management
	
	Project tracking included:
	• Policy statement
	• Procedures:
	  - Cost and schedule tracking
	  - Technical metrics tracking
	  - Project reviews
	  - Risk management
	• Instructions
		1. Lotus Notes database:
		• Document library
		  - Program A development methodology
		  - standards and procedures
		  - guidebooks
		• Process assets
		  - process improvement initiatives
		  - technology management
		  - reference documents
		  - lessons learned
		• Software Measurement System
		  - collected data
		  - data analysis
		  - collection status
		  - tools/help
		• ISO/CMM Discussion
		  - deployment team meeting minutes
		  - CMM/ISO briefings
		  - process briefings
		2. Automated workflow management tools

signed. ... I used to be an independent developer for about three years. I never even created a flow chart of my work! The only documentation I needed was a 'to do' list. So I had to change a lot of habits when I got here. (B developer)

To some extent, this formalization was due to size. The projects in the programs under study here were not huge (see details below), but were large enough to require a level of formalization and standardization that was noticeably higher than some employees had experienced in prior positions in smaller establishments. Moreover, government clients typically imposed more documentation requirements than commercial sector clients. And in Programs A and C, formalization was further increased due to the life-threatening risks associated with the products that the software was supporting.

These were, of course, differences in the degree of routineness across the programs and across the departments within the programs; however, all the departments in all four programs—from the most routine to the least—had come under great pressure to adopt a more mature process orientation. Partly this was due to pressure to conform to the expectations of key customers, and partly it was because progress towards higher CMM Levels appeared to at least some influential insiders as a valuable opportunity for technical process improvement. As a result of these external and internal pressures, all four programs had considerably increased the degree of standardization and formalization of all the aspects of the development process. The two high-maturity programs (A and C) had gone significantly further than Programs B and D, with detailed Instructions specifying the work of even the development functions.

It is particularly noteworthy that this drive to bureaucratization took place in organizations devoted to relatively innovative tasks. While the degree of innovativeness was not as high as we might find in a pure research environment, it was substantial since each project represented a novel challenge: all these programs delivered fully customized systems as well as maintaining current systems. Moreover, over recent years, even as they were bureaucratizing, the programs were becoming more rather than less innovative. In all four programs, customer requirements were becoming more complex; new technologies and languages were being introduced at an accelerating rate; and the programs were being pushed to show ever-greater flexibility in responding to customer demands. As a result, training budgets had increased in all four programs in recent years. A program manager at Program C noted, 'Our main challenge has been to transition a staff of 400 plus to new languages and technologies. That has engaged us in a large-scale training effort.'

A common human resource management challenge

Software development relies primarily on relatively 'professional' personnel. It is true that software developers' claim to professionalism is limited because they have not established an accreditation monopoly such as that accorded physicians and lawyers, and because their knowledge base is not as theoretical (although a discipline of 'software engineering'—of which CMM is a direct reflection—has begun to change this).[35] Nevertheless, two factors encouraged a professional status and outlook. First, software development depends critically on the capabilities of the staff, and these capabilities are more occupation specific and less firm specific than is the case with less-professionalized occupations. As evidence, I would cite the fact that in the four focal units, two-thirds of the personnel held a bachelor's, master's, or Ph.D. degree. And second, notwithstanding the discipline created by process maturity, developers needed to exercise considerable discretion in their work to ensure quality and efficiency. Developers thus had considerable power in their relations with management. This excerpt illustrates:

Buy-in is important in this kind of business. Take an example: programming languages. The DoD was very enthusiastic a few years ago about Ada. It was a great language from a management point of view, since it specified things in a way that gave management a lot of control over the process. But the programmers preferred C because it was less constraining and more open. They simply refused to get on board with Ada, and management lost the fight. (A program manager)

Given this relatively professional character of the work, and given also the persistent imbalance of supply and demand in the labor market for software personnel, staff retention had long been a high priority for GCC and an important consideration in the management of process rationalization efforts. As government contractors, these GCC programs had little control over salary levels, and salaries tended to be lower than in the commercial sector. Moreover, by policy, GCC offered only modest financial incentives to staff below senior management levels; symbolic rewards were more common. So managers understood that retaining talented employees depended above all on making GCC a good place to work, with both good employment conditions and challenging tasks. Program D illustrates the resulting climate:

The turnover figures don't show you how many people come back. We've had six or seven people leave then return. They realized that we have a pretty good environment. You don't get crucified for mistakes, for one thing. The 'blame game' is pretty much non-existent. If someone underperforms, we usually find another job for them that's a better fit. They aren't humiliated. (D department manager)

In the programs studied, annual staff turnover in recent years had been significantly lower than the industry average.

Key findings

To analyze the evolution of software development, we need a theoretical framework that allows us to recognize the mutual influence of community, identity, and the other factors internal and external to the collectivity that affect the organization of software development. To this end, this chapter relies on cultural-historical activity theory (CHAT). CHAT's key ideas are summarized in Appendix 5.2. We take from CHAT the framework summarized in Fig. 5.1.

In the sections below, I will discuss each of the elements of the software development activity system in turn. In each case, we will see the contradiction between valorization and socialization at work. By way of introduction, I begin with an overview.

Traditionally, at the lowest levels of process maturity, Level 1, developers enjoyed high levels of autonomy, task variety, and task identity. Recall the interview quoted in the introduction. The activity systems within which developers worked were largely local. As another study of programmers of that period noted, 'Programmers (and analysts) followed a logic and procedures which were largely of their own making.'[36] Being tacit rather than codified, tools and rules were difficult to communicate across locales. Working knowledge was in these senses private rather than social.

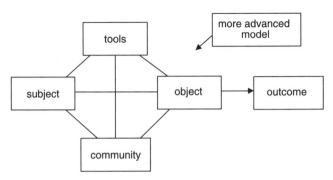

Fig. 5.1 The structure of an activity system (adapted from Engeström 1987)

At higher levels of process maturity, developers were embedded in larger, more complex organizations, and encountered approaches that were the fruit of a complex, organized, large-scale process design and development effort—recall the second interview quoted in the introduction. Tools, models of the development process, and the structuring of the work community were no longer naturally emergent phenomena grounded in local experience. They were formalized, standardized, bureaucratized. Developers were aware that their effectiveness was not only the result of their own individual effort and skill and of informally shared tricks of the trade, but also and increasingly the result of this social, rather than private, accumulation of working knowledge.

At first, this socialization took a form many developers experienced as alienating and coercive. Discussing the Military Standards for software quality assurance that came into force in the mid-1980s, one veteran noted that: '[Military Standard] 2167A was supposed to make coding a no-brainer' (C development manager). In the civilian Program A too, the initial experience with process was top down, oriented to conformance, and 'most managers felt that it was just a matter of ensuring that people were implementing it' (A program manager).

But by the time of my study a decade or more later, the Level 5 programs had pushed the socialization of the production process further, and it had taken a more enabling form. Recall the GCC interview quoted in the Introduction: 'But I can see the need now.' Another developer said:

I came from a background in industrial process computers and the organization I worked for was much less structured in how they handled all this. The process was basically just define the requirements, write the code, then do a final test. Apart from that, you were basically on your own. Here the processes tell you a lot more about how to do the work. By formalizing things, they make it easier to incorporate lessons-learned a lot faster. Previously, it was more like a 'hand-me-down'—you learned how to do your work with some help from other people on the job, or just by yourself. (B developer)

Overall, my interviews suggest that the bureaucratization represented by CMM-style process maturity had broadly positive effects, both technical and attitudinal. Technically, the more routine tasks in software development were rendered more efficient by standardization and formalization, leaving the non-routine tasks relatively unstructured to allow more creativity in their performance. Moreover, non-routine tasks benefited from the guidance afforded by well-designed process controls, and from the elimination of 'noise' and overload created by unnecessary rework in routine tasks.

Attitudinally, process maturity was experienced by many developers as enabling and empowering rather than coercive and alienating. Process maturity did mean a loss of autonomy. Higher CMM Levels drew people into broader and tighter webs of interdependence, both horizontally and vertically. The individualistic 'hacker' model of software development was displaced by a new understanding of work as a collective endeavor. In that collective endeavor, process discipline, even though a constraint on individual autonomy and a burden on individual productivity, was often seen as a functional necessity in the pursuit of individually and collectively valued goals.

The key to ensuring a positive response to process discipline was extensive participation: As several interviews summarized it, 'People support what they help create.' These organizations had both formalized processes supporting participation and strong normative commitments to participative rather than autocratic styles of leadership. The resulting organizational form corresponded to the 'enabling bureaucracy' type, combining a dense web of rules and a finely differentiated vertical and horizontal division of labor with high levels of trust and collective cohesion—combining the community and hierarchy principles of organization.[37] Thus, not only did community become more salient, but the form of community changed—from the guildlike traditional form of professional community to the collaborative community discussed in this volume's Introduction.

On the other hand, however, as we will see below, the forces at work also reflected valorization pressures, and these pressures simultaneously stimulated and limited socialization. Socialization appeared to be the dominant tendency; but the progress of socialization was hesitant and uneven. In each of the following subsections, I first identify the dominant tendency and then one or more accompanying tensions that reflect the various contradictions at work.

Object: an expanded object

Common English usage captures the dual nature of the object of work—both raw materials and purpose. My interviews suggest, first, that process maturity made the object of developers' work more stable and more intelligible. This object was less likely to mutate in unpredictable ways due to the poor quality of configuration control, requirements planning, or quality management:

Before I came to GCC, I worked for a small software firm doing business software. It was what the SEI folks would call a Level 1 organization—completely ad hoc. No documentation, no design reviews, no standardized testing. So there was a lot of chaos and rework. ... In a place like this, everything is more organized, and you know exactly where you are in the development process. I like the fact that you know where you're up to and how to do your work. It's more streamlined and there's less rework. (C testing)

Second, process meant that the object of developers' work expanded to include more paperwork. Process forced developers to document their work more thoroughly—to attach to the code or the test a description of its meaning, its intent, and the rationale of the design. The developer quoted immediately above went on to say: 'On the other hand, I don't like all the paperwork. Your work may be more streamlined, but after the work is done, there's more forms you have to fill out to document what you've done.'

On the one hand, this paperwork could feel like a burden; but on the other hand, it represented welcome expansion of the object of work to include an imaginary dialogue with previous and future developers (a temporal expansion) and with other people who are working on the code (a social expansion): 'I think that our process—and even the paperwork part of it—is basically a good thing. My documentation is going to help the next person working on this code, either for testing or maintenance. And vice versa when I'm on the receiving end' (C developer).

Process also enabled a technical expansion of the object of work to include process itself. Developers were called upon to participate in process improvement efforts. The process itself thus became an object of their work:

Perhaps the biggest change as we've become more process mature is that it makes everyone more interested in process improvement. Take an example: now I'm working on a new software utility. Top management asked us to evaluate it, to see if we should all use it. So I've been facilitating a series of meetings with all the managers, where everyone is talking about the utilities they are using and the problems they're having. It's been great to see this kind of problem-solving work going on. That's the effect of having a defined technology change management process [a CMM Level 5 KPA]. CMM got this process going for us. (D logistics)

TENSIONS: 'IN THE END, IT'S ALL ABOUT PROFIT AND MEETING SCHEDULES!'

The object of work is never simply an unproblematic, technical given. When the object of work expands to include CMM certification, tensions appear between competing priorities, between short- and long-term goals, and between technical and business needs:

Lower-level managers juggle the needs of the customer and the pressures from GCC upper management. And upper management is focused primarily on things that strengthen GCC's position for obtaining future work rather than what we need to retain current work. So even though the requests for things like CMM ratings may have no value-added for our immediate assignment, we do them anyway. (A developer)

I understand why we need the CMM evaluations. But it's added a lot to the amount of documentation we need and the number of interviews we have to go through. I suppose that in the long term, this documentation might help us improve, but for the developers, it's added a lot of paperwork. (C developer)

Clearly, part of the CMM effort was 'for show,' responding to symbolic legitimacy pressures rather than technical performance pressures. As such, it sometimes led to a decoupling between formal process and daily practice.[38] Comments such as these were common in the two Level 3 programs but less so in the two Level 5 programs:

We do have written processes, but some are not always used consistently. They are not always being used by the developers. They are not always used by the program managers in their regular reviews. (B process engineering, formerly with A)

The evaluation and CMM SCE forced us to update our documents. We didn't really change anything in how we work though. (D developer)

In part, this symbolic/technical tension in the nature of the object reflected a deeper contradiction, between the use-value and exchange-value aspects of the object. Interviewees were often aware that their (use-value-oriented) process improvement efforts were at risk of being overridden by a higher (exchange-value) imperative:

As I see it, GCC is a corporation, and that means it's run for the benefit of the major stockholders. So top management is incentivized to maximize dollar profits. Quality is only a means to that end, and in practice, quality sometimes gets compromised. I used to be a technical person, so I know about quality. But now I'm a manager, and I'm under pressure to get the product out—come what may. I just don't have time to worry about the quality of the product. I have a manager of software development under me who's supposed to worry about that. (D development manager)

It's hard to convince people that improving the process will help us get or keep business. [Referring to the downsizing of Program A:] We had a world-class process, and look what happened to us! Jobs in an organization like this depend a lot more on the vagaries of contracting than on our process excellence. (A department manager)

The contradiction between use-value and exchange-value was particularly visible to the interviewees in the form of missed opportunities for process improvement:

One key challenge is maintaining buy-in at the top. Our top corporate management is under constant pressure from the stock market. The market is constantly looking at margins, but Government business has slim margins. That doesn't leave much room for expenditures associated with process improvement—especially when these take two or three years to show any payoff. (C developer)

We could do better at capturing and using lessons learned. We have all the vehicles for doing it—presentations, newsletters, databases. But it takes time. And there are so many competing priorities. In the end, it's all about profit and meeting schedules! (laughs) (A project manager)

In sum, the impact of the transformation of the object under mature process conditions was to make developers more conscious of their interdependence with other contributors in attempting to create a good product, even if the organization's profit imperative sometimes undermined those efforts.

Tools: better information

Under a more mature process, many interviewees felt that they had better tools for software development work. First, as we saw earlier, process was a tool that helped clarify the object of development work:

Our policies and procedures mean that I have better information on what we're trying to do because we have better requirements documents and better information on how to do it with Instructions etc. At Level 5 versus Level 1, I'm more confident we're all playing to the same sheet of music. Looking across the organization, process also means that managers understand better the way the whole system works, so they are all playing the same game. (C development manager)

Second, process functioned as a tool providing valued guidance in the work process:

Developers want above all to deliver a great product, and the process helps us do that. What I've learned coming here is the value of a well-thought-out process, rigorously implemented, and continuously improved. It will really improve the quality of the product. In this business, you've got to be exact, and the process ensures that we are. You have to get out of hacker mode! (A developer)

Process maturity assisted in this by creating a common vocabulary:

In a Level 1 organization, one without a common process, even one where there was a lot of goodwill between the functions, they wouldn't have the common vocabulary, or common definitions of key tasks, and everything would be subject to conflicting interpretation, so people would be fumbling in the dark. A common process greatly simplifies things. (C project manager)

Process maturity also provided tools in the form of objectified and collectively accessible memory:

Process gives people access to assets from prior work—for estimation, for standards and procedures, and for lessons learned. In our asset library, we keep the standards and procedures of all our projects, and project managers refer back to these to use as templates. We encourage people to share and borrow. (A quality assurance)

Take for example our internal software delivery procedure. At first, developers thought that this was just more burdensome paperwork. But soon they found it was a great memory system. (B quality assurance)

Overall, process did not appear to hinder creativity—or at least not the forms of creativity needed in these programs. This excerpt expresses the assessments made by several interviewees:

[E]ven when tasks are more innovative, you can still get a lot of advantage from process. You need to sit down and list the features you want in the system, and then work out which are similar and which are different from your previous work. And you need to make sure the differences are real ones. You'll discover that even in very innovative projects, most of the tasks are ones you've done many times before. Then, for the tasks that are truly novel, you can still leverage your prior experience by identifying somewhat related tasks and defining appropriate guidelines based on those similarities. They won't be precise instructions of the kind you'll have for the truly repetitive work: but these guidelines can be a very useful way to bring your experience to bear on the creative parts of the work. (B testing, formerly with A)

Automation of tools was a crucial precondition for process maturity, since developers needed to consult voluminous documentation and circulate work-in-process in a timely manner. GCC had therefore invested considerable resources into building not only a sophisticated 'development environment' for technical tasks but also an integrated suite of databases and tools for the associated management tasks. The software factory was thus highly automated—contrasting with the 'handicraft' or 'manufacturing' models that prevailed in software development in earlier decades.[39]

Alongside this automation, GCC also sought to streamline the remaining human tasks. Testing exemplified this trend:

Over the last ten years, we've refined the test procedures considerably. First, we have better tools. Documentation and reports that used to take two or three days each week to create can now be generated in an hour. Second, we streamlined some of the procedures for some projects. Now we have a generic template, which we can modify to suit the circumstances. We moved from prescribed, detailed test tables to simpler and voluntary guidelines based on historical examples. And with the benefit of experience and analysis, we are collecting more useful information and less of the kinds of information that proved to be not all that useful. (A testing)

TENSIONS: LESS 'PEOPLE DEPENDENCE' MEANS LESS (INDIVIDUAL) POWER

Sophisticated tools such as those offered by mature processes reduce the dependence of the organization on the individual:

When I arrived here, we had a lot of veterans with deep process knowledge. But as we lost those people, we lost their institutional knowledge. That's why I'm trying to document our process. That will make us less people dependent. (D department manager)

Our process makes us less people dependent. And that goes for managers too. We have promoted the three project managers we used to have, and now we have five new project managers. Bringing these new managers up to speed was much easier with a strong process. (C program manager)

While the direct business benefits were obvious, reducing people dependence also reduced the individual's power vis-à-vis the organization. A fear of vulnerability thus lurked in the background:

If you have a good process, then people become like widgets you can stick into it, and everyone knows what their job is. Obviously that's a big advantage for the organization. ... On the other hand, it also brings some fear for job security. It does make my job as a programmer easier to fill. (B department manager, formerly with A)

This vulnerability was moderated by the favorable labor-market situation of software professionals. Moreover, our discussion of the community will reveal that process gives more influence to subordinates as well as to managers.

TENSIONS: INSUFFICIENT AUTOMATION AND SIMPLIFICATION

Many interviewees argued that insufficient effort had been devoted to developing the tools needed to lighten the burdens of process. Comments such as these were common:

All these forms have a valid purpose, but it takes so long to fill them out that it just doesn't seem very efficient. We really need a lot more automation in doing all this. (B developer)

There's no doubt that more process maturity means more paperwork. Some of it is good, and some of it is an impediment, especially from a productivity point of view. Unless we have the tools to automate this documentation, it has to slow us down. We still don't have the right tools. (C project manager)

The object had expanded in the eyes of managers and developers, but management had not invested the resources needed to upgrade the tools to support the new, expanded tasks. Such tensions are inevitable when the object itself evidences the (primary) contradiction between use-value—great code, well produced—and exchange-value—'In the end, it's all about profit.' Under such conditions, resource investment decisions are inevitably somewhat inconsistent.

In sum, from the use-value point of view, the transformation of tools under mature process conditions not only helped developers in their daily work, but it did so in a way that made their interdependence increasingly visible. On the other hand, from an exchange-value point of view, developers were expendable variable capital and tools were expensive.

Community: beyond my cube

At higher levels of process maturity, the collective nature of software development work became more explicit as did the organizational architecture of this community:

A well-defined process gives you a kind of map of the whole enterprise. (B quality assurance)

The overall process is more intelligible now. All the organization charts, the people, the processes and documents, and the minutes of various groups are on the website. (C program manager)

Moreover, the boundaries of people's everyday reference group—the community with which people identified—broadened to encompass all the functions that contributed to the final product:

Some programmers here used to be very isolated. We had one fellow who just sat in his cube all day from six in the morning till two in the afternoon. Many of us didn't even know his name! But the process here drew him into team meetings and into new conversations. Eventually we even got him helping with training. (B developer)

The Improvement Team's work created a real sense of community. Each week it would be someone else's turn to present their process. Since you knew it would be your turn soon, we all helped each other. And everybody got to see how the rest of the organization functioned. All the data was shared. I compare that to the way the organization functioned a few years ago. One of our big problems was poor communications across the organization and up and down the organization. No one knew anything anyone else was doing. Now we're working in unison. Process makes for a more unified front for the customer. And it makes you feel important, because you're part of the process and you know where you're at in the process. I'm only a tiny part of the process, but I know that what I do is needed for the success of the whole thing. (D logistics)

Interviewee B-13 was one of the senior process staff at Program A before being transferred to Program B to help its process maturity efforts. His assessment reflected longer experience:

At Level 5, everyone feels part of the enterprise—versus feeling very good technically, in what they do, but hazy about their place in the whole business organization—for example, they can't explain the functions of QA. At Level 5, you understand what other people are doing and why. Everyone can discuss and are involved in improvement efforts, not only technical but also process, organizational problems—versus at Level 1, where the only improvements that people can talk about are local and technical. And at Level 5, measurement is a part of life. At worst, people tolerate it. The majority see it as an integral part of their work—versus at Level 1, where measurement is not part of the culture, where it's not seen as having value, and where it's seen as waste, bureaucratic overhead, and people feel 'Just leave me alone.' (B process engineering, formerly with A)

RULES: CONSTRAINTS THAT MAKE SENSE

Process maturity did mean that there were more procedural rules constraining developers in how they did their work, but it also meant that these constraints were largely seen as means by which the efforts of many contributors to the development activity could be coordinated more effectively:

Here, I'm just a small part of a bigger project team. So you don't do anything on your own. It's a collaborative effort. So there has to be a lot of communication between us. And the process is there to ensure that this communication takes place and to structure it. The process helps keep us all in sync. (C developer)

At higher levels of process maturity rules were more numerous, but developers had more opportunity to participate in defining and refining them. As quoted above, interviewees described the cultures of Programs A and C as having become more participative in recent years. In daily practice, rules took an enabling form. Through a formalized 'Tailoring Cycle,' software development standards and procedures ('S&Ps,' of which there were over 100 at Program A) were modified for each project with participation by the developers themselves:

People have to be a part of defining the process. We always say that 'People support what they help create.' That's why the Tailoring Cycle is so important. As a project manager, you're too far away from the technical work to define the S&Ps yourself, so you have to involve the experts. You don't need everyone involved, but you do need your key people. It's only by involving them that you can be confident you have good S&Ps that have credibility in the eyes of their peers. (A project manager)

When S&Ps are chosen for a project, the rule is that they have to be sent out to everyone affected for review. And sometimes we give some pretty negative feedback! I remember I wrote on one draft, 'Hey, you've forgotten to tell us how to get out of bed in the morning and how to brush our teeth!' It was way too detailed and rigid. Those kinds of things get shot down pretty quickly. Over a period of years, people learned how to write procedures that were reasonable for our work environment. ...

When I managed software development on one of our bigger projects, I asked all our software developers to help me tailor our S&Ps. The GCC people knew the drill, but we also had some other contractors working on this with us ... and they would say, 'No, just tell me how you want us to do this.' About a year into the project, I remember one of the contractors who had complained the most about this extra work coming to me to thank me, saying, 'If you'd have written these, I would have just ignored them. But since I helped write them, I've felt duty bound to follow them.' (A developer)

The Tailoring Cycle was not the only vehicle for participation in process definition. In Programs C and D, Software Engineering Process Groups (SEPGs) also served this purpose. In recent years, the SEPG at C, but less so at D, had put increasing weight on encouraging suggestions for process improvement from lower-level staff. Moreover, many departments had process improvement teams. Whereas these teams were sparse and temporary in the less mature programs, they were ubiquitous and ongoing in the more mature programs.

DIVISION OF LABOR: DIFFERENTIATION AND INTEGRATION

The division of labor at GCC differentiated various roles and subunits whose complementary capabilities were integrated both by superordinate goals and by strong process discipline. The following excerpt presents an assessment that is particularly interesting because the interviewee is a woman whose experience of a relatively mature process was recent:

A more mature process means you go from freedom to do things your own way to being critiqued. It means going from chaos to structure. It's a bit like streetball versus NBA basketball. Streetball is roughhousing, showing off. You play for your-self rather than the team, and you do it for the love of the game. In professional basketball, you're part of a team, and you practice a lot together, doing drills and playing practice games. You aren't doing it just for yourself or even just for your team: there are other people involved—managers, lawyers, agents, advertisers. It's a business, not just a game. You have to take responsibility for other people—your team-mates—and for mentoring other players coming up. (B developer)

Process maturity created both more differentiation and more systematic integration in three dimensions of the division of labor: horizontal, line/staff, and vertical. I take them in turn.

As the process became more mature and disciplined, the horizontal division of labor deepened. The span of integration became correspondingly broader: actors developed relations with a broader set of partners. These relations became tighter: the coordination across groups became more rigorous. And they became more collaborative: mutual indifference or rivalry was replaced by active collaboration. These changes were visible within departments as well as between them:

Process means that people play more specialized, defined roles, but also that these specialists get involved earlier and longer as contributors to other people's tasks. If we analyzed the way a coder uses their time, and compared it with comparable data from, say, 15 years ago, we'd find the coder doing less coding because of more automated tools. They'd be spending more time documenting their code, both as it was being built and afterwards in users' guides. They'd be spending more time in peer reviews. And they'd be spending more time in design meetings and test plan meetings. As for testers ... now the testers are more involved in system concept definition and requirement definition activities. (A quality assurance)

With process maturity, new staff functions such as Configuration Management and Process Engineering emerged, and new line/staff relations were created. QA exemplifies the trend.[40] In the past, QA was often remote from the daily work of developers, arriving on the scene at the end of the work cycle to inspect the output. QA's role evolved with process maturity to (a) a greater focus on process quality rather than only product quality, (b) greater responsibility for infusing process rather than only auditing it, and (c) a closer and more collaborative relation with the line departments. QA's role in the Tailoring Cycle is a good example:

First, QA sits down with project manager and his management team. I'll ask: what processes do you need? Do they exist? We come up with a process approach for the project. Second, project managers work with Process Engineering to resolve the action items out of the first step: what new S&Ps have to be written? Which have to be modified? The project managers, often assisted by their leads, then define the S&Ps they need. Third, this proposal comes to the CRB [Change Review Board] for discussion and approval. Fourth, we try to get the managers of each project to do the training for their S&Ps. Fifth, QA conducts a regular in-progress process audit to check the project's compliance with the process approach they've chosen. And there's also an End-of-life-cycle-phase audit. ... QA is not a policeman! QA is there to help the project identify the processes you need, tailor existing ones to your needs, learn that process, and do a check to see if you're using it. If I find a problem, it's my job to help the project work out how to address it and how I can help. (B quality assurance)

Finally, in the vertical dimension too, relations grew denser and more collaborative. Process brought greater specificity—clarity and detail—to planning and assessing the progress of work: 'With a more mature process, my manager has visibility into how I do my work and can challenge me on it—I can't just play excuses and he can't use brute force' (B developer).

Process also provided superior–subordinate relations with objective points of reference outside the dyadic authority relationship. Process thus reduced the 'people dependence' of these authority relations just as it reduced people dependence in technical relations. Several interviewees argued that the objective character of the data created in a more mature process gave the subordinate more power. This excerpt illustrates:

I think formalized process and metrics can give autocratic managers a club. But it also gives subordinates training and understanding, so it makes the organization less dependent on that manager: he can be replaced more easily. Before I came to GCC, I worked for one of the most autocratic managers you can find. It was always, 'And I want that report on my desk by 5 p.m. today,' with no explanation or rationale. Compared to that kind of situation, an organization with a more mature process leaves a lot less room for a manager to arbitrarily dictate how you should work and when work is due. And a more mature process also means that there are more formal review points, so any arbitrary autocratic behavior by a manager will become visible pretty quickly. (D program manager)

TRAINING: BEYOND APPRENTICESHIP

The acquisition of professional knowledge was rationalized. Process encouraged a shift from a traditional form of training—apprenticeship— towards something more systematic. Apprenticeship is a mode of learning that is appropriate and necessary when knowledge is the local, tacit, private property of the guild artisan-craftsman.[41] A more socialized production process relies on forms of knowledge that are more codified and on forms of training that can thus be more rationalized. Going back a couple of decades, this transformation began with the shift to formal university training requirements for development jobs; more recently, under the pressure of CMM, it continued in the further rationalization of the acquisition of firm-specific skills:

We've developed a formal mentoring program. There's a checklist of the key processes everyone needs to understand, and every new person is assigned a mentor whose job it is to explain each of these in turn. The checklist is audited by QA. (A testing)

We had an informal training and mentoring program, and when we got serious about the CMM, we wrote it down. Writing the process down has had some great benefits. It's made us think about how we work, and that's led to improvements. For example, formalizing the training program has helped bring some outliers into conformance. (C department manager, formerly with A)

TENSIONS: GENERAL VERSUS PAROCHIAL INTERESTS

Differentiation created local identities, which complicated the horizontal integration task. This excerpt illustrates:

On most of our projects, different people fill the two roles, systems engineering versus software engineering. (On smaller projects, the same person may have both roles.) As with any interaction between two groups, there have been communication gaps between them. There are a variety of reasons: the systems engineers point to the software engineers and say, 'They didn't read what I wrote,' and 'They don't understand what I mean,' and the software engineers point back and say, 'They didn't specify the requirements adequately,' 'The requirements are inconsistent,' and 'That wasn't in the requirements.' (D process engineer, also works with C)

Staff/line relations were not always easy:

By and large, we haven't had too much difficulty bringing our managers around to this more collaborative approach. . . . We did have a problem with one staff person. He had a very difficult relationship with the project people he was supposed to be helping. We got a lot of complaints that he was trying to force the projects to conform to his idea of how they should function. We tried to counsel him and get him to work in a more cooperative way. But he just wouldn't ease up. Eventually we just had to let him go. (A program manager)

Interviewees also discussed tensions in the vertical dimension: management did not always 'listen,' or if they listened, did not always 'hear.' Compared to the horizontal tensions, the vertical ones reflected a deeper, structural asymmetry of power and authority:

How managers react depends a bit on how you present your suggestion. If you present your idea constructively, they're more likely to react positively. If you come at them with complaints and negative criticism, they don't take it as well. Managers are people too! And sometimes how receptive they are depends on other things going on. For example, if they are under pressure from their bosses to move faster, they may not be very receptive to taking time out to redefine the process. (B developer)

Notwithstanding these tensions, it was striking that in its various dimensions, community appeared to be stronger and more cohesive in the Level 5 programs than in the Level 3 programs. A key factor explaining this result was the more extensive participation in process definition we saw in the discussion of rules, above.

TENSIONS: RULES, ENABLING VERSUS COERCIVE

Some rules appeared to developers as burdensome and coercive: 'The forms are all electronic, but we still have to print them out and sign them. Why all this overhead? The theory is that it will increase quality. But I'm not convinced it really helps quality. Sometimes it seems like it's more for accountability' (B developer).

However, the professional character of the workforce gave developers considerable power to resist coercive rules. Earlier, we saw how developers stopped the adoption of Ada. Another excerpt offers a second illustration:

Whenever you force programmers to do paperwork they don't want to do, they get sloppy. They will invent workarounds just to avoid it. And those workarounds can create problems. For example, if you want to create a new sub-routine versus add to an existing one, you have to write a whole new package. So programmers will go a long way to avoid creating a new sub-routine, even if it means that the quality of the code is affected. (B developer)

The importance of buy-in and the temptation of coercion were evidenced in the firmness with which senior management treats instances of autocratic behavior by managers. Among the several cases cited by interviewees in the various programs, this one was illustrative:

Executive management might impose on me as program manager a CMM rating goal without much dialogue, and they might even have a pretty coercive view of what process discipline consists of. But I can't let that flow downhill from me. We explain to our managers why the rating is important to our future. And once you see the heads nodding, then you have to find the right people for the implementation team—people who aren't going to dictate to the other levels how to proceed. We really can't afford an autocratic style of leadership. The risk of losing critical people is too high. ... We did have a pretty autocratic manager a while back in our software development organization. He had very strong technical skills and would often make decisions without consulting his staff. We heard a lot of complaints, and we saw some turnover too. But his technical skills made him very valuable to us, so we kept him on even after he offered to resign. We tried to get him to change his style, but he didn't, and eventually, after maybe two years of this, we just had to let him go. It was difficult. And he took a few loyal people with him too. (D program manager)

TENSIONS: 'WE STILL DON'T HAVE THE RESOURCES'

Several interviewees pointed to another persistent tension in the structure of community: the lack of dedicated resources for specialized staff departments. The following quotes were illustrative:

We do ask project teams to do a Lessons Learned report at the end of the project. We post the results on the database. But there's no staff support for the process. (A quality assurance)

The key issue moving forward, I think, is that we still don't have the resources we need to devote to process. A program of this size should have a full-time staff dedicated to our internal process maintenance. (C developer)

(As explained in Appendix 5.1, Program C, like D, did not have a dedicated Process Engineering group.) These concerns echo those relative to resources for better tools.

TENSIONS: COMMUNITY VERSUS CLASS

On the one hand, developers and managers were (and saw themselves as) part of a community, part of a collective endeavor. On the other hand, their interests sometimes put them in opposition to each other. We saw this in the earlier discussions of the conflict over Ada and the organization's interest in avoiding 'people dependence.' While senior management put considerable weight on building a sense of common destiny and community, the battle could never be won once and for all. This excerpt illustrates:

We didn't initially have any questions on the employee survey about your boss. Frankly, people were worried that managers might retaliate. But now we do, and we find the data very useful in surfacing management problems. The earlier rounds of the survey did show some big communications problems in some groups. Counseling often helped, and in some cases, we moved people out to other positions. (A program manager)

In sum, under mature process conditions developers experienced themselves more strongly connected in their communities; but the effect was sometimes undermined by conflicting interests. Process-mature organizations drew developers into collaborative efforts to define and refine their rules; but managers struggled to preserve this participation against the temptations of coercion. A more mature process augmented both differentiation and integration efforts, and as a result, developers saw themselves as part of a larger, more complex, and more interdependent endeavor, one that was often, but not always, collaborative in nature.

Outcome: collaborating with customers

The outcome of the software development activity system at these GCC programs was a market-mediated exchange, giving software in exchange for fees from a distinct activity system in the customer organization. Process was both influenced by and in turn influenced these relations.

As noted above, government agencies were increasingly making CMM Level 3 an important factor in awarding contracts. Program B's contract included an explicit Level 3 requirement, and customer pressure had been a critical impetus to process efforts in Programs A, C, and D too. For customers and suppliers alike, process maturity held the promise that the risks associated with arm's-length market transactions—the inevitable gap between the producer's supply and the customer's demand—could be moderated by mutual commitment to a process that set expectations and guided collaborative decision making. This drew developers into more conscious collaboration with people in the client organization. Instead of submitting to the conventional wisdom that 'The customer is always right,' GCC staff were encouraged to push back and open a dialogue:

There's a great focus now on 'accountability' all through the system. We are expected to be more aggressive in pushing back when things are inconsistent with our processes. And that goes down to our project managers. Instead of simply supporting our customer management counterparts, the project managers have to be willing to push back. That's changed the tone of some of our monthly program review meetings with the customer. This culture change goes right down to the staff. In general, we try to buffer the staff from these issues, but if they get instructions that violate our processes, they have to push back too. (C program manager)

TENSIONS: COORDINATION VERSUS MARKET ANARCHY

The fact that the customers were economically independent entities pursuing their own priorities sometimes undercut the cooperation needed to assure a high-quality custom software process:

The biggest problem here has been the customer and getting their buy-in. At Program A, our customer grew towards process maturity with us. Here [at Program B], we started with a less mature client. Some of the customer management even told us that they didn't want to hear about QA or our quality management system—they saw it as wasteful overhead. When you bid a project, you specify a budget for QA and so forth, but if they don't want to pay, you have a resource problem. And once you get the contract, then you start dealing with specific project managers within the customer organization, and these managers don't necessarily all believe in QA or simply don't want to pay for it out of their part of the budget. On the Y2K project, the customer kept changing standards and deadlines. Basically, we were dealing with a pretty process-immature customer, and that made it difficult for us to build our process maturity. Things have improved considerably since then. (B process engineer, formerly with A)

Even at high levels of maturity, the outcome node was the site of contradictions between activity systems. Program C illustrates:

Our customer has been rated a CMM Level 4, but they don't seem to implement their process. For example, in one of our recent projects, the requirements kept changing and the scope kept growing, but the customer wasn't following a disciplined process for controlling these changes and just didn't want to hear about the implications. The requirements kept drifting so much that it was very hard to even regularly update our estimate of the size of the project. They just ignored our concerns for nearly a year. Finally we issued a cost report that showed that we'd need 25% more staff-months. Putting it in dollars finally got their attention. But not before we had wasted a lot of work and time. (C project manager)

In sum, the transformation of the outcome under mature conditions made developers more conscious of their interdependence with clients in creating a good product, even if the competing objectives of organizations and subunits sometimes undermined that effort.

A more advanced model: the CMM as scaffolding

In all four programs, the CMM was seen by many as representing a more advanced model of software development work, a model that could guide improvement efforts. The challenge of CMM certification was to 'map' the program's existing practices to the CMM's KPAs. In some cases, existing practices were revealed to be satisfactory, and this mapping was therefore experienced as wasteful burden; but in most cases, the CMM provided guidance—the kind of guidance that builders receive from scaffolding—for ongoing process improvement efforts.[42]

Program C had long worked under Military Standards, so the discipline of the CMM was experienced against that backdrop, but its experience was otherwise representative. This excerpt expands on one quoted earlier:

Most of our CMM work has been focused on translating what we already do into the CMM KPAs. We were doing virtually all the KPAs anyway, just because you can't manage large-scale projects without doing something like what the SEI is recommending. The first SCE team told us they knew that we must have good procedures and that everyone followed them because everyone told us the same thing; but, they said, the process must have been tattooed on the inside of eyelids because they couldn't find them written down anywhere. So we spent the next year putting them down on paper. For example, we had an informal training and mentoring program, and when we got serious about the CMM, we wrote it down. Writing the process down has had some great benefits. It's made us think about how we work, and that's led to improvements. For example, formalizing the training program has helped bring some outliers into conformance. And we formalized the SEPG process, and that has helped stimulate improvement. (C training)

The CMM could function effectively as scaffolding—as a model of a more advanced activity system—because, and to the extent that, it was seen as an 'industry-validated approach':

The CMM is helping us move ahead. Just to take an example, even if the CMM didn't exist we would need a technology change management process [a Level 5 KPA]. Of our 450 people, we have about 50 people in CM, QA, and data management. To move them from one process to another is sometimes like herding cats! The CMM helps us in that by providing an industry-validated approach. (C program manager)

In their struggle against proponents of alternative organizational development scenarios, proponents of the CMM had the advantage of this cultural-historical validation.[43]

TENSIONS: SCAFFOLDING VERSUS LEARNER-CENTERED DEVELOPMENT

Notwithstanding the research evidence cited earlier, interviewees were nuanced in their assessments of the impact of CMM on process effectiveness. One concern was that the CMM prescribed certain features of the development process and, in doing so, substituted its own 'wisdom' for the results that might emerge from a more self-directed organizational learning process.[44] This excerpt illustrates:

SEI has encouraged people to think that progress will come from 'implementing' the KPAs, when you really need to decide which KPAs matter to your business and how you should pursue them. Many organizations, even some people in our

Government Systems Group, think they need to implement all the requirements of every Level. So the CMM ends up being seen as externally coercive rather than as an internally motivated improvement process. You can get a false sense of security when you force your way to certification—or a false sense of failure if you try to force your way and fail. (B process engineer, formerly with A)

As discussed above, part of the difficulty was how to juggle the goals of symbolically valuable certification with technically valuable process improvement. On the upside, external legitimacy pressure could facilitate internal change. However, CMM ratings seemed to play a somewhat different role in the different organizations. According to this same interviewee:

I can see that external evaluations are a very important learning tool. It's just like in college: 90% of what the student learns is in the week before the test! So we do need the test to create that incentive. But it's not an end in itself. The real issue is: Is passing the test just a veneer? That depends on how the managers treat the test—as an opportunity to put some banners on the walls, or as an opportunity to focus attention and get some real learning done. At Program A, we have reached (well, almost reached) the point where people like the tests as an opportunity to show off their improvements. (B process engineer, formerly with A)

TENSIONS: IS CMM REALLY A MORE ADVANCED MODEL?

Levels 4 and 5 address organization-wide, as distinct from project-specific, capabilities. Optimistically, one might imagine that once a basic level of discipline was established in the conduct of individual projects, even greater improvement might come from organization-wide cross-project discipline, since this would enable an organization to leverage lessons learned from any one project to the whole portfolio of projects. This would seem to be true of many hardware development improvement efforts.[45] So far, however, the experience of the two Level 5 programs was mixed. At Programs A and C, several interviewees—albeit a minority—assessed their skepticism in these terms:

We struggled to get past Level 3. Level 3 seems to give you most of the CMM's benefits. Frankly, Levels 4 and 5 haven't changed or helped much. Beyond 3, documenting the technology management process didn't really do much for us: we manage to change technology pretty effectively without formalizing that process. But on the other hand, defect prevention has been very useful. (A contract officer)

I think Level 3 was worth doing. But most of Levels 4 and 5 just don't seem to add much. It isn't about everyday stuff anymore. We are doing most of these processes, and documenting them adds a lot of cost but not much value. (C training)

Interviews suggested three possible reasons for this mixed reaction. First, the CMM might have been simply misguided in how it characterized Levels 4 and 5. After all, when the CMM was first elaborated, these levels, particularly Level 5, were essentially hypothetical, since so few software organizations had been shown to function in this manner. (As of 2001, however, there were over 130 organizations certified at Levels 4 or 5.) Second, and alternatively, perhaps Levels 4 and 5 were well conceived, but the hypothesized potential benefits would only materialize with further effort and experience. A third, related, possible reason is that the magnitude of the benefits of cross-project processes is related to the number of projects undertaken, and both Program A and Program C undertook a relatively small number of relatively large projects.

Overall, however, the interviews suggested that the CMM had been a valuable tool for organizational improvement, and in doing so, had drawn developers into more conscious collaborative improvement efforts— within their programs, with clients, and with the community behind the CMM.

Subject: a more interdependent self-construal

My interviews suggest that process maturity led to changes in the subjective identity of developers—towards a more interdependent self-construal. What mattered to these professionals' self-esteem and identity was now not so much their individual efficacy as their collective efficacy.[46] In my interviews, 'we' tended to replace 'I' as the subject of work, because people increasingly saw themselves as part of a collective effort. The ratio of mentions of 'we' to mentions of 'I' in my interview transcripts was 1.83 in Program A and 1.95 in Program C (the two Level 5 programs), and 1.29 in Program B and 1.44 in Program D (the two Level 3 programs).

The proximate cause of this change was the experience by developers of changes in the other nodes of the software production activity system. As argued a century ago by pragmatist philosophers and symbolic interactionist sociologists, and as further articulated by CHAT, the self is not an immutable spirit hovering above the material world, merely influenced, but never fundamentally changed, by an external context. The self is an identity whose contours and contents vary with—indeed, are constituted by—the networks of people and things within which the individual is located. The hacker self reflected the structure of CMM Level 1 activity systems. The effect of process maturity on the software development activity system was to socialize its objective elements and thereby to forge a different kind of self—a broader, more interdependent sense of one's identity. Some excerpts illustrate:

In a small organization doing small projects, you have a lot of flexibility, but there's not much sharing. You're kind of on your own. Here, I'm just a small part of a bigger project team. So you don't do anything on your own. It's a collaborative effort. (C developer)

We used to be a group of hackers. If we'd have had to rebuild a system, we simply wouldn't have been able to do it because we wouldn't have had the documents. We've come a long way from that! Now we function according to a defined process and we collect data on ourselves so we can do defect causal analysis to drive continuous improvement. (A quality assurance)

More concretely, this new self-construal emerged through a mix of adult socialization and attraction-selection-attrition processes.[47] On the effects of the former, we have the testimony quoted earlier of 'But I can see the need now.' In Program D, one interviewee described his experience in these terms:

I was not originally a believer in this process stuff. I remember seeing coding guidelines when I joined the Program D. I just threw them into a corner. But a year later, I found that my code didn't make it through the code checker, and that got me to reconsider. So I went to some CMM training a few years ago—and I've been converted! Most of the developers and leads are being dragged into process kicking and screaming. Any coder would rather just hack. (D process engineer)

On the importance of attraction-selection-attrition, two excerpts are illustrative:

You won't fit in well here if you don't like structure, you prefer working by yourself, you don't like getting suggestions from other people, or you don't like taking responsibility for your work and for making it better. (A project manager)

We still have to deal with the 'free spirits' who don't believe in process. . . . Most of them adapt, although some don't and they leave. (C process engineer)

COSMOPOLITANS VERSUS LOCALS

Professionals tend to have strong ties to and identify with their occupational community: they traditionally have little identification with the local, employer organization.[48] Interviews suggested that the greater process maturity strengthened both developers' cosmopolitan orientations and their local orientations.

First, process strengthened somewhat developers' cosmopolitan orientations. At higher CMM Levels, at least some staff spent more time reading industry journals and magazines and attending industry conferences:

In Program A, there was a focus on the big picture, and we tried to make development staff aware of other studies, findings, activities outside GCC. This sometimes prompted developers to become more interested in such conferences as the SEPG, DoD Tech conferences, and SEI affiliates symposia. (B process engineering, formerly with A)

The process-focused people certainly spend more time outside—the more you know, the more you know you don't know and need to learn. And probably some percentage of the general population spends more time outside as their awareness of things not-immediately-project increases and their interest is piqued. But my guess is that the John Q. project guy is still spending most of his time 'doing.' (D process engineering, also works with C)

At the same time, process maturity strengthened local orientations:

On the one hand, as higher levels of maturity are attained, many of the good developers realize their value and are now more marketable outside; on the other hand, they have 'bonded' with the organization and may be a bit more inclined to stay. (B process engineering, formerly with A)

Programs that don't have a process focus tend to have less of a formal connection with the larger GCC corporation. Programs focusing on advancing their process maturity tend to receive support from outside the immediate project, and tend to reach across GCC for best practices and lessons learned. The connection does create enhanced awareness, and in that sense perhaps both more 'professionalism' and more corporate identity. (D process engineering, also works with Program C)

A NEW PROFESSIONALISM

This more interdependent self implied a corresponding mutation in the nature of developers' notion of professionalism. Some aspects of professionalism were preserved, while some were significantly transformed.

On the one hand, process leveraged traditional values of professionalism, including the appeal to individual pride in the results of one's own work:

We appeal to people's sense of professionalism, saying something like, 'We're all professionals. And as professionals, we're both pretty mobile *and* committed to high quality work. Since I may leave here at some point, even soon, it's my duty as a professional to give the organization the documentation it needs to continue serving the customer.' (B quality assurance)

Our process makes for better testing, which means earlier detection of problems, which in turn makes the life of the programmer a lot easier and avoids a lot of embarrassment. (B department manager, formerly with A)

On the other hand, however, process seemed to encourage a mutation of professionalism. Whereas traditional conceptions of professionalism give great salience to the individual practitioner's judgement and thus to their autonomy—if not economic autonomy, at least technical decision-making autonomy—process encouraged the emergence of a more collective professional subject. This was expressed eloquently by this interviewee:

Think of bridge building. Back in the eighteenth century, there were some very beautiful bridges built, but quite a few of them collapsed because they were designed by artists without any engineering understanding. Software is like bridge building. Software developers think of software as something of an art, and yes, you need that artistry, but you better have the engineering too. Developers often don't like the constraining rules, but the rules are necessary if you want to build complex things that have to work together. If you have only two or three people, you don't need all these rules. But if you have hundreds of people, the way we have here, then you need a lot of rules and discipline to get anything done. (C training)

This mutation is particularly significant because it appeared to moderate the traditional tension between professional autonomy and bureaucratic authority:

Usually people run away from audits. But amazingly, recently we've seen several projects volunteering—they want to show off their accomplishments and process capabilities. (A process engineer)

The Improvement Team's work ... made everyone realize that there are real business benefits to sharing information—instead of just worrying about your own rice bowl. I'm your [internal] customer, so I need you to understand my requirements. And the effect has been to make people interested in improving their own operations on their own, even without management being involved or pushing them. (D logistics)

TENSIONS: INTERDEPENDENCE VERSUS DEPENDENCE AND INDEPENDENCE

Interviews revealed two main types of tensions that could provoke resistance to the more socialized development process and thus affect the emergence of a more interdependent self.

First, due to the use-value/exchange-value contradictions at each of the other nodes, there was the constant risk that the demand for interdependence would mutate into coercive dependence and provoke either resistance or apathy. Second, developers sometimes clung to their independence. This was due in part to the tension between the collective and collaborative requirements of effective process (the use-value aspect) and the individual and competitive nature of the employment contract (the exchange-value aspect). Ultimately, the capitalist employment relation recognizes individuals, not collectivities. Even in firms with extensive team- and organization-wide rewards—and as noted above, GCC had few—these are minor components of the individual rank-and-file employee's compensation. The 'collective worker'—the community as productive actor—is in contradiction with the individualistic and instrumental foundation of the wage relation. In part it was also due to the contradictions between prior socialization and the demands of the new model for a new self-construal. In the US context, the change from a more independent to a more interdependent self-construal means a change in deeply ingrained cognitions and emotions. Such a change challenges the subject's prior socialization, as effected in early childhood personality formation, and in subsequent education, training, and work experiences.

Together, these contradictions help explain a certain lack of interest and passivity on the part of several interviewees:

I follow the rules because they are there. (B developer)

By and large, people just accept the Instructions pretty passively. (C development manager)

The overall result of these tendencies and counter-tendencies was an uneven process of subjective socialization. Expanding on the excerpt above:

We still have to deal with the 'free spirits' who don't believe in process. These are typically people who have worked mainly in small teams. It's true that a small group working by itself doesn't need all this process. But we rarely work in truly independent small teams: almost all our work has to be integrated into larger systems, and will have to be maintained by people who didn't write the code themselves. These free spirits, though, are probably only between 2% and 4% of our staff. We find some of them in our advanced technology groups. We have some in the core of our business too, because they are real gurus in some complex technical area and we can't afford to lose them. And there are some among the new kids coming in too: many of them need convincing on this score. Most of them adapt, although some don't and they leave. (C process engineer)

Discussion

Several features mark the emerging form of community here as collaborative. In their values, structure, and identity, these organizations were constructing a form of community that was distinct from *Gemeinschaft* or *Gesellschaft*, and as distinct from the traditional, guildlike form of

237

professionalism. Clearly, the salience of this form of community in structuring real working relations was rendered precarious by the pressures of valorization; but just as clearly, these organizations had made considerable progress towards the new form.

Values: interdependent contribution

The guildlike form of professional identity expressed in the hacker ideal of technical autonomy was progressively replaced under more process-mature conditions by an ethos of collaborative contribution—the software engineer as bridge builder. What mattered was one's contribution to the success of a complex organization rather than one's individual prowess—being part of a successful NBA team rather than a creative streetball player.

In the classic terms of cross-cultural analysis, we would say that the values of developers had become considerably more 'collectivist'; but there was clearly something distinctive about this collectivism. The new value orientation can be described with the two-dimensional mapping of culture and values articulated by Triandis and others: on one dimension, collectivism is contrasted with individualism, and on the other dimension, 'horizontal' cultures and low power distance are contrasted with 'vertical' cultures and high power distance.[49] Hackers, like other traditional professionals, are typically high on individualism and low on power distance. By contrast, while high-maturity software developers remain low on power distance and relatively egalitarian, they are more collectivist, a constellation we can call 'horizontal-collective.'[50]

Organization: interdependent process management

We saw how process maturity transformed the coordination of work: As the process became more mature and disciplined, the horizontal division of labor deepened; the span of integration became correspondingly broader; but at the same time, these relations became both tighter and more collaborative. Guild independence was replaced by complex interdependence. Guild independence was also undermined by the rationalization of an apprenticeship process that formalized the acquisition of firm-specific know-how.

Crucially, this interdependence did not take the form of hierarchical domination. The community principle prevailed over—but did not eliminate—the importance of hierarchy. These GCC programs appeared to be engaged in an effort to simultaneously maintain a high level of influence by lower-level developers *and* dramatically increase the level of organizational control.

Organizational research often proceeds as if influence by the rank-and-file professional and organizational control were mutually exclusive, in a zero-sum relation.[51] This case reminds us that they are not. In the four programs studied here, and in particular the two Level 5 ones, Program A and Program C, both higher-level and lower-level influence were relatively strong:

- Control was achieved through a panoply of mechanisms. Higher levels of the management hierarchy made overall architectural choices. Standardization of processes allowed operational decision making to be safely decentralized (per March and Simon's model of premiss setting). Management exercised strong control over project schedules and plans. And management actively structured mutual adjustment between people and units. The autonomy of individuals and units was thus severely curtailed. Overall coordination and consistency of action was not accidental or emergent, but planned through centralized control.

- Lower-level influence was also strong, as witnessed by the extensive involvement of staff in decision making and in developing and refining the standards, plans, and mutual adjustment processes under which they all worked. Management was committed to the philosophy of 'People support what they help create.' In the Level 5 programs, lower-level staff often participated in process tailoring; in contrast, such participation was significantly less common in the Level 3 programs. The Level 5 programs had 'improvement teams' in every subunit; in contrast, such teams were only occasionally operative in the Level 3 programs.

Identities: interdependent self-construals

The self is always social, always the result of a socialization process. It was just as social, just as much the result of individual socialization, when it took the hacker form. The independent self of the hacker was the result of socialization under a division of labor that was (using Durkheim's terms somewhat metaphorically) 'mechanical'—each person working in parallel on a self-contained task—rather than 'organic'—each person contributing only a specialized component of the whole. This independent self was reinforced by the shared norms of the profession, by educational experience, and by its fit with the relatively primitive tools, rules, and division of labor that then characterized the software development activity system. With greater process maturity and more advanced means of production, the social character of the self is no longer merely an abstract proposition, but becomes concrete in the form of subjectively experienced interdependent self-construals. The self is socialized—as it always has been—but now this socialization is not merely a remote antecedent, but becomes a lived reality.

In the present case, the experience of work under process maturity appeared to promote, first, a more interdependent sense of self: people's reference groups broadened. Second, process maturity led to a richer, more complex set of identities: we saw a heightened identification both with the broader software profession and with the local GCC corporation. Third, process promoted values that were, I argued, horizontal-collectivist, and corresponding to these values, a distinctive self-construal that preserves a certain individual autonomy even within growing interdependence.

Most cultural psychology contrasts *independent* and *interdependent* self-construals—but does not distinguish carefully between the latter and what we might more properly call *dependent* self-construals. This distinction seems crucial to differentiate strongly 'group'-based cultures and the form of professionalism we saw at GCC. The interdependent self-construals we heard expressed at GCC provide a less conformist form of other-directedness—a form of caring.[52] Viewed developmentally, one might characterize this orientation as representing a dialectical synthesis (transcendence) of the contradiction between *Gemeinschaft*, with its associated 'engulfment' of the individual,[53] and the modern, alienated autonomous individual under *Gesellschaft* conditions, a synthesis Hirschhorn (1997) calls the 'post-modern' self. We could call it the collaborative self.

Conclusion

The motivation for the present study was to understand the transformations of professional work through an analysis of the case of software development. I found that progress towards CMM Level 5 process maturity prompted the emergence of a new, collaborative form of professional community and of identity.

Marx contrasted the isolation of individuals and communities in the pre-capitalist world with the growing interdependence fostered by capitalist development. He saw capital's civilizing mission to abolish 'rural idiocy' and 'craft idiocy,' and to augment humanity's capacity for large-scale, productive collaboration. According to Marx, the development of capitalism is shaped by the basic contradiction between, on the one hand, the growing socialization of the forces of production and, on the other hand, the persistence of private ownership in the relations of production. Few today have Marx's confidence about the final outcome. But the present study suggests that this basic contradiction continues to shape the evolution of work, as illustrated here by the path traced by process maturity efforts—taking software development beyond 'hacker idiocy.'

Appendix 5.1: Four programs

For the main part, my analysis abstracts from the differences between the four programs. But the programs differed in many ways, as did the departments within them. Some background is therefore useful.

Program A: CMM Level 5. Program A had had a continuous contractual relationship with its customer for thirty years. Many employees had been attracted to the program because of the high public profile of the customer. Historically, Program A had ten to twenty projects under way at any one time, each building mid-sized subsystems composed of 100,000–400,000 lines of source-code. Recent years, however, had seen a downsizing of the organization due to the changes in the customer's needs. Between 1995 and 1999, employment had shrunk from over 1,600 to around 450.

Program A relied mainly on established technology and was responsible for a considerable amount of software maintenance. Over time, however, the program's tasks had become more complex as the customer requirements and the associated technologies had evolved. The business environment had also become more demanding, with considerable pressure for more code reuse and tighter deadlines.

Discussing the history of process at Program A, one interviewee summarized the evolution in these terms:

The first phase, in the late 1980s, was conformance. We had developed our standard process—a big fat set of requirements and standards—and most managers felt that it was just a matter of ensuring that people were implementing it. The second phase, in the early 1990s, was enlightenment. This phase coincided with our big TQM push. We started getting working-level people involved in improving things. The third phase, running between about 1994 and 1998, was empowerment. The word might sound trite to some people, but we had the process framework, and we had the involvement, so we were really ready to delegate more autonomy down to the projects and the tasks. (A program manager)

Program A adopted the CMM in the early 1990s, and during the latter part of the decade used both CMM and ISO-9001 to help guide their improvement efforts. While their customer did not require CMM certification, external pressure played an important role in its adoption: 'We knew that other clients would require it and we felt it might be a good thing to do to help us improve' (B process engineering, formerly with A).

In 1991 the first formal, external Software Capability Evaluation (SCE) rated the organization a Level 1. The organization subsequently undertook several internal self-assessments. In 1996, the second evaluation rated them close to Level 3. In 1998, they were formally assessed as a Level 5 organization.

Program A was a 'poster child' for aggressive process improvement efforts at GCC. Analyzing some thirty projects over the 1994–2000 timeframe, Program A found that both productivity and quality improved on average by 10 per cent per year. They also saw dramatic improvement in the accuracy and speed with which they forecast costs and schedules for project proposals.

An internal survey of Program A personnel in 1999 asked whether they saw value in the effort associated with CMM certification. There were 260 responses from 850 surveys distributed. Opinions were largely positive, and more so among people who had personally participated in an audit. Of those not audited for the CMM, 58 per cent saw CMM as 'well worth the effort' and another 30 per cent as 'of some value.' Of those audited, 79 per cent thought CMM was 'well worth the effort' and another 18 per cent thought it was 'of some value.' The proportion who thought it was of little or no value was 12 per cent among the non-audited and 3 per cent among the audited.

Program B: CMM Level 3. Program B's mission was to build information management tools for its government client to use in operations around the world: internal accounting, management, IS resource management, and so on. Program B's staff developed new systems, maintained and upgraded old ones, and operated a Help Desk.

GCC won the contract in 1998 by promising to leverage GCC's experience in Program A to help Program B reach CMM Level 3 within eighteen months. GCC replaced nearly thirty contractor organizations that had worked largely independently of each other. Program B functioned as a prime contractor and system integrator, both developing systems itself and coordinating a small number of subcontractors.

Program B itself employed directly or indirectly about 275 people. The largest of its projects employed about ninety people. The overall system was composed of 700 files, comprising about 1 million lines of source-code (MSLOC).

To help reach Level 3, several people were transferred from Program A. The two largest projects were each led by former Program A people, and Program A veterans staffed several other key management and staff positions. Program B's process efforts were slowed down by a very difficult Y2K project, which strained relations with the client. Once that project was completed, relations improved. The program was officially assessed as Level 3 in early 2000.

Program C: CMM Level 5. This program, like Program A, had had a continuous contractual relationship with its Department of Defense (DoD) end-customer for some thirty years. But the relationship had always been mediated by other organizations serving as prime contractors. Program C undertook two or three major projects at a time, each representing about 2.5 MSLOC. These projects created new versions of the weapons system control software they provided to the DoD. Program C employed about 450 people. It was divided into four main units that developed and maintained the main modules of the system, plus several support departments.

In recent years, there had been a swing towards greater bottom-up participation and a corresponding effort to change management styles.

I think it's fair to say that our culture has not put a lot of weight on things like participation and empowerment. When I first came on board, I found levels of secrecy, need to know, and cones of silence. In part, that was due to the influence of the customer we worked with, and to the high proportion of senior people both there and here with military backgrounds. It was like, 'Don't ask questions; just do it,' and the ethos around here was more like 'Just do your job.' Even the TQM program in the early 1990s didn't make much of an impact. It was seen mainly as a passing fad. But in the last 18 months, the change has been dramatic. We've started to free up resources for symbolic and financial recognition. And we've emphasized communication more. (C process engineering)

The key drivers of process maturity at Program C had historically been the succession of Military Standards imposed by the end-customer (the government) in conjunction with the intermittent pressure of their immediate customer (the prime contractor) (see Schulmeyer 1998 for an overview of the evolution of the DoD software standards). Unlike Programs A and B, Programs C and D did not have dedicated process engineering groups driving process improvement, but relied instead on an expanded quality assurance staff and cross-functional management-level Software Engineering Process Groups (SEPGs). Nevertheless, by the middle of 1998, Program C was evaluated at Level 4, with all but some minor elements of Level 5 in place as well. Shortly thereafter, it was evaluated at Level 5. The quality of its products was widely recognized. The program had averaged 97 per cent of award fees, which is an unusually high rate among DoD contractors.

Program D: CMM Level 3. Program D began operations in 1991, developing infrastructure systems for the DoD. Program D was unusual within GCC because it covered the whole product life/cycle, offering complete solutions including hardware, the integration of hardware and software, warehousing, installation, and ongoing support. It had developed 2 MSLOC over the 1993–9 period. Program D was also unusual within GCC for its extensive use of commercial, off-the-shelf (COTS) hardware and software. Its systems incorporated over 200 commercial products. The program's systems were being used in about 100 sites, of which about 50 were interlinked. In 2000, Program D employed some 350 people directly, plus a further 120 contractors.

Until recently, software process had received less attention in this program than in the others studied. According to one interviewee:

The Program D system was billed as based on a prototyping approach rather than the traditional waterfall approach. At the time, this was pretty leading-edge stuff at GCC, and it attracted people who don't like the discipline associated with relatively routine projects of the kind GCC Government Systems had traditionally done. But the initial team of 30 people has grown to nearly 600, and the business really has to deliver, so they realized they needed at least some Level 2 discipline. Even some of the die-hards have had a kind of religious conversion, and have become quite committed to process now. (D process engineering, also works with Program C)

Process had recently moved into the foreground. As part of a bid for a very large DoD contract, Program D had to undergo an external process evaluation. In preparation for that evaluation, they conducted their own assessment, and discovered that the program would likely be rated no higher than a Level 1. The general manager chartered an Improvement Team and charged it with taking the program to Level 3. QA was significantly strengthened — the staff grew from three to eight people — and a broad effort at process documentation was undertaken throughout the organization by department-level Action Teams. By the end of 1999, the program was assessed as Level 3.

Differences across the programs. Contingency theory teaches us that the scope for process standardization and formalization such as recommended by the CMM is closely related to the degree of routineness of the organization's key tasks. Task routineness varied across these GCC programs — that is, people encountered more or fewer exceptions to established patterns of problem solving, and these exceptions were more or less difficult to resolve. And as predicted by contingency theory, the level of detail in the process varied across programs with this routineness. For example, in comparison with Program C, its sister program D dealt with a broader range of technologies and these technologies evolved more rapidly; so it is not surprising that Program C was considerably more mature in its process than Program D and its process was more controlled at finer degrees of granularity. Within programs too, the tasks of different departments differed in their degree of uncertainty and degree of process discipline. For example, at Program D, one department was responsible for defining site requirements, planning and procuring hardware, getting it to the site, and installing it, and this department, unlike development, did specify Instructions.

Appendix 5.2: Cultural-historical activity theory

This paper relies on cultural-historical activity theory (CHAT) and the broader Marxist theory on which CHAT is based. As developed primarily by Yjro Engeström and Michael Cole, CHAT is based largely on the work of Vygotsky, Luria, and Leont'ev.[54] CHAT is distinctive first in its unit of analysis, positing that the most appropriate unit of analysis for the study of work situations is the *activity*, understood as the system of relations established when a community pursues a common object. Leont'ev argues that in the study of work, the activity is the 'molar' unit of analysis, preferred over discrete psychological *operations* (quasi-automatic responses to stimuli) because work involves higher-order cognitive functions, and preferred over *actions* (discrete goal-directed behaviors) because work is best understood as a collective endeavor that unfolds over historical time.[55]

Adapting Engeström's development of CHAT, and summarized in Figure 5.1, the structure of an activity system can be understood as an interrelated set of functional nodes:

- Subject: The subject of activity can be an individual or a collective actor.

- Object: The object of an activity is not merely the behaviorist's stimulus, but (consistent with common usage, American Pragmatism, and Marx of the 1844 Manuscripts) both (*a*) something given to the mind or senses, and (*b*) a purpose. The gap between these two is the fundamental 'motivation' for the activity, and the object thus has a profound effect on the shape of the rest of the activity system.

- Tools: Human activity is distinctive in its extensive reliance on tools (including concepts and language) as culturally transmitted artifacts that partly mediate the subject's relation to the object of activity.

- Community: The subject's activity is embedded in the activity of community that shares the same object. At the community node, CHAT captures the contours of the subject's reference group, its internal division of labor, and the rules governing the behavior of individuals in the community.[56]

- Outcome: The result of the system's activity is an outcome, a product. This result will, in some cases, become an input to another activity system. Conversely, nodes of the focal system can themselves be the outcome of other activity systems: tools, for example, are often procured from specialized suppliers.

- More advanced model: In some circumstances, actors in the activity system are aware of a potentially more advanced model of their activity, and the contradiction between this ideal and the current form of the activity system—along with the other contradictions discussed below—can drive the evolution of the system.

Figure 5.1 is a model of what Marx calls 'production in general'—the generic structure of productive activity; as it stands, this is a trans-historical model that abstracts from the specific forms that activity takes in different social settings.[57] To understand any given activity, we need to augment this model with the more concrete determinations that reflect the nature of the specific cultural-historical context of activity. CHAT analyzes the resulting model in terms of its characteristic contradictions. Following Engeström, we can distinguish four types of contradiction, and in the analysis presented in the body of the chapter, we see examples of each:

- Each node is marked by a primary contradiction characteristic of all activities (but particularly business activities) conducted in capitalist social settings—the contradiction between use-value and exchange-value. I find that use-value considerations in the implementation of the CMM drive the software development activity system towards greater interdependence and greater efforts to master that interdependence through more collaborative community. Exchange-value considerations, on the other hand, sometimes stimulate these forces and sometimes impede them as unprofitable, replacing collaboration with competition and autocratic control.

- Secondary contradictions give rise to tensions between nodes. In the present study, I focus mainly on the contradictions that link the community and subject nodes to the others. These are the proximate cause of the emergence of a new form of professional community and new self-construals among developers.

- Tertiary contradictions are those between the form of the current activity system and a more advanced model of it. I find that the CMM functions in a manner akin to what activity-oriented psychologists have called 'scaffolding,'[58] guiding an organizational learning process that also contributes directly and indirectly to the emergence of new forms of community and identity.

- Quaternary contradictions are those between the given activity system and surrounding activity systems. On the outcome side, I find contradictions between the interests of development organizations and those of their clients. On the input side, I find contradictions between the prior socialization of developers and the subjective demands of more mature development processes.

CHAT offers a particularly fruitful path for understanding the mutations of software development by interpreting change as resulting from these various contradictions and their interactions.

References

Abbott, A. (1988). *The System of Professions: An Essay on the Division of Expert Labor.* Chicago: University of Chicago Press.

Adler, P. S. (1996). 'The dynamic relationship between tacit and codified knowledge: comments on Nonaka's "Managing innovation as a knowledge creation process." ' In G. Pogorel and J. Allouche (eds.), *International Handbook of Technology Management.* Amsterdam: North-Holland: 110–24.

—— (1999). 'Building better bureaucracies.' *Academy of Management Executive*, 13/ 4: 36–47.

—— (2001). 'Market, hierarchy, and trust: the knowledge economy and the future of capitalism.' *Organization Science*, 12/2: 214–34.

—— and Borys, B. (1996). 'Two types of bureaucracy: enabling and coercive.' *Administrative Science Quarterly*, 41/1: 61–89.

—— Kwon, S., and Singer, J. (2003). 'The "Six West" problem: an essay on the role of professionals in knowledge management, with particular reference to the case of hospitals.' USC working paper.

Azjen, I. (1991). 'The theory of planned behavior.' *Organizational Behavior and Human Decision Processes*, 50: 179–211.

Bach, J. (1994). 'The immaturity of CMM.' *American Programmer*, 7/9. Online at www.satisfice.com/articles/cmm.htm.

—— (1995). 'Enough about process: what we need are heroes.' *IEEE Software*, 12/2: 96–8.

Bakhurst, D., and Sypnowich, C. (1995). 'Introduction: problems of the social self.' In D. Bakhurst and C. Sypnowich (eds.), *The Social Self*. London: Sage: 1–17.

Bandura, A. (1997). *Self-Efficacy: The Exercise of Control*. New York: W. H. Freeman.

Barley, S. R. (1986). 'Technology as an occasion for structuring: evidence from observations of CT scanners and the social order of radiology departments.' *Administrative Science Quarterly*, 31/1: 78–108.

—— and Tolbert, P. S. (1997). 'Institutionalization and structuration: studying the links between action and institution.' *Organization Studies*, 18/1: 93–117.

Baronas, A., and Louis, M. (1988). 'Restoring a sense of control during implementation: how user involvement leads to system acceptance.' *MIS Quarterly*, 12/1: 111–24.

Bart, C. K. (1999). 'Controlling new products: a contingency approach.' *International Journal of Technology Management*, 18/5–8: 395–413.

Blackler, F. (1993). 'Knowledge and the theory of organizations: organizations as activity systems and the reframing of management.' *Journal of Management Studies*, 30/6: 863–84.

Blau, P. M. (1955). *The Dynamics of Bureaucracy*. Chicago: University of Chicago Press.

Boehm, B., and Turner, R. (2003). *Balancing Agility and Discipline*. Boston: Addison-Wesley.

Bollinger, T., and McGowan, C. (1991). 'A critical look at Software Capability Evaluations.' *IEEE Software*, 8/4: 25–41.

Bottomore, T. (ed.) (1983). *A Dictionary of Marxist Thought*. Cambridge, Mass.: Harvard University Press.

Braverman, H. (1974). *Labor and Monopoly Capital*. New York: Monthly Review Press.

Brown, S. L., and Eisenhardt, K. M. (1995). 'Product development: past research, present findings, and future directions.' *Academy of Management Review*, 20/2: 343–78.

Burkitt, I. (1991). *Social Selves: Theories of the Social Formation of Personality*. London: Sage.

Burns, T., and Stalker, G. (1961). *The Management of Innovation*. London: Tavistock.

Butler, D. L. (1998). 'In search of the architecture of learning: a commentary on scaffolding as a metaphor for instructional interactions.' *Journal of Learning Disabilities*, 31/4 (July): 374–85.

Butler, T., Standley, V., and Sullivan, E. (2001). 'Software configuration management: a discipline with added value.' *Crosstalk*, 14/7: 4–8.

Chaiklin, S., and Lave, J. (eds.) (1993). *Understanding Practice: Perspectives and Activity and Context*. New York: Cambridge University Press.

—— Hedergaard, M., and Jensen, U. J. (eds.) (1999). *Activity Theory and Social Practice*. Aarhus: Aarhus University Press.

Clark, B. (1999). 'Effects of process maturity on development effort.' Unpublished paper available at http://sunset.usc. edu/~bkclark/Research.

Cohen, G. A. (1974). 'Marx's dialectic of labor.' *Philosophy and Public Affairs*, 3/3: 235–61.

—— (1978). *Karl Marx's Theory of History: A Defense*. Princeton: Princeton University Press.

Cohen, Joshua (1982). Review of G. A. Cohen, *Karl Marx's Theory of History. Journal of Philosophy*, 79/5: 253–73.

Cole, M. (1996). *Cultural Psychology: A Once and Future Discipline*. Cambridge, Mass.: Belknap/Harvard University Press.

Conn, R. (2002). 'Developing software engineers at the C-130J software factory.' *IEEE Software* (Sept.–Oct.): 25–9.

Conradi, R., and Fuggetta, A. (2002). 'Improving software process improvement.' *IEEE Software* (July–Aug.): 92–9.

Cooper, D. J., Hinings, C. R., Greenwood, R., and Brown, J. L. (1996). 'Sedimentation and transformation in organizational change: the case of Canadian law firms.' *Organization Studies*, 17/4: 623–47.

Couger, J. D., and O'Callaghan, R. (1994). 'Comparing the motivation of Spanish and Finnish computer personnel with those of the United States.' *European Journal of Information Systems*, 3/4: 285–301.

Craig, T. (1995). 'Achieving innovation through bureaucracy: lessons from the Japanese brewing industry.' *California Management Review*, 38/1: 8–36.

Crocca, W. T. (1992). 'Review of *Japan's Software Factories: A Challenge to U.S. Management.' Administrative Science Quarterly*, 37/4: 670–4.

Crosby, P. B. (1979). *Quality is Free*. New York: McGraw-Hill.

Cusumano, M. A. (1991). *Japan's Software Factories: A Challenge to U.S. Management*. New York: Oxford University Press.

—— (2000). ' "Made in India": a new sign of software quality.' *Computerworld* (29 Feb.): 36.

Damanpour, Fariborz (1991). 'Organizational innovation.' *Academy of Management Journal*, 34: 555–91.

Dannefer, D. (1984). 'Adult development and social theory: a paradigmatic reappraisal.' *American Sociological Review*, 49: 100–16.

DeMarco, T., and Lister, T. (1987). *Peopleware: Productive Projects and Teams*. New York: Dorset.

Derber, C. (1982). *Professionals as Workers: Mental Labor in Advanced Capitalism*. Boston: G. K. Hall & Co.

Dewey, J. (1930). *Individualism Old and New*. New York: Minton, Balch & Co.

—— (1939). 'The individual in the new society.' In J. Ratner (ed.), *Intelligence in the Modern World: John Dewey's Philosophy*. New York: Random House: 405–33.

Dosi, G. (1996). 'The contribution of economic theory to the understanding of a knowledge-based economy.' In *Employment and Growth in the Knowledge-Based Economy*. Paris: Organization of Economic Cooperation and Development: 81–94.

Eisenhardt, K. M., and Tabrizzi, B. N. (1995). 'Accelerating adaptive processes: product innovation in the global computer industry.' *Administrative Science Quarterly*, 40/1: 84–111.

Elias, N. (1998). *On Civilization, Power, and Knowledge: Selected Writings*, ed. S. Mennell and J. Goudsblou. Chicago: University of Chicago Press.

—— (2000). *The Civilizing Process*. Malden, Mass.: Blackwell.

Engels, F. (1978). 'Socialism: utopian and scientific.' In R. C. Tucker (ed.), *The Marx-Engels Reader*. 2nd edn. New York: Norton: 683–717.

Engeström, Y. (1987). *Learning by Expanding: An Activity-Theoretical Approach to Developmental Research*. Helsinki: Orienta-Konsultit.

Engeström, Y. (1990). *Learning, Working and Imagining: Twelve Studies in Activity Theory*. Helsinki: Orienta-Konsultit.

—— (1999). 'Situated learning at the threshold of the new millennium.' In J. Bliss, R. Säljö, and P. Light (eds.), *Learning Sites: Social and Technological Resources for Learning*. Amsterdam: Pergamon.

—— Miettinin, R., and Punamaki, R.-L. (eds.) (1999). *Perspectives on Activity Theory*. Cambridge: Cambridge University Press.

Erez, M., and Earley, P. C. (1993). *Culture, Self-Identity, and Work*. New York: Oxford University Press.

Fiske, A. P., Kitayama, S., Markus, H. R., and Nisbett, R. E. (1998). 'The cultural matrix of social psychology.' In D. T. Gilbert, S. T. Fiske, and G. Lindzey (eds.), *The Handbook of Social Psychology*. 4th edn. Boston: McGraw-Hill: 915–81.

Freidson, E. (2001). *Professionalism: The Third Logic*. Cambridge: Polity.

Friedman, A. L., and Cornford, D. S. (1989). *Computer Systems Development: History, Organization and Implementation*. Chichester: John Wiley & Sons.

Galbraith, J. R. (1977). *Organization Design*. Reading, Mass.: Addison-Wesley.

Gibbs, G. G. (1994). 'Software's chronic crisis.' *Scientific American* (Sept.): 86–92.

Gibson, C. D., and Earley, P. C. (n.d.). 'Work-team performance motivated by collective thought: the structure and function of group efficacy.' Unpublished, University of Southern California.

Giddens, A. (1979). *Central Problems in Social Theory*. Berkeley and Los Angeles: University of California Press.

Goldstein, D. K., and Rockart, J. F. (1984). 'An examination of work-related correlates of job satisfaction in programmer/analysts.' *MIS Quarterly*, 8/2: 103–15.

Gordon, R. W., and Simon, W. H. (1992). 'The redemption of professionalism?' In R. L. Nelson, D. M. Trubek, and R. L. Solomon (eds.), *Lawyers' Ideals/Lawyers' Practice: Transformations in the American Legal Profession*. Ithaca, NY: Cornell University Press.

Gouldner, A. W. (1954). *Patterns of Industrial Bureaucracy*. New York: Free Press.

—— (1957). 'Cosmopolitans and locals: toward an analysis of latent social roles.' *Administrative Science Quarterly*, 2/3: 281–306.

Gramsci, A. (1971). *Selections from the Prison Notebooks*. New York: International Publishers.

Green, G., and Hevner, A. R. (1999). 'Perceived control of software developers and its impact on the successful diffusion of information technology.' Carnegie Mellon University, Software Engineering Institute, Special Report CMU/SEI-98-SR-013.

Greenbaum, J. M. (1979). *In the Name of Efficiency*. Philadelphia: Temple University Press.

Griffin, A., and Hauser, J. R. (1992). 'Patterns of communication among marketing, engineering and manufacturing: a comparison between two new product teams.' *Management Science*, 38/3: 360–73.

Griffin, P., and Cole, M. (1984). 'Current activity for the future: the Zo-Ped.' In B. Rogoff and J. V. Wertsch (eds.), *Children's Learning in the 'Zone of Proximal Development.'* New Directions for Child Development 23. San Francisco: Jossey-Bass: 45–63.

Griss, M. L. (1993). 'Software reuse: from library to factory.' *IBM Systems Journal*, 32/4: 548–66.

Hackman, J. R., and Oldham, G. R. (1980). *Work Redesign*. Reading, Mass.: Addison-Wesley.

Harter, D. E., Krishnan, M. S., Slaughter, S. A. (2000). 'Effects of process maturity on quality, cycle time, and effort in software development.' *Management Science*, 46/4: 451–66.

Henderson, J., and Lee, S. (1992). 'Managing I/S design teams: a control theories perspective.' *Management Science*, 38/6: 757–76.

Herbsleb, J., Zubrow, D., Goldenson, D., Hayes, W., and Paulk, M. (1997). 'Software quality and the Capability Maturity Model.' *Communication of the ACM*, 40/6: 30–40.

Hernandez, M., and Iyengar, S. S. (2001). 'What drives whom? A cultural perspective on human agency.' *Social Cognition*, 19/3: 269–94.

Hirschhorn, L. (1997). *Reworking Authority*. Cambridge, Mass.: MIT Press.

Hoch, D. J., Roeding, C. R., Purkert, G., and Linder, S. K., (2000). *Secrets of Software Success*. Boston: Harvard Business School Press.

Holt, G. R., and Morris, A. W. (1993). 'Activity theory and the analysis of organizations.' *Human Organization*, 52/1: 97–109.

Humphrey, W. S. (2002). 'Three process perspectives: organizations, teams, and people.' *Annals of Software Engineering*, 14: 39–72.

Hyman, R. (1987). 'Strategy or structure? Capital, labour and control.' *Work, Employment and Society*, 1/1: 25–55.

Jackson, S. E., and Schuler, R. S. (1985). 'A meta-analysis and conceptual critique of research on role ambiguity and role conflict in work settings.' *Organizational Behavior and Human Decision Processes*, 36: 17–78.

Jelinek, M., and Schoonhoven, C. B. (1993). *The Innovation Marathon*. San Francisco: Jossey-Bass.

Jones, C. (2002). 'Defense software development in evolution.' *CrossTalk* (Nov.): 26–9.

Kagitcibasi, C. (1997). 'Individualism and collectivism.' In J. W. Berry, M. H. Segall, and C. Kagitcibasi (eds.), *Handbook of Cross-Cultural Psychology*. Needham Heights, Mass.: Allyn & Bacon: 1–49.

Kahn, R., Wolfe, D., Quinn, R., Snoek, J. D., and Rosenthal, R. (1964). *Organizational Stress: Studies in Role Conflict and Role Ambiguity*. New York: John Wiley and Sons.

Kenney, M., and Florida, R. (1993). *Beyond Mass Production: The Japanese System and its Transfer to the U.S.* New York: Oxford University Press.

King, R. C., and Sethi, V. (1998). 'The impact of socialization on the role adjustment of information system professionals.' *Journal of Management Information Systems*, 14/1: 195–217.

Kogut, Bruce, and Metiu, Anca (2001). 'Open-source software development and distributed innovation.' *Oxford Review of Economic Policy*, 17: 248–64.

Kohn, M. L., and Schooler, C. (1983). *Work and Personality*. Norwood, NJ: Ablex.

Kraft, P. (1977). *Programmers and Managers: The Routinization of Computer Programming in the United States*. New York: Springer Verlag.

Krishnan, M. S., Kriebel, C. H., Kekre, S., and Mukhopadhyay, T. (2000). 'Productivity and quality in software products.' *Management Science*, 46/6: 745–59.

Kunda, G. (1992). *Engineering Culture: Control and Commitment in a High-Tech Corporation*. Philadelphia: Temple University Press.

Langer, E. (1983). *The Psychology of Control*. Beverly Hills, Calif.: Sage.

Lave, J. (1988). *Cognition in Practice*. New York: Cambridge University Press.

—— (1993). 'The practice of learning.' In S. Chaiklin and J. Lave (eds.), *Understanding Practice: Perspectives and Activity and Context*. New York: Cambridge University Press: 3–35.

—— (2001). 'Lines on social practice theory.' Unpublished manuscript, UC Berkeley.

Lawrence, P. R., and Lorsch, J. W. (1967). *Organization and Environment: Managing Differentiation and Integration*. Boston: Harvard University Graduate School of Business Administration.

Leont'ev, A. N. (1978). *Activity, Consciousness, and Personality*. Englewood Cliffs, NJ: Prentice-Hall.

Levine, A., and Wright, E. (1980). 'Rationality and class struggle.' *New Left Review*, 123: 47–68.

Lieberman, H., and Fry, C. (2001). 'Will software ever work?' *Communications of the ACM*, 44/3: 122–4.

Lillkrank, P. (2003). 'The quality of standard, routine and nonroutine processes.' *Organization Studies*, 24/2: 215–33.

Livingston, J. (2000). 'The strange career of the "social self." ' *Radical History Review*, 76: 53–79.

Luria, A. R. (1976). *Cognitive Development: Its Cultural and Social Foundations*. Cambridge, Mass.: Harvard University Press.

Lynn, L. H. (1991). 'Assembly line software development.' *Sloan Management Review*, 88:

McKinlay, J. B., and Arches, J. (1985). 'Toward the proletarianization of physicians.' *International Journal of Health Services*, 15/2: 161–95.

March, J., and Simon, H. (1958). *Organizations*. New York: Wiley.

Markus, H. R., and Kitayama, S. (1991). 'Culture and the self: implications for cognition, emotion, and motivation.' *Psychological Review*, 98: 224–53.

Marx, K. (1955). *The Poverty of Philosophy*. Moscow: Progress. Online version consulted 27 Dec. 2004 at www.marxists.org/archive/marx/works/1847/poverty-philosophy/ch026.htm.

—— (1973). *Grundrisse*. Harmondsworth: Penguin Books.

—— (1975). *Karl Marx: Early Writings*. New York: Vintage.

—— (1977). *Capital*. Vol. i. New York: Vintage.

—— and Engels, F. (1959). 'The Communist Manifesto.' In L. S. Feuer (ed.), *Marx and Engels: Basic Writings on Politics and Philosophy*. New York: Anchor: 1–41.

Mathieson, K. (1991). 'Predicting user intentions: comparing the technology acceptance model with the theory of planned behavior.' *Information Systems Research*, 2/3: 173–91.

Meyer, J. W., and Rowan, B. (1977). 'Institutionalized organizations: formal structure as myth and ceremony.' *American Journal of Sociology*, 83: 340–63.

Mintzberg, H. (1979). *The Structuring of Organizations: A Synthesis of the Research*. Englewood Cliffs, NJ: Prentice-Hall.

Mowery, D. C. (ed.) (1996). *The International Computer Software Industry*. New York: Oxford University Press.

Nardi, B. A. (1996). 'Studying context: a comparison of activity theory, situated action models, and distributed cognition.' In B. A. Nardi (ed.), *Context and Consciousness: Activity Theory and Human–Computer Interaction*. Cambridge, Mass.: MIT Press: 69–102.

Ngwenyama, O., and Nielson, P. A. (2003). 'Competing values in software process improvement: an assumption analysis of CMM from an organizational culture perspective.' *IEEE Transactions on Engineering Management*, 50/1: 100–12.

Organ, D. W., and Green, C. N. (1981). 'The effects of formalization on professional involvement: a compensatory process approach.' *Administrative Science Quarterly*, 26: 237–52.

Oyserman, D., Coon, H. M., and Kemmelmeier, M. (2002). 'Rethinking individualism and collectivism: evaluation of theoretical assumptions and meta-analyses.' *Psychological Bulletin*, 126/1: 3–73.

Paulk, M. C. (1995). 'The evolution of SEI's Capability Maturity Model for Software.' *Software Process: Improvement and Practice*, 1: 3–15.

—— Weber, Charles V., Garcia, Sonnne M., Chrissis, Mary Beth, and Bush, Marilyn W. (1993). 'Key practices of the capability maturity model, version 1.1.' Software Engineering Institute, CMU/SEI-93-TR-25, DTIC No. ADA263432, Feb.

Pinnington, A., and Morris, T. (2003). 'Archetype change in professional organizations: survey evidence from large law firms.' *British Journal of Management*, 14/1: 85–99.

Podsakoff, P. M., Williams, L. J., and Todor, W. T. (1986). 'Effects of organizational formalization on alienation of professionals and non-professionals.' *Academy of Management Journal*, 29/4: 820–31.

Rasch, R. H., and Tosi, H. L. (1992). 'Factors affecting software developers' performance: an integrated approach.' *MIS Quarterly* (Sept.): 395–413.

Rizzo, J. R., House, R. J., and Lirtzman, S. I. (1970). 'Role conflict and ambiguity in complex organizations.' *Administrative Science Quarterly*, 15: 150–63.

Sacks, M. (1994). *On-the-Job Learning in the Software Industry*. Westport, Conn.: Quorum.

Sagie, A. (1997). 'Leader direction and employee participation in decision-making: contradictory or compatible practices?' *Applied Psychology: An International Review*, 46: 387–416.

Schneider, B. (1987). 'The people make the place.' *Personnel Psychology*, 40: 437–54.

Schulmeyer, G. G. (1998). 'Standardization of software quality assurance: where is it all going?' In G. G. Schulmeyer and J. I. McManus (eds.), *Handbook of Software Quality Assurance*. Upper Saddle River, NJ: Prentice Hall: 61–90.

Smith, P. G., and Reinertsen, D. G. (1991). *Developing Products in Half the Time*. New York: Van Nostrand.

Software Engineering Institute (2002). 'Process maturity profile of the software community, 2002 mid-year update.' Download from www.sei.cmu.edu.

—— (2004). 'Process maturity profile software CMM, 2004 mid-year.' Download from www.sei.cmu.edu.

Sohn-Rethel, A. (1978). *Intellectual and Manual Labour: A Critique of Epistemology*. Atlantic Highlands, NJ: Humanities Press.

Spenner, K. I. (1990). 'Skill: meanings, methods, measures.' *Work and Occupations*, 17: 399–421.

Standish Group (1994). Chaos study report at www.standishgroup.com.

Steinmuller, W. E. (1996). 'The U.S. software industry: An analysis and interpretive history.' In D. C. Mowery (ed.), *The International Computer Software Industry*. New York: Oxford University Press: 15–52.

Stone, C. A. (1993). 'What is missing in the metaphor of scaffolding?' In E. A. Forman, N. Minick, and C. A. Stone (eds.), *Contexts for Learning: Sociocultural Dynamics in Children's Development*. New York: Oxford University Press: 169–83.

Strauss, A. L., Fagerhaugh, S., Suczek, B., and Wiener, C. (1985). *Social Organization of Medical Work*. Chicago: University of Chicago Press.

Suchman, L. (1987). *Plans and Situated Actions*. Cambridge: Cambridge University Press.

Swanson, K., McComb, D., Smith, J., and McCubbrey, D. (1991). 'The application software factory: applying Total Quality Techniques to systems development.' *MIS Quarterly* (Dec.): 567–79.

Tannenbaum, A. S. (ed.) (1968). *Control in Organizations*. New York: McGraw-Hill.

Taylor, C. (1989). *The Sources of the Self*. Cambridge: Cambridge University Press.

Taylor, S., and Todd, P. (1995). 'Understanding information technology usage: a test of competing models.' *Information Systems Research*, 6/2: 144–76.

Thompson, P. (1989). *The Nature of Work: An Introduction to Debates on the Labour Process*. London: Macmillan.

Triandis, H. C., and Gelfand, M. J. (1998). 'Converging measurement of horizontal and vertical individualism and collectivism.' *Journal of Personality and Social Psychology*, 74/1: 118–28.

—— and Suh, E. M. (2002). 'Cultural influences on personality.' *Annual Review of Psychology*, 53: 133–60.

—— Leung, K., Villareal, M., and Clack, F. L. (1985). 'Allocentric versus idiocentric tendencies: convergent and discriminant validation.' *Journal of Personality Psychology*, 19: 395–415.

van der Pijl, K. (1998). *Transnational Classes and International Relations*. London: Routledge.

Van Iterson, A., Mastenbroek, W., Newton, T., and Smith, D. (eds.) (2002). *The Civilized Organization: Norbert Elias and the Future of Organization Studies*. Philadelphia: John Benjamins.

Van Maanen, J., and Barley, S. R. (1984). 'Occupational communities: culture and control in organizations.' *Research in Organizational Behavior*, 6: 287–365.

Vygotsky, L. S. (1962). *Thought and Language*. Cambridge, Mass.: MIT Press.

—— (1978). *Mind in Society*. Cambridge, Mass.: Harvard University Press.

Weber, H. (ed.) (1997). *The Software Factory Challenge*. Amsterdam: IOS Press.

Wertsch, J. V. (ed.) (1979). *The Concept of Activity in Soviet Psychology*. Armonk, NY: M. E. Sharp.

—— Tulviste, P., and Hagstrom, F. (1993). 'A sociocultural approach to agency.' In E. A. Forman, N. Minick, and C. A. Stone (eds.), *Contexts for Learning: Sociocultural Dynamics in Children's Development*. New York: Oxford University Press: 136–56.

Wheelwright, S. C., and Clark, K. B. (1992). *Revolutionizing Product Development*. New York: Free Press.

Wood, D., Bruner, J., and Ross, G. (1976). 'The role of tutoring in problem-solving.' *Journal of Child Psychiatry and Psychology*, 17: 89–100.

Wright, E. O., Levine, A., and Sober, E. (1992). *Reconstructing Marxism: Essays on Explanation and the Theory of History*. London: Verso.

Yates, J., and Orlikowski, W. J. (1992). 'Genres of organizational communication: a structurational approach to studying communication and media.' *Academy of Management Review*, 17/2: 299–323.

Notes

1. Gordon and Simon (1992: 234).
2. The literature on professionals and the mutations of professional work is enormous. An excellent entry point is provided by Eliot Freidson (2001).
3. e.g. McKinlay and Arches (1985); Derber (1982).
4. Greenbaum (1979: 64–5).
5. Gibbs (1994); Lieberman and Fry (2001); Standish (1994).
6. Harter et al. (2000); Clark (1999); Cusumano (2000).
7. On the concept of the software factory and the associated debates, see Cusumano (1991); Swanson et al. (1991); Griss (1993): Weber (1997); Friedman and Cornford (1989).
8. The general argument for this position is articulated in the 'contingency theory' branch of organization studies—see Burns and Stalker (1961); Lawrence and Lorsch (1967); Galbraith (1977); Mintzberg (1979). The argument has been applied in the software development arena by authors such as Crocca (1992); Bach (1994, 1995); Conradi and Fuggetta (2002); Lynn (1991); Ngwenyama and Nielson (2003).
9. Marx (1973, 1977); Engels (1978).
10. Markus and Kitayama (1991).
11. Marx, following Hegel, takes contradictions as real—out there, in objective, independent reality—rather than purely notional, in the mind of the observer. Contradiction here is a relation between two real forces, not merely a logical relation between two propositions. As such, contradictions are the source of change.
12. Marx (1977: appendix); Thompson (1989); Bottomore (1983: 267–70).
13. Engels (1978). My reading of Marx is based on G. A. Cohen's (1978) presentation. Cohen's version has been criticized by, amongst others, Levine and Wright (1980) and Cohen (1982); see G. A. Cohen's (1988) reply, also Wright et al. (1992). This essay takes G. A. Cohen's interpretation from the general societal plane into the production process.
14. e.g. Marx (1973: 705; 1977: 1024).

15. See also van der Pijl (1998); Engels (1978).
16. Engels (1978: 702).
17. Marx (1977: ch. 13).
18. Marx (1977: 458); Gramsci (1971: 201–2).
19. Markus and Kitayama (1991).
20. Marx (1977: 447).
21. Marx and Engels (1959); Marx (1955).
22. Marx (1973: 704–6).
23. Hyman (1987).
24. Adler (2001).
25. See Cohen (1978); Levine and Wright (1980).
26. Humphrey (2002).
27. Jones (2002).
28. Paulk (1995: 11).
29. Crosby (1979); see Humphrey (2002); a bibliography on the CMM is available at www.sei.cmu.edu/docs/biblio.pdf.
30. Clark (1999).
31. Harter et al. (2000). Other multi-organization studies include Krishnan et al. (2000); Herbsleb et al. (1997).
32. For some observers, the bureaucratizing path of the CMM is a dead end, and the way forward is shown by the open-source movement and 'agile' methods. But close examination shows that these approaches are only feasible in narrow segments of the software industry. Open source is feasible only where interfaces can be standardized and systems can be modularized (Kogut and Metiu 2001); and its cost-effectiveness remains unproven. Agile methods have proven appropriate only where systems and development teams are small, where the customers and users are available for frequent consultation, and where requirements and the environment are particularly volatile—see Boehm and Turner (2003).
33. Autonomy is often presented as a key motivating characteristic of jobs (Hackman and Oldham 1980). A similar assumption underlies Ajzen's (1991) theory of planned behavior, with its focus on 'perceived behavioral control.' In labor process theory and the broader field of sociology of work too, autonomy is one of the two defining dimensions of skilled work, alongside complexity (see Braverman 1974; Spenner 1990). In the Information Systems field, a considerable body of research has focused on the role of perceived control and autonomy as determinants of the use of, and satisfaction with, new techniques and technologies (see for example Baronas and Louis 1988; Mathieson 1991; Taylor and Todd 1995; Henderson and Lee 1992; Green and Hevner 1999). This emphasis on autonomy seems particularly appropriate for programmers, who typically manifest low need for social interaction (Couger and O'Callaghan 1994).
34. On the software industry and its components and major players, see Hoch et al. (2000), and Mowery (1996). Notwithstanding the growth of the personal computer market and the associated mass-market pre-packaged 'software prod-

ucts' industry, the bulk of the rapidly expanding software industry resembles GCC and its competitors in delivering 'software services'—creating fully or partly customized, large-scale systems for specific clients. In 2000, according to data provided by IDC, software services in the USA accounted for revenues of $395 billion versus $171 billion for software products. Steinmuller (1996) notes that both these industry segments are small relative to the software developed for their own use by firms and public organizations.

35. See Abbott (1988).
36. Kraft (1977: 56).
37. Adler (2001).
38. As described by Meyer and Rowan (1977).
39. Using Marx's periodization (1977: pt. IV).
40. For discussion of the impact of process maturity on the role of another key staff function, Configuration Management, see Butler et al. (2001): many of the same conclusions apply.
41. See for example Sacks (1994); Lave (1988).
42. The metaphor of scaffolding refers to the temporary assistance provided by teachers/adults to students/children as they strive to accomplish a task in their 'zone of proximal development.' The metaphor was originally articulated by Wood et al. (1976). The concept of 'zone of proximal development' is one of Vygotsky's best-known contributions: see Griffin and Cole (1984).
43. In offering software development organizations a prescription for their future that was based on lessons drawn from the industry's past, the CMM functioned in precisely the 'proleptic' manner described by Cole (1996: 183 ff.).
44. This concern echoed critiques of the 'top-down' nature of the scaffolding metaphor: see Stone (1993); Butler (1998).
45. See Wheelwright and Clark (1992); Smith and Reinertsen (1991).
46. Bandura (1997).
47. On adult socialization, see e.g. Kohn and Schooler (1983); and see Conn (2002) for discussion of the process of developer socialization in another software factory. On 'attraction-selection-attrition,' see Schneider (1987).
48. Gouldner (1957); Van Maanen and Barley (1984).
49. See Triandis and Gelfand (1998).
50. An alternative—more provocative but also more confusing—formulation would be to argue that individualism and collectivism are orthogonal constructs and the new developers are high on both: see discussion in Oyserman et al. (2002: 8), and other contributors to that issue; also Kagitcibasi (1997).
51. This shallow view has persisted notwithstanding the strong case made by Tannenbaum's work on the 'control graph'—see, e.g., Tannenbaum (1968); more recently, Henderson and Lee (1992).
52. On the social-self thesis and other-directedness, see Livingston (2000).
53. See Cohen (1974).

54. Engeström (1987, 1990); M. Cole (1996); Vygotsky (1962, 1978); Luria (1976); Leont'ev (1978). Useful overviews of CHAT and discussion of its variants include: Engeström et al. (1999); Chaiklin et al. (1999); Wertsch (1979); Blackler (1993); Holt and Morris (1993).
55. Leont'ev (1978).
56. It is here that my presentation differs from Engeström: Engeström distinguishes rules and division of labor from community itself, whereas I have subsumed them under the one broader category. This eases the burden of exposition.
57. Marx (1973: 85).
58. Wood et al. (1976).

6

Health Care Organizations as Collaborative Learning Communities

Michael Maccoby

The troubling issues surrounding health care in the USA are well known: rising costs, 45 million people without insurance and increasing, variability in diagnosis and treatment, avoidable mistakes that cause harm to the patient. Solving these problems is proving extremely difficult. Many analyses focus on technical and financial aspects of the system; but the most difficult and most deeply rooted source of resistance to change lies in the structure, culture, and values of the medical profession. To a large degree, these issues are symptoms of a medical mode of production that is increasingly maladapted to the explosion of knowledge and the changing health care economy. The danger for the future of medicine is that in an effort to cut costs and improve quality of treatment, the craft mode of production will be replaced by a manufacturing mode of production, with a bureaucratic organization framework that makes the physician into a kind of factory worker. Based on research in health care organizations attempting to develop a new model, we argue that the most viable solution lies not in further bureaucratic control but in the development of collaborative processes and relations among health care providers and the creation of learning organizations.

The problem: the craft–bureaucracy conflict in medical delivery

We view health care as a total system, taking an anthropological perspective focused on its changing mode of production. A mode of production refers not only to the use of tools; it describes a productive system of values, beliefs, rules, and relationships in organizations. It may change over time due to new technology, knowledge, and innovations. For example, agriculture was characterized by a craft mode of production in 1840, when over 70 per cent of the US workforce tilled the soil using methods that had not radically changed for centuries. Today, however, agriculture is highly mechanized and organized in large farms run by agribusinesses. The mode of production, including work roles and relationships, has been transformed. In the process, most independent craft farmers fought the change as long as they could.

Traditionally, medicine has been much like a craft, organized like a cottage industry with sole proprietors and small partnerships, based on the physician's reputation and personal relationships with colleagues and patients within a guildlike structure that determines membership and monopolizes functions. There are, to be sure, some important differences: unlike crafts, medicine depends on a widely shared, relatively open and scientific knowledge base, imparted in formalized, socialized training rather than in apprenticeship. Yet the parallels are striking. The ideal leadership model, as with other crafts, is the most accomplished practitioner who represents the interests of his peers. The physician–patient relationship has depended on the patient's trust of the doctor's expertise and caring attitude. For centuries, the technology has been hand tools—stethoscope, scalpel, needles, etc.—and a limited number of useful medicines. The model of care has been biomedical with a strong dose of positive transference to the doctor as a parental figure to cement trust and strengthen a placebo effect that aids natural self-healing.

Historical studies have shown that the model of the autonomous professional physician in America has been deeply institutionalized through a long process, starting in the nineteenth century, driven in part by the need for doctors to establish a solid basis of prestige to replace the image of unregulated quackery of the nineteenth century. The establishment of medical education and licensing was crucial to creating a sense both among the public and among physicians themselves that they had a solid basis of scientific knowledge and professional ethics that warranted respect and financial reward. The American Medical Association during the twentieth century came to focus primarily on the maintenance of this professional autonomy, repeatedly fighting off regulatory incursions from the government.[1] Although physicians now use more complex tools, many remain in a kind of cottage industry type of organization. Even when specialists are located in academic health centers, these become like feudal kingdoms run by the university's vice president for health affairs.

Two major factors have worked to undermine this model in the last few decades. Most visible has been the escalating crisis of health care costs, which has given strength to cost-control efforts such as HMOs and medical protocols managed by insurance companies. The second is the growing sophistication and assertiveness of patients, fueled by an explosion of information available on the internet and finding an explosive outlet in medical malpractice claims, which has weakened doctors' claims to authority based on occult knowledge. Together, these have weakened the autonomy and prestige of physicians to the point that they find themselves increasingly constrained by external rules, forced to conform to regulated procedures, and drawn into group rather than individual practices.

Following the example of other industries, many health care organizations have moved towards a manufacturing mode of production based on bureaucratic control. The dominant form of the new regulation has been one of formal rule making—though the rule makers have been primarily large private insurance companies rather than government. Doctors increasingly have to go 'by the book' both to guarantee insurance reimbursements and to reduce exposure to malpractice suits. Physicians, less able to manage the complex regulatory systems or to assume the growing risks on their own, have been drawn to the protection of large hospitals and groups which further organize and rationalize the bureaucratic forces. Current trends increasingly turn physicians into employees in a bureaucracy or in 'focused factories' that specialize in a particular type of treatment. The physician becomes a 'provider' or else a manager who is engaged more in monitoring than mentoring and must ensure business profitability.

To be sure, there have been useful learnings from manufacturing, particularly quality management which can be used to address variability in practice and supply management. The use of statistical process control and the development of informatics show promise of both improving outcomes by constructing clinical pathways and controlling costs. However, physicians tend to resist any further limitation of their freedom to make medical decisions. Unless they are personally involved in decreasing variability, they may see these efforts as 'cookbook medicine' which does not take into account unique patient needs.

In recent years there has been criticism of this bureaucratic model from several directions. Many physicians tend to look backwards with nostalgia to the earlier era of individual autonomy. Patient care advocates sometimes do the same, citing the loss of personal relationships which can in themselves facilitate healing. A 2001 Harris Poll reports that 61 per cent of Americans believe that managed care has decreased the time doctors spend with patients.[2]

But others have moved in a different direction, laying emphasis on the increasing need for coordination among multiple specialties: the explosion of medical information and technology means that good health care has already largely gone beyond the capabilities of individual physicians and has become a matter of interdependent knowledge work. Coordination and communication among specialties, functions, and roles in hospitals plays a very large and generally unrecognized role in health care quality outcomes. Furthermore, due to the barriers of organizational boundaries, status, and expertise that divide health care providers from each other, the relationships that facilitate the coordination of interdependent work are particularly hard to achieve in health care. Studies have shown that communication problems are at the root of many medical errors; a review of the evidence by the Agency for Healthcare Research and Quality concludes:

Researchers now believe that most medical errors cannot be prevented by perfecting the technical work of individual doctors, nurses, or pharmacists. Improving patient safety often involves the coordinated efforts of multiple members of the health care team.[3]

From this perspective the problem for the health care system is neither to reassert the autonomy of the individual physician nor simply to control it through more detailed bureaucratic rule making; neither the craft nor the manufacturing model is appropriate to the task. Medical service delivery requires a novel organizational form based on a network of collaborative relations—in the language of this volume, a collaborative community capable of collective learning. This requires an orientation different from both the main existing alternatives, of hospital bureaucracy and physician craft autonomy—one that brings physicians and hospitals into a collaborative partnership coordinated through strong process discipline rather than tight bureaucratic control.

We know of no full-fledged models of this kind of collaborative practice in health care. The Mayo Clinic, which we will discuss shortly, provides some important learnings, but has not shown the capacity to efficiently manage large-scale systems. The difficulty is not just to get physicians to work together, though this can be difficult enough. A collaborative system in the sense of this volume must combine dialogue and involvement with process discipline and standardization on a large scale, in order to bring the best care to the largest number of patients. It must be based neither in a bureaucratic logic nor a craft logic, but in a third orientation that combines aspects of both (see Fig. 6.1).

Our research on best examples of health care practice shows the difficulty of this move, as well as bringing out aspects of current practice that show promise for the future.

Studying health care practice

In 1999 and 2000 I led a study, under the auspices of the Robert Wood Johnson Foundation, of not-for-profit health care organizations and academic health centers considered among the best in the country. We aimed to understand their leadership visions and implementation strategies,

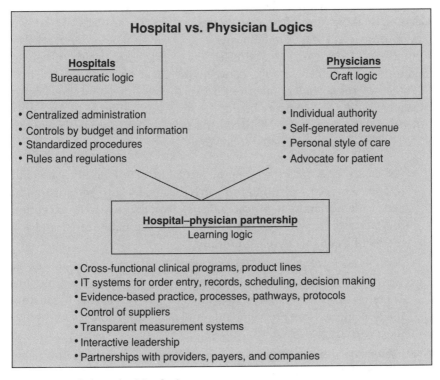

Fig. 6.1 Hospital vs. physician logics

and to elicit models of good organizational practice that could be used by other health care organizations.[4]

We began with two assumptions. The first was that organizations must be understood as social systems made up of people with their own values and purposes. To change a social system, it is not sufficient to install new technology and processes: leaders must understand how to motivate people to achieve the organization's mission. The second assumption was that in an ideal health care system, physicians should be able to be productive and creative and to develop trusting relationships with their patients. Without this freedom, the most qualified young people will go into professions other than medicine, where they can better realize their potential.

Our initial research included in-depth interviews with physician-leaders in order to understand their shared values or social character. We wanted to learn what kind of a health system they would consider ideal. Their responses largely gravitated towards nostalgia for a vanished age of craftlike autonomy, expressed as concern about the deterioration of the physician's professional freedom and ability to develop relations of trust with patients. However, they also believed that autonomy in medical decision making should be discouraged when the answers are known and routine (e.g. Class I guidelines).

In 1999, I led a workshop with leaders of academic health centers to determine the perceived gaps between the ideal and current practice. Eighteen of these leaders filled out a gap survey I prepared, and which was reviewed by the advisory board; the results are reported in Appendix 6.1 below. The largest gaps between the ideal and current practice indicated by these leaders were the following:

- *Patient service as the highest priority* was an ideal universally stated but seldom achieved. We found this gap indicated by both administration and academic chairs at all academic health centers with the exception of Mayo Clinic, which is organized to put the patient first and is a model of a collaborative community.

- *All of us are involved in continuously improving the cost and quality of our services* is a gap that reflects the prevailing craft mode of production. There is, in general, significant variability by physicians in treating the same presenting problem and physicians don't take responsibility for controlling costs.

- *Information systems support physician decision making* is a gap now being addressed by all the health centers we studied. But not all have built in the informatics that supports learning from best practice. (A notable positive model has been developed at Vanderbilt University Medical Center.)

- *Individual performance is evaluated regularly.* This again reflects the craft model. In general, physicians don't like to evaluate colleagues. However, we found some department chairs who have instituted evaluation systems based essentially on clinical and research productivity in economic terms. Some faculty members object to it, but it appears to result in improved productivity in these areas. However, these evaluations do not include the result of patient care and degree of collaboration among specialists.

- *Leaders develop relationships of trust.* A number of factors cause the trust gap. As health care leaders pressure their organizations to cut costs and improve performance, distrust increases. A large part of the problem has to do with a lack of dialogue between leaders and their organizations about the need for change and how best to achieve it. Such a dialogue must increase transparency about the flow of money since many physicians at academic health centers distrust the hospital system that collects revenue and allocates costs.

- *Leaders communicate a vision.* Even leaders indicated this was a gap. Their subordinates indicated an even larger gap. People want to know what the organization is trying to become and how they fit in this vision. Given the uncertainty in health care, people, especially the middle managers and chairs, want the leader not only to set a clear course but to explain the logic underlying it and help them to understand the meaning of change for them. If sacrifice is required, they need to know why this will pay off in the long run.[5]

In 1999, we made study trips to the University of Rochester Medical Center, Intermountain Health Care, Penn State Geisinger, Aetna US Health Care Southeastern Region, University of Michigan Medical Center, Shands-University of Florida, and Mayo Clinic, Rochester, Minnesota. In 2000, study trips were made to Scripps Health, Mayo Clinic, Scottsdale, Arizona, Vanderbilt University Medical Center, and Kaiser Permanente in Oakland, California. In November 2000, we facilitated a two-day workshop in Salt Lake City with leadership teams from Mayo Clinic Scottsdale (MCS) and Intermountain Health Care (IHC). The purpose was to bring together an organization representing the best in patient-focused service in a collaborative community (MCS) with an organization in the forefront of evidence-based medicine (IHC), to facilitate learning from each other. Each admired the other for these qualities and hoped to develop them. The results, which we will discuss later, were enlightening about both the possibilities and limits of interorganizational learning.

In December 2000 we met with members of the advisory board of distinguished physicians and discussed all our findings from the two-year study. A follow-up seminar, sponsored by the Association of Academic Health Centers, took place in May 2001. This report incorporates suggestions from the participants, led by Roger Bulger, MD, president of AHC, which subsequently published our final report to the Robert Wood Johnson Foundation and sent it to all its member academic health centers.

Culture and social character

Key to our approach was the exploration of social character, grounded in the theoretical claim—elaborated elsewhere in this volume—that modal patterns of personality dynamics both result from and reciprocally define the shape of organizational cultures. 'Culture' is in effect an interplay among social norms, organizational structures, and social character; attempts to change organization without recognizing the limits of character are likely to run aground on resistance and lack of motivational capabilities.[6]

Based on social character interviews and surveys of senior physicians and graduating doctors in the medical centers we studied, we found that the dominant personality type was what we termed *expert-helper*, a variant of the craft social character.[7] The dominant value for the expert is mastery, including the need for achievement. The expert's sense of self-esteem and employment security is achieved by gaining status and professional respect. Experts find pleasure at work in their craftsmanship and recognition by their peers and superiors. They have a strong need for autonomy. At their best, experts stand for high standards of service and scientifically proven knowledge. They value professionalism, a term with roots in the Calvinist concept of professing a calling to serve. For most of the physician-experts we interviewed, the meaning of their work is not only the excellence of their performance, but also helping people.

However, at their worst, their obsessive qualities may make experts into inflexible know-it-alls. They are rooted in a system of master and apprentice, where knowledge is based on experience, at a time when knowledge is quickly out of date and competence depends on continual learning. Thus the expert's character can be a major roadblock to change. Experts want control over their functions and they resist the empowerment of others, which they see as loss of control. This has been the complaint we heard repeatedly from nurses and administrators. Physician experts want health centers and hospitals to serve them and they do not appreciate the added value of an organization over what they do as individuals. Physicians, like other experts, relate best with mentors, peers, or younger high-potential apprentices who share their values.

Some of the most innovative physician leaders we interviewed, however, had a somewhat different personality, focused not on crafts-man-like service but on creating a great organization. These leaders were typically productive narcissists, the type described by Sigmund Freud as not impressed by the status quo but 'especially suited to act as a support for others, to take on the role of leaders, and to give a fresh stimulus to cultural development or damage the established state of affairs.'[8] While the craftlike experts see health care organizations as little more than a support for their individual work, innovative leaders understand that effective organizations are essential to achieve the goal of better health care in a cost-effective manner. This difference in thinking about the organization can cause a profound disconnection between leader and physicians.

Social character and the changing mode of production

The expert physician is comfortable within a craft mode of production. His ideal organization is his own craft shop or possibly a partnership. With some frustration, he can also fit into the semi-feudal academic health center where his identity as a member of the physicians' guild is more important than his identification with the institution. In the medical center, the vice president typically takes the role of feudal lord and the chairs become the barons who determine which of their physician vassals are most favored. To carry the analogy further, the academic faculty of specialists are often viewed by the local MDs, who are primary-care physicians, as superior beings who demand tribute and referrals but show little or no respect to the peasant-like local generalists. Many of the faculty members we interviewed seek to maintain their autonomy through research grants that allow them to set up their own shops. They can justify being part of an academic organization for the prestige it provides them as professors. Because independence, prestige, and promotions depend on research grants and publications, service to patients is not their first priority.

It is also the case that physicians are selected and trained to be autonomous craftsmen. There is little teaching about interdependence or the importance of organization. Physicians are not trained to look at work from the viewpoint of nurses, pharmacists, and technicians. The image of the independent decision maker which may have made the field attractive to them is reinforced by their education.

But the rise of the manufacturing mode of production, with increased emphasis on bureaucratic rule making, puts great strains on those with an expert social character. They often find themselves in a culture clash with hospital administrators; in a general sense, this is a conflict between a craft logic of individual authority, self-generated revenue, personal style of care, and being the patient's advocate as opposed to the bureaucratic logic of centralized administration, financial controls, standardized procedures, and rules based on principles of fairness where patients are treated according to the rules.

At the same time, this tension cannot be resolved, even in theory, by developing bureaucratic physicians who follow rules and stick to their jobs. Medicine is naturally purpose driven in a way that most manufacturing organizations are not: doctors are in constant contact with the patient, who is the goal and outcome of the work process.

In effect, then, neither of the two existing models—craft or manufacturing—is adequate to the task of applying modern medical knowledge to patient care: a half-conscious search is on for some way of combining cost discipline with patient focus, and professional knowledge with consistency of processes.

The Mayo group practice: a collaborative model

The closest to the collaborative model is the group practice culture as developed, most notably, by the Mayo Clinic. The Mayo Clinic was founded a century ago by two brothers who challenged the broad trend of individual professionalism which was then growing more entrenched in American medicine; William Mayo wrote: 'It [has become] necessary to develop medicine as a cooperative science; the clinician, the specialist, and the laboratory workers uniting for the good of the patient. Individualism in medicine can no longer exist.'[9] Long before current efforts to develop integrated information systems, Mayo pioneered a medical records system that facilitated the sharing of information. The clinic was among the first to develop organized medical specialties like orthopedics and pediatrics, and the first to organize those specialties in patient-focused teams. Today the first element of their 'core principles' is:

Practice medicine as an integrated team of compassionate, multi-disciplinary phys-icians, scientists and allied health professionals who are focused on the needs of patients from our communities, regions, the nation and the world.

At Mayo, as we observed in our visits to two of the clinics,[10] the patient comes first; research and teaching are important but secondary. Research is aimed at clinical utility. Furthermore, specialists cooperate across disciplines in a way seldom seen in other academic health centers. Mayo doctors are salaried and all departments are treated as cost centers. Phys-icians can take as much time with patients as they consider necessary. And administrators at Mayo see their role as serving doctors rather than struggling with them about costs. Of all the organizations we surveyed, Mayo was the only one in which most gaps between ideal and practice were small; whereas others particularly said that they espoused but did not practice 'Patient service as the highest priority,' Mayo doctors saw them-selves as constantly striving towards this ideal with the full support of the institution and the traditions.

The Mayo case offers a glimpse into a resolution of the clash between bureaucratic-hospital logic and the craft-physician logic: one that sustains a transparent learning culture where physicians become persuaded that principles and processes are good for all stakeholders.

For health care organizations to make full use of informatics and quality processes, they must become *learning organizations* within a knowledge-service mode of production. This means that professionals will act to further organizational purposes, not in response to command and control systems, but because they have internalized shared values and operative principles. They will not see any contradiction between their autonomy and the organization's goals. For example, physicians will be convinced that by addressing variability, they will be benefitting their patients as well as the organization.

Such a system also needs to use information technology to aid physician decision making and make the patient's experience free of hassles and respon-sive to individual needs. Thus, the system requires both advanced organiza-tional design, informatics, and committed, informed professionals—nurses, administrators, and technicians as well as physicians.

Such a system will ideally become a collaborative community, where specialists work together for the patient's well-being. This contrasts to the common practice of each specialist working independently, where it becomes the patient's job to make appointments separately with different specialists who may or may not communicate with each other.

Can collaboration be generalized? Exploring the implications of the model

The next question is whether the Mayo example can serve as a change model for other medical institutions. Effective though it is, it has some limitations that have resulted in its remaining rather isolated so far and confined to particular niches. The most important limitation is that it remains grounded in academic health centers; it has not fully entered the bare-knuckled world of large-scale competition. In general it is most effective in 'boutique' situations where patient problems require intensive customized solutions. Although physician interactions go beyond the individual-craft model, they remain quite personal and small scale. Thus it seems likely that some of the lessons from the bureaucratic-manufacturing model will need to be incorporated into the collaborative Mayo approach.

This fusion, however, is not a simple matter. We were able to document two cases of interaction between the team-based Mayo model and more bureaucratic systems; these bring out some of the issues involved in developing a collaborative model of modern medical practice.

THE GEISINGER–PENN STATE MERGER

The Geisinger Clinic is explicitly modeled after Mayo and uses a systematic multidisciplinary team approach. In 1998 it attempted to merge with the Penn State Medical Center, a much more traditional medical system organized into highly autonomous 'baronies' run by powerful physician chairs. At the time Geisinger was performing extremely well, and better than Penn State, on measures of both quality and cost efficiency. Their interest in merging was to achieve greater economies of scale and to reduce duplication of technology and facilities in the Pennsylvania area. But the merger was ultimately unsuccessful, primarily because of the clash of cultures. We were able to closely observe the process, including interviewing over 120 physicians and administrators from the two organizations. We had been asked by the leadership of the nascent Penn State–Geisinger partnership to help develop a common culture based to a large extent on the collaborative learning model. As long as this model remained abstract there was strong support for it: in questionnaires and in workshops, physicians and administrators from both cultures expressed attraction to it. However, as the process began to develop in practice, the leadership groups began to split. It became clear that the Geisinger and the Penn State leaders, especially at the top levels, saw the world very differently and fundamentally mistrusted each other.

The Geisinger chairs saw themselves as placing the highest value on patient service: they emphasized that since they received a fixed salary, financial incentives did not distort their clinical practice. They could take as much time as needed with each patient. They contrasted their cooperative interdependence with their view of Penn State faculty as individualistic and careerist. They affirmed their respect for primary-care physicians and the primary–tertiary care relationship and accused the Penn State faculty of being arrogant, controlling, and self-serving.

The Penn State chairs, by contrast, described themselves as individual entrepreneurs in the best sense—open to new ideas, innovative, active participants in decision making. They viewed the team approach of Geisinger as stifling and conformist. They were convinced that their clinical care was better, although data showed clearly that in some specialties, such as coronary artery bypass operation (CABG), Geisinger results were better than theirs and achieved at a lower cost.

In many respects this conflict of world views mirrors that of the software specialists described by Adler in Chapter 5: individualist physicians, like 'hackers,' experienced the process-based discipline of collaborative teamwork as a constraint on their autonomy and ability to innovate. The software industry, however, has moved far enough for the hackers to develop a greater appreciation of the power of bringing people together systematically through collaborative processes; the medical world continues for the most part to idealize the individualist model. With this cultural framework, the Penn State physicians could not accept what they felt would be the constraints of the Mayo-Geisinger model. Although younger physicians, in a meeting we held with the departments of medicine of both groups, clearly favored close cooperation and shared leadership, the effort foundered on the inability of top leadership to work together. In the end the board of directors voted to dissolve the merger.

Penn State then went through a major crisis in which the limitations of individualist professionalism were clearly exposed. It pulled out of these difficulties by hiring a strong director who 'broke' the individual physician baronies through the strong application of bureaucratic rule making. In our terms, the organization, having proved incapable of moving to a collaborative-learning mode, took the somewhat easier step of moving to a manufacturing-bureaucratic organization of production.

THE MAYO–INTERMOUNTAIN DIALOGUE

As part of our work we also organized a discussion between the Mayo Clinic in Scottsdale (MCS) and Intermountain Health Care (IHC), a large integrated health care system that has been repeatedly rated number 1 in the nation by independent ratings agencies.[11]

On the surface the organizations are very different. Intermountain is a large integrated delivery system with a health plan. To maintain its huge market share and not-for-profit status, it must demonstrate a commitment to 'the best clinical practice' at 'the lowest appropriate cost.' Their hospital charges are 15 per cent lower than the national average. Mayo-Scottsdale, by contrast, is part of a unique academic health center in which research and teaching are vital to the mission. Compared to Intermountain, Mayo-Scottsdale is a medical boutique for episodic treatment; their charges are among the highest in the Phoenix area.

Despite these differences, these organizations appeared to have complementary competencies. Intermountain is a leader in Evidence-Based Medicine, which is a systematic process of basing care on what research says is most effective, rather than tradition or instinct. Mayo was interested in learning how Intermountain leadership went about this. Reciprocally, some of the Intermountain physicians had asked us how they could create more of a Mayo group practice, with a patient-focused cross-disciplinary culture. We thought that by bringing leaders of the two organizations together, they might learn from each other, and the CEOs of both organizations agreed this could be very useful.

What emerged from this encounter between two of the best health care organizations in the world is that they are both approaching collaborative models, but from different directions. The Intermountain leadership came from the world of bureaucratic hospitals: they are comfortable with large scale and with practices like rule-based management and performance incentives, but sought to 'reinvent' it in a way which would create greater involvement of physicians and staff. The Mayo tradition comes originally from the craft world and has remained generally within a small-group, personalized framework. They were interested in each other because both see that their approaches need to be further developed to deal with the complex interdependence on a large scale. The Mayo physicians, like the Geisinger ones, are both interested in and wary of formalized process management of the type sketched in other cases in this volume; the Intermountain leaders are interested in (and also wary of) encouraging flexible local teamwork in the place of some of their top-down rules.

These differences emerged most clearly around two issues.

- *Evidence-Based Medicine.* Intermountain is one of the leaders of this approach, which advocates the practice of medicine according to formalized clinical guidelines, based on meta-analysis of published clinical and epidemiological research. They believe that this leads both to more consistent clinical excellence, reducing the rate of medical errors, and to maximum cost-effectiveness. In the dialogue the Mayo doctors, however, expressed resistance to EBM; they pointed out that they often deal with complex health problems that require cooperation across disciplines and do not fit standardized pathways. Although some Mayo chairs have begun to address systematic variability, the physicians as a whole are not yet convinced that the scientific literature is strong enough to provide consistent answers to many situations; they trust more in their peer interactions and mutual criticism focused on the patient to maximize quality.

- *The physician–administrator relation.* At Intermountain, there is a built-in conflict between administrators and physicians: the former focus on controlling costs and quality, while the latter continue to try to maximize their individual professional autonomy within the framework of a large organization. In our interviews we found that some Intermountain physicians complained that they felt stressed and powerless, and others complained that the culture discouraged open debate. Administrators, meanwhile, complained that physicians continued to resist standardized technology and protocols. Thus despite a major effort to develop coordinated information systems, the vice president of medical research at Intermountain has publicly complained that physician resistance has often 'stymied' his efforts, and that even successful trials too often fail to spread to other parts of the system.[12] And in our gap survey, the largest gap registered was 'Our information systems support physician decision making.'

At Mayo administrators explicitly serve physicians. The positive element in this is that the focus on patient welfare is unclouded; the negative element is that there is little opportunity to create a unified set of processes that would standardize the best learnings throughout the hospital and lead to continuous improvement of the whole.

One way of putting the problem is that the Mayo approach of physician interaction and consensus works very effectively to bring together varied resources around a specific problem; on a case-by-case basis it is unmatched. The problem is to scale this capability to a larger system where learnings cannot be expected to pass by informal means. At Mayo groups rely on peer review and discussion to work out consistency of procedures; but at Intermountain, as one leader pointed out to us, a nurse may need to deal with twenty surgeons with twenty different ways of doing things, which leads to a high probability of mistakes.

Intermountain leaders in our interviews and discussions seemed to be struggling to define an approach that reconciles the need for physician involvement and commitment with the need for procedural consistency and efficiency on a large scale. They are moving, with difficulty, towards a process in which medical protocols are developed through group consensus across the system. Though this is still in a nascent stage—only three of sixty-five protocols had achieved consensus at the time of our research—it may point the way to a resolution of the tension between collaboration based on case-focused discussion and more formalized processes.

Thus the two organizations show in different ways the difficulty of making the transition to a collaborative model for the health care system as a whole. The Mayo example involves high levels of collaboration but on a small and personal scale, with much use of informal mechanisms; the Intermountain case involves large scale and an attempt to create greater involvement, but continues to struggle with the tensions between administrators and physicians. Both are in early phases of exploring the kind of process-based norms described in Chapter 1, and in trying to define a set of values that move beyond individual craft performance to a focus on collective contribution.

As a result of the dialogue between these two systems, Intermountain intends to further develop the dialogue between leaders and physicians, to increase understanding of their mission and to respond to legitimate concerns. Mayo-Scottsdale plans to develop a leadership dialogue and to design a version of Evidence-Based Medicine that fits its culture and values.

Conclusions

Is there an alternative mode of production for health care? Is there one that addresses variability, improves outcomes and cost, yet allows physicians to be creative and retains the best of the craft tradition?

The exploration of this question must begin with the recognition that health care is, in the sense developed throughout this volume, a matter of complex coordination of knowledge work. It has become rapidly more specialized, but it cannot be delivered in pieces; successful care depends on the interaction of experts with different perspectives. Furthermore, it equally involves the production of *solutions*: the combination of knowledge aims not to create new inventions, but to resolve specific problems of unique patients. Indeed, it goes beyond this to involve communities: health involves the behaviors not just of individuals but of groups. Thus it ultimately requires an expansion from a purely biomedical focus—complex as that is—to the level of biopsychosocial and epidemiological ecosystems.

These are the conditions above all that require the kind of formalized norms and systems that we refer to as collaborative community, providing the basis of understanding and trust to enable highly differentiated specialists to work together efficiently and reliably. So far the medical system is still largely stuck in the traditional craft mode centered on individual professionals. The major alternative is bureaucratic control through large hospitals and insurance companies. The broad scene is one of a tug-of-war between these two logics, but neither is in fact adequate to deal with a mode of production founded on complex knowledge and solutions.

The Mayo case gets us part-way to an image of what a collaborative community would look like in health care, but not the whole way: it has not yet shown a capability for large-scale efficiency as well as small-scale responsiveness. We have suggested that some of the elements of bureaucratic hospital systems may contribute to the further development of the Mayo approach. But we should also look for clues at other related industries—knowledge-service production organizations.

At this early stage in the journey we can cite a few lessons from empirical efforts at transformation of health care:

- There is a strong affirmation from leaders of some of the nation's best health care organizations of the need to move to the learning mode of production and what is essentially a collaborative community. There are elements of this type of organization emerging in some of these organizations.

- There is resistance to change, particularly from physicians whose social character and training support the craft mode of production. Unless the education of physicians focuses on developing the values and competencies for a learning organization, resistance will continue to impede change to the learning organization.

- The dominant attempt to move from a craft to a manufacturing-bureaucratic model generally leads to alienation of doctors and inefficiency of organizations that ultimately depend on their commitment. Narcissistic leaders who try to impose a new vision of 'managed' care conflict too strongly with the professional-craft ethic of the medical profession.

- Policy makers need to understand that solving the problems of health care delivery is not just a matter of different incentives and new techniques, but rather of transforming a craft mode of production in a way that incorporates the best craft values in more, interactive learning organizations. This means that leaders should be selected not because they are distinguished experts, but because they understand the logics of business, quality, and leadership. They must also have the informed support of their boards which recognize that positive change will provoke resistance.

Appendix 6.1. Academic Health Center Leaders Survey Results, March 1999

How important are each of these elements of your organization and how well are you implementing them?	Importance					Level today					Mean Gap
	Low				High	Low				High	
	1	2	3	4	5	1	2	3	4	5	
Strategies											
• **Service is our highest priority.**	0	0	1	5	12	0	5	9	2	2	1.56
• Our culture, attitudes, and behavior support service.	0	0	1	9	9	0	7	7	5	0	1.53
• Our goal is to exceed expectations for service and cost by good management.	0	0	2	7	10	1	6	7	5	0	1.58
• We provide compassionate care that is appropriate and effective.	0	0	0	1	17	0	1	6	10	1	1.33
• We work to improve the health of individuals and communities.	0	0	1	5	12	0	5	5	6	2	1.33
• Population health needs and the market shape and size our clinical programs.	0	0	3	9	6	1	5	7	3	1	1.28
• **We function as a physician-led system that integrates all the elements of health services.**	0	0	3	8	7	1	3	8	4	2	1.06
• Physicians are leaders as well as care-givers.	0	0	2	8	8	0	5	8	3	2	1.22

How important are each of these elements of your organization and how well are you implementing them?	Importance					Level today					Mean Gap
	Low				High	Low				High	
	1	2	3	4	5	1	2	3	4	5	
• Physicians share leadership functions with other professionals.	0	0	2	8	8	0	6	5	4	3	1.11
• We collaborate with other organizations in order to better serve individuals and communities.	0	0	1	6	11	1	3	9	4	1	1.50
• **We are a learning organization.**	0	0	0	2	14	1	3	6	4	2	1.69
• Our research and education strengthens the clinical enterprise.	0	0	2	5	11	0	4	7	5	2	1.22
• We continually work to better understand the health needs of individuals and communities.	0	0	2	7	9	0	6	7	5	0	1.44
• All of us are involved in continuously improving the cost and quality of our services.	0	0	0	6	13	2	8	5	4	0	2.11
• We learn from and with other organizations.	0	0	3	7	9	1	4	10	2	2	1.32
• **We value people as partners for success.**	0	0	1	7	10	0	3	10	3	2	1.28
• We invest in people's development.	0	0	0	6	13	0	7	6	4	2	1.63
• We give people appropriate responsibilities that make full use of their capabilities.	0	0	0	4	15	0	3	12	2	2	1.63
• We provide meaningful rewards.	0	0	2	5	12	2	6	6	5	0	1.79
• We recognize accomplishment.	0	0	1	6	12	0	7	6	6	0	1.63
• We develop relationships of trust.	0	0	0	6	13	2	5	8	3	1	1.89
• Utilization management.	0	1	0	11	6	2	3	9	4	0	1.39
Systems That Support Strategies											
• Information systems that support physician decision-making	0	0	1	3	13	1	8	7	2	0	2.15
• Call center	0	0	4	6	6	3	2	6	4	1	1.25
• Clinical pathways and guidelines	0	0	3	7	8	3	6	6	3	0	1.78
• Continuous improvement	0	0	2	6	10	1	6	6	5	0	1.61

(*continues*)

How important are each of these elements of your organization and how well are you implementing them?	Importance					Level today					Mean Gap
	Low				High	Low				High	
	1	2	3	4	5	1	2	3	4	5	
• Periodic evaluation of individual performance	0	0	1	7	10	1	4	7	4	2	1.39
Style of Relationship among and by Leaders											
• Interactive dialogue	0	0	0	5	14	0	2	8	7	2	1.26
• Openness	0	0	0	5	14	1	5	2	9	2	1.42
• Systems Thinking	0	1	1	3	14	1	8	6	3	1	1.84
• Coaching/teaching	0	1	1	3	14	0	6	6	7	0	1.53
• Accountability	0	0	1	5	13	0	3	6	10	0	1.26
• Teaching	0	0	0	5	13	0	3	6	8	1	1.33
Skills											
• Leadership	0	0	0	2	16	0	1	9	7	0	1.54
• Financial	0	0	1	2	15	0	4	4	6	4	1.22
• Medical	0	0	0	2	16	0	1	1	9	7	0.67
• Teaching	0	0	0	3	15	0	1	5	9	3	1.06
• Research	0	0	2	3	13	0	5	5	6	2	1.33
• Human Resources	0	0	1	2	15	0	4	11	3	0	1.83
• Marketing	0	0	2	3	13	1	8	5	3	1	1.89
• Information Technology	0	0	0	3	15	2	3	11	1	1	2.06
Structure											
• Systems of Excellence/ product lines	0	1	1	8	8	1	7	7	2	1	1.56
• MD–administrator partnership	0	0	1	5	12	0	4	11	2	1	1.61
• Health Plans	1	0	2	8	7	3	2	10	3	0	1.39
• Support Services (e.g., HR, IT, Marketing, Finance)	0	0	1	4	13	1	4	8	5	0	1.72
Shared Values											
• Service to patients	0	0	0	0	18	0	3	6	8	1	1.61
• Service to students	0	0	0	3	15	0	2	5	8	3	1.17
• Service to colleagues	0	0	0	4	13	0	4	10	2	1	1.76
• Service to the university	0	0	0	7	11	0	3	6	5	4	1.06
• Service to the community	0	0	1	4	13	0	6	7	3	2	1.61
• Ethics	0	0	0	1	17	0	1	1	13	3	0.94
• Fiscal responsibility	0	0	0	2	16	0	2	4	7	5	1.06
• Innovation	0	0	0	0	18	0	3	6	9	0	1.67

References

Ackoff, Russell L. (1999). *Re-creating the Corporation: A Design of Organizations for the 21st Century.* Oxford: Oxford University Press.

Bulger, Roger (1998). *The Quest for Mercy, the Forgotten Ingredient in Health Care Reform.* Charlottesville, Va.: Garden Jennings Publishing Co.

Evans, H. Clyde, and Rubin, Elaine R. (1999). *Creating the Future.* Washington: Association of Academic Health Centers.

Griner, Paul, et al. (2000). *Managing Change.* Washington: Association of American Medical Colleges.

Maccoby, Michael (1988). *Why Work: Leading the New Generation.* New York: Simon & Schuster. 2nd edn. Alexandria, Va.: Miles River Press, 1995.

—— (2003). *The Productive Narcissist: The Promise and Peril of Visionary Leadership.* New York: Broadway Books.

Ramirez, Rafael, and Wallin, Johan (2000). *Prime Movers: Define your Business or have Someone Define it Against you.* Chichester: John Wiley & Sons.

Ritzer, George, and Walczak, David (1988). 'Rationalization and the deprofessionalization of physicians.' *Social Forces,* 67/1 (Sept.): 1–22.

Rosen, George (1983). *The Structure of the American Medical Profession, 1875–1941.* Philadelphia: University of Pennsylvania Press.

Rubin, Elaine R. (1988). *Mission Management: A New Synthesis.* Washington: Association of Academic Health Centers.

Stanbeck, Thomas M., Jr., Bearse, Peter J., Noyelle, Thierry J., and Karasek, Robert A. (1983). *Service: The New Economy.* Totowa, NJ: Allenheld, Osmun & Co.

Starr, Paul (1982). *The Social Transformation of American Medicine.* New York: Basic Books.

Notes

1. Starr (1982); Rosen (1983).
2. Reported in the *Wall Street Journal* (21 Feb. 2001).
3. Making health care safer: a critical analysis of patient safety practices: summary (July 2001). AHRQ Publication No. 01–E057. Agency for Healthcare Research and Quality, Rockville, Md. www.ahrq.gov/clinic/ptsafety/summary.htm.
4. The advisory board included Polly Bednash, Ph.D., RN, FAAN, executive director, American Association of Colleges of Nursing, Roger Bulger, MD, president, Association of Academic Health Centers, Paul Griner, MD, former president, American College of Physicians, and vice president and director, Center for the Assessment and Management of Change in Academic Medicine, Association of American Medical Colleges, Federico Ortiz Quesada, MD, director, International Relations, Mexican Ministry of Health, Stan Pappelbaum, MD, former CEO, Scripps Health, Richard Riegelman, MD, MPH, Ph.D., former

dean, School of Public Health and Health Services, George Washington University, Henry Simmons, MD, president, National Coalition on Health Care.

The research team included Richard Margolies, Ph.D., Barbara Lenkerd, Ph.D., and Doug Wilson, Ph.D.

5. Detailed data on these gap surveys is presented in Appendix 6.1.

6. For more on the theory of social character, see Chapter 3 above. The interaction among norms, structures, and character is elaborated in Chapter 1.

7. See Maccoby (1988) for a fuller description of the expert-bureaucrat.

8. On the productive narcissist character type, see Maccoby (2003).

9. From the Mayo clinic website: www.mayoclinic.org/about/history.html (viewed 2 Dec. 2004).

10. We conducted research at the Mayo sites in Rochester, Minnesota, and Scottsdale, Arizona; we did not visit the Mayo Clinic in Jacksonville, Florida.

11. Mayo's tax-exempt status is based on its research mission; IHC's is based on its willingness to serve patients without regard to their ability to pay.

12. Jennifer Fisher Wilson, 'Doctors are the main barrier to computerizing records.' From the Nov. 1997 *ACP Observer*, copyright © 1997 by the American College of Physicians. (Also at www.acponline.org/journals/news/nov97/barrier.htm, viewed 2 Dec. 2004.)

7

Hyperconnected Net Work

Computer-Mediated Community in a High-Tech Organization

Anabel Quan-Haase and Barry Wellman

Computer networks and work networks

The turn to networked collaborative work community

Computer-mediated communication (CMC) permeates organizations. The internet and internal intranets link managers, professionals, and even many line workers. These communication media provide speed, flexibility, and the ability to append germane documents, pictures, and audio.

Yet there is more assertion than evidence about how CMC actually affects work relations and organizations. Have applications such as listserves, email, and instant messaging (IM) fostered new forms of organization that are less bounded than traditional bureaucratic hierarchies? Analysts have asserted that CMC aids rapid communication and information access among employees, providing easier inexpensive and convenient communication with far-flung communities of work. They argue that CMC provides the means for leaping over workgroup and organizational boundaries, communicating rapidly: locally or long distance; one to one, one to many, many to many. Coupled with a low operating cost and the ability to communicate while the other person is not immediately available, CMC can create an enhanced ability to maintain spatially dispersed, sparsely knit, and interest-based relationships.[1]

One consequence may be the rise of a new form of network organization, in which traditional hierarchical bureaucracies are short-circuited by employees who have direct access to all. Traditional solidary workgroups (and non-work communities) have featured densely interconnected relationships in physically compact spaces. By contrast, interactions in networked social systems occur with multiple others and relationships are specialized. As Manuel Castells argues:

Cooperation and networking offer the only possibility to share costs and risks, as well as to keep up with constantly renewed information.... Inside the networks, new possibilities are relentlessly created. Outside the networks, survival is increasingly difficult.[2]

Although social networks have always pervaded organizations, it is only recently that some analysts have proclaimed the proliferation of organizations structured around such networks. In Chapter 4, Jay Galbraith argues that organizational structures can be understood in terms of networks differentiated on the basis of the amount of power and authority vested in them. For Galbraith, companies today are faced with high levels of complexity and can only adapt successfully to the changes in their environments if they can create networks with differing characteristics that are appropriate for each component of a business reflecting its importance. Paul Adler and Charles Heckscher in Chapter 1 of this book usefully apply community theory to the nature of community at work: they argue that the need for complex interdependence of specialists has led to the exploration of norms and processes for a goal-oriented type of cooperation which they call a collaborative community. It is distinctive in three key dimensions: in its values, which emphasize contribution to a collective purpose; in its organization, which supports horizontal interdependence; and in the social character of its members which integrates multiple social identities and is tolerant of ambiguity and conflict.

This shift to networks affects the structure of work relations. For example, Adler and Heckscher suggest that collaborative community, based on social networks, is one of three ways of organizing work, along with hierarchies and markets. Their argument links with three contrasting models of community prevalent in analyses of non-work communities.

In the earliest model, analysts feared that community was withering away under the nineteenth–twentieth-century impact of urbanization and bureaucratization since the Industrial Revolution. More recently, Robert Putnam has argued that dual-career families and privatized television-based leisure have fostered a turn away from the voluntary organizations that are the putative Tocquevillian (1835) key to American democracy and community. Such 'mass society' arguments contend that the state of hyper-individualism takes the place of attenuated community ties of sociability, support, and social control.

The second model has responded to the alleged withering of community by repeatedly showing the persistence of contemporary neighborhood communities. Driven by data, ethnographers and survey analysts have documented the persistence of supportive relations.

The third model has developed since the 1970s, and has been built on social network analysis. Like Adler and Heckscher, it looks at community as consisting of social networks, rather than local solidarities. Researchers have shown that networked communities have developed—even before the coming of the internet. Like the second model, analysts have documented the persistence of community ties of sociability and support. However, unlike the local group orientation of the second model, they have shown that networked communities rarely are local or solidarities. This work suggests that while densely knit neighborhood and organizational groups may be diminishing, informal networks are flourishing under the group-focused radar. These networked communities consist of interdependent specialized relationships that are sparsely knit and often spatially dispersed. Under such circumstances, each person operates a personal community. Each person must maneuver through discrete ties to obtain social capital (rather than depending on communal support) and must construct identities out of often-fragmented sets of relationships. Wellman has recently called this 'networked individualism.'[3]

There are straightforward analogies to work relationships. Analogous to the first community model: are workers in organizations atomized, so that they respond individually to hierarchical direction and rewards? Although 'mass society' contentions abounded in early studies of industrialization, abundant research has been done to show the persistence of the second community model: village-like support, sociability, and control among white- and blue-collar workers. Yet, Adler and Heckscher contend in Chapter 1 that the third 'networked' model is more appropriate for understanding work relations among the growing population of knowledge workers, especially those who work individually but interdependently within organizations. For example, organizations assign managers, software programmers, or lawyers problems to be solved, but largely leave it to them to work out their own solutions and find appropriate colleagues with whom to consult.[4] They argue that in the last few decades cooperative norms have begun to crystallize in the corporate sphere in a goal-oriented form that they call collaborative community. 'The large corporation combining bureaucracy and loyalty-based community meets its limits in organizing the production of knowledge. Bureaucracy... is very effective at organizing routinized production, but it does very poorly at these complex interactive tasks involving responsiveness and innovation' (p. 28). Adler and Heckscher call this 'process management' that requires 'the deliberate and formal organization of cooperation' (p. 44). They comment:

Collaborative community in modern industry needs to coordinate interactions that span a wide range of competencies and knowledge bases, and that shift constantly to accommodate the evolving nature of knowledge projects. The challenges it faces cannot be met through 'teamwork' in the usual sense of small, homogeneous, and informal groups. Process management coordinates large, diverse communities and high levels of complexity (p. 44).

Computer-mediated communication and networked work

That is the theory; what is the practice? Although there has been much optimism about the value of network organizations for information flow, collaboration, and innovation, few studies have actually observed the extent to which relationships actually span workgroup and organizational boundaries. Yet, many managers are aware of the relevance of networking and, as Galbraith shows in Chapter 4, use boundary-spanning teams to stimulate interdepartmental networks. Managers see such boundary-spanning networks as important sources of information and innovation. They have seized upon CMC networks as key media for organizing work in loosely coupled ties across departmental, organizational, and physical boundaries. However, analysts are just now coming to grips with how people in CMC-intensive organizations actually network—online and offline.

Although there is general agreement as to the value of boundary-spanning communication, the actual functional ecology of groups and cross-cutting ties is unclear. Nor has there been much information about how the networking of communities—in both the organizational and the communication sense—affects trust and collaboration. As Galbraith points out, it is not desirable that everyone talks to everyone else in an organization. What matters is identifying communication gaps and establishing linkages to achieve desirable network structures. Where both trust and social control in traditional workgroups and communities have been both hierarchical and collective, networked communities rely more on dyadic, interpersonal relationships and negotiations. These take time and effort to build. Moreover, organizational power structures can be robust, so that an alternative consequence may be the use of CMC to increase connectivity while maintaining hierarchical bureaucratic structures.[5]

In this chapter, we use a case study of relations in a medium-size, high-tech firm to see how CMC actually affects communication, community, and trust in organizations. We analyze a high-tech firm of knowledge workers because its technologically savvy employees routinely and frequently use CMC. Hence, the case illustrates a leading edge of organizational form and behavior. We use social network analysis as a means to make visible the actual lines of communication within departments, between departments, and outside of the organization. We focus especially on three phenomena associated with CMC:

1. *Hyperconnectivity*: The availability of people for communication anywhere and anytime.
2. *Local virtuality*: The pervasive use of CMC for interaction with physical proximate people, even if located at the next desk at work or next door at home.
3. *Glocalization*: Constraint-free communication combining global and local connectivity. In addition to local virtualities, there often are virtual localities, in which spatially dispersed people use CMC to work and commune together on a common task or shared interest.

Debating the impact of CMC on community

A decade ago, the use of CMC was seen as neither routine nor normal, neither at work nor at leisure. Part of the early excitement over the internet was the debate over what CMC was doing to relationships.

The *dystopian* view argues that CMC hinders community—at work or elsewhere—because it disconnects people from 'authentic' face-to-face (FTF) relationships. It warns that CMC's limited capability for transmitting social cues—such as voice tone, facial expressions, body gestures, and smell—diminishes people's sense of connectivity.[6] This view sees only traditional community as valid, ignoring abundant evidence that people carry on copious and important communications online. It echoes the now-discredited fears since the early 1800s that industrialization and technological change would destroy solidary community. In two influential books, Sherry Turkle argued that people created different personas, 'second selves,' online, as they lost themselves in cyberspace and forgot the real world. Voicing a then-common fear, Texas commentator Jim Hightower warned over the ABC radio network: 'While all this razzle-dazzle connects us electronically, it disconnects us from each other, having us "interfacing" more with computers and TV screens than looking in the face of our fellow human beings.'

The *utopian* view argues that CMC fosters an enormous increase in cooperation by allowing far-flung people to interact. Rather than dystopian atomization, there would be unlimited communing and community. As John Perry Barlow, co-founder of the Electronic Frontier Foundation, dreamed early in the internet age:

[T]o feel the greatest sense of communication, to realize the most experience... I want to be able to completely interact with the consciousness that's trying to communicate with mine. Rapidly... we are now creating a space in which the people of the planet can have that kind of communication relationship.[7]

Both the utopian and dystopian views have privileged CMC, assuming that its very existence would radically affect community—at work and at leisure. Their prognostications have not taken into account the social patterning of community and trust: It is not solely a matter of easier communication. The Manichean fervor of both critics and enthusiasts has not been encumbered by evidence. Their fixation on the internet has ignored a century of research in community studies that has shown that technological change before CMC—planes, trains, telephones, and cars—neither destroyed community nor left it alone as remnant urban villages.

Well before the internet, community had become non-local—metropolitan and even transnational in scope—and partial, with people maneuvering among several networks of friends, relatives, neighbors, and workmates. Studies of non-work communities have shown that industrialization has not destroyed community, but has transformed its composition, practices, attitudes, and communication patterns away from local solidarities to far-flung, sparsely knit networks. Considering that socializing occurs beyond the boundaries of the local neighborhood, such analyses do not define community in terms of locality (or workgroup), but as social networks of interpersonal ties that provide sociability, support, information, a sense of belonging, and social identity.

Drawing upon this body of research, our own argument is neither dystopian nor utopian. Consistent with the theses developed by Wellman in previous writing and by Adler and Heckscher in the Introduction to this book, we argue that CMC has facilitated a mutation in the form of community. We argue that CMC facilitates collaboration that is both hyperconnected and glocal. Our findings are consistent with the findings of research in non-work communities: CMC—email, IM, chat, virtual communities, etc.—*adds on to* FTF communication with friends and relatives rather than destroying it or replacing it. Moreover, despite the globe-spanning ability of CMC, ties with neighbors seem to increase as online and offline communications reinforce each other symbiotically. Although CMC was originally envisioned as long-distance communication media, in reality it also supports *local virtualities*: physically proximate people extensively connected by CMC as well as by FTF (and the telephone) contact.[8]

Yet while people communicate online via electronic bits, they still consist of atoms embodied in flesh and blood. Hence, *glocalization* matters, with both physically proximate and long-distance communication. CMC is used to communicate between FTF visits, to share pictures and music, and to broadcast to large numbers. But it rarely replaces FTF contact where people smile, snarl, and sniff at each other, and exchange physical objects not reducible to email attachments.

Computer-supported social networks flourish in organizations where information represents a key asset, informal networks have supplemented traditional hierarchies, the flow of information has become critical for success, and communication often crosses workgroup and organizational boundaries. The underlying assumption is that geographical proximity, group membership, and simultaneous physical presence no longer limit communication and collaboration.

Changes in how people communicate have created a need to develop new models for conceptualizing, and hence measuring, community. While information and communication technologies have the potential to foster new forms of networked collaborative community in organizations, what is the reality? It is no longer sufficient to draw boxes representing workgroups and hierarchical tree diagrams representing intergroup relations.

Hence, this chapter investigates how CMC affects the networked nature of collaborative community at work. More specifically, it addresses the following questions: What is the nature of collaboration in such communities? Are work relations based on an interdependent, organic solidarity where people feel a sense of reciprocity toward other members of the community and make their information freely available? Are relations principally peer to peer or hierarchical? Are employees using CMC to bridge group and physical boundaries, as the champions of network organizations contend? Is communication across boundaries occurring at the expense of local, within-group communication?

Rather than isolating CMC as a separate social/communication system, we study it in the real-world context. CMC itself does not create hyperconnectivity, glocalization, and local virtuality in organizations and communities. Technologies themselves—including CMC—do not *determine* work relations. Rather, CMC provides possibilities, opportunities, and constraints for the formation and maintenance of work relations: what Erin Bradner has called *social affordances*.[9]

The social affordance perspective recognizes that CMC is embedded in a variety of ways in which workers actually communicate, including FTF and telephone communication. We show how CMC has become routinized and integrated in an organization, creating hyperconnected, glocalized, local virtualities of ubiquitous, multiple communication. We analyze how the different characteristics of specific CMCs afford somewhat different communication possibilities. For example, the store and forward nature of email supports asynchronous exchanges where sender and receiver do not have to be online simultaneously. By contrast, IM demands simultaneous presence for successful communication.[10]

Our principal research questions are:

1. How does a local virtuality use the internet?
2. Is hyperconnectivity associated with the lack of face-to-face contact?
3. Is hyperconnectivity associated with the weak departmental structure that characterizes a networked organization?
4. What form of work community is present in a hyperconnected organization? Do the market, hierarchical, or networked models hold?

To illuminate the situation, we use a case study of a high-tech, CMC-pervaded organization. Interactions in this organization are based on loosely coupled relationships of trust, where employees feel comfortable to ask others for help and values of reciprocity guide the exchange of knowledge. It is neither a bureaucratic hierarchy nor an individualistic marketplace. We discuss the consequences of this organization's hyperconnectivity for the negotiation of norms and rules. We show that hierarchy continues to exist, even in an organization pervaded with CMC. But we also show that the notion of hierarchy needs to be reconsidered in the context of knowledge-based settings.

KME: a case study

The organization

Knowledge Media Enterprise ('KME,' a pseudonym) is an eighty-employee high-tech corporation located in a major North American city. KME was founded in 1997 and expanded during the technology boom. Its involvement in knowledge-intensive activity and its high reliance on CMC make it a good place to study collaborative community in a network organization.

KME is a post-industrial firm that offers knowledge-based services and software to clients. A principal business is the hosting and facilitation of online communities, in which employees of other organizations can exchange information and work together. Besides hosting and facilitating business-to-business online communities, KME also supports business-to-consumer online communities, where a community is created around a specific product or service. For example, online communities that form to discuss soap operas or artists are considered business-to-community.

Within KME, the exchange of information and the creation of new knowledge are essential, as the firm is under constant competitive pressure to develop and improve its services and products. Moreover, KME operates in a rapidly changing environment, recalling the adage that 'an internet year is a dog year': change occurs much faster than in many traditional industries. Its work is heavily event driven: requests come from clients or from within the firm both to develop new features for the software and new ways to host online communities of practice. To remain innovative, KME relies heavily on collaboration among employees. The firm employs skilled workers who have diverse backgrounds ranging from computer science to sales to the arts.[11]

KME has received much media coverage since its founding. This attention both reflects and creates pressure on it. The media actively monitors new software releases or virtual community innovations for quality and sales levels. Numerous articles have appeared in newspapers, business and technology magazines, and Gartner Group business reports. Internal and external websites report on the firm's software and its functionality. Venture capitalists with a stake in the firm want to know about KME's financial and business situation. KME's innovations are watched and compared to those of other companies in the industry, increasing the pressure on managers and employees to deliver high-quality, innovative products in short periods. For example, during the data collection stage of this study, the firm was working on a new release of its software and the time-to-market pressures are clear.

KME relies heavily on CMC. As a high-tech firm, KME has the latest communication equipment. All employees are technologically savvy. They have high-speed internet connections and use CMC routinely. This makes KME a good place to investigate how CMC might facilitate collaborative community. With our interest in an organization already comfortable with CMCs, we deliberately chose a technology-intensive organization such as KME, rather than doing an 'adoption study' of how an organization has recently implemented new forms of CMC.[12]

Data collection

Survey: Data collection took place in 2002 through surveys, interviews, and observations. KME workers enthusiastically participated: 27 out of 28 departmental employees responded to the survey: 11 in the software development department (including 3 women) and 16 in the client services department (including 5 women). Survey participants had worked for KME an average of 28 months (range: 5–48 months). Six had a high-school diploma or less, 12 had completed an undergraduate degree, and 8 had a graduate degree. Survey participants included 3 managers, 5 supervisors, and 19 other department members.

The lengthy self-administered survey gathered information about communication at each of three sociolocational distances: within the department, with other colleagues in the organization, and with people outside the organization. At each distance, participants were asked to report how frequently they used three types of media: face to face (FTF) or telephone, email, and IM (instant messaging). Participants also reported on their social and instrumental networks. They were asked to indicate how often they sought information from and socialized with colleagues in both the software development and client services group. By focusing on the information and socializing networks of both groups simultaneously, we obtained a better picture of collaboration within and between departments. The survey also asked about employees' use of information sources, and how often they used each type of media to communicate with others in the organization and with colleagues and clients elsewhere.[13]

Interviews: Ten survey participants were interviewed by Quan-Haase in December 2002, with each interview lasting approximately 45 minutes. Five employees were recruited from each department, coming from a range of positions and roles. Semi-structured interviews provided flexibility to follow important leads while covering the same set of questions in all interviews. Transcribed interviews were sent to interviewees for review and approval. To guarantee the confidentiality of interviewees, pseudonyms are used throughout our research reports.

Observations: Quan-Haase also observed everyday work practices to learn about how people handled CMC and how they fit it into their relationships and communication. These one-on-one observations started at 9.00 a.m. and concluded when the employee left the office (at approximately 4.30 p.m.). Through one-on-one observations of a workday, all FTF, telephone, and online interactions can be observed and recorded, including email, IM, FTF, and telephone exchanges. The start and end time, duration, and content of interaction were recorded. Although participants were given the opportunity to have private conversations, no one did.

Comparing two KME departments

Software development and client services

We compare work roles and communication patterns in two main KME departments: *software development* and *client services*. While tasks are somewhat similar within each department, they are very different across the two departments. Each department had existed for at least one year, with stable patterns of communication and use of information sources. The twenty-eight employees in the two departments comprise 35 per cent of the total workforce at KME. Data from both departments enable comparisons of the extent to which task interdependency influences collaboration and the use of CMC.

The tasks, departmental structure, and milieus of the two departments can be found in thousands of firms, except for their great reliance on CMC. We do not describe the departments here for their uniqueness, but to set the stage in the next section to show how the structure of work in these two departments intersects with their CMC use in ways that build trust, social networks, community, and social capital.

The software development department had existed for 2.5 years and consists of twelve employees. The main task of the software development department is to create software packages that are largely used by customers in combination with services from the client services department. Some customization for special customers is also done. As it was fairly new at the time of our study, more revenues came from the client services side.

Table 7.1. Comparing the departments

	Software development	Client services
Performance measures	• Pressures: time-to-market; feature wars • Success measures: performance-to-schedule; profit, market share	• Pressures: cost; threat of in-sourcing by clients • Success measures: accept-ance; satisfaction, profit
Tasks	• Staff assigned to specific tasks • User is distant and less involved in development • Process is immature • Software development via coordination	• Staff assigned to specific projects • User is involved and pro-vides input • Process is more mature • Task accomplishment in-dependent
Cultural milieu	• Entrepreneurial • Individualistic • Long work hours	• More bureaucratic • Less individualistic • More set working hours
Groups	• Less likely to have matrix structure • Involved in entire development cycle • Cohesive, motivated, jelled • Evolving creative work • Small, co-located • Opportunities for large financial rewards • Large dispersion in income	• Matrix managed and pro-ject focused • People assigned to mul-tiple projects • Work together as needed • Rely on formal specifica-tions • Larger, somewhat dis-persed • Salary-based • Little dispersion in income

The client services department had existed as a functional department for 4.0 years and consists of sixteen employees. The client services department provides KME customers with planning and support services for communities of practice and other online communities that exchange information. Some of their clients are units of large, world-famous organizations. The department works hard and skillfully to create 'virtual localities': online places where participants would log on, come to know their electronic neighbors, and share best practices. (By contrast, physically compact KME is the opposite: a 'local virtuality.') Table 7.1 summarizes the characteristics of the two departments.[14]

Tasks and performance pressures

KME, like other high-tech firms, often has intense time-to-market pressure, competing on services and the functionality of its software. The competition exists in both the national and international market. KME serves clients in Europe, Asia, and North America.

The primary task of the software development department is to write code. The department is expected to develop and implement new functionalities quickly. As the industry is under intensive scrutiny, software must be innovative and high quality. While all department members know how to program, each person is responsible for specific components of the software that require specialized expertise. As Linda, a programmer, reports:

We are all programmers. We all know Java; we all know database Access stuff. I probably know a bit more the Access database program than other people. I know XML and database Access. I end up doing a lot of programming.

By contrast, the client services department is expected to work closely with clients and provide them with high-quality services. The client services department consists of experts in facilitating online communities. The tasks of a community facilitator include organizing relevant information for the site, keeping the site up to date, and monitoring exchanges between community members. These exchanges can occur asynchronously (i.e. on bulletin boards) or synchronously (i.e. in real-time chat rooms). If inappropriate material is posted to the site, the community facilitator is responsible for removing it. When people behave inappropriately (flaming, swearing, etc.), the offending individuals are banned from the community. While the tasks of online facilitators are similar across online communities, the nature of the online communities can vary considerably. Some online communities are focused around a product (e.g. car, computer, or food brand), while others revolve around common interests (e.g. soap operas or movies).

The client services department does not operate under as much time and innovation pressure as the software development department. Customer satisfaction is the most important measure of success for client services, while profit and market share are more important measures of success for software development. The department's focus on client satisfaction is reflected in management's work practices, as enunciated by Bridget, a supervisor: 'I talk the most with my community facilitators since everything revolves around client satisfaction. My source of information is people that interact with our clients most.'

Thus, time-to-market pressures have a stronger effect on the software development component of the business, while cost pressures have a stronger effect on the client services. Another key difference between the two departments is their relationship with users and customers. The software development department has no direct contact with users or customers. They rely on intermediaries—the marketing and sales units—to obtain information about users and their requirements. By contrast, the client services department needs to be in close contact with users and customers. Employees engage in frequent discussions with clients about content development, tracking and monitoring, and the evaluation of websites.[15] Community facilitators need to be attuned to the needs of their clients and develop the necessary expertise to keep clients satisfied, as Ben, one of the supervisors in the client services department, explains:

Trying to make sure that I know what the clients need from us and that is ever changing. Given the services we provide—we are kind of different and new in the business world—it is not a standard kind of service that we offer; it could be considered consulting services in a way. But, it is specific to something that still grows—a new phenomenon—and that is online marketing. It is using online communities as a marketing tool. So, constantly trying to figure out how we can make that work for the client. How are the client's needs or interests changing? How do we keep up with that, how do we stay ahead of the client on some respects, because our clients are very forward looking and always want to know the newest thing.

Cultural milieus

The work culture of the two departments is very different. The KME software development department consists of a highly qualified team of programmers that were formerly employed by companies such as Microsoft and SPSS. The work culture of the software development department is characterized by the highly individualistic work habits of programmers. Often, there is no predetermined work schedule. In the lead up to a release date, employees often work 50 hours or more per week. Two of the programmers have above-average incomes and excel in writing code and solving programming problems. One programmer described another ('Alex') as one of the best programmers in the country who is respected, and perhaps even revered, by his peers. This fits well with the description of *software cowboys* made by Constantine: brilliant geniuses who single-handedly create and develop clever new code in sleepless weekends of non-stop programming.

The presence of star software cowboys does not preclude the software development department from showing high levels of cooperation and cohesion. Employees at KME respect and value expertise, and they actively offer assistance to one other. The software development department also frequently socializes by going out for lunch or coffee. Many of the meetings are impromptu, taking place in a small meeting room in the middle of the office. A high level of communication and exchange between members of the software development department is necessary because of the interdependence of all components of the project. Moreover, consultation on design issues is also required because they affect the operability of the code.[16]

By contrast, the client services department works more independently. Community facilitators are not required to coordinate their activities because their work consists of interacting with individual clients. As such, community facilitators communicate primarily with clients and their respective facilitators. Thus, the work culture of the client services department is highly individualistic.

Departmental structure

The departments are structured differently in response to their work needs. The software development department functions as a cohesive, horizontal team.[17] Although one departmental manager and two supervisors oversee the development cycle and ensure compatibility of the software components, individual department members work independently. Furthermore, all members of the department are involved in decision making for the development cycle. This is essential because individual components must be successfully integrated.

The client services department has a different structure. There are two departmental managers who are responsible each for a cluster of clients and their corresponding online communities. In addition, there are three supervisors who help oversee the two clusters and are responsible for one or two clients and their respective communities. Each online community has a dedicated community facilitator (these are the department members) assigned to oversee the needs of the client and the users. This reporting structure means it is less necessary for community facilitators to collaborate or communicate frequently with other community facilitators. In some rare instances, two community facilitators are assigned to the same online community if the workload or demand is sufficient to warrant the added personnel. Andy, a community facilitator assigned to the same client as another facilitator, explains how he and his colleague collaborate: 'Even though we have different sites, we have the same client and we are dealing with many of the same kinds of issues. We work together essentially. We support each other on things.'

Physical spaces

The software development and client services departments are located on different floors of an office building. The floors are approximately three minutes from each other—either by elevator or staircase—creating a barrier for communication between departments.[18] Each employee in the two departments has a computer, desk, and telephone.

The key places for informal FTF interaction in each department are the kitchens, the printers, the photocopiers, and the washrooms. The common areas on both floors were very similar: they had a coffee machine, a water boiler for tea, and a microwave.

The software development department is isolated from the rest of the company, a separation that programmers regard as advantageously allowing them to concentrate on their work without being distracted by noise and interruptions from other departments. The programmers also feel that their work is different from that of the rest of the company and does not require much interaction with people from other departments.

The programmers work in a large open space, with a washroom and a small kitchen next to the meeting room. The open concept was adopted to help programmers to collaborate and engage in joint problem solving. The only person who had a closed office separate from the common working space was the departmental manager. However, most of the time, the manager keeps the office door open so that people can just walk in.

The client services department has more people and occupies a much larger space that is adjacent to the organization's marketing, sales, and head office departments. Community facilitators are in cubicles, with supervisors having a large common area, and the two departmental managers sharing a private office. There is a kitchen, with a large table where employees gather for breakfast or lunch, and free breakfasts encourage collegial mingling.

Social networks

Work networks. Connectivity within the two departments has quite distinct patterns.[19] The software development department is a densely knit network that resembles a core team. By contrast, the client services department is sparsely connected. Pairs of people in the software development department communicate more often on a daily and weekly basis. Moreover, people in the software development department communicate

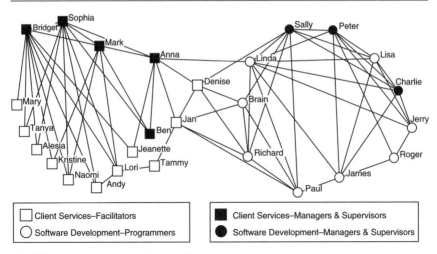

Fig. 7.1 Information network—weekly exchanges

with a higher percentage of fellow department members than do those in the client services department.

The software development department is relatively egalitarian, with managers and programmers having similar communication patterns. All department members are sought for information regardless of their hierarchical position. By contrast, most information exchanges in the client services department occur between facilitators and supervisors, or between supervisors and managers. There is little communication among department members. Fig. 7.1 shows that supervisors and departmental managers are clearly the most central persons in this department. Thus, managers in the client services department are more likely to be the harbingers of information in comparison to the software development department, where programmers are as likely to control the flow of information as managers.

Socializing networks. We asked KME employees how often they meet colleagues from their own department or from the client services department for lunch, coffee, dinner, and/or a drink. Like the work network, Fig. 7.2 shows that the socializing network of the software development department is more densely knit than the network of the client services department. In the software development department, there is no difference between hierarchical positions in terms of socializing.

By contrast, while department managers in the client services department are linked to each other, in the socializing network, they are not

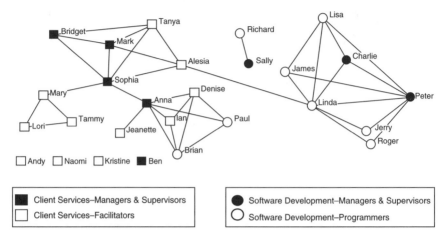

Fig. 7.2 Social network—annual interactions

linked to other department members. Thus, there is a disparity between the client services' socializing network and work network.

In the software development department, two department members are isolated from the rest of the department and only socialized with each other. Two other members do not socialize with members from the software development department at all, but instead socialize with members from the client services department. In the client services department, there are more isolates—a total of four department members. In addition, the department is divided into three clusters linked by a single person: Sophia.

In short, work exchanges on a weekly basis occur primarily within the boundaries of the departments, with few bridging ties. Information exchanges follow the hierarchical structure of communication of the organization in the client services department, but not in the software development department, where department members exchange information among themselves. In the client services department, managers and supervisors are central for the flow of information. Overall, socializing occurs less frequently than information exchange in both departments. Again, the software development department has denser socializing networks than the client services department. While socializing also primarily occurs within the boundaries of the departments, two members of the software development department are part of the socializing network of the client services department. Thus, important work and social linkages exist between the two departments.

Media ecologies in a high-tech organization

Face-to-face and computer-mediated communication

KME people communicate a great deal: informing, coordinating, and collaborating. Employees use CMC regularly as a convenient means of collaborative communication, creating a dense virtual network of exchange. Their frequent communications online have taught them whom they can trust—to respond, produce and provide reliable and valid information, and to keep confidences and commitments. Yet CMC does not function as an independent communication system at KME. CMC, FTF contact, and the telephone serve different communication purposes, often working in synergy and not in competition with one another. Although there are no formal rules at KME for which media to use for communication, employees have tacitly adopted conventions about which media to use for what purposes. FTF and the telephone are used for dealing with complex problems that require extensive discussion. Employees often use the telephone or walk to their colleagues' desks to ask questions. They see such encounters as good occasions to chat and connect on a more personal level. They often arrange via IM to meet at a nearby coffee shop for a break or go out for lunch.

Email and IM frequently lead to FTF encounters among colleagues. As shown in Fig. 7.3, employees often use IM to arrange to meet for lunch or coffee. Exchanges with a social purpose occur frequently between co-workers, and they create a sense of belonging to the organization, provide social support, and create meaningful work relationships. People build relationships, and their exchanges provide them with friendship, humor, and advice. Even though CMC currently does not have the capacity to transmit certain voice, visual, smell, or touch cues, it enables people to remain in contact and exchange social messages.[20]

CMC provides employees with a more convenient form of communication because it allows for cheap, fast and continuous exchanges. Communication occurs almost simultaneously over multiple media, and not just sequentially. Employees often answer an IM and glance at their email while holding a FTF conversation. Thus, employees do not switch between media and FTF for communication, but rather use various media simultaneously to interact with different people. When Charlie, a programmer, needed to fix a bug, he contacted people with various expertise and background via FTF and IM:

> Mark: coffee?
>
> **Sophie: ok, give me 5 minutes**
>
> Mark: now is better for me
>
> **Sophie: is Maureen in?**
>
> Mark: no
>
> **Sophie: let me finish up this email first and then we'll go**
>
> Mark: was my comment to you [about your project] not clear?
>
> **Sophie: it was but if you want my feedback**
>
> **you'll have to wait a few minutes**
>
> Mark: ok, ok
>
> **Sophie: I'll ping you in a few**
>
> **Sophie: almost done**
>
> **Sophie: ok, ready to go**
>
> **Sophie: meet at the elevator**

Fig. 7.3 Social exchange via CMC

Today they had an error in the internal community. So, I investigated the product by trying various things and to do that I sent an instant message to some people that it had an impact on—Brian and Sally they are experts. I had to ask and I had to compare it with something else to see if I can replicate it somewhere else. And I had to work with Linda when we had to do the command line stuff. So I worked with Linda face to face. And then, it happened to be in this case Paul and Denise who were emailing me and Brian. They were in this email thread that is going back and forth. It is very specific to what the problem is, though.

James, a programmer, notes the limitations of CMC for sending complex messages. When he felt that IM could not handle his problem, he immediately switched to telephone conversations:

If there is any complexity to it, I use the phone sometimes too. The phone and face to face, it is kind of similar in that if it is at all complex, I want it that way, just to have it back and forth. Last night I started communicating with Roger with IM and pretty quickly I just wanted to call him on the phone. It would just take too long to explain everything on IM. You can do a fair amount of back and forth. [Phone] is better than email: there is some back and forth. So I talk on the phone because it is too complex to try and sort out over IM.

CMC does not disrupt work as much as FTF and telephone calls in the crowded KME workspaces. Community facilitator Lori feels:

I don't want to be loud because there are all these people right there. So phone is OK, but I feel I am invading other people's privacy, if I am loud on the phone. So the best way for me is email. Plus, I like to keep a written record of everything that is going on.

All media are central at KME for getting work done. Employees do not use various media at random, and they are aware of differences in the suitability of various media for different types of messages, types of communication partners, and degrees of urgency and importance. Thus, understanding the appropriateness of media use is essential for KME's collaborative community. Employees trust that others will make the appropriate media choices, and they themselves are careful when selecting a medium. They have 'media etiquette.'

Instant messaging and email

Instant messaging. CMC is not a single homogeneous medium. This is clear at KME where two widely used forms of CMC—email and IM—are used differently.[21]

KME's culture and fast-paced environment emphasizes using IM. It takes priority over email, FTF, and the telephone. This is not only a matter of individual discretion, but also an important organizational norm. Employees rely on IM because of its speed and its real-time (almost synchronous) nature. Although employees can in principle ignore IM messages, in practice there is a norm of trying to reply within two minutes. This allows the senders of IMs to receive rapid feedback, at the cost of potentially interrupting their colleagues. We noticed that as soon as an IM message appeared on someone's screen, they would glance over and read the message. As part of the culture at KME, people feel compelled to reply, even if it is only to say that they are in a meeting and will respond later. Clearly, IM often comes before FTF, despite the more abundant media cues present in FTF.

Yet, sending an IM is perceived as a relatively polite way of asking a question: The IM appears on the communication partners' screens alerting them of an incoming request, but unlike a telephone call or FTF visit, the IM message does not force others to respond immediately—the norm of rapid response can be ignored at times.

IM serves as a meta-communication medium that affords informal talk about work, email exchanges, and other current organizational developments and concerns. As Linda notes, IM serves for chatting and discussing issues while email allows for the exchange of more detailed information:

I use IM a lot. IM is great if you have one question that you just need an answer to. When you need to explain something in detail—an outline, kind of a business case for doing something, or for getting somebody to take action—email is the best.

With people at their desktops, IM provides important information about the availability of others. In physical space, employees can see each other and communications are based on visual cues. If a person is on the telephone it is not appropriate to approach them until they become disengaged. However, when most communications occur via CMC, one never knows if a person is working on an important document, exchanging urgent IMs, writing an important email, or just chatting or daydreaming.

IM partially solves this problem by providing information about who is logged on to the communication system, usually at their desks.[22] People appear as present on IM when they are logged on or they are busy typing. Again, this type of information is only based on people's presence and not on their availability. IM provides the possibility to learn if people are busy, thereby postponing exchanges for a later, more convenient time. For example, Kristine, a facilitator, uses IM to time her requests for information: 'I see that they are online, I need an answer now, I need to talk to them now, I will ping them.' As Linda, a programmer, points out: 'I just know that if you call or send an IM, you will get a faster response than email.'

As IMs are not saved or archived, they represent a more transient, casual form of exchange. Often IM is used for short social exchanges providing an opportunity to greet others or to share jokes. This promotes closeness among department members and integrates them into a web of online exchanges—both work and social. Yet, such exchanges do not occur in the same manner with all employees. The type of relationship that connects two persons influences the frequency and content of their messages.[23] People with strong ties make more frequent use of IM than those with weaker ties. This difference between strong and weak ties is greater in IM than in email, telephone, or FTF contact. Thus, programmer Linda feels comfortable sending her colleague Liz an IM, even if she may be interrupting her. However, she would not send messages to other people in the office unless it was urgent or important:

I kind of IM Liz. I don't mind interrupting her as much. I don't think she minds it. I enjoy communicating with her: I can say: 'What is going on?' and by the way I have this technical question. Whereas other people, I wouldn't want to IM because I don't have the kind of relationship with them unless it is really important. Then I would. But, I would be less likely to IM because I would not want to disturb them without a real excuse.

IM can be disruptive, because of the information it provides about who else was around. As people knew who else was around, this created expectations for how quickly a response should come. When the expectations of rapid response are not met, conflict sometimes develops. For example, Ben sent an IM to one of his clients, but did not receive a reply. Yet, Ben knew the client was online as he could see the client on the IM buddy list. He resent the IM message the next day and asked the client whether he had received the previous message. The client responded that no IM message had been received. Ben does not believe that the message had not arrived, and he thought the client had ignored him. It is not surprising that when she wants to get a solo job done, one community facilitator, Denise, does not log on to avoid interruptions by others.[24]

Despite these tensions, at KME, IM contributes to hyperconnectivity and facilitates collaborative community. Knowing whether other department members are connected or not—and thus potentially available for communication—creates feelings of closeness and community. This is especially important in an environment where most employees spend the majority of their time sitting in front of computer screens. IM provides the basis for routine exchanges that maintain a community of work.

Email. Email is used differently than IM. Email provides a medium to state complex matters and obtain responses that can be archived and referred to later. It is less often dashed off or used socially. Email leaves a record: It can be stored, checked at a later point in time, and forwarded to other people in the department or organization.[25] Linda, a programmer, explains:

I use email, if it is something that I do not need immediate response to. I like using email because I can develop a well thought-through message, and the other person can respond to it at a different time. Instant messaging exists for immediate things, for quick exchanges, where you don't care about archiving. To me, I think that email should not substitute for face-to-face relationships.

At KME, email represents a more serious and instrumental (as distinct from expressive) form of communication. While IM is primarily used for one-on-one exchange of messages, email goes to a wider range of employees within the department and elsewhere in the organization. Employees are more likely to send email to someone with whom they do not have a close, trusting relationship because it is not as intrusive. Anna, a department manager in client services, says that unlike IM, she makes an effort for her email to be clear and logical: 'I like email because it allows you to put together a well-thought-out message. With my emails, I go back and I edit and I think about them a little bit before I send them off.'

James, a programmer, says he prefers people to communicate with him via email, which is less intrusive:

If it is trivial or it is just as easily handled by an email I'd much rather somebody communicate to me that way on email. Let me answer it on my own time. So, I extend the same courtesy to them. I don't interrupt them unless it is important or really simple, and I have a good relationship with them.

Programmer Linda makes a clear distinction among CMC forms of communication:

If you are communicating with someone who sits next to you only by email, that seems kind of a problem. Like if someone is sitting over here and you are only talking to him by email, there is something artificial about that. It does not seem quite healthy. I could say: 'Hey, what do you know about this?'

CMC has also become an electronic superego. Employees routinely keep IM and email windows open, using outstanding IM messages as a to-do list of reminders of what they need to respond to within minutes (or at most, hours) and outstanding email messages as reminders of what they need to respond to within hours (or at most, days).

Together, IM and email help shape work community and trust at KME. Propelled through CMC, employees are to a large extent connected in real time, opening the opportunity for a stream of constant exchanges. CMC has not only changed the speed of communication, but also its nature. Most obviously, both email and IM allow communication with spatially or temporally distant others, with email providing the additional ability to converse while not simultaneously logged on to the communication system. At KME, each employee would have multiple IM windows open at the same time. Moving between IM windows—and thus conversations—is common practice. Just like teenagers gossiping about each other, multiple relationships can be juggled, sometimes in small groups and sometimes in simultaneous one-to-one conversations. Each IM window represents a conversation with a distinct communication partner and addresses a different topic.

Hyperconnectivity

KME employees are hyperconnected, using CMC and FTF at high rates in their rapidly changing, technology-intensive work. In light of the text-only nature of CMC, its predominance is somewhat unexpected.[26] Yet it is task complexity and interdependency that are key factors in determining group structure and CMC use. Hyperconnectivity is more pronounced in the software development department, where tasks are interdependent, than it is in the client services department, where tasks are independent.

To a great extent, communication with other employees is the basis of work at KME. Employees must obtain information; they must coordinate. Although hyperconnectivity creates new opportunities for exchange and collaboration leading to denser networks, it also creates challenges. At times, hyperconnectivity has negative effects on work processes. Each employee must deal with a large number of requests that add up on a day-to-day basis. Norms require that KME employees be available for CMC, yet employees frequently feel overloaded—and at times overwhelmed—by the number of incoming requests for information and coordination. Hyper-connectivity stops them from getting their 'own work' done. Their densely knit, hyperconnected networks lead to interruptions in completing tasks. Employees are constantly multitasking, dealing simultaneously with their own work demands and others' requests for information. Employees say they do not mind being available to answer others' information requests, but they often feel unable to control when these interruptions occur. Clearly, the ease of CMC adds to the volume of communication.[27]

Local virtuality

Local virtuality—the use of CMC for local communication—is endemic in this high-tech organization,[28] where each employee has a computer ter-minal. Employees rely on CMC for the majority of their communications, even though they work in physical proximity. After all, they already are at their computers and staring at their screens. The time spent writing an email or an IM generally is shorter than the time it takes to lead a FTF or telephone conversation. As a consequence, workers can communicate with each of their communication partners more frequently and they can communicate with more partners. In this way, IM and email combine to create a hyperconnected local virtuality.

Despite the heavy use of CMC, KME is not a 'spaceless place': Locality as a physical place to meet and interact emerges as a key dimension for the formation of collaborative community.[29] At first sight, an observer might think that the fact that people are rarely interacting visibly—in meetings and informal FTF interactions—means that they are in isolation. However, they are going online to exchange emails and IMs with colleagues who are sitting next to them. In this local virtuality, fingers flying over keyboards are easier than walking to another desk or picking up a telephone. The physical setting is crowded, and people do not want to disturb others by moving about and talking. Moreover, people need to work with multiple others. CMC exchanges usually take less time than FTF conversations, allowing for a greater number of exchanges. Under these conditions, CMC is both more effective and less disruptive than FTF or telephone communication.[30] Communication has moved from the physical space to the virtual realm, where conversations consist of typed words.

Work relationships are often formed in the context of work itself. People collaborate on a project, work on the same account, or help each other solve bugs in the software. Andy, a community facilitator, thinks back to when he and fellow facilitator Lori developed a close and trusting work relationship:

I had chats at night where I needed more people and could not just handle it on my own. Lori worked with me on them. So we built a very strong working relationship that has remarkably, I think, carried over into a new area. Now we work on completely different accounts from each other. There is no relationship between my account and her account, or very little. But we still find each other a helpful source of information and knowledge sharing, which is weird. But it is only because we have built personal contact. We turn around and talk to each other all day long about stuff. And say: 'Hey look at what is going on.'

Glocalization

Is communication at KME spanning group boundaries? Because CMC facilitates communication at a distance overcoming barriers of space and time, it allows for easy and quick communication across group boundaries connecting colleagues in other KME departments and outside of the organization.

Most communication stays within a department (see Fig. 7.4). Employees report a mean of 285 days per year of within-department communication, which means that they communicate more than once per day, based on a 250-day work year (5 days × 50 weeks). Most exchanges within the department use CMC. Employees report communicating FTF with departmental colleagues an average of 240 days per year in comparison with 306

Table 7.2. Communication at KME (days per year)

	FTF and phone	Email	IM
Within department	240	306	306
Elsewhere in organization	99	213	215
Outside organization	21	103	72

days per year via CMC (see Table 7.2). KME employees use both email and IM frequently and at about the same frequency. Despite the boundary-spanning 'global village' properties of CMC, KME employees use CMC more for communication within their departments than for communication outside of their department or the organization. They use email and IM more than FTF or the telephone (Fig. 7.5). Within departments, email is used 1.3 times more frequently than FTF and the telephone, and IM is used also 1.3 times more frequently than FTF and the telephone. Thus, even in this high-tech organization, where employees have diverse CMC tools available to them for boundary-spanning communication, they continue to exchange information primarily with other department members.[31]

However, boundary spanning is also common at KME: a large proportion of communication is with colleagues elsewhere in the firm, with a mean of 178 communication days per year (see Table 7.2 and Fig. 7.5).[32] CMC is even more the predominant means of communication to elsewhere in KME than it is within departments. Communication to elsewhere in KME follows a similar pattern as within departments: Email (213 days per year) and IM (215 days per year) are used most frequently,

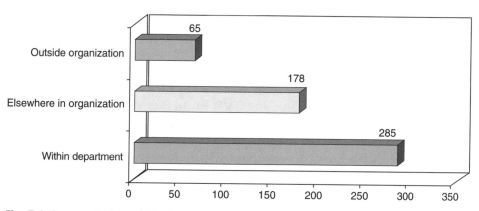

Fig. 7.4 Communication within departments, elsewhere in organization, and outside organization

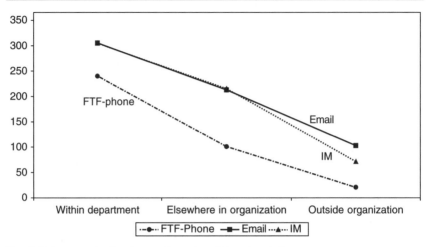

Fig. 7.5 Communication by media and sociolocational distance

while FTF and the telephone are used less for communication (101 days per year each). Although less frequent than communication within departments, the frequency of email and IM contact to elsewhere in the organization is about two-thirds of within-department contact, while FTF contact drops even more to about one-half (see Table 7.2). The ratio of communication with colleagues elsewhere in KME to within-department communication is 0.62.

CMC even more greatly dominates communication patterns for contact outside of KME, with email (103 days per year) and IM (72 days per year) used more frequently than FTF and the telephone (21 days per year). The difference between CMC and traditional means of communication for outside communication is large: email is used 4.9 times more frequently than FTF and the telephone, and IM is used 3.4 times more frequently than FTF and the telephone.

As in the comparison within and between KME departments, there is a much greater drop in the frequency of using FTF contact to people outside of KME than the drop in using CMC. Email is especially used for contact outside of the organization. Thus, employees communicate primarily within their departments even in this high-tech global organization permeated with boundary-spanning CMC. However, when they do span boundaries, either to elsewhere in KME or to outside the organization, they rely heavily on CMC. KME is both a local virtuality and a glocal organization, with CMC supporting communication with customers, partners, and users who are distributed nationally and globally.

Although the general pattern of communication is very similar in the two departments, they differ in their proportion of inward and outward communication and in their use of particular media. As is inherent in their job, the client services department is outwardly oriented. Communication with the client occurs on a regular basis as Kristine, one of the community facilitators, reports: 'I talk to someone at the client site almost every day.' Client communication relies heavily on CMC. For contact outside of KME, client services employees communicate an average of 159 days per year on email and 113 days per year on IM, but only 28 days per year by FTF and the telephone. For them, CMC supports boundary spanning and helps coordinate work with clients and partners, as facilitator Lori explains:

It is mostly just Megan that I talk to. Tuesdays I have a conference call with Megan for half an hour. . . . We communicate so often through email and IM that once the conference call comes around there is really not much else to talk about.

By contrast, the software development department communicates less frequently with people outside of KME: 22 days per year by email and 11 days per year by IM, in contrast to 10 days per year by FTF and the telephone. Although CMC makes boundary spanning possible, the type of work performed by the software development department does not call for as much boundary spanning as it does in the client services department.

Both departments rely heavily on CMC to communicate with colleagues in other departments. The client services group communicates more frequently with colleagues elsewhere in KME by email (186 days per year) and IM (232 days per year) than by FTF and the telephone (105 days per year). Similarly, in the software development group, employees communicate more frequently by email (251 days per year) and IM (191 days per year) than by FTF and the telephone (96 days per year).

The pattern of communication within departments is similar to that for communication with colleagues elsewhere in KME. Employees of both the client services and software development rely heavily on CMC for internal communication. In the client services department, the average employee emails internally 299 days per year and IMs 279 days per year, compared to 210 days per year for FTF and the telephone. In the software development department, email comprises 315 days per year and IM 344 as compared to 279 days per year for FTF and the telephone. Note that in both departments, employees are using email more than the number of workdays per year, indicating that they use email to communicate with each other even while off the premises, presumably while at home. Even though there is proportionally more FTF and telephone contact within departments, CMC is still used more frequently.

Five patterns are evident:

1. KME is a local virtuality, with CMC outweighing FTF and telephone conversations even though people are co-located.

2. In both departments, CMC is used more frequently than FTF and the telephone for communication. This becomes even more evident if we compare overall CMC communication—comprising email and IM—versus FTF and telephone exchanges.

3. There is a proportionally greater reliance on CMC for communicating outside of KME than for communicating with colleagues elsewhere in KME. This suggests that locality influences the choice of media as FTF and telephone interactions increase when people are co-located.

4. The practices and capabilities of people outside of KME affect the media use of KME employees. For example, KME employees use email heavily to communicate with one major client that 'lives on email' and never uses IM externally.

5. Differences in work function and tasks are driving the differences in communication. While CMC affords glocalized networks, it does not cause them. The types of tasks performed by the two departments also play an important role in creating different communication patterns.

Collaborative community in a high-tech organization

Formal meetings and informal exchanges

Formal meetings. Collaboration at KME operates through both formal meetings and informal exchanges. Formal meetings occur frequently in both departments. They are routinely scheduled in advance, or on an ad hoc basis to deal with emergencies. They are held in the two departments' meeting rooms that are equipped with speakerphones and audiovisual equipment.

All employees in the software development department are customarily present during formal meetings. Ad hoc meetings are more common in the software development department because decisions made about the software can influence various components and it is considered important that all members are aware of these changes. Developers need to be up to date with changes, decisions, or problems occurring with the software. Their expertise is valued, and their input is considered relevant. This

emphasis on participation is a key aspect of the way the software development department works as a collaborative community.[33]

Formal meetings also occur frequently in the client services department.
However, not all department members attend all meetings. The only ones
who attend routinely scheduled meetings are those working on a specific
account and the managers and supervisors. Ad hoc meetings typically take
place between two or three employees. The client services department's
large size makes it difficult to schedule meetings for the entire department.
The lack of common meetings creates fragmentary understanding of other
employees' tasks and accounts. This has led to lower levels of understanding among employees and to a collaborative community that is less densely
knit.[34] Ben, a supervisor, explains how the lack of department-wide meetings has reduced understanding of others' challenges and problems:

We used to have a weekly meeting with the entire community management
department, which we no longer have. . . . There are times when it feels like there
may be things going on with Alesia and Tanya's accounts that would help me, and I
don't know about them.

Informal encounters. Despite the importance of formal meetings, employees
usually communicate informally to share knowledge, coordinate activities, and collaborate on a project. Most informal collaborations take place
one on one rather than in groups, with one person contacting another.
The most common communication is asking questions to obtain clarifi-
cation or work lore about a specific matter. However, much communication is devoted to in-depth problem solving, where one person would
help another make sense of a problem and think through various strategies to find a solution. A third type of communication occurs when the
person originally contacted refers the questioner to others better equipped
to help. Charlie, a supervisor in software development, often cycles
through different sets of people and roles:

I probably would be communicating with Sally the majority of the day. Then Ian
and Denise would be probably the number two and three because they normally
are either helping me develop something or I am helping them. Then Alesia would
probably be the fourth most because she is the one who deals with the client, so,
designing or prioritizing the projects for me.

Commitment to collaborative community

Contrary to the early fears of dystopians, KME's heavy reliance on CMC
has not weakened its employees' sense of community. Although CMC

provides limited sensory cues, it nevertheless supports interpersonal trust, and active networks of socializing, information exchange, coordination, and collaboration. For example, James, one of the programmers, asked his colleague Jerry for help on an ill-defined programming problem and received a prompt response:

I looked at some of what we had in place, and it looked kind of promising, but I wasn't sure still what to do. So, then I emailed Jerry about an area that he is very knowledgeable about. And he responded within 20 minutes, probably. I had to go back and forth a couple of times over email, and I ended up calling him over the phone just to clarify some things. And then I implemented what he recommended and it worked.

Jerry responded quickly to James's request, using email and the telephone to give in-depth problem-solving advice. This close collaboration between employees reflects what Adler and Heckscher refer to in the introductory chapter of this volume as an ethic of contribution to the success of others. At KME, hyperconnected employees constantly help each other with their particular expertise, and they use CMC to pool their knowledge toward joint problem solving.

Commitment at KME is simultaneously interpersonal, departmental, and organizational. Frequent CMC has bred *interpersonal* awareness, understanding, and trust. FTF meetings and encounters provide a broad bandwidth of communication, enabling employees to assess voice tone, body language, and physical presentation of self. But while CMC does not allow people to smell each other, its highly frequent use provides a ubiquitous backdrop of communication. The combination of CMC, FTF, and telephone communication enables people to understand the concrete interests and identities of others in collaborative relationships, and to provide the communication auspices for creating and maintaining trust.

There are both strong and weak ties at KME. Opportunities to form strong, trusting relationships continue to exist in this hyperconnected local virtuality. Strong, trusting relationships are particularly relevant in the context of CMC because of the potential intrusiveness. When a close relationship links two people, interruptions are not seen as intrusive. Trust plays an important role because employees need to trust that others will use different media in appropriate ways, so that they do not unnecessarily interrupt others' work. Such computer-facilitated trust is a precursor for these active work networks. People interact more easily with those whom they trust and feel close with, and trust relationships are an important basis for knowledge sharing and joint problem solving—and ultimately, the success of the firm.[35]

As a *department*, the software development department is more committed to collective community than client services. Software development's small size and focus on a single goal fosters group cohesion. The developers feel they have ownership of the software, and they commit much time and effort to improving it. Software supervisor Charlie explains the need for sharing information under such circumstances:

The engineers need to talk to their partner about the module that they are working on, and documentation needs to know about every single module. Testing needs to know about every single module. Design needs to know about every single module.

By contrast, community facilitators in client services often work on different accounts. While most employees do similar work, their work does not contribute to a single effort: the success of one account is independent of the success of others. Thus, department members do not share a common goal and do not feel part of a team in the same way as programmers do. Andy, a facilitator, feels the absence:

We don't meet and we don't talk about stuff. So, it may not occur to the other community facilitators that anything that occurs with their clients may have any relevance to my client and vice versa. I think we need to be more aware of what each other's clients are like.

Nonetheless, frequent email and IM in the client services department support a sense of collaborative community where people advise and help each other. They readily share their expertise and best practices, and hyperconnectivity makes all easily reachable.

Employees in both departments are invested in the success of the *organization*. They have chosen to work in KME because it is a high-tech firm, and they believe that its products can lead to large revenues. Many of the employees identify with the firm and see their own personal success as closely linked to it. The ethic of contribution to the collective value is spurred by the involvement often found in start-up firms that struggle to find a niche in the marketplace and require the support of employees to be successful. Many KME employees had given up stable jobs in established companies with the hope that the start-up will be successful and they will directly benefit from earnings. They believe they have better chances for advancement than in established organizations, and often have potentially lucrative stock or options as part of their compensation packages. Their contribution to the collective value consists of high performance, long hours of work, and high commitment to the firm's goals. Thus, the ethic of contribution occurs through increasing the collective value as well as contributing to the success of others. For example, programmer Linda is so committed that:

Sometimes I just get up in the middle of the night and I am jotting stuff down, just so that I can get them out of my head. So I realize I don't have to think about them. But I am constantly thinking about the details of the job and what needs to get done. I constantly think of the things I need and then I write them down.

The commitment of employees to create a collaborative community has led to the development of a sense of identity that seamlessly merges a strong sense of individualism—based primarily on expertise—with feelings of obligation toward the organization as a whole—based primarily on collaboration and an ethic of contribution. As Adler and Heckscher suggest in the introductory chapter, work in the collaborative community consists not only of the uniqueness and high levels of expertise of workers, but also of workers using their expertise to contribute to the success of the organization. The KME employees' sense of individualism is linked to their seeing their jobs as unique and their expertise as having little overlap. The uniqueness of their jobs results from the independent types of tasks they need to accomplish. Employees see themselves as self-sufficient in that they can accomplish the tasks that are expected of them. Moreover, they have high levels of expertise that often have little overlap with that of others. They often feel that their expertise has reached such high levels that they can manage problems specific to their areas of expertise better than anyone else.

The employees' sense of obligation is a result of high commitment to the success of the organization as a whole. Employees are often working with various individuals at the same time and need to adapt to the demands of each of the projects in which they are involved. Although they are not involved to the same extent in each of the projects, their unique expertise may be a key to dealing with a problem at hand. James, a programmer, explains how he is involved in a number of projects, each demanding a different aspect of his expertise:

So, I did a little bit of that this week, reviewed some documentation that Kristy asked me to review, helped out Tom a little bit, he is making some changes to some other page. He needed some additions to the Java code and had some questions about that.

To be involved in various projects and with various sets of individuals, workers must be flexible in how they apply their expertise to a variety of demands. This creates a need to develop an identity that is simultaneously individual and collective.

Hierarchy

When we began studying KME, we expected to find a networked, post-bureaucratic organization where people worked in shifting teams with multiple others, with little structured departmentalization and hierarchy. Instead, we found a hybrid organization, what Adler and Borys call an 'enabling bureaucracy,' where rules about work and vertical and horizontal divisions of labor exist along with high levels of trust and community cohesion. How does a high-tech, hyperconnected company such as KME reconcile collaborative, networked community and bureaucratic hierarchy?

KME has an explicit hierarchy that relates people and functions. The hierarchy provides a way of organizing individuals around work tasks as well as coordination and communication. The roles and statuses of people at KME are clearly formalized. People know what their role is, to whom they report, and what the adequate type of engagement is. Decision making takes place at the top and decisions are then communicated to employees.

Yet, KME is also an enabling bureaucracy. Rules about work and vertical and horizontal divisions of labor support rather than displace trust and community cohesion. On the one hand, employees enjoy sufficient freedom to perform their jobs without reporting constantly to their supervisors and asking for permission. On the other hand, their meta-awareness of the reporting structure—combined with hyperconnectivity, trust, expertise, and experience—allows employees to work largely independently while connected to a larger departmental and organizational enterprise.

For example, Lisa is responsible for designing the interface of a specialized search engine to seek and mine information from a large database. Her work does not require direct input from any of the other programmers and has little overlap with their roles and functions. Although most of her work is done alone with little supervision, she often asks others in the team to look at her design. Meanwhile, others are developing the database itself. While each worker takes ownership of his or her own part of the software, these components must work together. Hence, software development is a constant switch between individual work on subcomponents and group work on the whole product. The process at KME fits nicely with Adler and Heckscher's discussion in the introductory chapter about work that creates in employees a sense of ownership of the whole project— an ethic of contribution to the success of the department/organization as a whole—while employees continue to take responsibility for their particular work. For example, community facilitator Lori says:

I used to report to Mark, but I do not report to him anymore; he does something else. I report directly to Bridget. All that Bridget does: if there is a problem, a huge problem or an issue coming up, then I'll ask her about it. Otherwise, it's pretty autonomous. They trust me enough; I have been doing it long enough; I don't need to run to Bridget or Mark for every little problem.

Lori has worked for her boss for nearly three years: long enough to develop a relationship of trust. She can evaluate when the situation requires the involvement of the boss. Otherwise, she deals with the arising problems herself. While the work is done independently, this does not create a problem in the hierarchy because the status of the players remains clear. What changes is the amount of consultations occurring among various levels.

Moreover, the type of work done by these high-tech employees has reached such complexity that the boss often cannot give much input for dealing with a technical problem. Such circumstances preclude direct hierarchical-bureaucratic supervision. As department manager Anna points out, management needs to trust and rely on their employees to provide them with the necessary information to make decisions because they are dependent on their expertise:

I have been on Ryan for a week to get me the help desk statistics in a way that I can look at them. And it has taken him this much time. Today I have started to see them. I get a little bit frustrated because I cannot get in and do it myself. And I really don't want to do it myself. So, I think the biggest thing for me is just getting people to get it to me in a timely enough fashion. So, it is more people management.

Although hierarchy and collaborative community exist side by side, one strain is an imbalance of expertise between management and employees. Programmers each have more specialized knowledge than their managers. As for client services, management has expertise with regards to the market, sales, and clients, but does not have a full understanding of the day-to-day tasks and problems of employees. In both departments, management cannot provide sufficient guidance in the execution of tasks. Employees must develop the expertise themselves, with management trusting that employees have the expertise to develop their own plan of action.

CMC supports both hierarchy and collaborative community. While CMC allows managers and employees to communicate, it is especially useful for communication among employees within and between depart-ments. This is especially the case in the software development department where programmers need to be in close contact and frequently share expertise. Although the hierarchy is explicit in this department, employ-ees communicate via email and IM with those who have the expertise they need, regardless of status in the hierarchy. Yet, employees remain aware of status differences. While this is not reflected in their interactions within the department—where people socialize and trust each other—it clearly affects their interactions with the organization's management. In this case, CMC supports communication with all employees within the department, but does not remove hierarchical structuring outside the department.

In the client services department, hierarchical position influences to a greater extent who talks to whom (see Fig. 7.1). A person's status within the hierarchy of the organization plays a key role in how messages are replied to. Employees of lower status feel compelled to reply to messages of employees of higher status because receivers of messages knew that senders are aware that they have received the message. Thus, the aware-ness of others' availability leads to expectations in the sender about how long it should take the recipient to reply. For example, Brian, a department manager in the client services department, received two IMs during our interview. Each time, when the message popped up on the screen, Brian glanced at his screen and quickly scanned it. Both times he excused himself and initiated an exchange that lasted for two or three minutes.

When asked what had happened, Brian replied, 'I usually do not answer messages while I am engaged in a face-to-face meeting unless they are short questions or are urgent.' Yet he answered these messages, because they were from his superior. With IM, the status of the communicator and the urgency of the message can be more compelling than the physical presence of someone FTF.

Conclusions

Social affordances of CMC

KME is *hyperconnected*. The adding on of CMC to FTF and telephone contact has created hyperconnectivity where community members—at work or elsewhere—are always connected to CMC and always available for communication. Employees can easily send an email or instant mes-sage (IM) to any other member of the organization, regardless of status or role. Hyperconnectivity affords new forms of collaboration, such as instant availability of contact and constant monitoring of IMs. Hyperconnectivity combines the traditional availability (and surveillance) of all-to-all characteristic of pre-industrial villages and workplaces with the flexible connectivity to socially and physically dispersed others characteristic of the networked internet age.

In this hyperconnected organization, and perhaps in many others, pervasive CMC has become the routine and practical means for contacting people within and outside workgroups, departments, and organizations. We may be observing a change in the use of CMC and traditional media unique to firms where work consists of sitting at desks. Organizations that have multiple and the latest technology available for communication may prefer to rely on CMC for communication. CMC is simply the *modus operandi* of the organization, with organizational norms outweighing social presence and message–media fit limitations.

CMC-fostered hyperconnectivity means that KME is a *local virtuality*. Most communication is via CMC, both email and IM, despite the physical proximity of fellow employees. People go online to exchange email and IM with colleagues who are sitting next to them. The high volume of CMC use, within a department and beyond it, strongly suggests that CMC does not weaken trust in this organization. It is the social structure and ethic of contribution of the organization that is important to the formation of collaborative community, and not the communication media alone.

KME is *glocalized*. Its members not only communicate by CMC with fellow department members on the same floor, but email is their predominant means of communication with people outside the organization. Rather than the utopian dream of CMC making community independent of distance, CMC has become the way to communicate, both locally and globally.

Task complexity and interdependency are key factors in determining the extent to which employees communicate with one another both via traditional media and CMC. Programmers have independent jobs, but they recognize and use each other's expertise, forming dense networks of collaboration. The KME way of working collaboratively involves the simultaneous independence of jobs combined with interdependencies. Although KME is not a thoroughly networked organization, people are often enmeshed in multiple work networks. They work simultaneously and sequentially with different members of their department.

For example, in the client services department, people work on different accounts that function independently of one another and thus have little incentive to share best practices. This leads to more sparsely knit networks than in the densely knit software development department. The differences in collaboration between the two departments show that while CMC affords the creation of collaborative community, task characteristics also have an influence on its formation.

In a nice illustration of the Adler–Heckscher model of collaborative community, the KME way of working collaboratively involves the simultaneous independence of jobs combined with interdependencies. There is a dynamic tension between shared and individual problem solving. Workers are given clear roles to deal with assigned tasks, and they are expected to fulfill these tasks independently. Yet, frequent meetings and discussions of product development accompany these independent tasks. Shared understandings develop during these meetings, with other department members providing input into the various components of the software development task. As Sabel argues in Chapter 2, when problems reach levels of urgency, volatility, and complexity where no single person can know the whole answer to a particular question, people will use their social network to locate someone who is already solving the problem or at least has worked on a similar problem. In this way, individuals have access through their social networks to experts that can help them identify potential solutions and compare various problem-solving strategies.

What makes KME particularly effective in locating experts who can help solve a problem is that hyperconnectivity in this local virtuality creates a dense network of exchange. Frequent communication helps employees create the shared understandings that are key for effective joint problem solving. Moreover, the availability of multiple CMC and the always-connected nature of KME provide flexibility and access for employees to solve problems quickly.

Contrary to the arguments of dystopians, CMC at KME attracts the attention of employees but does not *immerse* them in their computer screens. When Quan-Haase sat with KME employees at their workstations, she noticed how they were always glancing at their screens to check for incoming messages. They frequently interrupted their conversations with her to respond to an urgent message. Yet, they were not totally immersed, as they always turned back to Quan-Haase (and others) to resume chatting FTF, picking up the continuing conversational threads.

Nor *does CMC fragment identity*, another fear of dystopians. Although KME employees vary in how they use CMC, each employee has the same

319

persona online and offline. They are integrated personas, having nothing resembling Sherry Turkle's 'second self' online. Employees use CMC pragmatically as a tool and a social facilitator. They do not use CMC as therapeutic devices to get lost in cyberspace, away from the real world.

CMC at KME affords *trust*. Colleagues do not need to be in FTF contact to trust one another. There are frequent shorthand IM conversations, so much so that we marveled at their apparent intrusiveness. More structured emails are equally as frequent, with email leaving more time for thought, allowing attaching documents, and providing archives and paper trails. Emails are supplemented by FTF encounters, both formal meetings and casual conversations. It is clear that FTF contact is not the only trustworthy form of communication. In a milieu with much individual networking and little direct supervision, it is hyperactive CMC that fosters collaborative community and trust within and between departments.

Technology does *not determine* communication behavior at KME. Rather, technology creates possibilities for behavior. Norms and social structures of interdependency affect media use. For example, programmers use IM more than email, while client service employees use email. The needs of the two departments differ: there is close collaboration among the programmers and a culture that favors rapid IM exchanges. By contrast, client service people, oriented more to external relations, use the more formal email. It is the type of relationship—not the type of technology—that influences how employees interact.

Despite the fears of early pundits, the supposed limitations of CMC— low *social presence* and *media richness*—do not significantly affect communication. While people cannot physically hug online, they can maintain close social relations and offer social support. As people become technologically savvy and become routinely used to communicating over CMC, the range of their computer-mediated use expands. KME employees frequently use CMC for sociability and social support, with communication ranging from simple information messages to complex discussions.

There is *conservation of media choice* in this hyperconnected organization. People who are contacted by one medium routinely respond by that medium: IM will be answered by IM, email by email, voice-mail by return phone call, and real-time phone calls and FTF chats inherently use the same medium. Although media conservation is a strong norm, we hesitate to call it a media law, as there are enough situations where people switch from one medium to another out of complexity or convenience. It is to this limited extent that differences in media richness come into play. For example, in several instances employees switched from IM to phone to deal with complex situations and there were other situations where a phone call led to a request: 'Could you send me an email about that?' Media etiquette at KME is a complex product of local norms and more widespread understandings of when different media should be used. Thus, employees used more email—and less IM—when communicating with people outside of KME.

Organizational affordances of CMC

Overlaying the formal structuring of departments, KME is *networked*. It is a milieu of multiple work teams and multiple friendship networks. While networks have always been pervasive in organizations, they are now facilitated by the routinization and normalization of CMC that is making communication easier and quicker across departmental and organizational boundaries. People move in and out of different networks as needed. At KME, hyperconnectivity affords more fluid and active use of networked relationships within and between workgroups. Their links interconnect multiple networks, providing access to new information and possibly more creative problem solving. Employees work simultaneously and sequentially with shifting sets of others, in *networked individualism*: reflecting the shift of work and community structures away from solidary, comprehensive bounded groups to sparsely knit, partial social networks.

Ties in KME's networks are *neither randomly nor evenly distributed*. Interdependent work (in software development) and organizational efforts to build collegiality (in client services) creates clusters of densely knit relationships of work, and to a lesser extent, sociability. The two departments are quite different (see Figs. 7.1 and 7.2). The outwardly oriented client service facilitators connect less frequently with each other than do the programmers. Yet while the hyperconnectivity of the programmers creates a densely knit cluster of relationships, at any one time, relationships usually operate as dyads—two persons working on a problem—rather than operating in groups. Despite the networked basis of work at KME, its hyperconnected local virtuality fosters departmental and *organizational identity and loyalty*. Employees were always keenly aware of their colleagues, their organizational role, and their organization's mission.

Although networked in practice, communication at KME occurs within an organizational structure. Despite the widespread belief that CMC is fostering a wholesale transition to network organizations in high-tech firms, KME remains *hierarchical* in the form of an enabling bureaucracy.[36] Hierarchy and roles continue to exist even in this hyper-connected environment. Not all employees are equally connected to all other employees. Status differences continue to influence interactions in a computer-mediated work environment. The immediacy of responses to IM and email is driven by norms and power, as much as by techno-logy. All employees are connected, but some are more connected than others.

Hierarchy continues to play a dominant role in relationships among workers. At the same time, the meaning of hierarchy requires revisiting. Supervision does not occur in the same way as happens in a traditional bureaucratic organization, where employees report on a daily basis to their bosses and where bosses closely surveil the work of their employees. This is possible in production types of work, but when it comes to knowledge work, employees have unique expertise that is difficult to evaluate and supervise from the bosses' perspective.

Trust and hyperconnectivity in the local virtuality of KME play key roles in terms of employee independence. Employees' experience and expertise lead to what Levin and Cross have referred to as competence-based trust, which allows employees to make decisions without prior consulting.[37] This is important in these types of industries where time is a key resource and involving one's boss is a burden.

The evidence provides a view that is more routinized and stable than a 'network organization' but more flexible and hyperconnected than a trad-itional bureaucratic organization. Unlike Adler and Heckscher's opposition of hierarchical and networked models of organization, KME is a mixture of both forms. Neither is an overlay of the others. Employees are organized into departments. These departments significantly structure their work practices, and most communication occurs within departments—on and off the internet. Yet, KME is also a network—functioning as a hypercon-nected local virtuality. Within the stable framework of departments, its employees communicate frequently and widely. In this local virtuality, there is less need to go to meetings or to get up from desks. CMC provides employees with the flexibility and access to gain the information and coordination they need immediately—within and between departments. The ways in which CMC supports peer-to-peer communication within and between departments provide 'gangplanks' that facilitate informal coordination while maintaining formal hierarchical control.[38] In short, while KME is not a network organization, it is highly networked, with CMC networks providing the means for information and social net-working.

References

Adler, P. S., and Borys, B. (1996). 'Two types of bureaucracy: enabling and coercive.' *Administrative Science Quarterly*, 41/1: 61–89.

Ahuja, M., and Carley, K. (1999). 'Network structure in virtual organizations.' *Organization Science*, 10/6: 741–57.

Allen, T. J. (1977). *Managing the Flow of Technology: Technology Transfer and the Dissemination of Technological Information within the R&D Organization*. Cambridge, Mass.: MIT Press.

Barlow, J. P., Birkets, S., Kelly, K., and Slouka, M. (1995). 'What are we doing on-line?' *Harper's* (Aug.): 35–46.

Bimber, B. A. (2003). *Information and American Democracy: Technology in the Evolution of Political Power*. Cambridge: Cambridge University Press.

Borsook, P. (2000). *Cyberselfish: A Critical Romp through the Terribly Libertarian Culture of High Tech*. New York: Public Affairs.

Bradner, E. (2001). 'Social factors in the design and use of computer-mediated communication technology.' Unpublished doctoral dissertation, University of California, Irvine.

——Kellogg, W. A., and Erickson, T. (1998). 'Babble: supporting conversation in the workplace.' *SIGGROUP Bulletin*, 19/3: 8–10.

——————— (1999). 'Social affordances of Babble: a field study of chat in the workplace.' Paper presented at the ECSCW'99, the Sixth European Conference on Computer Supported Cooperative Work, Copenhagen, 12–16 Sept.

Brooks, F. P. (1974). *The Mythical Man-Month*. Reading, Mass.: Addison-Wesley.

Carmel, E. (1995). 'Cycle-time in packaged software firms.' *Journal of Product Innovation Management*, 12/2: 110–23.

——and Sawyer, S. (1998). 'Packaged software development teams: what makes them different?' *Information, Technology & People*, 11/1: 7–19.

Castells, M. (1996). *The Rise of the Network Society*. Cambridge, Mass.: Blackwell.

——(2000). *The Rise of the Network Society*. 2nd. edn. Oxford: Blackwell.

Choo, C. W. (1998). *The Knowing Organization: How Organizations Use Information to Construct Meaning, Create Knowledge, and Make Decisions*. New York: Oxford University Press.

Cohen, D., and Prusak, L. (2001). *In Good Company: How Social Capital Makes Organizations Work*. Cambridge, Mass.: Harvard Business School Press.

Constantine, L. L. (1995). *Constantine on Peopleware*. Englewood Cliffs, NJ: Prentice Hall/Yourdon Press.

Culnan, M. J., and Markus, M. L. (1987). 'Information technologies.' In F. M. Jablin, L. L. Putnam, K. H. Roberts, and L. W. Porter (eds.), *Handbook of Organizational Communication: An Interdisciplinary Perspective*. Beverly Hills, Calif.: Sage: 420–43.

Dabbish, L., and Kraut, R. (2004). 'Controlling interruptions: awareness displays and social motivation for coordination.' *Proceedings of CSCW2004 Conference* (Chicago, Nov.). New York: Association for Computing Machinery: 182–91.

Daft, R. L., and Lengel, R. H. (1986). 'Organizational information requirements, media richness and structural design.' *Management Science*, 32/5: 554–71.

————— and Trevino, L. K. (1987). 'Message equivocality, media selection and manager performance: implications for information systems.' *MIS Quarterly*: 355–66.

Davenport, T. H., and Prusak, L. (1997). *Information Ecology: Mastering the Information and Knowledge Environment*. New York: Oxford University Press.

————— (2000). *Working Knowledge: How Organizations Manage what they Know*. 2nd edn. Boston: Harvard Business School Press.

Davenport, T. O. (1999). *Human Capital: What it is and Why People Invest in it*. San Francisco: Jossey-Bass.

DeMarco, T., and Lister, T. (1987). *Peopleware: Productive Projects and Teams*. New York: Dorsett House.

DiMaggio, P., Hargittai, E., Neuman, W. R., and Robinson, J. P. (2001). 'Social implications of the internet.' *Annual Review of Sociology*, 27: 307–36.

Dimitrova, D. (2002). 'The telework mosaic: forms of corporate telework.' Unpublished doctoral dissertation, University of Toronto, Toronto.

Dubé, L. (1998). 'Teams in packaged software development: the software corp. experience.' *Information, Technology & People*, 11/1: 36–61.

Eppler, M. J., and Mengis, J. (2004). 'The concept of information overload: a review of literature from organization science, accounting, marketing, MIS, and related disciplines.' *Information Society*, 20/5: 325–44.

Erickson, T., and Kellogg, W. A. (2000). 'Social translucence: an approach to designing systems that support social processes.' *ACM Transactions on Computer–Human Interaction*, 7/1: 59–83.

Fayol, H. (1949). *General and Industrial Management*. London: Pitman.

Fischer, C. S. (1982). *To Dwell among Friends*. Berkeley and Los Angeles: University of California Press.

Fish, R., Kraut, R., Root, R., and Rice, R. (1992). 'Video as a technology for informal communication.' *Communications of the ACM*, 36/1: 48–61.

Fox, R. (1995). 'Newstrack.' *Communications of the ACM*, 38/8: 11–12.

Friedkin, N., and Johnsen, E. C. (2002). 'Control loss and Fayol's gangplanks.' *Social Networks*, 24/4: 395–406.

Gans, H. (1962). *The Urban Villagers*. New York: Free Press.

————— (1967). *The Levittowners*. New York: Pantheon.

Grannis, R. (1998). 'The importance of trivial streets: pedestrian-based communities, tertiary street networks, and geographic patterns of residential segregation.' Presented to the Sunbelt Social Networks Conference. San Diego, Feb.

Greer, S. (1962). *The Emerging City*. New York: Free Press.

Hampton, K., and Wellman, B. (2003). 'Neighboring in Netville: how the internet supports community and social capital in a wired suburb.' *City & Community*, 2/4: 277–311.

Handel, M., and Herbsleb, J. D. (2002). 'What is chat doing in the workplace?' Paper presented at the CSCW 2000, New Orleans, La., 16–20 Nov.

Haythornthwaite, C., and Wellman, B. (1998). 'Work, friendship and media use for information exchange in a networked organization.' *Journal of the American Society for Information Science*, 49/12: 1101–14.

Heckscher, C., and Donnellon, A. (eds.) (1994). *The Post-Bureaucratic Organization: New Perspectives on Organizational Change*. London: Sage.

Herbsleb, J. D., and Olson, G. (eds.) (2004). *Computer Supported Cooperative Work Conference Proceedings* (Chicago, Nov.). New York: ACM Publications.

——Atkins, D. L., Boyer, D. G., Handel, M., and Finholt, T. A. (2002). 'Introducing instant messaging and chat in the workplace.' Paper presented at the SIGCHI conference on human factors in computing systems, Minneapolis, 20–25 Apr.

Heydebrand, W. V. (1989). 'New organizational forms.' *Work and Occupations*, 16: 323–57.

Hillier, B. (1996). *Space is the Machine: A Configurational Theory of Architecture*. Cambridge: Cambridge University Press.

Hudson, J. M., Christensen, J., Kellogg, W. A., and Erickson, T. (2002). ' "I'd be overwhelmed, but it's just one more thing to do": availability and interruption in research management.' *Proceedings of the SIGCHI Conference on Human Factors in Computing Systems*, (Minneapolis, 20–25 Apr.). New York: ACM Press: 97–104.

Jarvenpaa, S. L., and Ives, B. (1994). 'The global network organization of the future: information management opportunities and challenges.' *Journal of Management Information Systems*, 10/4: 25–57.

Johnson, L. C. (1999). 'Bringing work home: developing a model residentially-based telework facility.' *Canadian Journal of Urban Research*, 8/2: 119–42.

Katz, J. E., and Rice, R. E. (2002). 'Syntopia: access, civic involvement, and social interaction on the net.' In B. Wellman and C. Haythornthwaite (eds.), *The Internet in Everyday Life*. Oxford: Blackwell Publishers: 114–38.

Keil, M., and Carmel, E. (1995). 'Customer–developer links in software development.' *Communications of the ACM*, 38/5: 33–44.

Keller, S. (1968). *The Urban Neighborhood*. New York: Random House.

Kling, R., and Gerson, E. (1978). 'The social dynamics of technical innovation in the computing world.' *Symbolic Interaction*, 1: 133–46.

Kling, R., and Scaachi, W. (1982). *The Web of Computing: Computer Technology as Social Organization*. San Diego: Academic Press.

Koskikallio, I. (2002). 'Empowering rural communities (by ICT).' Paper presented at the International Workshop, Helsinki, 22–23 Nov.

Krishnan, M. S. (1998). 'The role of team factors in software cost and quality: an empirical analysis.' *Information, Technology & People*, 11/1: 20–35.

Levin, D., and Cross, R. (2004). 'The strength of weak ties you can trust: the mediating role of trust in effective knowledge transfer.' *Informs*, 50 (Nov.): 1477–90.

Mantei, M., Baecker, R., Sellen, A., Buxton, W., Milligan, T., and Wellman, B. (1991). 'Experiences in the use of a media space: reaching through technology.' In *Proceedings of the CHI '91 Conference*. Reading, Mass.: Addison-Wesley: 203–8.

Miles, R. E., and Snow, C. C. (1986). 'Organizations: new concepts for new forms.' *California Management Review*, 28 (Summer): 62–73.

————(1992). 'Causes of failure in network organizations.' *California Management Review*, 34/4: 53–72.

Monge, P. R., and Contractor, N. S. (2000). 'Emergence of communication networks.' In F. M. Jablin and L. L. Putnam (eds.), *Handbook of Organizational Communication*. 2nd edn. Thousand Oaks, Calif.: Sage: 440–502.

————(2003). *Theories of Communication Networks*. Oxford: Oxford University Press.

Nahapiet, J., and Ghoshal, S. (1997). 'Social capital, intellectual capital and value creation in firms.' *Academy of Management Best Paper Proceedings*: 35–9.

————(2000). 'Social capital, intellectual capital, and the organizational advantage.' *Academy of Management Journal*, 23/2: 242–66.

Nardi, B. A. (2004). 'Objects of desire: power and passion in collaborative activity.' *Journal of Mind, Culture and Activity*, in press.

——Whittaker, S., and Bradner, E. (2000). 'Interaction and outeraction: instant messaging in action.' *Proceedings of Conference on Computer Supported Cooperative Work (CSCW)* (Philadelphia, 2–6 Dec.) New York: ACM, Inc.: 79–88.

Nisbet, R. (1953). *The Quest for Community*. Oxford: Oxford University Press.

Nohria, N., and Eccles, R. (1994). *Networks and Organizations*. Boston: Harvard Business School Press.

Orlikowski, W. J. (1996). 'Learning from notes: organizational issues in groupware implementation.' In R. Kling (ed.), *Computerization and Controversy: Value Conflicts and Social Choices*. 2nd edn. San Diego: Academic Press: 173–89.

Poe, R. (2001). 'Instant messaging goes to work.' *Business 2.0*, www.business2.com.

Putnam, R. (2000). *Bowling Alone: The Collapse and Revival of American Community*. New York: Simon & Schuster.

Quan-Haase, A. (2004). 'Information brokering and technology use: a case study of a high-tech firm.' Unpublished doctoral thesis, Faculty of Information Studies, University of Toronto.

——and Cothrel, J. (2003). 'Uses of information sources in an internet-era firm: online and offline.' In M. Huysman, E. Wenger, and V. Wulf (eds.), *Communities and Technologies*. Deventer: Kluwer Academic: 143–62.

——and Wellman, B. (2004). 'Networks of distance and media: a case study of a high-tech firm.' *Analyse und Kritik*, 26/2: 241–57.

————Witte, J., and Hampton, K. (2002). 'Capitalizing on the internet: social contact, civic engagement, and sense of community.' In B. Wellman and C. Haythornthwaite (eds.), *Internet and Everyday Life*. Oxford: Blackwell: 291–324.

Rheingold, H. (2000). *The Virtual Community: Homesteading on the Electronic Frontier*. Rev. edn. Cambridge, Mass.: MIT Press.

Rice, R. E. (1993). 'Influence of computer communication use and network structure on work networks and performance in a R&D organization.' International Sunbelt Social Network Conference, Tanepa (Feb.).

Salaff, J. W., Wellman, B., and Dimitrova, D. (1998). 'There's a time and a place for telework: how social networks affect telework.' Third International Workshop on Telework. Turku.

Sproull, L. S., and Kiesler, S. B. (1991). *Connections: New Ways of Working in the Networked Organization*. Cambridge, Mass.: MIT Press.

Stone, B. (2004). *Who Let the Blogs out? A Hyperconnected Peek at the World of Weblogs*. New York: St Martin's Griffin.

Strong, R., and Gaver, Bill (1996). 'Feather, scent, and shaker: supporting simple intimacy.' Presented at CSCW conference, Cambridge, Mass.

Taylor, P. (1999). *Hackers*. New York: Routledge.

Tilly, C. (1974). 'Introduction.' In C. Tilly (ed.), *An Urban World*. Boston: Little, Brown: 1–35.

Tocqueville, A. de (1835). *Democracy in America*. New York: Knopf.

Tönnies, F. (1887/1955). *Community and Organization*. London: Routledge & Kegan Paul.

Turkle, S. (1984). *The Second Self: Computers and the Human Spirit*. New York: Simon & Schuster.

—— (1995). *Life on the Screen: Identity in the Age of the Internet*. New York: Simon & Schuster.

Van Alstyne, M. (1997). 'The state of network organization.' *Journal of Organizing Computing and Electronic Commerce*, 7/3: 83–151.

Ward, R., Wamsley, G., Schroeder, A., and Robins, D. B. (2000). 'Networked organizational development in the public sector: a case study of the federal emergency management administration (FEMA).' *Journal of the American Society for Information Science*, 51/11: 1018–32.

Wellman, B. (1979). 'The community question: the intimate networks of East Yorkers.' *American Journal of Sociology*, 84: 1201–31.

—— (1988). 'Structural analysis: from method and metaphor to theory and substance.' In B. Wellman and S. D. Berkowitz (eds.), *Social Structures: A Network Approach*. Cambridge: Cambridge University Press: 19–61.

—— (1999a). 'The network community: an introduction.' In B. Wellman (ed.), *Networks in the Global Village*. Boulder, Colo.: Westview: 1–47.

—— (ed.) (1999b). *Networks in the Global Village*. Boulder, Colo.: Westview Press.

—— (2001a). 'The persistence and transformation of community: from neighbourhood groups to social networks.' Report to the Law Commission of Canada (Oct.).

—— (2001b). 'Physical place and cyberspace: the rise of personalized networks.' *International Urban and Regional Research*, 25/2: 227–52.

—— (2002). 'Designing the internet for a networked society.' *Communications of the ACM*, 45/5: 91–6.

—— and Gulia, M. (1999). 'Net surfers don't ride alone.' In B. Wellman (ed.), *Networks in the Global Village*. Boulder, Colo.: Westview Press: 331–66.

Wellman, B. and Haythornthwaite, C. (eds.) (2002). *The Internet in Everyday Life.* Oxford: Blackwell Publishers.

—— and Hogan, B. (2004). 'The immanent internet.' In Johnston McKay (ed.), *Netting Citizens: Exploring Citizenship in a Digital Age.* Edinburgh: St Andrew Press: 54–80.

—— and Leighton, B. (1979). 'Networks, neighborhoods and communities.' *Urban Affairs Quarterly*, 14: 363–90.

—— Salaff, J., Dimitrova, D., Garton, L., Gulia, M., and Haythornthwaite, C. (1996). 'Computer networks as social networks: virtual community, computer supported cooperative work and telework.' *Annual Review of Sociology*, 22: 213–38.

Wenger, E. (1998). *Communities of Practice: Learning, Meaning, and Identity.* Cambridge: Cambridge University Press.

—— (2000). 'Communities of practice: the key to knowledge strategy.' In E. L. Lesser, M. A. Fontaine, and J. A. Slusher (eds.), *Knowledge and Communities: Resources for the Knowledge-Based Economy.* Woburn, Mass.: Butterworth-Heinemann: 3–20.

—— McDermott, R. A., and Snyder, W. (2002). *Cultivating Communities of Practice: A Guide to Managing Knowledge.* Boston: Harvard Business School Press.

Wired. (2002). *Born Digital: Children of the Revolution*, 10 Sept. Retrieved 16 Oct. 2004, from the World Wide Web: www.wired.com/wired/archive/10.09/borndigital.html.

Zachary, G. P. (1998). 'Armed truce: software in an age of teams.' *Information, Technology & People*, 11/1: 62–5.

Notes

Support for the research underlying this chapter has been provided by BMO (the Bank of Montreal), Communication and Information Technology Ontario, the Institute of Knowledge Management (IBM), Mitel Networks, and the Social Science and Humanities Research Council of Canada. The first author acknowledges assistance from the Alumni Research Awards Program, Faculty of Social Science, the University of Western Ontario. We thank Paul Adler, Manuel Castells, Rob Cross, Charles Heckscher, Lynne Howarth, Richard Livesley, and Larry Prusak for their advice, and Julie Wang for her editorial assistance. We particularly want to thank Joseph Cothrel for facilitating our research and for thoughtful comments on an earlier draft. We especially want to thank all those employees at KME who completed the survey, and even more so, those who gave generously of their time with interviews and observations.

1. The changes from hierarchical to networked organizations have been discussed in such texts as: Heydebrand (1989); Jarvenpaa and Ives (1994); Miles and Snow (1986); Miles and Snow (1992); Nohria and Eccles (1994); Monge and

Contractor (2000, 2003); Davenport and Prusak (1997, 2000); Ward et al. (2000); Wellman (2002); Castells (1996). Sproull and Kiesler's *Connections* (1991) was one of the first books to discuss how organizations are changing as a consequence of CMC. See also Howard Rheingold's description of the online community The WELL (2000) and Bradner et al.'s (1998) portrayal of work groups on Babble.

2. The quotation is from Castells (1996: 171). See also Adler and Heckscher's introductory chapter; Adler and Borys (1996); Ahuja and Carley (1999); Castells (2000); Choo (1998); Davenport and Prusak (1997, 2000); Heckscher and Donnellon (1994); Heydebrand (1989); Jarvenpaa and Ives (1994); Monge and Contractor (2003); Nohria and Eccles (1994); Sproull and Kiesler (1991); Van Alstyne (1997).

3. Withering away of community in mass society: Tönnies (1887/1955); Nisbet (1953); Putnam (2000); Tocqueville (1835). Persistence of community: For case studies, see Gans (1962, 1967) Grannis (1998); for a synthesis, see Greer (1962); Keller (1968). For networked community, see Tilly (1974); Wellman (1979, 1999*a*, 1999*b*); Wellman and Hogan (2004); Wellman and Leighton (1979); Fischer (1982). 'Networked individualism' is discussed in Wellman (2001*b*).

4. Telework, where organizational employees work from home using CMC, takes this model one step further as employees are no longer under the visual control of supervisors. See Johnson (1999); Dimitrova (2002); Salaff et al. (1998).

5. See the discussion of how the creation and maintenance of social relationships are a major investment for organizations in Nahapiet and Ghoshal (1997, 2000).

6. See Cohen and Prusak's discussion in chapter 7 on 'The Challenge of Virtuality' (2001). The lack of social cues in CMC compared to FTF is discussed in Rice (1993) as well as in Fish et al. (1992).

7. Turkle's work (1984, 1995) is based on observations of children and teenagers in the early days of CMC. Hightower is quoted in Fox (1995: 12). Barlow is in a *Harper's* symposium (1995: 40).

8. Adler and Heckscher's introductory chapter summarizes the evidence adduced by Fischer (1982), Wellman (1999*a*, 2001*a*, 2001*b*); Wellman and Gulia (1999); and others. For how the internet adds on to existing forms of communication, see Quan-Haase and Wellman (2002); DiMaggio et al. (2001); Wellman and Haythornthwaite (2002); Katz and Rice (2002). For how the internet affects local use, see Hampton and Wellman (2003).

9. This work is presented most thoroughly in Bradner's doctoral dissertation (2001). See also Bradner et al. (1999).

10. Asynchronous communication is also starting to become more popular on IM as teenagers and adolescents leave each other messages when not online.

11. See Bruce Bimber's *Information and American Democracy* (2003) for a description of the shift in American organizations and institutions towards rapid, event-driven processes. Also see the chapter in this book by Paul Adler and Charles

Heckscher, and the books by Davenport and Prusak (1997, 2000) and Davenport (1999).

12. A number of studies in the literature report on challenges that employees confront when adopting a new tool (see Orlikowski 1996; Kling and Gerson 1978).

13. For an analysis of the use of information sources and working relationships in KME, see Quan-Haase and Cothrel (2003), Quan-Haase (2004), and Quan-Haase and Wellman (2004). The scale for the instrumental, social, and media networks was: 1='never'; 2='a few times a year'; 3='1/month'; 4='1/week'; 5='several times a week'; 6='1/day'; 7='several times a day.'

14. For discussions of communities of practice and their relevance to knowledge sharing in organizations, see Wenger (1998, 2000); Wenger et al. (2002). The conceptual framework to compare the software development and client services departments is adapted from Carmel and Sawyer's typology (1998).

15. For time to market pressures, see Carmel (1995); Carmel and Sawyer (1998); Dubé (1998); Krishnan (1998); Zachary (1998). For client relationships, see Keil and Carmel (1995) and Constantine (1995).

16. The work of programmers reflects many attributes of the entrepreneurial legend: long hours, grit and determination, and high risk. (See Boorsook 2000; Carmel and Sawyer 1998; Taylor 1999.) The term 'software cowboys' was coined by Constantine (1995: 48). By contrast to the KME situation, Adler's chapter provides evidence of the industrialization of software programming: routinized, coordinated work with bureaucratically regulated divisions of labor. See also Kling and Scaachi (1982). Brooks (1974) in his investigation of how IBM developed the Systems 360 operating system documented how team behavior is the driver of software development. While this is also the case at KME, where employees work on a single software package that requires high levels of integration, not all software development depends on highly interrelated tasks.

17. Carmel (1995) calls this a 'core team.'

18. Thomas J. Allen (1977) describes in his studies that as people are physically further away from each other, the less they communicate and hence the fewer opportunities they have to build trusting relationships. Hillier (1996) describes how the design of a workspace influences the possibilities for communication.

19. To investigate the instrumental networks of the two departments, weekly exchanges of information among department members and between departments are examined.

20. Although not used at KME, internet phones provide voice contact that mimics traditional telephones. They may develop additional capacity at a later time. Desktop videoconferencing systems have been around since the early 1990s (see, for example, Mantei et al. 1991; Herbsleb and Olson 2004). There have even been prototypes of remote transmission of smell and touch (Strong and Gaver 1996).

21. The fact that various media are used for different purposes suggests that a single dimension ranging from lean to rich is not sufficient to describe and predict media choice and adequacy, as message–media fit theory has attempted (Daft and Lengel 1986; Daft et al. 1987). Various media serve different purposes in different social contexts. Thus, while message–media fit theory is not refuted by the observations at KME, it needs to be expanded to include other relevant dimensions. In many organizations employees are now collaborating via IM, either as a complement to email or a replacement: see Handel and Herbsleb (2002); Herbsleb et al. (2002); Poe (2001); Nardi (2004).

22. The first study to our knowledge on the use of IM in the workplace as a tool to identify other communication partners is conducted by Nardi et al. (2000).

23. This is in accord with the findings by Haythornthwaite and Wellman (1998) who showed that when more types of social relationships connect two individuals, the more types of media are used to communicate and the more frequent the communication.

24. Erickson and Kellogg (2000) describe how information about a user that is transmitted by a communication system can be used for making social inferences about the status of the communication partner, including inferences about awareness, availability, and accountability.

25. The need for a recorded trail of messages has increased in the USA with the passage of the Sarbenes-Oxley legislation in 2002, requiring archiving of all organizational correspondence. Folklore has it that some organizations use IM precisely because current software does not archive messages.

26. Although 'hyperconnected' is not a newly coined word, we give it a new meaning as social systems in which people are always on: available for communication anywhere and anytime. The word is rarely defined. A search on Google provided a number of hits and multiple usages for 'hyperconnected.' Some websites refer to a use in mathematics. In the context of technology, hyperconnected is used to refer to the connections between websites. Biz Stone (2004) uses 'hyperconnected' to refer to the linkages between weblogs. *Wired* magazine (2002) used the word to describe children who are born in the digital age. The pervasiveness of hyperconnectedness at KME calls into question message–media fit theory which argues that the characteristics of media lead to different media choices (Daft and Lengel 1986; Daft et al. 1987). Messages that are complex or equivocal are transmitted via rich media, such as FTF and the phone, because lean media, such as email, are not adequate.

27. These findings are similar to those of a study of interruptions and availability in managerial jobs that found that managers want to be accessible to others, yet maintain control over these interruptions (Hudson et al. 2002). See also the experiment done by Dabbish and Kraut (2004) showing that frequent monitoring of availability displays affects attention and Eppler and Mengis's guide to overload research (2004).

28. 'Local virtualities' is not new. We use the term here to describe local work settings where people are physically near each other and use CMC to exchange information, share best practices, and socialize. See Quan-Haase and Cothrel (2003) for a more detailed description and a more extensive discussion of the emergence of local virtualities at KME. The term 'local virtuality' also has been used in the study of rural communities, where it is defined as the use of email as a communication tool among non-anonymous parties and contrasted with global virtuality, which refers to exchanges among anonymous parties (Koski-kallio 2002).

29. Manuel Castells argues that information and communication technologies create spaceless places where information is stored, shared, and exchanged in virtual space. He contends that even in a technological and networked society, place continues to be a relevant dimension for the formation and maintenance of culture.

30. CMC is usually thought of as an alternative way of communication for long-distance, boundary-spanning exchanges (see Sproull and Kiesler 1991). Among the few studies of IM at work are Nardi et al. (2000). At KME, CMC is used for local exchanges as a result of a crowded workspace and ease of use.

31. The original 7-point scale has been transformed into days per year: 'never'=0; 'a few times a year'=5; '1/month'=12; '1/week'=52; 'several times a week'= 130; '1/day and several times a day'=365. Much social network research has shown that while specific metrics of communication frequency tend to be unreliable, comparative metrics tend to be valid. The ratios have been obtained by calculating the proportion of communication between distances. For example, the ratio 'Colleagues Inside Organization/Work Group' is 178/ 285=0.62. In this example, the mean days per year communication with colleagues elsewhere in the organization is divided by the mean days per year communication within the workgroup. For more details on glocal communication in KME, see Quan-Haase and Wellman (2004).

32. Robin Teigland's (2000) investigation of a high-tech firm showed that external sources of information help programmers find creative solutions to their problems, in particular online communities of practice that span the globe. External sources are reported to be critical as key information is often not available within the department or organization. Employees at KME similarly report using external sources of information when critical knowledge is not available within the organization and relying on CMC to access these external sources.

33. The high degree of collaboration among the software development department reflects previous arguments that the most important factor in software development is the team interaction, which has been referred to as 'people-ware' (DeMarco and Lister 1987; Constantine 1995).

34. Cohen and Prusak (2001) see the creation of shared understandings among coworkers as a key organizational process. They see shared understandings as a

prerequisite for the development of trust. Unless people can develop shared understandings, it will be difficult for them to trust each other.

35. Cohen and Prusak (2001) refer to the sum of relationships among coworkers that facilitate the flow of resources (information, knowledge, social support, etc.) in a firm as social capital. Social capital constitutes the key factor for success in a knowledge economy. See also Adler and Heckscher's introductory chapter for a discussion of trust and community in organizations.

36. In enabling bureaucracies, procedures provide organizational memory encoding best practices and providing a stable environment for innovation (Adler and Borys 1996). See Wellman (1988) for a discussion of why ties in networks are never randomly distributed.

37. Levin and Cross (2004). See also Adler and Heckscher's introductory chapter and Adler and Borys (1996).

38. The notion of cross-cutting, coordinating 'gangplanks' comes from Fayol (1949) and is developed as a social network concept by Friedkin and Johnsen (2002).

8

Collaborative Community and Employee Representation

Saul A. Rubinstein

Introduction

A collaborative community must provide voice and influence to all its members. Unions are the primary mechanism available today for assuring—institutionalizing—such voice and influence in business organizations. However, in many unionized organizations, management and labor are locked in adversarial rather than cooperative relations. This chapter discusses the much smaller number of organizations in which management and labor have committed to partnership in the pursuit of their common goals. The experience of these partnerships suggests several lessons concerning their potential benefits, the changes in unions required to pursue these benefits, and the significance of the fact that so many of them eventually fail. In summary, the benefits of partnership appear to be potentially large—large enough to outweigh the extra 'overhead' they require. The changes required of unions are extensive, most notably: new skills, a new understanding of their mission, and more democratic internal processes. Analysis of the reasons for the limited life-spans of these partnerships implicates some of the enduring features of the capitalist economy. The prospects for democratization of business organizations remain uncertain.

The impact of collaborative community on unions

Over the past twenty-five years, while many firms have taken the 'low road' of aggressive pursuit of short-term cost advantage, a growing number have shifted in the other direction, toward team-based structures, more horizontal coordination, and greater opportunities for involvement of the workforce in problem solving and decision making.[1] In these latter firms, the principle of collaborative community has become more salient as an organizing principle. Some of these firms are unionized. This chapter addresses the role of unions in these settings and the impact of this shift for the internal functioning of unions.

Unions have traditionally represented employees' collective interests through bargaining with management, and employees' individual interests through grievance procedures aimed at contract enforcement. These relationships typically place unions and their leaders in the role of adversaries of management and advocates for their members. In this role, unions have typically been organized internally as *Gemeinschaft* collectivities with strong internal hierarchies: the former aspect provides solidarity and the latter provides direction.

In the period that Adler and Heckscher (Chapter 1) have described as that of 'paternalist bureaucracy,' this definition of roles was acceptable to management. In fact, companies took the lead in shaping labor law so as to make unions formally responsible only for member interests, with companies retaining the sole 'prerogative' for determining strategy and representing shareholders. This was in accord with the top-down model that viewed strategy as the preserve of top management and boxed all employees into defined and delimited roles.

As shown throughout this volume, this arrangement has been brought increasingly into question by management itself. The growing knowledge intensity and solutions orientation increasingly require all employees to understand and actively contribute to the overall strategic purpose. In this emergent collaborative logic, the idea of the union as an adversarial body representing employees against management and trying to police the enforcement of contractual provisions becomes an obstacle to, rather than a facilitator of, business success. It is therefore not surprising that in those companies where both unions and the knowledge/solutions competitive pressures are strong, there are also strong pressures to reshape labor relations.[2]

Forms of union involvement and associated challenges

Unions have had considerable difficulty responding to this challenge. Most frequently, management wants greater employee participation in front-line operations but holds the union at arm's length. Some unions have tried a 'militant' approach of rejecting such programs out of hand, as snares designed to weaken worker loyalty to their unions; but this has been a difficult position to maintain in the face of members' generally favorable view of these initiatives. The majority have adopted an uncomfortably defensive attitude—allowing management to introduce worker participation, but vigilantly monitoring these programs for violations of contract clauses. This is uncomfortable because it can easily bring unions in conflict with their own members who propose work changes that impinge on contractual provisions.

In a much smaller number of cases, management and unions have sought to go beyond front-line participation and to give union representatives voice and influence in the broader strategic decision-making process. Such 'partnership' arrangements bring unions into deliberations about strategy, capital investment, product development, technology selection and implementation, quality assurance, budgeting, finance, personnel recruitment, selection and allocation, supplier relations, and operations management.[3] Compared to the issues posed by front-line participation, involvement in such strategic decisions poses even greater challenges to the traditional functioning of unions.

One way to conceptualize these different forms of labor/management collaboration is presented in Fig. 8.1.[4] The columns differentiate between direct participation of union members on the right and those where participation relies on union leaders and representatives on the left. This distinction corresponds to the operational/strategic distinction just discussed because worker involvement in strategic decision making relies on representative rather than direct participation mechanisms (at least in any but the very smallest organizations). The rows reflect the embeddedness of the collaboration in the work process or day-to-day management of the business—'offline' focuses on intermittent problem solving as distinct from 'online,' continuous influence.

Over the last eight years, in conjunction with scholars from Rutgers University, the Massachusetts Institute of Technology, and Harvard University, we have studied approximately fifty cases of such strategic partnerships involving participation on the left-hand side of Fig. 8.1 (see Appendix 8.1 for a partial list of cases). These cases span a wide variety of industries including airlines, automotive, communications, defense, health care, papermaking, pharmaceuticals, and steel.[5] This research program also included a series of workshops with a network of local union leaders, as well as extensive interviews, case studies, surveys, and direct observations.

336

	Representative/indirect—through union representatives	*Direct*—through member participation
Offline	**Governance** through union–management committees	**Consultative** through problem-solving teams
Online	**Co-management** through union–management partnerships	**Operational** through self-directed work teams

Fig. 8.1 Forms of labor–management collaboration

In the cases we studied, partnerships extended beyond front-line participation and beyond occasional meetings between leaders at the top of the respective union and management hierarchies: we focused on cases where partnership characterized the entire structure of relations throughout the organization. This kind of structure arguably represents the most fully developed form of collaborative community in a corporate setting. The following broad patterns emerged from these studies:

1. These unions attempt to represent their members' collective interests through increased involvement in managerial decision making. This involves union representatives in greater horizontal and vertical collaboration. They increasingly have come to see management not as a specific class of employees, but as a function or set of tasks the firm must accomplish—and that managers should not monopolize.

2. Union participation in managerial decision making adds economic value to the organization and in this way provides power that can be leveraged to produce tangible gains.

3. The shift to collaborative partnership relations between union and management requires new capacities and skills among union leaders and members, and requires new ways to organize the membership, structure the local, and allocate union resources. This shift to partnership requires that union leaders move beyond the adversarial role of representing their constituents' separate interests. They must

learn to combine the firm defense of employees' separate interests with the active pursuit of integrative bargaining around the interests that are common between workers and management.

Broader horizontal and vertical involvement

Most of the unions in these studies reported expanding their influence vertically to include joining with management in decision making in areas such as development of business strategy, new investments, product development, choice and introduction of technology, training, job design, quality assurance, subcontracting, business planning, supplier selection, and work reorganization. In some cases, this influence has extended beyond that afforded by occasional, offline conferences, and has become a more continuous affair, bringing union influence to bear on the online, day-to-day managerial decision making. And in the most interesting cases, this online influence has extended down into the management hierarchy, so that unions have influence across the full range of strategic and operational decisions. At American Axle the influence ranges from participation in decisions regarding business strategy, to customer contact, to running departments. At Union Camp Paper the union has been involved in managerial decision making including strategy, product development, work design, technology, facilities supplier selection, quality, and customer relations. In addition, union members have taken on many of the operations jobs formally held by management.

These unions also report broader horizontal involvement. In traditional bureaucratic organizations, managers construed their responsibility in rather parochial ways: union stewards in turn had responsibilities rather narrowly circumscribed by the department whose workers they represented. In organizations where the collaborative principle has assumed greater importance, managers and employees alike are drawn into broader webs of horizontal interdependence across functions and divisions: union representatives in such organizations must follow suit.

This can be seen in the new leadership roles and structures put in place by the unions involved in these collaborative partnership arrangements. For example, many of the unions created new positions within the union for the administration of the partnership. In these unions, representatives are selected by the leaders to facilitate and administer the involvement of union members in the partnership. These leaders have responsibility across the organization, not just in one department as stewards typically do. They attempt to improve the participation and voice opportunities for the entire membership on areas of common organizational interest with management. This stands in sharp contrast to the traditional focus of stewards who pay attention to contract violations in their own department. In some cases, like Saturn, the partnership agreement called for fewer stewards than a traditional UAW plant and more positions for union leaders in partnership roles. These leaders, both appointed and elected, came together every other week in a forum called Congress where they discussed union strategy and partnership concerns across the entire company. In other cases (Acme, Republic, Xerox) the partnership leaders/facilitators gained power within the union at the expense of the stewards because of their ability to work on problems that addressed the concerns of the majority of members who did not have grievances, and because their attention was at the level of the organization, not the department.

The union leaders involved in these partnerships, unlike many of their colleagues in the union movement, see the opportunity to advance the collective economic and social interests of their members by participating in decisions about how the business can respond effectively to competitive demands. (By economic interests, I refer to wages and benefits and income security; by social, I refer to the interest many workers feel in the dignity associated with voice and influence.) These leaders have concluded that given the opportunity to participate in a partnership relationship, they should take up the associated challenges and difficulties.

Adding economic value

Structural changes in the economy have put a premium on the ability of firms to respond rapidly to changes in the marketplace and the competitive environment. Unions can be of considerable economic value in helping firms respond to these challenges.

Unions can have significant benefits for the development of collaboration and trust at the firm level. Unions have been shown to improve managerial performance by creating checks and balances and exerting institutional discipline, and by creating a voice option that increases efficiency by decreasing turnover and channeling important information to management.[6] Unions can also improve firm performance by facilitating the participation of employees in problem solving and organizational improvement activities, and improving motivation and effort.[7] Unions create social networks that provide a highly effective infrastructure for communications and coordination laterally and vertically across the organization. This social network also creates solidarity—trust and identification with the union. If union and management are working in partnership and if workers see that their union has a beneficial influence in management decisions, this trust and identification will extend to the business organization. In this way, unions can add significant economic value to the organization that management alone cannot replicate.[8]

A number of studies have shown that as unions have expanded their roles in management, they have added economic value to the firm specifically through their ability to provide leadership, internal organization, and networking that brings effective coordination and implementation capability to the shop floor.[9] Part of this implementation capability is the higher level of trust workers have for leaders they elect. Unions have also demonstrated greater effectiveness in organizing worker participation in problem solving than management acting alone.

At Saturn, for many years one of the most advanced collaborative partnerships—with workers involved in managerial decision making at all levels—we were able to document the contribution of union-led involvement to product quality. We used social network analysis to model and analyze the labor–management and cross-department collaboration. We found that the union functioned as a dense communication and coordination network among the leaders who filled managerial roles, solving problems and co-managing the operations departments across three plants—engine and transmission, body, and assembly. Using social network analysis to model the communication patterns and multiple regression to isolate the union contribution, we found that communication by the union-represented co-managers was the most significant predictor of first-time quality performance at the department level, explaining 30 per cent of the variation across the company. Further, 53 per cent of the variation in quality improvement was explained by the communication and behavior of these union managers, and the dynamics of their relationship with their non-represented (management) partner.[10]

Similar results emerged in a recent study in the pharmaceutical industry. A longitudinal social network analysis of the impact of collaborative work systems at the laboratory services and facilities divisions of Bristol-Myers Squibb showed positive effects on economic performance of changes in the pattern and structure of employee communications. Horizontal coordination among workers increased as did communication between labor and managers. Centralization measures at Bristol-Myers Squibb declined over time as collaboration increased. Vertical communications between labor and management also increased as employees reported more input into departmental decisions and influence over daily work activities. Direct vertical communication increased not only with management but also across organizational boundaries with research scientists. At the same time company measures of internal customer satisfaction with the laboratory services and facilities divisions improved across all categories measured by management—reliability, responsiveness, timeliness, professionalism, and overall customer satisfaction.[11]

The economic value added by union representatives comes not only from their expertise and independent perspective but also from their credibility with the workforce which greatly enhances the implementation of decisions once made. It is unlikely that this value can be created in organizations without some form of credible employee representation.

We have found that as union representatives collaborate in making managerial decisions with worker interests in mind, they often take a broader firm-based perspective than do their counterparts in middle management. Many managers' careers depend on their ability to demonstrate performance improvement in their own area of responsibility—which, in traditional bureaucracies, often inclines them to ignore the needs of the broader organization. Union representatives are often less parochial. At the more senior strategic level of business units, we found that union leaders often have a longer time horizon than their management counterparts, since the union representatives do not have career paths that take them to higher corporate levels: instead, they typically see their futures as tied to the success of that division. Both generalizations admit many exceptions of course: some stewards are very parochial and some union leaders can be very focused on the short term; but when organizations are attempting to make the difficult transition from traditional bureaucracy to something closer to collaborative community, they may find union representatives to be strong allies.

Part of the value unions offer is a way to surface an alternative perspective in decision making which can supplement that of non-represented management. Non-union employee representation plans that simply align employee goals with those of management lose this opportunity. Diversity of perspective in decision making does not necessarily lead to adversarialism or dual loyalty. Rather, it can enrich the decision-making process and bring greater commitment to the implementation of decisions once they are reached. Thus, when unions engage in designing and administering employee participation efforts they not only add value to the firm, but also help create systems that can potentially outperform non-union forms of participation.

Further, a union's participation in decision making creates an atmosphere where workers are more likely to support those decisions and facilitate their implementation. Coordination and communication is also decentralized which allows information to flow more easily to those employees who can make the decision and are closest to the point of implementation.[12]

Local unions involved in managerial decision making have also added value by reducing the level of grievances.[13] Lockheed Martin reported a drop in annual grievances from 300 to 12, and American Axle reported a similar drop from 150 to 15.[14] In the past unions took on grievances whether or not they believed in their merits. Unions have a legal responsibility to protect the interests of their members both collectively and individually; like defense attorneys, unions often defend their clients without regard to larger considerations of what might be in the best interests of the organization. In these partnerships, unions advance workers' interests both by defending their separate interests and by pursuing the common interests they share with management—and here the union must consider whether filing a grievance contributes to the union's broader goals. The union may be reluctant to pursue grievances that it might have pursued under a more traditional system. On the one hand, this means frivolous grievances are less likely; on the other hand, there is some risk that the individual's rights might be inappropriately sacrificed. At the same time, the shift to partnership opens up a broader range of conflict resolution mechanisms. Union leaders in our research workshops argued that if grievances declined, it was not because union leaders were trying to avoid conflict but because partnership (a) reduced bad behavior by managers, (b) encouraged unions to avoid frivolous grievances by first exploring the nature of the issue rather than first filing the grievance, and (c) created alternative means to resolve conflict.

The ability to contribute to economic value has given unions increased power and influence.[15] Some of this power comes from the acquisition of new managerial skills, access to information networks, the demonstration of managerial competency of union leaders, and the ability to effectively mobilize the workforce. While the union can still exercise traditional tactics such as strike threats, it can also publicly challenge management's decisions that it does not see as in the best long-term interests of the company or its stakeholders. Further, if the union organization is essentially embedded in the management organization as was the case with Saturn, management can no longer direct the operation without union support. For example, during a weakening of the small car market in

1997–8, the union was able to force a negotiation to change the bonus formula by its unwillingness to continue to manage the operation under the incentives of the old formula while curtailing production and therefore bonuses. By continuing the production levels until a new formula was reached the union in effect put in place a reverse strike, producing more than management wanted in order to force management to the1 bargaining table. This was possible only because the union was so embedded in managerial roles in the operations organization.[16]

New union priorities, structures, and leadership

This shift toward collaborative partnership has necessitated deep and difficult shifts in the functioning of local unions. We see in these cases a new set of values governing organized labor—a shift from loyalty to value-adding contribution, from adversarial grievance handling to facilitating collaboration in problem solving, from job focus to building relationships, balancing individual and collective needs, representation, and management. There has also been an increase in union leaders taking on responsibilities that used to be the domain of management—from team leaders taking over the jobs of supervisors, to union leaders taking on managerial responsibilities in a partnership arrangement which breaks the line of demarcation between traditional labor and management roles.

More concretely, one can observe in these cases a significant shift in resources: more union leaders are engaged in collaborative activities and fewer in the traditional roles providing individual representation through administering the contract and grievance procedure and collective representation through bargaining. At Saturn there were more than 400 full-time union leaders out of a membership of 7,300—some elected, some appointed—filling positions that in any other division of General Motors would have been occupied by management. These positions ranged from operations management in departments of self-directed work teams, to engineering, to sourcing, to training, to quality assurance, to product design. Union leaders participated on joint labor–management governance bodies at the department, plant, and strategic levels of Saturn.

The union leadership developed a selection process for these partnership positions by which members could apply and a committee would decide on the most qualified candidates. The union leadership took the position that elections would politicize the partnership and would compromise the ability of these individuals to balance the needs of the membership with the needs of the business. Further, the leadership wanted skills, knowledge, and ability—not popularity—to be the determining factors. Elections were seen as a return to the traditional grievance committee structure and an increase in adversarialism. Members of an opposition caucus within the local argued that since the union was a democratic institution, all of these positions should be maximally accountable to union members and therefore subject to election by the rank and file. The opposition did not see elected union representatives' responsibilities as including such 'balancing'; they saw their role as representing members' interests, both their separate interests and their common interests with management.

The debate about internal union democracy continued for years within the Saturn local. Eventually an increased number of partnership positions were subject to rank-and-file election. This issue found its way into the 1999 local elections when the incumbent president and his caucus were defeated in part due to a perception that they had acquired too much power through their ability to approve the selection of 400 full-time union positions in the partnership, and that political loyalty rather than capability and contribution was becoming the most important consideration.

Alongside this broader ideological and political debate were more pragmatic issues. When an increasing number of rank-and-file members complained that they were not receiving adequate individual representation the union shifted resources from the collaborative partnership and increased the number of more traditional grievance committee positions who worried only about representing individual members' concerns, not balancing union needs with the need to co-manage the business.[17]

The shift to partnership also encourages a shift toward greater democracy within the union. Strengthening democracy seems to involve both direct and representative mechanisms. Saturn illustrates again.

First, the Saturn local strengthened direct participation in governance. Shop-floor team leaders at Saturn are elected by the team members and become union officials after their election with responsibilities for representation. If we consider the 700 elected team leaders, the 400 selected partnership leaders, and the elected union officers and grievance committee, almost one member in five had a position of leadership in the Saturn local—an extraordinary level of participation in the affairs of the union and movement toward increased union democracy.

Second, the Saturn local created a whole panoply of ways to improve the effectiveness of its representative mechanisms: The bi-weekly Congress, mentioned earlier, that included all elected and appointed union leaders holding positions in the partnership met to discuss the union's agenda and priorities, and its role in managerial collaboration. The leadership team comprised of the 50 top union leaders met every week to discuss union strategy, the partnership, and business issues. Weekly block meetings were conducted in each department between local union leaders and shop-floor team leaders to discuss problems and improve communication in each area. Rap sessions were held in each business unit between the union president and members in an open forum. Monthly Town Hall union membership meetings were held twice during the work day so that each shift could participate. And annual member-to-member surveys were conducted in which team leaders would hold personal interviews with every union member about the issues, concerns, and needs they would like to see addressed by the union. All of these mechanisms increased the input by members in running and setting the agenda of the union.

Capitalism and collaboration: the tension between managerial control and union influence

Despite the demonstrated economic potential of collaborative partnerships, there is an enduring tension between the forces within capitalism that put a premium on the flexibility and responsiveness that partnership provides, and competing forces that limit or undermine unions.

There are three main ways in which the capitalist nature of the firm can undermine partnership. First, in the absence of strong, constraining legislation, managers can simply pull back. My study of collaboration and partnership in the steel industry makes this clear: even when the parties had reached contractual agreement for collaboration, the single greatest obstacle was managerial resistance.[18] Looking back over the past twenty-five years we can see many examples of the creation of collaborative work systems where over time management, or in some cases the union, was unable to maintain its commitment to the process and the collaborative systems could not be sustained.[19]

Second, in some cases the demise of partnership was due to upheavals in the larger economic context: under capitalism, market trumps community, even in the best cases where partnerships have achieved a significant

level of local institutional embeddedness. For example, in the steel industry the United Steel Workers of America included Cooperative Partnership
Agreements in their 1993 and 1999 negotiations in the basic steel. These
agreements established joint labor–management planning, problem-solving, and decision-making processes at every level of the organization—from union appointees for each company board of directors to
corporate, division, plant, department, and shop floor committees. However, worldwide overcapacity in the late 1990s led to falling prices and by
2003 twenty-eight companies were in bankruptcy. This economic context
undermined the full implementation of the collaborative partnership
agreements in much of the industry. The partnership between ATT and
CWA—the Workplace of the Future—has suffered in a similar way as the
company cut operations and jobs in the face of increased competition
after deregulation. Sustaining a meaningful partnership arrangement
under these circumstances has proven to be extremely difficult.[20]

Third, in yet other cases, partnerships have faltered because of decisions
made higher in the corporate hierarchy. For example, at Saturn, although
collaborative systems at the manufacturing plant level have continued to
function, at the strategic level General Motors has centralized decision
making on product development and supplier sourcing decisions that the
local union and Saturn management used to control. This has significantly
eroded the level of collaboration achieved a decade earlier (though the
level still exceeds that in comparable plants throughout the General Motors system). American Axle was part of a division that was spun off by
General Motors as it shed some of its parts-making operations. Fortunately
for the United Auto Workers, the new owners were willing to continue the
collaborative relationship. New management is typically in a position to
decide this for themselves because even with contractual provisions for
partnerships, unions have a hard time sustaining collaboration with
unwilling partners.

Notwithstanding these pressures, there have been significant increases
in the implementation of *some* forms of collaborative work systems. In
particular, there has been an increase in front-line participation in operational decisions—but nowhere near a commensurate increase in union
involvement in strategic decisions (i.e. a much greater increase on the
right-hand side than the left-hand side of Fig. 8.1). And among the
forms of front-line involvement the offline forms are more common and
have proliferated faster compared to the online forms. For example, Osterman (1994, 2000) found in 1992 that 27.4 per cent of U.S. firms nation-
wide had implemented offline problem-solving teams (upper right-side

quadrant in Fig. 8.1) with at least 50 per cent of their employees. That proportion grew to 57.7 per cent by 1997. He also found that 40.5 per cent of firms claimed to use self-directed work teams (lower right-side quadrant in Fig. 8.1) with at least 50 per cent of their employees in 1992. That number declined slightly by 1997 to 38.4 per cent.[21] Osterman's 1997 survey also revealed that unionized firms were more likely to have self-directed work teams (45 per cent) than were non-union firms (37 per cent). He also estimated that unionized firms were more likely to have offline problem-solving teams (65 per cent) than were non-union firms (56 per cent).[22] By contrast, using data from the early 1990s Lawler et al. (1995) estimated that only 14 per cent of employees in the unionized firms among the Fortune 1,000 had unions that were engaged in even offline collaborative arrangements through union–management committees.

What I called in Fig. 8.1 'co-management'—that is, comprehensive partnership—is even rarer still. No recent national survey provides us with an indication of the extent of union institutional participation in managerial decision making. However, in a recent study focusing on collective bargaining agreements covering more than 1,000 employees, Gray et al. (1999) found that while 46.6 per cent have some 'cooperative' provisions, only 15.7 per cent established joint labor–management committees (upper left quadrant) and 14.8 per cent provide for offline employee problem-solving groups (upper right quadrant), and a mere 2.6 per cent were found to establish 'strategic'-level labor–management partnerships. We might also note, in a skeptical vein, that the presence of contract language establishing collaborative partnership institutions does not necessarily mean that they are in fact implemented by the local parties.

Increased strategic collaboration (in the left column of Fig. 8.1) necessitates more power sharing with labor: while there are important potential gains for this as illustrated above, management appears unwilling to pay the price of shared power in order to reap these gains. Management appears satisfied with the substantial yet more limited gains from operations-level participation. We need to track the evolving forms of collaboration more systematically in the decade ahead.

If management continues to promote schemes to involve members directly but continues too to resist power sharing with unions, the long-term gains for management will be limited and unions will have increasing difficulty coping with pressures from management to support work reorganization. The danger is real that politics will continue to trump economics when it comes to power sharing. The Saturn case illustrates this point, as management appears willing to forgo the valued added by the strategic-level partnership as General Motors recentralizes decision making. Direct shop-floor level participation both offline and online continues but representative participation has eroded significantly. Since management can get most of what it believes it needs directly from the workforce, it attempts to bypass the union and thereby avoids significant power sharing, which disadvantages the workforce and management itself in the long run as opportunities for higher levels of performance are left on the table.

It seems very clear that institutionalizing these partnership arrangements will depend on changes in the broader institutional context, particularly legal and regulatory reforms. While institutional changes are in the long run enlightened self-interest of management, they do not appear to be sustainable absent government support: the spontaneous functioning of the market does not generate the institutional context optimal for capitalist development. Left to their own devices, too few firms will take the high road, and the race down the low road—the race to the bottom—will continue. Given the current political climate in the United States these types of changes are unlikely in the near future, and so development of collaborative community with institutions of employee representation will necessarily be limited.

Appendix 8.1: Cases—Partial List Due to Non-Disclosure Agreements

- Acme Steel/United Steel Workers of America (USWA)—2 Plants
- Allina Health Systems/Minnesota Nurses' Association (ANA)
- American Axle/United Auto Workers (UAW)
- AT&T/Communication Workers of America (CWA)
- Bethlehem Steel/United Steel Workers of America (USWA)—3 Plants
- Bristol-Myers Squibb/Oil Chemical and Atomic Workers (OCAW)
- Corning/The American Flint Glass Workers Union
- Greater Metropolitan Hospital System/National Health and Human Service Union (SEIU/1199)
- Harvard University/Harvard Union of Clerical and Technical Workers (AFSME)
- Ispat-Inland Steel/United Steel Workers of America (USWA)
- J&L Specialty Steel/United Steel Workers of America (USWA)
- Kaiser Permanente and the Coalition of Kaiser Permanente Unions
- Lockheed Martin/International Union of Electrical Workers (IUE)

- LTV Steel/United Steel Workers of America (USWA)
- LTV-Sumitomo Metals Electro-galvanizing (LSE)/United Steel Workers of America (USWA)
- National Steel/United Steel Workers of America (USWA)—4 Plants
- NUMMI/United Auto Workers (UAW)
- Republic Engineered Steels/United Steel Workers of America (USWA)—4 Plants
- Saturn/United Auto Workers (UAW)
- Seattle/Laborers International Union of North America (LIUNA)
- Union Camp/United Paperworkers International Union (UPIU)
- United Airlines/Airline Pilots Association (ALPA)/International Association of Machinists and Aerospace Workers (IAM)
- US Federal Government/American Federation of Government Employees (AFGE) and National Treasury Employees Union (NTEU)
- US Steel(USX)/United Steel Workers of America (USWA)—7 Plants
- Xerox/Union of Needletrades, Industrial and Textile Employees (UNITE)

References

Bailey, Thomas (1994). ' "High performance" work organization and the apparel industry: the extent and determinants of reform.' New York: Columbia University, Institute on Education and the Economy, Oct.

Eaton, Adrienne E., and Rubinstein, Saul A. (forthcoming). 'Tracking local unions involved in "co-management." ' Manuscript under review.

—— and Voos, Paula (1994). 'Productivity enhancing innovations in work organization, compensation, and employee participation in the union vs. non-union sectors.' *Advances in Industrial and Labor Relations*, 6. Greenwich, Conn.: JAI Press: 63–109.

Eaton, Susan, Rubinstein, Saul, A., and McKersie, Robert (2004). 'Building and sustaining labor–management partnerships: recent experiences in the U.S.' In David Lewin and Bruce Kaufman (eds.), *Advances in Industrial and Labor Relations*, 13: 137–56.

Freeman, Richard B., and Medoff, James L. (1984). *What Do Unions Do?* New York: Basic Books.

—— and Rogers, Joel (1999). *What Workers Want*. Ithaca, New York: ILR Press.

Gittell, Jody Hoffer (1996). 'Paradox of coordination and control.' Working paper, Harvard Business School, Boston.

Gittleman, Maury, Horrigan, Michael, and Joyce, Mary (1998). ' "Flexible" workplace practices: evidence from a nationally representative survey.' *Industrial and Labor Relations Review*, 52/1: 99–115.

Gray, George R., Myers, Donald W., and Myers, Phyllis, S. (1999). 'Cooperative provisions in labour agreements: a new paradigm.' *Monthly Labor Review*, 122/1: 29–45.

Heckscher, Charles (2001). 'Living with flexibility.' In Lowell Turner, Harry C. Katz, and Richard W. Hurd (eds.), *Rekindling the Movement: Transforming the Labor Movement in the 1990s and Beyond*. Ithaca, NY: Cornell University Press: 59–8.

——Maccoby, Michael, Ramirez, Rafael, and Tixier, Pierre-Eric (2003). *Agents of Change: Crossing the Post-Industrial Divide*. Oxford: Oxford University Press.

Ichniowski, Casey, Kochan, Thomas A., Levine, David, Olson, Craig, and Strauss, George (1996). 'What works at work: overview and assessment.' *Industrial Relations*, 35/3 (July): 356–74.

Kaufman, Bruce E. (2001). 'The employee participation/representation gap: an assessment and proposed solution.' *University of Pennsylvania Journal of Employment and Labor Law*, 3: 491–550.

Kochan, Thomas A., Katz, Harry C., and McKersie, Robert B. (1987). *The Transformation of American Industrial Relations*. New York: Basic Books.

Kruse, Douglas, and Blasi, Joseph (2000). 'The new employee/employer relationship.' In David Ellwood, T. Rebecca, M. Blank, Joseph Blasi, Douglas Kruse, William A. Niskanen, and Karen Lynn-Dyson, *A Working Nation: Government Work and the Economy*. New York: Russell Sage Foundation: ch. 2.

Lawler, Edward E., Ledford, Gerald, and Mohrman, Susan (1989). *Employee Involvement in America: A Study of Contemporary Practice*. Houston: American Productivity and Quality Center.

——————(1992). *Employee Involvement and Total Quality Management: Practices and Results in Fortune 1000 Companies*. San Francisco: Jossey-Bass, Inc.

——————(1995). *Creating High Performance Organizations*. San Francisco: Jossey-Bass, Inc.

Levine, David I., and Tyson, Laura D'Andrea (1990). 'Participation, productivity, and the firm's environment.' In Alan S. Blinder (ed.), *Paying for Productivity: A Look at the Evidence*. Washington, DC: Brookings Institution: 183–237.

MacDuffie, John Paul (1995a). 'Human resource bundles and manufacturing performance: organizational logic and flexible production systems in the world auto industry.' *Industrial and Labor Relations Review*, 48/2 (Jan.): 197–221.

————(1995b). 'Workers' roles in lean production: the implications for worker representation.' In Steve Babson (ed.), *Lean Work: Empowerment and Exploitation in the Global Auto Industry*. Detroit: Wayne State University Press: 54–69.

Osterman, Paul (1994). 'How common is workplace transformation and who adopts it?' *Industrial and Labor Relations Review*, 47/2: 175–88.

——(2000). 'Work organization in an era of restructuring: trends in diffusion and impacts on employee welfare.' *Industrial and Labor Relations Review*, 53/2 (Jan.): 179–96.

——Kochan, Thomas, Locke, Richard, and Piore, Michael (2001). *Working in America*. Cambridge, Mass.: MIT Press.

Pil, Frits K., and MacDuffie, John Paul (1996). 'The adoption of high involvement work practices.' *Industrial Relations*, 35/3 (July): 423–55.

Rubinstein, Saul A. (1996). 'The Saturn Partnership: management and governance in team-based high performance manufacturing.' Ph.D. dissertation, MIT, Boston.

—— (2000). 'The impact of co-management on quality performance: the case of the Saturn Corporation.' *Industrial and Labor Relations Review*, 53/2 (Jan.): 197–218.

—— (2001*a*). 'The local union revisited: new voices from the front lines.' *Industrial Relations*, 40/3 (July): 405–35.

—— (2001*b*). 'A different kind of union: balancing co-management and representation.' *Industrial Relations*, 40/2 (Apr.): 163–203.

—— (2001*c*). 'Unions as value-adding networks: possibilities for the future of U.S. unionism.' *Journal of Labor Research*, 22/3 (Summer): 581–98.

—— and Heckscher, Charles (2003). 'Partnerships and flexible networks: alternatives or complementary models of labor–management relations?' In Thomas Kochan and David Lipsky (eds.), *Negotiations and Change: From the Workplace to Society.* Ithaca, NY: Cornell University Press 189–204.

—— and Kochan, Thomas A. (2001). *Learning from Saturn: Possibilities for Corporate Governance and Employee Relations.* Ithaca, NY: Cornell University Press.

—— Bennett, Michael, and Kochan, Thomas (1993). 'The Saturn partnership: co-management and the reinvention of the local union.' In B. Kaufman and M. Kleiner (eds.), *Employee Representation: Alternatives and Future Directions.* Madison, Wisc.: Industrial Relations Research Association: 339–70.

Notes

1. See Bailey (1994); MacDuffie (1995*a*); Osterman (1994, 2000); Ichniowski et al. (1996).
2. See Kochan et al. (1986).
3. Rubinstein (2001*a*, 2001*b*); Rubinstein and Kochan (2001).
4. See Rubinstein et al. (1993); Rubinstein (2000).
5. See Rubinstein (2001*a*, 2001*c*); Eaton et al. (2004); Eaton and Rubinstein (forthcoming).
6. See Freeman and Medoff (1984); Levine and Tyson (1990).
7. See Freeman and Rogers (1999) where they estimate that workplace transformation that increases employee collaboration results in productivity increases of 2–5%; Kaufman (2001).
8. See Rubinstein (2000, 2001*c*).
9. See Levine and Tyson (1990); Eaton and Voos (1994); Rubinstein (1996, 2000, 2001*b*); Gittell (1996).
10. See Rubinstein (2000); Rubinstein and Kochan (2001).
11. See Eaton and Rubinstein (forthcoming). While the company provided us with the results of their surveys, we were not given standard deviations and thus

were not able to conduct statistical tests for differences. However, while we could not determine whether the changes in customer satisfaction were statistically significant, they are suggestive of interesting trends.

12. See MacDuffie (1995*b*); Rubinstein (1996).
13. Rubinstein (2001*b*).
14. Rubinstein (2001*a*).
15. Osterman et al. (2001); Kaufman (2001); Heckscher (2001); Rubinstein (2001*b*).
16. Rubinstein (2001*b*).
17. Rubinstein (2001*b*).
18. See Rubinstein and Heckscher (2003).
19. See Eaton et al. (2004); Rubinstein and Heckscher (2003).
20. See Heckscher et al. (2003).
21. Gittleman et al. (1998) produced a similar estimate of work teams in establishments with 50 employees or more (32%), but reported a lower level (15.8%) of offline problem-solving groups. Lawler et al. (1989, 1992, 1995) found that while 28% of employees reported the use of self-directed teams in their companies in 1987, by 1995 the proportion had increased to 68%. Pil and MacDuffie (1996) reported similar results in their extensive study of worldwide auto assembly. They estimated that in 1989 28.9% of employees were involved in offline problem-solving teams. By 1993/4 that proportion had increased to 48.8%. They also found that while 15.7% of the automotive workforce was involved in self-directed work teams in 1989, by 1993/4 the level had reached 46.3%. While most studies rely on managerial informants, Freeman and Rogers (1999) obtained similar estimates in their national survey of workers. Fifty-two per cent of the workers they surveyed reported offline problem-solving teams in their firms.
22. These results were provided by Osterman but were not published in his 2000 *Industrial & Labor Relations Review* article. In an analysis of the National Employer Survey data, Kruse and Blasi (2000) found that unionized establishments were slightly more likely to have self-directed teams (38.9%) than were non-union establishments (34.3%).

Part III

Community across Firms

9

Building Inter-Firm Collaborative Community
Uniting Theory and Practice

Lynda M. Applegate

> If the old model of organization was the large, hierarchical organization, the new model that is considered characteristic of the New Competition is a network of lateral and horizontal interlinkages within and among firms.
>
> (Nohria and Eccles 1992: 2)[1]

Today's executives are both fascinated by—and often skeptical of—the new business models that they read about in the business press. Some academics and business futurists argue that we are in the midst of an economic transition from the industrial economy to a global network economy that promises to be just as profound as the transition from the agrarian economy to the industrial economy during the latter half of the nineteenth century.[2] Others prefer to avoid such far-reaching predictions. But, no matter what their position, most agree that traditional industrial economy intra- and inter-firm hierarchies are becoming increasingly less effective in today's turbulent and increasingly networked world.

The collaborative community model provides important framing for understanding the nature of this transformation. This chapter extends that analysis to examine changes in ownership, design, and governance among players within *inter-firm* business networks. Consider the following three examples that will be discussed in more depth in this chapter:[3]

1. In early 2004, the board of directors of Global Health Care Exchange (GHX) gathered at company headquarters in Westminster, Colorado.

Seated around the boardroom table were the world's most important players in the health care industry, including suppliers (Abbott, Baxter, Becton Dickinson, B. Braun, CR Bard, GE Medical, Guidant, Johnson & Johnson, Siemens, and Tyco), distributors (AmeriSource-Bergin, Cardinal Health, Fisher Scientific, and McKesson), and providers (HCA and Premier). As global health care costs are squeezed, these fierce competitors within each industry segment battle to increase share. Across segments, suppliers, distributors, and providers struggle to prevent margin erosion. Yet all have joined together to invest in GHX to achieve a common goal—to drive over $11 billion in annual cost from the industry supply chain and provide common standards and a common operating platform upon which all can do business as they innovate to improve the health and productivity of society. While over ninety health care industry exchanges were competing in early 2000, by 2003 GHX was one of the few survivors.

2. In early 2004, the board of directors of Covisint gathered in Detroit Michigan to approve the sale of Covisint to Compuware—a software and services firm located nearby. Founded four years earlier by three large automakers (DaimlerChrysler, Ford, and General Motors), Covisint's vision of becoming the 'world's biggest, fastest, and largest exchange,' and of going public shortly after launch, had crashed with the stock market and the economy. While the commitment to the goal of increasing efficiency of the global automotive supply chain remained strong, distrust slowed buy-in until even the founders began using internal supply-chain solutions to hedge their bets.[4] In late 2003, Covisint's CEO sold, shut down, or returned software applications that were not widely used across the industry to its automaker investors and then sold the remaining assets to Compuware.[5] Analysts hailed the new CEO's strategy for Covisint. Under its new *neutral* owners, Covisint planned to redirect its efforts toward unique business opportunities that provided equal value to suppliers and automakers and solved true sources of 'pain that all industry participants were experiencing.',[6] By early 2005, participation was on the rise.

3. On 24 May 2004, executives at Nasdaq announced they had entered into a definitive agreement to acquire Brut LLC, the owner and operator of the BRUT ECN, for $190 million. It was hoped that the acquisition of Brut would enable Nasdaq to respond to competitive threats from an aggressive new breed of competitor, called ECNs, that used a sophisticated internet-based trading platform to trade Nasdaq

securities on behalf of large institutional investors. Between 1998 and 2003, ECNs siphoned off almost 40 per cent of the most highly liquid and high-margin trading volume of Nasdaq-listed stock. The acquisition of Brut not only provided Nasdaq with the technology to win back share from the ECNs, it also brought Nasdaq the trading volumes of the BRUT ECN. Bob Greifeld, president and chief executive officer of NASDAQ, stated, 'The addition of the BRUT ECN to NASDAQ's market center is just one more step in NASDAQ's multi-pronged strategy to...reinforce NASDAQ's status as the premier U.S. equity market [with a goal to] serve investors better.'

These examples highlight the promise and challenges of building inter-firm cooperation in a complex, rapidly changing, uncertain, and hyper-competitive environment. While this chapter focuses in depth on these three cases, the insights presented are drawn from longitudinal field research on emerging network economy business models conducted over the past nine years in twenty-nine companies that represent a variety of industries (including financial services, health care, consumer packaged goods, retail, and the automotive industry), geographic locations (including Asia, Europe, Latin America, and the USA), size, and age. Common features of the three cases discussed in this chapter include:

1. Each is operating in a complex, uncertain, rapidly changing, and hyper-competitive business environment that demands that business networks be optimized for both efficiency *and* innovation.

2. Each has established or is in the process of establishing a common platform and processes for managing interdependencies among intra- and inter-firm members. These interdependencies include: task, information/expertise, and affiliation/identity.

3. Each is developing a central coordinating role that is designed to facilitate coordination and control, manage complexity, and improve network efficiency and effectiveness. We adopt the term 'orchestrator' for this role as defined by John Seely Brown, John Hagel, and others.[7] In each case, ownership of the orchestrator is shared among aggressive competitors who must cooperate to succeed.

4. Each is developing hybrid forms of governance that blend features of market, hierarchy, and community. In GHX and Nasdaq, we see an emerging model where hierarchy and market reinforce and enable collaborative capability and trust, which, in turn, enables community to become the dominant governance model. In Covisint we see

attempts to maintain hierarchical power perpetuate distrust. In the end, collaboration without trust proves unsustainable.

While there are many similarities, there are also important differences that provide a rich and nuanced description of the challenges and opportunities that executives face as they attempt to build cooperative business networks. The Nasdaq case, having been launched by a business cooperative, the National Association of Securities Dealers (NASD), enables analysis of the design features of a collaborative community within a favorable business context where high levels of trust are already present. It also provides an opportunity to examine the challenges (for example, free rider and control problems) that traditional business cooperatives face as changes in the business context, coupled with diverging interests and affiliations over time, weaken relationships and trust among members.[8] In contrast, Covisint and GHX are launched within much less supportive business contexts. While the goals of the two exchanges are similar, we see two different governance models emerge over time. For example, the automaker owner-founders of Covisint attempted to use their market power to achieve cooperation without trust.[9] In contrast, GHX's owner-founders designed inter-firm governance structures and systems that fostered the development of trust. They determined that equity ownership by all stakeholders—suppliers, health care providers, and distributors—was a precondition for gaining cooperation. Once all parties were represented on the governing board of directors, trust and collaborative community design features evolved as the board struggled to find common ground. By examining the struggles and successes of these three organizations, we gain insight into design features of emerging collaborative models and the challenges of building them.

The chapter begins with an overview of the fundamental theory that frames analysis and understanding of business networks. Attention then turns to deep exploration of the evolution of the Nasdaq Stock Market as an example of a collaborative community that was built *de novo* in 1971. This is followed by a comparison of Covisint and GHX and a discussion of key insights.

Understanding business networks

At the most basic level, organizations and the industries and markets within which they operate can be defined as networks of specialized nodes that perform specific activities required to achieve a common purpose.[10] These nodes are united through relationships that manage interdependencies.[11]

Organizational solutions are designed to enable the attainment of goals that require coordinated efforts. Interdependence and uncertainty make goal attainment more difficult and create the need for intra- and inter-firm organizational solutions.[12] Two overarching principles play a key role in the design of intra- and inter-firm business networks.[13]

- *Differentiation* defines how individuals, groups, and organizations are subdivided into specialized work units (nodes). This differentiation may include horizontal division of work into specialized 'operating units,' vertical division into power/authority levels, and spatial division into geographic or product groups. Differentiation enables the network to manage complexity, develop specialized expertise and assets, and focus attention and resources on accomplishing specific goals and tasks.

- *Integration* defines the relationships and links between nodes that are required to unite specialized, differentiated groups, units, and organizations to enable them to achieve a common purpose and create shared value.

A myriad of different types of relationships unite specialized nodes in a business network as they work together to achieve shared goals.[14] For example, *task-based relationships* unite individuals, groups, or organizations that work together or sequentially to perform one or more activities in a process that creates economic output; *information- or expertise-based relationships* unite individuals, groups, or organizations that provide information or expertise required by the network to accomplish tasks and achieve shared goals; and *social relationships* unite individuals, groups, or organizations to enable them to develop strong bonds of affiliation and identity.

Sociologists have found that stronger, deeper relationships among differentiated nodes in a network are required in environments characterized by increased complexity, uncertainty, and turbulence—especially in networks characterized by a large number of highly differentiated nodes that must work closely together to achieve common goals.[15] Stronger, deeper relationships are also required in the presence of:

- Increased task interdependence secondary to the need to:
    - produce customized products or deliver shared services; and
    - develop and deliver innovative and creative products, services, and solutions.
- Increased information/expertise interdependence secondary to the need to:
    - share large amounts of real-time information; and

- unite the perspectives of various actors to make sense of the information to support decisions and actions;

- Increased social interdependence secondary to:
  - incentives that reward cooperation and collaboration across highly differentiated subunits;
  - a large number of divergent subcultures that must develop shared beliefs and a sense of trust to work together; and
  - leader preferences for shared vision and action.

While network relationships tend to be stronger among people and groups who are in close physical contact and are most 'like' one another (e.g. within a single highly differentiated node such as a functional unit within a hierarchy), network performance in complex, uncertain, and turbulent environments requires a dense network of diverse specialized assets (physical products and services, information and expertise, etc.) and the ability to quickly and effectively deploy those assets to create value for all members and the network as a whole.[16] This is balanced, of course, by the cost of developing and maintaining a broad range of specialized nodes and the relationships among them. As such, redundant relationships that lead to the same resources may help to mitigate risk and increase the speed with which resources and assets can be leveraged and used, but they do so at an increased cost. Table 9.1 summarizes the relationships between the three levels of interdependency and network performance in terms of efficiency and effectiveness.[17]

One core proposition of this book is that new network configurations are emerging that permit large, diverse networks to manage task, information/expertise, and social interdependencies required for innovation and knowledge creation. These new configurations of business networks can represent a wide range of ownership dimensions. For the purpose of this chapter, three dominant forms of ownership have been identified. However, it is recognized that any given business network may incorporate a wide variety of ownership models across different subnets. The three dominant forms of ownership include:

1. Nodes may be located inside a *corporation* or other legally defined organization form;
2. An *alliance* may be formed between two (or a small number of players); or
3. A diverse and fluid *consortium* of players representing different industry roles (e.g. suppliers, distributors, buyers) and ownership work together to achieve shared goals.

Table 9.1. Sample measures of business network efficiency and effectiveness

Type of interdependency	Benefit category	Performance measures	Link to value
Task	Efficiency related to tasks and processes involved in the development of product/service offerings	*Productivity* (process inputs)—(process outputs)	Economic capital
		Cycle time time to complete a task or process	
		Cost absolute and relative cost of completing a task or process in terms of money, effort, opportunity cost	
	Effectiveness related to product/service offerings and task-based goals	*Quality* (customer value delivered)—(value expected)	
		Loyalty customer recruitment, retention, and defection rates	
		Goal attainment level to which goals are achieved or exceeded (on time, under budget, high-quality deliverables)	
Information/expertise	Efficiency related to accessing, storing, analyzing, and using information and expertise	*Productivity* (information inputs)—(information outputs)	Knowledge capital
		Cycle time time to access, analyze or share, and use information cycle time for key decisions	

Table 9.1. Sample measures of business network efficiency and effectiveness (*Cont'd*)

Type of interdependency	Benefit category	Performance measures	Link to value
	Effectiveness related to accessing, storing, analyzing, and using information and expertise	*Cost* absolute and relative cost of accessing, storing, analyzing, sharing, and using information in terms of money, effort, opportunity cost *Quality* (customer value delivered)—(value expected) *Loyalty* customer recruitment, retention, and defection rates	
Affiliation/identity	Efficiency related to developing and maintaining relationships, shared values, and identity	*Productivity* (relationship inputs)—(relationship outputs) *Cycle time* time to build a shared purpose, identity, an ethic of contribution, etc. *Cost* absolute and relative cost to in terms of money, effort, opportunity cost	Social capital
	Effectiveness related to developing and maintaining relationships, shared values, and identity	*Quality* (customer value delivered)—(value expected) *Loyalty* network member recruitment, retention, and defection rates	

Collaborative community blends features of three governance models for coordinating and controlling interdependent action among specialized nodes (see Chapter 1 in this volume). The three governance models are:[18]

1. *Markets* coordinate short-term transaction-based relationships primarily through supply, demand, and price;

2. *Hierarchies* coordinate long-term transaction-based relationships primarily through standardization, structure, contracts, and authority; and

3. *Communities* coordinate long-term partnership-based relationships primarily through frequent interactions, communication, and information sharing and trust.

As we will see later in this chapter, while features of all three models may coexist within any relationship, one model often becomes the dominant governing principle. Of interest in this chapter are the mechanisms through which community gains in richness and strength, rising to become the dominant principle. More importantly, we examine how market and hierarchy do not compete with community but actually *enable it to emerge as a dominant form*.

The two perspectives of ownership and governance are framed in Fig. 9.1 with examples from my research that show various hybrid combinations.

As can be seen, emerging collaborative community models represent a wide range of ownership and governance structures. Other chapters in this book discuss examples of emerging models within a corporation or alliance. The following section of this chapter focuses on the challenges of building inter-firm consortia.

Uniting theory and practice

Executives spent much of the twentieth century building and perfecting hierarchies—and the last few decades tearing them down. During the 1980s and 1990s, downsizing, delayering, and re-engineering swept through large companies. Rigid intra- and inter-firm boundaries were shattered to enable firms to focus on core competencies while also delivering customized solutions in global markets. Strategic partnerships and alliances were formed to ensure access to capabilities and expertise that could not be efficiently and

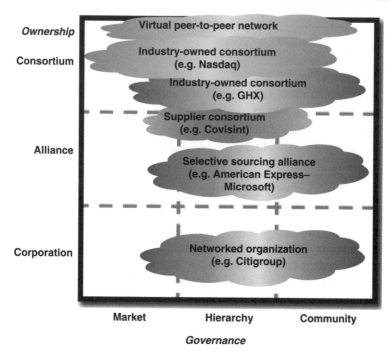

Fig. 9.1 Emerging hybrid governance models

effectively built and managed inside and, in the extreme, networked consortia of independent firms emerged.

The vision of eliminating hierarchy was compelling, and the change initiatives—many of them enabled by emerging information technologies—shook business markets and the organizations within them to their foundations. But take a walk around most large, established firms, or talk with executives from established industries, and it soon becomes clear that the 'hierarchy' is far from dead. Yet, when asked what their companies or industries should look like, most executives call immediately for new capabilities that enable them to work more effectively and efficiently within a more diffuse and fluid business network that increasingly has become known as an 'ecosystem.'[19] The problem confronting these executives, they report, is that they do not wish to sacrifice efficiency for speed nor can they abandon authority and control as they empower others—be they employees, partners, or other loosely connected network members—to make decisions that directly influence real-time customer needs and business performance.

In the mid-1990s, Jack Welch, CEO of General Electric (GE) at the time, summarized the dilemma his company faced. 'Our dream and our plan well over a decade ago was simple,' he said. 'We set out to shape a global enterprise that preserved the classic big company advantages while eliminating the big company drawbacks. What we wanted to build was a hybrid enterprise with the...power, resources, and reach of a large firm and the hunger, spirit and fire of a small one.'[20] Nor was this just a US point of view: Percy Barnevik, CEO of Switzerland-based Asea Brown Boveri (ABB), was one of many in other countries who echoed Welch's comments. 'ABB is an organization with three internal contradictions,' he explained. 'We want to be global and local, big and small, and radically decentralized with centralized reporting and control. If we resolve those contradictions, we create real competitive advantage.'[21] Fig. 9.2 summarizes the dilemma that drove these executives and countless others to search for new organizational solutions.

We believe that the collaborative community model is emerging as a hybrid form that is ideally suited for creating the lean, yet agile, extended enterprises that executives have been struggling to design. This section provides three examples of business networks that are attempting to build and sustain effective inter-firm collaboration. We begin with a discussion

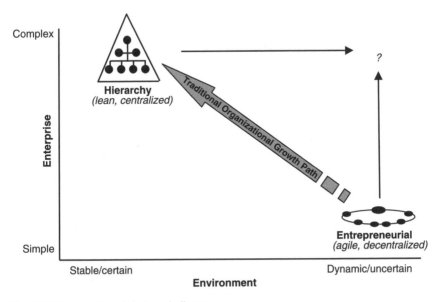

Fig. 9.2 Organizational design challenge

Source: Adapted from *Nolan Norton Research Report* (1988).

of the Nasdaq Stock Market as a model of an inter-firm business network that was designed as a collaborative community from its inception. As a result, compromises were not made to fit the design to an established power base and governance model. Other *de novo* collaborative communities discussed in the literature include Visa's credit card network[22] and Li and Fung's global trading network.[23]

We then discuss the challenges of transforming established business networks by describing Covisint (a consortium established within the hierarchically structured automotive industry that did *not* adopt a collaborative community model) and GHX (a consortium within the health care industry that is struggling to adopt a model similar in design to the one at Nasdaq but with a unique form of governance). More detailed discussion of all three business networks is available in published cases referenced at the end of the chapter.

Nasdaq Securities Exchange: a collaborative community in action

Nasdaq mission: To facilitate capital formation in the public and private sectors by developing, operating and regulating the most liquid, efficient and fair securities market for the ultimate benefit and protection of the investor.

Nasdaq vision: To build a worldwide market of markets built on a worldwide network of networks . . . assuring the best possible price for securities at the lowest possible cost.[24]

Nasdaq was created in 1971 by the National Association of Securities Dealers (NASD) as an online securities market that enabled a widely dispersed network of independent broker-dealers to trade securities on behalf of individual and institutional investors. By early 2005, Nasdaq listed over 22.5 billion shares of stock compared to 100 in 1971. These shares were offered by over 3,000 issuers (companies that list on the Nasdaq exchange) and were traded by over 500 broker-dealers. Nasdaq had also expanded its network to link to strong competitors in the USA (for example, NYSE and AMEX) and to stock exchanges around the world (for example, stock exchanges in Tokyo and London).[25] In addition, Nasdaq linked to a variety of online trading platforms—also called Electronic Communication Networks or ECNs (for example, Instinet and Archipelago).

The mission and vision that unites Nasdaq's business network is to be a worldwide *'market of markets'* built on a worldwide *'network of networks.'* Unlike the physical trading floor for most traditional securities exchanges, the Nasdaq Stock Market is not located in a single place, nor is it owned by a single entity. Instead, it is a diffuse, interdependent network; success requires that everyone participate and strictly adhere to the policies and procedures required to ensure a fair, transparent, and orderly market that delivers value to all members. Over the years, Nasdaq has adopted a complex governance model that combines features of market, hierarchy, and community. Examination of the organizational solutions that have been adopted provides an excellent starting point for analysis of two emergent consortia—Covisint and GHX.[26]

BUILDING NASDAQ

The operating core of a securities exchange is focused on the buying and selling of securities. The easiest way to understand how the Nasdaq market organizes its operating core is to compare it with the New York Securities Exchange (NYSE). Until recently, the NYSE was a physical place located on Wall Street in New York City where specialists (who act as agents for companies that list stocks for sale on the NYSE—also called *issuers*) sell stocks to NYSE floor brokers who, in turn, buy and sell stocks for broker-dealers. These broker-dealers (who are licensed by NASD to buy and sell stocks for *investors*) may be independents working out of their home or they may work for the securities trading unit of a large investment firm, like Merrill Lynch or Citigroup's Smith Barney.

On the NYSE floor, specialists and floor brokers usually serve as an agent in the buy–sell transaction between an issuer who wants to sell and an investor who wants to buy. As an agent, they do not commit their own capital in the transaction although the law permits and, at times even requires them to act as a principal to ensure an orderly market. By contrast, Nasdaq broker-dealers act as principals in the transaction. NASD regulations require broker-dealers to commit their own capital to buy stocks that they wish to sell. In practice, NASD broker-dealers post a price at which they will buy a given stock and a price at which they will sell the stock. They then buy and sell blocks of stock from investors. As such, each broker-dealer in the NASD network operates as an independent market maker—an orchestrator of a subnetwork that is reconfigured in real time to complete specific transactions on behalf of the Nasdaq members. See Fig. 9.3.

Given that the price for each buy–sell transaction is determined in real time based on supply and demand, the Nasdaq market is an excellent example of using a market model of governance to coordinate short-term task and information interdependencies among competing broker-dealers.

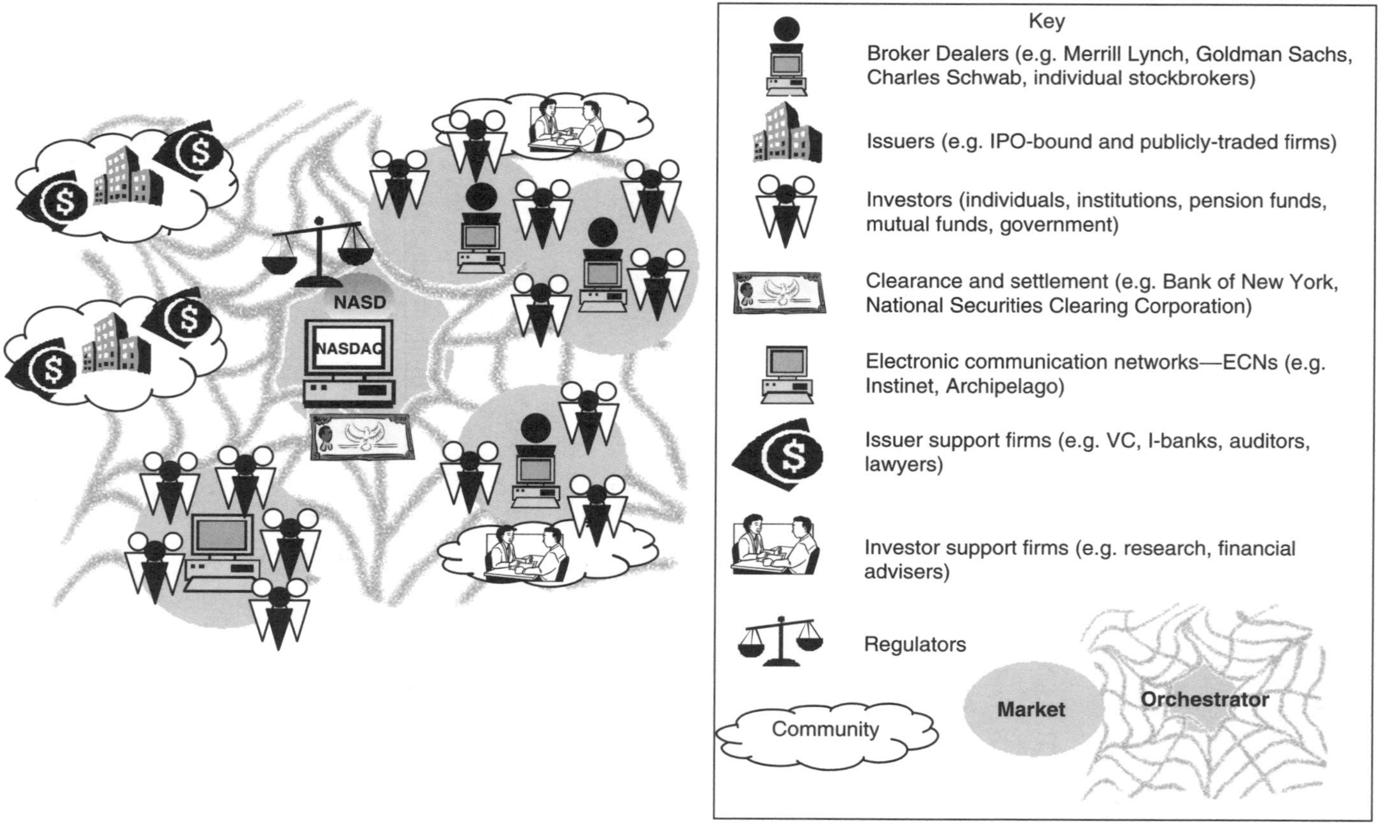

Key

Broker Dealers (e.g. Merrill Lynch, Goldman Sachs, Charles Schwab, individual stockbrokers)

Issuers (e.g. IPO-bound and publicly-traded firms)

Investors (individuals, institutions, pension funds, mutual funds, government)

Clearance and settlement (e.g. Bank of New York, National Securities Clearing Corporation)

Electronic communication networks—ECNs (e.g. Instinet, Archipelago)

Issuer support firms (e.g. VC, I-banks, auditors, lawyers)

Investor support firms (e.g. research, financial advisers)

Regulators

Market

Orchestrator

Community

Fig. 9.3 Nasdaq business network

Thus, at its core, the Nasdaq worldwide network of networks can be thought of as an *organizational solution that supports horizontal relations among peers using a combination of technology-embedded procedures, policies, and controls and market-based inter-firm governance*. Because the transactions take place online, the Nasdaq market is able to capture information on each transaction and provide its members with a sophisticated trading workstation that provides the information transparency needed to set price interactively and in real time.

As a legal entity, the Nasdaq Stock Market serves as an orchestrator to enable the buy–sell transaction between broker-dealers and investors that buy and sell stocks offered by issuers. Over time, a number of specialized roles have emerged to support the basic buy–sell transactions: *issuer support firms* (e.g. investment banks, accountants, lawyers, and public relations firms) help issuers prepare public offerings of stock to be listed on a public securities exchange, set the initial price at which the shares will be sold, and then help an issuer communicate its strategy and capabilities to potential investors; *investor support firms* (e.g. financial planners, information providers, and research firms) provide information and advice to investors to help them decide whether to buy or sell a given security at a given price and also help them manage their overall portfolio of investments to increase personal wealth; and finally, *clearance and settlement firms* (e.g. banks, electronic funds transfer firms) ensure that payments are made and credited and that ownership rights are transferred. Nasdaq works in partnership with these information and service providers to ensure that all members can achieve personal and shared goals.

While routine trading transactions take place online using primarily market-based governance mechanisms, knowledge-based and creative tasks among Nasdaq members take place in highly interactive, self-managing teams. These teams are formed to complete a specific project or to define and execute a strategic initiative that requires a customized, creative solution. They primarily utilize a community form of governance model, although all operate within a legislative framework defined by NASD and various other regulatory agencies and groups. Examples of these teams are:

- *Initial public offering (IPO) teams* are composed of senior executives and board members from companies that wish to offer their stock for sale on the Nasdaq Stock Market and issuer support professionals from investment banks, legal and accounting firms, and advertising firms that provide customized services and expertise. Nasdaq plays a role on these teams by developing the rules by which a company can become a member (as an issuer) on the Nasdaq Stock Market. It also sets the price of membership and provides professional consulting, advisory, and marketing services.

- *Financial planning and portfolio management teams* are composed of investors and the registered financial advisers, information providers, lawyers, and accountants that support them. These teams work together to make decisions about securities to buy and sell with the goal of optimizing the value of a personal or institutional portfolio.

- *New product development teams* are composed of technology professionals and economists employed by Nasdaq and members of key stakeholder groups. These groups convene to define the requirements for new market-based products and services and to manage implementation.

- The Nasdaq *Technology Advisory Council (TAC)* is composed of operating leaders who run trading operations within Nasdaq stakeholder organizations and industry/government experts. The council meets several times per year to provide feedback on Nasdaq's product/service offerings and plans and to oversee progress on key initiatives.

- The Nasdaq *board of directors* is composed of senior executives from key issuer and broker-dealer stakeholder groups and independent directors that represent investor interests. While the TAC serves Nasdaq in an advisory role, the board of directors plays a legal and fiduciary role in defining and overseeing the governance process for the Nasdaq Stock Market on behalf of NASD and its members. Recent corporate scandals called into question whether Nasdaq's corporate governance process continued to serve the interests of all stakeholders. New corporate governance rules and processes were approved in July 2002 to ensure that the Nasdaq board represented the interests of all stakeholders in the buy–sell and support transactions.[27] In addition to its formal governance role, the Nasdaq board of directors also sets the strategy of the Nasdaq Stock Market and approves and monitors resource use and progress on new strategic initiatives.

The capacity to create these innovative teams that function reliably despite the diversity of their members is a distinctive capability of a successful complex, global business cooperative, like Nasdaq. These organizational solutions embrace a community model of governance as the dominant principle but they are enabled by features of the market and hierarchical models upon which they are built. The community model enables flexibility and innovation; the market model enables efficiency; and the hierarchical model enables stability over time.

The complexity of the Nasdaq governance model is summarized in Table 9.2. The table highlights how features of market, hierarchy, and community models combine to play a role in enabling members of the Nasdaq business network to unite together to create a trusted, fair, and transparent market where members can perform their distinct (differentiated) roles and manage interdependencies to achieve both personal and shared goals.

The legitimacy of Nasdaq as a trusted orchestrator for trading securities initially came from the legitimacy of the NASD. As a membership organization, NASD was granted authority by its members to set and enforce the rules of conduct, standards, and procedures. NASD defined the licensing procedure to determine who could become a broker-dealer and also the conditions for revoking the license. Additional authority and controls were imposed by the Securities and Exchange Commission (SEC) and other Federal agencies formed to oversee commerce and protect investors.

Within the Nasdaq electronic market, the standards and rules for buying and selling stock and for clearance and settlement of transactions are embedded within the information technology and automated transaction processing systems (IT) that all members use. These market standards and rules are clearly communicated, closely monitored, and consistently enforced through mandatory information reporting procedures. Information is created as a by-product of the information systems used to process transactions in the online market. This information enables all members to self-monitor transactions to ensure the market is operating according to agreed-upon standards and rules.

This *information transparency* not only promotes consistency and confidence in the repeated interactions among members—a necessary precondition to the development of process-based trust—but it also enables members to learn how the dynamics of the market link to positive or negative outcomes. As a result, common data standards and information transparency also enable both individual and team learning—a necessary precondition to creativity and innovation.

This form of what Adler and Heckscher call 'interdependent process management' is a key organizational feature. Hierarchical coordination, control, and authority are granted by members, mandated by law, and embedded within procedures and information systems used to process day-to-day routine transactions and control systems.[28]

Many suggest that the simple act of embedding standards and procedures into the information systems used to process day-to-day routine

Table 9.2. Features of the traditional (pre-ECN) Nasdaq governance model

	Market	Hierarchy	Community
Operating core	Discrete, easily understood, short-term, buy–sell transactions.	Activities have been grouped into differentiated roles. Standardized procedures have been defined and embedded in IT to enable efficiency and consistency of routine buy–sell transactions.	Customized solutions are 'co-designed' by community members that perform specialized value-added roles to support issuers and investors.
Coordination and control	Information needed to set price and complete transactions is readily available to all members. Members set price through online postings of bids and offers.	Coordination and control of task interdependencies are embedded within IT to ensure that routine processes take place efficiently and effectively. Routine online and offline reporting and monitoring ensure compliance. Vertical differentiation of authority is present within a flat hierarchy.	Long-term coordination and control are based on commitment to shared purpose and trust in the Nasdaq Stock Market as a transparent, fair, highly efficient, and effective place to do business that creates value for all members and distributes it equitably.
Infrastructure and supporting processes	Nasdaq provides a standardized platform for buy–sell transactions and information sharing. Information needed to participate fully in the market is available to all and is easy to access and use.	Routine and customized reports are generated automatically from data in transaction systems and databases and are made available to support both lateral processes among peers and vertical control within a flat hierarchy.	While product councils and issuer/investor support teams primarily meet face to face to interact and work, shared high-bandwidth information and communication-processing infrastructure provides support.
Culture and affiliation	Individual interests dominate during routine trading.	The emphasis on individual beliefs, values, and interests is modified by loyalty that is often based on status, past experience, and long-term incentives.	An ethic of contribution and active participation binds members to the group. Shared purpose and mission link individual and community interests. Process-based trust provides the foundation for collaborative community values.
Leadership	Routine trading transactions occur within seconds. Formal leadership is not required, given the structured, short-term nature of interdependency. Authority is embedded in the transactions and systems that support them.	Transactional leadership—oversight of operations—is embedded within the systems that automate routine transactions. Early warning systems alert executives to non-routine problems and events. Standardized performance reporting communicates progress toward meeting goals.	Transformational leadership communicates Nasdaq's vision for a global network of networks. After the 2002 reform, Nasdaq's board of directors represented the interests of all stakeholder groups. Nasdaq's Technology Advisory Council ensures that all members have a voice in the development and execution of product strategy and priorities.

transaction and control systems will automatically lead to vertical distribution of power and an unequal distribution of value (as we would expect in the evolution to a hierarchical form of governance). Yet Nasdaq's legitimacy and authority has been used to create a fair, transparent market, to ensure equality of access, to fairly apportion value among all members, and to create process-based trust.

Why do the same design features lead to vertical hierarchical power in a consortium such as Covisint and to horizontal loosely coupled processes in a collaborative community of peers such as Nasdaq? As we will see later in this chapter, the source of the legitimacy for those who have been granted authority to set policy and standards is a key factor. So, too, is the purpose and intent that frames how standards and rules are defined and administered. Finally, Nasdaq's non-profit status and its governance through an interlocking set of boards, councils, and self-managing teams ensures that all members of the network play an active role and have a voice in how value is created and apportioned.

Thus Nasdaq was granted the authority to provide a shared platform (infrastructure, information, supporting processes) to enable all parties to manage task, information/expertise, and social interdependencies in real time. It works with members to define standards and processes and embeds them within the technology platform. Nasdaq's authority was granted *by network members* and the value created is *delivered back to those members*.

The organizational solutions adopted by the Nasdaq business network enable examination of the link between design choices and the development of trust among members of an inter-firm business network. Zucker (1986) suggests three different approaches for building trust in business networks: *Process-based trust* emerges from recurrent transactions as parties manage task interdependencies; *affiliation-based trust* rests on strong feelings of identity and social similarity within a specific group; and *institution-based trust* is tied to formal organizational and social structures.[29] While other authors in this book argue that the move to collaborative community involves the strengthening of process-based trust at the expense of the other two, this research suggests that affiliation- and institution-based trust continue to play a role in the creation and maintenance of process-based trust, which, in turn, plays a key role in the transition to collaborative community.

Stewart (2003) shows that trust can be transferred from a trusted party to an unknown party.[30] The willingness to transfer trust from one person or institution to another has been shown to be important when deciding how much, if at all, to trust an 'unknown other.' In this research, mechanisms by which trust transfer takes place become increasingly important. This is especially true as our attention turns to the discussion of Covisint and GHX and the approaches that these newly launched companies take to build trust in an increasingly distrustful industry. Key approaches used in trust transfer include: (1) developing a relationship with a trusted party who will vouch for the unknown party; and (2) providing verifiable evidence (including direct observation, monitoring, and information) of trustworthiness.[31] Research has shown that trust can be transferred from a single individual to a group,[32] and it can be transferred directly or across network ties,[33] including online network ties.[34] Institutional structures, standards, and safeguards provide important conditions for building and transferring trust.[35] As shown below, Nasdaq executives drew upon these approaches to building trust as their governance model evolved over time.

- NASD was formed by its member-owners, independent broker-dealers, to enable them to work together to buy and sell securities on behalf of investors. As such, the *shared purpose and mission of NASD was set by its broker-dealer members and provided the foundation for affiliation-based trust.*

- NASD was granted authority by its members to work on their behalf to develop, perform, and oversee: the licensing process that would enable all members to trust that the broker-dealers involved in a transaction were reputable and knowledgeable; the procedures and information-sharing standards required to price and trade securities; the clearance and settlement system that ensured that ownership of the security was transferred; and that the agreed-upon price was paid etc. As such, *the authority, duties, and obligations of NASD were defined and granted by its members and provided the foundation for institution-based trust.*

- NASD granted Nasdaq the authority to embed these agreed-upon processes, information-sharing standards, and controls in technology systems that all members of the industry would use to do business. As such, *NASD transferred its authority, duties, and obligations to NASDAQ along with the trust of its members and Nasdaq created institutional structures, standards, and safeguards that further increased willingness to trust.*

- Once everyone was connected and business was being conducted online, information was generated that enabled the *development of a reliable market that consistently met the expectations* of members. Further, market transparency enabled all members to *access real-time information that confirmed and strengthened perceptions of trustworthi-*

ness. As such, Nasdaq was able to develop *process-based trust*, which, in turn, provided the *foundation for collaborative community.*

CHALLENGES TO NASDAQ

For most of its existence, the collective and individual interests of Nasdaq members were closely aligned and there was a tight fit between contribution to value and benefits received for all members of the Nasdaq communities. This picture changed, however, in the mid-1990s when legislation and technology enabled new entrants (called ECNs) to emerge as both members of the Nasdaq Stock Market and also strong competitors.

As members of Nasdaq, ECNs were classified as individual market makers. They could trade stocks based on their own buy–sell positions without posting their trading positions on the public Nasdaq market. While all market makers were able by law to do this, traditional broker-dealer market makers rarely had an interest in doing so as the volume of trades and liquidity on the Nasdaq offered access to a wider range of buy and sell positions—also called the 'best bid and offer.'

ECNs, however, used emerging internet-based technologies to build highly sophisticated trading networks that rivaled—and for large institutional investors often surpassed—the performance and cost of the Nasdaq's platform. In addition, since ECNs were not legally obliged to ensure an efficient, fair, and transparent network for all, they were able to offer special services (for example, the ability to trade anonymously) that were very attractive to large block traders. As large institutional traders shifted more of their trading volume to ECNs, the ability to find the best bid and offer without leaving the ECN network increased. As a result, ECNs were able to complete an increasing number of large, high-margin block trades within their own networks. Free rider problems soon emerged. Because ECNs were also classified as Nasdaq market makers, when a trade did not take place immediately on the internal ECN network it could be posted on the Nasdaq. These trades were harder to execute and more expensive and thus provided much lower margins and returns to Nasdaq and its members.

During the late 1990s, as the ECNs were first gaining power and share, Nasdaq total volumes and the value delivered to members were growing exponentially, fueled by 'dot-com' exuberance. But early signs of problems could be seen as total market share began to decline. Nasdaq lobbied for regulations that would prevent fragmentation of the market. They invested in new customized workstations for high-volume traders and decreased the price for transactions to remain competitive with ECN pricing. However, the legal restrictions that mandated that Nasdaq provide a fair, transparent market for all limited the ability to compete with ECNs. Between 1995 and 2003, Nasdaq market share dropped significantly as two large ECNs effectively launched competitive private securities markets that built on the investments and assets of the Nasdaq, but did not contribute to its shared value.

The current competitive problems faced by Nasdaq highlight threats to the success of the collaborative community model that have been well documented in the literature on business cooperatives. Katz and Boland (2002) define a cooperative as a membership organization composed of individuals and/or firms that unite to achieve a common purpose or mission.[36] A cooperative exists to serve the business needs and interests of its members and to provide a *means for collective action*. Finally, a cooperative is owned by its members who contribute not just capital (as is the case for investor-owned firms) but also 'patronage'—the latter of which is often tied to active participation in achieving the shared purpose for which the cooperative was formed. From the above description, it is clear that NASD and Nasdaq embody many of the features of a business cooperative.

But cooperatives have also been shown to suffer from a common set of problems (see Table 9.3). Given that NASD was formed as a cooperative, Nasdaq's collaborative governance structure and many of its current problems can be traced to the business cooperative model.

Over the past ten years, Nasdaq has indeed seen a dramatic increase in problems with free riders, increased power of dominant coalitions, lengthy processes for assuring member buy-in, and failure of authority and control. Difficulty of gaining access to capital to fund effective response and lack of agreement among members on changes to strategic direction hamper the speed with which Nasdaq can respond to competition.

In 2002, Nasdaq received permission from the SEC to launch its own ECN-style market model and, in 2004, it acquired an established ECN, BRUT, to speed penetration and adoption. The GHX case, discussed later in this chapter, provides an opportunity to discuss potential solutions to the problems that collaborative communities commonly face as the business context becomes more turbulent, complex, uncertain, and hyper-competitive.

The Nasdaq case illustrates the design features of an inter-firm consortium that, until recently, had adopted features of collaborative

Table 9.3. Cooperatives: problems and solutions

Problem	Traditional cooperatives	New generation cooperatives
Free rider: Individuals or groups use shared resources for individual benefit without contributing equal or greater benefits to the community.	Few mechanisms to prevent free riding given that each member has equal voice without regard to level of contribution.	Ongoing investment and contributions determine share of benefits received and voice in decision making. Opportunities for free riding are decreased.
Investment liquidity: Owner/members are unable to sell their membership at a price that reflects both investments to date and future value of the assets.	Lack of a secondary market for investments limits members' willingness to invest in building the future value of the community.	Members receive a share of ownership tied to the level of investments and contributions. Members are allowed to trade 'shares' to allow entry and exit.
Risk: Investments are tied to the development of assets required to fulfill purpose and mission. Risks increase since owner/members cannot diversify investment across a portfolio of businesses.	Owner/members often force the cooperative to make less risky decisions which limits overall returns and competitive positioning.	Level of investment in assets is determined on an ongoing basis. Sale or transfer of ownership is allowed to enable owners to manage risk.
Access to capital: Owner/member capital availability and preferences determine the amount of capital to fund longer-term strategy and growth.	Owner/members tend to be driven to increase short-term benefits and may sacrifice long-term success and survival. This is especially problematic as cooperatives mature and interests diverge.	If it does not threaten the alignment with shared purpose, the ability to create a portfolio of assets within a collaborative can allow members to invest in the development of specialized assets and capabilities that meet their individual goals.
Control: Limited controls available. Problems increase as cooperatives grow and/or as interests diverge.	Factions can create subnets that act in ways that promote individual interests. Lack of formal control systems (e.g. information reporting, oversight, authority, sanctions) may make it difficult to detect and correct problems.	Contribution-based voting helps align individual and collective benefits and interests. Automation of transactions can enable better information reporting to provide transparency on community operations, benefits, and contributions.
Influence: Members and/or groups of members attempt to influence decisions and actions.	One vote per member, irrespective of contribution, enables coalitions to pursue self-interest at the expense of collective good.	Contribution-based voting replaces membership voting on decisions, actions, and priorities.

Note: See Katz and Boland (2002); Harris et al. (1996); Cook (1995) for a comparison of traditional and new generation cooperatives.

community. As a cooperative, Nasdaq's members sought to promote collective action through a shared value and identity that stressed an ethic of contribution and collective action. Organizational solutions were designed to support horizontal processes among peers. The Nasdaq case also highlights the challenges that collaborative communities face as interests diverge over time.

Given that Nasdaq was originally formed as an inter-firm collaborative community, it does not enable us to study the challenges of transforming established industries toward a collaborative community model. The next section uses the Covisint case to discuss what happens when collaboration develops within a hierarchically structured industry, and the limitations of systems that do not achieve high levels of trust and community.

Covisint: testing the limits of hierarchy

Can a networked consortium built upon a hierarchical governance model survive and prosper? This was the research question that prompted field research at Covisint between 2001 and 2004.

If we review the Nasdaq case, we see that features of hierarchical governance were a critical component to the development of process-based trust, which has been found to be a foundation of the collaborative community model.[37] Yet, within the Nasdaq collaborative community, these hierarchical features (for example, authority, standards, and structured processes) were crafted by the members to achieve common purpose, enable collective action, and serve as a foundation for community.

Early in its history, community—if present at all at Covisint—existed in 'the shadow of the hierarchy' (Chapter 1). In Chapter 10, MacDuffie and Helper identify a similar pattern of formal collaboration with high levels of control in some alliances within the automotive industry. They call this 'collaboration without trust.' Can automakers successfully impose supply-chain standards and structured processes from a position of power in a hierarchical relation? Or is a more communal form of collaboration likely to emerge as the dominant form in inter-firm consortia? To answer these questions, it is necessary to begin with a brief description of the hierarchical design of the traditional automotive industry.

COVISINT BUSINESS CONTEXT

Many point to the US automotive industry as the model of a hierarchically organized value chain. After all, the founder of the industry, Henry Ford, created many of the features of the hierarchy as he built his company and the industry during the early twentieth century. By the mid-1900s in the USA, most of the small, local, fragmented collaborative communities that characterized business markets in the agrarian economy had been replaced by large, hierarchically dominated consolidated business markets. This was especially true in industries that produced physical products, like the automotive industry, and for those portions of the industry directly related to production of products and services that would be sold to consumers.

The automotive industry of the mid-1950s represented an interesting mix of ownership and governance models. Production activities were organized within large, vertically integrated hierarchies—dominated by the automakers. Distribution activities—less amenable to scale economies—were organized within a hybrid market/hierarchy model (between automakers and dealers) and market/community model (between dealers and consumers). See Fig. 9.4.

During the 1970s, Japanese industrial giants entered a number of US industries with products that were much cheaper to build and of higher quality. As fierce competitors slashed prices and increased quality across many industrial economy industries, market share tumbled and with it industry stability and complacency. In the US auto industry, the threat from Japanese competitors was magnified by the Middle East oil embargoes that dramatically lowered demand.

The response of the 'Big Three' US automakers—Chrysler, Ford, and General Motors—was to slash costs and re-engineer supply chains. The first target for restructuring was to reduce the size of bloated middle management hierarchies and to 'empower' self-managing teams of workers by expanding roles and authority. The second target for restructuring was to break up tightly vertically integrated organizational structures and spin out suppliers. For example, Delphi—formerly the supply unit of GM—was incorporated in 1998 and became independent in 1999; similarly, Visteon, formerly the supply unit of Ford Motor Company, became independent in 2000.[38] While these large independent suppliers adopted increasingly market-focused relationships with automaker customers, the hierarchical power of the automakers remained strong. In fact, the power of the automakers was so strong that industry participants frequently referred to the automotive supply chain within 'tiers.' Tier 1 suppliers provided integrated solutions to automotive manufacturers worldwide (for example, power trains, electronics, climate controls, chassis, interiors, and exteriors); Tier 2 suppliers supplied specialized parts and components

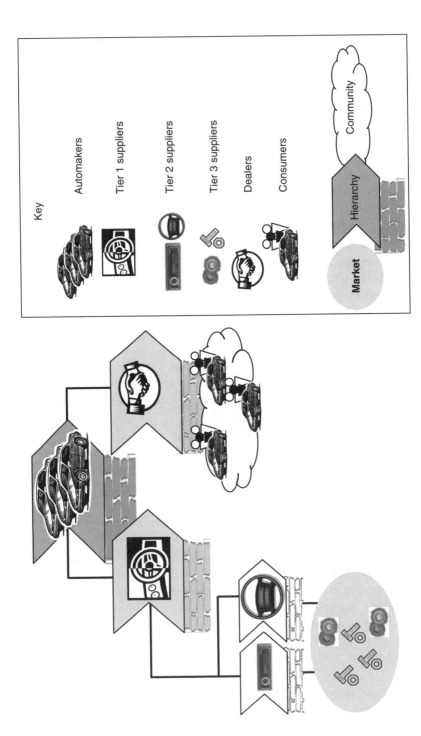

Key

Automakers

Tier 1 suppliers

Tier 2 suppliers

Tier 3 suppliers

Dealers

Consumers

Community

Hierarchy

Market

Fig. 9.4 US auto industry hierarchical value chain (pre-Covisint)

to Tier 1 suppliers; and Tier 3 through 'n' suppliers provided increasingly more commoditized supplies and parts to higher-tier suppliers.

BUILDING COVISINT

The commercialization of the internet in 1994 served as the spark that ignited a firestorm of changes in the technologies used to support how individuals and organizations did business in countries around the world. While the 'dot.com' crash and global economic recession during 2000 and 2001 slowed the pace at which new businesses were started to exploit internet-based technology, it did not halt the penetration and use of the technologies.[39]

Even as the internet captured the imagination of consumers, it also sparked the interest of the business community. Just as mechanical technologies provided the platform to build market power within industrial economy *production systems*, many viewed emerging internet-based technologies as the platform upon which to build market power in network economy *distribution* channels. During the late 1990s, capital flowed to create powerful network orchestrators that investors hoped would emerge as the dominant power within network economy industries of the twenty-first century.

As they entered the twenty-first century, automakers witnessed over 150 well-capitalized independent online exchanges enter the market determined to come between them and their suppliers. Covisint was launched in early 2000 by three of the world's largest automakers—DaimlerChrysler, Ford, and General Motors—to block the growth of independent internet entrants within automotive supply chains and to dramatically decrease the cost associated with over $300 billion in purchasing transactions each year.[40] Within months other large European and Asian automakers had contributed equity to the new venture in return for a voice in the development and launch of what was being billed as the 'industry supply-chain solution.'

Opinions differed concerning why the Big Three agreed to abandon their individual supply-chain initiatives and join in this 'unnatural marriage,' as the agreement was called at the time.[41] Certainly the suppliers had painted a vivid picture of the technological nightmare they would have faced interacting with three different exchanges, each using different standards. Others saw the impetus as purely monetary: 'Such turnabouts are natural when so much money is at stake.'[42] 'Everyone at the table understood that this was the largest deal in e-commerce history by a factor of about 100,' an industry consultant explained.[43]

At the time of Covisint's launch, the founders announced their intent to sell shares of the company on the public securities markets within one to two years of launch. Given the size of its founders, the potential volume of orders that could flow through Covisint was huge. At the time of the announcement, Ford spent $80 billion annually on procurement of parts; GM, $85 billion; and DaimlerChrysler, $73 billion. Combined, the three founders represented 44 per cent of the $379 billion in goods sold in the global automotive industry supply chain and 91 per cent of the $20 billion in profit.[44] Handling even a small percentage of these volumes would instantly make Covisint the dominant supply-chain exchange in the world, surpassing approximately 2,000 other business-to-business exchanges in operation at the time and all of the fledgling automotive industry start-ups. The potential size, scope, and power of Covisint caused two more automakers (Renault of France and Nissan of Japan) to join as investors and twenty-five auto suppliers joined as members within months of the announcement.[45]

But the dot.com crash shortly after Covisint was announced delayed the dream of rapid return on investment, and the distrust in the industry delayed the dream of driving efficiencies, flexibility, and cost savings. A Covisint executive explained the business context within the industry at the time of the launch.[46]

At the same time that automakers were striving to get leaner and more flexible, automobiles were becoming more highly engineered and complex. This put increasing pressure on inefficient supply chains that were already struggling to keep up with the relentless pace of competition and changing consumer demands. Covisint was envisioned as a hub that would sit within the network of industry relationships to simplify and decrease the cost of coordinating and managing the increasing pace and complexity. There's tremendous value in making it easier to do business and share information within this network. But we won't be able to achieve this vision if we can't get everyone to participate. The lack of trust in this industry will be a real barrier for us.

Not surprisingly, the culture of distrust, coupled with the lack of information and market transparency and shared purpose, caused problems for the fledgling company. These problems manifested themselves most directly in a lack of active participation. Suppliers complained that Covisint would further strengthen the automakers' power in the industry and would further enable automakers to extract what many believed was *more than their share of value.*[47] This prediction appeared to be borne out when one of the first applications launched by Covisint required suppliers to use a reverse auction process to submit bids for automaker contracts. Suppliers resisted, stating that the new online bidding process further eroded their margins, already squeezed by decades of fierce competition.[48] In addition, they worried that bidding on price would commoditize their products and services and destroy their ability to differentiate them on any criteria other than low price.

By 2002, participation among suppliers remained low. Given the uncertainty of Covisint's future success, even automaker participation—including the participation of original founders—remained well below the levels required for Covisint to fulfill its mission as the dominant supply-chain platform for doing business in the global automotive industry. In June 2002, Covisint's CEO resigned and Harold Kutner, former General Motors group vice president of Worldwide Purchasing and founding chairman of the board of directors of Covisint, assumed the CEO role. At GM Kutner was well known as a razor-sharp negotiator with suppliers. Many agreed that suppliers would view Kutner's appointment as an attempt by the automakers to increase their power over the supply chain. One analyst remarked: 'Kutner has the clout and power to convince both automakers and suppliers to use Covisint.'[49]

Yet, Kutner's power and influence were insufficient to gain widespread industry adoption. Kutner remained as CEO for ten months, grooming his successor, who then resigned after only thirty-one days on the job. At that time, Covisint had burned through hundreds of millions of dollars in cash. In 2003, the board accepted the proposal of Covisint's new CEO that many of Covisint's software assets be returned to investors, sold, or shut down and that the remainder of the software assets (which included the network infrastructure and collaborative portal) be sold to Compuware[50]—an information technology software and services firm. With the sale, Covisint's business model changed from a supplier-owned inter-firm consortium to a third party inter-firm consortium. While it is too early to tell whether Covisint will evolve toward a collaborative community model under this new ownership structure, early results suggest that participation within supplier and automaker networks has increased and the foundation for trust is being established under its new ownership model.

Fig. 9.5 and Table 9.4 provide a summary of the Covisint business network configuration and design features. Comparison of Figs. 9.3 and 9.5 and Tables 9.2 and 9.4 highlight the similarities and differences between Nasdaq and Covisint. Both were created to fill the role of a network orchestrator within their industry and both were owned by a coalition of players that represented a single role within the industry. Nasdaq was

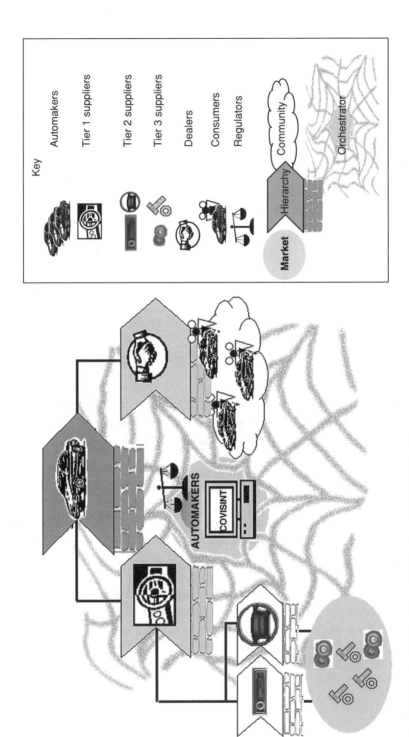

Fig. 9.5 US auto industry hierarchical value chain (2003)

Key

Automakers

Tier 1 suppliers

Tier 2 suppliers

Tier 3 suppliers

Dealers

Consumers

Regulators

Market

Hierarchy

Community

Orchestrator

Table 9.4. Features of the Covisint governance model (2000–2002)

	Market	Hierarchy	Community
Operating core	Automakers took actions to 'commoditize' transactions through reverse auctions and short-term market-based transactions.	Supply-chain activities are grouped into a hierarchical, tier-based structure. Automakers sit at the top of the tier and buy components (for example, the interior) from a Tier 1 supplier, who in turn sources individual components from Tier 2 suppliers who source parts from Tier 3 and smaller suppliers.	As products become more complex and as technological innovation increases, cooperation has increased—especially at upper tiers—but there is little trust among the parties. US automakers are considering connecting the customer into the supply chain to enable them to directly order a customized vehicle.
Coordination and control	Information needed to set price and complete transactions is readily available to all members for commodity parts and supplies. Reverse auction process is attempting to provide all members of the supplier community with real-time feature/price information to enable bidding on complex, customized solutions.	Automakers attempted to define standards and procedures and embed them within IT systems that would be adopted by the industry. Limited agreement and adoption by suppliers and automakers prevented Covisint from achieving its goals.	High levels of distrust prevented formation of community forms of coordination and control.
Infrastructure and supporting processes	Years of creating proprietary platforms, processes, and information systems have caused the industry to operate in silos. Since its sale to Compuware, Covisint has achieved increasing success in developing a common platform, standards, and applications required to support market-based transactions.	Fear of increasing the power of automakers prevented members of the automotive supply chain from granting Covisint the legitimate authority to fulfill the hierarchical roles of a network orchestrator.	Adoption of Covisint's portal application has increased since the sale to Compuware. The portal enables individual members to create communities of interest. Because they are built on a common, shared platform using shared data standards, the ability to link communities across the industry is also present.
Culture and affiliation	Self-interest predominates.	Loyalty is low.	Community affiliation and identity are low but may be increasing within portal communities.
Leadership	Market power rests with automakers, although large Tier 1 suppliers are gaining power.	Covisint's legitimate authority was unclear. Informal power led to manipulation. Lack of information transparency made monitoring difficult.	Initially, there was a lack of a clear, compelling vision that united all members of Covisint.

owned by an association of broker-dealers and Covisint was owned by the automakers. Yet, the purpose and intent of the two networks were decidedly different and, as a result, so too were the designs.

COMPARING NASDAQ AND COVISINT

Just as the initial high levels of trust within the Nasdaq community became a powerful foundation for success, the lack of trust among players in the automotive industry became a powerful barrier to success when Covisint was owned by suppliers. This finding is consistent with the findings of other authors in this book: MacDuffie and Helper, for example, find similar problems in networks of 'collaboration without trust' (see Chapter 10).

As we saw earlier, the intent of Nasdaq founders was to enable collective action among NASD members. As such, it was designed as a cooperative dedicated to sharing benefits equally among all members. In contrast, Covisint was launched as a for-profit investor-owned firm and, as such, at least one of its goals was to create wealth for its owners/investors. Covisint's automotive investors sought to perpetuate hierarchical power within the industry. Yet, if value were to be created, commitment of all industry participants would be required to break down the operating silos that decreased network efficiency and effectiveness. As a result, while they sought to achieve wide participation, Covisint's owner/founders failed to break the strong culture and identity of individualism that permeated the industry. The *organizational solutions designed by Covisint's founders stressed vertical authority-based process management rather than horizontal processes and relationships among peers.*

At Nasdaq, trust developed through a long history of repeated interactions that validated the expectations and confidence of members. In Chapter 2, Sabel refers to this as 'iterated co-design' a process that is supported by both learning and self-monitoring. A 'thick form of trust' developed before the launch of Nasdaq through association with NASD. This trust persisted over time to create a stable and structured community. Standards for action and performance embedded within the Nasdaq systems and processes structured interdependencies and provided the foundation for ensuring that members could rely on the behavior of others. Coordination and control systems stressed transparency and openness to enable everyone to monitor that rules were being fairly and consistently applied and that value was being fairly apportioned. This transparency also enabled members of the Nasdaq community to understand the dynamics of the market in real time and to link those dynamics to outcomes (value created or lost). Thus, transparency also became a foundation for learning. Finally, legitimacy for Nasdaq's and NASD's authority in enforcing rules and procedures was granted by the members.

In contrast, having been launched within a culture of distrust, Covisint was unable to generate commitment to standards that were set by the automakers and embedded within Covisint's IT-enabled operating processes. While market power could force some level of adoption of online systems within which standards and procedures were embedded, it could not force commitment to use those systems in a manner that would improve network efficiency and effectiveness. The real-time transparency that was essential for enabling Nasdaq members to rely on the behavior of others was also missing—although it is important to highlight that the high levels of complexity and interdependence in the automotive operating processes made transparency extremely difficult to achieve.[51] Given the lack of consistent, repeated interactions that met expectations, it is no surprise that Covisint did little to increase members' confidence that they could rely on the behavior of others. Lacking trust, there was little commitment to work together to develop horizontal processes.

The GHX case, discussed next, provides a third view of the challenges of building collaborative community. GHX, like Covisint, was launched within an industry that was in the throes of transformational change that threatened entrenched interests and power bases and created a sense of distrust among participants. Unlike Covisint, however, GHX made design decisions that promoted collaboration rather than perpetuating—and even increasing—silos and distrust. As such, it provides insights on how to use the lessons from our examination of Nasdaq to address the challenges experienced by Covisint.

GHX: designing the foundations for trust

The Covisint case provides a compelling view of the challenges of building a successful industry-owned consortium when a foundation of trust among members and potential members is not present. Research at GHX sought to deepen understanding of how trust might be produced among members of a newly formed consortium within an industry in which relationships were becoming increasingly distrustful. Specifically the research sought to identify organizational solutions and social structures that provided a 'foundation for trust' as a precursor for the development of collaborative community.

GHX BUSINESS CONTEXT

GHX was launched as pressures to reduce health care costs broke apart the strong bonds of trust in what had been a fragmented and dispersed but tightly cohesive network of local service providers. This important point bears emphasis when comparing the experience at Covisint and GHX. While distrust had a long history in the automotive industry, it was not firmly entrenched in the US health care industry. This may help explain the willingness of the founders of GHX to search for ways to create community rather than taking a strong stance to preserve hierarchy.

GHX evolved in the context of an industry moving from local ties to a much wider range of complex interdependencies. Until the 1970s, the physician served as network orchestrator at the center of small, local, collaborative health care communities. The physician not only delivered care (which could be considered highly complex, knowledge-intensive customized solutions) but also coordinated and controlled access by patients and their families (the consumers of health care) to a wide variety of local care providers (hospitals, pharmacists, radiologists, long-term care) and to the many products sold by suppliers (pharmaceutical, medical devices, and hospital supplies). (See Fig. 9.6.) Strong bonds of trust developed within these local communities. This trust was built on recurring interactions and strong identification with the local community within which members lived and worked (affiliation-based trust).[52]

The small size of the local community not only ensured repeated personal interactions at work, but also enabled friendships to develop outside of work. The relationships that developed not only served as 'reference points for resolving disputes,' but also as the foundation for the development of social norms that, in turn, provided the foundation for future 'trustworthy' relationships within the closely knit community (affiliation-based and institution-based trust).[53] Granovetter (1985) and others have shown that the hazards of opportunism (including the free rider, control, and influence problems that emerged within the Nasdaq business network) are diminished when economic transactions are embedded in close personal relationships and stable communities that influence behavior through strong social norms and a desire to maintain status and reputation.[54]

Until the 1980s, health care payers (primarily corporations and governments that bought insurance on behalf of individuals) played a role analogous to the clearance and settlement firms in the Nasdaq business market. Once a transaction was complete, payers settled the accounts. But, unlike

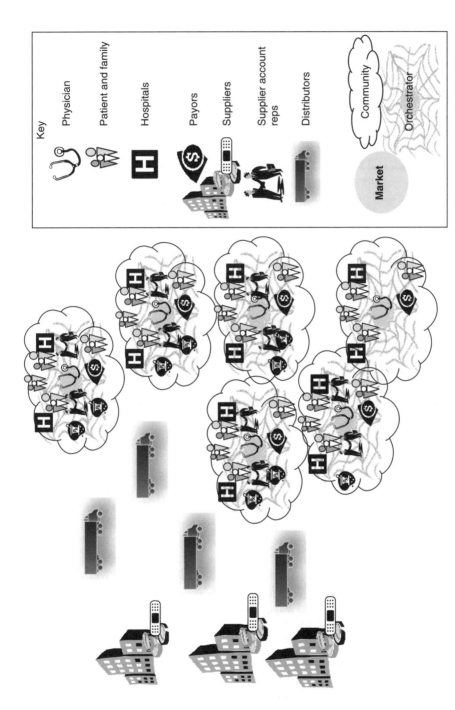

Fig. 9.6 US health care industry (pre-1980s)

389

the Nasdaq where prices were negotiated in real time to maintain a competitive, fair, and transparent market, prices in the health care marketplace were set by individual players based on *actual costs incurred* in the design, production, marketing, selling, and delivery of health care products and services. This 'retrospective pricing' model provided little incentive to control costs and, after the launch of Medicare and Medicaid in the 1960s, health care costs began to spiral upward—from 5 per cent of gross domestic product (GDP) in 1960 to 9 per cent in 1980.[55]

During the 1980s, a 'prospective pricing' model was introduced that tied health care reimbursement to a standardized price that reflected payers' agreed-upon 'willingness to pay' for delivery of care in the treatment of a specific disease or condition. In essence, the payer transitioned from a role of providing clearance and settlement services to vying with physicians for the role of controlling and coordinating access to care. This change in reimbursement sparked wide-scale industry restructuring and consolidation. The goal was to take massive costs out and streamline the industry while not destroying its ability to develop and deliver the innovative technologies and treatments required to achieve a higher purpose of improving the health and productivity of individuals, families, and society. This commitment to preserving health in an age of rapidly advancing technology caused the cost of innovation to outpace the efficiencies gained through consolidation and restructuring. By 2002, US health care expenditures had risen to over 13 per cent, or approximately $1.3 trillion, of the US GDP.

By the late 1990s, payers had embarked on a program of even more stringent cost control. A hallmark of the new programs was the need for care providers to collect and report objective data that would quantify both the cost of care and its benefits. To do this, providers of care would need to join with suppliers of drugs, medical devices, etc., and with patients and families, payors, and other members of the health care industry to share information, manage costs, and quantify benefits. This would require a significant increase in the level of market transparency to enable industry participants to link the cost of health care to treatment outcomes. It was within this environment, that five of the largest global health care suppliers joined together to launch GHX.

BUILDING GHX/BUILDING TRUST

Established within weeks of Covisint in early 2000, GHX was originally launched to provide a 'worldwide online, open, and neutral electronic trading exchange to facilitate the real-time transfer of information, money, goods, and/or services in the medical equipment, products, and services industry.'[56] Its founders were among the largest, most powerful health care suppliers in the world, including Johnson & Johnson (J&J), General Electric (GE) Medical Systems, Baxter Healthcare, Abbott Laboratories, and Medtronic. Within two weeks, seven additional large, global suppliers joined as investors and two additional supplier-investors joined several months later. James T. Lenehan, vice chairman and president of J&J, explained the motivation for these fierce competitors to come together to form GHX. 'Every health care system around the world is under enormous pressure to create efficiency and take out costs. This exchange is a big part of the solution, providing access to state-of-the-art supply chain management and clinical content [while dramatically lowering the cost of doing business].'[57] Thus the value of GHX would not only come from the efficiencies that would be gained by creating a common, state-of-the-art platform upon which the industry could do business, but also by providing a common platform for *sharing information* to enable all members of the global health care industry to work together to define standards of care that would reduce costs while also improving outcomes and increasing benefits for patients, families, and society. This latter goal highlights Sabel's concept of creating transparency in co-design as both a tool for monitoring and a tool for learning. (See Chapter 2.)

Like Covisint, the founders initially intended to run GHX as a supplier-owned exchange and within months of the launch of its first product—an online catalog—over fifty suppliers joined as members. Within a short time, GHX provided access to equipment and supplies that accounted for over 90 per cent of the transaction volume in the health care industry. But 'you can't have a viable marketplace with only one side participating,'[58] a GHX executive remarked as it became clear that other industry participants were reluctant to join a 'supplier exchange.'

Initially, executives at GHX defined the problem as one of access to groups on the purchasing side. They sought to achieve this access through alliances with the orchestrators for the largest online group purchasing organizations (GPOs) for the large integrated health care delivery networks (IDNs) that were rapidly consolidating the industry's fragmented, local health care providers. In summer 2001, GHX signed its first such alliance with Neoforma, an online GPO exchange owned by two of the largest US IDNs, Voluntary Hospitals of America (VHA) and University Healthcare Consortium (UHC). By uniting their respective exchanges, the alliance with Neoforma allowed GHX to gain instant access to the buying power of Neoforma's vast network of health care providers, while Neoforma received instant access to the online catalogs of the leading GHX suppliers. In November 2001, GHX formed an alliance with Amer-iNet, a GPO that represented over 14,000 independent health care providers. This was quickly followed by alliances with Broadlane, a GPO that represented hospitals in the Tenet, Kaiser Permanente, and Universal Health Services IDNs, and MedAssetsHSCA, one of the largest GPOs in the USA.

While these alliances gave instant reach to a broad network of providers, GHX executives soon realized that they did not enable the level of process integration, real-time interactions, and information sharing needed to achieve the learning and monitoring that come with co-design. As was seen in the Nasdaq case, co-design requires a seamless flow of information that enables the market transparency needed to create deep insights on the relationship between market dynamics and outcomes. For its core trading transactions, the Nasdaq Stock Market supports relatively simple transactions and the information needed for co-design can be created online. GHX, like Covisint, supported a much more complex transaction. As a result, co-design would require both online transparency and the ability for all members to communicate and collaborate in real time. The alliances enabled visibility of supply and demand but did not provide the seamless flow of information and interactivity needed for members to work collaboratively to lower costs while also improving quality of care.

Another important distinction between the design of the Nasdaq broker-dealer network and the initial GHX network of alliances involved the roles of the network orchestrators. Recall that the Nasdaq network connects broker-dealers in short-term 'alliances' that enable them to buy and sell stocks on behalf of investors and issuers. Thus, each Nasdaq broker-dealer can be thought of as a network orchestrator that connects *both buyers and sellers*. Contrast this with the GHX network of alliances discussed above. The GHX alliances connected the network orchestrators for specialized consortia—each of which represented only one party in the transaction (e.g. GHX represented suppliers and Neoforma, AmeriNet, Broadlane, and MedAssets represented different networks of buyers). In effect, the alliances perpetuated the industry silos and distrust between buyers and suppliers.

The Nasdaq case highlighted that willingness to trust was grounded in bottom-up development and legitimization of industry standards that encompassed *all* parties to a transaction. GHX found that its alliances with network orchestrators (each of which represented entrenched groups in the industry) failed to induce all parties in the health care supply transactions to work together to develop the shared industry standards needed to streamline and integrate horizontal processes that would enable the seamless flow of information.

In fall 2001, GHX and HealthNexis announced the decision not just to ally, but to merge companies and operations. HealthNexis was a health care information and technology solutions company formed as a joint venture between four of the largest and most powerful US health care distributors, including AmeriSourceBergen, Cardinal Health, Fisher Scientific, and McKesson. Given that the large distributors had already established direct online links to health care providers and suppliers, the stage was now set to develop horizontal processes.

Interestingly, executives at GHX believed that its earlier alliances played a critical role in developing the trust needed for the merger. A GHX executive explained:

The partnership deals we did early on with AmeriNet, Neoforma, and large health care providers and GPOs provided us with the credibility we needed to bring HealthNexis to the table. However, we still had to deal with the issue of trust. We needed to prove to the distributors that our goal was to work with them, not against them. Developing mutual understanding and trust was a long process, but eventually we were able to strike a deal that was beneficial to the industry.[59]

Less than one year later, GHX used the successful merger with HealthNexis as evidence of trustworthiness during its merger with MediBuy—an online health care exchange owned by several of the largest IDNs and GPOs in the USA, for example, Premier, HealthTrust Purchasing Group (HPG), and Hospital Corporation of America (HCA).

The merger with MediBuy transformed GHX, and the industry, by creating a *network orchestrator that was owned by all members of the industry.* (See Fig. 9.7.) This provided the foundation for developing and legitimizing shared industry standards that would enable the development of end-to-end horizontal relationships and processes across the industry and created a platform for the repeated transactions and market transparency needed to achieve process-based trust among all members.

The mergers also enabled GHX to rapidly bring scale efficiencies to the industry while also leveraging operating synergies and broadening product scope. 'Over the past several years, [GHX, HealthNexis, and Medibuy] have been working on parallel tracks to deliver on the same market promise: a more efficient healthcare supply chain,' a GHX board member

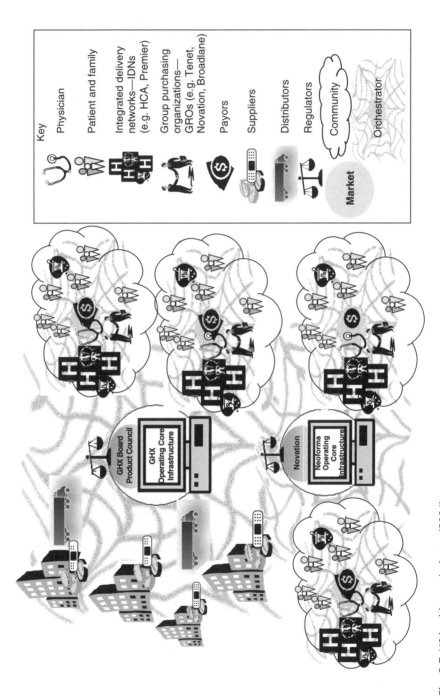

Fig. 9.7 US health care industry (2004)

Key

Physician

Patient and family

Integrated delivery networks—IDNs (e.g. HCA, Premier)

Group purchasing organizations— GROs (e.g. Tenet, Novation, Broadlane)

Payors

Suppliers

Distributors

Regulators

Community

Orchestrator

Market

GHX Board Product Council

GHX Operating Core Infrastructure

Novation

Neoforma Operating Core Infrastructure

explained. 'Each [company] provides valuable technology solutions. Together, we have an opportunity to eliminate redundancy and improve business processes for all participants.'[60] An executive for one of Medibuy's key customers, HCA, agreed.

Medibuy's products and services played a significant role in the achievement of HCA's supply chain efficiency objectives over the past few years, and we anticipate that the combined resources of the new company will deliver even greater value. HCA hospitals have utilized Medibuy's software to streamline the requisitioning process. Now, as a result of the merger, HCA will be able to improve the accuracy of their purchase orders by using product data, maintained and verified by suppliers, in the GHX catalog and Content Intelligence⒯ systems.

Within one year of completing the HealthNexis and Medibuy mergers, GHX had successfully achieved end-to-end horizontal process integration among over 1,600 of the largest health care providers and 300 suppliers, thereby enabling them to seamlessly do business online and access the full power of GHX's value-added information and services. In addition, it allowed all members of the health care industry in the USA and increasingly in Europe and Canada to connect to a much broader network of providers through its own web-based subscription purchasing service and its ongoing alliances with Neoforma, AmeriNet, Broadlane, and MedAssets HCSA.

Within two years of its formation GHX became the dominant internet-based global health care marketplace and the only industry supply-chain consortium with equity ownership by key participants representing all major industry players: health care providers, suppliers, distributors, GPOs, and IDNs. A GHX executive explained: 'Investors quickly recognized that the chances for success were slim given the commitment of the leading companies to create a neutral, third-party exchange.' In an open letter to customers, Harry Kraemer, CEO and chairman of Baxter, stressed: 'With [hundreds of years] of combined experience in the healthcare industry, this new company combines our proven record of quality and trust with the agility of an Internet technology company.'[61]

Clearly, the ability of GHX to bring together trusted members of each participant group within the health care value chain and to offer representatives of those groups both a share of the equity in GHX and a seat on the company's board of directors signaled to the industry that all interests would be considered. Thus the trust that each group of participants had as respected members of their group (affiliation-based trust) was transferred to the GHX board of directors (and company) as a whole.

A look at the inner workings of the GHX board, including the legal agreements that were hammered out at each step in the company's formation, provides a deeper understanding of the governance model that enabled GHX to manage competing interests over time. A GHX operating manager explained.

While most companies in the dot-com era were trying to extend their influence and dominate all positions in the value chain, we chose a very different approach. We knew we would never try to take over the operations and [technology] systems *within* our customers, manufacturers, or distributors—nor did we want to. What we could offer was a complementary set of offerings that would serve as a nerve center, connecting all parties but stopping at the doors to their organization. This was consistent with our Vision, Mission, and Guiding Principles—all of which were formally specified in our LLC Agreement.

EVOLVING THE GHX GOVERNANCE MODEL

GHX vision. To grow as the global leader in business-to-business supply chain management solutions and services for the health care industry, providing superior member satisfaction, delivered by energized employees who are driven to meet commitments.

GHX goals. To transform health care by dramatically improving the efficiency of healthcare delivery through information exchange and by maximizing efficiencies in the supply chain; and to facilitate continuous improvement in the relationship between all stakeholders in the health care supply chain resulting in collaborative communication, reduced costs, and better patient care.

One of the initial challenges that the GHX founders faced was to prove that it was possible for competing supplier organizations to work together collaboratively. Initial discussions helped clarify a common vision, mission, and goals. These shared purposes, beliefs, and values stressed the commitment not only to improve the efficiency of the industry but also to *improve relationships and collaborative communications among all industry participants to achieve the goal of reduced costs and better patient care.*

While most new firms go through the exercise of creating a shared vision and mission, for GHX founders it was a critical first step in enabling these fierce competitors to develop an interdependent form of identity that would motivate and engage active participation and affiliation over time. Thus while Adler and Heckscher (Chapter 1) note that process-based trust is dominant in collaborative community, the GHX and Nasdaq cases suggest that affiliation- and institution-based trust may be important *precursors* to its development. How did this work? The merger negotiations brought the various industry interest groups together, face to face around a table. The negotiation process enabled the development of shared purpose and goals that, in turn, formed the foundation for the development of industry standards needed to develop horizontal processes and information transparency. These, in turn, provided the foundation for the development of process-based trust.

The GHX founders believed that the development of shared values and identity were so critical to the industry's success that they formalized their shared purpose and vision, which had been hammered out over months of negotiation, into wording that was added to the Global Healthcare Exchange Limited Liability Corporation (LLC) Agreement. While all corporate legal agreements specify the obligations among owners and investors that are required by law, the GHX founders sought to go beyond the standard legal agreement and capture the unique nature of GHX's obligations and commitments to its investors, the health care industry, patients and families, and society. As a result, the founders decided to add the agreed-upon vision, mission, and goals in the LLC Agreement as a way of 'capturing the intent of the founders.' In addition, specific clauses were inserted to cover key negotiated agreements. For example, the LLC Agreement explicitly stated that the company did not plan to pursue an initial public offering (IPO). Instead, the firm would seek to 'generate revenue and distribute excess profits back to its investing members and its customers through fee reductions.' The GHX general council explained how this legal agreement was reached and evolved as new equity owners with different interests joined the company's board:

The initial L.L.C. Agreement formalized many hours of discussion among the founders. We tried to provide a legal framework for corporate governance and for the partnership that would protect all members yet be flexible enough to deal with uncertainty. A key area of uncertainty in the beginning involved the eventual equity ownership structure. For example, the initial L.L.C. Agreement only considered the interests of suppliers since, at the time, we did not anticipate that we would have non-supplier equity owners. We soon realized, however, that it would be more difficult than we expected to gain the trust of distributors, GPOs, and healthcare providers if we did not formalize their interests in our agreements. [Gaining the trust of other industry participants] was essential to gaining the critical mass needed to become the industry-wide exchange we envisioned. For example, during the discussions leading up to the acquisition, HealthNexis owners stated three basic strategic risks that they wanted us to address. First, they wanted us to agree that GHX would not become a distributor or a GPO. They also wanted us to state that we wouldn't aggregate demand, and they wanted us to insure that we wouldn't try to influence pricing. These concepts were very consistent with our intent, and we thought that it was a great idea to formalize our *Guiding Principles* and to include statements covering these areas as an Exhibit in the L.L.C. Agreement.[62]

Given that the company did not plan an IPO, the LLC Agreement also specified that each founder would be issued 'Membership Units,' with each unit equivalent to $1 of capital contributed by a founding member during the Initial Capital Call. Subsequent equity investors were also issued Membership Units at a price per unit that was determined by the board based on the value of the company. The Membership Units were used to determine voting rights, decision authority, and distribution of profits and loss. This enabled the company to *directly tie investment and participation to influence and value received while also providing investors with liquidity, thereby avoiding key problems associated with traditional cooperatives* (refer back to Table 9.2).

Another key issue that needed to be hammered out during negotiations by members of the GHX board concerned ownership of the flow of products, services, and information across the integrated system. These agreements formed the foundation for 'Data Ownership Standards' that were also added as an appendix in a revised LLC Agreement. These data standards clarified areas of interdependency. But, more importantly, they also clarified what would not be shared. A GHX operating manager explained: 'Consistent with our vision and mission, each supplier "owned" its product data and the buyer owned its procurement data. Each buyer and supplier jointly "owned" data on their respective transactions.'

A GHX product developer explained that, when GHX was first formed, few standards existed. GHX, like NASD and Nasdaq, used the legitimization provided by its members and its position at the center of the industry to form an operating council that enabled operating managers to collaborate in the development of industry standards and horizontal processes. As such, collaborative co-design took place, not just at the executive level, but also at the operating level.

[When GHX was first formed], distributors, manufacturers and providers still referred to identical products by different numbers. There was also no agreement on how customers should be identified since every supplier, GPO, and distributor had their own unique customer identifiers. Agreement on transaction standards for common processes such as placing purchase orders, sending invoices, and electronically transferring funds would enable us to develop value-added industry solutions—lowering the cost for the entire industry and improving quality of care. The delay in reaching agreement on standards was that everyone was waiting for someone else to go first. Hospitals wouldn't push the issue because manufacturers weren't, and manufacturers wouldn't push the issue because their customers weren't. Until now, no one has had the critical mass to break through the obstacles. We're in a great position to accelerate the adoption of standards. We recently formed a Product Council, composed of representatives from the supplier, distributor, GPO, and provider communities. The Council meets regularly to provide input on GHX product offerings. This will be a great forum to help us discuss standards that can be embedded in our product offerings.

The Guiding Principles and legal agreements were not static documents. Instead, they evolved over time along with the governance model of the firm. See Table 9.5 for a summary of the GHX governance model.

Rather than remaining as a formal document sitting in a lawyer's file cabinet, the legal agreements, Guiding Principles, and Data Standards also became an important mechanism for institutionalizing culture and values—not only inside GHX but also throughout the industry. A GHX operating manager explained:

The Guiding Principles evolved over time as we learned more about the needs and expectations of our expanding membership base and ownership structure. They provided a tangible statement of our shared expectations and became a powerful tool for marketing and selling the exchange to new members.

As such, the legal agreements among members created institution-based trust that was then transferred to the company's salespeople and used as evidence of trustworthiness.

The LLC Agreement also specified other governance mechanisms, for example, the composition of the board of directors, change of control, and decision authority. Once again, standard legal agreements proved insufficient for capturing the unique requirements of the GHX board and the interests they represented. For example, decision-making authority was also specified in the LLC Agreement. The levels of board approval for key decisions included:

1. The *Guiding Principles* set the strategic direction and parameters to guide key decisions. Any changes in the Guiding Principles required super majority shareholder approval (see below).

2. *Ultra/Super Majority Shareholder Approval* decisions required greater than 95 per cent approval of all shareholders with equity interests greater than 5 per cent. The decision to revise the LLC Agreement to allow GHX to become a public company (IPO) was an example of a decision that required this level of approval.

Table 9.5. Features of the GHX governance model

	Market	Hierarchy	Community
Operating core	Prices for routine health care supplies are negotiated by GPOs on behalf of IDNs. GHX provides access to supplier catalogs reflecting negotiated prices and to IT-enabled transactions systems that enable market transactions to take place efficiently and reliably.	Activities have been grouped into differentiated roles. Standardized procedures have been defined and embedded in IT to enable efficiency and consistency of routine buy–sell transactions.	Customized solutions and innovative medical devices are 'co-designed' by suppliers, providers, and academic researchers. Teams of suppliers and care providers deliver highly customized and complex care routines.
Coordination and control	Information needed to set price and complete routine supply-chain transactions is readily available to all members that participate in a transaction. Anonymity and privacy are maintained across transactions.	GHX aggregates data on behalf of individual owner/members and provides customized reports. In addition, on behalf of its members GHX provides routine online and offline reporting and monitoring to ensure compliance with agreed-upon standards. Vertical differentiation of authority is present within a flat hierarchy.	Long-term coordination and control are based on commitment to shared purpose and trust that GHX is operating on behalf of its broad membership. Membership units determine each member/owner's voice in community governance.
Infrastructure and supporting processes	GHX provides a standardized platform for routine buy–sell transactions and information sharing. Information needed to actively participate is available to all and is easy to access and use.	Routine and customized reports are generated automatically from data in GHX transaction systems and databases and are made available to support both lateral processes among peers and vertical control within a flat hierarchy.	While product councils and health care delivery teams primarily meet face to face to interact and work, shared high-bandwidth information and communication processing infrastructure provides support.

Culture and affiliation	Individual interests, captured in negotiated agreements, dominate during routine supplier–distributor– provider interactions.	Increasing power of payers has resulted in an increasing culture of distrust and polarization of interests and values. Some health care provider groups have developed their own payment plans and have 'exited' from payer networks.	Strong ethic of contribution to shared purpose and values to provide high-quality health care to all members of society. Shared purpose and mission link individual and community interests. Affiliation- and process-based trust provide the foundation for collaborative community values.
Leadership	Formal leadership is not required, given the structured, short-term nature of interdependencies in routine transactions. Authority is embedded in the transactions and systems that support them.	The LLC Agreement formalizes governance processes, including shared mission, purpose, and values. Transactional leadership—oversight of operations—is embedded within the systems that automate routine transactions. Early warning systems alert GHX executives to non-routine problems and events. Standardized performance reporting communicates progress toward meeting goals.	GHX's board of directors is made up of member/owners and independents that represent the interests of all stakeholder groups. GHX's Product Council ensures that all members have a voice in the development and execution of product strategy and priorities.

3. *Super Majority Shareholder Approval* decisions required greater than 85 per cent approval of equity shareholders. Examples of decisions that required this level of approval included changes to Guiding Principles, liquidation, mergers, and alliances.

4. *Majority Shareholder Approval* decisions required greater than 50 per cent approval of equity shareholders. Examples of decisions that required this level of approval included capital calls and issuance or redemption of stock.

5. *Majority Board Approval* decisions required greater than 50 per cent approval of the board of directors. Board members approved budgets, contracts, expenditures over a specified amount, executive compensation, auditor selection, and the launch of new lines of business that fell within the Guiding Principles.

As the GHX case demonstrates, trust and the collaborative community governance model required to maintain it did not emerge fully formed. Instead, it was built over time through a process that began with a search for shared purpose and a vision for the future by individuals that represented the interests of important stakeholder groups. If successful, these discussions and negotiations resulted in the formation of personal, affiliation-based trust among the negotiating group that was then *transferred* to the represented stakeholder groups who, in turn, *legitimized* the consortium to act on their behalf. This legitimization of authority carried with it obligations and rights. GHX's founding members had the foresight to capture, not just the legal obligations and rights, but also the intent, purpose, vision, and goals in the legal documents that formalized authority, obligations, and the governance process through which they would be ensured. In the process, they developed institution-based trust. As such, affiliation- and institution-based trust were required to support the transition toward process-based trust that, in turn, formed the foundation for moving toward the collaborative community form of governance discussed in this book.

The GHX case is valuable in that it also shows how trust, collaborative community, and the governance processes required to build and maintain them over time are diffused and institutionalized throughout a company (GHX) and the industry. Using the Guiding Principles and LLC Agreement, the GHX board, executives, and employees were able to create a *shared, interdependent identity and values* that stressed *an ethic of contribution and motivated and engaged active participation and affiliation over time.* Organizational configurations and solutions—including a Product Council of industry representatives that developed shared standards that, in turn, became embedded in end-to-end operating processes and systems—supported horizontal relations among peers. These inter-firm organizational solutions further enhanced process-based trust. Once everyone was connected and business was being conducted online, information began to be generated that would enable the development of a reliable business network that consistently met the expectations of members, which, in turn, provided evidence that confirmed and strengthened perceptions of trustworthiness.

Building collaborative community: lessons from the field

Throughout the second half of the twentieth century, advances in IT—coupled with the rapid evolution of management theory and tools (for example, total quality management, business process re-engineering, self-managing teams, and networking and negotiation skills)—made it increasingly easier for *independent* companies to coordinate *interdependent* activities. Consultants championed the rise of the 'virtual corporation'—a network of focused businesses that would come together as free agents to design, build, market, sell, and support products and services within a wide variety of old and new economy industries.[63] The proposed benefits: greater efficiency, increased responsiveness, the ability to share specialized assets (including physical assets, knowledge, and relationships), and to tap into high-powered market incentives. Indeed, the business literature has provided numerous examples of virtually integrated firms, like Dell, that outperformed much larger vertically integrated competitors and rose to the number one position in the industry.[64]

But, as we see from the three cases discussed here, the same factors that make virtual business networks so powerful can also leave them vulnerable. Increased inter-firm coordination costs can destroy hoped-for efficiency gains; self-interest and opportunism can lead to free-riding; and lack of trust can delay adoption of the shared standards and horizontal processes required to enable collective action. The Nasdaq, Covisint, and GHX cases provide insight into how these problems arise. They also show how they can be addressed through organizational solutions that enable coordination of interdependencies, alignment of interests, and development of trust. Key insights from the three cases are summarized below.

Key Insight: Community is emerging from the shadow of hierarchy and market to become a dominant form of governance.

For decades, academics have recognized the power of hybrid forms of governance that unite hierarchy, market, and community.[65] The three cases discussed here suggest that emerging hybrid governance models do not need to eliminate hierarchy or market for community models to become the distinctive and dominant governance model. Instead, GHX and Nasdaq show that *market and hierarchy can actually facilitate and enable collaborative capacity and trust*—which, provide an important foundation for community. These two cases highlight how standards, policies, and procedures—all governance mechanisms typically associated with hierarchy—can be embedded in transaction-processing systems that enable market-based transactions to take place consistently, reliably, and efficiently. More important, these automated transactions capture information on each transaction and, when associated with outcomes, enable self-monitoring to occur which increases trust.

While routine transactions are governed primarily through market transactions and self-monitoring by market participants, the information about transactions can also be captured and made available to other parties. At Nasdaq we saw that this information could be used to support routine reporting to regulators that ensure compliance with policies and laws (a hierarchical governance feature and a requirement in any stable community). We also saw that the same information was made available to teams of experts from many disciplines that formed to develop highly customized, knowledge-based solutions. These self-managing, highly creative teams could form anywhere on the network and could unite multiple independent agents. An example is the teams of investment bankers, lawyers, accountants, advertising agencies, Nasdaq listing agents, and issuer executives that come together to complete an initial public offering (IPO). All share common information, all submit to common standards and procedures, yet the output is highly creative and innovative. And, unless team self-interest overpowers network interests, value can be created—not just for the members of the team working on the deal, but also for all members of the Nasdaq business network. Thus, community features increased the innovative and collaborative capacity by building on a foundation of hierarchical and market governance.

How did Nasdaq and GHX create this unique and distinctive governance model? The cases provide deep insight on the interplay among organizational solutions, trust, and governance models over time. This is discussed in more detail later in this section.

Key Insight: A network orchestrator role is emerging to coordinate inter-firm interdependencies within industry consortia.

Given the complexity of the transactions carried out and the sheer number of highly differentiated yet interdependent parties involved, a network orchestrator was required to coordinate task, information/expertise, and affiliation/identity interdependencies within the three industry consortia discussed in this chapter. Within the securities industry, NASD—an industry cooperative—launched Nasdaq to fulfill the orchestrator role. Within the health care industry, suppliers, distributors, and health care providers contributed both equity and patronage to build GHX to fulfill the network orchestrator role. Within the automotive industry several of the most powerful automakers launched Covisint. In this latter case, we see that it is exceedingly difficult to motivate collective action and engaged participation when the interests of all parties involved in the transactions to be carried out are not represented 'at the governance table.' The recent sale of Covisint to Compuware was designed to provide the neutral, third-party governance and ownership missing when the interests of only one side of the transaction were represented.

Both GHX and Nasdaq built consortia that were owned and governed by industry members involved in both the buy and sell side of the transaction. The founders of these consortia believed that shared ownership was critical to ensuring active commitment to collective action and participation. They also believed that a 'cooperative' association membership model would best align member interests and contributions to value created and received.

Key Insight: Network orchestrators design organizational solutions that reflect the interests of all parties.

The Nasdaq case provides an initial view of how a network orchestrator ensures that all interests in a buy–sell transaction are represented. The identification of obligations and responsibilities begins with the board of directors responsible for defining direction, setting priorities, and overseeing the actions taken to ensure that the collective interests of the members are supported. Nasdaq received its legitimacy to act on behalf of its members from NASD—an industry association that represented the interests of the broker-dealer community. Given that broker-dealers bought *and* sold stocks on behalf of investors, NASD was in a unique position to represent both the buy side and the sell side of the market transaction through representation of one participant in the market.

Over time, however, the securities industry transactions became more complex and so too did the interests of Nasdaq members. Specialized roles developed to support issuers and investors in more complex transactions, such as listing stock for sale through a public offering and providing research and financial planning advice to investors. Eventually, ECNs emerged that used new technologies to create alternative securities markets that both collaborated and competed with the Nasdaq Securities Market. While Nasdaq expanded its role and services to meet these needs, its governance process failed to reflect the rapidly diverging interests. In 2002, rocked by scandals and competitive threats, NASD and Nasdaq overhauled its board and governance processes.

In contrast to the Nasdaq case, which looks back in time, the Covisint and GHX cases provide the rare opportunity for a researcher to observe first-hand how two network orchestrators experimented with governance models that would represent the complex—and often competing—interests of an industry consortium. Unlike Nasdaq, both GHX and Covisint were originally launched to support only one position in the buy–sell transaction. Executives in both companies soon learned that they would need to broaden their base of support to effectively represent the interests of all parties in the transaction and gain the necessary participation. Covisint, which represented the buyer in the automotive supply chain, tried adding suppliers to its board of directors but prevented them from becoming equity owners. When board positions alone failed to motivate the participation required, Covisint was sold to a neutral, third-party player.

GHX, which represented the seller in the health care supply chain, initially attempted to link its network of suppliers to independent networks of buyers. While this approach enabled routine transactions to take place, no one party was granted the authority and legitimacy to represent the interests of the industry. As a result, there was little progress in developing the common standards and horizontal processes required to achieve the dual goals of driving efficiencies while also enabling the technological innovation needed to improve the quality of care delivered. To reach this deeper level of collaboration, GHX merged its operations and organizations with consortia that represented the interests of distributors and health care providers. These mergers provided the foundation upon which process-based trust and a collaborative community model of governance could be built.

Key Insight: Trust, collaborative community, market, and hierarchy co-evolve over time.

GHX began as a consortium of suppliers. The case details how months of face-to-face negotiation among senior executives representing five of the most powerful competitors in the health care industry enabled these competitors to achieve a common understanding and 'hammer out' the governance framework that would serve as the foundation for collective action. Recognizing that most legal agreements were inadequate, the founders had the foresight to capture not just their legal obligations, but also the purpose and goals that united them in seeking a collective solution to problems that plagued the industry.

While none had read about 'New Age Cooperatives,' the governance framework they developed embodied many of its key features. Examples include: (1) tying decision making and value received to contribution by assigning Membership Units; (2) formalizing decision processes to avoid hold-up problems; (3) developing a formal process through which interests could be clarified and conflicts resolved; and (4) engaging all stakeholders in a process of ongoing negotiations to ensure that interests are reflected in both the development and execution of business strategy and resource decisions.

The intent and governance processes were formalized in the legal agreements that served as the charter for the consortium. The charter became a 'manifesto'—a dynamic document that evolved to incorporate the months of discussion and the agreements that united the supplier, distributor, and health care provider interests. It contained Guiding Principles and Data Standards that were used to frame decision making and action. The manifesto was also used as evidence of trustworthiness as new members were recruited. Finally, it became a clear statement of the shared values that all members were expected to uphold.

The standards, policies, and values were also embedded within IT-enabled horizontal processes that supported the collective action among members. These systems also provided the information transparency needed for each member to participate fully and the self-monitoring required for the development of 'process-based trust' among all members.

The GHX case also provides deep insight into the interplay between the evolving governance model and evolving trust. While these insights are presented based on data in a single case study, they have been supported by evidence from the broader research program. Additional research is currently under way to determine the generalizability of the findings. With this caveat in mind, the approach used by GHX is presented below.

Trust initially developed within a small team of individuals as they engaged in months of face-to-face negotiation around the initial launch of GHX. These individuals became the governing board that represented the interests of their respective companies in the GHX consortium. Trust was transferred from the board to each member's respective organization through affiliation-based trust and, given the reputation of each board member for trustworthy behavior, trust was also transferred in a limited way to other members of the supplier community. As new members representing other segments of the industry negotiated to merge with GHX, a similar process was used to expand affiliation-based trust and trust transfer within companies representing buyer and distributor interests.

Once interests and benefits were aligned at the board of directors level, GHX formed a Product Council made up of operating managers that mirrored the membership of the board and the interests of the broad-based constituency. The board transferred authority for product strategy and its execution to the Product Council, and the council worked with all members to develop the common standards and processes required to coordinate interdependencies. These standards, procedures, and rules were then embedded in a shared platform and common IT-enabled horizontal processes.

These standards and processes, like the agreements of the board, were hammered out through frequent face-to-face negotiations. This approach to using interlocking boards and councils was also seen at Nasdaq. In both cases, this inter-firm organizational governance mechanism enabled all members of the consortium to have their interests represented and their voices heard as strategy was developed and executed, resources were prioritized and deployed, and benefits and value were apportioned among the members.

At Nasdaq, we saw how agreed-upon standards and processes related to routine transactions were embedded within a shared platform upon which members came together to buy and sell securities. These buy–sell transactions were enabled by IT systems that formalized agreements worked out by the board and product council. These horizontal processes enabled members of the industry to leverage shared assets and create efficiency benefits that all could share. Further, once all industry transactions were taking place on a common platform using common systems, information was generated and made available to all members. This real-time information provided the market transparency that members needed to ensure that Nasdaq was living up to its obligations to establish a fair, reliable, and trustworthy place to do business. The transaction-level information transparency also enabled members to learn how their actions and decisions related to outcomes. This learning enabled them to continually innovate to drive greater efficiency and effectiveness. Until recently, the strict reporting enabled the governing bodies to ensure that these innovations continued to serve the interests of all members.

The insights from these three cases provide important lessons that can be used to guide future research. Especially critical next steps are action-based research programs that enable other emerging industry consortia to build on the experiences and lessons of others.

Closing thoughts

Executives around the world, including the ones discussed in this chapter, spent significant effort during the 1990s transforming their companies and industries to meet the challenges of operating in a more dynamic, hyper-competitive world. But as the millennium drew to a close, many were forced to face the grim reality that the twenty-first century would demand even more radical change. As disruptive technologies, regulatory environments, and societal norms destabilized markets, industries, and organizations, these executives found that they needed to respond even more quickly, to deliver even higher-quality products and services, and to cut costs even more deeply. Intra- and inter-firm boundaries were shattered and authority expanded to the point where many worried that their organizations and industries would spin out of control. In the process, the assumptions of traditional organizational and economic models of governance were pushed to the limit.

Thomas Kuhn's analysis of scientific revolutions suggests that crisis is a necessary precondition to the emergence of a new theory or model.[66] But when presented with crisis, most people do not immediately reject existing models. Instead, they attempt incremental adjustments that, over time, begin to blur the fundamental structure and assumptions upon which the old models were based. Practitioners are often the first to lose sight of old models as the familiar rules for solving problems become ineffective. At some point, total reconstruction is required. During the transition, however, there is frequently an overlap between the problems that can be solved by the old and new models. But no matter which is used, there is a decisive difference in the modes of solution.

This appears to be the point at which we find ourselves. A crisis, largely driven by a fundamental mismatch between environmental demands and

organizational capabilities, has called into question many of the fundamental assumptions of traditional organizational and economic models.
As we can see in the case studies of Nasdaq, Covisint, and GHX, academic
thinking is being framed by practice. The lessons from the field suggest
that a new collaborative community model is emerging that harnesses the
power of today's technologies in the hands of a more knowledgeable
workforce to offer fundamentally new approaches to organizing and managing in a networked world. Understanding this evolution will be a fruitful
area of research for decades to come.

References

Books and articles

Adler, P. (2001). 'Market, hierarchy, and trust: the knowledge economy and the
future of capitalism.' *Organization Science*, 12/2: 215–34.

Applegate, L. M. (1999*a*). 'Electronic commerce.' In Richard C. Dorf (ed.), *The
Technology Management Handbook*. New York: CRC Press: 11-22–11-31.

——(1999*b*). 'In search of a new organizational model: lessons from the field.' In
Shaping Organizational Form: Communication, Connection, and Community. Thousand Oaks, Calif.: Sage Publications: 33–70.

——(1999*c*). 'Time for the big small company.' *The Financial Times Mastering Information Management Series*, 1 Mar.

Baker, W. (2002). 'Network organizations in theory and practice.' In N. Nohria and
R. Eccles (eds.), *Networks and Organizations: Structure, Form, and Action*. Boston:
Harvard Business School Press: 397–429.

Bennett, J. (2002). 'Covisint reshapes workforce.' *Detroit Free Press*, 4 Apr.

Ben-Porah, Y. (1980). 'The f-connection: families, friends, and firms and the
organization of exchange.' *Population Development Review*, 6: 1–30.

Best, M. (1990). *The New Competition*. Cambridge, Mass.: Harvard University
Press.

Bradach, J., and Eccles, R. (1989). 'Price, authority and trust.' *Annual Review of
Sociology*, 15: 97–118.

Burt, R. (1992). *Structural Holes: The Social Structure of Competition*. Cambridge,
Mass.: Harvard University Press.

Chutkow, P. (2001). *Visa: The Power of an Idea*. New York: Harcourt Press.

Cook, M. (1995). 'The future of US agricultural cooperatives: a neoinstitutional
approach.' *American Journal of Agricultural Economics*, 77: 1153–9.

Dell, M., and Magretta, J. (1998). 'The power of virtual integration: an interview
with Dell Computer's Michael Dell.' *Harvard Business Review* (Mar.): 72–84.

Drucker, P. (1988). 'The coming of the new organization.' *Harvard Business Review*
(Jan.–Feb.): 3–11.

Eiler Communications (2002). 'Q&A with Covisint's Shankar Kiru: creating a successful electronic exchange.' 19 Mar.

Galbraith, J. (2001). *Designing Organizations: An Executive Guide to Strategy, Structure, and Process Revised*. New York: Jossey Bass.

Garretson, W. (2002). 'Building tier zero auto collaboration.' *Forrester Research Reports* (Jan.).

Granovetter, M. (1985). 'Economic action and social structure: the problem of embeddedness.' *American Journal of Sociology*, 1: 451–510.

Gulati, R. (1995). 'Does familiarity breed trust? The implications of repeated ties for contractual choice in alliances.' *Academy of Management Journal*, 38: 85–112.

Häcki, R., and Lighton, J. (2001). 'The future of the networked company.' *McKinsey Quarterly*, 3: 26–39.

Harris, A., et al. (1996). 'New generation cooperatives and cooperative theory.' *Journal of Cooperatives*, 11: 15–28.

Heckscher, C., and Donnellon, A. (1994). *The Post-Bureaucratic Organization: New Perspectives on Organizational Change*. Palo Alto, Calif.: Sage Publications.

Inkpen, A., and Tsang, E. (2005). 'Social capital, networks, and knowledge transfer.' *Academy of Management Review*, 30/1: 146–65.

Katz, J. and Boland, M. (2002). 'One for all and all for one? A new generation of co-operatives emerges.' *Long Range Planning*, 35: 73–89.

Krackhardt, D. (1992). 'The strength of strong ties: the importance of Philos in organizations.' *Networks and Organizations*. Boston: Harvard Business School Press: 216–39.

Kuhn, T. (1970). *The Structure of Scientific Revolution*. Chicago: University of Chicago Press.

Lawrence, P., and Lorsch, J. (1986). *Organization and Environment: Managing Differentiation and Integration*. Boston: Harvard Business School Press.

Macauley, S. (1963). 'Non-contractual relations in business: a preliminary study.' *American Sociological Review*, 72: 854–906.

McEvily, B., Perrone, V., and Zaheer, A. (2003). 'Trust as an organizing principle.' *Organization Science*, 14/1: 91–103.

McKnight, D. et al. (2003). 'Initial trust formation in new organizational relationships.' *Academy of Management Review*, 23: 473–90.

Milliman, R., and Fugate, D. (1988). 'Using trust transference as a persuasion technique: an empirical field investigation.' *Journal of Personal Selling and Sales Management*, 8: 1–7.

Mintzberg, H. (1979). *The Structuring of Organizations*. New York: Prentice-Hall.

——et al. (2003). 'The structuring of organizations.' In *The Strategy Process*. Englewood Cliffs, NJ: Prentice-Hall: 209–25.

Moran, N. (2004). 'Survivors of the dotcom era regroup to fight another day.' *FT.com*, 11 May.

Mullen, B. (1991). 'Group composition, salience, and cognitive representations: the phenomenology of being in a group.' *Journal of Experimental Social Psychology*, 27: 297–323.

Nohria, N., and Eccles, R. (1992). *Networks and Organizations: Structure, Form, and Action*. Boston: Harvard Business School Press.

Ostroff, F., and Smith, D. (1992). 'The horizontal organization.' *McKinsey Quarterly*, 1: 148–68.

Paul, L. (2001). 'B2B e-commerce: the biggest gamble yet.' *IDG*, 5 Feb.

Powell, W. (1990). 'Neither market nor hierarchy: network forms of organization.' *Research on Organizational Behavior*, 12: 295–336.

Quinn, J. (1992). *The Intelligent Enterprise*. New York: Free Press.

Scott Morton, M. (1991). *The Corporation of the 1990s: Information Technology and Organizational Transformation*. Oxford: Oxford University Press.

Sedgwick, D., et al. (2002). 'Kutner has tough task at Covisint.' *Automotive News*, 30 June.

Seely Brown, J., and Hagel, J. (2003). 'Flexible IT, better strategy.' *McKinsey Quarterly*, 4: 51–9.

——et al. (2002). 'Loosening up: how process networks unlock the power of specialization.' *McKinsey Quarterly*, special edition: 59–69.

Stewart, K. (2003). 'Trust transfer on the World Wide Web.' *Organization Science*, 14/1: 5–17.

Stinchcombe, A. (1985). 'Contracts as hierarchical documents,' in Strinchcombe and Heimer (eds.), *Organization Theory and Project Management*. Bergen: Norwegian University Press: 121–71.

Strub, P., and Priest, T. (1976). 'Two patterns of establishing trust: the marijuana users.' *Sociological Focus*: 399–411.

Sullivan, L. (2004). 'Compuware drives away with Covisint.' *InformationWeek*, 5 Feb.

Taylor, S., et al. (1978). 'Categorical and contextual bases of person memory and stereotyping.' *Journal of Personality and Sociology*, 36: 778–93.

Temkin, B. (2001). 'The industry consortia lifeline.' *Forrester Research Reports* (Aug.).

Uzzi, B. (1996). 'The sources and consequences of embeddedness for the economic performance of organizations: the network effect.' *Sociological Review*, 61: 674–98.

Webster, F. (1984). *Industrial Marketing Strategy*. New York: Wiley.

Welch, J. (1995). 'Letter to Shareholders.' *General Electric Annual Report*.

Zucker, L. (1986). 'Production of trust: institutional sources of economic structure, 1840–1920.' *Research in Organization Behavior*, 8: 53–111.

Published Cases

Applegate, L. (1994). *Business Transformation Self-Assessment: Summary of Findings, 1992–1993*. Harvard Business School Publishing #194–013.

——(2000). *QuickenInsurance: The Race to Click and Close*. Harvard Business School Publishing #800–295.

—— (2001*a*). *The Intellectual Property Exchange*. Harvard Business School Publishing #801–350.

—— (2001*b*). *Submarino.com (A)*. Harvard Business School Publishing #801–350.

—— (2002*a*). *American Express Interactive*. Harvard Business School Publishing #802–022.

—— (2002*b*). *Nasdaq Japan: E-Merging Markets*. Harvard Business School Publishing #802–056.

—— (2002*c*). *Understanding Securities Markets in the U.S. and Japan*. Harvard Business School Publishing #802–093.

—— (2004*a*). *Global Healthcare Exchange*. Harvard Business School Publishing #804–002.

—— (2004*b*). *Citigroup 2003: Testing the Limits of Convergence*. Harvard Business School Publishing #804–041.

—— and McFarlan, F. W. (2003). *Charles Schwab in 2002*. Harvard Business School Publishing #803–070.

—— et al. (2001*a*). *Amazon.com: 1994–2000*. Harvard Business School Publishing #801–176.

—— et al. (2001*b*). *National Logistics Management*. Harvard Business School Publishing #801–110.

—— et al. (2003). *PSA: The World's Port of Call*. Harvard Business School Publishing #803–003.

—— et al. (2005). *IBM's Decade of Transformation: A Vision for on Demand*. Harvard Business School Publishing #805–018.

Loveman, G. (1995). *Li & Fung (Trading) Ltd*. Harvard Business School Publishing #396–075.

Perold, A. (2002). *The Nasdaq Stock Market, Inc*. Harvard Business School Publishing #202–803.

Rivkin, J., and Porter, M. (2003). *Matching Dell (Condensed)*. Harvard Business School Publishing #704–440.

Simons, R., and Bartlett, C. (1992). *Asea Brown Boveri*. Harvard Business School Publishing #192–139.

Notes

1. This quote references a model of New Competition that was defined by Best (1990) as networks of small entrepreneurial firms and geographic 'competitive clusters' such as those in Silicon Valley, California, and the *keiretsu* model popularized in Japan.

2. During the late 1980s and early 1990s, academics and business futurists predicted the demise of the hierarchy and the rise of a more networked, intelligent, and agile organizational model. For examples, see Drucker (1988); Powell (1990); Ostroff and Smith (1992); Hecksher and Donnellon (1994).

3. Published cases are listed in the bibliography for those who desire deeper analysis.

4. See Moran (2004).

5. See *Wall Street Journal Business Brief*, 6 Feb. 2004, for an announcement of the sale. On 11 May 2004, *FT.com* reported that Covisint had been valued at $5 billion in early 2002 when it became an independent company.

6. See *Gartner/G2 Research Report*, 6 Jan. 2004.

7. Hacki and Lighton (2001), Seely Brown et al. (2002), and Seely Brown and Hagel (2003) state that loosely coupled processes are the building blocks of networked companies. They state that network orchestrators establish a platform upon which network participants do business and interact.

8. See Katz and Boland (2002).

9. See Chapter 10 for further discussion of the automotive industry and approaches that are being used to support collaboration with trust and collaboration without trust.

10. McEvily et al. (1998) discuss the role of trust as an organizing principle.

11. Baker (2002).

12. See McEvily et al. (1998).

13. Pioneering work on differentiation and integration as core organizational design principles was developed by Lawrence and Lorsch (1986), among others. Baker (2002) applied these principles to the design of intra-firm and inter-firm networks.

14. See Granovetter (1985); Krackhardt (1992); Burt (1992).

15. See Granovetter (1985).

16. See Burt (1992).

17. See Gulati (1995); Inkpen and Tsang (2005).

18. See Stinchcombe (1985); Bradach and Eccles (1989); Powell (1990); Adler (2001).

19. Applegate (1999c) describes the features of early attempts at building intra-firm collaborative community. Also see Applegate (1994) for results of a survey of business executives who were asked to describe changing governance models during the early 1990s and expectations for future changes.

20. See Welch (1995).

21. See the Asea Brown Boveri case study by Simons and Bartlett (1992).

22. See Chutkow (2001).

23. See the Li & Fung case study by Loveman (1995).

24. Background for the discussion of the Nasdaq Stock Exchange is from two cases and a note. See Perold (2002); Applegate (2002a, 2002b). This quote is taken from Perold (2002: 2).

25. In some cases, issuers dual-listed their stock on more than one exchange. More frequently, electronic linkages allowed investors to trade stocks listed on exchanges around the world.

26. In his 1979 book *The Structuring of Organizations*, Henry Mintzberg defined typologies of organizational configurations, including the hierarchy, entrepreneurial form, adhocracy, professional services form, and missionary organization. Mintzberg's typologies are examined across six dimensions that are used here to compare Nasdaq, Covisint, and GHX. In some cases, the name of one of Mintzberg's dimensions has been changed to reflect the more horizontal nature of a collaborative community network of peers. For example, Mintzberg's 'middle line' dimension has been changed to 'coordination and control' and strategic apex to leadership. In addition, the definition of an 'organizational configuration' has been extended to encompass organizational solutions required to manage interdependencies across intra- and inter-firm business networks.

27. Visit the Nasdaq corporate website (www.nasdaq.com/investorrelations/ir_governance.stm) to review current governance rules and processes.

28. For further discussions of interdependent process management and process-based trust, see especially Chapters 1, 2, and 5 in this book.

29. See Zucker (1986).

30. See Stewart (2003).

31. See Uzzi (1996); Milliman and Fugate (1988); Strub and Priest (1976).

32. See Mullen (1991); Taylor et al. (1978).

33. See Gulati (1995); Krackhardt (1992).

34. See Stewart (2003).

35. See McKnight (2003).

36. See Katz and Boland (2002).

37. See Chapter 1.

38. See the Delphi (www.delphi.com) and Visteon (www.visteon.com) websites.

39. See Jupiter Research Online Behavior and Demographics report (2004).

40. See 'FTC clears car firms' online parts venture,' Washingtonpost.com, 12 Sept. 2000.

41. See Paul (2001).

42. See Paul (2001).

43. Paul (2001).

44. See Eiler Communications (2002).

45. Covisint Press Releases, downloaded from company website, Apr. 2002.

46. Covisint onsite interview, conducted Jan. 2003. Also discussed in Garretson (2002).

47. See Temkin (2001).

48. See Bennett (2002).

49. See Sedgwick et al. (2002).

50. See Sullivan (2004).

51. In Chapter 10, MacDuffie calls the tightly linked task and information interdependencies in the auto industry 'integrality' and points to a shift toward 'modularity' as a potential, yet partial, solution.

52. Large drug and medical device manufacturers tied into these local communities by using key account representatives as their agents within a local community. These salespeople worked alongside doctors in the operating room and routinely visited their offices, participating as a full partner within a closely knit team.
53. See McEvily, Perrone, and Zaheer (2003).
54. See Ben-Porah (1980); Webster (1984); Macauley (1963).
55. See Standard & Poor's Industry Surveys: Healthcare (19 Mar. 2003; 20 Mar. 2003; and 11 May 2003).
56. Details of the Global Healthcare Exchange Limited Liability Company Agreement, 25 Aug. 2000, are available in the case study by Applegate (2004a).
57. Global Healthcare Exchange, News Desk, 29 Mar. 2000.
58. See Global Healthcare Exchange case study (Applegate 2004: 15).
59. Author interview, 2003, as quoted in Applegate (2004: 11).
60. GHX Press Release, 11 Dec. 2002.
61. Open Letter to Customers (29 Mar. 2000), Baxter Corporation website (downloaded on 27 June 2003).
62. Author interview as quoted in Applegate (2004).
63. See Seely Brown et al. (2002); Seely Brown and Hagel (2003).
64. See Dell and Magretta (1998) and the case study by Rivkin and Porter (2003).
65. See Bradach and Eccles (1989); Powell (1990); Adler (2001).
66. See Kuhn (1970).

10

Collaboration in Supply Chains
With and Without Trust

John Paul MacDuffie and Susan Helper

The growth of collaboration has occurred over the last few decades not only within firms but also across firms, through elaboration of complex supply-chain and alliance relationships. The automobile industry has long been used as an exemplar of important economic phenomena involving supply chains. For most of the first two-thirds of the twentieth century, mass production was dominant and the automotive industry was highly vertically integrated. During this period, economists dating back to Coase focused on determining why and when a given component would be procured outside the firm, in a market transaction, rather than supplied internally from a wholly owned subsidiary, through hierarchical coordination governed by transfer pricing. (See for example Coase 1937; Klein et al. 1978.)

Oliver Williamson's (1975, 1985) answer to the question primarily involved 'asset specificity'—when investments in firm-specific assets were required, economic logic pointed towards maintaining vertical integration, i.e. internal manufacturing, of those components. Under conditions of low asset specificity—commodity parts of one sort or another—transactions in spot markets or short-term contracts based on low-bid competition were superior for obtaining the best price for a given level of quality. The shorthand for this decision process was 'make vs. buy,' highlighting the differentiated advantages of hierarchy and market as methods of coordinating economic activity.

Roughly fifty years ago, another supply-chain phenomenon reappeared on the global automotive scene. Certain automakers procured parts externally, rather than through vertical integration, but not in spot markets or through short-term contracting. Instead, they relied upon a small number of supplier firms with whom they had long-term business relationships (often including an equity stake)—'relational' contracts governed by understandings about sharing both pain and gain, and large amounts of asset-specific knowledge on both sides. This approach allowed the close coordination on design and manufacturing tasks usually associated with vertical integration, while maintaining the potential for price pressure and supplier competition associated with market transactions.[1]

This development shifted attention from 'make vs. buy' to the different issue of 'how to buy,' which deals centrally with the terms of the relationship among the parties. Hirschman (1970) famously distinguished between economic relationships managed by the constant threat of 'exit' from those managed by 'voice,' an exchange of views within an ongoing relationship.[2] Helper and Sako (Helper 1991; Sako 1992; Helper and Sako 1995) apply these terms to the dominant modes of supply-chain management associated with the USA, whose 'exit' approach involves arm's-length relationships, selection based on low bid, frequent switching among suppliers, and reliance on contracts for governance. In contrast, the 'voice' approach dominant in Japan involves long-term relationships, selection based on supplier capabilities, frequent collaboration within stable supplier partnerships, and reliance on normative understandings for governance.

In the language of Chapter 1, the buy–exit option relies on market, and the buy–voice option relies on community; the make option could rely either on hierarchy (as in a traditional vertically integrated organization), or on community (in a network-based firm).

The application of 'exit' and 'voice' to supplier relations captures the orientation of the parties towards their relationship (as opposed to just a single transaction) and frames the issues of information sharing that crucially affect the relationship beyond transaction-specific costs. 'Exit' is characterized by the creation and exploitation of information asymmetries by both parties, even when the relationship endures over long periods of time. 'Voice' requires shared norms of reciprocity that balance the willingness of the customer to undertake investments in the supplier's capabilities against the supplier's responsibilities to invest in new technology and capacity. As we discuss below, both exit and voice have been profit-maximizing strategies in the past, depending on such conditions as firm strategy and market structure.

Yet the 'exit' vs. 'voice' distinction is no longer as clear as it was just twenty years ago. On the 'voice' side, the closed *keiretsu* system of suppliers characteristic of Japanese industry has been considerably opened to market pressures, requiring more formalization and cost justification of the relationships. On the other side, the hard-nosed 'exit' approach of US firms has faced pressure for increased collaboration to achieve the increased levels of quality demanded in the market. There has been a wide range of responses to these pressures, often mixed and contradictory. In the USA there are frequent attempts to achieve the necessary levels of collaboration *without* trust; but this approach is marked by internal contradictions which, we believe, make it unlikely that it can stabilize as a lasting model. Thus, we will argue, the industry is converging from all sides on a form of pragmatic collaboration, involving substantial levels of trust, though more open and formalized than the traditional Japanese system.

The transformation in supplier relations

Over the last half-century four trends—each characterized by a different rate of change—have had a profound effect on relations between automakers and suppliers.

First, global competition brought Japanese vehicles (beginning in the 1960s) and Japanese manufacturing facilities (beginning in the 1980s) to the USA. The need to compete with Japanese automakers on quality and the gradual diffusion of lean production created incentives for US automakers to increase product quality. Achieving this increased quality required a more closely coordinated relationship with suppliers vis-à-vis design, subassembly, and parts production.

Second, there was a trend away from vertical integration (deverticalization) in the USA, starting in the 1970s. Outsourcing of manufacturing was the initial focus, given a growing gap between wages and benefits at the automakers' in-house parts divisions (which were unionized) and at non-union independent suppliers. The subsequent decision that many design tasks should also be outsourced resulted in a much more rapid pace of deverticalization (as measured by the percentage of value-added outsourced by the automakers) and the creation of a new breed of megasupplier. Automakers also turned away from vertical integration for strategic reasons, perceiving increased competitive advantage from focusing on core competencies. By outsourcing both manufacturing and design, automakers could rely on specialized supplier expertise, rather than maintaining that expertise in-house, while also reducing labor costs.

The third factor is less a trend than a continuing reality amid other dramatic changes. Since establishing a dominant design in the 1930s, the product architecture of the automobile has been primarily integral, requiring a great deal of ongoing communication among the designers of different parts. Starting in the mid-1990s, automakers and mega-suppliers alike began determined efforts to move towards a more modular approach. However, vehicle architecture has proved stubbornly resistant to these efforts and retains a high level of integrality, thus defying expectations of more independence for suppliers during the design process.

Fourth, global overcapacity in automotive assembly and the parts sector has increased price pressure on both automakers and suppliers. In the US context, this has given automakers greater leverage over most suppliers in price negotiations. Given a greater availability of parts from newly sophisticated suppliers in less-developed countries, automakers have more options for exit and hence a more credible threat in demanding that their existing suppliers meet, for example, a 'China price.' This reinforces the apparent value of US automakers' long-standing purchasing routines built around exit, and has contributed to organizational inertia with respect to moving towards a more collaborative mode of exchange.

The net result of these four trends is that the level of collaboration between automakers and suppliers has increased. Despite some developments during this same period that have appeared to push the auto industry in the direction of reduced collaboration, we find the underlying forces affecting supply chains have in fact made collaborative relations more important rather than less.

Yet we have been surprised to see that, contrary to customary expectations for collaboration, these supply-chain relationships do not always involve high levels of trust. That is, in response to these developments, some firms, especially in the USA, collaborate on certain core engineering, manufacturing, and product design tasks while at the governance level, where suppliers are selected and contracts are written, there is an adversarial relationship and lack of trust. We will explore to what extent this model of 'collaboration without trust'[3]—task-level collaboration without the underlying relational and value base that cements longer-term relationships—is a viable model.

This phenomenon poses two questions: (1) Can organizations with an exit-oriented tradition create effective forms of collaboration?; and (2) Does collaboration necessarily require trust? These questions bear on the central question of this volume. Other authors here, particularly Adler and Heckscher in Chapter 1, argue that effective collaboration requires trust and institutions of community to support it. To the extent that the benefits of collaboration, such as flexible resource allocation and response to change, can be achieved *without* trust, that thesis is called into question.

Global competition, quality, and lean production

To an ever-increasing extent in the post-war era, the US industry operated in exit mode, with production of simple parts done by outside suppliers under short-term (one-year) contracts, often with multiple suppliers per part. The key consideration for US automakers was maintaining a credible threat of exit, to prevent 'hold-up' by suppliers taking advantage of asset-specific knowledge developed over time. Therefore, automakers created a large supply of potential suppliers, partly by outsourcing only simple manufacturing tasks (more complicated tasks like subassembly and design stayed in-house) and partly by standardized specifications and bidding procedures.

This short time horizon and extreme division of labor resulted in inefficiency and poor quality. For example, since suppliers usually did not design their own products, they could not optimize them for their own production processes.[4] Since each supplier produced only a small component (e.g. one bracket rather than an entire headrest assembly), it was difficult to optimize across components. However, since each of the Big Three US automakers had similar practices, consumers did not have the ability to buy higher-quality cars. Despite their inefficiency, exit relationships therefore maximized automaker profits by making it easy to switch suppliers (Helper 1991; Helper and Levine 1992).

However, when the Japanese entered the US market, first with imports in the late 1960s and early 1970s and soon with local manufacturing plants in the early 1980s, consumers did gain access to more reliable cars. The Japanese quality advantage was based on thoroughgoing adoption of 'lean production' practices governed by voice supplier relationships.[5] To compete with the Japanese, the Big Three had to improve quality by reuniting design and production and increasing the size of subassemblies. To do this, they needed more capable suppliers that combined a variety of skills, instead of the 'bend and send', 'shoot and ship' firms with few design or management skills, capable only of doing one narrow production process.

Deverticalization and the emergence of 'mega-suppliers'

In the 1970s, component design was largely done by the automakers in-house, although production was done by a mix of vertically integrated divisions and financially independent firms. The reintegration of design and production could have occurred by taking more production back in-house. Instead, the opposite occurred—design gradually moved to suppliers, and the Big Three spun off their parts divisions.

Why did vertical integration decline? Three factors seem to be responsible:

1. A new breed of purchasing executive, exemplified by Ignacio (Inaki) Lopez at General Motors, promoted the idea that in-house parts production had become inefficient during years of Big Three quasi-monopoly of the US automotive market and that long-standing relationships with outside suppliers were 'cozy' and riddled with waste. To remedy this, purchasing moved towards a more aggressive use of market mechanisms—more outsourcing to reduce reliance on in-house divisions and intensified bidding procedures to force greater price competition among suppliers.

2. The wage gap between non-union independent suppliers and unionized in-house supply divisions grew during the 1970s, as suppliers grew more bold in their union-avoidance strategies and inflation eroded the purchasing power of non-union workers. The UAW was able to maintain its strength at the Big Three by threatening to shut down assembly plants, but did not have such leverage over independent parts suppliers, which were able to expand their non-union operations rapidly. By the mid-1980s, the wage gap between a worker in a Big Three component plant and an independent plant ranged from 2:1 to 3:1 (Herzenberg 1991).

3. Managers perceived an increase in returns to specialization. As automakers began to take advantage of innovations in electronics and plastics in the 1980s, they chose to rely on the expertise of outside suppliers from those industries rather than expanding their in-house knowledge. This increased reliance on outsiders was bolstered by new management theories (e.g. Prahalad and Hamel 1990) which argued that firms sticking to narrow core competencies performed better.[6]

The pace of deverticalization increased dramatically when first GM and then Ford spun off their captive parts divisions, creating Delphi (1999) and Visteon (2000), respectively. Delphi and Visteon immediately became the first 'mega-suppliers' (also known as Tier 0.5). More mega-suppliers were soon on the way, formed from horizontal merger and acquisition activity in order to compete for larger subassemblies, i.e. aggregations (or 'chunks') of components. These were mostly existing automotive suppliers (Johnson Controls Inc., Lear, Magna, Denso, Eaton, Dana, TRW Automotive, Federal Mogul) now growing larger and taking over critical design and engineering tasks, handling more complex manufacturing and logistics tasks, and assuming a larger role in the management of second- and third-tier suppliers.[7]

More subcontracting does not necessarily mean more collaboration. The interface between design and production can be organized in three ways (Clark and Fujimoto 1991): supplier proprietary (supplier designs and manufactures the part and sells it through a catalog); OEM (original equipment manufacturer) detail controlled (all design specifications are predetermined by the OEM, the supplier has no design role and only manufactures the part), or 'black box' (the OEM provides performance requirements and basic parameters of size, weight, etc. and the supplier provides the rest of the design). From this perspective, 'black box' subcontracting involves the greatest collaboration of the sort that we term (below) 'pragmatic.'[8]

In data from the late 1980s, Clark and Fujimoto find marked differences between US and Japanese companies in how subcontracts are organized, with 62 per cent of all procurement cost handled in 'black box' mode in Japan vs. 16 per cent in the USA and 81 per cent of procurement cost handled in OEM detail controlled in the USA vs. 30 per cent in Japan; European firms were in between, with 54 per cent detail controlled parts and 39 per cent 'black box.'

As these percentages suggest, the Japanese subcontracting system never achieved the same level of vertical integration in the auto industry as the USA and Europe. In that context, a low level of vertical integration was synonymous with a high level of 'black box,' collaborative subcontracting. The US case, in contrast, reveals that even as vertical integration dropped from its peak in the mid-1950s, the resulting subcontracting was not often collaborative; the detail-oriented approach has been quite consistent with the exit mode of exchange. Tables 10.1 and 10.2 reveal levels of vertical integration over time for the USA and Japan, respectively; the Japanese data are more recent (and more precise), the US data are chosen to reflect the impact of the Delphi and Visteon spin-offs.

The recent wave of deverticalization increases the reliance on 'black box' subcontracting as a replacement for the OEM detail-oriented approach. The decision by OEMs to pursue lower labor costs and to focus on core knowledge and capabilities initiated this move, and the resulting creation of mega-suppliers with enhanced design capabilities accelerated the trend.

Table 10.1. Vertical integration—US Big Three

Company	1975(%)	1995(%)	2005[a]
General Motors	75	66	[b]
Ford	66	50	[c]
Chrysler	50	33	[d]

Note: Estimates, includes bought-in materials for in-house produced parts (Nishiguchi 1994; Rubenstein 2001).

[a] Rubenstein (2001) estimates that GM, Ford, and Chrysler levels of vertical integration were similar—around 30%—after Delphi and Visteon spin-offs.

[b] Delphi Corporation, when spun off from GM in 1999, was immediately the world's largest supplier, with worldwide sales of $27 billion ($21 billion in North America). 78% of its sales were to GM (54% in 2004).

[c] Visteon Corporation, when spun off from Ford in 2000, had worldwide sales of $12 billion, with 88% of its sales to Ford (70% in 2004).

[d] Chrysler was purchased by Daimler-Benz in 1999; a few parts plants have been sold or closed.

Table 10.2. Vertical integration—Japan

Company	1984	1990	1996	2002
Toyota	12%/60%	11%/62%	10%/62%	10%/62%
Nissan[a]	10%/56%	10%/53%	8%/56%	4%/36%
Honda	5%/39%	5%/46%	5%/48%	4%/41%

Notes: Based on IRC data on component transactions for 200 key components, analyzed by Takeishi and Noro (2005), supplemented by Nobeoka and Manabe (forthcoming, see under references below) survey on nature of components. These time series data reflect 72 components that are the same for the entire period.

Figures on the left are purchases from in-house (vertically integrated) parts suppliers, for car and light truck manufacturing only.

Figures on the right are purchases from *keiretsu* suppliers, as defined by IRC based on financial affiliation, sales dependency, and historical relations.

[a] Nissan figures in 1999 are 7% in-house and 55% *keiretsu* suppliers. Restructuring of Nissan's *keiretsu* began in 2000, reflecting the new strategy after the alliance with Renault.

Table 10.3 documents the growth of mega-suppliers beginning in the mid-1990s and Table 10.4 lists the top ten mega-suppliers as of 2003.

'Modularity' and the predicted decline of collaboration

One rationale for the creation of mega-suppliers was a prediction about the future of automotive product architecture. Influenced by the example of information technology, automakers and suppliers began anticipating the rise of 'modularity' as the new basis for designing automotive products. 'Modules' as a basis for product architecture are defined as elements that are 'interdependent within, and independent across,' whereas 'integral' product architecture is based on interdependence *both* within and across elements. Put differently, modules can be developed independently

Table 10.3. The rapid increase in automotive 'mega-suppliers'

	1992	1995	1997	2000	2004
# of suppliers with:					
>$10bn global sales	3	3	4	8	11
$5–10bn global sales	2	11	10	10	12
$2–5bn global sales	11	36	33	35	41

Source: Automotive News.

Table 10.4. Top ten global suppliers (sales in 2003)

1. Delphi ($26.2 billion)
2. Robert Bosch ($23.2 billion)
3. Denso Corp. ($16.9 billion)
4. Visteon Corp. ($16.5 billion)
5. Lear Corp. ($15.7 billion)
6. Magna Internat'l ($15.3 billion)
7. Johnson Controls ($15.2 billion)
8. Aisin Seiki Co. ($13.5 billion)
9. Faurecia ($12.7 billion)
10. TRW Automotive ($11.3 billion)

Source: Automotive News.

from one another and connected via standardized interfaces, established by the architecture's predetermined 'design rules,' while an integral architecture requires intensive coordination throughout the design process.[9]

Thus modularity, according to its proponents, is efficient in part because it requires little collaboration. Because a module provides one predefined function and its interface compatibility with other modules is assured through standardization, innovation within modules can proceed independently, without extensive coordination with innovations in other modules (Langlois 2002). Modularity may also reduce asset specificity. Any PC manufacturer can hypothetically use any hard drive from any supplier, as long as the predefined function is fulfilled and the standardized interface is present.

Beginning in the late 1990s (and influenced by the success of companies like Dell that take advantage of modular product architecture to 'build to order'), automakers began to think of how they could divide up the vehicle into discrete modules, some of which could be fully outsourced to mega-suppliers. At the same time, mega-suppliers brought proposals for module designs to their customers.

But the move towards modularity has been much less decisive than its advocates predicted a decade ago. Automotive product architecture, unlike that of computers, has proved resistant to moving away from integrality. Though the term 'module' is often used today in the auto industry, it means something quite different than in the information technology world (Sako 2004). What is called a 'module' could be more accurately described as a chunk of physically proximate components that could be subassembled independently from the rest of the vehicle, tested for functionality after subassembly, and then installed on the final assembly line in a single step. This violates formal definition of 'modularity' in multiple ways: more than one function is mapped to the 'chunk,' there is no standard definition of the functions performed by a module (certainly not within the industry, but usually not even across models designed by the same automaker), and there is no standardized interface allowing interchangeable connectivity of modules.[10]

Why has it been so hard to modularize the car? First, in today's dominant design, space is at a premium, so components are designed to conform tightly to model-specific physical constraints. Related to this is the need to avoid problems that result from the interaction of the parts, problems that can result in noise, vibration, and harshness of ride. Similarly, laptop computers are more integral than desktop PCs because of the need to utilize scarce space efficiently.

Second, the 'look and feel' of a given vehicle is important to brand image and the emotional connection to the customer, and designers fear loss of distinctiveness from moving to the use of standardized modules, even within a single automaker.

Third, many important functions or subsystems are geographically distributed around the vehicle, such as safety, electrical, braking, steering. Achieving systemic integrity for these functions requires precise coordination across components to meet requirements for a vehicle of a particular size, weight, center of gravity, etc. Furthermore, when various companies began trying to divide up the vehicle into a set of standard modules, differences in design philosophy meant widely different numbers of defined modules and no agreement on modular boundaries.

Finally, the costs of automobile modules—although predicted to be lower due to economies of scale from standardization—have often proven to be higher than the collection of components, individually installed, that they were meant to replace. Engineering costs for modules can be higher. Some reasons are: OEMs preserve a 'shadow engineering' presence to monitor supplier engineers; OEMs are reluctant to allow a first-tier supplier to choose second- and third-tier suppliers due to the volume-based contracts the automakers have negotiated directly with these suppliers, thus constraining product innovation and cost reduction; and supplier capabilities are in some cases not adequate to the design responsibilities given them, even as current purchasing routines prevent suppliers from including investment costs for those capabilities in their piece price.

Even aside from these industry-specific reasons, there is now a greater realism about the inherent limits of modularity, even for products whose architecture is easily decomposable into modules, because of the requirements of achieving advance agreement about module boundaries and a standardized interface.[11] Such agreement may be impossible to achieve (or to sustain over time) at any meaningful level of aggregation, given ongoing changes in underlying technologies and consumer demands for functionality, or simply a lack of willingness in a competitive context to sacrifice proprietary or brand-influential architectural features in order to achieve the gains from standardization.

Despite this litany of problems, the importation of the concept of 'module' has had value for automakers and suppliers by causing them to think about larger chunks of components as the relevant unit for design and sourcing decisions. It has also provided the rationale for changes that ultimately, we would argue, have more to do with deverticalization than with any change in product architecture—including the very formation, through mergers and acquisitions, of the mega-suppliers.[12]

Whatever can be said about the changes wrought by the arrival of 'modules' in the automotive industry, one thing that definitely did *not* occur was any reduction in task interdependence and coordination requirements between automakers, first-tier suppliers, and (by extension) lower-tier suppliers as well. In fact, due to the combination of the shift in design responsibility for components associated with deverticalization and the move towards designing and manufacturing bigger 'chunks' as discrete units, these requirements have, if anything, increased. The persistent integrality of automotive product architecture has made necessary continued intensive collaboration between assemblers and suppliers.[13]

Legacies of exit and global overcapacity

Although the shift towards collaboration was noteworthy during the 1990s, it was far from complete; legacies of exit remained in incentive systems and compartmentalized organization. Purchasing agents continued to be rewarded for their ability to cut suppliers' piece prices, and not so much for their ability to ensure the on-time delivery of high-quality parts.

The temptation to return to exit was intensified by overcapacity, particularly among parts makers. Japanese automakers frequently brought their suppliers with them to the USA, often finding this easier than to train US firms in the techniques of lean production; in the 1980s over 300 Japanese auto suppliers came to the USA (Kenney and Florida 1993). Meanwhile, improvements in transportation and communication combined with low wages in less-developed countries made it attractive for multinational firms to build new plants in nations such as Mexico, China, and India (Sturgeon 2002).

This increase in new capacity was not matched by shutdowns of old capacity. Despite wage cuts, many workers, particularly those with high-school educations, found that staying in the industry was their best alternative. Much of the equipment used by plants that did go out of business was not scrapped, but rather was sold cheaply at auction to firms that continued to produce.

Eventually, supply and demand will come more into balance, but given the long life of both workers and equipment, it may take another decade. In the meantime, automakers will find themselves with a variety of suppliers to choose from, making exit on some occasions tempting even for practitioners of voice. As we discuss below, this excess supply does not obliterate the tendency toward collaboration that results from greater global competition in final product markets, but it does temper it.

The shift towards collaboration

To summarize: due to the four trends described above, we see an increasing degree of collaboration in automotive supply chains over the past ten to fifteen years. Given the higher costs (both perceived and real) of vertically integrated suppliers and the persistent integrality of vehicle product architecture, automakers found the pursuit of quality took a form that required more coordination and collaboration on design and production with financially independent first-tier suppliers.

This form of collaboration no longer fits cleanly into the 'exit' and 'voice' strategies that characterized the earlier phase. The typically American 'exit' pattern has been pushed in the direction of longer-term relationships; conversely, the typically Japanese 'voice' pattern has been confronted with greater competition from new entries into the once-closed group of suppliers, greater demands from the global expansion of existing customers, and unfamiliar demands from new customers—in short, a wider and more open range of relationships than the traditional *keiretsu*. Thus firms with an 'exit' legacy find themselves needing to develop collaborative capability in response to deverticalization; and firms with a 'voice' legacy must be more prepared to face competitive pressure.

Table 10.5 elaborates this hybrid collaborative mode of exchange in relation to 'exit' and 'voice.' The fundamental orientation of the parties is long term and relational, as with voice. However, customers are open to establishing relationships with new suppliers. Selecting a supplier does not involve bidding, as in exit, but nor is it based entirely on assessment of capabilities within a closed group of suppliers, as in voice. Rather suppliers are competitively evaluated and cessation of business is not uncommon, although less frequently and speedily than under 'exit.' This assessment continues even after the relationship is established. Carried over from voice is the manner in which performance problems are handled. Poor performance by Supplier A may not cause exit but a reduction in the share of the customer's business, mirrored by an increased share for Supplier B.

Table 10.5. From 'exit' and 'voice' to hybrid collaborative mode of exchange

Exit	Voice	Hybrid Collaborative
Arm's length and transactional	Long term and relational	Long term and relational
Open for new suppliers to bid	Set of potential suppliers mostly closed	Open to new suppliers, after a vetting period
Competitive selection by low bid—frequent and speedy exit	Selection based on capabilities—exit rare and slow	Competitive assessment—intermediate frequency and speed of exit
Design simplified by customer to enlarge pool of suppliers	Design controlled by customer, supplier involved via resident engineer	Larger design role for supplier, attention to supplier design capabilities
No equity stake	Often an equity stake	Equity stake depends on criticality of technology
Contracts for governance	Norms/dialogue for governance	Norms + process management routines for governance
Codified procedures	Tacit procedures	Process management routines make procedures explicit

While design under exit is simplified in order to generate a larger pool of potential suppliers, design under voice is typically organized so that supplier engineers can be 'resident' at the customer's design facility; yet the supplier role in developing new designs is limited. Under the hybrid mode, the supplier's design role is much larger, to the extent that customers express high concern about the level of a supplier's design capabilities—which was very unusual in the past.

While equity stakes are common under voice and not under exit, the hybrid mode finds variation. Automakers frequently take equity stakes in suppliers who are expert in technologies that are assuming an increased importance in vehicle design (e.g. electronics, composite materials), but otherwise this is not common. While the hybrid mode relies more heavily upon dialogue than formal contracts for governance, it also relies upon extensive use of formalized process management routines affecting problem solving in manufacturing and design rather than simply upon tacit understandings based on long-term relationships. Similarly, while exit codifies procedures and voice relies on tacit understandings, the hybrid mode relies on process management routines that make procedures explicit. These more general (less customer-specific) techniques make it easier for customers and suppliers to collaborate effectively even when the relationship is relatively new.

Types of collaboration: with and without trust[14]

It is our contention that convergence towards this hybrid mode of collaboration has characterized automotive supply chains over the past ten years and that this trend will continue. Within this general move towards increased collaboration, however, there remains substantial variation. Here we describe the range of responses and below we provide interpretations of the US patterns, where the most variation is found.

The greatest continuity with previous practice can be seen in Japan. Given the tradition of working closely with suppliers as collaborative partners, the hybrid mode takes the form of 'collaboration with trust,' a relatively small departure from the history of 'black box' subcontracting within a voice mode of exchange—although at some companies, the implications for the traditional *keiretsu* structure of the supply chain are quite significant. We explore the situation in Japan in greater detail as one of three case studies below.

The American Big Three's interpretation of collaboration has often been to impose increasing demands, on suppliers, resulting in suppliers having less trust in OEMs than was the norm for the exit mode previously. For example, with suppliers taking a larger role in providing component designs as part of their bid, OEMs have been caught taking those incipient designs and sending them to another supplier to get a competitive bid. Breaking from a long tradition of paying for tooling as part of a supply contract, OEMs began telling suppliers they would now be responsible for those costs. Other extreme examples include OEMs demanding immediate 5 per cent price cuts, regardless of contractual terms already established; using online 'reverse auctions' in which some of the bids pushing prices to record low levels could not be verified as coming from credible suppliers; and, most recently, confronting suppliers with a 'China price' and demanding they meet it or lose the business, even in the midst of established contracts.

Such hard-nosed, transaction-based behaviors have at times provoked strong public reactions—to the point where any suggestion that collaborative activity might exist between these adversaries can seem absurd. One noteworthy speech was made by the CEO of a medium-sized supplier at the annual industry briefing meetings in Traverse City, Michigan, in August 2002.[15] This excerpt captures the strong emotions stirred up by these developments:

> There is little chance that beating the hell out of the supplier base and breaking contracts . . . is going to get to the root cause of your problem, Big Three. You know that the suppliers raked over the coals and used as a whipping boy to explain the Big Three's cost problem are the same suppliers investing, building partnerships, and earning a good return with the vehicle producers that have the growing market share. There is a discontinuity here. But it is also very clear that our futures are inextricably tied and neither can afford the other to fail. (Tim Leuliette, president/ CEO of Metaldyne, 12 Aug. 2002)

Responding to this cry from the heart a few days later, GM's CEO Rick Wagoner had a ready answer: 'Stop whining!'[16]

Leuliette's speech points out a powerful underlying dynamic: When given the choice, suppliers will readily choose collaboration with trust over collaboration without trust. Gradually, but steadily, US suppliers have been learning to prefer working with the Japanese transplant manufacturers who operated in 'voice' mode when establishing supplier contracts—even as their Big Three customers came to adopt more and more of the design and manufacturing practices long in place at companies such as Toyota, Honda, and Nissan. Yet few suppliers can afford to turn their back on Big Three business, so many of them have adapted as best they can to operating under these new conditions.

Task-level convergence, governance-level divergence

The descriptions above suggest that our earlier statement about a convergent trend towards collaboration must be qualified. While supplier relations at the level of specific design and manufacturing tasks may be responding similarly to the forces analyzed above, these tasks are carried out within differing transactional contexts.

At the governance level, the policies that govern the transaction—the process of awarding work to a supplier (or, from the supplier's perspective, bidding for work), the negotiations over price, the responsibility for investments in tooling and other capabilities, who is responsible for warranty and product liability costs, and the way that disputes are handled—can all vary widely. Some firms are choosing a greater reliance on market mechanisms to keep price pressure on their suppliers, while others are choosing to pursue a small number of longer-term relationships within which various issues are resolved. Interestingly, at the firm level, past history of 'exit' or 'voice' doesn't necessarily determine which path is chosen.

At times these pressures can lead to contradictory behavior in different arenas. At one limit, we find instances where collaborative activity occurs at the task level, while at the governance level, OEMs subject suppliers to severe versions of 'exit' behavior.

Reflecting on these developments, some thoughtful observers suggest that there is no single emerging pattern but rather a portfolio of viable OEM–supplier relationships whose diversity is motivated by various things: risk hedging; the differential importance of one criterion (price vs. quality vs. design) for that particular part; internal lack of coordination at the OEM; suppliers' protective moves.[17] Herrigel (2004) summarizes this perspective:

Are the new relations cooperative and collaborative, or are they still essentially about cost and price? . . . [It] is important to avoid the urge to choose between these hard alternatives. This is because neither the actors in OEMs nor the actors in component producing firms make such drastic choices. Indeed, both seem to distribute their strategies to accommodate as broad an array of (even contradictory) sourcing strategies as possible. Within OEMs, it is both the case that managers in charge of sourcing seek to maintain a diversity of in-house capacities and subcontracting relations and that different strategic sourcing practices compete with one another for dominance. In reaction to this de facto multiplicity of OEM sourcing strategies, component producers are developing a broad range of strategies that take advantage of the (sometimes quite unpredictable) variety of OEM sourcing practices. (pp. 45–6)

We have two objections to this view. First, inherent in our view of 'voice' (and of the hybrid mode) is the idea that the parties can actively circumvent any necessary trade-off between collaboration and efficiency. Collaborative 'cost-down' activities can achieve both. Second, we are skeptical that supplier relationships can be constructed or maintained by 'mixing and matching' contradictory strategies. Like cars, patterns of relationships are integral.

To explore the problems of 'mix and match' strategies, consider that economic relationships are based on mutual expectations resulting from past experience: if a pattern of low-trust expectations is established it cannot easily be shifted to high trust for a new transaction. Furthermore, any given pattern of relationships leads to differences all the way through the organizational system. For example, exit and voice require different criteria for choosing and compensating purchasing agents: exit strategies benefit from financially oriented purchasing agents who are compensated based on their ability to keep prices low; voice benefits from agents with engineering backgrounds and complex compensation schemes that balance multiple objectives.[18]

Indeed, the choice of strategy affects not just purchasing but the entire corporation. For example, maintaining a credible threat of exit is facilitated by an ability to make 'apples-to-apples' price comparisons. This in turn requires designs to be well documented (so suppliers know what they are bidding on), and suggests that purchasing will act as a gate-keeper, limiting suppliers' access to the engineering department, where they might succeed in obtaining design changes that would limit purchasing's ability to compare prices. In contrast, under voice much knowledge can remain tacit (not documented) since relationships change infrequently, and collaboration with engineering is considered a good thing.

Thus, while there can be some variation in how individual suppliers are treated, we question whether the pattern of task-level convergence and governance-level divergence can be explained by deliberate efforts by firms to sustain a portfolio of different purchasing strategies.

Emerging alternatives: pragmatic collaboration, with and without governance trust

Rather than a panoply of strategies, we see two emerging alternatives that account for the range of observations above: a convergent trend towards 'pragmatic collaboration' at the task level that can be found within divergent approaches at the governance level.[19] The distinction we draw

between collaboration 'with trust' and 'without trust' reflects the consequence of superimposing the new reality of iterated co-design upon the
legacies of 'voice' and 'exit' modes of exchange that continue to exert
inertial influence on purchasing routines and governance arrangements.
Fig. 10.1 displays the underlying logic generating this pattern.

In this view, the interdependent design and manufacturing practices
linking automakers and their suppliers at the task level are *pragmatic* in
that they confront the uncertain and changing nature of knowledge with a
continuing willingness to question current routines and past choices and
to explore alternatives. Collaboration emerges naturally during this exploration, partly because the process of dialogue and debate allows 'learning by
monitoring' (see Chapter 2). Those individuals engaged in interdependent
design and manufacturing tasks can assure themselves that even as they are
advancing completion of the task, they are able to ascertain whether the
other party is behaving in trustworthy, non-opportunistic fashion. Thus,
the very process of pragmatic collaboration generates the levels of task-
level trust necessary for the process of iterated co-design—and for persistence of task-level relationships.

The pragmatic evolution of collaboration opens the door, in our view,
for participation in such collaborations by firms with an 'exit' history,
since they too recognize the gains in the face of technological change
and unpredictable market demand. The problem for such firms is the
absence of trust at the governance level, and the difficulty of developing
a form of pragmatic collaboration at that level capable of generating trust
over time. We do not expect that this internal contradiction can be viable

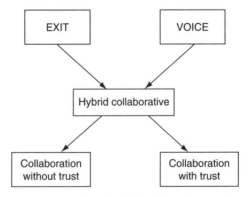

Fig. 10.1 Two patterns emerging from hybrid collaborative mode

over the long term, although we see a number of reasons why it will not disappear quickly. We return to these issues below.

Case examples

We turn now to consider three individual case examples: (1) the continuing phenomenon of 'collaboration with trust' in Japan, as practiced by firms like Toyota and Honda and the recently different approach of Nissan; (2) the coping strategy of Stoneridge, a small second-tier supplier faced with heavy downward pressure on profit margins from its Big Three customers; and (3) the effort by mega-supplier Delphi (formerly part of GM and hence with a strong legacy of 'exit') to change its purchasing and supply-chain management practices in order to move towards the 'collaboration with trust' model.

Starting from the premise that the pace and extent of deverticalization and lean production are requiring more collaborative interdependence between automakers and suppliers, the first case considers how Japanese firms have updated their former 'voice' approach to what we are calling 'collaboration with trust.' The second and third cases consider the USA, where OEMs and suppliers alike have a legacy of 'exit' relations with low trust. Here we find contradictions, with an increase in trust-destroying behaviors by OEMs on the one hand—as in the second case of Stoneridge, a small US electronics supplier—while on the other hand some mega-suppliers attempt to move towards 'collaboration with trust'—as in the third case of Delphi. The cases will set the stage for a final discussion of what kind of supplier relationships we are most likely to see in the future, both in the US context and beyond.

'Collaboration with trust' as work in progress—supply-chain management at Toyota, Honda, and Nissan

Toyota and Honda are rightly regarded as the leading practitioners of 'collaboration with trust' in their relationship with suppliers, although the earlier characterization of the 'voice' mode of exchange was often applied to all Japanese firms. We include Nissan in this assessment because of its much-heralded recovery from near-bankruptcy after an alliance with Renault and the importation of a Western CEO (Carlos Ghosn) who set out energetically to dismantle key aspects of the old supplier system. Taking a current snapshot of these firms is a good way to consider 'collaboration with trust' as a work in progress.

We will argue that current manifestations of 'collaboration with trust' are not simply the previous 'voice' mode of exchange, whose Japanese form was highly intertwined with the industrial structure of interlinked firms known as *keiretsu*. Rather, they are a modern adaptation reflecting the forces and pressures affecting the entire industry, as described above, as well as the very substantial foreign direct investment by leading Japanese automakers in establishing a manufacturing footprint and building local supply chains all over the world. Globalization has required collaborative processes that are considerably more accessible to out-of-network suppliers and contain more explicit articulation of norms and values as well as specific guidance in how to approach task interdependencies.

Japan's prolonged recession in the 1990s—what some observers call the 'lost decade'—put tremendous strains on both first-tier and lower-tier suppliers in Japan. First-tier suppliers were often asked to join their OEM customers in expansion efforts overseas, opening new plants first in the USA and then in Europe. At the same time, these firms were investing heavily in South-East Asia in order to reduce their production costs, but this severely strained the lifetime employment commitments at their domestic plants and sparked social criticism of their role in the 'hollowing out' of the Japanese economy. Smaller second- and third-tier suppliers faced a starker challenge. Japanese OEMs typically pledged to invest heavily in supply base development when entering a new country and they (and their first-tier partners) could easily replace the small Japanese supplier by sourcing their parts from domestic suppliers near their new overseas manufacturing plants. While these small suppliers were not cut off completely, many struggled to stay in business. The general economic conditions are somewhat improved now, but the fundamental challenge to small Japanese suppliers to justify their continued place in the supply chain remains.

During this same period, the past pattern of strong vertical control of design activities and production coordination by the OEM has begun to change. This raises the same fundamental dilemma: OEMs want suppliers to take a larger role in design and in managing lower tiers of the supply chain, but they also want to maintain their knowledge and power; they recognize that they must 'know more than they make.'[20] Suppliers must therefore make more investment (in capacity and knowledge), which is potentially redundant and not paid for by OEMs.

Japanese OEMs have also put suppliers under growing pressure for cost reduction. Nissan took the lead, with Carlos Ghosn setting forth a drastic cost-cutting plan that aimed to shock the old *keiretsu* system into changing past patterns. Toyota, determined not to let Nissan gain any cost structure advantage, followed soon with its CCC 21 program (Construction of Cost Competitiveness for the Twenty-First Century) that aimed for 30 per cent reductions in parts prices—targets much higher than the usual incremental 'cost-down' targets.[21]

Akira Takeishi (2003) and his colleagues argue that Japanese OEM–supplier relations must move into a new fourth phase, after three previous phases that emphasized cost, quality, and engineering input for individual components respectively. The newest phase emphasizes horizontal coordination with suppliers of other components for improved design, greater system integrity, and more innovation at both component and system levels, as well as exploration of more modular design principles.

The Japanese word *kyogyo* is used to describe this phase; it means 'collaborative division of labor.' OEMs have shown a willingness to turn more design responsibilities over to suppliers who can manage these horizontal collaborations most successfully. Certain examples of *kyogyo* are well publicized in Japan, e.g. an instrument panel console for a new Lexus model that resulted from the self-initiated collaboration of Sumitomo Denko (an electronics firm) and Toyota Gosei (a plastics firm) and that achieved sizeable improvements in terms of lighter weight, lower parts count, and lower overall cost.

Initial expectations were that *kyogyo* might be the first step towards modularization, but this particular example suggests otherwise, for the Lexus console is completely idiosyncratic to a single Lexus model. It is possible that these suppliers will attempt a more standardized design that they can offer to multiple customers, in order to spread their fixed costs over more units. Within the Japanese context, where the integrality of product architecture is accepted as fundamental to how product development is organized, we think it more likely that these horizontal collaborations will continue to result in highly integral designs that still require high vertical design interdependence with OEMs. Thus 'collaboration with trust' within Japanese supply-chain structures is likely to take on more of this 'first horizontal, then vertical' coordination flavor in the future.

Within overseas operations, Toyota and Honda continue to strengthen their local supply chains in terms of systematic production capabilities to reduce cost, improve quality, increase logistical accuracy, and shorten lead times, often through direct supplier development activities that began in the 1990s and continue to the present day. Slower to develop have been supplier-to-supplier working groups, called *Jishuken* in Japan; these are considered to be a better method of supplier development in terms of sustainability, since the direct supplier assistance by the OEM often produces too much dependency.[22]

Overall, supplier development in the USA has been a slower and more difficult process than originally envisioned by the Japanese OEMs. At first, it was difficult for Toyota and Honda to find suppliers who would agree to participate in their collaborative approach. Dyer and Singh (1998) quote Toyota's VP for purchasing Koichiro Noguchi from Dyer's interview with him in 1992:

Many U.S. suppliers do not understand our way of doing business. They do not want us to visit their plants and they are unwilling to share the information we require. This makes it very difficult for us to work with them effectively; we also can't help them improve. (p. 673)

More recently, Hajime Ohba, head of Toyota's Supplier Support Center in Kentucky, locates the reason in the overwhelmingly financial orientation of many US suppliers; they emphasize short-term fixes that produce immediately visible savings, typically through inventory reduction, and don't persist with more fundamental changes in how they approach manufacturing.[23]

As noted above, US suppliers are increasingly vocal about their preference for working with Toyota and Honda rather than the Big Three, with evidence that overall costs are lower and the amount of innovation contributed is higher. As these automakers localize more design activity to their R&D facilities in the USA and Europe, more design involvement by local suppliers will result.

Nissan's situation demonstrates some of the gains and losses that occur when a company with a 'voice' tradition resorts to 'exit' behavior. In early 1999, Nissan was in deep financial crisis, with both Moody's and Standard and Poor's announcing plans to reduce its credit rating to 'junk' status unless it received outside investment.[24] Renault provided that investment in March 1999, assuming a 36.8 per cent stake in Nissan and thus freeing up $5.4 billion in capital and retaining 'investment grade' bond status.[25] Carlos Ghosn from Renault, already well known for his success in cost cutting and turning around troubled operations, became the new CEO.

One target of Ghosn's cost cutting was Nissan's *keiretsu* ties with suppliers. Nissan had followed a traditional *keiretsu* approach, cultivating extensive financial and personnel interconnections with its suppliers. Retained earnings were typically invested in purchasing shares of these affiliated companies and supplier CEOs were routinely appointed from among the ranks of senior Nissan executives approaching retirement. By 1999, Nissan held equity stakes in *keiretsu* companies totaling over $4 billion. Yet these cross-sharing holdings and personal relationships did not yield the cost advantages achieved by Nissan's competitors, such as Toyota. At the time of the alliance, Nissan's purchasing costs were estimated to be 20–25 per cent higher than Renault's costs.

Ghosn and the Nissan board reached an early decision to end its equity participation in *keiretsu* supplier companies and to accept competitive bids from outside suppliers, as part of the Nissan Revival Plan (NRP), which also included internal plant closings. This freed up billions in capital for investments in new products and debt servicing. *Keiretsu* suppliers were still encouraged to compete for Nissan's business, but with high expectations for ongoing cost reductions. With this introduction of 'exit' mechanisms, Nissan's purchasing costs declined by 20 per cent by March 2002, one year ahead of the NRP schedule. The number of suppliers shrank by 40 per cent overall. One reason was platform consolidation; prior to NRP, Nissan had seven plants producing vehicles based on twenty-four platforms, while after NRP, four plants produced vehicles based on fifteen platforms.

From most accounts, this change of policy was implemented remarkably quickly and smoothly. Although Ghosn was criticized heavily at first by the Japanese media and government officials, he won internal support for these policy changes by creating a set of cross-functional teams that reported directly to the Executive Committee and were given access to all company information. These teams, rather than external consultants, had primary responsibility for developing recommendations for how to achieve the goals of the turnaround. Supplier companies often made dramatic changes in response to Nissan's new policy; for example, one long-time supplier of brake systems chose to focus on just one group of components, divesting itself of all other businesses and hence moving from a first-tier to a second-tier position in Nissan's supply chain.[26]

Ghosn's next plan—called Nissan 180 to reflect an increase of sales by 1 million vehicles, an 8 per cent operating margin; and zero debt—was even more ambitious. To be achieved by April 2005, Nissan 180 called for a further 15 per cent reduction in purchasing costs while also developing twenty-eight new models for release by 2007—including seven completely new products. Soon signs of strain began to emerge. In May 2003, Nissan opened a new plant in Canton, Mississippi (completed in a speedy $2\frac{1}{2}$

years) with three brand-new vehicles, a new workforce, and new sup-pliers—defying the conventional wisdom that new plants should build existing products to reduce start-up risks. By April 2004, quality problems from this plant (as revealed in J. D. Power's initial quality survey of consumers) dragged Nissan down to eleventh place, from sixth place the previous year, with 147 defects per 100 vehicles—greatly exceeding the industry average of 119. While the plant itself had start-up problems, many observers attributed the problems to 'cheap parts' from suppliers that couldn't be installed precisely (Bremner et al. 2004).

Is this quality decline an inevitable consequence of Nissan's switch to exit mechanisms? Ghosn's actions in response to this crisis suggest that he is returning to a more collaborative approach. Dramatically, he flew to Mississippi in May 2004 with over 200 Nissan engineers to undertake extensive examination of quality problems at the Canton plant and at suppliers; changes in product and process design followed, as well as operational problem solving and extensive worker training.[27]

Then in November 2004, Ghosn held a meeting with Nissan suppliers at which he reportedly changed his position on the value of *keiretsu* relation-ships, saying, 'Not everything about the keiretsu was wrong. It simply did not function properly at Nissan in the past. With Nissan's subsidiaries, the *keiretsu* system was too cozy, but at Toyota, the system seems to be func-tioning very well. From now on, we need stronger ties with our suppliers.'

Nissan, immediately thereafter, raised its stake in Calsonic Kansei Corp., a maker of dashboard modules, from 27.6 per cent to 41 per cent (more than a controlling share). In order to support the high number of new product launches, Ghosn announced a new 'project partnership system' in which collaborative teams of Nissan and supplier engineers would 'review parts from scratch and aim to achieve higher quality at low cost.' A new plant, built on the grounds of a former university, will take the 'supplier park' concept of co-location one step further by putting supplier operations under the same roof with Nissan assembly lines. Furthermore, Nissan recognizes that its suppliers have not been keeping up with the R&D investments made by Toyota's main suppliers. According to Calsonic Kansei's CEO, Nissan's increased financial stake recognized that 'we needed financial assistance to oversee the process from R&D to extending our worldwide production and supply chain.'[28]

Thus Nissan appears to be moving back towards 'collaboration with trust' as rapidly as possible, following its restructuring-driven move away from the voice-without-exit world of the traditional Japanese *keiretsu*. Nissan's new approach emphasizes extensive supplier involvement in design, close collaboration on a project basis, and investments in supplier capabilities. How much these collaborations can flourish against the backdrop of Nissan's extensive shift to exit mechanisms in recent years remains to be seen. Nissan may be tempted to resort to exit threats to gain continued price reductions.

Toyota's CCC21 program may also contain indications of where 'collaboration with trust' is headed—not least because its architect, purchasing vice president Katsuaki Watanabe, has become the next CEO of the company, as of 1 July 2005. Many of the savings achieved since the program's launch in 2000 have come from teams of Toyota engineers working with suppliers on design issues, in particular the reduction of part counts and product variants. Often a supplier is asked not only to implement improvements in their own operations but also to help identify where Toyota's design and manufacturing process for a part increases costs. In one much-publicized example, Toyota once had thirty-five different versions of the interior assist grip installed above each door. After a joint investigation by a CCC21 team and suppliers, now only three grip styles cover all of Toyota's ninety models (Dawson 2005). This required as much—if not more—change on Toyota's side as it did from the supplier.

This type of collaborative problem solving—involving careful study and mutual adjustment—is also how Toyota hopes to cope with the challenge of meeting the 'China price' for many components. CCC21 is identifying global benchmarks for 180 key components on price and quality, including those established by major US and European competitors with extensive manufacturing facilities in China like Robert Bosch and Delphi. The goal is to come as close as possible to the benchmark price without any sacrifice in quality.

Where benchmarking reveals that an outside supplier has the best price, Toyota may award them a portion of its growing business for that component—providing competitive pressure while also giving its own group of suppliers more time and opportunity to make further improvements. This mix of continuity of relationship with competitive pressure amid growth in demand is characteristic of Toyota's approach with suppliers. The prospect that the China price may be so low that it takes considerable time for suppliers to match it will test Toyota's commitment to this strategy, though we predict that they will not switch towards exit despite the potential for short-term cost gains. In any case, those gains may be less substantial if these new suppliers do not have the strong problem-solving capabilities upon which Toyota relies.[29]

Survival strategies at Stoneridge: scrambling to keep ahead of commoditization

This case considers how Stoneridge, a small American second-tier supplier, has coped with the 'exit'-oriented supply chain restructuring by US auto companies in recent years as of 2004.

Stoneridge is a supplier of highly engineered, application-specific, electrical and electronic products to automotive OEMs, including control devices, sensors, power distribution, and system management components. It operates twenty-four manufacturing plants in the USA, Mexico, Brazil, Europe, and Asia, and has 6,000 employees and approximately $682 million in annual sales.

Jerry Pisani, Stoneridge's President and chief executive officer, provided these reflections on the demands placed on his firm by the Big Three OEMs during an International Motor Vehicle Program (IMVP) conference session on 'Building Tomorrow's Supplier Capabilities Amid Today's Pressures.' He enumerated a long list of additional expectations placed on suppliers by their customers, which we have grouped into four categories:

1. Costs to absorb (program management; inventory management, longer payment terms);
2. Investments to make (supplier-owned tools; advanced IT; advanced R&D and prototypes);
3. Liabilities to assume (warranty indemnification; charge-back for quality defects by customer plants); and
4. Rights to waive (intellectual property rights; established contractual provisions).

In response, Pisani argued, Stoneridge is pursuing multiple survival strategies.

1. The management culture must promote lean production/six sigma thinking in order to achieve operational excellence, both in manufacturing but also through involvement in iterated co-design; this is necessary but not sufficient because of convergence in performance on this dimension across the industry.
2. The product life cycle must be carefully managed. Both product differentiation (through features or associated services) and planned product obsolescence are needed to keep a few steps ahead of the threat of commoditization. By seizing on technical inflection points as a time to introduce new advanced features, margins can be boosted

on newer products even as prices are being reduced on older products. Deep knowledge of the customer is required to support this survival strategy, as is the relentless pursuit of cost reduction described above.

3. Even a small supplier must be mindful of operating in a global industry. Sales to multiple countries and automakers help build the volume that is necessary to amortize product development investments. A diversified customer base provides some protection against firm-specific volatility in demand and currency fluctuations. Working with partner firms (particularly for joint venture overseas investments) reduces financial risk, even as it raises coordination costs/risk. Participation in emerging markets provides option value with respect for future demand growth.

4. Investments must be carefully monitored to ensure adequate returns and to avoid the trap of maximizing revenues at the expense of profits. Profitability should be tracked at a micro-level, tied to product lines through activity-based costing. Inventory turns should be benchmarked against competitors to ensure that industry standards are met or exceeded. The balance sheet should be kept relatively unleveraged to retain maximum flexibility with regard to future investments.

5. Stoneridge's own suppliers must be carefully managed through disciplines of cost management, with an effort to focus on a small group of 'best in class' suppliers with whom relationships are long-term. These suppliers should be global in their manufacturing footprint but also in their strategic orientation. Stoneridge should work to educate them and directly develop their capabilities.

6. Learning should be maximized through selective use of consultants (as trainers, not doers); centralized corporate-level training (more focused and cost-effective than outside training); and attentive migration of best practices across facilities and divisions.

It is striking that even for a supplier like stoneridge operating in a situation where its customers focus myopically on price and trust is minimal, many of these survival strategies involve collaboration—externally with OEM engineers, with joint venture partners, with their own suppliers, and internally across divisions and within plants. Evidence from Helper and Stanley's recent survey of small and medium-sized second- and third-tier suppliers in the northern Midwest states suggests that even competitors are exchanging information and technical assistance; 37 per cent responded affirmatively to a statement that 'my firm receives technical assistance from competitors,' in contrast with only 17 per cent who said they received such assistance from their customers.[30]

At one level, the Stoneridge survival strategies seem to point towards developing the most collaborative relationship with customers that can be achieved. Understanding customer needs and differentiating products to offer unique sources of value are two approaches consistent with the 'collaboration with trust' mode.

Yet for the most part, these survival strategies are self-protective vis-à-vis customers. The only remedy for operating in the face of a low-trust relationship with key customers is to manage product life cycles strictly to keep ahead of commodity pricing pressures. Financial survival requires avoidance of commitments that build volume and revenue but have low return on investment (ROI). Suppliers must be prepared to make quick moves to phase out product lines where pressures are strong to cut prices below actual costs.

Although Pisani did not say so, it is easy to imagine that he would prefer working with customers who are not entirely focused on price; and that he would be more likely to offer the fruits of Stoneridge's investments in advanced R&D and product innovation to those customers. This suggests that one dynamic over time for suppliers who have some customer relationships characterized by trust and some that are not, will be to shift effort and contribution (in design insight, technological innovation, and willingness to forward-invest) to the former group. The question for the 'collaboration without trust' group of customers is whether they will perceive this risk—of suppliers withholding contribution and shifting commitments—in time to remedy it, or whether they will find new sources of suppliers and new means—presumably market based, since reverticalization seems highly unlikely—of acquiring the knowledge and innovation that they would be losing.

Toyota comes to Delphi—cost management in the land of exit

This case study examines the efforts of one US-based 'mega-supplier'—Delphi Corporation[31]—to introduce 'collaboration with trust' into the US context where the 'exit' mode still prevails. The focus of the case study is Delphi's efforts to shift how it manages its own suppliers, because it is here that the firm's intention to move towards a more collaborative approach is most evident.

Delphi has undertaken a serious effort to implement the Delphi Manufacturing System (DMS) that is closely modeled on the Toyota Production System (TPS) in order to overcome its problematic cost structure, change mindsets, and diversify its customer base. For the purchasing function, this means implementing two core TPS processes known as 'cost management' and 'cost profit planning'.

One of Delphi's primary methods for developing DMS is to hire senior people—*sensei*, or teachers in Japanese—from Toyota and Honda, two of the world's best lean producers. Kaz Nakada, a member of the famed OMCD (operational methods and cost management division) at Toyota—the internal 'consulting' group created by Taiichi Ohno and the guardians/ stewards of TPS—is now a lean *sensei* at Delphi. Where he has a similar role. With his help, Delphi has hired other Toyota people who are skilled in cost management and cost profit planning. Delphi also hired Dave Nelson, who was VP of purchasing at Honda of America for ten years.[32]

Delphi's approach to changing supplier relations draws heavily from Toyota and Honda's approach with their US suppliers. For the small group of suppliers identified as 'core,' Nelson starts Delphi's lean supplier development process with a face-to-face meeting that includes the top executives at the supplier's location.

We do the meetings one by one; it's a time to set expectations. I explain that Delphi wants them to be a strategic supplier and is willing to work closely with them. We expect them to be committed to being the best supplier in the industry. I tell them it won't be easy but they'll be glad they made the effort. I explain how cost management works and that if the process works right, the margin of both companies will improve. We ask them to work with us on achieving the best possible understanding of cost and explain that developing this cost standard will take the place of the multiple rounds of bidding they are accustomed to. Then we help them become more competitive through lean implementation.[33]

The next step is to educate the supplier in how the cost management process works. Materials from a Delphi lean supplier development session provide insights into how these TPS disciplines foster a 'collaboration with trust' approach.[34] Suppliers are told at the start that the remedy for dealing with relentless pressure on margins is achieving ongoing cost reductions. This is achieved through a strategic sourcing policy at Delphi that relies on both a cost management methodology and on lean supplier development activities; the former identifies the opportunities for cost reduction while the latter develops supplier capabilities to take advantage of those opportunities. Cost management is presented as a 'new paradigm'—the 'modern agriculture' approach that relies on science, logic, and facts vs. the old

445

paradigm ('hunters and gatherers') that relies on 'playing poker' through 'multiple bidding rounds.'

Suppliers are told what cost management is *not*: not a one-time cost-down method, not a tool to use against suppliers by squeezing their profits or sharing their proprietary data with others. Rather it is an explicitly collaborative pursuit of the 'ideal' cost, defined as the 'lowest total unit cost in the world that is achievable with effort.' (Tables 10.6a and 10.6b.)

Beginning with 'supplier cost' (from the original supplier quote or industry benchmarks), the first goal is 'agreed-upon cost.' This is achieved through discussion after the customer compares the supplier cost with its book of cost standards, developed through exhaustive study of all currently available versions of a component along with a similarly detailed assessment of current and future raw material and commodity prices. This cost standard takes the place of a multiple bid system; only very occasionally are multiple bids taken as a check on the cost standards. The cost standard provides a starting point for reaching the 'agreed-upon cost'; this is also where a short-term cost reduction target is applied. But the 'agreed-upon cost' does not define the parameters of the improvement efforts. That is set by the 'ideal cost'—the ultimate goal—which takes the minimal cost for each factor achieved anywhere in the world to construct a hypothetical target that is kept as a visible goal to avoid complacency as 'agreed-upon' cost targets are reached. (Table 10.3)

'Reality-based' price reductions are contrasted with the 'arbitrary price-downs' often inflicted upon suppliers by 'exit'-oriented OEMs. Arbitrary price-downs erode profits because they are mandated independent from progress on cost reduction. 'Reality-based' price reductions closely track cost reductions so that margins are preserved rather than eroded. Customers help suppliers achieve these cost reductions first by identifying the gap between 'supplier cost' and 'ideal cost' and then by drawing up 'creative improvement plans' to apply countermeasures to each identified gap.

This problem-solving approach of working collaboratively towards cost reduction is an archetypal example of interdependent process management. Delphi has a process for charting 'creative improvement plans (Fig. 10.2).' When completely filled out, such a chart is crammed with information and symbolic markers of a collaborative effort—names of champions on the customer and supplier sides, an explicit statement of the Delphi's 'savings sharing percentage' that is applied to each cost savings achieved (making it clear that the supplier retains a percentage as well); and very detailed breakdowns of cost savings for every factor of production and for every part number, reinforcing norms of information sharing and transparency.

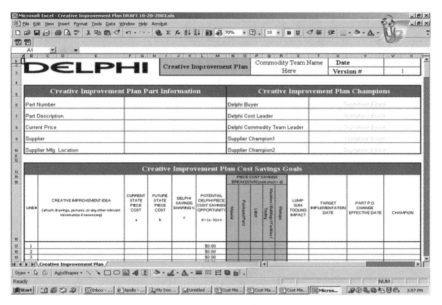

Fig. 10.2 Delphi form for charting creative improvement plans

In many cases, these cost reduction processes carried out by Delphi together with its suppliers yield savings. Table 10.6 shows one example that produced a 25 per cent reduction in supplier unit cost. The means for achieving the savings included changes in production layout that improve flow and eliminate wasted motion, thus reducing direct labor costs; improvements in the accuracy of material and cycle time specifications; and improved packaging. This process emphasizes identifying cost elements accurately by eliminating faulty specifications and erroneous assumptions, even if the more accurate assessment of a given cost element is higher than the original estimate.

If cost management is the short-term, real-time discipline for achieving cost reduction, cost profit planning is the long-term approach to eliminating cost at the source. Cost profit planning views the sources of manufacturing cost differently, in comparison with traditional manufacturing cost accounting. In the traditional view, design accounts for 5 per cent of costs; materials for 50 per cent; labor for 15 per cent; with 30 per cent allocated to indirect and overhead costs. In contrast, cost profit planning views design decisions as affecting 70 per cent of cost, vs. only 5 per cent for labor, 5 per cent for overhead, and 20 per cent for materials.[35]

Table 10.6a. Cost management example

Before	After	Cost (%)
	Machining	
– 1 operator running 1 CNC station	– 1 operator running 3 CNC stations	**8.1**
	Part stacking	
– 1 operator running 1 stacker	– 1 operator running 2 stackers	**5.3**
– Manual stacking performed as needed	– No manual stacking required	
	Assembly	
– Straight line layout	– U-shaped module	**8.9**
– No communication	– Improved communication	
– 5 piece flow	– 1 piece flow	
– 6.5 operators	– 6 operators	
– 90 pieces/hour	– 126 pieces/hour	
25% reduction in overall cost with improvement to supplier margins		

Source: Delphi Corporation.

How can design affect so much of cost? Decisions made during design lock in certain requirements for labor and materials and logistics. Hence the primary way to tackle reducing those costs on a long-term basis is to go back to the point in the design process where alternative choices could be considered.

The cost profit planning process developed by Toyota proceeds in the following way. Each aspect of cost is tracked back to that point in the design process where it is locked in, and a lower cost target is assigned. Where does this cost target come from? Unlike cost management, which focuses on what is hypothetically attainable from best possible manufacturing practice, this cost target is calculated following the opposite of a cost-plus logic. The desired market price for the entire vehicle is set by the OEM based on analyses of consumer perceptions of value, the desired level of profit is subtracted, and what remains is the target cost for the vehicle. This is then decomposed, following the same logic, to come up with a target cost for each component, and then for each design element of the component. Value engineering activities during product development then attempt to achieve that cost target.

The implications for collaborative and iterative co-design are enormous. Through supplier involvement with value engineering activities, costs can be taken out before the manufacturing process even begins, making it much easier to envision reaching the hypothetical ideal cost, or at least closing the gap substantially. This supplier involvement represents a blend of design ideas and operational ideas; suppliers are primarily expected to

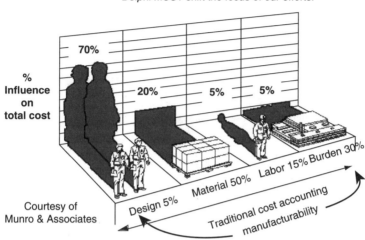

Since *DESIGN impacts 70% of the Total Cost,*
Delphi MUST shift the focus of our efforts.

Fig. 10.3 Cost profit planning at Delphi

contribute their input on how to make the manufacturing process easier (what is sometimes called 'design-for-manufacturing'), but at the same time, they are learning far more about the design aspects than they would under the traditional 'black box' system.

Supplier impact on costs during design can be substantial. We saw a summary of one such example that first identified the expected cost from the cost standards set by external research; next showed the range of supplier quotes, including the quote from the recognized cost leader; and then indicated that the cost leader, during the design process, recommended a switch from a two-step to a one-step manufacturing process. This change reduced the part cost 45 per cent below the cost leader's cost with the old design. This dramatic cost reduction was achieved without any adverse impact on the supplier's profit margins.

Delphi summarizes, for its suppliers, what is different about this approach in the following way. Prices are set not by multiple rounds of bidding but by comparing the 'supplier cost' with the cost standard and having discussions to get to an 'agreed-upon cost.' Further improvements upon the 'agreed-upon' cost are achieved through the 'creative improvement plan' in the short term and by cost profit planning—to eliminate costs during the design stage—in the long term. After starting with a negotiated already low cost, Delphi works with the supplier on cost reductions and

Table 10.6b. Cost profit planning example

Product:	Oil Control Valve
Project:	OCV
Division:	E&C
Annual Volume:	2 million +
SOP:	November 2005
Component:	Frame
Design:	2-piece stamping with spot welding
Costbook:	0.80 euros
Supplier quotes:	0.28–0.75 euros
Cost leader estimate:	0.33 euros
VE activities:	Cost leader and suppliers recommend 1-piece
Status:	1-piece design in process
New cost leader estimate:	0.18 euros (45% avoidance over 2-piece)

Source: Delphi Corporation.

price reductions follow as a matter of course, consistent with norms of sharing cost savings.

Delphi then tells suppliers what changes in customer and supplier roles are required to make this collaborative mode a reality. The customer must: (1) become experts on commodity pricing and manufacturing processes in order to develop effective cost standards; (2) focus on cost discussions vs. multiple rounds of bidding and negotiating; (3) get the lowest upfront ('agreed-upon') cost through reliance on cost standards and benchmarking; (4) establish 'creative improvement plans' with suppliers and document their 'reality'—their actual progress—in implementing these plans; (5) work to help suppliers develop capabilities and pursue ideal cost, focusing on their manufacturing realities rather than price; and (6) share cost improvement savings with the supplier.

The supplier, in turn, must: (1) provide cost breakdown/cost standard information; (2) discuss operational issues with the customer; (3) identify where the customer's decisions (design, scheduling, commodity purchasing) are adding cost and tell the customer; (4) take ownership of the creative improvement plan and identify opportunities for cost reduction; (5) assign target costs to specific design and manufacturing steps and pursue those cost savings aggressively; and (6) share cost improvement savings with the customer.

It is worth noting the extent to which these Toyota-derived processes of cost management and cost profit planning capture the essential elements of collaborative community as defined in this volume. Disciplined processes and a focus on facts ('realities') provide reliable and valid performance outcomes marked by ongoing improvements that build common purpose between the customer and supplier and, over time, trust. An ethic of contribution permeates the customer–supplier relationship, from the joint development of creative improvement plans to joint involvement in design to achieve target cost goals: the core value or standard for trust is not performance to preset targets, but the willingness and capability to engage in discussion about how to work towards solutions of problems. There is a strong expectation that all parties will frame problems as opportunities for mutual gain. Both sides take responsibility for gathering and sharing relevant information and vow to avoid gaming behavior that exploits information asymmetries.

What success has Delphi had implementing this system? The potential impact is certainly huge. As of the end of 2004, Delphi has 4,000 suppliers and purchases $14 billion in parts annually. This number of vendors is greatly reduced from the roughly 9,000 suppliers in place when Dave Nelson arrived but is still judged to be too high, given the intention to have more long-term collaborative relationships. The intention is to focus purchases on 1,000–1,500 suppliers. Three years after his arrival at Delphi, Nelson has completed ninety-two expectation-setting meetings with senior executives at this core group.

This patient one-at-a-time approach seems to be bearing fruit. Under the direction of a former Toyota cost management *sensei*, cost standards are steadily being developed for all the Delphi commodities and manufacturing processes. Quality levels have improved from 10,000 defective parts per million in 1995 to 28 PPM in 2003. The director of Delphi's lean production activities told me that in 2003, Delphi saved $500 million from lean-derived improvements in design, manufacturing, and purchasing.[36]

This effort to remake Delphi's relationship with its own suppliers has certainly run into obstacles. Paul Brent, director of Delphi's supplier development program, said,

I spend a lot of my time making sure that our purchasing guys act in ways consistent with the relationship we're building with the supplier through cost management and lean supplier development. We acknowledge to the suppliers that we are in the midst of our own lean transformation. It helps that with the lean supplier development process, we are already starting to build good relationships and trust. We don't even deal with price. We assess the state of their operations at the beginning and get the benchmarking in place to capture improvements, and then we begin working on creative improvement plans.[37]

When we asked Dave Nelson what he sees in the future, he said,

We're moving rapidly in this new direction. We're working more and more closely with Toyota and getting more business from them; they are lending us some of their best lean supplier development engineers. I see a one-way evolution in the move towards cost management. Once we get past a certain point, it will be impossible to unravel. Suppliers won't want to do conventional bidding on parts. A customer that insists on bids will end up paying significantly more.

Evidence of various kinds is emerging to suggest that those following the 'collaboration with trust' approach are reaping real economic gains. Delphi provides its suppliers with data on the profits achieved by companies that follow cost profit planning vs. those that do not; the difference is roughly 2 to 1. A 2004 consulting study[38] finds evidence from surveys that suppliers working with Toyota and Honda achieve costs that are, on average, 8 per cent lower than those working with other North American OEMs, mostly attributable to the avoidance of time and cost during multiple bidding rounds and to the elimination of design-influenced cost based on supplier input during the product development process.

Finally, in recent interviews, the authors are hearing some suppliers saying, privately, that they are increasingly reserving their most advanced technological innovations for their Japanese customers. While they can't afford to refuse business from the Big Three, they can refuse to provide their best knowledge and effort to customers who relentlessly squeeze their margins and violate trust by taking advantage of having access to proprietary supplier information.

The Delphi case shows that it is possible for a first-tier supplier with historical roots in the traditional US approach of 'exit' to move towards 'collaboration with trust' in its relationships with both customers and second- and third-tier suppliers. Delphi's progress has depended on senior management commitment to putting 'lean processes' in place throughout the company; on the presence of knowledge resources (*sensei*); and on the growing willingness of suppliers to differentiate among their customers in their level of contribution to design innovation and cost improvement.

Even amid its current financial difficulties, we believe that enough people at Delphi have seen the benefits of collaboration with trust—both senior management and the middle ranks of design and manufacturing engineers and purchasing staff—to sustain the commitment to this approach.

Implications of collaboration with and without trust

This section discusses implications of the above analysis for our understanding of collaborative community. We address the dynamics of collaboration in this context by addressing four questions: (1) Is trust needed for

Table 10.7. Collaboration with and without trust

	Collaboration without trust	Collaboration with trust
Legacy mode of exchange	Exit	Voice
Governance level (purchasing regime)	Adversarial/short term and arm's length	Long term and relational
Task level (design/engineering)	• Iterative co-design • Interdependent process management • Low discretionary effort (?)	• Iterative co-design • Interdependent process management • High discretionary effort
Information exchange	Low at governance level; high at task level	High at governance and task level
Trust	Low governance; ? task	Emergent → High

collaboration? (2) Can the gains from collaboration with trust be appropriated by other firms that are practicing collaboration without trust? (3) What are the micro-level social and economic dynamics of collaboration without trust? (4) What constraints are faced over time by collaboration with trust?

Before doing so, we summarize similarities and differences between collaboration with and without trust in Table 10.7. The difference in legacy mode primarily affects the purchasing regime at governance level. At the task level, we see similar reliance on iterative co-design and interdependent process management regardless of the level of trust at the governance level. However, we speculate that the level of discretionary effort applied to making the economic relationship work effectively (including solving emergent problems) may differ even at a task level, as a consequence of a 'trickle-down' effect of the lack of trust at the governance level.

With respect to information exchange, we see similarly high amounts at the task level but a striking feature of low trust at the governance level is a constricted and formalized flow of information—something that should have long-term consequences for quality. Finally, with respect to trust at the task level, we believe that empirical investigation will be needed to determine the conditions under which this is possible. We now address a series of questions on the dynamics of collaboration with and without trust.

Is trust needed for collaboration?

The evidence of this chapter suggests that trust is not a *precondition* for collaboration. We argue that a shift of knowledge-intensive design work from OEMs to suppliers is under way, as part of a move to deverticalize the automotive industry. This work requires collaboration by necessity, particularly given a (still) largely integral product architecture and the diffusion of innovations of iterated co-design and shop-floor problem solving associated with lean production (Toyota Production System). The evidence of this chapter is that firms are being pushed in the direction of collaboration whether or not they have prior traditions of trust-based supplier relations. Collaboration without trust can emerge where 'exit' approaches to purchasing routines and governance mechanisms persist.

However, we predict that collaboration will prove to be more successful if it takes forms that allow for the emergence of trust over time. Given a volatile set of external circumstances and ongoing advances in technology that must be absorbed, collaborative co-design—when well executed—will lead to superior outcomes and provide experiences of success that will help build trust. This trust is likely to be fragile at first, easy to destroy with a single exploitative act during the purchasing process, such as the customer sending the supplier's proprietary design information to competitors seeking a competitive bid. It may also exist primarily at a micro-level of personal relationships among engineers and managers who have worked together during co-design and may not diffuse readily to individuals who are not part of the co-design experience such as purchasing agents.

Can the gains from collaboration with trust be appropriated?

Since, increasingly, suppliers work with multiple customers, some of which help the supplier improve through supplier development activities, there is a risk that other customers might 'free ride.' Imagine that a supplier has improved its design and manufacturing capabilities through collaborative interaction with Customer A. Now suppose that Customer B, not willing to make such investments in supplier capabilities and operating under a low-trust purchasing regime, can gain the benefits of this supplier's superior capabilities simply by awarding it some business, under the assumption that the supplier capabilities will diffuse naturally within the firm. Or, Customer B could demand to receive the same annual cost reduction offered to Customer A, figuring that the only way the supplier could attain these reductions would be through the same process improvements.

Many observers do make an argument of this kind, claiming that the improvement of supplier capabilities in the USA, prompted by the Japanese transplants, has given their Big Three competitors a considerable upgrading in cost and quality—a 'rising tide lifts all boats' hypothesis. Yet Dyer's (1997) evidence suggests that this may be only partially true: he found that the diffusion of best practices within the same supplier can be remarkably low. Two production lines side by side within the same supplier plant, one dedicated to a Big Three customer and the other to a Japanese transplant, had widely different performance. His explanation was partly based on organizational barriers to diffusion of knowledge and partly on differences in production philosophy that affected manufacturing outcomes. For example, Toyota worked with the supplier plant to implement one-piece flow of parts through the production process, emphasizing the use of small containers that could be moved by hand and short lead times. These techniques were not useful to the GM line in the same plant, because GM mandated the use of standard containers, containers that were so large that forklifts were required to move them.

Our view is that while some capabilities are generic and all customers will benefit from a supplier's improvement, others are relationship and context specific. Even without deliberate intent, a supplier drawing on deep knowledge of Customer A achieved through a long-term relationship governed by trust and frequent interactions will be able to provide more innovative designs and insightful process improvements than it will be able to provide to customer B with whom it has an arms-length relationship applying generic process management routines. The consequences over time will be a growing gap between what Customer A and Customer B are receiving, even from the very same supplier.

What are the micro-dynamics of collaboration without trust?

One way to describe the micro-level motivations and dynamics of collaboration without trust is by focusing on the typical culture and experiences of different professions. For example, consider a general hypothesis that the engineers want to collaborate, but the automaker purchasing agents are so intent on squeezing suppliers for every last nickel that they are eliminating the prospect of effective collaboration. In the absence of direct evidence, we would speculate that value and personality differences are important: that an 'ethic of contribution' among engineers inclines them more positively towards collaborative activity than purchasing agents. Unlike quality control/improvement, which is often a win-win situation between workers and managers in a manufacturing setting, parts sourcing may lack a task that would pull automaker purchasing agents and supplier salespeople into greater interdependence and help develop norms of reciprocity.

Another framing would use the language of incentives: 'Engineers and automaker purchasing agents are each responding rationally to the incentives they face.' Engineers are evaluated on completion of interdependent tasks (such as whether designs are finished on time and pass crash tests) that require collaboration between counterpart engineers at automaker and supplier. Automaker purchasing agents are rewarded for reducing piece prices, causing them to evaluate the benefits of collaboration (vs. trust-undermining price-reducing actions) in each period for which they are rewarded. They thus ignore a potential lost stream of future benefits from collaboration.

Both framings contribute to an explanation of why the cost management/cost profit planning approach used by Toyota (and being adopted by Delphi) can be successful at the governance level, facilitating collaboration with trust. First, it provides a different set of goals and experiences for purchasing agents that over time changes their culture. The Toyota approach involves coming to an agreement upon an initial cost based on careful preparation of cost standards and then pursuing cost reduction to reach the target cost. This decision to focus on the 'reality' faced by the supplier's manufacturing plant, and hence to reduce prices only after reducing costs, provides the basis for norms of mutual gain and reciprocity and builds trust. Second, purchasing agents are judged based on their ability to contribute to these tasks, giving them an incentive to think about the value of collaboration over a longer period.[39]

What constraints are faced over time by collaboration with trust?

Long-term collaborative relationships with little or no threat of exit can certainly face constraints in the form of complacency, rigidity, 'groupthink' tendencies, etc. Meta-routines for examining skeptically all current practices may be important to avoid stagnation. Furthermore, sudden environmental changes or financial pressures may require rapid response that might not allow fulfillment of the commitments of collaboration—a tension between flexibility and the market as mentioned early in the volume. However, as long as all unexpected shocks—whether from external or internal sources—are approached according to collaborative norms of information sharing, reciprocity of effort, shared distribution of gains and losses, firms following these norms should possess a greater adaptability than firms which are able to make very quick short-term decisions. It is for this reason that MacDuffie (1995) describes the Toyota Production System in terms of 'flexible production' rather than 'lean production.' This perspective is supported by empirical evidence that flexible production plants can achieve high levels of product variety without suffering a decrement in cost or quality performance.

Predictions about the future of 'collaboration without trust'

Above, we predict that collaboration without trust will not perform as well as collaboration with trust, and also predict that suppliers will prefer to deal with customers operating collaboratively with trust. This would suggest a steady evolution towards collaboration with trust as the dominant mode.

Yet we do not expect that collaboration without trust will disappear any time soon. From the perspective of transaction cost analysis with which we began this chapter, it may seem surprising that suppliers would make investments in assets tied to one customer (e.g. 'free' design work absent any contract) with so few safeguards. However, suppliers have assets they need to pay off, in plant and equipment, technology etc., and if they can cover part of these costs, they are still better off than they would be without any sales. Customers know this, and can bid commodity producers down to their marginal costs. To the extent they are willing to accept less than perfect substitutes for their first-choice product, they have bargaining power over non-commodity producers as well.

This transition could last for a long time. The overcapacity situation affecting the parts sector is not likely to change quickly; indeed, the forces promoting the addition of capacity in low-wage countries (their large direct-labor cost advantage) as well as those slowing the removal of existing capacity in high-wage countries (the long-lived nature of capital equipment) remain strong.

It is also possible that some future trends affecting supply chains in the automotive industry could decrease the necessity for collaboration. To the extent that tasks relatively predictable in their frequency, timing, and informational requirements can be automated (relying on sophisticated software that can be contextually responsive), the total requirement for collaboration may decrease, even as the proportion of non-automated tasks that are collaborative—and that would benefit from trust—would increase. Furthermore, if fundamental technological shifts—towards alternate fuels, new drive train designs such as fuel cells, new materials, new uses of information technology within the vehicle—break the dominant design sufficiently for a more modular product architecture to become possible, collaborative activity could shift towards module definition and interface standardization and away from high interdependence during design, with more market-based modes of module procurement.

Even in the presence of dramatic technological change, we predict that collaborative activity between automakers and suppliers will remain high and might even increase. It is tempting to speculate that customers would benefit from relationships with less commitment when 'radical' or 'disruptive' innovations (Abernathy 1978; Christensen 1997) make their current suppliers' capabilities obsolete.

This seems plausible, but does not in practice seem to have been the case in the auto industry. The industry has over the last twenty years adopted a number of such innovations (such as the change from mechanical to electrical control of carburetion, suspension, etc., and experimentation with alternative power trains). But it is not clear that automakers using more collaboration were slower than others, and in fact most of the new technologies are supplied in partnership with existing suppliers. Perhaps this continuity is due to features of the auto industry (such as the integrality of its products, high volumes, and high demand for reliability) that mean even a new supplier of a radically new product must take a lot of time to learn about unchanging features of the industry, giving existing suppliers a chance to learn about (or buy) the new technology.

What we can assert with confidence is that the automotive industry will continue to be a fruitful context for examining modes of inter-firm economic exchange, since its global scale, technological scope, and overwhelming product and process complexity generate such a challenging and diverse set of decisions about purchasing strategy. The important intangibles of 'look and feel' associated with automotive products and brands will resist any sweeping move towards modularization and preserve the knowledge intensity and idiosyncratic requirements for systemic integrity that place collaboration at the heart of this industry.

References

Abernathy, William J. (1978). *The Productivity Dilemma: Roadblock to Innovation in the Automobile Industry.* Baltimore: Johns Hopkins University Press.

Axelrod, Robert (1984). *The Evolution of Cooperation.* New York: Basic Books.

Baldwin, Carliss Y., and Clark, Kim B. (2000). *Design Rules, i: The Power of Modularity.* Cambridge, Mass.: MIT Press.

Bremner, Brian, Edmondson, Gail, and Dawson, Chester (2004). 'Nissan's boss.' *Business Week* (4 Oct.): 50.

Brusoni, Stefano, Principe, Andrea, and Pavitt, Keith (2001). 'Knowledge specialization, organizational coupling, and the boundaries of the firm.' *Administrative Sciences Quarterly*, 46/4: 597–621.

Chandler, Alfred D. (1962). *Strategy and Structure: Chapters in the History of the American Industrial Enterprise*. Cambridge, Mass.: MIT Press.

—— (ed.) (1964). *Giant Enterprise: Ford, General Motors, and the Automobile Industry.* New York: Harcourt, Brace & World.

Chesborough, Henry (2002). 'Towards a dynamics of standards: their emergence, dominance, and death.' Working paper, Harvard Business School.

Christensen, Clayton M. (1997). *The Innovator's Dilemma*. Boston: Harvard Business School Press.

Clark, K. B., and Fujimoto T. (1991). *Product Development Performance: Strategy, Organization, and Management in the World Auto Industry.* Boston: Harvard Business School Press.

Coase, Ronald (1937). 'The nature of the firm.' *Economica*, 4/16: 386–405.

Dawson, Chester (2005). 'A "China" price for Toyota.' *Business Week* (21 Feb.): 50–1.

Dyer, Jeffrey H. (1997). 'Does governance matter? Keiretsu alliances and asset specificity as sources of Japanese competitive advantage.' *Organization Science*, 7/6: 649–66.

—— (2000). *Collaborative Advantage: Winning through Extended Enterprise Supply Networks*. Boston: Harvard Business School Press.

—— and Singh, Harbir (1998). 'The relational view: cooperative strategy and sources of interorganizational competitive advantage.' *Academy of Management Review*, 23/4: 660–79.

Fine, Charles (1999). *Clockspeed*. Reading, Mass.: Perseus Books.

Fixson, Sebastian (2005). 'Product architecture assessment: a tool to link product, process, and supply chain design decisions.' *Journal of Operations Management*, 23/3–4: 345–69.

—— Ro, Y., and Liker, J. (forthcoming). 'Modularization and outsourcing: a study of generational sequences in the U.S. automotive cockpit industry.' *International Journal of Automotive Technology and Management*.

Fujimoto, Takahiro (1999). *The Evolution of the Toyota Manufacturing System*. Oxford: Oxford University Press.

Ghosn, Carlos (2002). 'Saving the business without losing the company.' *Harvard Business Review*, 80/1: 37–45.

—— (2004). *Shift: Inside Nissan's Historic Revival*. New York: Currency Publishing.

Helper, Susan (1991). 'Strategy and irreversibility in supplier relations: the case of the US automobile industry.' *Business History Review*, 65/4: 781–824.

—— and Kiehl, Janet (2004). 'Developing supplier capabilities: market and non-market approaches.' *Industry and Innovation*, 11/1–2: 89–107.

—— and Levine, David (1992). 'Long-term supplier relations and product–market structure.' *Journal of Law Economics and Organization*, 8/3: 561–81.

—— and MacDuffie, John Paul (2001). 'E-volving the auto industry: e-business effects on consumer and supplier relationships.' In R. Litan and A. Rivlin (eds.), *Tracking a Transformation: E-Business and the Terms of Competition in Industries.* Washington, DC: Brookings Institution: 178–213.

Helper, Susan, and MacDuffie, John Paul (2003). 'Suppliers and intermediaries.' In Bruce Kogut (ed.), *The Global Internet Economy*. Cambridge, Mass.: MIT Press: 331–80.

—— —— and Sabel, Charles (2000). 'Pragmatic collaborations: advancing knowledge while controlling opportunism.' *Industrial and Corporate Change*, 10/3: 443–83.

—— and Sako, Mari (1995). 'Supplier relations in Japan and the United States: are they converging?' *Sloan Management Review*, 36/3: 77–84.

—— and Stanley, Marcus (2004). 'Industrial clusters, social capital, and international competition in the U.S. component manufacturing industry.' Conference paper for Clusters, Industrial Districts and Firms: The Challenge of Globalization, Modena, Italy, 4 Aug.

Herrigel, Gary (2004). 'Emerging strategies and forms of governance in high-wage component manufacturing regions.' *Industry and Innovation*, 11/1–2: 45–79.

Herzenberg, Stephen (1991). 'Towards a cooperative commonwealth? Labor and restructuring in the U.S. and Canadian auto industries.' Ph.D. dissertation, MIT.

Hirschman, Albert (1970). *Exit, Voice, and Loyalty*. Cambridge, Mass.: Harvard University Press.

Hochfelder, David, and Helper, Susan (1996), 'Joint product development in the early American auto industry.' *Business and Economic History* (best papers volume), 25/2: 39–51.

Jacobides, Michael (2002). 'The shifting boundaries of the firm: a case for information, coordination, and modularity conditions.' Working paper, London Business School.

Kenney, M., and Florida, R. (1993). *Beyond Mass Production: The Japanese Lean System and its Transfer to the U.S.* Oxford: Oxford University Press.

Klein, B., Crawford, R. A., and Alchian, A. (1978). 'Vertical integration, appropriable rents, and the competitive contracting process.' *Journal of Law and Economics*, 21/2: 297–326.

Langlois, Richard N. (2002). 'Modularity in technology and organization.' *Journal of Economic Behavior and Organization*, 49/1: 19–37.

Liker, Jeffrey (2004). *The Toyota Way*. New York: McGraw-Hill.

MacDuffie, John Paul (1995). 'Human resource bundles and manufacturing performance: organizational logic and flexible production systems.' *Industrial and Labor Relations Review*, 48/2: 197–221.

—— (1997). 'The road to root cause: shop-floor problem-solving at three automotive assembly plants.' *Management Science*, 43/4: 479–502.

—— (2005). 'Modularity and the automobile: what happens when the concept hits the road.' Working paper, International Motor Vehicle Program.

—— and Helper, Susan (1998). 'Creating lean suppliers: diffusing lean production through the supply chain.' In J. K. Liker, W. M. Fruin, and P. S. Adler (eds.), *Remade in America: Transplanting and Transforming Japanese Management Systems*. Oxford: Oxford University Press: 154–202.

Mackintosh, James (2004). 'Nissan lifts oversight in U.S.' *Financial Times* (30 Sept.): 28.

Mikawa, Tadahisa, and Okudaira, Kazuyuk (2005). 'Ghosn recasting keiretsu suppliers.' *Nikkei Weekly* (24 Jan.).

Millikin, John P., and Fu, Dean (2005). 'The global leadership of Carlos Ghosn at Nissan.' *Thunderbird International Business Review,* 47/1: 121–37.

Nishiguchi, Toshihiro (1994). *Strategic Industrial Sourcing: The Japanese Advantage.* Oxford: Oxford University Press.

Nobeoka, Kentaro and Manabe, Seiji (forthcoming) 'Jidousya Buhinn Tokusei no Sokutei (Measuring properties of automobile parts)', Yokohama National University Working Paper, in Japanese.

Prahalad, C. K., and Hamel, Gary (1990). 'The core competence of the corporation.' *Harvard Business Review,* 68/3: 79–91.

Rubenstein, James M. (2001). *Making and Selling Cars: Innovation and Change in the U.S. Automotive Industry.* Baltimore: Johns Hopkins University Press.

Sabel, Charles F., and Zeitlin, Jonathan (2004). 'Neither modularity or relational contracting: inter-firm collaboration in the new economy.' *Enterprise and Society: The International Journal of Business History,* 5/3: 388–403.

Sako, Mari (1992). *Prices, Quality, and Trust: Inter-Firm Relations in Britain and Japan.* Cambridge: Cambridge University Press.

——(2002). 'Cooperative capitalism: self-regulation, trade associations, and the antimonopoly law in Japan.' *Journal of Economic Literature,* 40/3: 952–3.

——(2003). 'Supplier development at Honda, Nissan, and Toyota.' Working paper, International Motor Vehicle Program, http://imvp.mit.edu/pub0304.html (forthcoming in *Industrial and Corporate Change*).

——(2004). 'Modularity and outsourcing: the nature of co-evolution of product architecture and organizational architecture in the global automotive industry.' In Andrea Principe, Andrew Davies, and Michael Hobday (eds.), *The Business of Systems Integration.* Oxford: Oxford University Press: 229–53.

Sawyer, Christopher A. (2004). 'Speed and quality.' *Automotive Design and Production,* 116/12: 26.

Sturgeon, Timothy (2002). 'Modular production networks: a new American model of industrial organization.' *Industrial and Corporate Change,* 11/3: 451–96.

Takeishi, Akira (2003). 'Structural changes of Japanese supplier system.' Presentation at Japan Auto Industry Symposium and Sponsors Meeting (co-hosted by IMVP, Hose University and REITI), Tokyo, 12 Sept.

——and Noro, Yoshihisa (2005). 'Structural changes in Japanese supplier system.' Presentation at IMVP Spring Researchers Meeting, Philadelphia, 2–3 June.

Ulrich, Karl (1995). 'The role of product architecture in the manufacturing firm.' *Research Policy,* 24/3: 419–40.

Welch, David (2004). 'Nissan: the squeaks get louder.' *Business Week* (17 May): 44.

White, Lawrence J. (1971). *The Automobile Industry since 1945.* Cambridge, Mass.: Harvard University Press.

Whitford, Josh, and Zeitlin, Jonathan (2004). 'Governing decentralized production: institutions, public policy, and the prospects for inter-firm collaboration in U.S. manufacturing.' *Industry and Innovation,* 11/1–2: 11–44.

Williamson, Oliver (1975). *Markets and Hierarchies.* New York: Free Press.

Williamson, Oliver (1985). *The Economic Institutions of Capitalism*. New York: Free Press.

Womack, James P., Jones, Daniel, and Roos, Daniel (1990). *The Machine That Changed the World*. New York: Rawson Associates.

Notes

The authors are grateful for comments received from the editors; to colleagues from the International Motor Vehicle Program (IMVP), particularly Mari Sako, Takahiro Fujimoto, Akira Takeishi, Sebastian Fixson, and Frits Pil; to participants in the Jones Center seminar, Wharton School; the ICOS seminar, University of Michigan, and to the individuals at various OEMs and suppliers whom we interviewed. We are also grateful to IMVP for providing the funding for this research.

1. Collaboration between automakers and their suppliers was not invented by the Japanese. Until the 1920s, US suppliers played a key role in product design and innovation in the industry. Gradually, vertically integrated divisions came to take on this role, and suppliers (except for a few large independents) played the role of 'cheap capacity.' Vertical integration fell in the 1930s, then rose in the 1950s before falling again in the 1980s and 1990s. See Hochfelder and Helper (1996); Helper (1991); White (1971).

2. Hirschman offers a third category, 'loyalty,' which affects the relationship between exit and voice by discouraging those who are dissatisfied with an economic relationship from leaving it immediately. With less likelihood of 'exit,' there is an increased likelihood they will resort to 'voice,' thus providing valuable information to improve the relationship. This addresses the situation in which the presence of both exit and voice options yields a net bias towards exit; the possibility of exit may, in Hirschman's words, 'atrophy the development of voice.' The implication, in the supply-chain context, is that a supplier will benefit when its customer displays some loyalty and pursues voice mechanisms. Indeed, choosing to display such loyalty is central to the strategy associated with this mode of exchange, since especially at the beginning of relationships, there are often bumpy periods in which the benefits of switching (often tangible, such as a lower price) seem to outweigh the loss of the ongoing relationship (which entails costs that are often hard to measure, such as loss of trust).

3. We define both 'collaboration' and 'trust' below. Susan Helper coined this phrase in connection with a presentation at an International Motor Vehicle Program (IMVP) conference in Sept. 2002. See also Helper and Stanley (2004).

4. For example, a supplier with small stamping presses might want to design small parts and weld them together, while a supplier with larger presses would prefer to produce fewer, larger parts.

5. These practices include: simultaneous engineering during product development, involving iterated communication about a design space that is steadily narrowed to reflect emergent understandings of which choices will optimize the design

across multiple dimensions of performance; continuous improvement routines that pursue 'root-cause' solutions to cost and quality problems through rigorous, comprehensive experimentation with different manufacturing approaches; and just-in-time inventory practices that interlink supplier and automaker factories in a minimal-buffer regime that requires precise coordination and well-developed logistics capabilities. See Fujimoto (1999); Womack et al. (1990); MacDuffie (1997); Helper et al. (2000).

6. It is unclear how much of an independent effect the new theories had, or whether they were rationalizations of decisions taken due to labor cost differentials. Attention to these differentials was magnified due to automakers' accounting systems, which focused on direct labor costs and did not capture other kinds of costs as effectively.

7. Ironically, the mega-suppliers often became *more* vertically integrated, as they strived to provide one-stop shopping for their deverticalized customers.

8. The Clark and Fujimoto typology isn't comprehensive from the perspective of this chapter. Black box subcontracting could be purely market based; the OEM could essentially say to the supplier 'here are the parameters, meet them, if you don't we'll go somewhere else.' Indeed, this approach is what some observers imagine will be commonplace with a modular product architecture, as discussed below. In practice, the category of 'black box' in Clark and Fujimoto's data collection did involve considerable interactive deliberation between OEM and suppliers over the parameters of a component and how they were to be achieved. Perhaps a closer concept to our description of 'pragmatic collaboration' is relational subcontracting (the term used in transaction cost economics). Certainly the issue of how extensively the parties work together on determining parameters, identifying design problems, and jointly solving them is central to the issue of collaboration in supply chains.

9. See Ulrich (1995) for the classic definition of modules as involving a one-to-one mapping from component (design element) to function. For a useful reconceptualization of product architecture that challenges and extends the Ulrich definition, see Fixson (2005).

10. Fixson et al. (forthcoming) track the evolution of cockpit designs over three periods while also tracking the extent of outsourcing of design and manufacturing tasks from automakers to suppliers. They find that outsourcing is much more extensive than any change in product architecture; indeed, the changes described as 'stage 1 modularity' are primarily to allow one-step installation during assembly and do not reflect any of the more fundamental attributes of modularity.

11. See Langlois (2002); Chesborough (2002); Jacobides (2002); Brusoni et al. (2001); Sabel and Zeitlin (2004).

12. For an expanded treatment of this line of argument, see MacDuffie (2005).

13. A similarly incorrect prediction of an inevitable decline in collaboration due to increasing standardization was made by proponents of e-business in the late 1990s. See Helper and MacDuffie (2001).

14. By 'collaboration,' we mean undertaking tasks that require ongoing discussion; the outcome of these discussions is frequently a contingent action not anticipated or provided for in a contract. In contrast, in a non-collaborative arm's-length or 'exit' mode, a division of labor is agreed on in advance and little discussion occurs across the agreed-upon interface. By trust, we mean taking actions that leave oneself vulnerable to another party, with the expectation that one will not be taken advantage of. This definition corresponds to Sako's (1992) definition of 'goodwill' trust.

15. This speech was reported in the 12 Aug. 2002 issue of *Automotive News*; the entire text is available at www.autonews.com/article.cms?articleId=40392.

16. www.thefabricator.com/Articles/Fabricating_Exclusive.cfm?ID=25.

17. Herrigel (2004); Whitford and Zeitlin (2004).

18. In future research we will investigate the relationship between changing incentives and changing attitudes. Top management frequently expresses frustration that their subordinates do not react quickly to changes in strategy. For the case of purchasing, we would like to understand better the extent to which this slow reaction is due to some inherent resistance to change, a difficulty in changing habits, and/or reward structures not changing to reflect the changed strategy. This transition seems particularly difficult when a firm moves from the relatively clear and measurable incentives of exit (minimize piece prices and the costs of switching suppliers) to the more multifaceted, subjective requisites of voice (nurture suppliers, but don't accept substandard performance).

19. See Helper et al. (2000); Helper and MacDuffie (2001).

20. See Brusoni et al. (2001).

21. By most accounts, Toyota has largely succeeded in reaching this goal, saving nearly $10 billion over its five-year span, a reduction of approximately one-third in procurement costs. The target of $1.7 billion in cost savings for the fiscal year ending in March 2005 has not been met, however, falling short by 15% because of high steel prices. In response, Toyota is aiming to reduce the number of steel parts in an average vehicle from 610 to 500. See Chester Dawson, *Business Week*, 21 Feb. 2005.

22. See Sako (2002).

23. Ohba seminar, Institute for International Economic Studies Seminar Series #9706, Toyota Motor Corporation, 1997; cited in Sako (2003). See also Liker (2004).

24. This account of the Nissan turnaround is based primarily on Milliken and Fu (2005), supplemented by articles from *Business Week, Fortune, Forbes*.

25. This was not an acquisition but an alliance: Nissan retained its name and board of directors, the Nissan board continues to choose the CEO, and Nissan took the primary responsibility for implementing a revival plan.

26. Ghosn's account is captured in various interviews and in a *Harvard Business Review* article (Ghosn 2002), with an extended treatment of the Nissan turnaround in a book titled *Shift: Inside Nissan's Historic Revival* (Ghosn 2004).

27. See Welch (2004); Mackintosh (2004); Bremner et al. (2004); Sawyer (2004).

28. See Mikawa and Okudaira (2005).

29. In contrast, the exit-based legacies of documentation and codification (plus lower quality standards) may mean that a firm like GM can more quickly incorporate new suppliers with weak management skills.

30. See Helper and Stanley (2004).

31. Delphi is a world leader in mobile electronics and transportation components and systems technology. Multinational Delphi conducts its business operations through various subsidiaries and has headquarters in Troy, Mich., Paris, Tokyo, and São Paulo. Delphi's two business sectors—Dynamics, Propulsion, Thermal, and Interior Sector, and Electrical, Electronics, and Safety Sector—provide comprehensive product solutions to complex customer needs. Delphi has approximately 184,000 employees and operates 167 wholly owned manufacturing sites, 42 joint ventures, 53 customer centers and sales offices, and 33 technical centers in 40 countries. Delphi can be found on the internet at www.delphi.com as (data as of 13 May 2005).

32. The supplier development program that Nelson directed at Honda is analyzed in detail in MacDuffie and Helper (1998).

33. MacDuffie interview with Dave Nelson, Jan. 2005.

34. This account is drawn from presentation materials from a Delphi meeting with its suppliers in Nov. 2004.

35. Munro & Associates, industry average, cited in Delphi presentation to suppliers, Nov. 2004.

35. MacDuffie interviews at Delphi, Dec. 2003 and Jan. 2005.

36. MacDuffie interview with Paul Brent, Jan. 2005.

37. MacDuffie interview with Paul Brent, Jan. 2005.

38. 2004 Global Supply Management Survey, Planning Perspectives, cited in *Automotive News*, 10 Jan. 2005. When suppliers rank OEM–supplier working relationships, Toyota is first ranked, followed closely by Honda while Ford is ranked next-to-last and GM is ranked last. The gap between Toyota and GM has widened each year from 2002 to 2004.

39. Why do suppliers continue to participate in collaboration without trust? As we have discussed, in these relationships suppliers (*a*) pay for things that OEMs used to pay for (such as program management), without an increase in the piece price they receive, and (*b*) make specific investments in design without perfect safeguards (to use Williamsonian language). That is (to take a real example from our interviews), they invest sometimes millions of dollars to create a complete design for the interior of a minivan, a design that was not used because the automaker decided not to make that particular model, and that could not be adjusted to fit another model.

Suppliers' willingness to take on new variable costs (as in (*a*)), is a disguised price cut, which is possible due to increased bargaining power by OEMs due to supplier excess capacity. Suppliers accept these new terms because they have sunk investments; the new price is still greater than their marginal cost.

Suppliers might make investments in 'non-redeployable assets' (Williamson 1975) (case (*b*)) for a variety of reasons. These investments (e.g. in design engineer time) might allow them to earn a return on other assets (a factory). Or, there might be uncertainty about the buyer's ability to hold up the supplier. (In contrast, in transaction cost theory, if a firm invests in a specific asset without contractual safeguards, there is a 100% probability that it will not recoup the fixed cost of this investment. In our case, this isn't always true—the OEM might not have an alternative supplier that can step in immediately, the purchasing agent might have a longer discount rate than most, or other factors might make the net present value of cooperation greater than that of defection.)

This scenario also differs from that of Axelrod (1984) and of Helper et al. (2000) in that there is not necessarily an increasing payoff to collaboration as the number of periods of collaboration increases. As we have argued, engineers may see this payoff increase due to greater familiarity with each other's design practices, etc., but purchasing agents often have no way of valuing this familiarity.

Part IV

The Process of Change

11

A Note on Leadership for Collaborative Communities

Michael Maccoby and Charles Heckscher

The role of leadership in the move to collaborative community is referred to frequently in this volume, but generally as a paradox or mystery: leaders must give up their familiar tools of imperative authority, yet they must continue to play a strong role. Adler and Heckscher (Chapter 1) write that collaboration is compatible with continued hierarchy, though subsumed under the principle of community; but they do not explain how leaders can navigate this seeming contradiction. Heckscher and Foote explore the difficulties faced by organizational leaders who confront a demand from their subordinates to justify their decisions in terms of the organization's purposes. Bonchek and Howard point to an even more difficult problem: 'How do the leaders of major business organizations exercise their leadership in an environment where, arguably, many of the most important business relationships exist outside the organization he or she leads?'

The existing literature on leadership is highly fragmented, with many competing paradigms and many exploratory studies. Here we draw on the theory proposed in this volume to suggest one way to bring order to this area. First, it is essential to make clear the differences among three categories of leadership: leadership in paternalist bureaucracies, leadership in collaborative communities, and leadership required in the *transition* from one to the other. The failure to make these distinctions sows confusion in the field, because propositions that appear true in one arena suddenly break down in another. Second, we focus on the role of leadership in connecting values and *personalities*. Leadership requires the development of commitment to values, but also must link these values to the character of followers, the motivational patterns of those to whom they appeal.

Paternalist-bureaucratic leadership

Historically, we have seen a broad progression in workplace leadership that maps the evolution from traditional to modern to collaborative communities. In the traditional frame the major form of leadership was that of the master craftsman, who carried on age-old ways of organizing and justified decisions on the basis of the past. The leaders of emerging businesses in the eighteenth and nineteenth centuries broke sharply with this traditional legitimization, initially by viewing the organization as an extension of the owner's will. In the modern era the evolution of corporate leadership has followed the 'zigzag' path between the poles of individualist rationality and solidarity sketched in Chapter 1. In the late nineteenth century visionary leaders like John D. Rockefeller and Andrew Carnegie recognized the importance of orderly rules for a growing bureaucracy and began to hand over the reins of authority to professional managers; Frederick Taylor's 'scientific management' was one pivotal step in establishing a form of leadership based on impersonal rules. The scientific basis of management, however, proved insufficient: it became clear at least by the 1920s that even large corporations needed cultures that fostered commitment and cooperation. The purely rule-based form of bureaucracy left individuals adrift in a state of anomie or alienation—or at times finding meaning through participation in solidary groups that approached revolutionary intensity.

Thus was born, from leaders like Henry Ford and Chester Barnard, the model of the leader as father figure—reintroducing, as described in Chapter 1, a contradictory element of traditional relationships to bolster the thin connections of modern culture. Elton Mayo promoted the ideal of the caring boss who listened to employees before telling them what to do. Thomas Watson, IBM's founder, further reinforced a childlike transference of the father image to bosses by outlawing team decision making; he decreed that authority relationships were to be strictly hierarchical and one to one.

Collaborative leadership

The bureaucratic-paternalist leadership style, like any leadership, appeals only to certain kinds of followers. In the bureaucratic environment, in which people are expected to focus on doing a defined job accurately and repeatedly, followers are primarily *obsessive* types; when connected to bureaucratic values, the obsessive personality becomes the bureaucratic social character well described by Merton.[1] The leader appeals primarily to an emotional transference drawn from the relation to a strong father in a traditional family.

Collaborative environments, in which people are expected to work with others in flexible teams with shifting responsibilities, attract and select for a different social character: the *interactive* type. People with the interactive social character no longer idealize father-figure managers. Raised in families where authority is shared by parents and where at an early age they become more socialized by peer relationships, often starting with early childcare in collective environments like day-care centers, the interactive social character is less likely to have unconscious transferential feelings to managers as protective father figures. They are more likely to evaluate authority rationally, according to the value it adds.[2]

Leaders within established collaborative systems—a situation still rare today—therefore need to abandon paternalist symbols and attitudes and move towards a peer-based leadership with followers whose transference is to siblings or childhood buddies. This can be difficult to manage: siblings can easily band together rebelliously against authority. But in a game with clear rules and processes, a respected 'older sibling' can gain a powerful form of authority by acting as a role model and by justifying decisions in terms of contribution to the group. By operating 'within' the group rather than 'above' the group, such a leader reinforces the connections of mutual help and understanding that are at the core of collaborative relationships.

The sibling transference has remained largely unexplored in the psychological literature: Freud and his followers focused on parental dynamics, as was appropriate in that era before the emergence of a collaborative ethic as a key social bond. When they discussed sibling relations, it was always in the shadow of the parent in a traditional family. In this frame the major focus was on the dynamics of *rivalry*, competition for favor and attention from above—exemplified in the ancient story of Cain and Abel. These are dynamics that are very visible in corporations, in competition for the blessing of the boss that is the main fuel of corporate 'politics.'

Jean Piaget was one of the few psychologists to explore the positive dynamics of peer groups separate from parental transferences. In his study of morality in children's games, he distinguished hierarchical attitudes of 'unilateral respect' from peer attitudes of 'mutual respect,' and showed how the latter coalesced in a 'common morality' that stabilized trust in what we would call a collaborative community.

...common morality does not consist in a 'thing' given to individuals from without, but in a sum of relationships between individuals. Common morality would thus be defined by the system of laws of perspective enabling one to pass from one point of view to the other, and allowing in consequences the making of a map or objective representation of the mountain or country.[3]

This sort of community involves strong leadership, though of a very different kind from that based on parental imagos—building attachment not to an authoritative figure but to a collective task or mission. The difference can be most clearly seen around criticism of the leader. For a traditional father figure, criticism fundamentally undermines the strength of leadership, because the role depends on the claim to know more and to be 'closer to God' than subordinates. The strength of the expectation of deference in most traditional corporations has reflected this authoritative conception. For a collaborative leader, by contrast, criticism is *strengthening* if it is from the perspective of the shared task: the leader's openness signals that she is truly committed to contributing to that effort and therefore worthy of trust.

Within this general type of collaborative leader there are a number of subcategories; successful systems require a *combination* of leadership capacities. Based on observation of what is still a developing and incomplete form, we would bring out four roles in particular:

1. *Transformational visionaries* are the leaders who, envisaging the need for a new organization, prod, push, and persuade others to follow. Such visionaries are of course needed in traditional systems as well: Henry Ford was an archetype of the paternalist variant. The collaborative visionary, however, seeks to build the vision through discussion, education, and mutual criticism rather than through authoritative pronouncements from on high. The history of IBM shows the contrast in sharp terms. When Thomas Watson wanted to establish the values for IBM to live by, he wrote them down and promulgated them. But when Sam Palmisano, nearly a century later, wanted to update them for a modern era, he rejected such an approach: instead he opened the company's intranet to all employees for a frank, freewheeling discussion, in which he participated as an equal, and from which new values emerged.[4]

2. *Operational executors* are also needed in any organization, but likewise gain new characteristics. There are a number of examples of successful partnerships between this type of leader and visionaries, including Herb Kelleher and Colleen Barrett of Southwest Airlines, or Andy

Grove and Craig Barrett of Intel. The operational types may take responsibility for architecting the processes that sustain the new system, but they work less through tight controls and organization charts, and more through process alignment and cross-boundary communications. The leader of the alliance group in the Citibank case described in Chapter 1 was an example of this type, widely recognized for his ability to work out effective implementation processes through evolving process discussions in order to bring about the broader vision of e-commerce.

3. *Bridge builders*: In Chapter 4, Jay Galbraith shows how advanced solutions companies like IBM and Nestlé need network leaders with the ability to develop trusting relationships across organizational boundaries. These leaders may do more than sustain networks; they may build bridges, not only across different functional organizations, but also different national cultures. DAI, an international development consulting firm, uses bridge-building leadership to bring together pharmaceutical companies with development consultants and national governments to address the problem of AIDS in African communities. Clearly, this is a role better filled by the interactive social character who is used to bringing people together to solve problems than by a bureaucratic expert who is used to directing people to follow instructions.

4. *Heterarchical team leaders*: Collaborative community requires leadership for many teams and projects. Leaders may facilitate the interaction of specialists, but ideally, these teams become heterarchies: in contrast to hierarchies in which a single individual has authority over a group, all or most members of a heterarchical group share leadership skills and the leadership role shifts according to which specialist has the relevant knowledge for addressing the task at hand. Leadership thus results not from position or even from personality, but rather from the relevance of individuals' capabilities and contributions to the task.

Leading the transition

Most of the leadership task today, however, is not about leading collaborative organizations, but rather about leading the *transition* from bureaucratic systems. The conflicting motivations and visions involved in this shift can lead to extraordinary leadership challenges. In this volume, Adler describes an instance of a collaborative software team that rejected a bureaucratic boss (Chapter 5); and Heckscher and Foote (Chapter 12) detail several instances of intense emotional confrontations between top teams and task forces charged with reporting on the state of the organization. It is notable in these latter cases that the Strategic Fitness Process they describe goes to great lengths to develop the peer transference within the task force—and to raise its intensity above the deference to leaders. Thus when, in early efforts, the task force reported directly to their leaders they tended to soften and distort honest criticisms; when they instead were asked to speak to each other in a 'fishbowl,' with top management listening on the outside, they were able to focus much more consistently on assessing contributions to the collective purpose.

The dangers of this transition are keenly felt by leaders and would also be familiar to psychologists. While rivalry among siblings for the parents' attention usually stabilizes a group, it can when destabilized swing to an opposite dynamic of peer bonding to attack the father—the subject of some of humankind's oldest myths. In the ancient Greek account, two successive fathers at the dawn of time—Uranus and Chronos—were killed by their children in particularly grisly ways. Echoes of this primal fear are heard whenever top managers consider opening up dialogue with their subordinates, particularly when the latter can talk to each other and band together as well as communicating upward to the boss. Most leaders of the Strategic Fitness Process admit that 'it's scary,' and the same words are sounded in other instances, such as the IBM values discussion process mentioned above. Indeed, these processes often do trigger at least mini-revolutions, moments that 'go too far,' in which subordinates express intense emotions of betrayal and anger against their leaders, before they can settle into more 'rational' debates about future directions. In our experience, no leader has in fact suffered in the long run from an open attitude to employee criticism. In a number of cases, by responding with a bit of courage, the leader has stimulated trust.

Apart from the exaggerated danger of primal upheaval, the transition towards collaboration faces more prosaic sources of resistance. A crucial one is traditional motivational patterns grounded in personality—both bureaucratic personalities and professional specialists with a pre-bureaucratic craft social character who resist organizations that rob them of the autonomy and the status they seek. These attitudes pose a particularly difficult challenge to leaders of professional specialist organizations like academic health centers and legal partnerships where it is not so easy to replace resistant actors.

Given these dangers and resistances, transformational leadership often takes the dramatic form described by Weber as 'charismatic,' focusing on the reformulation of shared values. In psychoanalytic terms, such leaders tend to be narcissists of the productive type.[5] This type is driven, not just to succeed, but to change the world according to their vision. The most successful are able to engage others in their visions and to partner with the operational executors. These are usually productive obsessives who develop the processes that institutionalize the new system.

However, all transitional leaders are not narcissists. Some are productive personalities who represent the prototypical interactive social character at its best. Like the e-Citi leadership, they show a radar-like sensitivity to changing customer needs and are able to engage like-minded colleagues in the campaign to create value with new business process. Once the vision-aries have created new models of collaboration, it becomes easier for the marketing-interactive personalities to copy a successful prototype.

However, to be effective for the collaborative transition, transformational leaders must be responsive to both the bureaucratic and the interactive social character. This means that they must show understanding for the traditional symbols of authoritarian protection and security, and *at the same time* reinterpret shared values in terms of collective purpose. Steering too close to either one of these poles is a recipe for failure. On one side, leaders who focus too heavily on presenting a systematic and compelling strategic vision will not find followers among those with a bureaucratic orientation, who are unused to grappling with that point of view and have never been motivated by it; they view the market not as a purpose or opportunity, but as a threat to their ability to do the job 'right.' The top of the organization has traditionally found its satisfaction in creating visions, but the rest have been asked to be conscientious, autonomous craft workers in defined spheres; they are less moved by dramatic and coherent strategies. Many efforts have run aground on this reef of misunderstanding.

On the other side, the danger is in failing sufficiently to challenge bureaucratic and craft expectations. Many chief executives, in dealing with their employees, have tried to soft-pedal the magnitude of the changes they face; the result is that the traditional types have continued to hold to the hope that if they just put their heads down and survive till the crisis passes, everything will return to the good old days. This leads to even greater isolation and game playing than in the old paternalist com-munity, which at least created some sense of common destiny.

Steering between this Scylla and Charybdis is difficult at best, and perhaps never fully successful. In all these change processes there seems to be at least a minority of people who never adjust to the new values and who have to leave the community. Furthermore, the transformational leaders are often damaged in the process—viewed by the old guard as destructive, or by the new as insufficiently decisive, or both—and like Moses are unable to finish the journey to the new land.

How can leaders deal with the resistance of loyalists, with their motivational patterns of obsessive experts and craftsmen? Perhaps the most effective transformative leaders are those who live in both worlds—who have earned their spurs in the traditional system but are capable of articulating the systematic vision and purpose that appeals to the interactive type. Since such people are rare, however, another route may be to create a sequence that combines the two types. The recent history of IBM is instructive. John Akers, the first CEO to try to transform the traditional culture, failed almost completely to rally employees behind the need for serious change. His successor, Lou Gerstner, took the reins just as the company was going into an abrupt death spiral; with this crisis he was able to break the old culture and put forward new strategies of network computing and integrated services. But while new employees were excited by these concepts, most of the old ones did not grasp them and continued to hope for the return of the old order. Sam Palmisano, following Gerstner, is an IBM old-timer who thoroughly understands the traditional culture and is trusted by those who believe in it, while also being a powerful and persuasive advocate of a new business vision which he has developed further. He is seeking to knit the old and new together through a process of open discussion of values throughout the company.

At times the old guard can be won over by an appeal to their own values: a demonstration that a collaborative approach results in higher quality and more craftsmanlike outcomes. The software coders described by Adler in Chapter 5 went through this transition: the formal process maps they had to follow at first seemed like an intrusion on their autonomy and ability to do their jobs, but later were seen by these same people as producing better coding and helping them to perform more effectively. Similarly, Bill Nelson, CEO of Intermountain Health Care, successfully persuaded physician, nursing, and administrative leaders to work with informatics experts to develop and test best medical practice. Most medical facilities, including this one, run into fierce resistance from doctors at any effort to cut into their autonomy; but Intermountain was able to appeal to them on their own terms, those of better patient care. Thus when Maccoby interviewed professionals at one of Intermountain's hospitals in Salt Lake City, the head nurse in the operating room (OR) said that before shared processes had been established, each of the fifteen surgeons who used the OR presented nurses with a different process. This inevitably resulted in errors affecting patients and increasing costs.

It is also vital to keep the common purpose—the strategy, the market demands, the views of constituents—in the foreground at all times, so that it becomes a common point of reference for all the players. The demands of the outside world must be used not as a club to justify increased pressure and threats to security, but rather as a focus of learning and discussion. In this way the majority even of bureaucratic-crafts types can engage over time with the excitement of building a shared enterprise.

This push towards purpose goes beyond the usual conception of 'facilitative' leadership or the creation of dialogue. One major strand of literature about good leadership practice has focused almost exclusively on facilitation or 'openness' as the catalyst for change. However, facilitation alone does not move bureaucratic or craft-oriented experts to develop a collaborative community. We have seen a number of facilitated expert meetings end in compromises where each actor gets something she wants, but there is no movement to a common view of strategy or direction. Leadership that moves experts with a craft or bureaucratic social character toward collaborative community needs to facilitate learning as well as dialogue. The purpose—establishing best practice processes or solving a customer's problem—must be made clear and the leadership role should be fully legitimized by team members. This may include the authority to cut off actors who obsessively repeat themselves and challenge those who insist on a position without supporting evidence. Effective leaders have found that with this approach and data that supports change, they can effectively appeal to the pride of experts in excellence and engage them in change.

Given these leadership tensions, the fact remains that almost all organizations moving toward collaborative community have great difficulty in overcoming patterns of bureaucratic deference and control. Leaders need to act not purely as transformational visionaries, operational executors, bridge builders, and team organizers, they must also act to satisfy continuing needs for authoritative protection and direction. Ideally, leaders in these roles can encourage the move toward community, including the empowerment of teams that share their purpose, while showing their understanding of the motivations of those whose orientation throughout their lives has been towards protective parental figures.

References

Maccoby, Michael (2000). 'Narcissistic leaders: the incredible pros, the inevitable cons.' *Harvard Business Review* (Jan.–Feb.): 69–77.

—— (2003). *The Productive Narcissist: The Promise and Peril of Visionary, Leadership.* New York: Broadway Books.

—— (2004). 'Why people follow the leader: the power of transference.' *Harvard Business Review* (Sept.): 76–85.

Merton, Robert K. (1940). 'Bureaucratic structure and personality.' *Social Forces*, 17: 560–8. Reprinted in Clyde Kluckhohn and Henry A. Murray (eds.), *Personality in Nature, Society and Culture.* New York: Knopf, 1961: 376–86.

Palmisano, Samuel J., Hemp, Paul, and Stewart, Thomas A. (2004). 'Leading change when business is good: the HBR interview—Samuel J. Palmisano.' *Harvard Business Review* (1 Dec.): 60–70.

Piaget, Jean (1932/1965). *The Moral Judgment of the Child.* New York: The Free Press. Original edn. *Le Jugement moral chez l'enfant.* Neuchâtel: ed. Delachaux & Niestlé, 1932.

Notes

1. Merton (1940). See also the discussion above in Chapter 3.
2. Maccoby (2004).
3. Piaget (1932/1965: 151).
4. See Palmisano et al. (2004).
5. On productive narcissists, see Maccoby (2000, 2003).

12

The Strategic Fitness Process and the Creation of Collaborative Community

Charles Heckscher and Nathaniel Foote

Introduction

If, as this volume has argued, collaborative community is necessary as a foundation for knowledge-based organizations, there remains the question of how to get there—whether and how existing bureaucratic systems can be *transformed* in this direction. It is an important problem because efforts to build participation and involvement in corporations have often, perhaps usually, ended in failure. In the last thirty years the range of 'programs' designed to increase communication and teamwork has been dizzying, and in many companies has resulted in nothing more than heightened cynicism.

The transition involves apparent magic. We have seen that the performance of complex tasks requires a great deal of trust: in order to combine different capabilities in a constantly changing competitive environment, people need to act in the expectation that others will respond in effective and productive ways. All organizations are in effect held together by such webs of mutual expectations. When those webs begin to tear—when, for example, companies begin to act in ways that violate what employees expect, through layoffs and new performance demands—the overall level of trust declines and people withdraw into self-protective individualism.

The problem is that in order to regenerate trust in a new form, people somehow need to understand and put their faith in an untried, complex system before it actually exists, and to act with each other *as if* it existed—as if others will know how to respond appropriately, and as if those who fulfill the new norms will be rewarded. In the 'before' state of bureaucratic culture, the core expectation was that employees would do their jobs and please their superiors, and that, if they did that, the organization would function well and they would be rewarded. But in the 'after' state, employees are expected to act on different principles—to do more than their jobs, to jump across levels and organizational boundaries, to take initiative, to challenge superiors. Yet there is at first no solid reason to believe that if they do so the organization will work better or they will be rewarded. If they play it safe and do what experience shows to be successful, a vicious circle will result in which everyone reinforces everyone else's 'old' behavior. To break out of this circle appears to require a collective leap of faith.

The 'Strategic Fitness Process' (hereafter 'SFP') developed by the Center for Organizational Fitness attempts to perform this magic by involving participants at all levels in 'conversations that matter,'[1] thus increasing the capacity for cross-boundary dialogues that link all levels to unifying strategies and purposes. Though its advocates have not used the language of 'collaborative community,' the affinities are striking. SFP first of all seeks to break down traditional barriers around jobs and individuals and to create a norm of contribution to a common cause. To this end it seeks to reduce the obstacles of suspicion and fear resulting from the hierarchy of power, and to create an openness in which knowledge trumps power. In short, though it does not use this language, it seeks to create a transition from bureaucratic to collaborative norms.[2]

A close examination of SFP interventions can therefore bring out evidence about the dynamics of transformation: the nature of the resistances to collaboration, the ways in which people react when put into a situation of open dialogue, some of the 'tricks' that make the switch possible—and, perhaps, a way of sorting out surface obstacles from possible deeper problems that could block the transition altogether.

One of the advantages of focusing on this process is that there is an unusual amount of data. The Center for Organizational Fitness has arranged with independent case writers to document many of the efforts, capturing the evolution and dynamics of each story; several of these descriptions have been made public. For this chapter we have reviewed detailed material, public and private, on sixteen SFP interventions. In addition, we have conducted new research on Veridian, described in more detail in Appendix 12.1.[3]

Challenges in the transition to collaborative community

The difficulty of changing bureaucracies

In the last few decades many companies have tried to modify their bureaucratic cultures, primarily through restructuring and culture change efforts. These moves have in the main shown how difficult the task is. Instead of breaking through to a new level of capability, bureaucracies have often turned, under such stress, into distorted and defensive forms. This is why numerous studies have shown that the massive changes of the late 1980s and 1990s largely failed to produce sustained performance improvements.[4]

Traditional bureaucracies, as we described in Chapter 1, pp. 33–4, depended heavily on a form of collaboration which became known as the 'informal organization.' This worked primarily through exchanges of favors—networks helping each other to get their jobs done. That type of negotiation creates enough flexibility to deal with everyday fluctuations and unexpected events of corporate life in relatively stable industries. But it is limited: the cooperative links, though widespread, are not well organized, they are not 'managed' by the organization as a whole, and they are not oriented to shared strategic objectives.

As a result, when traditional organizations face fundamental strategic challenges, this network of cooperation breaks down in recognizable ways. Most visibly, when informal networks are disrupted by reorganizations and downsizings, people no longer know whom to go to when they have a problem. Since the bureaucratic community is built around specific jobs rather than around shared purposes and vision, major strategic shifts leave everyone feeling confused and powerless: their job descriptions no longer fit the situation, and they have no other point of reference. Employees at all levels retreat to the safety of their defined jobs, put their heads down, and hope they can survive the turmoil around them. Thus the restructurings of the 1980s and 1990s often not only failed to move towards more flexibility and internal cooperation, but actually increased bureaucratic rigidity.[5]

REQUIREMENTS FOR CHANGE AND THE NATURE OF RESISTANCE

The analysis in this volume (especially Chapter 1) suggests some requirements for the creation of collaborative community. The focus on shared purpose, in the sense we have used it, is unfamiliar in a classic bureaucratic environment.[6] In the organizational view developed by Sloan and carried through to the 1980s in almost all organizations, such strategic issues were the concern only of the topmost layers, and it was indeed viewed as dangerous to share them more widely for fear of compromising company secrets. In virtually every one of the SFP cases, education about strategy at lower levels of the organization, and open discussion of its meaning, has been a vital piece of the process and often unfamiliar.

In order for the purpose to stabilize as a common point of orientation, to draw all parties into a shared focus, moreover, some of the core patterns of bureaucratic organization must be *undone*. The bureaucratic organization has coalesced over time as a system of mutual and interdependent norms or patterns of expectation. In the move towards collaboration, these bureaucratic norms become sources of resistance to change:

1. *The norm of deference.* One key value of bureaucracy which enables it to remain unified is deference: employees lower in the hierarchy are supposed to give way to their superiors and not to challenge their authority. This expectation is built deeply into everyday interactions in all traditional firms that we know of.[7] It is mixed, of course, with a strong tendency to criticize bosses privately—sometimes to peers, sometimes only to oneself; but *public* challenge and criticism has always been a 'career-killer.' The other side of the norm is that bosses are supposed to care for and protect 'their people.' In terms of whether deference is a *good* thing or not—in other words, whether it is a shared value as well as a pragmatic expectation—there is much more ambivalence: most people have traditionally believed on the one hand that the stability of the hierarchy is a good thing and should not be undermined, while at the same time—reflecting the tensions in the modern ethic—they have trumpeted their own independence and the value of rugged individualism against any and all hierarchy.

   The norm of deference is particularly powerful around purpose: bosses may sometimes be willing to be criticized for their operational style, but rarely to be challenged on the strategic direction; and subordinates are rarely willing to push.

2. *The norm of autonomy.* On the 'horizontal' dimension, bureaucracy depends on a norm of autonomy: each player is supposed to be left alone within a defined sphere, and with dedicated resources, to do a defined job. Thus the expectation is that peers will not invade each other's 'turf' or challenge their competence and expertise within their own areas—the core of the bureaucratic notion of 'respect.' In com-

bination with the norm of deference this creates a very strong norm of not 'ratting out' peers to the boss—shutting off all open discussion of performance issues.

Autonomy is often reinforced by the development of local subcultures—engineers vs. marketers, operational managers vs. human resources—in which each group reinforces its particular view of right and wrong and denigrates others. This makes the crossing of barriers even harder and can deeply distort open discussion: each group may act respectful in the public forum but maintain its private belief that others are not worthy of respect.

These two very powerful norms are barriers to open discussion and sharing of knowledge across boundaries. While people remain focused on their own jobs and willing to leave strategic issues to those above them, they will remain closely bound to their 'local' points of view and interests. It thus becomes extremely difficult to overcome disagreements and find common ground during a process of change.

When organizations restructure and downsize, moreover, these two norms typically emerge even more strongly as obstacles to trust. For all the talk of openness and teamwork, there is a strong tendency for employees to defer ever more to their bosses from fear of becoming the next victims of seemingly uncontrollable forces, and to avoid cooperative entanglements with peers who may be gone tomorrow and who are in any case in an increasingly bitter fight for position in an unstable world. This is why companies under pressure may become parodies of bureaucracy, with 'games'—the distorted variety of normal organizational politics—moving to the forefront: empire building, self-protection, pandering to the boss, secret undermining of peers, and avoidance of conflict.[8]

The final obstacle which emerges from the analysis of collaborative community is at a different level:

3. *Bureaucratic character and motivation.* Even in organizations where patterns of deference and autonomy have broken down—where it is widely seen as right, in the interests of the whole, to challenge authority and to get involved in issues outside one's own formal sphere of authority—there are people who seem to have a hard time adapting. In our experience of many attempts to create participatory programs and groups it is very common to hear that 20 per cent of the people can't 'get it.'

This seems to be more than a matter of changing the social environment: it involves patterns rooted in the dynamics of individual personality. This means that even when the organizational norms and expectations have clearly changed—when the leader signals clear expectations, and sanctions, both formal and informal, back them up—certain people continue to resist.

The difficulty centers on the acceptance of ambiguity and conflict. The bureaucratic organization is designed for the minimization of conflict: problems are escalated to the next level of authority, and priorities are clearly established and ranked. Robert Merton's famous 1940 analysis of the 'bureaucratic personality,' focused on mastery within a defined job sphere, fits well with this environment. In the more fluid collaborative community, by contrast—lacking the clear guidelines provided by the principles of deference and autonomy—individuals are constantly faced with dilemmas between competing priorities, and by a need to negotiate with peers who have differing perspectives on how to solve a problem. Earlier in this volume Maccoby argues that this requires a new motivational structure which he calls the 'interactive personality,' grounded in early childhood experiences and socialization. The bureaucratic character develops in families with a single strong center of control, and is therefore profoundly uncomfortable with ambiguous power and conflicting role expectations; interactive character, emerging from more fluid family structures, is less threatened by such uncertainties. The selection process for top corporate leaders, which tends to reward decisiveness and the appearance of strength, may weed out interactive types with particular effectiveness.

The limitations of classic interventions

Corporate leaders have generally tried to transform bureaucracy by using the levers of the bureaucratic system itself: that is, they try to use their power and status to require changes in roles and behaviors down the line. The majority of these efforts can be grouped into two categories—though in many cases both are under way at once:

1. Many organizations have tried top-down redefinitions of values spread through the organization by 'cascading': the top team goes offsite to redefine the company's core values, then runs workshops on the new values for their direct reports, who do the same for their reports, and so on down the line.

2. On the other hand, many companies have tried breaking the organization into small independent pieces in the hope of generating wide-

spread experimentation and gaining the benefits of small-group trust and cooperation.

The top-down 'cascade' has been well documented in the case of Xerox, which ran a very elaborate process of this type in the 1980s.[9] Xerox tried to make moves that rhetorically match in almost every respect the shift we have described—towards a more open, collaborative, cross-functional, customer-focused, flexible organization. The values definition process tried to make these values common currency in the organization through a particularly systematic process of cascading training. It became clear in the subsequent decade, however, that this effort had not penetrated far. Very much like IBM at that stage, Xerox was unable to implement the customer-focused values, remaining bound to its traditional high-margin proprietary-technology model of strategy; it remained internally focused, with only a fuzzy view of the competition even at the top levels;[10] it failed to build effective bridges among units or to find ways to utilize new technologies and ideas; as its business collapsed, an outsider CEO was fired and a longtime insider returned to leadership. That this is not an unusual type of failure has been documented by Mike Beer and colleagues in extensive studies of corporate change processes.[11]

The decentralization approach seems like an attractive alternative, as a way to break through excessive control and to encourage greater initiative; but it regularly runs aground because of a lack of overall coordination. Lucent and ABB are textbook cases of this difficulty in the past decade, though there are many other candidates. At Lucent, the CEO broke the organization into eleven highly autonomous divisions; at ABB it was 2,000. In both cases innovation appeared initially to increase, but deep problems quickly emerged: divisions developed innovative ideas that did not mesh with each other; they were unable to draw effectively on resources of other divisions; they confused customers with overlapping and poorly integrated offerings; they duplicated resources. Both have sought to increase coordination across divisional lines, with at best modest success. The fundamental problem of creating a collaborative system has been made, if anything, more difficult by the increase in autonomy.

Interactive intervention theory: testing the limits

Such experiences suggest that the move to collaborative culture cannot be 'managed' through top-down programs and initiatives, but must in some way involve more radical shifts in relationships. This reflection has led to a range of approaches which may be called 'interactive,' though there is as yet no widely accepted theory. Interactive interventions are not linear but iterative: whatever the starting point, and whatever leaders think they are doing initially, there are provisions for reviewing and modifying even the most basic principles through a process of open discussion with diverse interests and stakeholders; those lower in the organization are treated not as a source of data, but as active participants and contributors in defining and resolving the organization's concerns.[12]

This represents a far more fundamental break with the logic of bureaucracy: it does not treat those who are 'higher' as necessarily 'better,' and it requires people to argue through differences, to engage in integrative discussions, rather than withdrawing into zones of autonomy. The difference between the bureaucratic and interactive approach is further linked to fundamental views of the learning process. Chris Argyris (e.g. 1990) famously distinguished 'single-loop' from 'double-loop' learning: the former goes in a straight line from identifying errors to taking action to solve them; the latter 'loops' back to basic principles and governing values before deciding on what to do. The interactive approach usually involves this kind of discussion of the systemic basis for errors, which therefore draws a wide range of actors into open discussion. Similarly, classical cognitive theory has developed elaborate linear approaches to dealing with problems by breaking them down into 'chunks' or 'nearly decomposable' parts; but many have pointed out that such an approach cannot achieve breakthrough learnings that re-examine fundamental assumptions or processes.[13] In this volume, Sabel (Chapter 2) develops the contrasting 'holistic' tradition that breaks with the linear view and seeks a continued questioning of basic principles.

The interactive approach, however, is not without challengers itself. A fundamental criticism of all such efforts has been that they cannot overcome fundamental differences in interests, and therefore are likely if they work at all only to cover over and hide such differences. Reviewing actual experiences, Heckscher et al. (2003) found that many disputes in highly competitive markets cannot lastingly be resolved through discourse.

The Strategic Fitness Process

Four essential characteristics of the SFP approach should be underlined at the start. First, it focuses on the creation of discourse—the core element of collaborative community—by taking people from different areas and levels of the organization and creating a context that encourages open dialogue. Second, it structures this discourse around the collective purpose—the organization's strategy; there is a discipline around bringing the participants into a shared focus on the question of how best to achieve the organization's goals. Third, it leverages existing hierarchy by reinforcing the integrating role of the general manager and the senior team in leading the conversation around the collective purpose and then in shaping an organizational context which is aligned to support achievement of that purpose. Fourth, it embeds the principles of 'advocacy and enquiry'—in effect what Sabel (Chapter 2) calls 'iterative search'—into the structure of the interactions between the leadership and the rest of the organization, as a way of increasing the capacity to productively resolve the conflicts that more open communication inevitably surfaces.

The attempt to create open forums is not in itself unique (though it remains unusual): a number of companies have developed processes of one kind or another in which employees are encouraged to speak freely to their superiors, or to work as teams to develop ideas and proposals that skip the usual lines of authority. But SFP creates a context for the dialogue that is particularly systematic in overcoming the resistances and fears that are usually encountered in such groups, and that creates a powerful mandate for leadership actions to address the issues that are surfaced.

The essential steps in SFP are:

1. The top team gathers to develop a clear definition of the company's strategic mission—its competitive challenges and key initiatives by which it hopes to meet them.

2. A task force of influential middle managers is appointed—the main criterion being that they be credible both to the top team and to their peers throughout the organization. They conduct a set of interviews in all areas around a simple question: 'What are the strengths to build on and the barriers to address in implementing this strategy?' To enhance objectivity, task force members interview outside their area of responsibility.

3. This task force reports to top management. But they do not stand at the front of a room with a Powerpoint presentation—rather, they use a 'fishbowl': they sit in a circle, with top management observing from outside the circle, and discuss *with each other* the issues they have

identified. This then evolves into a back-and-forth in which the top team tries to fully understand the views distilled from the interviews.

4. The top team retreats to make modifications in its strategic vision and to develop a plan for change, based on their analysis of the strengths and barriers identified by the task force.

5. The top team presents the revised plan to the task force members, who (after some time for consideration) respond as to whether the modifications and the change process have effectively addressed the issues they identified. Frequently the answer is 'no'—which triggers another back-and-forth between top management and the task team about the source of the misunderstandings and what should be done about them.

6. The senior team continues to meet with the task force during the year to get feedback about their perception of progress.

7. The entire process is repeated on a regular basis—normally every year—as a critical link in the annual planning cycle between strategy and operational planning.

The dynamics of change in the Strategic Fitness Process

SFP has achieved some remarkable transformations. The best-documented one is the Hewlett-Packard Santa Rosa Systems Division, detailed in a Harvard Business School case (Beer and Rogers 1997). There, the move towards more complex customer relations led to internal tension and resistance. When these issues were raised through the Strategic Fitness Process, the top leaders at first reacted with denial, until at a crucial moment one of the top group accepted responsibility for contributing to the problems; this opened the way for much more open criticism and significant organizational change. Similar breakthroughs are documented in other accounts of the process.[14] But there are also many stories that are more mixed, and even a few that largely failed to penetrate the organization culture; these can be as instructive as the successes.

(Here we offer the reader a choice. Some may prefer now to get a concrete picture of a particular intervention; they should review Appendix 12.1, containing a case description of an intervention at Veridian Corporation, a technology-rich defense and national security contractor, seeking to leverage its capabilities more fully across its entire business. The analysis that follows refers at times to the case but does not depend on it.)

If we look at successful SFP interventions as a whole we can see a pattern of movement among three types of conversation.

- The starting point is the discussion of the shared sense of purpose;
- this raises debates around values and commitments;
- these are in turn worked through into detailed processes and role expectations.

Since these types of discussion are interdependent, each move on one of these dimensions requires review and development on the others to maintain alignment. In the best cases a virtuous circle is set up, in which each step in one area—of purpose, values, or processes—forces further progress on the others.

The dialogue about shared purpose is the starting point for SFP. First, the top team is asked to come up with a statement of strategic direction; this may surface conflicts and disagreements among the top team. Then the circle is widened through the task force interviews, which ask people at all levels to reflect on this direction. This consistent focus on purpose—or, in corporate terms, strategy—is distinctive to this method of intervention, contrasting with more common change efforts that focus on other dimensions—on 'human resource' or quality-of-life issues, or on corporate values, or on implementation (how to do the work better).[15] The experience has been that this focus on strategy works better than the others. A focus on values may generate energy but remain disconnected from 'real' work; a focus on implementation is more tied in to the daily work of the enterprise, but it allows the top leadership's definition of *what* should be implemented to remain unchallenged, thus shutting off many avenues of exploration and understanding and reinforcing the existing hierarchy.

The achievement of basic consensus understanding on the collective strategy seems to be an inescapable condition for progress beyond the initial steps. In a few instances the process has been unable to move past this stage, because people have not been convinced of the value of a unified strategy. At one company, the feedback from the task force put into question the top management's logic for synergies across the major businesses; the interviewees saw significant costs to trying to run as an integrated corporation. The net effect was that the senior management team decided to split up the company. They stopped the three-day meeting on day 2, and instead of following through with the task force called in their investment bankers.

More often, however, there is a growing agreement on the need for unity. Frequently the initial discussions have a powerful educational effect, shifting people from the usual focus on their own jobs to a focus on how to get the *collective* task done. At Veridian a conventional strategic planning process held before the beginning of SFP had highlighted the need to broaden the kind of work the company pursued, but failed to produce clarity and consensus among the top team on the relative priority and pacing of the change—some still felt that the traditional strategy of smaller projects, executed primarily within existing divisional boundaries, was working well. The initial SFP interview process, by contrast, helped build a consensus on the need for a wider collaborative unity: by getting people to think through the whole picture, the reasons for collaboration may become clear. As one task force member put it: 'When you really got people to think and talk through and walk through what our future looked like, there was no way we could be successful as [a set of] small companies.'

The urgency of moving towards the shared purpose raises and provides the motivation for a second type of conversation: the examination of values and mindsets—whether everyone has the same basic idea of what the organization *should* look like and how they should behave in it. Thus the participants spend time talking explicitly about the need for collaboration, debating the proper role of leadership, and defining the obligations of members towards each other and towards the organization. These value discussions help to pull everyone together, with a sense that they are moving in the same direction—a shared sense that is essential to the 'leap of faith' required in the creation of a new system. At Veridian, as in other cases, the value of 'collaboration' began to be generally accepted as defining how people should act—for example, that they should not duplicate capabilities found in other parts of the organization in order to keep full control of a contract. People became more concerned not to be seen as having put their own unit's interests ahead of those of the company as a whole; this provided the motivation for working through the difficult task of shifting focus from particular interests to collective goals.

Even more time is spent in a third kind of discussion, that of specific structures, processes, and behaviors to make the values work. Veridian set up, as discussed above, cross-functional teams for business development and initiated open discussions of resources among division leaders. In one of the most dramatically successful cases—the Agilent division described in a *Harvard Business Review* article—the leadership team initiated a move away from a functional, geographically decentralized structure and revamped the rules of interaction within their own team.[16]

But this description of the change process as a simple positive loop leaves out the main difficulty, which is that all these discussions are happening in the midst of a set of interlocked expectations, norms, and values that are based on the *old* bureaucratic pattern of behavior. Thus the process is not merely one of gradual discovery and enlightenment; the discovery happens in the context of overcoming and dismantling accepted ways of thinking, ones locked in place by years of habits and mutual accommodations. This brings us back to the three core aspects of the bureaucratic community described above—the norm of deference, the norm of autonomy, and the bureaucratic character—in order to consider how they can hamper progress and how they can be overcome.

TRANSCENDING NORMS OF DEFERENCE

A highly visible problem in most interactive interventions is that those lower in the hierarchy are unwilling to speak honestly to their superiors—and the superiors are unwilling to hear even the partial truths that are surfaced. If there is one distinctive, possibly unique strength of SFP—something it can do that other processes of change cannot—it is that it reliably breaks this norm of deference on the part of the lower-level employees on the task force. The feedback session with their managers is almost always remarkably honest and unvarnished, often including criticisms of top leaders by name. Even after the top team has formulated an action plan in response, the task force in numerous instances has continued its criticism and rejected the proposals as missing the point: in the Agilent SGDU case, for instance, the leaders were accused of failing to take on powerful resisters within their own ranks that needed to be challenged in order for the organization to proceed together. This is absolutely remarkable in traditional corporate settings, where openly disagreeing with the bosses is almost always seen as 'career limiting,' and challenges of this sort are a kind of *lèse-majesté* that threaten the legitimacy and security of the whole system.

The process accomplishes this through two very important tools. First, the task force is asked not to present its members' own views as direct stakeholders, but to do real research through interviews in a different part of the company and to present the objective results of that research. Second, they develop a very strong group identity—not as a channel for complaints, but as a mechanism for helping the organization to achieve its goals. This identity is strengthened through initial training and through their discussions during the interview process; it is cemented as they prepare to present to the top team. When they make the actual presentation, they talk to each other rather than directly to their bosses, reinforcing the norms of direct discussion rather than deferential reporting.

The emotional currents during this phase are very strong. The task force members are well aware they are exposing hitherto undiscussible issues. Equally, the challenge of understanding and taking part in the hitherto sacrosanct domain of strategic purpose raises considerable excitement and anxiety: excitement at being allowed into a formerly hidden preserve, and anxiety about whether top management will punish the sacrilege. At that point there is always a great deal of nervousness and joking around themes of suicide. There may also be half-conscious concern that the top management will be revealed as not knowing what they're doing, which is a frightening possibility to those used to depending on their direction.

What gives the task force the strength to overcome all this and to break their own habits is the sense that they are making a difference to a larger purpose that they care about. Through this process, they become in effect the first and strongest representatives of an ethic of contribution: the structure of discussion turns them into representatives not of particular interests or opinions, but of the problem of achieving the collective purpose. They bring objective data about to what extent the strategy is being accomplished and what major obstacles impede it. Their moral authority in relation to the top team comes not from a paternalistic sense that subordinates should be taken care of, but from a collaborative sense that only by pulling together can the organization accomplish its goals. This positioning allows the task force to be *legitimately* tough and critical with their bosses.[17]

The expectation of deference, however, has two sides, and the top team does not as reliably make a change on its side. The senior leaders are almost always shocked initially by the openness of the task force's criticism, which goes far beyond the traditional limits; when they meet after the task force feedback there is usually a highly emotional period swinging between hurt and rage. Normally they then try to 'get control of the situation' again by formulating an authoritative action plan (and perhaps telling themselves that this was what they had planned all along); they are then often shocked a second time when the task force tells them they have failed to address key points.

In a number of cases, this exchange has led to a kind of standoff: the top team maintains the view that they are in control and that the task force is merely bringing useful information to them to consider. In these instances, they do not see the need for any significant shift in their role as leaders. The SFP experience is, in effect, assimilated to the old expectations. The leaders see it as a good way to open up communication and to identify blocks to implementation of their strategy, to improve the relation between bosses and subordinates so that they can each play their roles better—but not to build a collaborative culture. Thus, one CEO who has made extensive use of SFP says to this day that his experience in the military taught him that leaders decide, and that he finds the fishbowl feedback useful as input so he can make decisions. In that organization, managers in general have failed to keep the task force involved as partners in the change process; and when this was pointed out to the CEO, he snorted, 'What partnership?' The consultants believe that this attitude has meant that the organization has gotten only partial value from the experience.

In such cases, the task force may become deeply frustrated and alienated: they themselves have made the switch to a mindset in which the value of a behavior is judged by its contribution to the shared purpose, but they find that their bosses continue to evaluate behaviors by the position of the actors. In one such instance, six of the nine task force members had left the organization within fifteen months of the SFP.

There are, however, some cases where the top does go through its own conversion experience that complements that of the task force: they begin to accept more clearly that their actions are legitimate only to the extent that they help the organization function well, and that the comments of their subordinates can contribute just as much as their own. The crucible of the meeting with the task force, where they are presented with objective data by respected employees who talk to them as equals, can sometimes create a sense that they need not just to gather information from below, but to *convince* the task force that their decisions are right and bring the subordinates along in a shared effort. And that realization can be very humbling. It is even possible for a moment to arrive at which the question is put: Is this leader capable of leading this organization forward in its next stage? And at that point he or she may offer to resign. Indeed, in three of the most successful SFP cases, leaders have taken this remarkable step, in effect saying that if they could not bring the organization along, could not persuade the task force that their view of how to proceed was right, that they could no longer lead. In each case, this unblocked a very open conversation about the leadership requirements of the organization, and ultimately, in each case, also led to a significant strengthening of the position of the leader.

But this initial conversion is still incomplete, because the problem then is to fill in the emerging values with substance: Just how is the top team supposed to lead in a collaborative order? When leaders try to embody values of involvement and collaboration, they may feel they have to go to the other pole and back off entirely from the use of authority.[18] The task force members, too, may feel contrary pulls—on the one hand a desire for decisive action, on the other a sense that any intervention from above violates the expectations of participation. Thus Veridian interviewees were still conducting a debate, at times with themselves, about whether the top leadership was too controlling or too lax—or both.

The leadership role in a collaborative process is something *new*, and no one knows what to expect; everyone tends to assimilate back to old patterns. SFP provides a context in which a new set of expectations is gradually established and worked through: *not* that the top team will withdraw or allow pure 'democracy,' but that it will take decisions to address the issues raised by the organization through the vehicle of the task force. Thus SFP explicitly seeks to create both a mandate for and an expectation of significant management decision making. It does not remove management power but legitimizes and mobilizes it in a different way. The entire idea of strategy and purpose, in effect, shifts from that of 'grand vision' to one of 'grand vision *that can be implemented*'—that is, the leader's view of the future is not legitimate unless those who have to carry it out understand it and believe that it makes sense in terms of their own areas of knowledge.

The meeting with the task force, connecting 'operational' and 'strategic' functions in a single dialogue, creates a forum for discussing questions like: Do we have the organizational capabilities to execute the strategic vision? What are the actual practical consequences for the organization? Do we recognize and embrace those consequences, or do they make us want to rethink the strategy? At that point, the conversation has been transformed from one of passing information up and down the chain to a collaborative one. The members of the task force *know* things that their leaders do not know, and vice versa; when the multiple types of knowledge come together, the problem of strategy is redefined.

This pattern of leadership and authority has not been fully worked out in any SFP case, and there are always continuing areas of debate about the nature of the top team role. In a broad sense the pattern of expectations— the notion of interactive leadership—has not yet crystallized conceptually, so it is still a subject of experimentation. But a number of the SFP cases have moved far enough to see the outlines of a collaborative notion of authority.

TRANSCENDING NORMS OF AUTONOMY

A second type of problem faced in Strategic Fitness Processes is the traditional expectation that each part of the organization will have its own zone of control, managing its own resources, and that peers should not interfere with each other in their own domains. Bureaucracies inevitably end up carved into distinct 'fiefdoms,' with strong internal cultures. Most of the companies involved in SFP—like most in the economy as a whole—have sought to change this: to create greater cross-unit coordination in order to achieve more flexibility and better allocation of resources.

SFP seeks to address this issue by reinforcing the integrating role of the senior team, and by ensuring that the task force brings a holistic perspective. Task force members are selected to represent a broad cross-section of the key areas across the company, are intentionally assigned to interview in areas outside of their normal responsibility, and then need to work together as a single team to craft a representative picture of all they have learned from their interviews. At the same time, many of the most important mechanisms for improving horizontal teamwork are expected to emerge as a consequence of the initial strategic dialogue: as people become aware of the *need* for collaboration they will focus their action plan on removing the barriers and developing the mechanisms to make it happen—cross-unit task forces, training, and so on.

The Veridian case shows how difficult this can be. Before the Strategic Fitness Process, the company was performing very strongly, and central ingredients of its success were clear divisional accountability for performance and full control of the dedicated resources required to deliver the results. To take the company to the next level, however, the leadership saw the need to expand to new types of work that would require greater cross-divisional collaboration. In particular, the CEO, two division managers, and the head of strategy were very clear in their support of integration and unity, but deeply embedded organizational barriers made it difficult to make progress. In addition, the third main division manager protected his territory with 'sharp elbows,' and the others felt they had to respond in kind in order to avoid losing out.

The initial SFP round did lead to an expressed consensus on the key idea that there should be 'One Veridian,' and task forces were established to review the allocation of opportunities and resources and to coordinate customer relations. But these coordinating systems were of limited effectiveness in the first year because of ongoing structural barriers to sharing resources, rooted in the rigidities of government cost accounting, as well as a classic problem in changing peer expectations: it is impossible for anyone to really change behavior until all the others do. Those who offer to share resources, if they are dealing with people who still want to control, will find that they have given without getting anything back;

and the system will quickly fall back into the old web of expectations based on autonomy.[19]

SFP does add in subtle but important ways to the leverage of those trying to change the system. The primary thing it does is to create a public discussion of the need for unity and (when appropriate) a public commitment to it. The Veridian interview process helped to create throughout the organization a clear enthusiasm around the potential to pursue larger projects requiring greater cross-business leveraging of resources, and this in turn helped the CEO get a verbal agreement from his top team. That did not mean, of course, that behaviors changed instantaneously or that the division heads were eager to see their resources reallocated to support corporate projects; but the SFP discussions provided a way to shine a light on breakdowns in coordination or instances of overt 'division first' behavior, and the agreement on values meant that those who engaged in those behaviors could be called to account.

The problem of autonomy is not confined to lower-level units of the organization, but is a major factor within the top team as well and determines to a large degree how effectively it operates as a team. The shift to greater collaboration requires, as some of the participants put it, a move from 'baseball' to 'volleyball'—from a game with well-defined positions and roles, to one that is far more fluid and interactive, with priorities and roles that shift depending on the context of the play. In successful cases, it mirrors the shift in the organization as a whole: rather than each unit leader controlling a particular area and the organization head managing all the interactions, the members of the top team begin to argue among themselves about how best to allocate resources and to maximize synergies among them. In a few notable instances at Veridian, members of the leadership group began to re-examine some of their own policies and practices and to call each other out for behaviors that violated collaborative norms.

This shift, to the extent that it occurred, was a slow one. Unlike the transformation of values, the recalibration of lateral relations does not involve a dramatic moment of conversion; it is more of a slow reordering of a network pattern, full of trial and error and correction. Some interviewees at Veridian felt that the move was still being fundamentally blocked by key players who were stuck in the old game; others felt that progress, though slow, was continuing, and that talk about unit identities had been to some degree replaced by talk about Veridian's identity. Among the other cases, there are several in which territoriality remained a strong force to the end, and none where it had been entirely driven from the field.

Like the problem of deference, one of the issues here is that it is not clear even to theorists and consultants exactly what collaborative relations should look like. The norms and expectations of the old order were generally clear and well understood: don't criticize peers in public and don't challenge their expertise on their own turf; in cases of conflict escalate to the next level; if you make a deal there has to be a pretty clear mutual benefit; and so on. But in a more collaborative system people are asked to give up control of resources not in exchange for a return favor, but for the good of the whole; it isn't clear who will recognize that and reward it, or what will happen if others don't reciprocate. As long as these and other issues are not worked through there will be a constant pull back to the simpler, established system. It takes a long, equally constant push back to overcome it.

DEALING WITH PERSONALITY AND MOTIVATIONAL RESISTANCES

We don't have direct evidence from SFP interventions about to what extent individual personality dynamics—images of parents, ego strength, and other factors of this type—may affect people's ability or willingness to participate in collaborative processes. It does seem clear, however, that some people always remained as outliers even in the more successful cases; or as one Veridian manager put it, 'You can't force people to see if genetically they're blind.' Interviewees from the task force and top team at Veridian were vociferous in their conviction that several key members of management just could not deal with the increased challenge and ambiguity of a collaborative approach: they felt at a visceral level unhappy in situations where there were no clear answers, where courses of action had no identifiable person in charge, where conflicting things might be going on at once. They fit Merton's description of the bureaucratic personality more than Maccoby's description of interactive personality.

Unlike the other two issues we have discussed, the Strategic Fitness Process does not tackle this dimension even indirectly: there is no attempt to do psychotherapy, or even extensive personal counseling, with resistant leaders. The result is that one of three things may happen with those who can't go along: they are fired, they successfully block change, or they find their standing and power eroding. In some SFPs, the changes set in train have indeed resulted in a senior executive being fired. In a larger number of cases, people who didn't get fired managed to block or limit change. Just one severely resistant and bureaucratic type at a key position can undermine the move to greater coordination, at least for a period, because he will force others with whom he deals to play the bureaucratic game as well. We have no evidence from this data about whether, under what conditions, and to what degree personal counseling might help to overcome this particular obstacle without the traumatic event of a firing.

THE CONTEST FOR LEGITIMACY

Given the weight of old communal patterns, SFP—as should be clear from these descriptions—is anything but a smooth and logical process, working from first principles through to inevitable consequences. It is in virtually all cases full of drama, emotion, and conflict—more so to the degree in which it involves a significant cultural shift towards collaboration rather than merely operational improvements. In the transformative cases the process can best be described as a *contest* for legitimacy, a battle between conflicting ways of viewing the world—a battle which sways back and forth, and in which the winner is not necessarily clear for a long time. The battle does not usually have clearly defined sides: it occurs as much within the minds and habits of individual players as between factions; but at particular moments groups may coalesce around one interpretation or another, feeling that 'we need to involve people more' or 'we need to restore clarity and control.'

In this sort of transformation the old order has a lot on its side: it is supported by established habits, reliable expectations, and systems of formal and informal rewards. The collaborative vision has at first nothing on its side except frustration with how things are actually working, and a rather nebulous sense of a better way. There is no chance that it will win unless the fight is a fair one, conducted on the open ground in full view of all, and connected to values that have weight for the group as a whole.

The debate begins in the first meeting between the top team and the task force. Frequently when the top team retreats to discuss the feedback, there is a roaring debate about the core values: whether the dialogue is a good thing or whether the leaders should reassert control. This basic conflict is then replayed at many levels and in many forms—from arguments over the action plan to the design of new cross-boundary structures to specific conflicts in which principles of bureaucratic autonomy run up against the goals of unified action. In these debates the idea of collaboration is transformed from a rhetorical shell to a living body of practice.

The success of SFP depends on its ability to keep this conflict of views out in the open, where everyone can examine it and make a judgement about what makes more sense. When it disappears from the public domain—when individuals start acting covertly to maintain their autonomy, without challenges from those who advocate collaboration—change will stop.

The battles are fought in countless skirmishes over how to allocate credit and blame and how to manage joint responsibility. Without the initial commitment to shared values and purpose the outcome would be a foregone conclusion: there would be absolutely no leverage against the force of local self-interest and established procedure. It is in the interplay between the values and the processes, with shared purpose as the guiding principle, that the contest is won or lost, and the outcome is far from assured at the outset.

The iterations of the SFP discussions are critical for keeping the process moving forward. The task force does not simply report to the top and then go its way; it stays around to critique the top team's first effort, and the latter then go back for another try. This second attempt is in many cases the crucial one, where the real issues are engaged. Then the entire SFP is repeated on an annual basis. At this level, too, it is often the second round that makes the difference in catalyzing deeper shifts in culture: the new norms of openness and dialogue begin to really take hold at this time. Conversely, when the top leaders feel that they are 'done' after one round, the organization may make operational reforms but always falls back into territorial rigidity.

Thus as Sabel stresses in his discussion of 'iterated co-design' in Chapter 2, the process does not follow a 'classic' linear pattern where general directions are defined from the top and progressively narrowed down; instead, the top's initial definition acts as a way of getting the discussion going rather than a framework within which everyone must operate. Though the top leaders may not fully realize it at first, it is in the critique and modification of the initial definition that much of the power of the process develops. In fact, as management teams gain experience with the process they typically find it is more powerful to engage earlier with the organization when their ideas and plans are more fluid.

The iterative discussions provide a forum for systematic learning— 'looping' back to the fundamental values and purposes, identifying points of conflict between practices and values, structuring public discussion around these. A key role of the consultants is to repeatedly raise these connections for enquiry, until the positive loop of purposes, values, and process becomes ingrained in the normal conversations of the organization, and learning becomes part of the political process. Thus conflict, rather than being avoided by segmenting the organization and sealing off autonomous units, is engaged through such learning conversations. The

Hewlett-Packard-SRSD case is probably the best-documented example of movement in this direction—though it cannot be said of any case that the contest is finished.

Conclusion

We began with the problem of how a group could make a collective leap of faith—from one network of solidly established interrelated expectations, to another which can only be vaguely imagined. The answer, it becomes clear, is that there can be no successful leap without a slog. Both are necessary: a powerful shared emotional conversion to a set of values and purposes that can only be defined in general terms, and a long struggle to bring practices into line with those visions.

SFP falls into the general category of interactive rather than expert-driven change processes: involving all participants in dialogue in a series of iterative loops that 'self-organize' a new pattern, rather than trying to impose a predefined pattern. The wealth of experience surveyed here brings out a few distinctive characteristics of this approach and suggests some lessons for further exploration.

- The consistent focus on shared purpose seems to be an effective driver that can keep the process moving through a continued loop between values and behaviors; whereas a focus on either of the latter dimensions risks becoming encapsulated and losing touch with the 'real' life of the organization.

- The process is a deeply emotional one, and it provides a way for emotions to be worked through in a constructive way—by providing various parties with room to discuss among themselves as well as in the charged venue of open dialogue, and by encouraging a slow and constant expansion of the domain of change.

- The violation of the norm of deference by the task force is a powerful disruptive moment. The positioning of the task force as an objective body with a stake only in the pursuit of shared purpose, furthermore, makes it in effect a living model of a new ethic of contribution that can pull the organization together.

- There is an emphasis on *formalized process* in the place of informal or individualized approaches. SFP does not focus on direct 'cultural' intervention such as value statements or new symbolism, nor does it attempt to modify 'leadership' styles. Rather, it sets out a process which brings diverse parties into a structured interaction according to rules designed to maximize dialogue. This is one pillar of the collaborative community as defined in this book.

These aspects of the approach create the possibility of major cultural transformation—but only the possibility. We have seen some key barriers that create drama and difficulty along the way, and may at least partially block the process. The top leadership often have difficulty accepting a culture in which subordinates can challenge and criticize them; if they push back or shut down the process, subordinates may fall back into traditional attitudes of deference or leave the company. The various parts of the organization that are used to their own area of autonomy and respect may have difficulty accepting the 'interference' of cross-boundary coordinating mechanisms and shared accountabilities. And even if the organization as a whole accepts these radical changes, some individuals may not be able to overcome their anxiety about complex, ambiguous, and interdependent systems; if these individuals are in key positions they could kill the process entirely.

It is also important to note some limits of the process. Companies that enter it already meet key preconditions that put them into a special category. First, they are formal organizations with a top team that represents the collective purpose: SFP has not been tried with looser confederations of stakeholders. Second, top management is necessarily motivated from the start by a sense that greater engagement of the organization is central to successful implementation of their strategy. Third, the head of the organization almost always has at least a general value-driven belief in the importance of collaboration. Where the top team and its commitment have been relatively weak within the SFP companies, the process has generally been less successful, at least from the view of creating a sustained culture of collaboration.

Yet despite these obstacles and limits the Strategic Fitness Process has achieved an impressive record. It is remarkable among change processes in that it is both rich, encompassing many dimensions of organizational functioning, and reliably structured—it has proved that it can be consistently reproduced in a wide variety of settings. It gets beyond the level of pure intuitive change leadership which characterizes so much of the field, without falling into the opposite error of a rigid cookbook approach. Because there is now a set of cases that can be compared within this overall framework, it teaches us a great deal about the possibility of change through structured dialogue; although it has not shown itself to be a total solution, it does show a hopeful path towards collaborative community.

Appendix 12.1: The Veridian story: overcoming resistances, developing collaboration[20]

Veridian was a defense and national security contractor built primarily by acquisition. Founded in the early 1980s to focus on space commercialization, by the mid-1990s it had evolved into a small, but respected player serving the military in Research, Development, Test, and Evaluation. Anticipating the shift in military thinking from a physical platform-centered view to a network-centric view, and the resulting needs of the military and intelligence services for increasingly integrated information system solutions, Veridian acquired a number of niche players who brought increasingly sophisticated information systems and knowledge management capabilities.

By 2001, Veridian had become a $700 million company, respected both for its distinctive technical capabilities and for the quality of its management. It was at the cutting edge of some of the most advanced areas of network security, sensor technology, and knowledge discovery and decision support, with nearly 20 per cent of its business coming from government-funded R&D. Customer loyalty was extremely high, with win rates on project 'recompetes' over 90 per cent—among the very best in the industry. Financially, earnings (EBITDA) had more than tripled over the previous three years, from $16 million in 1998 to $56 million in 2001, reflecting both rapid revenue growth and an improvement in margins from 5.9 per cent to 8.2 per cent.

Veridian's leadership believed they were now in a position to aim even higher— to set a new competitive standard for national security contractors. Their vision was to become a more nimble and responsive prime contractor than the traditional, hardware-based integrators like Boeing and Lockheed Martin, where Veridian's advantages would lie in earlier anticipation of military needs, greater customer responsiveness, and greater capacity to integrate capabilities across Veridian to develop superior customer solutions.

In order to achieve this vision, the company needed to make some fundamental changes in the management approach and cultures of its constituent parts. The acquired companies had been built around specific technologies, and generally had worked on small contracts. Annual revenues per contract were, on average, under $1 million per year, and only a handful of contracts or task orders generated revenues over $10 million per year. In the initial stage of integrating the acquisitions, Veridian management focused on restructuring the seven heritage companies into three divisions, and on driving business results through each of those divisions primarily on a stand-alone basis. In this, they were similar to most companies in the defense sector, which typically structure into divisions that are separate profit centers, build the necessary capability into each division, and expect limited interdivisional co-operation. Now, however, Veridian corporate managers saw the potential for the divisions to start to collaborate together more extensively in pursuit of larger contracts, in which they would provide their customers with more integrated solutions.

Early moves in that direction, however, caused significant conflict and dissension. Operating policies and practices varied widely across the divisions, reflecting the divergent heritages of the acquired companies. These were often entrenched by the complexities of government contracting where different parts of the company had different contracting structures (cost-plus vs. time and materials vs. fixed price), and changes in rate pools, overhead rates, and accounting treatments required government approval. The corporate HR, finance, and IT areas, which were charged with creating the platform of common approaches and shared services that would enable greater cross-divisional collaboration, found themselves instead ground down by a frustrating, recurring pattern: ideas for moving to a more common approach would be agreed to in principle in collective meetings with the division presidents and then stymied by divisional objections at a detailed, working level. In turn, the division presidents saw these corporate initiatives as poorly executed and lacking in operational understanding, and became increasingly resistant to further initiatives as early ones failed to deliver as promised.

Feelings became particularly heated and frustrated in the critical area of business development. Corporate managers saw the divisions as largely persisting with the old pattern of pursuing smaller contracts ('big acting small'), rather than stepping up to target larger contracts that their combined capabilities should have enabled them to pursue. In turn, the division presidents were troubled about the addition of corporate integrating roles—explicitly out of concern for costs, and also out of a less public concern about incursions into their autonomy. Thus a new key account process was created to coordinate across the divisions, but was seen by the corporate managers as intentionally under-resourced by the division presidents so as not to be effective. Similar disagreements plagued discussions about how to organize to pursue large-scale bids.

Behind these issues was the reality of an organization fragmented into competing interest groups. Since most of the company's units had started as independent entities, their sense of the whole was weak; divisions at times competed with each other for contracts, sometimes in ways that were directly harmful to the overall goals.

By early 2002, the CEO forged a consensus among the management team that strategy execution was their highest priority and that, to achieve their aspirations to create a new competitive model, they needed to address these natural internal barriers to collaboration in a more fundamental way, through the Strategic Fitness Process.

The Strategic Fitness Process enabled the management team to address these problems with considerable success. While the ending is ambiguous—less than twelve months after the first round of SFP, the company was acquired by General Dynamics—during that time there was much movement that bears on the types of issues and resistances cited above.

At the time of the SFP, in the summer of 2002, the management team was very stretched. They had just successfully taken the company public in June 2002, and agreed in late July on a major new acquisition that took the company above $1 billion in annual revenues. Significant issues among the management team were simmering, but had not had a chance to be aired: disagreements about the appropriate emphasis on large vs. small contracts and on the appropriate target rate of growth, and widespread concern that games were being played that put the interests of divisions above the interests of the company as a whole. Most felt that these games were illegitimate, but they could not on their own redefine the game or get out of it: if they did not protect their own divisions and interests, others would simply run over them, in effect rewarding and solidifying the illegitimate behavior.

The task force identified these issues immediately in its initial internal discussions and its field interviews. It uncovered instances, for example, in which different divisions had developed conflicting projects; and rather than discussing the potential conflict with each other or with the corporate level, each part had tried to push ahead quietly, hoping to trump the sister division by presenting a *fait accompli*. Other troubling cases involved units that used sister divisions to help them get contracts, but then worked to shut the collaborating division out of sharing in the economic benefit by staffing the projects with their own people; and units that insisted on developing their own resources and capabilities rather than using those already available in other parts of the organization.

At this stage, as in virtually all SFP cases, the main obstacle was around the culture of deference: Would the task force be able to raise the issue honestly, and would the leadership team be able to take the criticism from its subordinates? There was, as always, a great deal of nervousness in the task force, often expressed in gallows humor. But the more they met among themselves, the more clear they became in their understanding that certain behaviors of the top team did not match up with the goals and ideals that they professed. They were strengthened both by their increasing emotional commitment to their task force colleagues, and by the clear evidence of their coworkers expressed in interviews. The statement of direction from the leadership team articulated a vision of 'One Veridian.' In their interviews, the task force tested this, asking whether their interviewees genuinely believed the company should work to become 'One Veridian' or whether it should be a holding company for different divisions. The answer they brought back was clear: We want to be one Veridian, that's why we came here, but it's very hard to work in this environment. With this support the task force was able to distinguish between their commitment to the company mission and their deference to the company leaders, and were able to ask the question of whether the latter were really contributing to the former.

Thus in the first 'fishbowl' meeting the task team brought the particularistic games into the open. They also issued a direct challenge to the leadership team for failing to act on their rhetoric of unity and integration. They told the Executive Committee (EC): You say one thing in public and then you go back to your divisions and do something different. You represent your own areas, but are not seen as a collective team. They told the CEO: you are a visionary leader but you don't follow up to hold the division presidents accountable to make it happen. Their remarkably blunt overall assessment, as summarized in the meeting notes: 'The EC as a whole [is] not seen as effective.'

The task force also connected the dots to the question of the basic strategy of the organization: Could the company actually carry out its announced strategy of adding high-end integrated projects, or did it need to fall back on its demonstrated capabilities in division-specific smaller projects? The task force members challenged their leaders to live up to the grander vision.

This issue had previously been debated in the top team without clear resolution. The CEO was clear in his own mind that the move to high-end integration was essential, but some of the division leaders felt that this would strain the organization's capability and lead to lower performance, by undermining divisional accountability and relative autonomy. One of them had told the consultants privately, 'I don't think in my heart of hearts that my [division president] colleagues want an integrated company.'

Emotions ran high; disagreements that had previously been hidden came into the open. The leadership engaged in an open debate of the merits of the One Veridian strategy. As the espoused value of integration was reinforced in open discussion, division leaders who had behaved in ways that undermined it—by hiding their projects or boosting their own division's share of project profits by biasing staffing toward their own divisional resources—were 'outed' in a particularly embarrassing way, and others denounced this kind of behavior.

This intense exchange led to a complex set of responses. Some of the senior leadership grasped the message as a revelation—in particular the CEO and one division head who had been strongly preaching the need for integration. On the other hand, the chief financial officer seemed to embody the resistance to the disruption of hierarchy, despite being a strong advocate for the move towards larger contracts and a stronger corporate role in business development. Before the task force report, his view had been that, although it was true that there needed to be more unity, the top leadership should just tell everyone to get in line rather than going through this complex dialogue. During the first leadership meeting after the session with the task force, he blew up in a defensive tirade: What is this crap, why are they dredging up all these complaints, they don't have any answers, they're not even consistent about what they're saying. The CEO, however, supported by other members of the team, insisted on moving forward. They felt a moral accountability to the task team, even though the latter were formally subordinates, and a sense that genuine dialogue was worth pursuing.

In response to the task force feedback, the top leadership undertook a major initiative to translate the concept of 'One Veridian' into a five-year strategy that would articulate the specific customer, capability, and project areas where greater collaboration was required across the business. In parallel, they also commissioned a branding initiative to distill the shared characteristics and values common to the identity of all parts of the company. These two initiatives culminated in a leadership conference for the top 350 employees of the company in March 2003, roughly seven months after the task force had provided their initial feedback. In leading off the conference, the CEO was open and transparent in sharing the SFP process, its rationale, the feedback from the task force (negative as well as positive), the resulting action plan, and the progress in the intervening months. The event was extremely well received and generated considerable 'buzz' and energy across the top three to four layers of the company. The event itself, as well as the preparatory work leading up to it, contributed to a partial collective conversion experience to a different mindset—one that put contribution to the company over performance at the division or individual level, and that increased the degree of emotional commitment to Veridian as a whole rather than to the particular divisions.

But this shift was a partial one on both the horizontal and vertical dimensions. The vertical dimension required a move from a norm of deference. Though there was some movement towards more open discussion in the months following the SFP meeting, there was also clearly—in this case as in others—a continuation of old expectations and confusion about how the new ones would work. This was particularly visible in the challenges facing the CEO. He was criticized by the task force and others, during and after the SFP meeting, for not acting forcefully enough, making tough decisions, getting rid of people who did not fit the strategy and expectations of the company.

> It was sort of trench warfare . . . and this process only accentuated that warfare because it surfaced those issues that we were never able to get over. And our CEO

was never willing to go that next step and decide between these groups and define it.

The CEO's own view, by contrast, was that his approach reflected the realities of an organization in transition, where divisional focus remained important to delivering results, even as they sought to remove barriers to cross-divisional collaboration. He also believed his encouragement of collective dialogue, rather than simply taking decisive action, was consistent with the values of involvement and trust he was seeking to instill. Thus, he viewed the actions of the chief financial officer, for example—his periodic eruptions about the need for more control, his criticisms of the task force—not as fundamentally harming the process, but rather as useful contrary and cautionary pieces in the total puzzle that were rooted in some important business realities about the difficulties of change in a government contracting environment. From the CEO's perspective, he saw himself modeling a new type of leadership appropriate to an emerging culture; but clearly many others continued to act, and to expect him to act, within the rules of the old one.

On the horizontal dimension the problem is to move away from the norm of autonomy. Again, there was substantial movement, but again only partial. The movement can first be seen in the description of the interview process by one of the task force members. They asked people about whether they thought it was important for Veridian to operate as a single company or to maintain the separate cultures and capabilities of the heritage companies:

> What I remember overwhelmingly was it was an emotional topic when we asked people, but there was widespread consensus that we ought to be one company. I think the senior leadership team was surprised by that because there was so much dedication to our heritages. But when you really got people to think and talk through and walk through what our future looked like, there was no way we could be successful as small companies . . . When you got people to really get beyond the emotion and think strategically—and not everyone was there clearly, but for the most part when you got people to work themselves through that logic, people thought we should be one company.

On the other hand, this emotional shift was not fully incorporated into behaviors:

> the interesting thing in that was that while everyone thought we should be one company, everyone wanted their niche described in the vision—which was ridiculous.

> We had—especially from a business development point of view and who's going to take prime responsibility for opportunities—the biggest sandbox fights that there ever were. And so while we all said 'Yes we want to be one company Yes we want to be one company,' everyone wanted to take ownership of an opportunity

so that they'd get the sales credit even if it didn't fit into what their charter was. And that continued to be a problem up until the day we were sold.

In terms of observable structures and processes, the division managers began a process to implement the One Veridian vision: going through each division to identify its capabilities, feeding fact-based discussions on where there were unneeded overlaps, where there were gaps, how to realign, and what was needed or not needed. A forum of business development people from different divisions was also established with the responsibility for surfacing potential conflicts. And a corporate business development role was created, filled by an influential manager with a very strong collaborative capacity, with responsibility for coordinating across units for major projects of corporate strategic significance. But all of these efforts ran into continuing resistance as well. A member of the business development team said:

> I don't believe that team worked very well. Everyone had their own stovepipes, felt that they should have their own stovepipes . . . especially [two members], I mean I believe they never got over it—it was all about them, and saying the 'I' word.

One division head in particular was clearly unhappy with the growing set of cross-functional overlays, like the key account management system and the cross-divisional capability review. Though he expressed clear understanding and support for the value of One Veridian, he preferred to implement it by going back and working with his own people rather than by setting up another layer that would cut across his domain. There was certainly an element of turf protection, to preserve the authority and resource control to deliver on divisional accountabilities, and also a wider philosophical position that integration should be achieved through the hierarchy rather than by specifically collaborative systems.

It should be emphasized again that this intervention to move the company towards greater integration and greater capacity to pursue larger, more complex contracts (in addition to the traditional work) was a process in motion when it was prematurely terminated by the acquisition of Veridian. The company's leaders were about to begin a second round of the SFP process, and the CEO felt that either this would result in the level of Executive Council teamwork he was seeking, with the division presidents fully operating with a 'double hat' as corporate officers forming a unified senior team, or it would lead to his appointing a Chief Operating Officer to provide the required level of coordination.

It is clear that, during the entire eleven-month period of the intervention, there was a continuing struggle—with the CEO and several of the key executives clearly committed to increased collaboration, and, in large measure, the process of dialogue; at least one, and probably two, members of the top team highly skeptical, still essentially believing that clearly delineated divisional accountability and a top-down style were a better way to operate; and the largest number in between—liking the idea of collaboration but not clear what it would mean in many concrete situations, and not entirely willing to take the risk, in their own behaviors, of depending on it as a basis of trust and interaction.

At the same time, despite these continuing conflicts, Veridian made significant progress during the year towards its strategic objectives. The company continued its success rate with small contracts. It also achieved some notable wins of larger contracts, with several involving significant cross-divisional collaboration. Organic growth accelerated from 10 per cent a year earlier to 17 per cent, while margins continued to improve. Its external reputation also grew, and several of the very large defense contractors began to pursue it as a live acquisition target, despite management's desire to remain independent. The ultimate sale to General Dynamics valued the company at roughly double the figure at which it had gone public just one year earlier.

References

Aguilar, Francis J., and Bhambri, Arvind (1983). *Johnson & Johnson (A)*. Harvard Business School case study 384053 (19 Aug.).

Argyris, C. (1990). *Overcoming Organizational Defenses*. Boston: Allyn and Bacon.

Autier, Fabienne, and Ryan, Joe (1998). 'The document company: the social construction and enactment of strategic change.' Paper presented at the 18th Strategic Management Society Annual International Conference, Nov.

Axelrod, Robert (1997). *The Complexity of Collaboration: Agent-Based Models of Competition and Collaboration*. Princeton: Princeton University Press.

Beer, Michael (2002). *Merck Latin America*. Harvard Business School case study #401029.

—— and Eisenstat, Russell A. (1996). 'Developing an organization capable of strategy implementation and learning.' *Human Relations*, 49/5: 597–619.

—— —— (2004). 'How to have an honest conversation about your business strategy.' *Harvard Business Review*, 82/2 (Feb.): 82–9.

—— and Rogers, Gregory C. (1997). *Hewlett-Packard's Santa Rosa Systems Division: The Trials and Tribulations of a Legacy*. Harvard Business School case study #9-498-011 (rev 8–11).

—— and Weber, James (2003). *Whitbread Hotel Company*. Harvard Business School case study #403102, Feb.

—— Eisenstat, Russell A., and Spector, Bert (1990). *The Critical Path to Corporate Renewal*. Boston: Harvard Business School Press.

Bennett, A. (1991). 'Downsizing doesn't necessarily bring an upswing in corporate profitability.' *Wall Street Journal* (6 June): B1, B4.

Bianco, Anthony, and Moore, Pamela L. (2001). 'Xerox: the downfall.' *Businessweek Online* (5 Mar.).

Cameron, K. S. (1998). 'Strategic organizational downsizing: an extreme case.' *Research in Organizational Behavior*, 20: 185–229.

—— Kim, M. U., and Whetten, D. A. (1987). 'Organizational effects of decline and turbulence.' *Administrative Science Quarterly*, 32: 222–40.

Cascio, W. F., Young, C. E., and Morris, J. (1997). 'Financial consequences of employment change decisions in major U.S. corporations.' *Academy of Management Journal*, 40: 1175–89.

Cole, R. E. (1993). 'Learning from learning theory: implications for quality improvement in turnover, use of contingent workers, and job rotation policies.' *Quality Management Journal*, 1: 9–25.

Davis, Stanley M. (1984). *Managing Corporate Culture*. Cambridge, Mass.: Ballinger.

Heckscher, Charles (1995). *White-Collar Blues: Management Loyalties in an Age of Corporate Restructuring*. New York: Basic Books.

—— Maccoby, Michael, Ramirez, Rafael, and Tixier, Pierre-Eric (2003). *Agents of Change: Crossing the Post-Industrial Divide*. Oxford: Oxford University Press.

Henkoff, R. (1990). 'Cost cutting: how to do it right.' *Fortune* (9 Apr.): 17–19.

Jackall, Robert (1988). *Moral Mazes: The World of Corporate Managers*. New York: Oxford University Press.

McKinley, W., Sanchez, C. A., and Schick, A. G. (1995). 'Organizational downsizing: constraining, cloning, learning.' Working paper, Southern Illinois University Department of Management.

Mishra, Aneil K., and Mishra, Karen E. (1994). 'The role of trust in effective downsizing strategies.' *Human Resource Management*, 33/2 (Summer): 261–78.

Palmisano, Samuel J., Hemp, Paul, and Stewart, Thomas A. (2004). 'Leading change when business is good: the HBR interview—Samuel J. Palmisano.' *Harvard Business Review* (1 Dec.): 60–70.

Schlesinger, Len, Jick, Todd, Johnson, Amy B., and MacIsaac, Lori Ann (1991). *Xerox Corporation: Leadership through Quality (A) & (B)*. Harvard Business School case study #9-490-008.

Simon, Herbert A. (1973). 'The organization of complex systems.' In Howard H. Pattee (ed.), *Hierarchy Theory: The Challenge of Complex Systems*. New York: George Braziller: ch. 1.

Simons, Robert (1991). 'How new top managers use formal systems as levers of strategic renewal.' Presented to 11th Annual International Strategic Management Society Conference, Toronto, Oct.

Williamson, Alistair D., and Beer, Michael (1991). *Becton-Dickinson (A): Corporate Strategy*. Harvard Business School case study #9-491-151.

Notes

1. Beer and Eisenstat (2004).
2. The Strategic Fitness Process (formerly known as 'organizational profiling') has been described by its inventors in several publications and cases: see note 3 below.
3. Documented SFP cases include:
   In the public domain:

   - Agilent's Systems Generation and Delivery Unit (Beer and Eisenstat 2004)
   - Hewlett-Packard's Santa Rosa Systems Division (Beer and Rogers 1997)
   - Whitbread Hotel Company (Beer and Weber 2003)
   - Merck Latin America (Beer 2002), with specific subcases on
     - Merck-Brazil
     - Merck-Argentina
     - Merck-Mexico
   - Becton Dickinson (Williamson and Beer 1991)

   Private cases commissioned by the consultants, but carried out by independent investigators – in addition to those above:

   - Agilent Signal Sources
   - Agilent WSTS
   - Chase Auto Finance
   - Isenbeck Argentina
   - Isenbeck BCA
   - Mattel Canada
   - Mattel UK
   - Millipore
   - NAVCanada
   - Steak n Shake Corporate
   - Steak n Shake Grand Rapids Restaurant

4. For evidence of failure of restructuring initiatives to lead to sustained performance improvement, see Bennett (1991); Cameron et al. (1987); Cameron (1998); Cascio et al. (1997); Cole (1993); Henkoff (1990); Mishra and Mishra (1994); McKinley et al. (1995) (with thanks to Jody Hoffer Gittell for this compilation).

   For a particularly illuminating account of the pathological patterns of bureaucracy under pressure, see Jackall (1988: 75–100). His close observations of two companies are particularly rich in showing how rapid change, in interaction with bureaucratic systems of accountability, results in distorted behaviors such as 'outrunning your mistakes'—taking bold managerial initiatives and moving on quickly before the consequences become apparent.

5. For more detail on the 'rebureaucratization' of restructured firms, see Heckscher (1995).

6. The idea of 'purpose' has been defined at more length in Chapter 1. Here, to head off a possible objection, we should just reiterate that shared purpose is different from a diffuse feeling of 'family' unity: it is task focused, involving common understanding of the corporate strategy—the major competitive challenges, the company's position in relation to competitors, how it proposes to gain market advantage, and so on. Classic large bureaucracies of the 20th century like IBM and GM certainly had a sense of shared family, but not of purpose in this sense.

7. This daily culture of deference is documented in Heckscher (1995).

8. Here once again Jackall (1988) provides rich detail and evidence.

9. On Xerox, see Schlesinger et al. (1991); Autier and Ryan (1998).

10. In 1997 Rick Thoman, the new CEO, challenged his staff's report that showed that Xerox was 'world class' in manufacturing and development costs; it turned out their data was old and excluded many of their key competitors (Bianco and Moore 2001).

11. For a critique of the cascade approach, see Beer et al. (1990). Robert Simons has also studied cascades and concluded that they do not work (personal communication; the study is documented in Simons 1991, though the conclusions do not focus on this aspect).

   For a strong advocacy of the cascade approach, see Davis (1984).

12. On the literature of interactive intervention, see Heckscher et al. (2003: chs. 7–8).

13. On classical cognitive theory, see for example Simon (1973).

14. For example, Beer and Eisenstat (2004); Beer and Rogers (1997).

15. Johnson & Johnson and IBM have conducted elaborate dialogues around values (Palmisano et al. 2004; Aguilar and Bhambri 1983); other companies, in Quality Circles and similar efforts, have focused on implementation, asking people to analyze how they can do their work better.

16. Beer and Eisenstat (2004).

17. The emotional charge carried by this change in behaviors does, however, often lead to distortions. One common problem is that the task force becomes overly aggressive, attacking top leaders personally—a kind of overcompensation for the prior deference. Part of the consultants' role is to bring the parties back to a sustainable pattern.

18. Another good example of this dynamic is the description of John Bailey's role in the Mod IV case described above in Chapter 1.

19. This is a form of the classic 'Prisoner's dilemma'; see for example Axelrod (1997).

20. This case is based on a review of the original records and presentations during the intervention and interviews with the chief consultant and four members of the top team and task force.

13

'The Power to Convene':

Creating Collaborative Community with Strategic Customers

Mark Bonchek and Robert Howard

One of the most powerful forces pushing large business organizations to experiment with new forms of collaborative community is the desire—and the need—to develop closer relations with their customers. This trend is present across the global economy, but it is especially prominent for a particular segment of the economy: industries such as information technology, telecommunications, and business services where companies are providing technologically complex products and knowledge-intensive services to other large corporate customers.[1]

These sectors share some common characteristics. New technologies and the increasingly rapid diffusion of knowledge are producing a major business discontinuity, disrupting traditional ways of doing business. In particular, companies find themselves called upon to provide not stand-alone 'products' but complex and often highly customized 'end-to-end business solutions.' Many of these solutions require a significant up-front investment of time and capital, and feature a high degree of ongoing interdependence between the customer and solution provider. In such businesses, establishing deep customer relationships is increasingly critical to success in the marketplace. And this imperative is forcing companies to explore more collaborative kinds of relationships with key customers than they have typically pursued in the past.

A case in point, and the focus of this chapter, is the recent effort of Avaya Inc. to create an Executive Advisory Council consisting of senior executives from its most important customers. Avaya is a \$4 billion Fortune 500 company that designs, builds, deploys, and manages business communications, particularly voice applications such as telephony and call centers, doing much of its business with other Fortune 500 corporations. Created in 2000 in a spin-off from Lucent Corporation, Avaya traces its origins all the way to Western Electric, the equipment arm of the Bell System. Avaya is a major player in its industry. For example, it is the leading provider of call-center systems in both Europe and the United States, with more than 30 per cent of the market, and the worldwide leader in both automated 'interactive voice response' and voice-messaging systems. Avaya has been number one in the US private-branch exchange (PBX) market, and is also taking the lead in the rapidly growing market for internet protocol (IP) telephony.

At the same time, Avaya is experiencing a major transformation in its traditional business model. Due to its spin-off from Lucent, the company has gone from being a division of a larger corporation to being a major company in its own right. This shift has forced it to build an independent infrastructure in key areas such as sales, marketing, information technology, and distribution. Even more important, the technological shift from PBX to IP telephony is causing customers to demand more integrated solutions and forcing Avaya to become more agile and more integrated in how it serves customers. The Executive Advisory Council is an attempt on the part of the company's senior management both to respond to the rapid transformation of its industry and to accelerate its own organizational transformation.

Our perspective on the Avaya experience, and the broader trend of which it is a part, comes from our involvement with Tapestry Networks, a specialized professional services firm that helps organizations design, orchestrate, and manage senior-executive relationship networks.[2] These networks allow a company's top executives to engage in trusted dialogues with their peers on issues of mutual interest or problems of mutual concern. In some cases, the networks that Tapestry helps create are designed to allow companies to realize the full value of existing relationships with strategic customers, partners, and suppliers. In other cases, the goal is to create new networks where they have not existed in the past. And in still others, the purpose is to bring together diverse players in an industry in order to address challenges that none can address on its own.

Although the networks created by Tapestry come from diverse sectors of the economy and have different purposes, they all have two things in common. First, like Avaya, the sponsors are market *leaders*. They possess what Tapestry calls 'the power to convene'—i.e. the ability to bring together the key players in an industry and define shared interests and goals in a way that can have a decisive impact on the performance of the member companies and on the market as a whole. Second, like the Avaya Executive Advisory Council, the relationship networks are *leader-to-leader* networks, consisting of individuals at the senior-most levels of their respective organizations. In both respects, Tapestry's relationship networks represent an interesting laboratory for collaborative, trust-based modes of leadership and models of business community.

Avaya's experience is only one example. Still, we think it is illustrative of a far broader trend. A key theme of the recent literature on industrial organization has been the growing centrality of so-called inter-firm networks.[3] Such networks raise important questions for scholars and senior executives alike. What is the role of the senior executive in a more fluid and more 'networked' economy? How do the leaders of major business organizations exercise their leadership in an environment where, arguably, many of the most important business relationships exist outside the organization he or she leads? What kinds of behavior are most appropriate in organizational settings where traditional models of command and control, on the one hand, and market-oriented transactional relationships, on the other, are either irrelevant or incomplete?

The rich literature on inter-firm networks is not much help in answering these questions. Most descriptions of interfirm networks tend to focus on the interactions on the 'front line' of organizations.[4] To the degree that much of the most recent literature on networks is influenced by complexity theory and focuses on phenomena of 'emergence' and 'self-organization,' there is a tendency to underestimate, and sometimes even dismiss, the role of senior executives.[5] Although there is an emerging theoretical literature (of which this volume is an important part) on the complex organizational dynamics of interfirm networks, for the most part this work still awaits its concrete application in management practice.[6]

In the pages that follow, we will use Avaya's experience as a case study to explore the emerging managerial disciplines of the networked economy. We begin by exploring some of the trends in the business world that are making customer collaboration not just desirable but absolutely critical for companies like Avaya. We then turn to a detailed description of the Avaya Executive Advisory Council, which we analyze in terms of some of the theoretical concepts introduced in other chapters in this volume:

specifically, Adler and Heckscher's three-part model of collaborative community and Sabel's concept of the 'pragmatic organization.' Next, we consider some of the limits of the advisory council model at Avaya and how the company is trying to manage the tensions inherent to it. Finally, we conclude by discussing the potential generalizability of the model to other key stakeholders both within organizations and across inter-firm networks.

To anticipate our conclusion here at the beginning: we believe that even as inter-firm networks become an increasingly important part of the economy, the organizations participating in these networks remain, in important respects, traditional hierarchies. And, in an economy that is becoming a 'network of hierarchies,' there is unique leverage in bringing together the senior-most people from organizations across the network. But the way executives function and behave in such networks is fundamentally different from the way they behave in traditional hierarchies— less 'transactional,' and more 'collaborative.' In helping to lay the foundations of collaborative community at the senior-most levels of its customer networks, Avaya is laying the groundwork of an institutional and managerial infrastructure for the networked economy. And its advisory council model is an important new mechanism of strategy formulation, through which business organizations are, as Sabel explains, 'applying the core principle of iterated co-design to the choice of strategy or goals itself.'[7]

The strategic logic of customer collaboration

Of course, efforts on the part of corporations to get 'closer to the customer' are anything but new. From the quality movement's early focus on the 'voice of the customer' in the 1980s, to the more recent emphasis on programs and systems for 'customer relationship management,' the importance of developing closer relationships with customers has been a persistent theme of the strategy literature for nearly thirty years. In the past decade, however, three trends in particular have highlighted the critical importance of building trust and fostering collaboration with strategic customers in complex knowledge-intensive businesses.

The 'new economics of relationships.' Since the early 1990s, a growing literature has demonstrated that building stronger and deeper customer relationships has powerful economic benefits. The early work of Earl Sasser and Frederick Reicheld of the Harvard Business School argued that profitability isn't driven by market share (the prevailing assumption of much of the early strategy literature) but by customer loyalty.[8] In his subsequent work on loyalty at Bain & Company, Reicheld observed that across a wide range of industries, a 5 per cent improvement in customer retention rates will yield anywhere from 25 to 100 per cent increase in profits.[9] He argued that increased customer retention led to a variety of beneficial effects, including a 'customer volume effect' in which increased loyalty leads to the growth of the firm's customer inventory, and a 'profit-per-customer effect' in which 'the profit earned from each individual customer grows as the customer stays with the company.'[10]

This and other research gave birth to a cluster of new business concepts, variously described as 'customer life-cycle economics,' 'lifetime value of the customer,' 'customer equity,' 'loyalty economics,' etc.[11] It has also contributed to a shift in mindset on the part of at least some executives—*from* a situation where, as Reicheld described it in his book, 'firms overvalue transactions and undervalue relationships' *to* a new awareness of customer relationships as an important financial asset to be managed.[12]

And yet, the evidence seems to suggest that for all the focus on customer loyalty, many companies have yet to achieve it. In a 2002 survey of more than 2,200 information-technology buyers at major corporations, for example, more than 80 per cent said they were 'satisfied' with their technology vendors—but less than half described themselves as truly 'loyal,' i.e. predisposed to place their next order with the same company.[13]

The shift from 'products' to 'solutions.' A second important trend underlying the growing economic importance of deep customer relationships is the shift in many industries from 'products' to 'solutions.' In a wide variety of businesses, the product is increasingly something that is 'co-created' with customers.[14] This trend takes many different forms. One example is the increasing service component in even the most traditional manufacturing products.[15] And in complex technology-driven industries such as information technology and telecommunications, customers are demanding that companies provide not stand-alone products but integrated business solutions.[16] Increasingly, most of the value is in the solution, not in the (increasingly commoditized) product.

When companies provide solutions, the quality of their relationships with leading customers becomes central to competitive success. 'In the new world of manufacturing,' write Richard Wise and Peter Baumgartner of Mercer Management Consulting, 'the sturdiest barrier to competition is customer allegiance. The goal is not necessarily to gain the largest share of customers but to gain the strongest relationships with the most profitable customers.'[17] What Arnoldo Hax and Dean Wilde have termed 'customer bonding' allows companies to better anticipate customer needs and work jointly to develop new products.[18]

To succeed at customer bonding, however, presents new organizational challenges. Sales personnel on the front line of the customer relationship need to learn how to operate, in effect, more like consultants.[19] They must coordinate the many aspects of the customer offering, providing a customized bundle of not only technical but also business services. In the process, they are called upon to exhibit what, in a different context, Michael Useem and Joseph Harder have termed 'lateral leadership'[20]—in particular, orchestrating a broader array of more complicated relationships, with their customers certainly (in order to understand their business needs) but also with suppliers (who are often the most knowledgeable about the latest technology solutions) and even with their colleagues around the world (who may have already encountered a particular business problem and devised an effective solution for it that the salesperson can borrow).

Customer bonding also poses major challenges for senior executives. Increasingly, a company's most important strategic relationships are *outside* the firm. It is people outside the company who have the knowledge or experience a company needs to understand where the market is going and whom a company has to influence in order to shape the evolution of the market. As strategy consultant James Moore put it in his 1996 book *The Death of Competition: Leadership and Strategy in the Age of Business Ecosystems*, in the new networked environment, 'the job of ... top management is to seek out potential centers of innovation where, by orchestrating the contributions of a network of players, they can bring powerful benefits to bear for customers and producers alike.'[21]

The transformation of strategy in an era of discontinuity. These changes put the development of close customer relationships at the center of sales and marketing for many companies. A final 'meta-change' puts it at the center of business strategy as well. As companies struggle with major discontinuities due to technological change, deregulation, globalization, and other factors, what were once relatively stable businesses have become more fluid. Traditional strategic contexts are disrupted. There is a sharp increase in uncertainty—and, therefore, the need for timely and accurate knowledge about customers, competitors, new technologies, market trends, etc.

In this respect, a company's external relationships are becoming a key knowledge asset—but involving a fundamentally different type of knowledge than in the past. In a less complex and more certain business

environment, the answers to key business questions may have been difficult to discover but they were fundamentally knowable. An entire industry, management consulting, grew up around doing the hard analytical
work of getting the 'right' answer.

But in a business environment characterized by high levels of complexity
and uncertainty, there seem to be fewer 'knowable' answers. And, therefore,
a new type of knowledge comes to the fore. Call it *interpretive* rather than
analytical: the ability to detect weak signals, connect bits of fuzzy information, 'make sense' of poorly defined business problems and challenges.[22]

In such an environment, strategy ceases to be what David Lane and
Robert Maxfield have termed 'optimized precommitment.'[23] Rather, a central task of strategy becomes to develop and manage a set of 'generative
relationships' that 'can induce changes in the way the participants see their
world and act in it.'[24] For Lane and Maxfield, the development and coordination of generative relationships lies at the very center of strategy in
environments of high uncertainty where the 'foresight horizon' is complex
(i.e. the future evolution of the technology or market is impossible to
predict). 'As foresight horizons become even more complicated,' they
argue, 'the strategist can no longer foresee enough to map out a course of
action that guarantees desired outcomes. Strategy must include provisions
for actively monitoring the world to discover unexpected consequences, as
well as mechanisms for adjusting projected action plans in response to what
turns up.'[25] In other words, strategy is 'a process consisting of a set of
practices, in which agents inside and outside the firm structure and interpret the relationships, inside and outside the firm, through which they
both act and gain knowledge about their world.'[26]

In this respect, strategy becomes more like a mutual learning process. And
as Hax and Wilde point out, learning can itself be an important enabler of
customer bonding.[27] Deep customer relationships are not only essential to
success in the new marketplace of solutions selling; they are also critical to
defining and executing a company's evolving competitive strategy in an
increasingly uncertain competitive environment.

The Avaya Executive Advisory Council

For an illustration of how these trends play themselves out at a specific
company, consider the example of Avaya. Despite its clear position as a
market leader, from the moment of its spin-off from Lucent in 2000, Avaya
confronted some major competitive challenges.

One legacy of its origin in the quasi-monopolistic Bell System was an uncompetitive cost structure. Since its founding, Avaya has had to reduce its workforce by some 7,000 employees to bring its costs into line with rivals in what has become a more competitive business environment. And the majority of its revenues come from traditional product lines such as PBX maintenance and voice messaging, where growth has flattened and where commoditization has put margins under pressure.

At the same time, Avaya's business is confronting a major technological discontinuity. With the growing convergence of communications with computing, new technologies like internet protocol (IP) telephony are providing Avaya's customers with new options for organizing their internal communications networks. On the one hand, these technological changes provide Avaya with an opportunity to participate in promising new high-growth markets. Over the next decade, more than a hundred million phone lines are likely to move to IP telephony.

On the other hand, the convergence of telecommunications and computing has exposed the company to new competitors. In addition to traditional telecom rivals such as Nortel Networks, for example, Avaya now competes regularly with Cisco Systems and other companies that are trying to leverage their expertise in data networks to get into communications through the provision of so-called 'voice over internet protocol' (VoIP) networks. Perhaps most important, to succeed in these new markets, Avaya must migrate from being primarily a product and technology company to become a solutions company that provides customers with an integrated communications capability encompassing hardware, software, and services.

Parallel to the technological transformation in Avaya's business is a transformation in the relationships that matter with Avaya's customers. Traditionally, the company's account teams have developed good relationships with the telephony organizations at Avaya's customers. But with convergence, selling to the telephony organization is no longer good enough. Avaya has had to develop a whole new set of relationships inside its customers' IT organizations.

Even more important, the buying decision for complex communications networks has steadily migrated to more senior levels in the customer organization. Because telephony was never considered a strategic capability (with the possible exception of call centers), Avaya's relationships were not very senior, usually at the director level. But as intelligent communications networks become a critical component of a company's key business processes and as the decisions about what kind of networks to buy and how to configure them become more complex and require increasingly bigger bets, buying decisions are being made by more senior management.

In one of the paradoxes of the networked economy, decision making is becoming increasingly centralized even as organizations are becoming increasingly distributed. Companies are focusing on a few critical 'strategic' suppliers. Suddenly, Avaya finds itself having to influence decisions at the very top of its customers' IT organizations. And yet, until recently, the company has had few strong relationships with its customers' chief information officers (CIOs).

All these changes—from a regulated business environment to a highly competitive environment, from products to solutions, from the 'voice' organization to the IT organization, from mid-level relationships to senior-management relationships—take Avaya out of its traditional comfort zone. To begin to address those challenges, in 2002 Avaya CEO Donald K. Peterson proposed the creation of an Executive Advisory Council consisting of CIOs from some of the company's most important customers. Peterson's vision for the council was simple: to develop more personal and more strategic relationships with leading executives at its top customers in order to inform them of Avaya's innovation and thought leadership and to bring the 'voice of the customer' inside Avaya.

In the fall of 2002, Avaya hired Tapestry Networks to help shape the agenda and orchestrate the meetings of the council. As of October 2004, the advisory council has met for three major one-to-two-day meetings, with occasional teleconferences on specific issues conducted in between. In the little more than a year that the council has been in existence, it has had a major impact on the evolution of Avaya's strategy, been a catalyst for the creation of two additional executive relationship networks at the company (one focused on customer contact centers and the other focused on communications security in government agencies), and led Avaya to establish a full-fledged 'executive relationship management' program to extend the reach of the councils by building relationships with a broader range of customers and disseminating Avaya's ideas and innovations to a wide audience.

But for the purposes of this chapter, Avaya's Executive Advisory Council may be most interesting as an illustration of how new forms of collaborative community are taking shape at the senior-most levels of business organizations. It is to that story that we now turn.

Defining the 'shared journey': design rules for collaborative community

In Chapter 1 of this book, Adler and Heckscher propose a three-part model to characterize the new form of community that they see emerging in modern business organizations: a 'shared ethic of contribution' to ensure reciprocity and shared value in the relationship; formalized norms of 'interdependent process management' to coordinate activities in the absence of hierarchy; and an 'interactive social character' that encourages individuals to look for opportunities to collaborate.[28]

The first part of the model concerns how these new collaborative communities conceive of value. Unlike traditional 'loyalty-based' organizations, Adler and Heckscher argue, the new form of community is founded on an 'ethic of value contribution' or a commitment on the part of all its members to contribute to the collective value of the group and to the mutual success of all its members. But unlike the stability of the traditional loyalty model, this commitment is highly provisional, informed by a continuous calculation as to whether the community is providing enough value to make it worthwhile to keep participating. Maintaining this delicate balance requires the capacity 'to understand the concrete interests and identities of others in a collaborative relationship.'[29]

The designers of Avaya's Executive Advisory Council faced this challenge from the outset. Company executives were convinced that it was imperative for Avaya to forge closer bonds with senior customer executives. But it was not self-evident that the executives themselves would participate. Many of the target CIOs they hoped to attract had only a cursory understanding of Avaya and its strategy. They were not aware of how Avaya had overcome the financial challenges created by the spin-out or that it possessed differentiation and capability that would distinguish it in the fast-evolving world of enterprise communications. How to persuade busy executives that participating in the council would be worth their effort and their time?

To address this question, council organizers developed a three-part value proposition that they described as the 'shared journey.' First, the council would be about *learning, not selling*. Although the CIOs that Avaya was hoping to attract were key influencers in the buying process, they were often not direct buyers themselves. What's more, they tended to be less interested in product-focused marketing pitches than in a strategic dialogue about market trends and the ways the technology could be used to create business value. Organizers understood that before they could credibly sell to the CIOs, they needed to establish 'share of mind' first. So, they made clear that the council would be an opportunity for the CIOs to gain insight into where the market was going at a time of major uncertainty and change for everyone, and also a chance to get to know Avaya's senior management team (and, implicitly, assess for themselves whether they were a real player in the emerging new business of 'converged communications').

A key part of this mutual learning was what organizers called *reciprocal value*—the idea that there would be as much, if not more, value for participants in learning from each other as in learning from Avaya. The council would be an occasion for participants to share best practices, problems, and issues. And participants from the customer organizations would play a lead role in shaping the agenda and determining what the council would address. The commitment to reciprocal value was embedded in the design of council meetings. For example, all participants were interviewed before each meeting to understand what they hoped to get out of it and to gather input on the agenda. No more than one half of participants at any meeting would be from Avaya. Participants would be encouraged to present on their own experiences, initiatives, and business problems.

Finally, and most important, the council would be an occasion for the customer executives to participate in a real-time *strategic dialogue* that would help shape Avaya's emerging strategy. Avaya's leaders wanted the council to be a basic input into their strategy-making process. And they were determined to make the meetings action oriented—to listen and then change direction based on the input they received. Finally, from the beginning, they recognized that they would need to hold themselves accountable to the council. As a sign of its commitment to the strategic dialogue, the company's entire senior-management team, including Peterson, two group vice presidents, the CIO, the head of strategy and technology, and the head of sales and marketing, committed to attending every council meeting.

This delicate balance between Avaya's goals and those of its target participants raises the question, 'Who owns the network?' Who decides what it will address at any particular moment in time? The answer is clear: Avaya as the sponsor of the network and the institution that pays the bills is the owner and, in the end, decides what it will and will not support. This has the advantage of avoiding the typical dynamics one often sees in inter-firm networks which can disintegrate into factionalism, coalition building, and politicization. By the same token, participants in the council can always 'vote with their feet' by not attending a meeting or leaving the council, so it is incumbent on Avaya to make sure that the network's focus remains of direct interest to a broad enough subset of its members. This serves to keep the network squarely focused on value.

The second dimension of Adler and Heckscher's model of collaborative community is 'interactive process management' or norms and rules governing relations among peers. These norms are ways of structuring how people relate to each other, and how sanctions are applied when they deviate. Creating such norms requires, on the one hand, 'understanding'—i.e. helping 'participants to grasp the logic and sympathize with the feelings of other actors by putting them "in their shoes."' On the other hand, it requires 'commitment,' or the ability of members to count on future acts in a situation where such commitment does not follow automatically from the formal structure of the status order.[30]

In the Avaya Executive Council, perhaps the most important structural norm concerns the strict definition of who does—and does not—constitute a 'peer.' The organizers were convinced that, in order for the council to work, the participating companies needed to be comparable in terms of their scale and scope and strategic importance to Avaya. Even more important, the individuals involved had to be at the same executive level in their organizations—i.e. CIOs or their equivalent in seniority, responsibility, and scope of managerial challenges.

This *peers-only* rule was not so much an issue of *status*, as one might expect in a more traditional hierarchical organization. Rather, it was more a matter of *context*. In order to stimulate the kind of discussions Avaya wanted, it was essential that participants be working on the same kind of problems and face the same day-to-day issues and challenges. They also needed to share a strategic perspective—to be passionate not so much about the technology itself but about its potential to create business value. Only if participants shared a similar mindset and the same level of risk would they be likely to speak freely and engage in the kind of frank exchange of views that was a prerequisite to delivering on the council's potential value.

Another structural norm that council organizers emphasized was *professional intimacy*. In effect, they wanted to give the council the look and feel of a membership club, a club in which Avaya's target audience would feel comfortable and privileged. Membership would be kept small: only fifteen to twenty customer executives. The venues for council meetings would be selected to reinforce this sense of membership and professional intimacy. Working sessions would be designed to maximize discussion over presentation, with expert facilitation and the latest technologies for real-time anonymous polling. Time would be set aside for informal social inter-action in the evenings. Finally, all communications about council pro-ceedings would be governed by the 'Chatham House' rule, which specifies that the membership of the council is kept private and, although lessons and insights may be freely shared, no comments can be attributed to specific individuals or company identities be disclosed.

It's easy to characterize—and perhaps dismiss—such details as mere 'event planning.' And yet, in many respects, they are essential to creating the necessary context of confidentiality and trust so that the right inter-actions emerge. Think of them as elements of an 'interaction infrastruc-ture' designed to encourage real conversation and a frank exchange of views.

The third and final element of Adler and Heckscher's model is the emergence of what Maccoby calls a new 'interactive social character,' or a personality structure that values more collaborative forms of interaction over more traditional interaction styles elicited by bureaucratic or hier-archical organizations.[31] At Avaya, there was a strong focus on the type of behaviors that would make the council successful and how they differed from the 'default behaviors' that managers typically bring to exchanges with customers. For example, in order to create a true strategic dialogue, Avaya executives understood that they would have to behave differently than most executives do in their interactions with customers. Instead of making decisions about strategy and then announcing them, they wanted to bring these strategic partners into the dialogue on certain decisions and solicit their input and counsel. Executives talked about 'developing an open mindset' about the meetings and 'putting their strategic assump-tions on the table' for real-time reactions and review from their chief customers.

To promote interactive dialogue, the company has provided consider-able preparation for those Avaya executives who participate in council events. One member of the design team describes the message to execu-tives this way: 'In general, you will learn more by asking questions and listening to what customers have to say than by explaining or defending your own point of view. Before you say something, first ask yourself: "Is what I have to say more important than what I can learn from the cus-tomers here?" If so, then by all means say it. But choose your shots carefully.' Based on our experience to date, we would say that while some individuals do take to the collaborative style of council interactions more readily than others (and a few have never really been comfortable with it at all), the right context and coaching can go a long way toward eliciting collaborative interactions.

Strategy as 'iterative co-design'

The evolution of the dialogue in the Executive Advisory Council is a striking example in the domain of strategy of the kind of 'iterative co-design' that Sabel describes as characteristic of 'pragmatic organizations.' Indeed, during council meetings participants engage in something akin to what Sabel describes as 'metaphoric benchmarking'—in which deliberation about a given problem or challenge produces 'something "like" a provisional taxonomy or map of accessible solution strategies in relation to each other.' In such a process, he goes on to explain, 'the revision of categories is a desirable and expected outcome, not a failure of intelligence.'[32]

At the first meeting of the council in June 2003, Avaya executives described their high-level vision of the technological shift transforming enterprise communications. They emphasized the many opportunities made possible by what they called 'converged communications' and put a critical question on the table. Would companies first build the technological infrastructure to enable converged communications, and then find specific applications to take advantage of it? Or would they focus first on new applications in order to justify the investment in the infrastructure?

The CIOs were clear. Given the downturn in the world economy and the cost pressures that many companies were facing, the days when companies would invest in new technological infrastructure because of its long-term potential were over. As one participant explained, technology providers like Avaya needed to understand that IT itself was 'in the crosshairs.' The only investments that were being approved were those associated with specific business applications that had a near-term return on investment. What really mattered was not 'infrastructure push' but 'applications pull.' Avaya's proposals to its customers would need to demonstrate a business case with immediate financial payoff. Promises of 'new capabilities' and 'long-term revenue growth,' long the cornerstone of typical infrastructure proposals, had become less important, merely 'nice to have.'

On some level, Avaya's executives already knew that applications and near-term returns were important—but they had not realized how important. The frank feedback from senior executives at major customers had a way of concentrating the mind and producing a new degree of alignment around tangible action. Avaya's senior team came away from the first meeting realizing that they had to tackle the business case and applications issues directly. They also now had critical ammunition, in the form of direct testimony from leading customers, to drive the internal changes necessary in order to make these adjustments.

By the time of the second meeting of the Executive Advisory Council in December 2003, Avaya's senior team had some concrete changes to announce. The company had added an applications group to start focusing on critical business applications, and had identified three key areas of focus: branch offices, customer contact centers, and mobile workers. The sales and service organizations had also redoubled their efforts to demonstrate near-term cost savings, in addition to long-term revenue growth. What's more, the company had purchased a professional services company to improve its capabilities in providing business solutions.

The new plans were a major step forward, but in the discussion at the December 2003 meeting, council members identified additional weaknesses in Avaya's strategy. The new applications group was an improvement, they said, but the company in general was still too focused on technology and not enough on business value. Even the domains chosen for applications development were fundamentally based on technologies, rather than starting from a clear understanding of business needs. 'You're still selling us technical solutions and not asking us about our business problems,' said one participant.

What's more, although the company had begun to talk about integrated solutions, its own organizational structure was not integrated. There was a separate products group and services group, each with its own sales, marketing, and product development (the new applications unit was located in the product group). Avaya was still organized in product silos with no single face to the customer. As one participant put it, 'I want one global throat to choke.'

The December meeting was a tough one for the Avaya participants. The reactions of the customer members served to blow up some key strategic assumptions about how well Avaya was articulating a compelling value proposition to CIOs and how well Avaya was organized to bring solutions to the marketplace. But to their credit, the Avaya executives were able to listen and to engage with the criticisms. This openness made an impression. 'The way in which Avaya listens to customers says a lot about Avaya as a company,' said one participant. 'I had some concerns about a product company trying to become a services company,' said another, 'but I'm impressed with the degree to which Avaya listens and have seen evidence of movement since last time. Celebrate this progress.'

Coming out of the second meeting, Avaya took two major steps. First, it reorganized all its go-to-market activities under a single leader. In effect, the company created a customer-facing sales, channels, and marketing organization to bring products and services to market. To head this new organization, the company called on its former head of services, who had been hired from IBM and had helped lead that company's transition from a product organization to a more solutions-oriented company. One of his first actions was to thoroughly re-examine Avaya's global value proposition. With the assistance of a leading consulting company, Avaya conducted over one hundred interviews in a thorough re-examination of its go-to-market strategy. The result was a more compelling set of messages and value propositions, a more streamlined model for channel distribution, and a more strategic sales organization focused on targeted segments and verticals.

The third of the Executive Advisory Council's meetings took place in May 2004. Avaya presented its new go-to-market strategy and new organization, and elaborated on its evolving vision. What converged communications was really all about, from a business perspective, company executives now explained, was the ability to draw people more seamlessly into a company's business processes, through the automatic provision of information at just the right moment.

The company called this development 'communications-enabled business processes.' In manufacturing, for example, exceptions in the manufacturing process could automatically trigger notifications to those with the authority and expertise to remedy the situation. In financial services, a major change in a company's stock price could automatically trigger the communications system at a brokerage firm to locate and notify investors whose portfolios had been affected. The systems would contact investors through their medium of choice, ask if they would like to speak to their broker, and immediately arrange a conference call—all without any human intervention. In general, such communications-enabled processes remove the delays that result from people trying to connect with each other or gather required information.

On the one hand, participants strongly confirmed that Avaya's customer strategy was on the right track. On the other, they became engaged in an animated discussion about what communications-enabled business processes would mean for them. Two critical insights, one for Avaya, one for its customers, emerged from this discussion.

First, despite all the talk about the convergence of voice and data networks, some of the companies present, among them some of Avaya's most technologically sophisticated customers, were not really running their voice communications over their data networks. Rather, they were creating separate IP voice and IP data networks. This contradicted the conventional wisdom that the value of IP telephony was in the ability of companies to create low-cost multifunctional networks. These companies were willing to incur the extra cost of multiple networks because of the value they could derive from more applications-specific network designs. 'Don't talk about converged *networks*,' said one participant. 'Talk about converged *communications*.' Such comments, coming from leading-edge customers, suggested an emerging market trend that had the potential of playing directly to Avaya's strength in the market, i.e. its deep expertise in voice-specific applications and networks (and of differentiating Avaya from its primary competitor, Cisco, whose strength is in the world of hardware and data).

At the same time, Avaya's vision of communications-enabled business processes got the CIOs thinking of all the ways they could use the technologies to, as one participant put it, 'take human latency out of our business processes.' In effect, the new systems had the potential to radically reduce the transaction costs of collaboration. 'This changes everything,' said one participant. The group began to explore the implications of this change for their current business models. A focus of the next council meeting will be to explore these implications across a variety of core business processes.

As the evolution of the advisory council dialogue suggests, the council's deliberations have helped bring Avaya and its customers closer to each other and to the marketplace. Council proceedings have, in effect, become an arbiter for prioritizing issues inside the company and making decisions about strategy and positioning. Internal discussions are informed in a direct way by the viewpoints and reactions of some of the company's leading customers. At the same time, the council has allowed Avaya to educate its customers and influence the way they think about their business, their use of technology, and the value of Avaya not only as a solution provider but also as a trusted adviser.

Tensions in the model

Like any emerging institutional form, the advisory-council model has some inherent tensions and limitations. There are three, in particular, that Avaya has had to manage carefully.

Balancing 'learning' and 'selling.' For all the focus on mutual learning in the advisory council, Avaya remains, of course, a commercial organization. How to maintain the integrity of the council process while still leveraging the new relationships being developed for commercial ends?

The organizers of the council program have found that they have to actively manage the boundary between learning and selling. As soon as the Executive Advisory Council became active, for example, organizers received numerous requests from account teams for access to the participating customer executives and for information from council proceedings about their accounts. It was only natural that Avaya account teams sought greater access to the senior-level individuals that were joining the council. But council planners had to carefully protect the company's budding new CIO relationships. For example, while each individual account team knows that its customer CIO is participating, the complete list of participating individuals and companies remains confidential.

The irony, of course, is that the more the deliberations of the council have focused on mutual learning, the more Avaya has created the conditions of trust that ultimately allow it to sell in the new telecom environment. Here's how one Avaya executive involved in the council describes this evolution:

'After the first meeting of the council, a participant told me, "the worst thing you could have done was to sell to us. You didn't." I knew we were on the right track. Then, after the second meeting, someone said, "you know, you could sell to us more." At first, I was confused. But then I realized that they were really starting to trust us enough to give us permission to sell.'

At the limit, genuine learning turns out to be the best way to sell. Another Avaya executive described an event at the first meeting of the Customer Contact Council, a spin-off of the initial Executive Advisory Council that focuses on the specific issues facing call centers (the Customer Contact Council is described in more detail on p. 532 below). A participant said, 'this is the first time I've sat in an Avaya meeting where you didn't talk about your products. You talked about my business.' Then, after a presentation on IP telephony, the executive made a call to his management team to ask them to develop a comprehensive plan for implementing IP telephony in their business. 'Our account team had been urging them to do that for eight months,' the Avaya executive reflected. 'He made it happen after one day.'

As the council evolves, Avaya has also taken steps internally to make sure there is a constructive relationship between learning and selling and to creatively leverage its new senior-level relationships in its day-to-day business interactions with its customers. For example, the company has created an executive sponsor program which matches each of the Avaya senior executives participating in the Executive Advisory Council with an Avaya account team responsible for the customer organization participating in the council. These executive sponsors serve as a source of strategic advice to the account teams and also function as an 'escalation path' to help resolve any problems that emerge in the customer relationship. In this way, Avaya is trying to leverage the relationships that executives have developed in the council in their day-to-day business interactions outside the council.

Managing the trade-off between 'intimacy' and 'reach.' The Executive Advisory Council is designed to maximize the 'intimacy' of exchanges among members. But this intimacy comes at the cost of limited reach. As important as it has become for Avaya to have an advisory council in which senior executives from some of its key customers weigh in on the future strategic direction of the company, there are still many other customers that, by definition, the council cannot reach.

To reach that broader audience, Avaya is working with Tapestry to develop a far broader and more systematic program for 'executive relationship management' that reaches far beyond the initial participants in the Executive Advisory Council. The company has appointed a dedicated staff to lead the program and is looking to institutionalize connections between the new program and other business functions, including sales, marketing, R&D, and corporate strategy.

For example, Avaya has recently explored ways to allow a broader number of CIOs at customer organizations to benefit from the networked interactions of the council. The company is currently considering creating a program for CIOs who would not have the hands-on advisory role that the council has but would nevertheless have access to the learning coming out of the council's interactions. Of course, the more executives the Avaya program reaches, the more likely that its initiatives will resemble traditional broadcast marketing, rather than the participatory co-design and dialogue that defines the advisory council itself. This suggests an interesting new segmentation of the company's customer base, based in part on the capacity of a customer to contribute to Avaya's own learning and strategic development.

A nested 'hierarchy' of networks. A potential limitation of Avaya's strict focus on peer networks is to exclude those critical issues that emerge in interactions up and down the hierarchy in the participating business organizations. After all, one of the major lessons of the new industrial organization has been the value of working collaboratively across levels and creating new kinds of collaboration up and down the traditional hierarchy.[33] Doesn't the decision to limit participation in the advisory council to peers automatically limit the potential reach of the council model and undermine its effectiveness as a model for collaboration and community? Put another way, is Avaya's success at inter-firm collaboration with customers at the senior-most level inadvertently creating a 'collaboration gap' inside the firm itself?

So far, the company has created two mechanisms to ensure that the strategic shift defined in the Executive Advisory Council is translated into action on the front lines of the company's business. The mechanism inside Avaya is the executive sponsorship program described above. By placing a senior Avaya executive into the communications flow of a major customer account team, the program creates a new opportunity for customer-focused interaction between account teams and the company's senior leadership.

The mechanism for Avaya's customers is the creation of similar peer networks at different levels of the organizational hierarchy. For example, early in the deliberations of the Executive Advisory Council, a number of participants spoke about the value of getting their direct reports involved in the conversation. In the words of one, 'don't assume that my direct reports get this.' After considerable discussion and a careful search for a focus that would attract broad interest and justify the investment, Avaya created a Customer Contact Council to focus on the challenges of designing and managing customer contact centers.

Like the Executive Advisory Council, the Customer Contact Council is a peers-only network. But unlike the advisory council, the peers in question are one step down in their respective organizations: vice presidents or senior vice presidents, about half from customer IT organizations with responsibility for contact center technology, the other half from customer business units and responsible for actually running centers. Companies participating in the Executive Advisory Council make up about a quarter of the companies participating in the Customer Contact Council. And in some cases, the CIOs at these companies have selected the actual individuals who participate.

The creation of the Customer Contact Council, as well as the recent creation of yet another network focused on Avaya's business in the public sector, suggests an intriguing model. It may well be that in an economy that is increasingly a 'network of hierarchies,' a key design element of the 'pragmatic organization' will be a 'hierarchy of networks'—i.e. a portfolio of loosely coupled networks at various organizational levels with different but related areas of focus. Of course, precisely how these networks interact with each other and what characterizes the flow of information among them is a critical question for the future.

It is too early to tell what impact either of these innovations will have on Avaya's own organization. It is possible that the success of external networks with customers will generate new best practices for more participatory forms of collaboration inside the company as well.

Generalizing from the Avaya model

How generalizable is the Avaya model of collaborative leader-to-leader executive networks? The experience of Tapestry Networks to date suggests that the basic approach can be adapted to a relatively wide variety of business issues, organizational settings, and stakeholder groups.

As we have already discussed, at Avaya itself the model has spread from the Executive Advisory Council and the Customer Contact Council to a new initiative known as the Federal Government Leadership Forum. The forum, whose members include the CIOs of federal government agencies and the leaders of the public-sector practices at the largest IT solution providers, seeks to improve public–private partnership in the area of assured communications for homeland security.

Tapestry has also advised the Society of Thoracic Surgeons on the creation of multi-stakeholder forums to address the future of cardiac surgery.[34] It has helped the accounting firm Ernst & Young create a network consisting of the chairs of audit committees from the board of directors of leading corporations, in order to identify best practices for improving corporate governance. And it has created a network in the private-equity sector to address operational issues having to do with growth and succession planning.

Although these networks have different structures and different goals, we can recognize an emerging pattern of critical success factors that applies to all of them, specifically:

- A set of *stakeholder relationships* vital to the sponsoring company;
- A sponsor important enough to possess the *'power to convene'* this stakeholder group;
- *Shared strategic issues* that confront, with some degree of urgency, both the sponsor and the stakeholders—typically relating to market disruption, regulatory change, or new competitive forces;

- The potential for the network to produce *tangible benefits* to the sponsor and to individual stakeholders;
- The potential for the network to produce *clear public benefits* beyond the specific interests of individual members; and finally
- A group of *committed senior executives and leaders* who, as peers, can *make change happen.*

Of course, leader-to-leader networks are not the only form of collaborative community in the modern business organization. But as the Avaya case suggests, it is likely to become an especially useful, and therefore popular, organizational alternative—especially for companies whose technologically complex products and knowledge-intensive services require investing in collaborative relationships with customers. For such companies, the 'power to convene' is fast becoming an essential aspect of the power to compete.

References

Bettencourt, Lance A., et al. (2002). 'Client co-production in knowledge-intensive business services.' *California Management Review*, 44/4 (Summer): 100–28.

Bonchek, Lawrence I., et al. (2003). 'The STS Future Planning Conference for Adult Cardiac Surgery.' *Annals of Thoracic Surgery*, 76 (Dec.): 2156–66.

Dyer, Jeffrey H., and Hatch, Nile W. (2004). 'Using supplier networks to learn faster.' *MIT Sloan Management Review*, 45/3 (Spring): 57–63.

Foote, N., Galbraith, J., Hope, Q., and Miller, D. (2001). 'Making solutions the answer.' *McKinsey Quarterly*, 3: 84–97.

Gupta, Sunil, Lehmann, Donald R., and Stuart, Jennifer Ames (2003). 'Valuing customers.' Harvard Business School Marketing Research Paper 03–08 (Feb.).

Halbherr, Michael, and Howard, Robert (1999). 'Knowledge-based competition: closing the gap between strategy and knowledge management.' Working Paper, The Boston Consulting Group (Dec.).

Hax, Arnoldo C., and Wilde, Dean L., II (1999). 'The Delta model: adaptive management for a changing world.' *Sloan Management Review*, 40/2 (Winter): 11–28.

Hout, Thomas M. (1999). 'Are managers obsolete?' *Harvard Business Review* (Mar.): 161–8.

Lane, David, and Maxfield, Robert (1997). 'Foresight, complexity, and strategy.' In Brian Arthur et al. (eds.), *The Economy as a Complex Evolving System*, II. Reading, MA.: Addison-Wesley: 169–98.

Moore, James (1996). *The Death of Competition: Leadership and Strategy in the Age of Business Ecosystems*. New York: HarperBusiness.

Piore, Michael J., and Sabel, Charles F. (1984). *The Second Industrial Divide: Possibilities for Prosperity*. New York: Basic Books.

Porter, Michael E. (1998*a*). 'Clusters and the new economics of competition.' *Harvard Business Review* (Nov.–Dec.): 77–90.

——(1998*b*). 'Clusters and competition: new agendas for companies, governments, and institutions.' In *On Competition*. Boston: Harvard Business School Press: 197–288.

Powell, Walter W., et al. (1999). 'Network position and firm performance: organizational returns to collaboration in the biotechnology industry.' In Steven Andrews and David Knoke (eds.), *Networks in and around Organizations*, a special volume in the series Research in the Sociology of Organizations. Greenwich, CT.: JAI Press.

Reicheld, Frederick F. (1996). *The Loyalty Effect: The Hidden Force behind Growth, Profits, and Lasting Value*. Boston: Harvard Business School Press.

——and Sasser, W. Earl, Jr. (1990). 'Zero defects: quality comes to services.' *Harvard Business Review* (Sept.–Oct.): 105–11.

Reinartz, Werner J., and Kumar, V. (2000). 'On the profitability of long-life customers in a noncontractual setting: an empirical investigation and implications for marketing.' *Journal of Marketing*, 64 (Oct.): 17–34.

Sabel, Charles F. (1982). *Work and Politics: The Division of Labor in Industry*. Cambridge: Cambridge University Press.

——(1993). 'Studied trust: building new forms of cooperation in a volatile economy.' *Human Relations*, 46/9 (Sept.): 1133–70.

——(1995). 'Intelligible differences: on deliberate strategy and the exploration of possibility in economic life.' Paper presented to the 36th Annual Meeting of the Societá Italiana degli Economisti, (20–21 Oct.).

Sandberg, Robert, and Werr, Andreas (2003). 'The three challenges of corporate consulting.' *Sloan Management Review*, 44/3 (Spring): 59–66.

Saxenian, Annalee (1994). *Regional Advantage: Culture and Competition in Silicon Valley and Route 128*. Cambridge, MA.: Harvard University Press.

Stabell, Charles B., and Fjeldstad, Øystein D. (1998). 'Configuring value of competitive advantage: on chains, shops, and networks.' *Strategic Management Journal*, 19: 413–37.

Useem, Michael, and Harder, Joseph (2000). 'Leading Laterally in Company Outsourcing.' *Sloan Management Review* 41/2 (Winter): 25–36.

Wise, Richard, and Baumgartner, Peter (1999). 'Go downstream: the new profit imperative in manufacturing.' *Harvard Business Review* (Sept.–Oct.): 133–41.

535

Notes

1. According to one estimate, 'knowledge-intensive business services' contribute roughly 30% of the total value-added from services in the United States and United Kingdom. See Bettercourt et al. (2002: 100).

2. Bonchek is managing director of Tapestry and chief consultant to the Avaya executive relationship management program described in this chapter. Howard is an independent consultant and has conducted interviews with Tapestry personnel, Avaya executives, and Advisory Council members for this chapter.

3. The literature on inter-firm networks is extensive. Four lines of research are worth noting here: Charles Sabel's early work has emphasized the surprising persistence (at least, from the perspective of the traditional paradigm of the vertically integrated corporation) and ongoing strategic relevance of decentralized networks of firms in 'industrial districts.' (See Sabel (1982); Piore and Sabel (1984).) Subsequent work has highlighted the importance of the network model in cutting-edge new industries such as computing and biotechnology. See for example Saxenian (1994); Powell et al. (1999). Other researchers have pointed out the increasing centrality of the network model even in traditional vertically integrated industries such as the auto industry. For example, a recent article argues that Toyota's network-based model of supplier relations has been central to the firm's success in the global auto industry; see Dyer and Hatch (2004). Finally, some prominent business academics have argued that regional networks of firms can be a distinctive source of competitive advantage. In particular, see Porter (1998*a*, 1998*b*).

4. See for example the interesting description of the interactions between salespeople and customers in the fledgling PBX market in Lane and Maxfield (1997: 169–98).

5. For a review of this tendency and an interesting contrary view, see Hout (1999).

6. See, in particular, Sabel (1993, 1995); and Chapter 2 in this volume.

7. Sabel, Chapter 2, p.134 *et passim*.

8. See Reicheld and Sasser (1990).

9. See Reicheld (1996).

10. Reicheld (1996). Some researchers have challenged the universality of this relationship. See Reinartz and Kumar (2000).

11. More recently, researchers have extended the concept of 'customer lifetime value' to the arena of financial valuation. For example, one recent working paper argues that customer value is 'a useful metric to assess the overall value of a firm.' The authors found that improving customer retention by 1% is likely to improve customer and firm value by 3 to 7% and has almost five times greater impact than a 1% improvement in the discount rate of capital. See Gupta et al. (2003).

12. Reicheld (1993: 50).

13. See Robert Weisman, 'Quality products alone won't retain customers,' *Boston Globe*, (8 Aug. 2004), E2.
14. See Bettencourt et al. (2002).
15. According to one estimate, in many manufacturing sectors, revenues from downstream activities now represent ten to thirty times the annual dollar volume of the underlying product sales. See Wise and Baumgartner (1999: 134).
16. On the competitive dynamics of providing customer solutions, see Halbherr and Howard (1999); Hax and Wilde (1999); Foote et al. (2001).
17. Wise and Baumgartner (1999: 136).
18. Hax and Wilde (1999: 13).
19. For an interesting analysis of this broad trend, see Sandberg and Werr (2003).
20. See Useem and Harder (2000).
21. Moore (1996: 12). For another interesting take on these challenges, see also Stabell and Fjeldstad (1998).
22. The strategy literature is beginning to recognize the central role of a company's external relationships to meeting the new strategic challenges found in more complex business environments. Indeed, one can see a trend from the classical era with its primary focus on market position (roughly from Bruce Henderson through Michael Porter) to the focus of the late 1980s and 1990s on (mainly internal) capabilities and competencies (Hamel and Prahalad; re-engineering; and, in the academic world, the 'resource-based view of the firm') to recent attempts to devise a network-based view of strategy.
23. Lane and Maxfield (1997: 170).
24. Lane and Maxfield (1997: 171).
25. Lane and Maxfield (1997: 190).
26. Lane and Maxfield (1997: 189).
27. Hax and Wilde (1999: 13).
28. Adler and Heckscher, Chapter 1, this volume.
29. Ibid., p. 40.
30. Ibid., pp. 53–4.
31. Ibid., pp. 54–9. See also Maccoby, Chapter 3 in this volume.
32. Sabel, Chapter 2 in this volume, pp. 125–6.
33. For an example, see Heckscher and Foote, Chapter 12 in this volume.
34. See Bonchek et al. (2003).

Index